D0125339

W9-AZI-595

The

New Testament

with

Psalms & Proverbs

KING JAMES VERSION

Dear Sophia,
I'm so proud of you!
Read this little Bible
a few minutes each
day and you will always
be on the right path.
I love
you,
Uncle Dave

HENDRICKSON
BIBLES

THE NEW TESTAMENT
WITH PSALMS & PROVERBS
KING JAMES VERSION

Hendrickson Publishers Marketing, LLC
P.O. Box 3473
Peabody, MA 01961-3473

Seventh Printing Hendrickson Publishers Edition — March 2017

ISBN 978-1-59856-242-2	Blue Flexisoft
ISBN 978-1-59856-808-0	Espresso Flexisoft
ISBN 978-1-59856-811-0	Lilac Flexisoft
ISBN 978-1-59856-244-6	Tan Flexisoft
ISBN 978-1-61970-154-0	Black Flexisoft
ISBN 978-1-61970-155-7	Light Pink Flexisoft
ISBN 978-1-61970-871-6	Black Imitation Leather

Design and typesetting by Blue Heron Bookcraft, Battle Ground, WA

Printed in China by R. R. Donnelley

Preface to the King James Version
1873 Edition

The most time-honored and widely used edition of the English Bible is the translation of 1611, commonly known as the Authorized Version or King James Version (KJV). But though it has served as the standard translation for millions of users through nearly four centuries, there has never been a standard edition to which all printings are conformed.

No two early printings of the KJV were identical—not even the two printings of 1611—and no two modern settings are identical, either. These differences are due to accidental human error as well as to intentional changes by printers and editors, who sought to eliminate what they judged to be the errors of others and to conform the text to their standards of English usage. This said, most differences involve only spelling, punctuation, and italics, and few variations materially affect the meaning of the text.

As early as 1616 there were systematic attempts to revise and standardize the KJV. Other important early editions were issued by Cambridge in 1629 and 1638. In the eighteenth century, the two great English universities (who were also officially chartered printers) commissioned thorough and systematic revisions. The edition of Dr. F. S. Paris was published by Cambridge in 1762 and that of Dr. Benjamin Blayney by Oxford in 1769. Though far from perfect, these remained the standard editions until

The Cambridge Paragraph Bible of 1873.

The Cambridge Paragraph Bible began with the simple plan of arranging the text of the KJV according to the sense of the literature: arranging the prose sections into paragraphs and the poetic sections into parallel lines. This simple plan, however, was enhanced by the editor's desire to create the most thorough standardization of the text ever attempted. To this task Dr. F. H. A. Scrivener devoted seven laborious years: 1866 to 1873.

Because the translators' original manuscript no longer exists, the KJV text must be established by consulting the earliest settings. Dr. Scrivener compared at least 15 early settings and important revisions, including both settings of 1611; Bibles of 1612, 1613, 1616, 1617, 1629, 1630, 1634, 1638, 1640; and the significant editions of Drs. Paris (1762) and Blayney (1769).

In his 120-page introduction, Dr. Scrivener addressed the various features of the KJV he worked to standardize:

Italic type. Italic type was used in the KJV, as in the Geneva Bible, to indicate words in the English translation that have no exact representative in the original language. Dr. Scrivener, following many earlier scholars, noted that the KJV translators were noticeably inconsistent in their use of italics, sometimes even in the same paragraph and verse. To cite one small pattern from the

1611 edition, Leviticus 11:20 has "upon all foure," while for the same Hebrew 11:21 and 42 have "upon *all* foure," and 11:27 has "on *all* foure."

Dr. Scrivener carefully analyzed why italic type was used throughout the KJV, reduced this analysis to 14 major principles, and then applied these principles with meticulous consistency throughout the entire Bible. A substantial portion of the editor's "seven laborious years" was devoted to this significant improvement.

Punctuation. Later printings of the KJV added a great deal of punctuation to the editions of 1611. Dr. Scrivener restored the major punctuation (periods, colons, parentheses, question marks) of 1611, and used commas and semicolons to help divide longer sentences into more manageable units for reading.

Spelling and capital letters. Spelling of proper names and common words was very fluid in the sixteenth and seventeenth centuries: "Inquire" and "enquire" were interchangeable, as were "ceiling," "cieling," and "sieling." Most differences between modern settings of the KJV and early settings involve standardization of spelling. Dr. Scrivener's general rule was that whenever a word was spelled more than one way, he conformed all occurrences to the standard spelling of the late nineteenth century. Proper names, on the other hand, vary according to their spelling in the original languages, so "Elijah" throughout 1 and 2 Kings and in Malachi 4:5 becomes "Elias" throughout the New Testament, as in Matthew 11:14

and 17:3. For the benefit of modern readers, three spelling patterns are changed in this edition that are not changed in Scrivener's edition: twenty-nine occurrences of "mo" and "moe" are conformed to "more"; four occurrences of "unpossible" are conformed to "impossible"; and "neesed" in 2 Kings 4:35 is spelled "sneezed."

Paragraphs. According to Dr. Scrivener and other scholars, the paragraph marks (¶) were unequally and inconsistently distributed, and they disappear altogether after Acts 20:26. So, while consulted, the original marks were not always followed in *The Cambridge Paragraph Bible.* Since *The KJV Reference Bible: Compact Edition* is a paragraphed Bible, paragraph marks are not used.

In *The KJV Reference Bible: Compact Edition,* Hendrickson Publishers conforms its setting of the King James or Authorized Version to its most highly regarded edition: *The Cambridge Paragraph Bible* of 1873, edited by F. H. A. Scrivener. As in the case of the first edition of the version of 1611, this is done out of "zeal to promote the common good, whether it be by devising any thing ourselves, or revising that which hath been laboured by others" ("The Translators to the Reader," the preface to the version of 1611). With the original translators, we hope our efforts will be "welcomed," not "with suspicion" but with "love," and that the reissue of this edition will contribute to improvement of this great treasure of the English-speaking church.

John R. Kohlenberger III

Epistle Dedicatory

TO THE MOST HIGH AND
MIGHTY PRINCE
JAMES
BY THE GRACE OF GOD
KING OF GREAT BRITAIN,
FRANCE, AND IRELAND
DEFENDER OF THE FAITH, &c.

The Translators of the Bible wish
Grace, Mercy, and Peace
through JESUS CHRIST our Lord

Great and manifold were the blessings, most dread Sovereign, which Almighty God, the Father of all mercies, bestowed upon us the people of *England,* when first he sent Your Majesty's Royal Person to rule and reign over us. For whereas it was the expectation of many, who wished not well unto our *Sion,* that upon the setting of that bright *Occidental Star,* Queen *Elizabeth* of most happy memory, some thick and palpable clouds of darkness would so have overshadowed this Land, that men should have been in doubt which way they were to walk; and that it should hardly be known, who was to direct the unsettled State; the appearance of Your Majesty, as of the *Sun* in his strength, instantly dispelled those supposed and surmised mists, and gave unto all that were well affected exceeding cause of comfort; especially when we beheld the Government established in Your Highness, and Your hopeful Seed, by an undoubted Title, and this also accompanied with peace and tranquility at home and abroad.

But among all our joys, there was no one that more filled our hearts, than the blessed continuance of the preaching of God's sacred Word among us; which is that inestimable treasure, which excelleth all the riches of the earth; because the fruit thereof extendeth itself, not only to the time spent in this transitory world, but directeth and disposeth men unto that eternal happiness which is above in heaven.

Then not to suffer this to fall to the ground, but rather to take it up, and to continue it in that state, wherein the famous Predecessor of Your Highness did leave it: nay, to go forward with the confidence and resolution of a Man in maintaining the truth of Christ, and propagating it far and near, is that which hath so bound and firmly knit the hearts of all Your Majesty's loyal and religious people unto You, that Your very name is precious among them: their eye doth behold You with comfort, and they bless You in their hearts, as that sanctified Person who, under God, is the immediate Author of their true happiness. And this their contentment doth not diminish or decay, but every day increaseth and taketh strength, when they observe, that the zeal of Your Majesty toward the house of God doth not slack or go backward, but is more and more kindled, manifesting itself abroad in the farthest parts of *Christendom,* by writing in defence of the Truth, (which hath given such a blow unto that man of sin, as will not be healed,) and every day at home, by religious and learned discourse, by frequenting the house of God, by hearing the

Word preached, by cherishing the Teachers thereof, by caring for the Church, as a most tender and loving nursing Father.

There are infinite arguments of this right Christian and religious affection in Your Majesty; but none is more forcible to declare it to others than the vehement and perpetuated desire of accomplishing and publishing of this work, which now with all humility we present unto Your Majesty. For when Your Highness had once out of deep judgment apprehended how convenient it was, that out of the Original Sacred Tongues, together with comparing of the labours, both in our own, and other foreign Languages, of many worthy men who went before us, there should be one more exact Translation of the holy Scriptures into the *English Tongue;* Your Majesty did never desist to urge and to excite those to whom it was commended, that the work might be hastened, and that the business might be expedited in so decent a manner, as a matter of such importance might justly require.

And now at last, by the mercy of God, and the continuance of our labours, it being brought unto such a conclusion, as that we have great hopes that the Church of *England* shall reap good fruit thereby; we hold it our duty to offer it to Your Majesty, not only as to our King and Sovereign, but as to the principal Mover and Author of the work: humbly craving of Your most Sacred Majesty, that since things of this quality have ever been subject to the censures of illmeaning and discontented persons, it may re-

ceive approbation and patronage from so learned and judicious a Prince as Your Highness is, whose allowance and acceptance of our labours shall more honour and encourage us, than all the calumniations and hard interpretations of other men shall dismay us. So that if, on the one side, we shall be traduced by Popish Persons at home or abroad, who therefore will malign us, because we are poor instruments to make God's holy Truth to be yet more and more known unto the people, whom they desire still to keep in ignorance and darkness; or if, on the other side, we shall be maligned by self-conceited Brethren, who run their own ways, and give liking unto nothing, but what is framed by themselves, and hammered on their anvil; we may rest secure, supported within by the truth and innocency of a good conscience, having walked the ways of simplicity and integrity, as before the Lord; and sustained without by the powerful protection of Your Majesty's grace and favour, which will ever give countenance to honest and Christian endeavours against bitter censures and uncharitable imputations.

The Lord of heaven and earth bless Your Majesty with many and happy days, that, as his heavenly hand hath enriched Your Highness with many singular and extraordinary graces, so You may be the wonder of the world in this latter age for happiness and true felicity, to the honour of that great GOD, and the good of his Church, through Jesus Christ our Lord and only Saviour.

The
New Testament

S. Matthew

The genealogy of Jesus

1 The book of the generation of Jesus Christ, the son of David, the son of Abraham. ²Abraham begat Isaac; and Isaac begat Jacob; and Jacob begat Judas and his brethren; ³And Judas begat Phares and Zara of Thamar; and Phares begat Esrom; and Esrom begat Aram; ⁴And Aram begat Aminadab; and Aminadab begat Naasson; and Naasson begat Salmon; ⁵And Salmon begat Booz of Rachab; and Booz begat Obed of Ruth; and Obed begat Jesse; ⁶And Jesse begat David the king; and David the king begat Solomon of *her that had been the wife* of Urias; ⁷And Solomon begat Roboam; and Roboam begat Abia; and Abia begat Asa; ⁸And Asa begat Josaphat; and Josaphat begat Joram; and Joram begat Ozias; ⁹And Ozias begat Joatham; and Joatham begat Achaz; and Achaz begat Ezekias; ¹⁰And Ezekias begat Manasses; and Manasses begat Amon; and Amon begat Josias; ¹¹And Josias begat Jechonias and his brethren, about the time they were carried away to Babylon: ¹²And after they were brought to Babylon, Jechonias begat Salathiel; and Salathiel begat Zorobabel; ¹³And Zorobabel begat Abiud; and Abiud begat Eliakim; and Eliakim begat Azor; ¹⁴And Azor begat Sadoc; and Sadoc begat Achim; and Achim begat Eliud; ¹⁵And Eliud begat Eleazar; and Eleazar begat Matthan; and Matthan begat Jacob; ¹⁶And Jacob begat Joseph the husband of Mary, of whom was born Jesus, who is called Christ. ¹⁷So all the generations from Abraham to David *are* fourteen generations; and from David until the carrying away into Babylon *are* fourteen generations; and from the carrying away into Babylon unto Christ *are* fourteen generations.

The birth of Jesus

18 Now the birth of Jesus Christ was on this wise: When as his mother Mary was espoused to Joseph, before they came together, she was found with child of the Holy Ghost. ¹⁹Then Joseph her husband, being a just *man,* and not willing to make her a publick example, was minded to put her away privily. ²⁰But while he thought on these *things,* behold, *the* angel of the Lord appeared unto him in a dream, saying, Joseph, *thou* son of David, fear not to take unto *thee* Mary thy wife: for that which is conceived in her is of the Holy Ghost. ²¹And she shall bring forth a son, and thou shalt call his name JESUS: for he shall save his people from their sins. ²²Now all this was done, that it might be fulfilled which was spoken of the Lord by the prophet, saying, ²³Behold, a virgin shall be with child, and shall bring forth a son, and they shall call his name Emmanuel, which being interpreted is, God with us. ²⁴Then Joseph being raised from sleep did as the angel of the Lord had bidden him, and took unto *him* his wife:

25 And knew her not till she had brought forth her firstborn son: and *he* called his name JESUS. [Ex. 13:2; Luke 2:7,21]

The coming of the wise men

2 Now when Jesus was born in Bethlehem of Judea in the days of Herod the king, behold, there came wise men from the east to Jerusalem, 2 Saying, Where is he that is born King of the Jews? for we have seen his star in the east, and are come to worship him. 3 When Herod the king had heard *these things,* he was troubled, and all Jerusalem with him. 4 And when he had gathered all the chief priests and scribes of the people together, he demanded of them where Christ should be born. 5 And they said unto him, In Bethlehem of Judea: for thus it is written by the prophet, 6 And thou Bethlehem, *in* the land of Juda, art not the least among the princes of Juda: for out of thee shall come a Governor, that shall rule my people Israel. 7 Then Herod, when he had privily called the wise men, inquired of them diligently what time the star appeared. 8 And he sent them to Bethlehem, and said, Go and search diligently for the young child; and when ye have found *him,* bring me word again, that I may come and worship him also. 9 When they had heard the king, they departed; and lo, the star, which they saw in the east, went before them, till it came and stood over where the young child was. 10 When they saw the star, they rejoiced *with* exceeding great joy. 11 And when they were come into the house, they saw the young child with Mary his mother, and fell down, and worshipped him: and when they had opened their treasures, they presented unto him gifts; gold, and frankincense, and myrrh. 12 And being warned of God in a dream that *they* should not return to Herod, they departed into their own country another way. [ch. 1:20]

The flight into Egypt

13 And when they were departed, behold, *the* angel of the Lord appeareth to Joseph in a dream, saying, Arise, and take the young child and his mother, and flee into Egypt, and be thou there until I bring thee word: for Herod will seek the young child to destroy him. 14 When he arose, he took the young child and his mother by night, and departed into Egypt: 15 And was there until the death of Herod: that it might be fulfilled which was spoken of the Lord by the prophet, saying, Out of Egypt have I called my son. 16 Then Herod, when he saw that he was mocked of the wise men, was exceeding wroth, and sent forth, and slew all the children that were in Bethlehem, and in all the coasts thereof, from two years old and under, according to the time which he had diligently inquired of the wise men. 17 Then was fulfilled that which was spoken by Jeremie the prophet, saying, 18 In Rama was there a voice heard, lamentation, and weeping, and great mourning, Rachel weeping for her children, and would not be comforted, because they are not.

From Egypt to Nazareth

19 But when Herod was dead, behold, an angel of the Lord appeareth in a dream to Joseph in Egypt, 20Saying, Arise, and take the young child and his mother, and go into the land of Israel: for they are dead which sought the young child's life. 21And he arose, and took the young child and his mother, and came into the land of Israel. 22But when he heard that Archelaus did reign in Judea in the room of his father Herod, he was afraid to go thither: notwithstanding, being warned of God in a dream, he turned aside into the parts of Galilee: 23And he came and dwelt in a city called Nazareth: that it might be fulfilled which was spoken by the prophets, He shall be called a Nazarene. [John 1:45; Judg. 13:5; 1 Sam. 1:11]

John the Baptist

3 In those days came John the Baptist, preaching in the wilderness of Judea, 2And saying, Repent ye: for the kingdom of heaven is at hand. 3For this is he that was spoken of by the prophet Esaias, saying, The voice of one crying in the wilderness, Prepare ye the way of the Lord, make his paths straight. 4And the same John had his raiment of camel's hair, and a leathern girdle about his loins; and his meat was locusts and wild honey. 5Then went out to him Jerusalem, and all Judea, and all the region round about Jordan, 6And were baptized of him in Jordan, confessing their sins. 7But when he saw many of the Pharisees and Sadducees come to his baptism, he

said unto them, O generation of vipers, who hath warned you to flee from the wrath to come? 8Bring forth therefore fruits meet for repentance: 9And think not to say within yourselves, We have Abraham to *our* father: for I say unto you, that God is able of these stones to raise up children unto Abraham. 10And now also the axe is laid unto the root of the trees: therefore every tree which bringeth not forth good fruit is hewn down, and cast into the fire. 11I indeed baptize you with water unto repentance: but he that cometh after me is mightier than I, whose shoes I am not worthy to bear: he shall baptize you with the Holy Ghost, and *with* fire: 12Whose fan *is* in his hand, and he will throughly purge his floor, and gather his wheat into the garner; but will burn up the chaff with unquenchable fire. [Mal. 3:3; 4:1; ch. 13:30]

The baptism of Jesus

13 Then cometh Jesus from Galilee to Jordan unto John, to be baptized of him. 14But John forbad him, saying, I have need to be baptized of thee, and comest thou to me? 15And Jesus answering said unto him, Suffer *it to be so* now: for thus it becometh us to fulfil all righteousness. Then he suffered him. 16And Jesus, when he was baptized, went up straightway out of the water: and lo, the heavens were opened unto him, and he saw the Spirit of God descending like a dove, and lighting upon him: 17And lo a voice from heaven, saying, This is my beloved Son, in

whom I am well pleased. [John 12:28; Ps. 2:7; Is. 42:1; ch. 17:5; Mark 1:11; Luke 9:35; Eph. 1:6; Col. 1:13; 2 Pet. 1:17]

The temptation in the wilderness

4 Then was Jesus led up of the Spirit into the wilderness to be tempted of the devil. ²And when he had fasted forty days and forty nights, he was afterward a hungred. ³And when the tempter came to him, he said, If thou be the Son of God, command that these stones be made bread. ⁴But he answered and said, It is written, Man shall not live by bread alone, but by every word that proceedeth out of the mouth of God. ⁵Then the devil taketh him *up* into the holy city, and setteth him on a pinnacle of the temple, ⁶And saith unto him, If thou be the Son of God, cast thyself down: for it is written, He shall give his angels charge concerning thee: and in *their* hands they shall bear thee up, lest at any time thou dash thy foot against a stone. ⁷Jesus said unto him, It is written again, Thou shalt not tempt the Lord thy God. ⁸Again, the devil taketh him *up* into an exceeding high mountain, and sheweth him all the kingdoms of the world, and the glory of them; ⁹And saith unto him, All these *things* will I give thee, if thou wilt fall down and worship me. ¹⁰Then saith Jesus unto him, Get thee hence, Satan: for it is written, Thou shalt worship the Lord thy God, and him only shalt thou serve. ¹¹Then the devil leaveth him, and behold, angels came and ministered unto him. [Heb. 1:14]

The beginning of Jesus' ministry

12 Now when Jesus had heard that John was cast into prison, he departed into Galilee; ¹³And leaving Nazareth, he came and dwelt in Capernaum, which is upon the sea coast, in the borders of Zabulon and Nephthalim: ¹⁴That it might be fulfilled which was spoken by Esaias the prophet, saying, ¹⁵The land of Zabulon, and the land of Nephthalim, *by* the way of the sea, beyond Jordan, Galilee of the Gentiles; ¹⁶The people which sat in darkness saw great light; and to them which sat in the region and shadow of death light is sprung up. [Is. 42:7; Luke 2:32]

Jesus calls four disciples

17 From that time Jesus began to preach, and to say, Repent: for the kingdom of heaven is at hand. ¹⁸And Jesus, walking by the sea of Galilee, saw two brethren, Simon called Peter, and Andrew his brother, casting a net into the sea: for they were fishers. ¹⁹And he saith unto them, Follow me, and I will make you fishers of men. ²⁰And they straightway left *their* nets, and followed him. ²¹And going on from thence, he saw other two brethren, James the *son* of Zebedee, and John his brother, in a ship with Zebedee their father, mending their nets; and he called them. ²²And they immediately left the ship and their father, and followed him.

23 And Jesus went about all Galilee, teaching in their synagogues and preaching the gospel of the kingdom, and healing all *manner of* sickness and all *manner of* disease

among the people. ²⁴And his fame went throughout all Syria: and they brought unto him all sick people that were taken with divers diseases and torments, and those which were possessed with devils, and those which were lunatick, and those that had the palsy; and he healed them. ²⁵And there followed him great multitudes *of people* from Galilee, and *from* Decapolis, and *from* Jerusalem, and *from* Judea, and *from* beyond Jordan. [Mark 3:7]

The Beatitudes

5 And seeing the multitudes, he went up into a mountain: and when he was set, his disciples came unto him: ²And he opened his mouth, and taught them, saying, ³Blessed *are* the poor in spirit: for theirs is the kingdom of heaven. ⁴Blessed *are* they that mourn: for they shall be comforted. ⁵Blessed *are* the meek: for they shall inherit the earth. ⁶Blessed *are* they which do hunger and thirst after righteousness: for they shall be filled. ⁷Blessed *are* the merciful: for they shall obtain mercy. ⁸Blessed *are* the pure in heart: for they shall see God. ⁹Blessed *are* the peacemakers: for they shall be called the children of God. ¹⁰Blessed *are* they which are persecuted for righteousness' sake: for theirs is the kingdom of heaven. ¹¹Blessed are ye, when *men* shall revile you, and persecute *you,* and shall say all manner of evil against you falsely, for my sake. ¹²Rejoice, and be exceeding glad: for great *is* your reward in heaven: for so persecuted they the prophets which

were before you. [Luke 6:23; Acts 5:41; 1 Pet. 4:13; Neh. 9:26; Acts 7:52]

Teaching about salt and light

13 Ye are the salt of the earth: but if the salt have lost his savour, wherewith shall it be salted? it is thenceforth good for nothing, but to be cast out, and to be trodden under foot of men. ¹⁴Ye are the light of the world. A city that is set on a hill cannot be hid. ¹⁵Neither do men light a candle, and put it under a bushel, but on a candlestick; and it giveth light unto all that are in the house. ¹⁶Let your light so shine before men, that they may see your good works, and glorify your Father which is in heaven. [1 Pet. 2:12; John 15:8; 1 Cor. 14:25]

The higher righteousness

17 Think not that I am come to destroy the law, or the prophets: I am not come to destroy, but to fulfil. ¹⁸For verily I say unto you, Till heaven and earth pass, one jot or one tittle shall in no wise pass from the law, till all be fulfilled. ¹⁹Whosoever therefore shall break one of these least commandments, and shall teach men so, he shall be called the least in the kingdom of heaven: but whosoever shall do and teach *them,* the same shall be called great in the kingdom of heaven. ²⁰For I say unto you, That except your righteousness shall exceed *the righteousness* of the scribes and Pharisees, ye shall in no case enter into the kingdom of heaven. [Rom. 10:3]

Anger and reconciliation; adultery and divorce

21 Ye have heard that it was said by them of old time, Thou shalt not kill; and whosoever shall kill shall be in danger of the judgment: 22But I say unto you, That whosoever is angry with his brother without a cause shall be in danger of the judgment: and whosoever shall say to his brother, Raca, shall be in danger of the council: but whosoever shall say, *Thou* fool, shall be in danger of hell fire. 23Therefore if thou bring thy gift to the altar, and there rememberest that thy brother hath ought against thee; 24Leave there thy gift before the altar, and go thy way; first be reconciled to thy brother, and then come and offer thy gift. 25Agree with thine adversary quickly, whiles thou art in the way with him; lest at any time the adversary deliver thee to the judge, and the judge deliver thee to the officer, and thou be cast into prison. 26Verily I say unto thee, Thou shalt by no means come out thence, till thou hast paid the uttermost farthing. 27Ye have heard that it was said by them of old time, Thou shalt not commit adultery: 28But I say unto you, That whosoever looketh on a woman to lust after her hath committed adultery with her already in his heart. 29And if thy right eye offend thee, pluck it out, and cast *it* from thee: for it is profitable for thee that one of thy members should perish, and not *that* thy whole body should be cast into hell. 30And if thy right hand offend thee, cut it off, and cast *it* from thee: for it is profitable for thee that one of thy members should perish, and not *that* thy whole body should be cast into hell. 31It hath been said, Whosoever shall put away his wife, let him give her a writing of divorcement: 32But I say unto you, That whosoever shall put away his wife, saving for the cause of fornication, causeth her to commit adultery: and whosoever shall marry her that is divorced committeth adultery. [Luke 16:18; Rom. 7:3]

Oaths and retaliation

33 Again, ye have heard that it hath been said by them of old time, Thou shalt not forswear thyself, but shalt perform unto the Lord thine oaths: 34But I say unto you, Swear not at all; neither by heaven; for it is God's throne: 35Nor by the earth; for it is his footstool: neither by Jerusalem; for it is the city of the great King. 36Neither shalt thou swear by thy head, because thou canst not make one hair white or black. 37But let your communication be, Yea, yea; Nay, nay: for whatsoever is more than these cometh of evil. [Col. 4:6; Jas. 5:12]

38 Ye have heard that it hath been said, An eye for an eye, and a tooth for a tooth: 39But I say unto you, That *ye* resist not evil: but whosoever shall smite thee on thy right cheek, turn to him the other also. 40And if any man will sue thee at the law, and take *away* thy coat, let him have *thy* cloke also. 41And whosoever shall compel thee to go a mile, go with him twain. 42Give to him that asketh thee, and from

him that would borrow of thee turn not thou away. [Deut. 15:8; Luke 6:30]

Neighbours and enemies

43 Ye have heard that it hath been said, Thou shalt love thy neighbour, and hate thine enemy. 44But I say unto you, Love your enemies, bless them that curse you, do good to them that hate you, and pray for them which despitefully use you, and persecute you; 45That ye may be the children of your Father which is in heaven: for he maketh his sun to rise on the evil and *on* the good, and sendeth rain on the just and *on* the unjust. 46For if ye love them which love you, what reward have ye? do not even the publicans the same? 47And if ye salute your brethren only, what do ye more *than others?* do not even the publicans so? 48Be ye therefore perfect, even as your Father which is in heaven is perfect. [Gen. 17:1; Lev. 11:44; 19:2; Luke 6:36; Col. 1:28; 4:12; Jas. 1:4; 1 Pet. 1:15; Eph. 5:1]

Piety and almsgiving

6 Take heed that *ye* do not your alms before men, to be seen of them: otherwise ye have no reward of your Father which is in heaven. 2Therefore when thou doest *thine* alms, do not sound a trumpet before thee, as the hypocrites do in the synagogues and in the streets, that they may have glory of men. Verily I say unto you, They have their reward. 3But when thou doest alms, let not thy left hand know what thy right hand doeth: 4That thine alms may be in secret: and thy Father which seeth in secret himself shall reward thee openly. [Luke 14:14]

Prayer and fasting

5 And when thou prayest, thou shalt not be as the hypocrites *are:* for they love to pray standing in the synagogues and in the corners of the streets, that they may be seen of men. Verily I say unto you, They have their reward. 6But thou, when thou prayest, enter into thy closet, and when thou hast shut thy door, pray to thy Father which is in secret; and thy Father which seeth in secret shall reward thee openly. 7But when ye pray, use not vain repetitions, as the heathen *do:* for they think that they shall be heard for their much speaking. 8Be not ye therefore like unto them: for your Father knoweth what *things* ye have need of, before ye ask him. 9After this manner therefore pray ye: Our Father which art in heaven, Hallowed be thy name. 10Thy kingdom come. Thy will be done in earth, as *it is* in heaven. 11Give us this day our daily bread. 12And forgive us our debts, as we forgive our debtors. 13And lead us not into temptation, but deliver us from evil: For thine is the kingdom, and the power, and the glory, for ever. Amen. [ch. 26:41; 1 Cor. 10:13; 2 Pet. 2:9; Rev. 3:10; John 17:15; 1 Chr. 29:11]

14 For if ye forgive men their trespasses, your heavenly Father will also forgive you: 15But if ye forgive not men their trespasses, neither will your Father forgive your trespasses. [ch. 18:35; Jas. 2:13]

16 Moreover when ye fast, be not as the hypocrites, of a sad countenance: for they disfigure their faces, that they may appear unto men to fast. Verily I say unto you,

They have their reward. ¹⁷But thou, when thou fastest, anoint thine head, and wash thy face; ¹⁸That thou appear not unto men to fast, but unto thy Father which is in secret: and thy Father, which seeth in secret, shall reward thee openly.

Possessions and masters

19 Lay not up for yourselves treasures upon earth, where moth and rust doth corrupt, and where thieves break through and steal: ²⁰But lay up for yourselves treasures in heaven, where neither moth nor rust doth corrupt, and where thieves do not break through nor steal: ²¹For where your treasure is, there will your heart be also. ²²The light of the body is the eye: if therefore thine eye be single, thy whole body shall be full of light. ²³But if thine eye be evil, thy whole body shall be full of darkness. If therefore the light that is in thee be darkness, how great *is* that darkness?

Anxiety and God's kingdom

24 No *man* can serve two masters: for either he will hate the one, and love the other; or else he will hold to the one, and despise the other. Ye cannot serve God and mammon. ²⁵Therefore I say unto you, Take no thought for your life, what ye shall eat, or what ye shall drink; nor yet for your body, what ye shall put on. Is not the life more than meat, and the body than raiment? ²⁶Behold the fowls of the air: for they sow not, neither do they reap, nor gather into barns; yet your heavenly Father feedeth them. Are ye not much better than they?

²⁷Which of you by taking thought can add one cubit unto his stature? ²⁸And why take ye thought for raiment? Consider the lilies of the field, how they grow; they toil not, neither do they spin: ²⁹And yet I say unto you, That even Solomon in all his glory was not arrayed like one of these. ³⁰Wherefore, if God so clothe the grass of the field, which to day is, and to morrow is cast into the oven, *shall he* not much more *clothe* you, O ye of little faith? ³¹Therefore take no thought, saying, What shall we eat? or, What shall we drink? or, Wherewithal shall we be clothed? ³²(For after all these *things* do the Gentiles seek): for your heavenly Father knoweth that ye have need of all these *things.* ³³But seek ye first the kingdom of God, and his righteousness; and all these *things* shall be added unto you. ³⁴Take therefore no thought for the morrow: for the morrow shall take thought for the *things* of itself. Sufficient unto the day *is* the evil thereof.

Judging and hypocrisy

7 Judge not, that ye be not judged. ²For with what judgment ye judge, ye shall be judged: and with what measure ye mete, it shall be measured to you again. ³And why beholdest thou the mote that is in thy brother's eye, but considerest not the beam that is in thine own eye? ⁴Or how wilt thou say to thy brother, Let me pull out the mote out of thine eye; and behold, a beam *is* in thine own eye? ⁵*Thou* hypocrite, first cast out the beam out of thine own eye; and then shalt

thou see clearly to cast out the mote out of thy brother's eye.

6 Give not that which is holy unto the dogs, neither cast ye your pearls before swine, lest they trample them under their feet, and turn *again* and rent you. [Prov. 9:7,8; 23:9; Acts 13:45]

Prayer and the Golden Rule

7 Ask, and it shall be given you; seek, and ye shall find; knock, and it shall be opened unto you: 8For every one that asketh receiveth; and he that seeketh findeth: and to him that knocketh it shall be opened. 9Or what man is there of you, whom if his son ask bread, will he give him a stone? 10Or if he ask a fish, will he give him a serpent? 11If ye then, being evil, know how to give good gifts unto your children, how much more shall your Father which is in heaven give good *things* to them that ask him? 12Therefore all *things* whatsoever ye would that men should do to you, do ye even so to them: for this is the law and the prophets. [Luke 6:31; Lev. 19:18; ch. 22:40; Rom. 13:8; Gal. 5:14; 1 Tim. 1:5]

The strait and wide gates

13 Enter ye in at the strait gate: for wide *is* the gate, and broad *is* the way, that leadeth to destruction, and many there be which go in thereat: 14Because strait *is* the gate, and narrow *is* the way, which leadeth unto life, and few there be that find it.

The test of false prophets

15 Beware of false prophets, which come to you in sheep's clothing, but inwardly they are ravening wolves. 16Ye shall know them by their fruits. Do *men* gather grapes of thorns, or figs of thistles? 17*Even* so every good tree bringeth forth good fruit; but a corrupt tree bringeth forth evil fruit. 18A good tree cannot bring forth evil fruit, neither *can* a corrupt tree bring forth good fruit. 19Every tree that bringeth not forth good fruit is hewn down, and cast into the fire. 20Wherefore by their fruits ye shall know them.

21 Not every one that saith unto me, Lord, Lord, shall enter into the kingdom of heaven; but he that doeth the will of my Father which is in heaven. 22Many will say to me in that day, Lord, Lord, have we not prophesied in thy name? and in thy name have cast out devils? and in thy name done many wonderful works? 23And then will I profess unto them, I never knew you: depart from me, ye that work iniquity. [ch. 25:12; Luke 13:25; 2 Tim. 2:19; Ps. 5:5; 6:8; ch. 25:41]

The wise and foolish builders

24 Therefore whosoever heareth these sayings of mine, and doeth them, I will liken him unto a wise man, which built his house upon a rock: 25And the rain descended, and the floods came, and the winds blew, and beat upon that house; and it fell not: for it was founded upon a rock. 26And every one that heareth these sayings of mine, and doeth them not, shall be likened unto a foolish man, which built his house upon the sand: 27And the rain descended, and the

floods came, and the winds blew, and beat upon that house; and it fell: and great was the fall of it. 28And it came to pass, when Jesus had ended these sayings, the people were astonished at his doctrine: 29For he taught them as *one* having authority, and not as the scribes. [John 7:46]

The leper cleansed

8 When he was come down from the mountain, great multitudes followed him. 2And behold, there came a leper and worshipped him, saying, Lord, if thou wilt, thou canst make me clean. 3And Jesus put forth *his* hand, and touched him, saying, I will; be thou clean. And immediately his leprosy was cleansed. 4And Jesus saith unto him, See thou tell no *man;* but go thy way, shew thyself to the priest, and offer the gift that Moses commanded for a testimony unto them. [ch. 9:30; Mark 5:43; Lev. 14:3,4,10; Luke 5:14]

The centurion's servant healed

5 And when Jesus was entered into Capernaum, there came unto him a centurion, beseeching him, 6And saying, Lord, my servant lieth at home sick of the palsy, grievously tormented. 7And Jesus saith unto him, I will come and heal him. 8The centurion answered and said, Lord, I am not worthy that thou shouldest come under my roof: but speak the word only, and my servant shall be healed. 9For I am a man under authority, having soldiers under me: and I say to this *man,* Go, and he goeth; and to another, Come, and he cometh; and to my servant, Do this, and he doeth *it.* 10When Jesus heard *it,* he marvelled, and said to them that followed, Verily I say unto you, I have not found so great faith, no not in Israel. 11And I say unto you, That many shall come from the east and west, and shall sit down with Abraham, and Isaac, and Jacob, in the kingdom of heaven. 12But the children of the kingdom shall be cast out into outer darkness: there shall be weeping and gnashing of teeth. 13And Jesus said unto the centurion, Go thy way; and as thou hast believed, *so* be it done unto thee. And his servant was healed in the selfsame hour.

Peter's mother-in-law healed

14 And when Jesus was come into Peter's house, he saw his wife's mother laid, and sick of a fever. 15And he touched her hand, and the fever left her: and she arose, and ministered unto them. 16When the even was come, they brought unto him many *that* were possessed with devils: and he cast out the spirits with *his* word, and healed all that were sick: 17That it might be fulfilled which was spoken by Esaias the prophet, saying Himself took our infirmities, and bare our sicknesses. [Is. 53:4; 1 Pet. 2:24]

Teaching about discipleship

18 Now when Jesus saw great multitudes about him, he gave commandment to depart unto the other side. 19And a certain scribe came, and said unto him, Master, I will follow thee whithersoever thou goest. 20And Jesus saith unto him, The foxes have holes, and the birds

of the air *have* nests; but the Son of man hath not where to lay *his* head. 21And another of his disciples said unto him, Lord, suffer me first to go and bury my father. 22But Jesus said unto him, Follow me; and let the dead bury their dead.

The storm stilled

23 And when he was entered into a ship, his disciples followed him. 24And behold, there arose a great tempest in the sea, insomuch that the ship was covered with the waves: but he was asleep. 25And his disciples came to *him,* and awoke him, saying, Lord, save us: we perish. 26And he saith unto them, Why are ye fearful, O ye of little faith? Then he arose, and rebuked the winds and the sea; and there was a great calm. 27But the men marvelled, saying, What manner of man is this, that even the winds and the sea obey him?

Devils cast out

28 And when he was come to the other side into the country of the Gergesenes, there met him two possessed with devils, coming out of the tombs, exceeding fierce, so that no *man* might pass by that way. 29And behold, they cried out, saying, What have we to do with thee, Jesus, *thou* Son of God? art thou come hither to torment us before the time? 30And there was a good way off from them a herd of many swine feeding. 31So the devils besought him, saying, If thou cast us out, suffer us to go away into the herd of swine. 32And he said unto them, Go. And when they were come out, they went into the herd of swine: and behold, the whole herd of swine ran violently down a steep place into the sea, and perished in the waters. 33And they that kept *them,* fled, and went their ways into the city, and told every *thing,* and what was befallen to the possessed of the devils. 34And behold, the whole city came out to meet Jesus: and when they saw him, they besought *him* that he would depart out of their coasts. [See Deut. 5:25; 1 Ki. 17:18; Luke 5:8; Acts 16:39]

A man with palsy healed

9 And he entered into a ship, and passed over, and came into his own city. 2And behold, they brought to him a man sick of the palsy, lying on a bed: and Jesus seeing their faith said unto the sick of the palsy; Son, be of good cheer; thy sins be forgiven thee. 3And behold, certain of the scribes said within themselves, This *man* blasphemeth. 4And Jesus knowing their thoughts said, Wherefore think ye evil in your hearts? 5For whether is easier, to say, *Thy* sins be forgiven thee; or to say, Arise, and walk? 6But that ye may know that the Son of man hath power on earth to forgive sins, (then saith he to the sick of the palsy,) Arise, take up thy bed, and go unto thine house. 7And he arose, and departed to his house. 8But when the multitudes saw *it,* they marvelled, and glorified God, which had given such power unto men.

Matthew called

9 And as Jesus passed forth from thence, he saw a man, named

Matthew, sitting at the receipt of custom: and he saith unto him, Follow me. And he arose, and followed him. 10And it came to pass, as Jesus sat at meat in the house, behold, many publicans and sinners came and sat down with him and his disciples. 11And when the Pharisees saw *it,* they said unto his disciples, Why eateth your Master with publicans and sinners? 12But when Jesus heard *that,* he said unto them, They that be whole need not a physician, but they that are sick. 13But go ye and learn what *that* meaneth, I will have mercy, and not sacrifice: for I am not come to call *the* righteous, but sinners to repentance. [Hos. 6:6; Mic. 6:6-8; ch. 12:7; 1 Tim. 1:15]

The question about fasting

14 Then came to him the disciples of John, saying, Why do we and the Pharisees fast oft, but thy disciples fast not? 15And Jesus said unto them, Can the children of the bridechamber mourn, as long as the bridegroom is with them? but the days will come, when the bridegroom shall be taken from them, and then shall they fast. 16No *man* putteth a piece of new cloth unto an old garment; for that which is put in to fill it up taketh from the garment, and the rent is made worse. 17Neither do *men* put new wine into old bottles: else the bottles break, and the wine runneth out, and the bottles perish: but they put new wine into new bottles, and both are preserved.

A ruler's daughter raised

18 While he spake these *things* unto them, behold, there came a *certain* ruler, and worshipped him, saying, My daughter is even now dead: but come and lay thy hand upon her, and she shall live. 19And Jesus arose, and followed him, and *so did* his disciples. 20(And behold, a woman, which was diseased with an issue of blood twelve years, came behind *him,* and touched the hem of his garment: 21For she said within herself, If I may but touch his garment, I shall be whole. 22But Jesus turned him about, and when he saw her, he said, Daughter, be of good comfort; thy faith hath made thee whole. And the woman was made whole from that hour.) 23And when Jesus came into the ruler's house, and saw the minstrels and the people making a noise, 24He said unto them, Give place: for the maid is not dead, but sleepeth. And they laughed him to scorn. 25But when the people were put forth, he went in, and took her by the hand, and the maid arose. 26And the fame hereof went abroad into all that land.

27 And when Jesus departed thence, two blind men followed him, crying, and saying, *Thou* Son of David, have mercy on us. 28And when he was come into the house, the blind men came to him: and Jesus saith unto them, Believe ye that I am able to do this? They said unto him, Yea, Lord. 29Then touched he their eyes, saying, According to your faith be it unto you. 30And their eyes were opened; and Jesus straitly charged them, saying, See *that* no *man* know *it.* 31But they, when they

were departed, spread abroad his fame in all that country. [Mark 7:36]

The need for labourers

32 As they went out, behold, they brought to him a dumb man possessed with a devil. **33** And when the devil was cast out, the dumb spake: and the multitudes marvelled, saying, It was never so seen in Israel. **34** But the Pharisees said, He casteth out the devils through the prince of the devils. **35** And Jesus went about all the cities and villages, teaching in their synagogues, and preaching the gospel of the kingdom, and healing every sickness and every disease among the people. **36** But when he saw the multitudes, he was moved with compassion on them, because they fainted, and were scattered abroad, as sheep having no shepherd. **37** Then saith he unto his disciples, The harvest truly is plenteous, but the labourers *are* few; **38** Pray ye therefore the Lord of the harvest, that he will send forth labourers into his harvest. [2 Thes. 3:1]

The mission of the twelve

10 And when he had called unto *him* his twelve disciples, he gave them power against unclean spirits, to cast them out, and to heal all *manner of* sickness and all *manner of* disease. **2** Now the names of the twelve apostles are these; The first, Simon, who is called Peter, and Andrew his brother; James the *son* of Zebedee, and John his brother; **3** Philip, and Bartholomew; Thomas, and Matthew the publican; James the *son* of Alpheus, and Lebbeus, whose sur-

name was Thaddeus; **4** Simon the Canaanite, and Judas Iscariot, who also betrayed him. **5** These twelve Jesus sent forth, and commanded them, saying, Go not into the way of the Gentiles, and into *any* city of the Samaritans enter ye not: **6** But go rather to the lost sheep of the house of Israel. **7** And as ye go, preach, saying, The kingdom of heaven is at hand. **8** Heal the sick, cleanse the lepers, raise the dead, cast out devils: freely ye have received, freely give. **9** Provide neither gold, nor silver, nor brass in your purses; **10** Nor scrip for *your* journey, neither two coats, neither shoes, nor yet staves: for the workman is worthy of his meat. **11** And into whatsoever city or town ye shall enter, inquire who in it is worthy; and there abide till ye go thence. **12** And when ye come into a house salute it. **13** And if the house be worthy, let your peace come upon it: but if it be not worthy, let your peace return to you. **14** And whosoever shall not receive you, nor hear your words, when ye depart out of that house or city, shake off the dust of your feet. **15** Verily I say unto you, It shall be more tolerable for the land of Sodom and Gomorrha in the day of judgment, than for that city. [ch. 11:22]

16 Behold, I send you forth as sheep in the midst of wolves: be ye therefore wise as serpents, and harmless as doves. **17** But beware of men: for they will deliver you up to the councils, and they will scourge you in their synagogues; **18** And ye shall be brought before governors and kings for my sake, for a testimony against them and the Gentiles. ¹⁹But when they deliver you up, take no thought how or what ye shall speak: for it shall be given you in that *same* hour what ye shall speak. ²⁰For it is not ye that speak, but the Spirit of your Father which speaketh in you. ²¹And the brother shall deliver up the brother to death, and the father the child: and the children shall rise up against *their* parents, and cause them to be put to death. ²²And ye shall be hated of all *men* for my name's sake: but he that endureth to the end shall be saved. ²³But when they persecute you in this city, flee ye into another: for verily I say unto you, Ye shall not have gone over the cities of Israel, till the Son of man be come. ²⁴The disciple is not above *his* master, nor the servant above his lord. ²⁵*It is* enough for the disciple that he be as his master, and the servant as his lord. If they have called the master of the house Beelzebub, how much more *shall they call* them of his household? ²⁶Fear them not therefore: for there is nothing covered, that shall not be revealed; and hid, that shall not be known. ²⁷What I tell you in darkness, *that* speak ye in light: and what ye hear in the ear, *that* preach ye upon the housetops. ²⁸And fear not them which kill the body, but are not able to kill the soul: but rather fear him which is able to destroy both soul and body in hell. ²⁹Are not two sparrows sold for a farthing? and one of them shall not fall on the ground without your Father. ³⁰But the very hairs of your head are all numbered. ³¹Fear ye not therefore, ye are of more value than many sparrows. ³²Whosoever therefore shall confess me before men, him will I confess also before my Father which is in heaven. ³³But whosoever shall deny me before men, him will I also deny before my Father which is in heaven. [Luke 9:26; 2 Tim. 2:12]

34 Think not that I am come to send peace on earth: I came not to send peace, but a sword. ³⁵For I am come to set a man at variance against his father, and the daughter against her mother, and the daughter in law against her mother in law. ³⁶And a man's foes *shall be* they of his own household. ³⁷He that loveth father or mother more than me is not worthy of me: and he that loveth son or daughter more than me is not worthy of me. ³⁸And he that taketh not his cross, and followeth after me, is not worthy of me. ³⁹He that findeth his life shall lose it: and he that loseth his life for my sake shall find it. [Luke 17:33; John 12:25]

40 He that receiveth you receiveth me, and he that receiveth me receiveth him that sent me. ⁴¹He that receiveth a prophet in the name of a prophet shall receive a prophet's reward; and he that receiveth a righteous *man* in the name of a righteous *man* shall receive a righteous *man's* reward. ⁴²And whosoever shall give to drink unto one of these little ones a cup of cold *water* only in the name of a disciple, verily I say unto you, he shall in no wise lose his reward. [ch. 25:40; Mark 9:41; Heb. 6:10]

Tribute to John the Baptist

11 And it came to pass, when Jesus had made an end of commanding his twelve disciples, he departed thence to teach and to preach in their cities. ²Now when John had heard in the prison the works of Christ, he sent two of his disciples, ³And said unto him, Art thou he that should come, or do we look for another? ⁴Jesus answered and said unto them, Go and shew John again *those things* which ye do hear and see: ⁵The blind receive their sight, and the lame walk, the lepers are cleansed, and the deaf hear, the dead are raised up, and the poor have the gospel preached to them. ⁶And blessed is *he*, whosoever shall not be offended in me. [Is. 8:14,15; Rom. 9:32; 1 Pet. 2:8]

7 And as they departed, Jesus began to say unto the multitudes concerning John, What went ye out into the wilderness to see? A reed shaken with the wind? ⁸But what went ye out for to see? A man clothed in soft raiment? behold, they that wear soft *clothing* are in kings' houses. ⁹But what went ye out for to see? A prophet? yea, I say unto you, and more than a prophet. ¹⁰For this is *he*, of whom it is written, Behold, I send my messenger before thy face, which shall prepare thy way before thee. ¹¹Verily I say unto you, Among *them that are* born of women there hath not risen a greater than John the Baptist: notwithstanding he that is least in the kingdom of heaven is greater than he. ¹²And from the days of John the Baptist until now the kingdom of heaven suffereth violence, and the violent take it by force. ¹³For all the prophets and the law prophesied until John. ¹⁴And if ye will receive *it*, this is Elias, which was for to come. ¹⁵He that hath ears to hear, let him hear. [ch. 13:9; Luke 8:8; Rev. 2:7,11,17,29; 3:6,13]

16 But whereunto shall I liken this generation? It is like unto children sitting in the markets, and calling unto their fellows, ¹⁷And saying, We have piped unto you, and ye have not danced; we have mourned unto you, and ye have not lamented. ¹⁸For John came neither eating nor drinking, and they say, He hath a devil. ¹⁹The Son of man came eating and drinking, and they say, Behold a man gluttonous, and a winebibber, a friend of publicans and sinners. But wisdom is justified of her children. [ch. 9:10; Luke 7:35]

The judgment of the unrepentant

20 Then began he to upbraid the cities wherein most of his mighty works were done, because they repented not. ²¹Woe unto thee, Chorazin, woe unto thee, Bethsaida: for if the mighty works which were done in you, had been done in Tyre and Sidon they would have repented long ago in sackcloth and ashes. ²²But I say unto you, It shall be more tolerable for Tyre and Sidon at the day of judgment, than for you. ²³And thou, Capernaum, which art exalted unto heaven, shalt be brought down to hell: for if the mighty works, which have been done in thee, had been done in Sodom, it

would have remained until this day. 24But I say unto you, that it shall be more tolerable for the land of Sodom in the day of judgment, than for thee. [ch. 10:15]

Jesus reveals the Father

25 At that time Jesus answered and said, I thank thee, O Father, Lord of heaven and earth, because thou hast hid these *things* from the wise and prudent, and hast revealed them unto babes. 26Even so, Father: for so it seemed good in thy sight. 27All *things* are delivered unto me of my Father: and no *man* knoweth the Son, but the Father; neither knoweth any *man* the Father, save the Son, and *he* to whomsoever the Son will reveal *him*. [ch. 28:18; Luke 10:22; John 3:35; 13:3; 17:2; 1 Cor. 15:27; John 1:18; 6:46; 10:15]

28 Come unto me, all *ye* that labour and are heavy laden, and I will give you rest. 29Take my yoke upon you, and learn of me; for I am meek and lowly in heart: and ye shall find rest unto your souls. 30For my yoke *is* easy, and my burden is light. [1 John 5:3]

Jesus the Lord of the sabbath

12 At that time Jesus went on the sabbath day through the corn; and his disciples were a hungred, and began to pluck the ears of corn, and to eat. 2But when the Pharisees saw *it*, they said unto him, Behold, thy disciples do *that* which is not lawful to do upon the sabbath day. 3But he said unto them, Have ye not read what David did, when he was a hungred, and they that were with him; 4How he entered into the house of God, and did eat the shewbread, which was not lawful for him to eat, neither for them which were with him, but only for the priests? 5Or have ye not read in the law, how that on the sabbath days the priests in the temple profane the sabbath, and are blameless? 6But I say unto you, That in this place is *one* greater than the temple. 7But if ye had known what *this* meaneth, I will have mercy, and not sacrifice, ye would not have condemned the guiltless. 8For the Son of man is Lord even of the sabbath day.

9 And when he was departed thence, he went into their synagogue: 10And behold, there was a man which had *his* hand withered. And they asked him, saying, Is it lawful to heal on the sabbath days? that they might accuse him. 11And he said unto them, What man shall there be among you, that shall have one sheep, and if it fall into a pit on the sabbath day, will he not lay hold on it, and lift *it* out? 12How much then is a man better than a sheep? Wherefore it is lawful to do well on the sabbath days. 13Then saith he to the man, Stretch forth thine hand. And he stretched *it* forth; and it was restored whole, *like* as the other.

Jesus heals many

14 Then the Pharisees went out, and held a council against him, how they might destroy him. 15But when Jesus knew *it*, he withdrew himself from thence: and great multitudes followed him, and he healed them all, 16And charged them that they should not make

him known: 17That it might be fulfilled which was spoken by Esaias the prophet, saying, 18Behold my servant, whom I have chosen; my beloved, in whom my soul is well pleased: I will put my spirit upon him, and he shall shew judgment to the Gentiles. 19He shall not strive, nor cry; neither shall any *man* hear his voice in the streets. 20A bruised reed shall he not break, and smoking flax shall he not quench, till he send forth judgment unto victory. 21And in his name shall the Gentiles trust.

The Pharisees' slander

22 Then was brought unto him one possessed with a devil, blind, and dumb: and he healed him, insomuch that the blind and dumb both spake and saw. 23And all the people were amazed, and said, Is this the son of David? 24But when the Pharisees heard *it,* they said, This *fellow* doth not cast out devils, but by Beelzebub the prince of the devils. 25And Jesus knew their thoughts, and said unto them, Every kingdom divided against itself is brought to desolation; and every city or house divided against itself shall not stand: 26And if Satan cast out Satan, he is divided against himself; how shall then his kingdom stand? 27And if I by Beelzebub cast out devils, by whom do your children cast *them* out? therefore they shall be your judges. 28But if I cast out devils by the Spirit of God, then the kingdom of God is come unto you. 29Or else how can one enter into a strong *man's* house, and spoil his goods, except he first bind the strong *man?* and then he will spoil his house. 30He that is not with me is against me; and he that gathereth not with me scattereth abroad. 31Wherefore I say unto you, All *manner of* sin and blasphemy shall be forgiven unto men: but the blasphemy against the *Holy* Ghost shall not be forgiven unto men. 32And whosoever speaketh a word against the Son of man, it shall be forgiven him: but whosoever speaketh against the Holy Ghost, it shall not be forgiven him, neither in this world, neither in the *world* to come. 33Either make the tree good, and his fruit good; or else make the tree corrupt, and his fruit corrupt: for the tree is known by *his* fruit. 34O generation of vipers, how can ye, being evil, speak good *things?* for out of the abundance of the heart the mouth speaketh. 35A good man out of the good treasure of the heart bringeth forth good *things:* and an evil man out of the evil treasure bringeth forth evil *things.* 36But I say unto you, That every idle word that men shall speak, they shall give account thereof in the day of judgment. 37For by thy words thou shalt be justified, and by thy words thou shalt be condemned.

Warning against seeking signs

38 Then certain of the scribes and of the Pharisees answered, saying, Master, we would see a sign from thee. 39But he answered and said to them, An evil and adulterous generation seeketh after a sign; and there shall no sign be given to

it, but the sign of the prophet Jonas: ⁴⁰For as Jonas was three days and three nights in the whale's belly; so shall the Son of man be three days and three nights in the heart of the earth. ⁴¹*The* men of Nineveh shall rise in judgment with this generation, and shall condemn it: because they repented at the preaching of Jonas; and behold, a greater than Jonas *is* here. ⁴²*The* queen of the south shall rise up in the judgment with this generation, and shall condemn it: for she came from the uttermost parts of the earth to hear the wisdom of Solomon; and behold, a greater than Solomon *is* here. [1 Ki. 10:1; 2 Chr. 9:1; Luke 11:31]

43 When the unclean spirit is gone out of a man, he walketh through dry places, seeking rest, and findeth none. ⁴⁴Then he saith, I will return into my house from whence I came out; and when he is come, he findeth *it* empty, swept, and garnished. ⁴⁵Then goeth he, and taketh with himself seven other spirits more wicked than himself, and they enter in and dwell there: and the last *state* of that man is worse than the first. *Even* so shall it be also unto this wicked generation. [Heb. 6:4; 10:26; 2 Pet. 2:20-22]

Jesus' true family

46 While he yet talked to the people, behold, *his* mother and his brethren stood without, desiring to speak with him. ⁴⁷Then one said unto him, Behold, thy mother and thy brethren stand without, desiring to speak with thee. ⁴⁸But he answered and said unto him that told him, Who is my mother? and who are my brethren? ⁴⁹And he stretched forth his hand toward his disciples, and said, Behold my mother and my brethren! ⁵⁰For whosoever shall do the will of my Father which is in heaven, the same is my brother, and sister, and mother. [See John 15:14; Gal. 5:6; 6:15; Col. 3:11; Heb. 2:11]

The parable of the sower

13 The same day went Jesus out of the house, and sat by the sea side. ²And great multitudes were gathered together unto him, so that he went into a ship, and sat; and the whole multitude stood on the shore. ³And he spake many *things* unto them in parables, saying, Behold, a sower went forth to sow; ⁴And when he sowed, some *seeds* fell by the way side, and the fowls came and devoured them up: ⁵Some fell upon stony *places,* where they had not much earth: and forthwith they sprung up, because *they* had no deepness of earth: ⁶And when the sun was up, they were scorched; and because *they* had not root, they withered away. ⁷And some fell among thorns; and the thorns sprung up, and choked them: ⁸But other fell into good ground, and brought forth fruit, some an hundred*fold,* some sixty*fold,* some thirty*fold.* ⁹Who hath ears to hear, let him hear. [ch. 11:15; Mark 4:9]

10 And the disciples came, and said unto him, Why speakest thou unto them in parables? ¹¹He answered and said unto them, Be-

cause it is given unto you to know the mysteries of the kingdom of heaven, but to them it is not given. 12For whosoever hath, to him shall be given, and he shall have *more* abundance: but whosoever hath not, from him shall be taken away even that he hath. 13Therefore speak I to them in parables: because they seeing see not; and hearing they hear not, neither do they understand. 14And in them is fulfilled the prophecy of Esaias, which saith, By hearing ye shall hear, and shall not understand; and seeing ye shall see, and shall not perceive: 15For this people's heart is waxed gross, and *their* ears are dull of hearing, and their eyes they have closed; lest at any time they should see with *their* eyes, and hear with *their* ears, and should understand with *their* heart, and should be converted, and I should heal them. 16But blessed *are* your eyes, for they see: and your ears, for they hear. 17For verily I say unto you, That many prophets and righteous *men* have desired to see *those things* which ye see, and have not seen *them;* and to hear *those things* which ye hear, and have not heard *them.* 18Hear ye therefore the parable of the sower. 19When any one heareth the word of the kingdom, and understandeth *it* not, then cometh the wicked one, and catcheth away that which was sown in his heart. This is he which received seed by the way side. 20But he that received the seed into stony *places,* the same is he that heareth the word, and anon with joy receiveth it; 21Yet hath he not root in himself, but dureth for a while: for

when tribulation or persecution ariseth because of the word, by and by he is offended. 22He also that received seed among the thorns is he that heareth the word; and the care of this world, and the deceitfulness of riches, choke the word, and he becometh unfruitful. 23But he that received seed into the good ground is he that heareth the word, and understandeth *it;* which also beareth fruit, and bringeth forth, some an hundred*fold,* some sixty, some thirty.

Parables about the kingdom

24 Another parable put he forth unto them, saying, The kingdom of heaven is likened unto a man which sowed good seed in his field: 25But while men slept, his enemy came and sowed tares among the wheat, and went his way. 26But when the blade was sprung up, and brought forth fruit, then appeared the tares also. 27So the servants of the householder came and said unto him, Sir, didst not thou sow good seed in thy field? from whence then hath it tares? 28He said unto them, An enemy hath done this. The servants said unto him, Wilt thou then *that* we go and gather them up? 29But he said, Nay; lest while ye gather up the tares, ye root up also the wheat with them. 30Let both grow together until the harvest: and in the time of harvest I will say to the reapers, Gather ye together first the tares, and bind them in bundles to burn them: but gather the wheat into my barn. [ch. 3:12]

31 Another parable put he forth unto them, saying, The kingdom of

heaven is like unto a grain of mustard seed, which a man took, and sowed in his field: 32Which indeed is the least of all seeds: but when it is grown, it is the greatest among herbs, and becometh a tree, so that the birds of the air come and lodge in the branches thereof.

33 Another parable spake he unto them; The kingdom of heaven is like unto leaven, which a woman took, and hid in three measures of meal, till the whole was leavened. 34All these *things* spake Jesus unto the multitude in parables; and without a parable spake he not unto them: 35That it might be fulfilled which was spoken by the prophet, saying, I will open my mouth in parables; I will utter *things which have been* kept secret from the foundation of the world. [Ps. 78:2; Rom. 16:25,26; 1 Cor. 2:7; Eph. 3:9; Col. 1:26]

Parable of the tares explained

36 Then Jesus sent the multitude away, and went into the house: and his disciples came unto him, saying, Declare unto us the parable of the tares of the field. 37He answered and said unto them, He that soweth the good seed is the Son of man; 38The field is the world; the good seed are the children of the kingdom; but the tares are the children of the wicked one; 39The enemy that sowed them is the devil; the harvest is the end of the world; and the reapers are *the* angels. 40As therefore the tares are gathered and burnt in the fire; so shall it be in the end of this world. 41The Son

of man shall send forth his angels, and they shall gather out of his kingdom all things that offend, and them which do iniquity; 42And shall cast them into a furnace of fire: there shall be wailing and gnashing of teeth. 43Then shall the righteous shine forth as the sun in the kingdom of their Father. Who hath ears to hear, let him hear. [Dan. 12:3; 1 Cor. 15:42,43,58; ver. 9]

Further parables of the kingdom

44 Again, the kingdom of heaven is like unto treasure hid in a field; the which when a man hath found, he hideth, and for joy thereof goeth and selleth all that he hath, and buyeth that field. [Phil. 3:7,8; Is. 55:1; Rev. 3:18]

45 Again, the kingdom of heaven is like unto a merchant man, seeking goodly pearls: 46Who, when he had found one pearl of great price, went and sold all that he had, and bought it. [Prov. 2:4; 3:14,15; 8:10,19]

47 Again, the kingdom of heaven is like unto a net, *that was* cast into the sea, and gathered of every kind: 48Which, when it was full, they drew to shore, and sat down, and gathered the good into vessels, but cast the bad away. 49So shall it be at the end of the world: the angels shall come forth, and sever the wicked from among the just, 50And shall cast them into the furnace of fire: there shall be wailing and gnashing of teeth.

51 Jesus saith unto them, Have ye understood all these *things?* They say unto him, Yea, Lord. 52Then said he unto them, There-

fore every scribe *which is* instructed unto the kingdom of heaven is like unto a man *that is* a householder, which bringeth forth out of his treasure *things* new and old. [Sol. 7:13]

Jesus rejected at Nazareth

53 And it came to pass, *that* when Jesus had finished these parables, he departed thence. 54And when he was come into his own country, he taught them in their synagogue, insomuch that they were astonished, and said, Whence hath this *man* this wisdom, and *these* mighty works? 55Is not this the carpenter's son? is not his mother called Mary? and his brethren, James, and Joses, and Simon, and Judas? 56And his sisters, are they not all with us? Whence then hath this *man* all these *things?* 57And they were offended in him. But Jesus said unto them, A prophet is not without honour, save in his own country, and in his own house. 58And he did not many mighty works there, because of their unbelief. [Mark 6:5,6]

Death of John the Baptist

14 At that time Herod the tetrarch heard of the fame of Jesus, 2And said unto his servants, This is John the Baptist; he is risen from the dead; and therefore mighty works do shew forth themselves in him. 3For Herod had laid hold on John, and bound him, and put *him* in prison for Herodias' sake, his brother Philip's wife. 4For John said unto him, It is not lawful for thee to have her. 5And when he would have put him to death, he feared the multitude, because they counted him as a prophet. 6But when Herod's birthday was kept, the daughter of Herodias danced before them, and pleased Herod. 7Whereupon he promised with an oath to give her whatsoever she would ask. 8And she, being before instructed of her mother, said, Give me here John Baptist's head in a charger. 9And the king was sorry: nevertheless for the oaths' sake, and them which sat with him at meat, he commanded *it* to be given *her.* 10And he sent, and beheaded John in the prison. 11And his head was brought in a charger, and given to the damsel: and she brought *it* to her mother. 12And his disciples came, and took up the body, and buried it, and went and told Jesus.

The five thousand fed

13 When Jesus heard *of it,* he departed thence by ship into a desert place apart: and when the people had heard *thereof,* they followed him on foot out of the cities. 14And Jesus went forth, and saw a great multitude, and was moved with compassion toward them, and he healed their sick. 15And when it was evening, his disciples came to him, saying, *This* is a desert place, and the time is now past; send the multitude away, that they may go into the villages, and buy themselves victuals. 16But Jesus said unto them, They need not depart; give ye them to eat. 17And they say unto him, We have here but five loaves, and two fishes. 18He said, Bring them hither to me. 19And he

commanded the multitude to sit down on the grass, and took the five loaves, and the two fishes, and looking up to heaven, he blessed, and brake, and gave the loaves to *his* disciples, and the disciples to the multitude. 20And they did all eat, and were filled: and they took up of the fragments that remained twelve baskets full. 21And they that had eaten were about five thousand men, beside women and children.

Jesus walks on the sea

22 And straightway Jesus constrained his disciples to get into a ship, and to go before him unto the other side, while he sent the multitudes away. 23And when he had sent the multitudes away, he went up into a mountain apart to pray: and when the evening was come, he was there alone. 24But the ship was now in the midst of the sea, tossed with waves: for the wind was contrary. 25And in the fourth watch of the night Jesus went unto them, walking on the sea. 26And when the disciples saw him walking on the sea, they were troubled, saying, It is a spirit; and they cried out for fear. 27But straightway Jesus spake unto them, saying, Be of good cheer; it is I, be not afraid. 28And Peter answered him and said, Lord, if it be thou, bid me come unto thee on the water. 29And he said, Come. And when Peter was come down out of the ship, he walked on the water, to go to Jesus. 30But when he saw the wind boysterous, he was afraid; and beginning to sink, he cried, saying, Lord, save me. 31And im-

mediately Jesus stretched forth *his* hand, and caught him, and said unto him, O thou of little faith, wherefore didst thou doubt? 32And when they were come into the ship, the wind ceased. 33Then they that were in the ship came and worshipped him, saying, Of a truth thou art the Son of God. [Ps. 2:7; ch. 16:16; 26:63; Mark 1:1; Luke 4:41; John 1:49; 6:69; 11:27; Acts 8:37; Rom. 1:4]

34 And when they were gone over, they came into the land of Gennesaret. 35And when the men of that place had knowledge of him, they sent out into all that country round about, and brought unto him all that were diseased; 36And besought him that they might only touch the hem of his garment: and as many as touched were made perfectly whole. [ch. 9:20; Mark 3:10; Luke 6:19; Acts 19:12]

What defiles a man

15 Then came to Jesus scribes and Pharisees, which were of Jerusalem, saying, 2Why do thy disciples transgress the tradition of the elders? for they wash not their hands when they eat bread. 3But he answered and said unto them, Why do you also transgress the commandment of God by your tradition? 4For God commanded, saying, Honour thy father and mother: and, He that curseth father or mother, let him die the death. 5But ye say, Whosoever shall say to *his* father or *his* mother, *It is* a gift, *by* whatsoever thou mightest be profited by me; 6And honour not his father or his mother, *he shall be free.* Thus have ye made the commandment of God of none effect by your tradition. ⁷Ye hypocrites, well did Esaias prophesy of you, saying, ⁸This people draweth nigh unto me with their mouth, and honoureth me with *their* lips; but their heart is far from me. ⁹But in vain they do worship me, teaching for doctrines the commandments of men. [Is. 29:13; Col. 2:18-22; Tit. 1:14]

10 And he called the multitude, and said unto them, Hear, and understand: ¹¹Not that which goeth into the mouth defileth a man; but that which cometh out of the mouth, this defileth a man. ¹²Then came his disciples, and said unto him, Knowest thou that the Pharisees were offended, after they heard *this* saying? ¹³But he answered and said, Every plant, which my heavenly Father hath not planted, shall be rooted up. ¹⁴Let them alone: they be blind leaders of the blind. And if the blind lead the blind, both shall fall into the ditch. ¹⁵Then answered Peter and said unto him, Declare unto us this parable. ¹⁶And Jesus said, Are ye also yet without understanding? ¹⁷Do not ye yet understand, that whatsoever entereth in at the mouth goeth into the belly, and is cast out into the draught? ¹⁸But those *things* which proceed out of the mouth come forth from the heart; and they defile the man. ¹⁹For out of the heart proceed evil thoughts, murders, adulteries, fornications, thefts, false witness, blasphemies: ²⁰These are *the things* which defile a man: but to eat with unwashen hands defileth not a man.

The faith of a Canaanite woman

21 Then Jesus went thence, and departed into the coasts of Tyre and Sidon. ²²And behold, a woman of Canaan came out of the same coasts, and cried unto him, saying, Have mercy on me, O Lord, *thou* Son of David; my daughter is grievously vexed with a devil. ²³But he answered her not a word. And his disciples came and besought him, saying, Send her away; for she crieth after us. ²⁴But he answered and said, I am not sent but unto the lost sheep of the house of Israel. ²⁵Then came she and worshipped him, saying, Lord, help me. ²⁶But he answered and said, It is not meet to take the children's bread, and to cast *it* to dogs. ²⁷And she said, Truth, Lord: yet the dogs eat of the crumbs which fall from their masters' table. ²⁸Then Jesus answered and said unto her, O woman, great *is* thy faith: be it unto thee *even* as thou wilt. And her daughter was made whole from that *very* hour. ²⁹And Jesus departed from thence, and came nigh unto the sea of Galilee; and went up into a mountain, and sat down there. ³⁰And great multitudes came unto him, having with them *those that were* lame, blind, dumb, maimed, and many others, and cast them *down* at Jesus' feet; and he healed them: ³¹Insomuch that the multitude wondered, when they saw the dumb to speak, the maimed *to be* whole, the lame to walk, and the blind to see: and they glorified the God of Israel.

The four thousand fed

32 Then Jesus called his disciples unto *him,* and said, I have compassion on the multitude, because they continue with me now three days, and have nothing to eat: and I will not send them away fasting, lest they faint in the way. 33 And his disciples say unto him, Whence should we have so much bread in the wilderness, as to fill so great a multitude? 34 And Jesus saith unto them, How many loaves have ye? And they said, Seven, and a few little fishes. 35 And he commanded the multitude to sit down on the ground. 36 And he took the seven loaves and the fishes, and gave thanks, and brake *them,* and gave to his disciples, and the disciples to the multitude. 37 And they did all eat, and were filled: and they took up of the broken *meat* that was left seven baskets full. 38 And they that did eat were four thousand men, beside women and children.

39 And he sent away the multitude, and took ship, and came into the coasts of Magdala. [Mark 8:10]

Pharisees ask for a sign

16 The Pharisees also with the Sadducees came, and tempting desired him that *he* would shew them a sign from heaven. 2 He answered and said unto them, When it is evening, ye say, It will be fair weather: for the sky is red. 3 And in the morning, *It will be* foul weather to day: for the sky is red and lowring. O *ye* hypocrites, ye can discern the face of the sky; but can ye not *discern* the

signs of the times? 4 A wicked and adulterous generation seeketh after a sign; and there shall no sign be given unto it, but the sign of the prophet Jonas. And he left them, and departed. [ch. 12:39]

5 And when his disciples were come to the other side, they had forgotten to take bread. 6 Then Jesus said unto them, Take heed and beware of the leaven of the Pharisees and *of the* Sadducees. 7 And they reasoned among themselves, saying, It is because we have taken no bread. 8 *Which* when Jesus perceived, he said unto them, O ye of little faith, why reason ye among yourselves, because ye have brought no bread? 9 Do ye not yet understand, neither remember the five loaves of the five thousand, and how many baskets ye took up? 10 Neither the seven loaves of the four thousand, and how many baskets ye took up? 11 How *is it that* ye do not understand that I spake *it* not to you concerning bread, that *ye* should beware of the leaven of the Pharisees and *of the* Sadducees? 12 Then understood they how that he bade *them* not beware of the leaven of bread, but of the doctrine of the Pharisees and *of the* Sadducees.

Peter's confession of faith

13 When Jesus came into the coasts of Cesarea Philippi, he asked his disciples, saying, Whom do men say that I the Son of man am? 14 And they said, Some *say that thou art* John the Baptist: some, Elias; and others, Jeremias, or one of the prophets. 15 He saith unto

them, But whom say ye that I am? 16And Simon Peter answered and said, Thou art the Christ, the Son of the living God. 17And Jesus answered and said unto him, Blessed art thou, Simon Bar-jona: for flesh and blood hath not revealed *it* unto thee, but my Father which is in heaven. 18And I say also unto thee, That thou art Peter, and upon this rock I will build my church; and the gates of hell shall not prevail against it. 19And I will give unto thee the keys of the kingdom of heaven: and whatsoever thou shalt bind on earth shall be bound in heaven: and whatsoever thou shalt loose on earth shall be loosed in heaven. 20Then charged he his disciples that they should tell no *man* that he was Jesus the Christ. [ch. 17:9; Luke 9:21]

Future events foretold

21 From that time forth began Jesus to shew unto his disciples, how that he must go unto Jerusalem, and suffer many *things* of the elders and chief priests and scribes, and be killed, and be raised *again* the third day. 22Then Peter took him, and began to rebuke him, saying, Be it far from thee, Lord: this shall not be unto thee. 23But he turned, and said unto Peter, Get thee behind me, Satan: thou art an offence unto me: for thou savourest not the *things* that be of God, but *those* that be of men. 24Then said Jesus unto his disciples, If any *man* will come after me, let him deny himself, and take up his cross, and follow me. 25For whosoever will save his life

shall lose it: and whosoever will lose his life for my sake shall find it. 26For what is a man profited, if he shall gain the whole world, and lose his own soul? or what shall a man give in exchange for his soul? 27For the Son of man shall come in the glory of his Father with his angels: and then he shall reward every man according to his works. 28Verily I say unto you, There be some standing here, which shall not taste of death, till they see the Son of man coming in his kingdom. [Mark 9:1; Luke 9:27]

The transfiguration

17 And after six days Jesus taketh Peter, James, and John his brother, and bringeth them up into a high mountain apart, 2And was transfigured before them: and his face did shine as the sun, and his raiment was white as the light. 3And behold, there appeared unto them Moses and Elias talking with him. 4Then answered Peter, and said unto Jesus, Lord, it is good for us to be here: if thou wilt, let us make here three tabernacles: one for thee, and one for Moses, and one for Elias. 5While he yet spake, behold, a bright cloud overshadowed them: and behold a voice out of the cloud, which said, This is my beloved Son, in whom I am well pleased; hear ye him. 6And when the disciples heard *it*, they fell on their face, and were sore afraid. 7And Jesus came and touched them, and said, Arise, and be not afraid. 8And when they had lift up their eyes, they saw no *man*, save Jesus only.

9 And as they came down from the mountain, Jesus charged them, saying, Tell the vision to no *man,* until the Son of man be risen again from the dead. 10And his disciples asked him, saying, Why then say the scribes that Elias must first come? 11And Jesus answered and said unto them, Elias truly shall first come, and restore all *things.* 12But I say unto you, That Elias is come already, and they knew him not, but have done unto him whatsoever they listed. Likewise shall also the Son of man suffer of them. 13Then the disciples understood that he spake unto them of John the Baptist. [ch. 11:14]

A demoniac boy healed

14 And when they were come to the multitude, there came to him a *certain* man, kneeling down to him, and saying, 15Lord, have mercy on my son: for he is lunatick, and sore vexed: for ofttimes he falleth into the fire, and oft into the water. 16And I brought him to thy disciples, and they could not cure him. 17Then Jesus answered and said, O faithless and perverse generation, how long shall I be with you? how long shall I suffer you? bring him hither to me. 18And Jesus rebuked the devil; and he departed out of him: and the child was cured from that *very* hour. 19Then came the disciples to Jesus apart, and said, Why could not we cast him out? 20And Jesus said unto them, Because of your unbelief: for verily I say unto you, If ye have faith as a grain of mustard seed, ye shall say unto this mountain, Remove hence to yonder place; and it shall remove; and nothing shall be impossible unto you. 21Howbeit this kind goeth not out but by prayer and fasting.

22 And while they abode in Galilee, Jesus said unto them, The Son of man shall be betrayed into the hands of men: 23And they shall kill him, and the third day he shall be raised *again.* And they were exceeding sorry.

The money in the fish's mouth

24 And when they were come to Capernaum, they that received tribute money came to Peter, and said, Doth not your master pay tribute? 25He saith, Yes. And when he was come into the house, Jesus prevented him, saying, What thinkest thou, Simon? of whom do the kings of the earth take custom or tribute? of their own children, or of strangers? 26Peter saith unto him, Of strangers. Jesus saith unto him, Then are the children free. 27Notwithstanding, lest we should offend them, go thou to the sea, and cast a hook, and take up the fish that first cometh up; and when thou hast opened his mouth, thou shalt find a piece of money: that take, and give unto them for me and thee.

The greatest in the kingdom

18 At the same time came the disciples unto Jesus, saying, Who is the greatest in the kingdom of heaven? 2And Jesus called a little child unto *him,* and set him in the midst of them. 3And said, Verily I say unto you, Except ye be converted, and become as lit-

tle children, ye shall not enter into the kingdom of heaven. 4Whosoever therefore shall humble himself as this little child, the same is greatest in the kingdom of heaven. 5And whoso shall receive one such little child in my name receiveth me. 6But whoso shall offend one of these little ones which believe in me, it were better for him that a millstone were hanged about his neck, and *that* he were drowned in the depth of the sea. 7Woe unto the world because of offences: for it must needs be that offences come; but woe to that man by whom the offence cometh. 8Wherefore if thy hand or thy foot offend thee, cut them off, and cast *them* from thee: it is better for thee to enter into life halt or maimed, rather than having two hands or two feet to be cast into everlasting fire. 9And if thine eye offend thee, pluck it out, and cast *it* from thee: it is better for thee to enter into life with one eye, rather than having two eyes to be cast into hell fire.

The parable of the lost sheep

10 Take heed that ye despise not one of these little ones; for I say unto you, That in heaven their angels do always behold the face of my Father which is in heaven. 11For the Son of man is come to save that which was lost. 12How think ye? if a man have an hundred sheep, and one of them be gone astray, doth he not leave the ninety and nine, and goeth into the mountains, and seeketh that which is gone astray? 13And if so be that he find it, verily I say unto you, he rejoiceth more of that *sheep,* than of the ninety and nine which went not astray. 14*Even* so it is not the will of your Father which is in heaven, that one of these little ones should perish.

Sin and forgiveness

15 Moreover if thy brother shall trespass against thee, go and tell him his fault between thee and him alone: if he shall hear thee, thou hast gained thy brother. 16But if he will not hear *thee, then* take with thee one or two more, that in the mouth of two or three witnesses every word may be established. 17And if he shall neglect to hear them, tell *it* unto the church: but if he neglect to hear the church, let him be unto thee as a heathen *man* and a publican. 18Verily I say unto you, Whatsoever ye shall bind on earth shall be bound in heaven: and whatsoever ye shall loose on earth shall be loosed in heaven. 19Again I say unto you, That if two of you shall agree on earth as touching any thing that they shall ask, it shall be done for them of my Father which is in heaven. 20For where two or three are gathered together in my name, there am I in the midst of them.

Parable of the unforgiving servant

21 Then came Peter to him, and said, Lord, how oft shall my brother sin against me, and I forgive him? till seven times? 22Jesus saith unto him, I say not unto thee, Until seven times: but, Until seventy times seven. 23Therefore is the

kingdom of heaven likened unto a certain king, which would take account of his servants. 24And when he had begun to reckon, one was brought unto him, which ought him ten thousand talents. 25But forasmuch as he had not to pay, his lord commanded him to be sold, and his wife, and children, and all that he had, and payment to be made. 26The servant therefore fell down, and worshipped him, saying, Lord, have patience with me, and I will pay thee all. 27Then the lord of that servant was moved with compassion, and loosed him, and forgave him the debt. 28But the same servant went out, and found one of his fellowservants, which ought him an hundred pence: and he laid hands on him, and took *him* by the throat, saying, Pay me that thou owest. 29And his fellowservant fell down at his feet, and besought him, saying, Have patience with me, and I will pay thee all. 30And he would not: but went and cast him into prison, till he should pay the debt. 31So when his fellowservants saw what was done, they were very sorry, and came and told unto their lord all that was done. 32Then his lord, after that he had called him, said unto him, O *thou* wicked servant, I forgave thee all that debt, because thou desiredst me: 33Shouldest not thou also have had compassion on thy fellowservant, even as I had pity on thee? 34And his lord was wroth, and delivered him to the tormentors, till he should pay all that was due unto him. 35So likewise shall my heavenly Father do

also unto you, if ye from your hearts forgive not every one his brother their trespasses. [Prov. 21:13; ch. 6:12; Mark 11:26; Jas. 2:13]

Marriage and divorce

19 And it came to pass, *that* when Jesus had finished these sayings, he departed from Galilee, and came into the coasts of Judea beyond Jordan; 2And great multitudes followed him; and he healed them there. 3The Pharisees also came unto him, tempting him, and saying unto him, Is it lawful for a man to put away his wife for every cause? 4And he answered and said unto them, Have ye not read, that he which made *them* at the beginning made them male and female, 5And said, For this cause shall a man leave father and mother, and shall cleave to his wife: and they twain shall be one flesh? 6Wherefore they are no more twain, but one flesh. What therefore God hath joined together, let not man put asunder. 7They say unto him, Why did Moses then command to give a writing of divorcement, and to put her away? 8He saith unto them, Moses because of the hardness of your hearts suffered you to put away your wives: but from the beginning it was not so. 9And I say unto you, Whosoever shall put away his wife, except *it be* for fornication, and shall marry another, committeth adultery: and whoso marrieth her *which is* put away doth commit adultery. 10His disciples say unto him, If the case of the man be so with *his* wife, it is not good to marry. 11But he said unto them, All

men cannot receive this saying, save *they* to whom it is given. 12For there are *some* eunuchs, which were so born from *their* mother's womb: and there are *some* eunuchs, which were made eunuchs of men: and there be eunuchs, which have made themselves eunuchs for the kingdom of heaven's sake. He that is able to receive *it,* let him receive *it.* [1 Cor. 7:32; 9:5,15]

Jesus blesses the little children

13 Then were there brought unto him little children, that he should put *his* hands on them, and pray: and the disciples rebuked them. 14But Jesus said, Suffer little children, and forbid them not, to come unto me: for of such is the kingdom of heaven. 15And he laid *his* hands on them, and departed thence.

The rich young ruler

16 And behold, one came and said unto him, Good Master, what good *thing* shall I do, that I may have eternal life? 17And he said unto him, Why callest thou me good? *there is* none good but one, *that is,* God: but if thou wilt enter into life, keep the commandments. 18He saith unto him, Which? Jesus said, Thou shalt do no murder, Thou shalt not commit adultery, Thou shalt not steal, Thou shalt not bear false witness, 19Honour thy father and *thy* mother: and, Thou shalt love thy neighbour as thyself. 20The young man saith unto him, All these *things* have I kept from my youth up: what lack I yet? 21Jesus said unto him, If thou wilt be perfect, go *and* sell that thou hast, and give to the poor, and thou shalt have treasure in heaven: and come *and* follow me. 22But when the young man heard *that* saying, he went away sorrowful: for he had great possessions.

23 Then said Jesus unto his disciples, Verily I say unto you, That a rich *man* shall hardly enter into the kingdom of heaven. 24And again I say unto you, It is easier for a camel to go through the eye of a needle, than for a rich *man* to enter into the kingdom of God. 25When his disciples heard *it,* they were exceedingly amazed, saying, Who then can be saved? 26But Jesus beheld *them,* and said unto them, With men this is impossible; but with God all *things* are possible. [Gen. 18:14; Job 42:2; Jer. 32:17; Zech. 8:6; Luke 1:37; 18:27]

The worker in the vineyard

27 Then answered Peter and said unto him, Behold, we have forsaken all, and followed thee; what shall we have therefore? 28And Jesus said unto them, Verily I say unto you, That ye which have followed me, in the regeneration, when the Son of man shall sit in the throne of his glory, ye also shall sit upon twelve thrones, judging the twelve tribes of Israel. 29And every one that hath forsaken houses, or brethren, or sisters, or father, or mother, or wife, or children, or lands, for my name's sake, shall receive an hundredfold, and shall inherit everlasting life. 30But many *that are* first shall be last; and *the* last *shall be* first. [ch. 20:16; 21:31,32; Mark 10:31; Luke 13:30]

20 For the kingdom of heaven is like unto a man *that is* a householder, which went out early in the morning to hire labourers into his vineyard. ²And when he had agreed with the labourers for a penny a day, he sent them into his vineyard. ³And he went out about the third hour, and saw others standing idle in the marketplace, ⁴And said unto them; Go ye also into the vineyard, and whatsoever is right I will give you. And they went their way. ⁵Again he went out about the sixth and ninth hour, and did likewise. ⁶And about the eleventh hour he went out, and found others standing idle, and saith unto them, Why stand ye here all the day idle? ⁷They say unto him, Because no *man* hath hired us. He saith unto them, Go ye also into the vineyard; and whatsoever is right, *that* shall ye receive. ⁸So when even was come, the lord of the vineyard saith unto his steward, Call the labourers, and give them *their* hire, beginning from the last unto the first. ⁹And when they came that *were hired* about the eleventh hour, they received every man a penny. ¹⁰But when the first came, they supposed that they should have received more; and they likewise received every man a penny. ¹¹And when they had received *it,* they murmured against the goodman of the house, ¹²Saying, These last have wrought *but* one hour, and thou hast made them equal unto us, which have borne the burden and heat of the day. ¹³But he answered one of them, and said,

Friend, I do thee no wrong: didst not thou agree with me for a penny? ¹⁴Take *that* thine *is,* and go thy way: I will give unto this last, even as unto thee. ¹⁵Is it not lawful for me to do what I will with mine own? Is thine eye evil, because I am good? ¹⁶So the last shall be first, and the first last: for many be called, but few chosen. [ch. 19:30; ch. 22:14]

Jesus foretells his death

17 And Jesus going up to Jerusalem took the twelve disciples apart in the way, and said unto them, ¹⁸Behold, we go up to Jerusalem; and the Son of man shall be betrayed unto the chief priests and *unto the* scribes, and they shall condemn him to death, ¹⁹And shall deliver him to the Gentiles to mock, and to scourge, and to crucify *him:* and the third day he shall rise again. [ch. 27:2; Mark 15:1,16; Luke 23:1; John 18:28; Acts 3:13]

The ambition of James and John

20 Then came to him the mother of Zebedee's children with her sons, worshipping *him,* and desiring a certain *thing* of him. ²¹And he said unto her, What wilt thou? She saith unto him, Grant that these my two sons may sit, the one on thy right hand, and the other on the left, in thy kingdom. ²²But Jesus answered and said, Ye know not what ye ask. Are ye able to drink *of* the cup that I shall drink *of,* and to be baptized *with* the baptism that I am baptized *with?* They say unto him, We are able. ²³And he saith unto them, Ye shall drink indeed *of* my cup, and be baptized *with* the bap-

tism that I am baptized *with:* but to sit on my right hand, and on my left, is not mine to give, but *it shall be given to them* for whom it is prepared of my Father. 24And when the ten heard *it,* they were moved with indignation against the two brethren. 25But Jesus called them unto *him,* and said, Ye know that the princes of the Gentiles exercise dominion over them, and they *that are* great exercise authority upon them. 26But it shall not be so among you: but whosoever will be great among you, let him be your minister; 27And whosoever will be chief among you, let him be your servant: 28Even as the Son of man came not to be ministered unto, but to minister, and to give his life a ransom for many. [John 13:4; Phil. 2:7; Luke 22:27; John 13:14; Is. 53:10,11; Dan. 9:24,26; John 11:51,52; 1 Tim. 2:6; Tit. 2:14; 1 Pet. 1:19; ch. 26:28; Rom. 5:15,19; Heb. 9:28]

Healing of two blind men

29 And as they departed from Jericho, a great multitude followed him. 30And behold, two blind men sitting by the way side, when they heard that Jesus passed by, cried out, saying, Have mercy on us, O Lord, *thou* Son of David. 31And the multitude rebuked them, because they should hold their peace: but they cried the more, saying, Have mercy on us, O Lord, *thou* Son of David. 32And Jesus stood still, and called them, and said, What will ye *that* I shall do unto you? 33They say unto him, Lord, that our eyes may be opened. 34So Jesus had compassion *on them,* and touched their eyes: and immediately their eyes received sight, and they followed him.

The triumphal entry

21 And when they drew nigh unto Jerusalem, and were come to Bethphage, unto the mount of Olives, then sent Jesus two disciples, 2Saying unto them, Go into the village over against you, and straightway ye shall find an ass tied, and a colt with her: loose *them,* and bring *them* unto me. 3And if any *man* say ought unto you, ye shall say, The Lord hath need of them; and straightway he will send them. 4All this was done, that it might be fulfilled which was spoken by the prophet, saying, 5Tell ye the daughter of Sion, Behold, thy King cometh unto thee, meek, and sitting upon an ass, and a colt the foal of an ass. 6And the disciples went, and did as Jesus commanded them, 7And brought the ass, and the colt, and put on them their clothes, and they set *him* thereon. 8And a very great multitude spread their garments in the way; others cut down branches from the trees, and strawed *them* in the way. 9And the multitudes that went before, and that followed, cried, saying, Hosanna to the Son of David: Blessed *is* he that cometh in the name of the Lord; Hosanna in the highest. 10And when he was come into Jerusalem, all the city was moved, saying, Who is this? 11And the multitude said, This is Jesus the prophet of Nazareth of Galilee. [ch. 2:23; Luke 7:16; John 6:14; 7:40; 9:17]

Cleansing of the temple

12 And Jesus went into the temple of God, and cast out all them that sold and bought in the temple, and overthrew the tables of the moneychangers, and the seats of them that sold doves, 13And said unto them, It is written, My house shall be called the house of prayer; but ye have made it a den of thieves. 14And *the* blind and *the* lame came to him in the temple; and he healed them. 15And when the chief priests and scribes saw the wonderful *things* that he did, and the children crying in the temple, and saying, Hosanna to the Son of David; they were sore displeased, 16And said unto him, Hearest thou what these say? And Jesus saith unto them, Yea; have ye never read, Out of the mouth of babes and sucklings thou hast perfected praise? 17And he left them, and went out of the city into Bethany; and he lodged there. [Mark 11:11; John 11:18]

The barren fig tree

18 Now in the morning as he returned into the city, he hungered. 19And when he saw a fig tree in the way, he came to it, and found nothing thereon, but leaves only, and said unto it, Let no fruit grow on thee henceforward for ever. And presently the fig tree withered away. 20And when the disciples saw *it,* they marvelled, saying, How soon is the fig tree withered away! 21Jesus answered and said unto them, Verily I say unto you, If ye have faith, and doubt not, ye shall not only do this which is done to the fig tree, but also if ye shall say unto this mountain, Be thou removed, and be thou cast into the sea; it shall be done. 22And all *things,* whatsoever ye shall ask in prayer, believing, ye shall receive. [ch. 7:7; Mark 11:24; Luke 11:9; Jas. 5:16; 1 John 3:22; 5:14]

Jesus' authority challenged

23 And when he was come into the temple, the chief priests and the elders of the people came unto him as he was teaching, and said, By what authority doest thou these *things?* and who gave thee this authority? 24And Jesus answered and said unto them, I also will ask you one thing, which if ye tell me, I in like wise will tell you by what authority I do these *things.* 25The baptism of John, whence was it? from heaven, or of men? And they reasoned with themselves, saying, If we shall say, From heaven; he will say unto us, Why did ye not then believe him? 26But if we shall say, Of men; we fear the people; for all hold John as a prophet. 27And they answered Jesus, and said, We cannot tell. And he said unto them, Neither tell I you by what authority I do these *things.* 28But what think you? A *certain* man had two sons; and he came to the first, and said, Son, go work to day in my vineyard. 29He answered and said, I will not: but afterward he repented, and went. 30And he came to the second, and said likewise. And he answered and said, I *go,* sir: and went not. 31Whether of *them* twain did the will of *his* father? They say unto him, The first.

Jesus saith unto them, Verily I say unto you, That the publicans and the harlots go into the kingdom of God before you. ³²For John came unto you in the way of righteousness, and ye believed him not: but the publicans and the harlots believed him: and ye, when ye had seen *it,* repented not afterward, that *ye* might believe him. [ch. 3:1; Luke 3:12,13]

The parable of the husbandmen

33 Hear another parable: There was a certain householder, which planted a vineyard, and hedged it round about, and digged a winepress in it, and built a tower, and let it out to husbandmen, and went into a far country: ³⁴And when the time of the fruit drew near, he sent his servants to the husbandmen, that *they* might receive the fruits of it. ³⁵And the husbandmen took his servants, and beat one, and killed another, and stoned another. ³⁶Again, he sent other servants more than the first: and they did unto them likewise. ³⁷But last *of all* he sent unto them his son, saying, They will reverence my son. ³⁸But when the husbandmen saw the son, they said among themselves, This is the heir; come, let us kill him, and let us seize on his inheritance. ³⁹And they caught him, and cast *him* out of the vineyard, and slew *him.* ⁴⁰When the lord therefore of the vineyard cometh, what will he do unto those husbandmen? ⁴¹They say unto him, He will miserably destroy those wicked *men,* and will let out *his* vineyard unto other husbandmen, which shall render him the fruits in their seasons. ⁴²Jesus saith unto them, Did ye never read in the scriptures, The stone which the builders rejected, the same is become the head of the corner: this is the Lord's doing, and it is marvellous in our eyes? ⁴³Therefore say I unto you, The kingdom of God shall be taken from you, and given to a nation bringing forth the fruits thereof. ⁴⁴And whosoever shall fall on this stone shall be broken: but on whomsoever it shall fall, it will grind him to powder. ⁴⁵And when the chief priests and Pharisees had heard his parables, they perceived that he spake of them. ⁴⁶But when they sought to lay hands on him, they feared the multitude, because they took him for a prophet. [ver. 11; Luke 7:16; John 7:40]

The marriage dinner

22 And Jesus answered and spake unto them again by parables, and said, ²The kingdom of heaven is like unto a certain king, which made a marriage for his son, ³And sent forth his servants to call them that were bidden to the wedding: and they would not come. ⁴Again, he sent forth other servants, saying, Tell them which are bidden, Behold, I have prepared my dinner: my oxen and *my* fatlings *are* killed, and all *things are* ready: come unto the marriage. ⁵But they made light of *it,* and went their ways, one to his farm, another to his merchandise: ⁶And the remnant took his servants, and entreated *them* spitefully, and slew

them. 7But when the king heard *thereof,* he was wroth: and he sent forth his armies, and destroyed those murderers, and burnt up their city. 8Then saith he to his servants, The wedding is ready, but they which were bidden were not worthy. 9Go ye therefore into the highways, and as many as ye shall find, bid to the marriage. 10So those servants went out into the *high*ways, and gathered together all as many as they found, both bad and good: and the wedding was furnished with guests. 11And when the king came in to see the guests, he saw there a man which had not on a wedding garment: 12And he saith unto him, Friend, how camest thou in hither not having a wedding garment? And he was speechless. 13Then said the king to the servants, Bind him hand and foot, and take him away, and cast *him* into outer darkness; there shall be weeping and gnashing of teeth. 14For many are called, but few *are* chosen. [ch. 20:16]

Tribute money to Cesar

15 Then went the Pharisees, and took counsel how they might entangle him in *his* talk. 16And they sent out unto him their disciples with the Herodians, saying, Master, we know that thou art true, and teachest the way of God in truth, neither carest thou for any *man:* for thou regardest not the person of men. 17Tell us therefore, What thinkest thou? Is it lawful to give tribute unto Cesar, or not? 18But Jesus perceived their wickedness, and said, Why tempt ye me,

ye hypocrites? 19Shew me the tribute money. And they brought unto him a penny. 20And he saith unto them, Whose *is* this image and superscription? 21They say unto him, Cesar's. Then saith he unto them, Render therefore unto Cesar the *things* which are Cesar's; and unto God the *things* that are God's. 22When they had heard *these words,* they marvelled, and left him, and went their way.

Sadducees and the resurrection

23 The same day came to him *the* Sadducees, which say that there is no resurrection, and asked him, 24Saying, Master, Moses said, If a man die, having no children, his brother shall marry his wife, and raise up seed unto his brother. 25Now there were with us seven brethren: and the first, when he had married *a wife,* deceased, and, having no issue, left his wife unto his brother: 26Likewise the second also, and the third, unto the seventh. 27And last of all the woman died also. 28Therefore in the resurrection whose wife shall she be of the seven? for they all had her. 29Jesus answered and said unto them, Ye do err, not knowing the scriptures, nor the power of God. 30For in the resurrection they neither marry, nor are given in marriage, but are as *the* angels of God in heaven. 31But as touching the resurrection of the dead, have ye not read that which was spoken unto you by God, saying, 32I am the God of Abraham, and the God of Isaac, and the God of Jacob? God is not the God of the dead, but of

the living. ³³And when the multitude heard *this,* they were astonished at his doctrine. [ch. 7:28]

The great commandment

34 But when the Pharisees had heard that he had put the Sadducees to silence, they were gathered together. ³⁵Then one of them, *which was* a lawyer, asked *him a question,* tempting him, and saying, ³⁶Master, which *is* the great commandment in the law? ³⁷Jesus said unto him, Thou shalt love the Lord thy God with all thy heart, and with all thy soul, and with all thy mind. ³⁸This is the first and great commandment. ³⁹And the second *is* like unto it, Thou shalt love thy neighbour as thyself. ⁴⁰On these two commandments hang all the law and the prophets. [ch. 7:12; 1 Tim. 1:5]

The question about David's son

41 While the Pharisees were gathered together, Jesus asked them, ⁴²Saying, What think ye of Christ? whose son is he? They say unto him, *The Son* of David. ⁴³He saith unto them, How then doth David in spirit call him Lord, saying, ⁴⁴The LORD said unto my Lord, Sit thou on my right hand, till I make thine enemies thy footstool? ⁴⁵If David then call him Lord, how is he his son? ⁴⁶And no *man* was able to answer him a word, neither durst any *man* from that day forth ask him any more *questions.* [Luke 14:6; Mark 12:34; Luke 20:40]

The woes upon the Pharisees

23 Then spake Jesus to the multitude, and to his disciples, ²Saying, The scribes and the Pharisees sit in Moses' seat: ³All therefore whatsoever they bid you observe, *that* observe and do; but do not ye after their works: for they say, and do not. ⁴For they bind heavy burdens and grievous to be borne, and lay *them* on men's shoulders; but they *themselves* will not move them with *one of* their fingers. ⁵But all their works they do for to be seen of men: they make broad their phylacteries, and enlarge the borders of their garments, ⁶And love the uppermost rooms at feasts, and the chief seats in the synagogues, ⁷And greetings in the markets, and to be called of men, Rabbi, Rabbi. ⁸But be not ye called Rabbi: for one is your Master, *even* Christ; and all ye are brethren. ⁹And call no *man* your father upon the earth: for one is your Father, which is in heaven. ¹⁰Neither be ye called masters: for one is your Master, *even* Christ. ¹¹But he that is greatest among you shall be your servant. ¹²And whosoever shall exalt himself shall be abased; and he that shall humble himself shall be exalted. [Job 22:29; Prov. 15:33; 29:23; Luke 14:11; 18:14; Jas. 4:6; 1 Pet. 5:5]

13 But woe unto you, scribes and Pharisees, hypocrites! for ye shut up the kingdom of heaven against men: for ye neither go in yourselves, neither suffer ye them that are entering to go in. [Luke 11:52]

14 Woe unto you, scribes and Pharisees, hypocrites! for ye devour widows' houses, and for a pretence make long prayer: therefore ye shall receive the greater

damnation. [Mark 12:40; Luke 20:47; 2 Tim. 3:6; Tit. 1:11]

15 Woe unto you, scribes and Pharisees, hypocrites! for ye compass sea and land to make one proselyte, and when he is made, ye make him twofold more *the* child of hell than yourselves.

16 Woe unto you, *ye* blind guides, which say, Whosoever shall swear by the temple, it is nothing; but whosoever shall swear by the gold of the temple, he is a debtor. 17 *Ye* fools and blind: for whether is greater, the gold, or the temple that sanctifieth the gold? 18 And, Whosoever shall swear by the altar, it is nothing; but whosoever sweareth by the gift that is upon it, he is guilty. 19 *Ye* fools and blind: for whether *is* greater, the gift, or the altar that sanctifieth the gift? 20 Whoso therefore shall swear by the altar, sweareth by it, and by all *things* thereon. 21 And whoso shall swear by the temple, sweareth by it, and by him that dwelleth therein. 22 And he that shall swear by heaven, sweareth by the throne of God, and by him that sitteth thereon. [Ps. 11:4; ch. 5:34; Acts 7:49]

23 Woe unto you, scribes and Pharisees, hypocrites! for ye pay tithe of mint and anise and cummin, and have omitted the weightier *matters* of the law, judgment, mercy, and faith: these ought ye to have done, and not to leave the other undone. 24 *Ye* blind guides, which strain out a gnat, and swallow a camel.

25 Woe unto you, scribes and Pharisees, hypocrites! for ye make clean the outside of the cup and of the platter, but within they are full of extortion and excess. 26 *Thou* blind Pharisee, cleanse first that *which is* within the cup and platter, that the outside of them may be clean also.

27 Woe unto you, scribes and Pharisees, hypocrites! for ye are like unto whited sepulchres, which indeed appear beautiful outward, but are within full of dead *men's* bones, and of all uncleanness. 28 *Even* so ye also outwardly appear righteous unto men, but within ye are full of hypocrisy and iniquity.

29 Woe unto you, scribes and Pharisees, hypocrites! because ye build the tombs of the prophets, and garnish the sepulchres of the righteous, 30 And say, If we had been in the days of our fathers, we would not have been partakers with them in the blood of the prophets. 31 Wherefore ye be witnesses unto yourselves, that ye are the children of them which killed the prophets. 32 Fill ye up then the measure of your fathers. 33 *Ye* serpents, *ye* generation of vipers, how can ye escape the damnation of hell? [ch. 3:7; 12:34]

34 Wherefore behold, I send unto you prophets, and wise *men,* and scribes: and *some* of them ye shall kill and crucify; and *some* of them shall ye scourge in your synagogues, and persecute *them* from city to city: 35 That upon you may come all the righteous blood shed upon the earth, from the blood of righteous Abel unto the blood of Zacharias son of Barachias, whom ye slew between the temple and the altar. 36 Verily I say unto you,

All these *things* shall come upon this generation.

37 O Jerusalem, Jerusalem, *thou* that killest the prophets, and stonest them which are sent unto thee, how often would I have gathered thy children together, even as a hen gathereth her chickens under *her* wings, and ye would not? 38 Behold, your house is left unto you desolate. 39 For I say unto you, Ye shall not see me henceforth, till ye shall say, Blessed is he that cometh in the name of the Lord. [Ps. 118:26; ch. 21:9]

Signs of the end of this age

24 And Jesus went out, and departed from the temple: and his disciples came to *him* for to shew him the buildings of the temple. 2 And Jesus said unto them, See ye not all these *things?* verily I say unto you, There shall not be left here one stone upon another, that shall not be thrown down. 3 And as he sat upon the mount of Olives, the disciples came unto him privately, saying, Tell us, when shall these *things* be? and what *shall be* the sign of thy coming, and of the end of the world? 4 And Jesus answered and said unto them, Take heed that no *man* deceive you. 5 For many shall come in my name, saying, I am Christ; and shall deceive many. 6 And ye shall hear of wars and rumours of wars: see that ye be not troubled: for all *these things* must come to pass, but the end is not yet. 7 For nation shall rise against nation, and kingdom against kingdom: and there shall be famines, and pestilences, and earthquakes in divers places. 8 All these *are* the beginning of sorrows.

9 Then shall they deliver you up to be afflicted, and shall kill you: and ye shall be hated of all nations for my name's sake. 10 And then shall many be offended, and shall betray one another, and shall hate one another. 11 And many false prophets shall rise, and shall deceive many. 12 And because iniquity shall abound, the love of many shall wax cold. 13 But he that shall endure unto the end, the same shall be saved. 14 And this gospel of the kingdom shall be preached in all the world for a witness unto all nations; and then shall the end come. [ch. 4:23; Rom. 10:18; Col. 1:6,23]

15 When ye therefore shall see the abomination of desolation, spoken of by Daniel the prophet, stand in the holy place, (whoso readeth, let him understand:) 16 Then let them which be in Judea flee into the mountains: 17 Let him which is on the housetop not come down to take any *thing* out of his house: 18 Neither let him which is in the field return back to take his clothes. 19 And woe unto them that are with child, and to them that give suck in those days. 20 But pray ye that your flight be not in the winter, neither on the sabbath day: 21 For then shall be great tribulation, such as was not since the beginning of the world to this time, no, nor ever shall be. 22 And except those days should be shortened, there should no flesh be saved: but for the elect's sake those days shall be shortened. 23 Then if any *man* shall say unto you, Lo, here *is* Christ, or there; be-

lieve *it* not. ²⁴For there shall arise false Christs, and false prophets, and shall shew great signs and wonders; insomuch that, if *it were* possible, *they shall* deceive the very elect. ²⁵Behold, I have told you before. ²⁶Wherefore if they shall say unto you, Behold, he is in the desert; go not forth: behold, *he is* in the secret chambers; believe *it* not. ²⁷For as the lightning cometh out of the east, and shineth *even* unto the west; so shall also the coming of the Son of man be. ²⁸For wheresoever the carcase is, there will the eagles be gathered together. [Job 39:30; Luke 17:37]

²⁹ Immediately after the tribulation of those days shall the sun be darkened, and the moon shall not give her light, and the stars shall fall from heaven, and the powers of the heavens shall be shaken: ³⁰And then shall appear the sign of the Son of man in heaven: and then shall all the tribes of the earth mourn, and they shall see the Son of man coming in the clouds of heaven with power and great glory. ³¹And he shall send his angels with a great sound of a trumpet, and they shall gather together his elect from the four winds, from one end of heaven to the other. ³²Now learn a parable of the fig tree; When his branch is yet tender, and putteth forth leaves, ye know that summer *is* nigh: ³³So likewise ye, when ye shall see all these *things,* know that it is near, *even* at the doors. ³⁴Verily I say unto you, This generation shall not pass, till all these *things* be fulfilled. ³⁵Heaven and earth shall pass away, but my

words shall not pass away. [Ps. 102:26; Is. 51:6; Jer. 31:35; Mark 13:31; Luke 21:33]

³⁶ But of that day and hour knoweth no *man,* no, not the angels of heaven, but my Father only. ³⁷But as the days of Noe *were,* so shall also the coming of the Son of man be. ³⁸For as in the days that were before the flood they were eating and drinking, marrying and giving in marriage, until the day that Noe entered into the ark, ³⁹And knew not until the flood came, and took *them* all away; so shall also the coming of the Son of man be. ⁴⁰Then shall two be in the field; the one shall be taken, and the other left. ⁴¹Two *women shall be* grinding at the mill; *the* one shall be taken, and *the* other left. ⁴²Watch therefore: for ye know not what hour your Lord doth come. [ch. 25:13; Luke 21:36]

Faithful and unfaithful servants

⁴³ But know this, that if the goodman of the house had known in what watch the thief would come, he would have watched, and would not have suffered his house to be broken up. ⁴⁴Therefore be ye also ready: for in such an hour as you think not the Son of man cometh. ⁴⁵Who then is a faithful and wise servant, whom his lord hath made ruler over his household, to give them meat in due season? ⁴⁶Blessed *is* that servant, whom his lord when he cometh shall find so doing. ⁴⁷Verily I say unto you, That he shall make him ruler over all his goods. ⁴⁸But *and* if that evil servant shall say in his

heart, My lord delayeth his coming; 49And shall begin to smite *his* fellowservants, and to eat and drink with the drunken; 50The lord of that servant shall come in a day when he looketh not for *him,* and in an hour that he is not ware of, 51And shall cut him asunder, and appoint *him* his portion with the hypocrites: there shall be weeping and gnashing of teeth. [ch. 8:12; 25:30]

The parable of the ten virgins

25 Then shall the kingdom of heaven be likened unto ten virgins, which took their lamps, and went forth to meet the bridegroom. 2And five of them were wise, and five *were* foolish. 3They that *were* foolish took their lamps, and took no oil with them: 4But the wise took oil in their vessels with their lamps. 5While the bridegroom tarried, they all slumbered and slept. 6And at midnight there was a cry made, Behold, the bridegroom cometh; go ye out to meet him. 7Then all those virgins arose, and trimmed their lamps. 8And the foolish said unto the wise, Give us of your oil; for our lamps are gone out. 9But the wise answered, saying, *Not so;* lest there be not enough for us and you: but go ye rather to them that sell, and buy for yourselves. 10And while they went to buy, the bridegroom came; and they *that were* ready went in with him to the marriage: and the door was shut. 11Afterward came also the other virgins, saying, Lord, Lord, open to us. 12But he answered and said, Verily I say unto you, I know you

not. 13Watch therefore, for ye know neither the day nor the hour wherein the Son of man cometh. [ch. 24:42,44; Mark 13:33,35; Luke 21:36]

The parable of the talents

14 For *the kingdom of heaven is* as a man travelling into a far country, *who* called his own servants, and delivered unto them his goods. 15And unto one he gave five talents, to another two, and to another one; to every man according to his several ability; and straightway took his journey. 16Then he that had received the five talents went and traded with the same, and made *them* other five talents. 17And likewise he that *had received* two, he also gained other two. 18But he that had received one went and digged in the earth, and hid his lord's money. 19After a long time the lord of those servants cometh, and reckoneth with them. 20And *so* he that had received five talents came and brought other five talents, saying, Lord, thou deliveredst unto me five talents: behold, I have gained besides them five talents more. 21His lord said unto him, Well *done, thou* good and faithful servant: thou hast been faithful over a few *things,* I will make thee ruler over many *things:* enter thou into the joy of thy lord. 22He also that had received two talents came and said, Lord, thou deliveredst unto me two talents: behold, I have gained two other talents besides them. 23His lord said unto him, Well *done,* good and faithful servant; thou hast been faithful over a few

things, I will make thee ruler over many *things:* enter thou into the joy of thy lord. 24Then he which had received the one talent came and said, Lord, I knew thee that thou art a hard man, reaping where thou hast not sown, and gathering where thou hast not strawed: 25And I was afraid, and went and hid thy talent in the earth: lo, *there* thou hast *that is* thine. 26His lord answered and said unto him, *Thou* wicked and slothful servant, thou knewest that I reap where I sowed not, and gather where I have not strawed: 27Thou oughtest therefore to have put my money to the exchangers, and *then* at my coming I should have received mine own with usury. 28Take therefore the talent from him, and give *it* unto him which hath ten talents. 29For unto every one that hath shall be given, and he shall have abundance: but from him that hath not shall be taken away even *that* which he hath. 30And cast ye the unprofitable servant into outer darkness: there shall be weeping and gnashing of teeth. [ch. 8:12; 24:51]

The judgment

31 When the Son of man shall come in his glory, and all the holy angels with him, then shall he sit upon the throne of his glory: 32And before him shall be gathered all nations: and he shall separate them one from another, as a shepherd divideth *his* sheep from the goats: 33And he shall set the sheep on his right hand, but the goats on the left.

34 Then shall the King say unto them on his right hand, Come, ye blessed of my Father, inherit the kingdom prepared for you from the foundation of the world: 35For I was a hungred, and ye gave me meat: I was thirsty, and ye gave me drink: I was a stranger, and ye took me in: 36Naked, and ye clothed me: I was sick, and ye visited me: I was in prison, and ye came unto me. 37Then shall the righteous answer him, saying, Lord, when saw we thee a hungred, and fed *thee?* or thirsty, and gave *thee* drink? 38When saw we thee a stranger, and took *thee* in? or naked, and clothed *thee?* 39Or when saw we thee sick, or in prison, and came unto thee? 40And the King shall answer and say unto them, Verily I say unto you, Inasmuch as ye have done *it* unto one of the least of these my brethren, ye have done *it* unto me. [Prov. 14:31; 19:17; ch. 10:42; Mark 9:41; Heb. 6:10]

41 Then shall he say also unto them on the left hand, Depart from me, ye cursed, into everlasting fire, prepared for the devil and his angels: 42For I was a hungred, and ye gave me no meat: I was thirsty, and ye gave me no drink: 43I was a stranger, and ye took me not in: naked, and ye clothed me not: sick, and in prison, and ye visited me not. 44Then shall they also answer him, saying, Lord, when saw we thee a hungred, or athirst, or a stranger, or naked, or sick, or in prison, and did not minister unto thee? 45Then shall he answer them, saying, Verily I say unto you, Inasmuch as ye did *it* not to one of

the least of these, ye did *it* not to me. ⁴⁶And these shall go away into everlasting punishment: but the righteous into life eternal. [Dan 12:2; John 5:29; Rom. 2:7]

The plot to kill Jesus

26 And it came to pass, when Jesus had finished all these sayings, he said unto his disciples, ²Ye know that after two days is *the feast of* the passover, and the Son of man is betrayed to be crucified. ³Then assembled together the chief priests, and the scribes, and the elders of the people, unto the palace of the high priest, who was called Caiaphas, ⁴And consulted that they might take Jesus by subtilty, and kill *him*. ⁵But they said, Not on the feast *day*, lest there be an uproar among the people.

Anointing of Jesus at Bethany

6 Now when Jesus was in Bethany, in the house of Simon the leper, ⁷There came unto him a woman having an alabaster box of very precious ointment, and poured *it* on his head, as he sat at meat. ⁸But when his disciples saw *it,* they had indignation, saying, To what purpose *is* this waste? ⁹For this ointment might have been sold for much, and given to the poor. ¹⁰When Jesus understood *it,* he said unto them, Why trouble ye the woman? for she hath wrought a good work upon me. ¹¹For ye have the poor always with you; but me ye have not always. ¹²For in that she hath poured this ointment on my body, she did *it* for my burial. ¹³Verily I say unto you, Wheresoever this gospel shall be preached in the whole world, *there* shall also *this,* that this *woman* hath done, be told for a memorial of her.

The bargain of Judas Iscariot

14 Then one of the twelve, called Judas Iscariot, went unto the chief priests, ¹⁵And said *unto them,* What will ye give me, and I will deliver him unto you? And they covenanted with him for thirty pieces of silver. ¹⁶And from that time he sought opportunity to betray him.

The last supper

17 Now the first *day* of the *feast of* unleavened bread the disciples came to Jesus, saying unto him, Where wilt thou *that* we prepare for thee to eat the passover? ¹⁸And he said, Go into the city to such a man, and say unto him, The Master saith, My time is at hand; I will keep the passover at thy house with my disciples. ¹⁹And the disciples did as Jesus had appointed them; and they made ready the passover.

20 Now when the even was come, he sat down with the twelve. ²¹And as they did eat, he said, Verily I say unto you, that one of you shall betray me. ²²And they were exceeding sorrowful, and began every one of them to say unto him, Lord, is it I? ²³And he answered and said, He that dippeth *his* hand with me in the dish, the same shall betray me. ²⁴The Son of man goeth as it is written of him: but woe unto that man by whom the Son of man is betrayed: it had been good for that man if he had

not been born. 25Then Judas, which betrayed him, answered and said, Master, is it I? He said unto him, Thou hast said.

26 And as they were eating, Jesus took bread, and blessed *it,* and brake *it,* and gave *it* to the disciples, and said, Take, eat; this is my body. 27And he took the cup, and gave thanks, and gave *it* to them, saying, Drink ye all of it; 28For this is my blood of the new testament, which is shed for many for the remission of sins. 29But I say unto you, I will not drink henceforth of this fruit of the vine, until that day when I drink it new with you in my Father's kingdom.

[Mark 14:25; Luke 22:18; Acts 10:41]

30 And when they had sung a hymn, they went out into the mount of Olives. 31Then saith Jesus unto them, All ye shall be offended because of me this night: for it is written, I will smite the shepherd, and the sheep of the flock shall be scattered abroad. 32But after I am risen *again,* I will go before you into Galilee. 33Peter answered and said unto him, Though all *men* shall be offended because of thee, *yet* will I never be offended. 34Jesus said unto him, Verily I say unto thee, That this night, before *the* cock crow, thou shalt deny me thrice. 35Peter said unto him, Though I should die with thee, *yet* will I not deny thee. Likewise also said all the disciples.

Jesus' agony in Gethsemane

36 Then cometh Jesus with them unto a place called Gethsemane, and saith unto the disciples, Sit ye here, while I go and pray yonder. 37And he took with *him* Peter and the two sons of Zebedee, and began to be sorrowful and very heavy. 38Then saith he unto them, My soul is exceeding sorrowful, *even* unto death: tarry ye here, and watch with me. 39And he went a little further, and fell on his face, and prayed, saying, O my Father, if it be possible, let this cup pass from me: nevertheless not as I will, but as thou *wilt.* 40And he cometh unto the disciples, and findeth them asleep, and saith unto Peter, What, could ye not watch with me one hour? 41Watch and pray, that ye enter not into temptation: the spirit indeed *is* willing, but the flesh *is* weak. 42He went away again the second time, and prayed, saying, O my Father, if this cup may not pass away from me, except I drink it, thy will be done. 43And he came and found them asleep again: for their eyes were heavy. 44And he left them, and went away again, and prayed the third time, saying the same words. 45Then cometh he to his disciples, and saith unto them, Sleep on now, and take your rest: behold, the hour is at hand, and the Son of man is betrayed into the hands of sinners. 46Rise, let us be going: behold, he is at hand that doth betray me.

Jesus' betrayal and arrest

47 And while he yet spake, lo, Judas, one of the twelve, came, and with him a great multitude with swords and staves, from the chief priests and elders of the people.

⁴⁸Now he that betrayed him gave them a sign, saying, Whomsoever I shall kiss, that *same* is he: hold him fast. ⁴⁹And forthwith he came to Jesus, and said, Hail, master; and kissed him. ⁵⁰And Jesus said unto him, Friend, wherefore art thou come? Then came they, and laid hands on Jesus, and took him. ⁵¹And behold, one of them which were with Jesus stretched out *his* hand, and drew his sword, and stroke a servant of the high priest's, and smote off his ear. ⁵²Then said Jesus unto him, Put up again thy sword into his place: for all they that take the sword shall perish with the sword. ⁵³Thinkest thou that I cannot now pray to my Father, and he shall presently give me more than twelve legions of angels? ⁵⁴*But* how then shall the scriptures be fulfilled, that thus it must be? ⁵⁵In that *same* hour said Jesus to the multitudes, Are ye come out as against a thief with swords and staves for to take me? I sat daily with you teaching in the temple, and ye laid no hold on me. ⁵⁶But all this was done, that the scriptures of the prophets might be fulfilled. Then all the disciples forsook him, and fled. [Lam. 4:20; See John 18:15]

Jesus before Caiaphas

57 And they that had laid hold on Jesus led *him* away to Caiaphas the high priest, where the scribes and the elders were assembled. ⁵⁸But Peter followed him afar off unto the high priest's palace, and went in, and sat with the servants, to see the end. ⁵⁹Now the chief priests, and elders, and all the council, sought false witness against Jesus, to put him to death; ⁶⁰But found none: yea, though many false witnesses came, *yet* found they none. At the last came two false witnesses, ⁶¹And said, This *fellow* said, I am able to destroy the temple of God, and to build it in three days. ⁶²And the high priest arose, and said unto him, Answerest thou nothing? what *is it which* these witness against thee? ⁶³But Jesus held his peace. And the high priest answered and said unto him, I adjure thee by the living God, that thou tell us whether thou be the Christ, the Son of God. ⁶⁴Jesus saith unto him, Thou hast said: nevertheless I say unto you, Hereafter shall ye see the Son of man sitting on the right hand of power, and coming in the clouds of heaven. ⁶⁵Then the high priest rent his clothes, saying, He hath spoken blasphemy; what further need have we of witnesses? behold, now ye have heard his blasphemy. ⁶⁶What think ye? They answered and said, He is guilty of death. ⁶⁷Then did they spit in his face, and buffeted him; and others smote *him* with the palms of their hands, ⁶⁸Saying, Prophesy unto us, *thou* Christ, Who is he that smote thee? [Mark 14:65; Luke 22:64]

Peter's denial of Jesus

69 Now Peter sat without in the palace: and a damsel came unto him, saying, Thou also wast with Jesus of Galilee. ⁷⁰But he denied before *them* all, saying, I know not what thou sayest. ⁷¹And when he

was gone out into the porch, another *maid* saw him, and said unto them that were there, This *fellow* was also with Jesus of Nazareth. 72 And again he denied with an oath, I do not know the man. 73 And after a while came unto *him* they that stood *by,* and said to Peter, Surely thou also art *one* of them; for thy speech bewrayeth thee. 74 Then began he to curse and to swear, *saying,* I know not the man. And immediately *the* cock crew. 75 And Peter remembered the word of Jesus, which said unto him, Before *the* cock crow, thou shalt deny me thrice. And he went out, and wept bitterly. [ver. 34; Luke 22:61; John 13:38]

The death of Judas Iscariot

27 When the morning was come, all the chief priests and elders of the people took counsel against Jesus to put him to death: 2 And when they had bound him, they led *him* away, and delivered him to Pontius Pilate the governor. [ch. 20:19; Acts 3:13]

3 Then Judas, which had betrayed him, when he saw that he was condemned, repented himself, and brought again the thirty pieces of silver to the chief priests and elders, 4 Saying, I have sinned in that I have betrayed *the* innocent blood. And they said, What *is that* to us? see thou *to that.* 5 And he cast down the pieces of silver in the temple, and departed, and went and hanged himself. 6 And the chief priests took the silver pieces, and said, It is not lawful for to put them into the treasury, because it is the price of blood. 7 And they took counsel, and bought with them the potter's field, to bury strangers in. 8 Wherefore that field was called, The field of blood, unto this day. 9 Then was fulfilled that which was spoken by Jeremie the prophet, saying, And they took the thirty pieces of silver, the price of him that was valued, whom they of the children of Israel did value; 10 And gave them for the potter's field, as the Lord appointed me.

Jesus before Pontius Pilate

11 And Jesus stood before the governor: and the governor asked him, saying, Art thou the King of the Jews? And Jesus said unto him, Thou sayest. 12 And when he was accused of the chief priests and elders, he answered nothing. 13 Then said Pilate unto him, Hearest thou not how many *things* they witness against thee? 14 And he answered him to never a word; insomuch that the governor marvelled greatly.

15 Now at *that* feast the governor was wont to release unto the people a prisoner, whom they would. 16 And they had then a notable prisoner, called Barabbas. 17 Therefore when they were gathered together, Pilate said unto them, Whom will ye *that* I release unto you? Barabbas, or Jesus which is called Christ? 18 For he knew that for envy they had delivered him. 19 When he was set down on the judgment seat, his wife sent unto him, saying, Have thou nothing to do with that just *man:* for I have suffered many *things* this day

in a dream because of him. 20 But the chief priests and elders persuaded the multitude that they should ask Barabbas, and destroy Jesus. 21 The governor answered and said unto them, Whether of the twain will ye *that* I release unto you? They said, Barabbas. 22 Pilate saith unto them, What shall I do then with Jesus which is called Christ? *They* all say unto him, Let him be crucified. 23 And the governor said, Why, what evil hath he done? But they cried out the more, saying, Let him be crucified. 24 When Pilate saw that he could prevail nothing, but *that* rather a tumult was made, he took water, and washed *his* hands before the multitude, saying, I am innocent of the blood of this just *person:* see ye *to it.* 25 Then answered all the people, and said, His blood *be* on us, and on our children. 26 Then released he Barabbas unto them: and when he had scourged Jesus, he delivered *him* to be crucified. [Is. 53:5; Mark 15:15; Luke 23:16,24,25; John 19:1,16]

Jesus crowned with thorns

27 Then the soldiers of the governor took Jesus into the common hall, and gathered unto him the whole band *of soldiers.* 28 And they stripped him, and put on him a scarlet robe. 29 And when they had platted a crown of thorns, they put *it* upon his head, and a reed in his right hand: and they bowed the knee before him, and mocked him, saying, Hail, King of the Jews! 30 And they spit upon him, and took the reed, and smote him on the head. 31 And after that they had mocked him, they took the robe off from him, and put his own raiment on him, and led him away to crucify *him.* 32 And as they came out, they found a man of Cyrene, Simon by name: him they compelled to bear his cross. [Num. 15:35; 1 Ki. 21:13; Acts 7:58; Heb. 13:12; Mark 15:21; Luke 23:26]

Jesus crucified

33 And when they were come unto a place called Golgotha, that is to say, a place of a skull, 34 They gave him vinegar to drink mingled with gall: and when he had tasted *thereof,* he would not drink. 35 And they crucified him, and parted his garments, casting lots: that it might be fulfilled which was spoken by the prophet, They parted my garments among them, and upon my vesture did they cast lots. 36 And sitting down they watched him there; 37 And set up over his head his accusation written, THIS IS JESUS THE KING OF THE JEWS. 38 Then were there two thieves crucified with him, one on the right hand, and another on the left. [Is. 53:12; Mark 15:27; Luke 23:32,33; John 19:18]

39 And they that passed by, reviled him, wagging their heads, 40 And saying, *Thou* that destroyest the temple, and buildest *it* in three days, save thyself. If thou be the Son of God, come down from the cross. 41 Likewise also the chief priests mocking *him,* with the scribes and elders, said, 42 He saved others; himself he cannot save. If he be the King of Israel, let him

now come down from the cross, and we will believe him. 43He trusted in God; let him deliver him now, if he will have him: for he said, I am the Son of God. 44The thieves also, which were crucified with him, cast the same in his teeth. [Mark 15:32; Luke 23:39]

45 Now from the sixth hour there was darkness over all the land unto the ninth hour. 46And about the ninth hour Jesus cried with a loud voice, saying, ELI, ELI, LAMA SABACHTHANI? that is to say, My God, my God, why hast thou forsaken me? 47Some of them that stood there, when they heard *that,* said, This *man* calleth for Elias. 48And straightway one of them ran, and took a spunge, and filled *it* with vinegar, and put *it* on a reed, and gave him to drink. 49The rest said, Let be, let us see whether Elias will come to save him.

The death of Jesus

50 Jesus, when he had cried again with a loud voice, yielded up the ghost. [Mark 15:37; Luke 23:46]

51 And behold, the vail of the temple was rent in twain from the top to the bottom; and the earth did quake, and the rocks rent; 52And the graves were opened; and many bodies of saints which slept arose, 53And came out of the graves after his resurrection, and went into the holy city, and appeared unto many. 54Now when the centurion, and they that were with him, watching Jesus, saw the earthquake, and *those things* that were done, they feared greatly, saying, Truly this was the Son of God.

55And many women were there beholding afar off, which followed Jesus from Galilee, ministering unto him: 56Among which was Mary Magdalene, and Mary the mother of James and Joses, and the mother of Zebedee's children. [Mark 15:40]

Jesus laid in the sepulchre

57 When the even was come, there came a rich man of Arimathea, named Joseph, who also himself was Jesus' disciple: 58He went to Pilate, and begged the body of Jesus. Then Pilate commanded the body to be delivered. 59And when Joseph had taken the body, he wrapped it in a clean linen cloth, 60And laid it in his own new tomb, which he had hewn out in the rock: and he rolled a great stone to the door of the sepulchre, and departed. 61And there was Mary Magdalene, and the other Mary, sitting over against the sepulchre.

The sepulchre guarded

62 Now the next day, that followed the *day of the* preparation, the chief priests and Pharisees came together unto Pilate, 63Saying, Sir, we remember that that deceiver said, while he was yet alive, After three days I will rise *again.* 64Command therefore that the sepulchre be made sure until the third day, lest his disciples come by night, and steal him *away,* and say unto the people, He is risen from the dead: so the last error shall be worse than the first. 65Pilate said unto them, Ye have a watch: go your way, make *it* as sure as you can. 66So they went, and made the

sepulchre sure, sealing the stone, and setting a watch. [Dan. 6:17]

The resurrection of Jesus

28 In the end of the sabbath, as it began to dawn towards the first *day* of the week, came Mary Magdalene and the other Mary to see the sepulchre. ²And behold, there was a great earthquake: for *the* angel of the Lord descended from heaven, and came and rolled back the stone from the door, and sat upon it. ³His countenance was like lightning, and his raiment white as snow: ⁴And for fear of him the keepers did shake, and became as dead *men.* ⁵And the angel answered and said unto the women, Fear not ye: for I know that ye seek Jesus, which was crucified. ⁶He is not here: for he is risen, as he said. Come, see the place where the Lord lay. ⁷And go quickly, and tell his disciples that he is risen from the dead; and behold, he goeth before you into Galilee; there shall ye see him: lo, I have told you. ⁸And they departed quickly from the sepulchre with fear and great joy; and did run to bring his disciples word. ⁹And as they went to tell his disciples, behold, Jesus met them, saying, *All* hail. And they came and held him by the feet, and worshipped him. ¹⁰Then said Jesus unto them, Be not afraid: go tell my brethren that they go into Galilee,

and there shall they see me. [See John 20:17; Rom. 8:29; Heb. 2:11]

The bribing of the soldiers

11 Now when they were going, behold, some of the watch came into the city, and shewed unto the chief priests all the *things* that were done. ¹²And when they were assembled with the elders, and had taken counsel, they gave large money unto the soldiers, ¹³Saying, Say ye, His disciples came by night, and stole him *away* while we slept. ¹⁴And if this come to the governor's ears, we will persuade him, and secure you. ¹⁵So they took the money, and did as they were taught: and this saying is commonly reported among the Jews until this day.

The Great Commission

16 Then the eleven disciples went *away* into Galilee, into a mountain where Jesus had appointed them. ¹⁷And when they saw him, they worshipped him: but some doubted. ¹⁸And Jesus came and spake unto them, saying, All power is given unto me in heaven and in earth. ¹⁹Go ye therefore, and teach all nations, baptizing them in the name of the Father, and of the Son, and of the Holy Ghost: ²⁰Teaching them to observe all *things* whatsoever I have commanded you: and lo, I am with you alway, *even* unto the end of the world. Amen.

John the Baptist

1 The beginning of the gospel of Jesus Christ, the Son of God; ²As it is written in the prophets, Behold, I send my messenger before thy face, which shall prepare thy way before thee. ³The voice of one crying in the wilderness, Prepare ye the way of the Lord, make his paths straight. ⁴John did baptize in the wilderness, and preach the baptism of repentance for the remission of sins. ⁵And there went out unto him all the land of Judea, and they of Jerusalem, and were all baptized of him in the river *of* Jordan, confessing their sins. ⁶And John was clothed with camel's hair, and with a girdle of a skin about his loins; and he did eat locusts and wild honey: ⁷And preached, saying, There cometh one mightier than I after me, the latchet of whose shoes I am not worthy to stoop down and unloose. ⁸I indeed have baptized you with water: but he shall baptize you with the Holy Ghost. [Acts 1:5; 11:16; 19:4; Is. 44:3; Joel 2:28; Acts 2:4; 10:45; 11:15,16; 1 Cor. 12:13]

Baptism and temptation of Jesus

9 And it came to pass in those days, *that* Jesus came from Nazareth of Galilee, and was baptized of John in Jordan. ¹⁰And straightway coming up out of the water, he saw the heavens opened, and the Spirit like a dove descending upon him: ¹¹And there came a voice from heaven, *saying,* Thou art my beloved Son, in whom I am well pleased. [Ps. 2:7; Mat. 3:17; ch. 9:7]

12 And immediately the Spirit driveth him into the wilderness. ¹³And he was there in the wilderness forty days, tempted of Satan; and was with the wild beasts; and the angels ministered unto him. [Mat. 4:11]

14 Now after that John was put in prison, Jesus came into Galilee, preaching the gospel of the kingdom of God, ¹⁵And saying, The time is fulfilled, and the kingdom of God is at hand: repent ye, and believe the gospel. [Dan. 9:25; Gal. 4:4; Eph. 1:10; Mat. 3:2; 4:17]

Jesus calls four disciples

16 Now as he walked by the sea of Galilee, he saw Simon and Andrew his brother casting a net into the sea: for they were fishers. ¹⁷And Jesus said unto them, Come ye after me, and I will make you to become fishers of men. ¹⁸And straightway they forsook their nets, and followed him. ¹⁹And when he had gone a little further thence, he saw James the *son* of Zebedee, and John his brother, who also *were* in the ship mending *their* nets. ²⁰And straightway he called them: and they left their father Zebedee in the ship with the hired servants, and went after him.

The unclean spirit cast out

21 And they went into Capernaum; and straightway on the sabbath day he entered into the synagogue, and taught. ²²And they were astonished at his doctrine: for he taught them as *one* that had authority, and not as the scribes.

23 And there was in their synagogue a man with an unclean spirit; and he cried out, 24 Saying, Let *us* alone; what have we to do with thee, *thou* Jesus of Nazareth? art thou come to destroy us? I know thee who thou art, the Holy One of God. 25 And Jesus rebuked him, saying, Hold thy peace, and come out of him. 26 And when the unclean spirit had torn him, and cried with a loud voice, he came out of him. 27 And they were all amazed, insomuch that *they* questioned among themselves, saying, What *thing* is this? what new doctrine *is* this? for with authority commandeth he even the unclean spirits, and they do obey him. 28 And immediately his fame spread abroad throughout all the region round about Galilee.

The sick healed; devils cast out

29 And forthwith, when they were come out of the synagogue, they entered into the house of Simon and Andrew, with James and John. 30 But Simon's wife's mother lay sick of a fever, and anon they tell him of her. 31 And he came and took her by the hand, and lift her up; and immediately the fever left her, and she ministered unto them. 32 And at even, when the sun did set, they brought unto him all that were diseased, and them that were possessed with devils. 33 And all the city was gathered together at the door. 34 And he healed many *that were* sick of divers diseases, and cast out many devils; and suffered not the devils to speak, because they knew him. [ch. 3:12; Luke 4:41; See Acts 16:17,18]

Jesus preaches in Galilee

35 And in the morning, rising up a great while before day, he went out, and departed into a solitary place, and there prayed. 36 And Simon and they that were with him followed after him. 37 And when they had found him, they said unto him, All *men* seek for thee. 38 And he said unto them, Let us go into the next towns, that I may preach there also: for therefore came I forth. 39 And he preached in their synagogues throughout all Galilee, and cast out devils. [Mat. 4:23; Luke 4:44]

The leper cleansed

40 And there came a leper to him, beseeching him, and kneeling down to him, and saying unto him, If thou wilt, thou canst make me clean. 41 And Jesus, moved with compassion, put forth *his* hand, and touched him, and saith unto him, I will; be thou clean. 42 And as soon as he had spoken, immediately the leprosy departed from him, and he was cleansed. 43 And he straitly charged him, and forthwith sent him away; 44 And saith unto him, See thou say nothing to any *man:* but go thy way, shew thyself to the priest, and offer for thy cleansing *those things* which Moses commanded, for a testimony unto them. 45 But he went out, and began to publish *it* much, and to blaze abroad the matter, insomuch that *Jesus* could no more openly enter into the city, but was without in desert places: and they came to him from every quarter. [Luke 5:15; ch. 2:13]

A man with palsy healed

2 And again he entered into Capernaum after *some* days; and it was noised that he was in the house. ²And straightway many were gathered together, insomuch that there was no room to receive *them*, no, not so much as about the door: and he preached the word unto them. ³And they come unto him, bringing one sick of the palsy, *which was* borne of four. ⁴And when they could not come nigh unto him for the press, they uncovered the roof where he was: and when they had broken *it* up, they let down the bed wherein the sick of the palsy lay. ⁵When Jesus saw their faith, he said unto the sick of the palsy, Son, thy sins be forgiven thee. ⁶But there were certain of the scribes sitting there, and reasoning in their hearts, ⁷Why doth this *man* thus speak blasphemies? who can forgive sins but God only? ⁸And immediately, when Jesus perceived in his spirit that they so reasoned within themselves, he said unto them, Why reason ye these *things* in your hearts? ⁹Whether is it easier to say to the sick of the palsy, *Thy* sins be forgiven thee; or to say, Arise, and take up thy bed, and walk? ¹⁰But that ye may know that the Son of man hath power on earth to forgive sins, (he saith to the sick of the palsy,) ¹¹I say unto thee, Arise, and take up thy bed, and go thy way into thine house. ¹²And immediately he arose, took up the bed, and went forth before *them* all; insomuch that *they* were all amazed, and glorified God, saying, We never saw *it* on this fashion.

Matthew called

13 And he went forth again by the sea side; and all the multitude resorted unto him, and he taught them. ¹⁴And as he passed by, he saw Levi the *son* of Alpheus sitting at the receipt of custom, and said unto him, Follow me. And he arose and followed him. ¹⁵And it came to pass, that as *Jesus* sat at meat in his house, many publicans and sinners sat also together with Jesus and his disciples: for there were many, and they followed him. ¹⁶And when the scribes and Pharisees saw him eat with publicans and sinners, they said unto his disciples, How *is* it that he eateth and drinketh with publicans and sinners? ¹⁷When Jesus heard *it*, he saith unto them, They that are whole have no need of *the* physician, but they that are sick: I came not to call *the* righteous, but sinners to repentance.
[Mat. 9:12,13; 18:11; Luke 5:31,32; 19:10; 1 Tim. 1:15]

The question about fasting

18 And the disciples of John and of the Pharisees used to fast: and they come and say unto him, Why do the disciples of John and of the Pharisees fast, but thy disciples fast not? ¹⁹And Jesus said unto them, Can the children of the bridechamber fast, while the bridegroom is with them? as long as they have the bridegroom with them, they cannot fast. ²⁰But the days will come, when the bridegroom shall be taken away from them, and then shall they fast in those days.

21 No *man* also seweth a piece of new cloth on an old garment: else the new piece that filled it up taketh away *from* the old, and the rent is made worse. 22 And no *man* putteth new wine into old bottles: else the new wine doth burst the bottles, and the wine is spilled, and the bottles will be marred: but new wine must be put into new bottles.

Jesus the Lord of the sabbath

23 And it came to pass, that he went through the corn fields on the sabbath day; and his disciples began, as they went, to pluck the ears of corn. 24 And the Pharisees said unto him, Behold, why do they on the sabbath day *that* which is not lawful? 25 And he said unto them, Have ye never read what David did, when he had need, and was a hungred, he, and they *that were* with him? 26 How he went into the house of God in the days of Abiathar the high priest, and did eat the shewbread, which is not lawful to eat but for the priests, and gave also to them which were with him? 27 And he said unto them, The sabbath was made for man, *and* not man for the sabbath: 28 Therefore the Son of man is Lord also of the sabbath. [Mat. 12:8]

3 And he entered again into the synagogue; and there was a man there which had a withered hand. 2 And they watched him, whether he would heal him on the sabbath day; that they might accuse him. 3 And he saith unto the man which had the withered hand, Stand forth. 4 And he saith unto them, Is it lawful to do good on the sabbath days, or to do evil? to save life, or to kill? But they held their peace. 5 And when he had looked round about on them with anger, being grieved for the hardness of their hearts, he saith unto the man, Stretch forth thine hand. And he stretched *it* out: and his hand was restored whole as the other. 6 And the Pharisees went forth, and straightway took counsel with the Herodians against him, how they might destroy him. [Mat. 12:14; 22:16]

Jesus heals many by the sea

7 But Jesus withdrew himself with his disciples to the sea: and a great multitude from Galilee followed him, and from Judea, 8 And from Jerusalem, and from Idumea, and *from* beyond Jordan; and they about Tyre and Sidon, a great multitude, when they had heard what great *things* he did, came unto him. 9 And he spake to his disciples, that a small ship should wait on him because of the multitude, lest they should throng him. 10 For he had healed many; insomuch that *they* pressed upon him for to touch him, as many as had plagues. 11 And unclean spirits, when they saw him, fell down before him, and cried, saying, Thou art the Son of God. 12 And he straitly charged them that they should not make him known. 13 And he goeth up into a mountain, and calleth unto *him* whom he would: and they came unto him. 14 And he ordained twelve, that they should be with him, and that he might send them forth to preach, 15 And to have power to heal sicknesses, and to

cast out devils: 16And Simon he surnamed Peter; 17And James the *son* of Zebedee, and John the brother of James; (and he surnamed them Boanerges, which is, The sons of thunder:) 18And Andrew, and Philip, and Bartholomew, and Matthew, and Thomas, and James the *son* of Alpheus, and Thaddeus, and Simon the Canaanite, 19And Judas Iscariot, which also betrayed him. And they went into a house. 20And *the* multitude cometh together again, so that they could not so much as eat bread. 21And when his friends heard *of it,* they went out to lay hold on him: for they said, He is beside himself. 22And the scribes which came down from Jerusalem said, He hath Beelzebub, and by the prince of the devils casteth he out devils. 23And he called them unto *him,* and said unto them in parables, How can Satan cast out Satan? 24And if a kingdom be divided against itself, that kingdom cannot stand. 25And if a house be divided against itself, that house cannot stand. 26And if Satan rise up against himself, and be divided, he cannot stand, but hath an end. 27No *man* can enter into a strong *man's* house, and spoil his goods, except he will first bind the strong *man;* and then he will spoil his house. 28Verily I say unto you, All sins shall be forgiven unto the sons of men, and blasphemies wherewith soever they shall blaspheme: 29But he that shall blaspheme against the Holy Ghost hath never forgiveness, but is in danger of eternal damnation. 30Because they said, He hath an unclean spirit.

Jesus' true family

31 There came then *his* brethren and his mother, and, standing without, sent unto him, calling him. 32And *the* multitude sat about him, and they said unto him, Behold, thy mother and thy brethren without seek for thee. 33And he answered them, saying, Who is my mother, or my brethren? 34And he looked round about on them which sat about him, and said, Behold my mother and my brethren. 35For whosoever shall do the will of God, the same is my brother, and my sister, and mother.

The parable of the sower

4 And he began again to teach by the sea side: and there was gathered unto him a great multitude, so that he entered into a ship, and sat in the sea; and the whole multitude was by the sea on the land. 2And he taught them many *things* by parables, and said unto them in his doctrine, 3Hearken; Behold, there went out a sower to sow: 4And it came to pass, as *he* sowed, some fell by the way side, and the fowls of the air came and devoured it up. 5And some fell on stony ground, where it had not much earth; and immediately it sprang up, because *it* had no depth of earth: 6But when the sun was up, it was scorched; and because *it* had no root, it withered away. 7And some fell among thorns, and the thorns grew up, and choked it, and it yielded no

fruit. ⁸And other fell on good ground, and did yield fruit that sprang up and increased; and brought forth, some thirty, and some sixty, and some an hundred. ⁹And he said unto them, He that hath ears to hear, let him hear.

10 And when he was alone, they that were about him with the twelve asked of him the parable. ¹¹And he said unto them, Unto you it is given to know the mystery of the kingdom of God: but unto them that are without, all *these things* are done in parables: ¹²That seeing they may see, and not perceive; and hearing they may hear, and not understand; lest at any time they should be converted, and *their* sins should be forgiven them. ¹³And he said unto them, Know ye not this parable? and how *then* will you know all parables? ¹⁴The sower soweth the word. ¹⁵And these are they by the way side, where the word is sown; but when they have heard, Satan cometh immediately, and taketh away the word that was sown in their hearts. ¹⁶And these are they likewise which are sown on stony ground; who, when they have heard the word, immediately receive it with gladness; ¹⁷And have no root in themselves, and so endure but for a time; afterward, when affliction or persecution ariseth for the word's sake, immediately they are offended. ¹⁸And these are they which are sown among thorns; such as hear the word, ¹⁹And the cares of this world, and the deceitfulness of riches, and the lusts of other *things*

entering in, choke the word, and it becometh unfruitful. ²⁰And these are they which are sown on good ground; such as hear the word, and receive *it,* and bring forth fruit, some thirty*fold,* some sixty, and some an hundred.

Parables about the kingdom

21 And he said unto them, Is a candle brought to be put under a bushel, or under a bed? *and* not to be set on a candlestick? ²²For there is nothing hid, which shall not be manifested; neither was *any thing* kept secret, but that it should come abroad. ²³If any *man* have ears to hear, let him hear. ²⁴And he said unto them, Take heed what you hear: with what measure ye mete, it shall be measured to you: and unto you that hear shall more be given. ²⁵For he that hath, to him shall be given: and he that hath not, from him shall be taken even *that* which he hath. [Mat. 13:12; 25:29; Luke 8:18; 19:26]

26 And he said, So is the kingdom of God, as if a man should cast seed into the ground, ²⁷And should sleep, and rise night and day, and the seed should spring and grow up, he knoweth not how. ²⁸For the earth bringeth forth fruit of herself; first the blade, then the ear, after that the full corn in the ear. ²⁹But when the fruit is brought forth, immediately he putteth in the sickle, because the harvest is come. [Rev. 14:15]

30 And he said, Whereunto shall we liken the kingdom of God? or with what comparison shall we compare it? ³¹*It is* like a grain of

mustard seed, which, when it is sown in the earth, is less than all the seeds that be in the earth: ³²But when it is sown, it groweth up, and becometh greater than all herbs, and shooteth out great branches; so that the fowls of the air may lodge under the shadow of it. ³³And with many such parables spake he the word unto them, as they were able to hear *it.* ³⁴But without a parable spake he not unto them: and *when they were* alone, he expounded all *things* to his disciples.

The storm stilled

³⁵ And the same day, when the even was come, he saith unto them, Let us pass over unto the other side. ³⁶And when they had sent away the multitude, they took him *even* as he was in the ship. And there were also with him other little ships. ³⁷And there arose a great storm of wind, and the waves beat into the ship, so that it was now full. ³⁸And he was in the hinder part of the ship, asleep on a pillow: and they awake him, and say unto him, Master, carest thou not that we perish? ³⁹And he arose, and rebuked the wind, and said unto the sea, Peace, be still. And the wind ceased, and there was a great calm. ⁴⁰And he said unto them, Why are ye so fearful? how *is it that* you have no faith? ⁴¹And they feared exceedingly, and said one to another, What *manner of* man is this, that even the wind and the sea obey him?

Devils cast out

5 And they came over unto the other side of the sea, into the country of the Gadarenes. ²And when he was come out of the ship, immediately there met him out of the tombs a man with an unclean spirit, ³Who had *his* dwelling among the tombs; and no *man* could bind him, no, not with chains: ⁴Because that he had been often bound with fetters and chains, and the chains had been plucked asunder by him, and the fetters broken in pieces: neither could any *man* tame him. ⁵And always, night and day, he was in the mountains, and in the tombs, crying, and cutting himself with stones. ⁶But when he saw Jesus afar off, he ran and worshipped him, ⁷And cried with a loud voice, and said, What have I to do with thee, Jesus, *thou* Son of the most high God? I adjure thee by God, that thou torment me not. ⁸For he said unto him, Come out of the man, *thou* unclean spirit. ⁹And he asked him, What *is* thy name? And he answered, saying, My name *is* Legion: for we are many. ¹⁰And he besought him much that he would not send them away out of the country. ¹¹Now there was there nigh unto the mountains a great herd of swine feeding. ¹²And all the devils besought him, saying, Send us into the swine, that we may enter into them. ¹³And forthwith Jesus gave them leave. And the unclean spirits went out, and entered into the swine: and the herd ran violently down a steep place into the sea, (they were about two thousand,) and were choked in the sea. ¹⁴And they that fed the swine fled, and told *it* in the city, and in the country. And they went out to see what it was that was done. ¹⁵And they come to Jesus, and see him that was possessed with the devil, and had the legion, sitting, and clothed, and in his right mind: and they were afraid. ¹⁶And they that saw *it* told them how it befell to him that was possessed with the devil, and *also* concerning the swine. ¹⁷And they began to pray him to depart out of their coasts. ¹⁸And when he was come into the ship, he that had been possessed with the devil prayed him that he might be with him. ¹⁹Howbeit Jesus suffered him not, but saith unto him, Go home to thy *friends,* and tell them how great *things* the Lord hath done for thee, and hath had compassion on thee. ²⁰And he departed, and began to publish in Decapolis how great *things* Jesus had done for him: and all *men* did marvel.

Jairus' daughter raised

21 And when Jesus was passed over again by ship unto the other side, much people gathered unto him: and he was nigh unto the sea. ²²And behold, there cometh one of the rulers of the synagogue, Jairus by name; and when he saw him, he fell at his feet, ²³And besought him greatly, saying, My little daughter lieth at the point of death: *I pray thee,* come and lay *thy* hands on her, that she may be healed; and she shall live. ²⁴And Jesus went with him; and much

people followed him, and thronged him. ²⁵And a certain woman, which had an issue of blood twelve years, ²⁶And had suffered many *things* of many physicians, and had spent all that she had, and was nothing bettered, but rather grew worse, ²⁷When she had heard of Jesus, came in the press behind, and touched his garment. ²⁸For she said, If I may touch but his clothes, I shall be whole. ²⁹And straightway the fountain of her blood was dried up; and she felt in *her* body that she was healed of *that* plague. ³⁰And Jesus immediately knowing in himself that virtue had gone out of him, turned him about in the press, and said, Who touched my clothes? ³¹And his disciples said unto him, Thou seest the multitude thronging thee, and sayest thou, Who touched me? ³²And he looked round about to see her that had done this *thing.* ³³But the woman fearing and trembling, knowing what was done in her, came and fell down before him, and told him all the truth. ³⁴And he said unto her, Daughter, thy faith hath made thee whole; go in peace, and be whole of thy plague. ³⁵While he yet spake, there came from the ruler of the synagogue's *house certain* which said, Thy daughter is dead: why troublest thou the Master any further? ³⁶As soon as Jesus heard the word *that was* spoken, he saith unto the ruler of the synagogue, Be not afraid, only believe. ³⁷And he suffered no *man* to follow him, save Peter, and James, and John the brother of James. ³⁸And he cometh to the house of the ruler of the synagogue, and seeth *the* tumult, and them that wept and wailed greatly. ³⁹And when he was come in, he saith unto them, Why make ye *this* ado, and weep? the damsel is not dead, but sleepeth. ⁴⁰And they laughed him to scorn. But when he had put *them* all out, he taketh the father and the mother of the damsel, and them that were with him, and entereth in where the damsel was lying. ⁴¹And he took the damsel by the hand, and said unto her, TALITHA CUMI; which is, being interpreted, Damsel (I say unto thee) arise. ⁴²And straightway the damsel arose, and walked; for she was *of the age* of twelve years. And they were astonished with a great astonishment. ⁴³And he charged them straitly that no *man* should know it; and commanded that *something* should be given her to eat. [Mat. 8:4; 9:30; 12:16; 17:19; ch. 3:12; Luke 5:14]

Jesus rejected at Nazareth

6 And he went out from thence, and came into his own country; and his disciples follow him. ²And when the sabbath day was come, he began to teach in the synagogue: and many hearing *him* were astonished, saying, From whence hath this *man* these things? and what wisdom *is this* which is given unto him, that even such mighty works are wrought by his hands? ³Is not this the carpenter, the son of Mary, the brother of James, and Joses, and of Juda, and Simon? and are not his sisters here with us? And they were offended at him. ⁴But Jesus said unto them, A prophet is not without honour, but in his own country, and among his own kin, and in his own house. ⁵And he could there do no mighty work, save that he laid *his* hands upon a few sick *folk*, and healed *them*. ⁶And he marvelled because of their unbelief. And he went round about the villages, teaching. [Is. 59:16; Mat. 9:35; Luke 13:22]

The mission of the twelve

7 And he calleth unto *him* the twelve, and began to send them forth by two and two; and gave them power over unclean spirits; ⁸And commanded them that they should take nothing for *their* journey, save a staff only; no scrip, no bread, no money in *their* purse: ⁹But *be* shod with sandals; and not put on two coats. ¹⁰And he said unto them, In what place soever ye enter into a house, there abide till ye depart from that place. ¹¹And whosoever shall not receive you, nor hear you, when ye depart thence, shake off the dust under your feet for a testimony against them. Verily I say unto you, It shall be more tolerable for Sodom and Gomorrha in the day of judgment, than for that city. ¹²And they went out, and preached that *men* should repent. ¹³And they cast out many devils, and anointed with oil many *that were* sick, and healed *them*. [Jas. 5:14]

Death of John the Baptist

14 And king Herod heard *of him;* (for his name was spread abroad:) and he said, That John the Baptist was risen from the dead,

oft, eat not, holding the tradition of the elders. ⁴And *when they come* from the market, except they wash, they eat not. And many other *things* there be, which they have received to hold, *as* the washing of cups, and pots, brasen vessels, and of tables. ⁵Then the Pharisees and scribes asked him, Why walk not thy disciples according to the tradition of the elders, but eat bread with unwashen hands? ⁶He answered and said unto them, Well hath Esaias prophesied of you hypocrites, as it is written, This people honoureth me with *their* lips, but their heart is far from me. ⁷Howbeit in vain do they worship me, teaching for doctrines the commandments of men. ⁸For laying aside the commandment of God, ye hold the tradition of men, *as* the washing of pots and cups: and many other such like *things* ye do. ⁹And he said unto them, Full well ye reject the commandment of God, that ye may keep your own tradition. ¹⁰For Moses said, Honour thy father and thy mother; and, Whoso curseth father or mother, let him die the death. ¹¹But ye say, If a man shall say to *his* father or mother, *It is* Corban, that is to say, a gift, *by* whatsoever thou mightest be profited by me; *he shall be free.* ¹²And ye suffer him no more to do ought for his father or his mother; ¹³Making the word of God of none effect through your tradition, which ye have delivered: and many such like *things* do ye.

14 And when he had called all the people unto *him,* he said unto them, Hearken unto me every one of you, and understand: ¹⁵There is nothing from without a man, that entering into him can defile him: but the *things* which come out of him, those are they that defile the man. ¹⁶If any *man* have ears to hear, let him hear. ¹⁷And when he was entered into *the* house from the people, his disciples asked him concerning the parable. ¹⁸And he saith unto them, Are ye so without understanding also? Do ye not perceive, that whatsoever *thing* from without entereth into the man, *it* cannot defile him; ¹⁹Because it entereth not into his heart, but into the belly, and goeth out into the draught, purging all meats? ²⁰And he said, That which cometh out of the man, that defileth the man. ²¹For from within, out of the heart of men, proceed evil thoughts, adulteries, fornications, murders, ²²Thefts, covetousness, wickedness, deceit, lasciviousness, an evil eye, blasphemy, pride, foolishness: ²³All these evil *things* come from within, and defile the man.

A Greek woman's faith

24 And from thence he arose, and went into the borders of Tyre and Sidon, and entered into a house, and would have no *man* know *it:* but he could not be hid. ²⁵For a *certain* woman, whose young daughter had an unclean spirit, heard of him, and came and fell at his feet: ²⁶The woman was a Greek, a Syrophenician by nation; and she besought him that he would cast forth the devil out of her daughter. ²⁷But Jesus said unto her, Let the children first be filled:

for it is not meet to take the children's bread, and to cast *it* unto the dogs. 28 And she answered and said unto him, Yes, Lord: yet the dogs under the table eat of the children's crumbs. 29 And he said unto her, For this saying go thy way; the devil is gone out of thy daughter. 30 And when she was come to her house, she found the devil gone out, and *her* daughter laid upon the bed.

A deaf mute healed

31 And again, departing from the coasts of Tyre and Sidon, he came unto the sea of Galilee, through the midst of the coasts of Decapolis. 32 And they bring unto him one *that was* deaf, and had an impediment in his speech; and they beseech him to put *his* hand upon him. 33 And he took him aside from the multitude, and put his fingers into his ears, and he spit, and touched his tongue; 34 And looking up to heaven, he sighed, and saith unto him, EPHPHATHA, that is, Be opened. 35 And straightway his ears were opened, and the string of his tongue was loosed, and he spake plain. 36 And he charged them that they should tell no *man*: but the more he charged them, *so* much the more a great deal they published *it*; 37 And were beyond measure astonished, saying, He hath done all *things* well: he maketh both the deaf to hear, and the dumb to speak.

The four thousand fed

8 In those days the multitude being very great, and having nothing to eat, Jesus called his disciples unto *him*, and saith unto them, 2 I have compassion on the multitude, because they have now been with me three days, and have nothing to eat: 3 And if I send them away fasting to their own houses, they will faint by the way: for divers of them came from far. 4 And his disciples answered him, From whence can a man satisfy these *men* with bread here in the wilderness? 5 And he asked them, How many loaves have ye? And they said, Seven. 6 And he commanded the people to sit down on the ground: and he took the seven loaves, and gave thanks, and brake, and gave to his disciples to set before *them;* and they did set *them* before the people. 7 And they had a few small fishes: and he blessed, and commanded to set them also before *them.* 8 So they did eat, and were filled: and they took up of the broken *meat* that was left seven baskets. 9 And they that had eaten were about four thousand: and he sent them away.

Pharisees ask for a sign

10 And straightway he entered into a ship with his disciples, and came into the parts of Dalmanutha. 11 And the Pharisees came forth, and began to question with him, seeking of him a sign from heaven, tempting him. 12 And he sighed deeply in his spirit, and saith, Why doth this generation seek after a sign? verily I say unto you, There shall no sign be given unto this generation. 13 And he left them, and entering into the ship again departed to the other side.

14 Now *the disciples* had forgotten to take bread, neither had they in the ship with them more than one loaf. 15And he charged them, saying, Take heed, beware of the leaven of the Pharisees, and *of* the leaven of Herod. 16And they reasoned among themselves, saying, *It is* because we have no bread. 17And when Jesus knew *it,* he saith unto them, Why reason ye, because ye have no bread? perceive ye not yet, neither understand? have ye your heart yet hardened? 18Having eyes, see ye not? and having ears, hear ye not? and do ye not remember? 19When I brake the five loaves among five thousand, how many baskets full of fragments took ye up? They say unto him, Twelve. 20And when the seven among four thousand, how many baskets full of fragments took ye up? And they said, Seven. 21And he said unto them, How *is it that* ye do not understand? [ver. 17; ch. 6:52]

A blind man healed

22 And he cometh to Bethsaida; and they bring a blind man unto him, and besought him to touch him. 23And he took the blind man by the hand, and led him out of the town; and when he had spit on his eyes, and put *his* hands upon him, he asked him if he saw ought. 24And he looked up, and said, I see men as trees, walking. 25After that he put *his* hands again upon his eyes, and made him look up: and he was restored, and saw every *man* clearly. 26And he sent him away to his house, saying, Neither go into the town, nor tell *it* to any in the town. [Mat. 8:4; ch. 5:43]

Peter's confession of faith

27 And Jesus went out, and his disciples, into the towns of Cesarea Philippi: and by the way he asked his disciples, saying unto them, Whom do men say that I am? 28And they answered, John the Baptist: but some *say,* Elias; and others, One of the prophets. 29And he saith unto them, But whom say ye that I am? And Peter answereth and saith unto him, Thou art the Christ. 30And he charged them that they should tell no *man* of him. 31And he began to teach them, that the Son of man must suffer many *things,* and be rejected of the elders, and *of* the chief priests, and scribes, and be killed, and after three days rise again. 32And he spake *that* saying openly. And Peter took him, and began to rebuke him. 33But when he had turned about and looked on his disciples, he rebuked Peter, saying, Get thee behind me, Satan: for thou savourest not the *things* that be of God, but the *things* that be of men. 34And when he had called the people unto *him* with his disciples also, he said unto them, Whosoever will come after me, let him deny himself, and take up his cross, and follow me. 35For whosoever will save his life shall lose it; but whosoever shall lose his life for my sake and the gospel's, the same shall save it. 36For what shall it profit a man, if he shall gain the whole world, and lose his own soul? 37Or what shall a man give in

exchange for his soul? 38Whosoever therefore shall be ashamed of me and of my words in this adulterous and sinful generation; of him also shall the Son of man be ashamed, when he cometh in the glory of his Father with the holy angels. [Mat. 10:33; Luke 9:26; 12:9; See Rom. 1:16; 2 Tim. 1:8; 2:12]

9 And he said unto them, Verily I say unto you, That there be some of them that stand here, which shall not taste of death, till they have seen the kingdom of God come with power. [Mat. 16:28; Luke 9:27; Mat. 24:30]

The transfiguration

2 And after six days Jesus taketh with *him* Peter, and James, and John, and leadeth them up into a high mountain apart by themselves: and he was transfigured before them. 3And his raiment became shining, exceeding white as snow; so as no fuller on earth can white *them.* 4And there appeared unto them Elias with Moses: and they were talking with Jesus. 5And Peter answered and said to Jesus, Master, it is good for us to be here: and let us make three tabernacles; one for thee, and one for Moses, and one for Elias. 6For he wist not what to say; for they were sore afraid. 7And there was a cloud that overshadowed them: and a voice came out of the cloud, saying, This is my beloved Son: hear him. 8And suddenly, when they had looked round about, they saw no *man* any more, save Jesus only with themselves.

9 And as they came down from the mountain, he charged them that they should tell no *man* what *things* they had seen, till the Son of man were risen from the dead. 10And they kept *that* saying with themselves, questioning *one* with *another* what the rising from the dead should mean. 11And they asked him, saying, Why say the scribes that Elias must first come? 12And he answered and told them, Elias verily cometh first, and restoreth all *things;* and how it is written of the Son of man, that he must suffer many *things,* and be set at nought. 13But I say unto you, That Elias is indeed come, and they have done unto him whatsoever they listed, as it is written of him. [Mat. 11:14; 17:12; Luke 1:17]

The demoniac boy cured

14 And when he came to *his* disciples, he saw a great multitude about them, and *the* scribes questioning with them. 15And straightway all the people, when they beheld him, were greatly amazed, and running to *him* saluted him. 16And he asked the scribes, What question ye with them? 17And one of the multitude answered and said, Master, I have brought unto thee my son, which hath a dumb spirit; 18And wheresoever he taketh him, he teareth him: and he foameth, and gnasheth with his teeth, and pineth away: and I spake to thy disciples that they should cast him out; and they could not. 19He answereth him, and saith, O faithless generation, how long shall I be with you? how long shall I suffer you? bring him unto me. 20And they brought him unto him: and

when he saw him, straightway the spirit tare him; and he fell on the ground, and wallowed foaming. 21And he asked his father, How long is it ago since this came unto him? And he said, Of a child. 22And ofttimes it hath cast him into the fire, and into the waters, to destroy him: but if thou canst do any *thing,* have compassion on us, and help us. 23Jesus said unto him, If thou canst believe, all *things are* possible to him that believeth. 24And straightway the father of the child cried out, and said with tears, Lord, I believe; help thou mine unbelief. 25When Jesus saw that the people came running together, he rebuked the foul spirit, saying unto him, *Thou* dumb and deaf spirit, I charge thee, come out of him, and enter no more into him. 26And *the spirit* cried, and rent him sore, and came out of *him:* and he was as one dead; insomuch that many said, He is dead. 27But Jesus took him by the hand, and lifted him up; and he arose. 28And when he was come into *the* house, his disciples asked him privately, Why could not we cast him out? 29And he said unto them, This kind can come forth by nothing, but by prayer and fasting.

30 And they departed thence, and passed through Galilee; and he would not that any *man* should know *it.* 31For he taught his disciples, and said unto them, The Son of man is delivered into the hands of men, and they shall kill him; and after that he is killed, he shall rise the third day. 32But they understood not *that* saying, and were afraid to ask him.

True discipleship

33 And he came to Capernaum: and being in the house he asked them, What *was it that* ye disputed among yourselves by the way? 34But they held their peace: for by the way they had disputed among themselves, who *should be* the greatest. 35And he sat down, and called the twelve, and saith unto them, If any *man* desire to be first, *the same* shall be last of all, and servant of all. 36And he took a child, and set him in the midst of them: and when he had taken him in his arms, he said unto them, 37Whosoever shall receive one of such children in my name, receiveth me: and whosoever shall receive me, receiveth not me, but him that sent me. [Mat. 10:40; Luke 9:48]

38 And John answered him, saying, Master, we saw one casting out devils in thy name, and he followeth not us: and we forbad him, because he followeth not us. 39But Jesus said, Forbid him not: for there is no *man* which shall do a miracle in my name, that can lightly speak evil of me. 40For he that is not against us is on our part. 41For whosoever shall give you a cup of water to drink in my name, because ye belong to Christ, verily I say unto you, he shall not lose his reward. 42And whosoever shall offend one of *these* little ones that believe in me, it is better for him that a millstone were hanged about his neck, and he were cast into the sea. 43And if thy hand offend thee, cut it off: it is better for thee to enter into life maimed, than having

two hands to go into hell, into the fire that never shall be quenched: 44Where their worm dieth not, and the fire is not quenched. 45And if thy foot offend thee, cut it off: it is better for thee to enter halt into life, than having two feet to be cast into hell, into the fire that never shall be quenched: 46Where their worm dieth not, and the fire is not quenched. 47And if thine eye offend thee, pluck it out: it is better for thee to enter into the kingdom of God with one eye, than having two eyes to be cast into hell fire: 48Where their worm dieth not, and the fire is not quenched. 49For every one shall be salted with fire, and every sacrifice shall be salted with salt. 50Salt *is* good: but if the salt have lost his saltness, wherewith will ye season it? Have salt in yourselves, and have peace one with another. [Mat. 5:13; Luke 14:34; Eph. 4:29; Col. 4:6; Rom. 12:18; 14:19; 2 Cor. 13:11; Heb. 12:14]

Marriage and divorce

10 And he rose from thence, and cometh into the coasts of Judea by the farther side of Jordan: and the people resort unto him again; and, as he was wont, he taught them again. 2And the Pharisees came to *him,* and asked him, Is it lawful for a man to put away *his* wife? tempting him. 3And he answered and said unto them, What did Moses command you? 4And they said, Moses suffered to write a bill of divorcement, and to put *her* away. 5And Jesus answered and said unto them, For the hardness of your heart he wrote you

this precept. 6But from the beginning of the creation God made them male and female. 7For this cause shall a man leave his father and mother, and cleave to his wife; 8And they twain shall be one flesh: so then they are no more twain, but one flesh. 9What therefore God hath joined together, let not man put asunder. 10And in the house his disciples asked him again of the same *matter.* 11And he saith unto them, Whosoever shall put away his wife, and marry another, committeth adultery against her. 12And if a woman shall put away her husband, and be married to another, she committeth adultery.

Jesus blesses the little children

13 And they brought young children to him, that he should touch them: and *his* disciples rebuked those that brought *them.* 14But when Jesus saw *it,* he was much displeased, and said unto them, Suffer the little children to come unto me, and forbid them not: for of such is the kingdom of God. 15Verily I say unto you, Whosoever shall not receive the kingdom of God as a little child, he shall not enter therein. 16And he took them up in his arms, put *his* hands upon them, and blessed them.

The rich young ruler

17 And when he was gone forth into the way, there came one running, and kneeled to him, and asked him, Good Master, what shall I do that I may inherit eternal life? 18And Jesus said unto him, Why callest thou me good? *there is*

none good but one, *that is,* God. 19Thou knowest the commandments, Do not commit adultery, Do not kill, Do not steal, Do not bear false witness, Defraud not, Honour thy father and mother. 20And he answered and said unto him, Master, all these have I observed from my youth. 21Then Jesus beholding him loved him, and said unto him, One *thing* thou lackest: go thy way, sell whatsoever thou hast, and give to the poor, and thou shalt have treasure in heaven: and come, take up the cross, and follow me. 22And he was sad at *that* saying, and went away grieved: for he had great possessions.

23 And Jesus looked round about, and saith unto his disciples, How hardly shall they that have riches enter into the kingdom of God! 24And the disciples were astonished at his words. But Jesus answereth again, and saith unto them, Children, how hard is it for them that trust in riches to enter into the kingdom of God! 25It is easier for a camel to go through the eye of a needle, than for a rich *man* to enter into the kingdom of God. 26And they were astonished out of measure, saying among themselves, Who then can be saved? 27And Jesus looking upon them saith, With men *it is* impossible, but not with God: for with God all *things* are possible. [Jer. 32:17; Mat. 19:26; Luke 1:37]

28 Then Peter began to say unto him, Lo, we have left all, and have followed thee. 29And Jesus answered and said, Verily I say unto you, There is no *man* that hath left house, or brethren, or sisters, or father, or mother, or wife, or children, or lands, for my sake, and the gospel's, 30But he shall receive an hundredfold now in this time, houses, and brethren, and sisters, and mothers, and children, and lands, with persecutions; and in the world to come eternal life. 31But many *that are* first shall be last; and the last first. [Mat. 19:30; 20:16; Luke 13:30]

Jesus again foretells his death

32 And they were in the way going up to Jerusalem; and Jesus went before them: and they were amazed; and as they followed, they were afraid. And he took again the twelve, and began to tell them what *things* should happen unto him, 33*Saying,* Behold, we go up to Jerusalem; and the Son of man shall be delivered unto the chief priests, and unto the scribes; and they shall condemn him to death, and shall deliver him to the Gentiles: 34And they shall mock him; and shall scourge him, and shall spit upon him, and shall kill him: and the third day he shall rise again.

The ambition of James and John

35 And James and John, the sons of Zebedee, come unto him, saying, Master, we would that thou shouldest do for us whatsoever we shall desire. 36And he said unto them, What would ye that I should do for you? 37They said unto him, Grant unto us that we may sit, one on thy right hand, and the other on thy left hand, in thy glory. 38But Jesus said unto them, Ye know not

what ye ask: can ye drink *of* the cup that I drink *of?* and be baptized *with* the baptism that I am baptized *with?* ³⁹ And they said unto him, We can. And Jesus said unto them, Ye shall indeed drink *of* the cup that I drink *of;* and *with* the baptism that I am baptized *withal* shall ye be baptized: ⁴⁰ But to sit on my right hand and on my left hand is not mine to give; but *it shall be given to them* for whom it is prepared. ⁴¹ And when the ten heard *it,* they began to be much displeased with James and John. ⁴² But Jesus called them to *him,* and saith unto them, Ye know that they which are accounted to rule over the Gentiles exercise lordship over them; and their great ones exercise authority upon them. ⁴³ But so shall it not be among you: but whosoever will be great among you, shall be your minister: ⁴⁴ And whosoever of you will be the chiefest, shall be servant of all. ⁴⁵ For even the Son of man came not to be ministered unto, but to minister, and to give his life a ransom for many. [John 13:14; Phil. 2:7; Mat. 20:28; 1 Tim. 2:6; Tit. 2:14]

Bartimeus receives his sight

46 And they came to Jericho: and as he went out of Jericho with his disciples and a great number of people, blind Bartimeus, the son of Timeus, sat by the *high*way side begging. ⁴⁷ And when he heard that it was Jesus of Nazareth, he began to cry out, and say, Jesus, *thou* Son of David, have mercy on me. ⁴⁸ And many charged him that he should hold his peace: but he cried the more a great deal, *Thou* Son of David, have mercy on me. ⁴⁹ And Jesus stood still, and commanded him to be called. And they call the blind man, saying unto him, Be of good comfort, rise; he calleth thee. ⁵⁰ And he, casting away his garment, rose, and came to Jesus. ⁵¹ And Jesus answered and said unto him, What wilt thou *that* I should do unto thee? The blind man said unto him, Lord, that I might receive my sight. ⁵² And Jesus said unto him, Go thy way; thy faith hath made thee whole. And immediately he received his sight, and followed Jesus in the way. [Mat. 9:22; ch. 5:34]

The triumphal entry

11 And when they came nigh to Jerusalem, unto Bethphage and Bethany, at the mount of Olives, he sendeth forth two of his disciples, ² And saith unto them, Go your way into the village over against you: and as soon as ye be entered into it, ye shall find a colt tied, whereon never man sat; loose him, and bring *him.* ³ And if any *man* say unto you, Why do ye this? say ye that the Lord hath need of him; and straightway he will send him hither. ⁴ And they went their way, and found the colt tied by the door without in a place where two ways met; and they loose him. ⁵ And certain of them that stood there said unto them, What do ye, loosing the colt? ⁶ And they said unto them even as Jesus had commanded: and they let them go. ⁷ And they brought the colt to Jesus, and cast their garments on him; and he sat upon him. ⁸And many spread their garments in the way: and others cut down branches off the trees, and strawed *them* in the way. ⁹And they that went before, and they that followed, cried, saying, Hosanna; Blessed *is* he that cometh in the name of the Lord: ¹⁰Blessed *be* the kingdom of our father David, that cometh in the name of the Lord: Hosanna in the highest. ¹¹And Jesus entered into Jerusalem, and into the temple: and when he had looked round about upon all *things,* and now the eventide was come, he went out unto Bethany with the twelve. [Mat. 21:12]

The cleansing of the temple

12 And on the morrow, when they were come from Bethany, he was hungry: ¹³And seeing a fig tree afar off having leaves, he came, if haply he might find any *thing* thereon: and when he came to it, he found nothing but leaves; for the time of figs was not *yet.* ¹⁴And Jesus answered and said unto it, No *man* eat fruit of thee hereafter for ever. And his disciples heard *it.*

15 And they come to Jerusalem: and Jesus went into the temple, and began to cast out them that sold and bought in the temple, and overthrew the tables of the money-changers, and the seats of them that sold doves; ¹⁶And would not suffer that any *man* should carry *any* vessel through the temple. ¹⁷And he taught, saying unto them, Is it not written, My house shall be called of all nations the house of prayer? but ye have made

it a den of thieves. ¹⁸And the scribes and chief priests heard *it,* and sought how they might destroy him: for they feared him, because all the people was astonished at his doctrine. ¹⁹And when even was come, he went out of the city.

The power of faith

20 And in the morning, as they passed by, they saw the fig tree dried up from the roots. ²¹And Peter calling to remembrance saith unto him, Master, behold, the fig tree which thou cursedst is withered away. ²²And Jesus answering saith unto them, Have faith in God. ²³For verily I say unto you, That whosoever shall say unto this mountain, Be thou removed, and be thou cast into the sea; and shall not doubt in his heart, but shall believe that *those things* which he saith shall come to pass; he shall have whatsoever he saith. ²⁴Therefore I say unto you, What *things* soever ye desire, when ye pray, believe that ye receive *them,* and ye shall have *them.* ²⁵And when ye stand praying, forgive, if ye have ought against any: that your Father also which is in heaven may forgive you your trespasses. ²⁶But if you do not forgive, neither will your Father which is in heaven forgive your trespasses. [Mat. 18:35]

Jesus' authority challenged

27 And they come again to Jerusalem: and as he was walking in the temple, there come to him the chief priests, and the scribes, and the elders, ²⁸And say unto him, By what authority doest thou these *things?* and who gave thee

this authority to do these *things?* 29And Jesus answered and said unto them, I will also ask of you one question, and answer me, and I will tell you by what authority I do these *things.* 30The baptism of John, was *it* from heaven, or of men? answer me. 31And they reasoned with themselves, saying, If we shall say, From heaven; he will say, Why then did ye not believe him? 32But if we shall say, Of men; they feared the people: for all *men* counted John, that he was a prophet indeed. 33And they answered and said unto Jesus, We cannot tell. And Jesus answering saith unto them, Neither do I tell you by what authority I do these *things.*

The parable of the husbandmen

12 And he began to speak unto them by parables. A *certain* man planted a vineyard, and set a hedge about *it,* and digged *a place for* the winefat, and built a tower, and let it out to husbandmen, and went into a far country. 2And at the season he sent to the husbandmen a servant, that he might receive from the husbandmen of the fruit of the vineyard. 3And they caught him, and beat *him,* and sent *him* away empty. 4And again he sent unto them another servant; and at him they cast stones, and wounded *him* in the head, and sent *him* away shamefully handled. 5And again he sent another; and him they killed, and many others; beating some, and killing some. 6Having yet therefore one son, his wellbeloved, he sent him also last unto them,

saying, They will reverence my son. 7But those husbandmen said amongst themselves, This is the heir; come, let us kill him, and the inheritance shall be ours. 8And they took him, and killed *him,* and cast *him* out of the vineyard. 9What shall therefore the lord of the vineyard do? he will come and destroy the husbandmen, and will give the vineyard unto others. 10And have ye not read this scripture; The stone which the builders rejected is become the head of the corner: 11This was the Lord's doing, and it is marvellous in our eyes? 12And they sought to lay hold on him, but feared the people: for they knew that he had spoken the parable against them: and they left him, and went their way. [Mat. 21:45,46; ch. 11:18; John 7:25,30,44]

Tribute to Cesar

13 And they send unto him certain of the Pharisees and of the Herodians, to catch him in *his* words. 14And when they were come, they say unto him, Master, we know that thou art true, and carest for no *man:* for thou regardest not the person of men, but teachest the way of God in truth: Is it lawful to give tribute to Cesar, or not? 15Shall we give, or shall we not give? But he, knowing their hypocrisy, said unto them, Why tempt ye me? bring me a penny, that I may see *it.* 16And they brought *it.* And he saith unto them, Whose *is* this image and superscription? And they said unto him, Cesar's. 17And Jesus answering said unto them, Render to

Cesar the *things* that are Cesar's, and to God the *things* that are God's. And they marvelled at him.

Sadducees and the resurrection

18 Then come unto him *the* Sadducees, which say there is no resurrection; and they asked him, saying, 19 Master, Moses wrote unto us, If a man's brother die, and leave *his* wife *behind him,* and leave no children, that his brother should take his wife, and raise up seed unto his brother. 20 Now there were seven brethren: and the first took a wife, and dying left no seed. 21 And the second took her, and died, neither left he *any* seed: and the third likewise. 22 And the seven had her, and left no seed: last of all the woman died also. 23 In the resurrection therefore, when they shall rise, whose wife shall she be of them? for the seven had her to wife. 24 And Jesus answering said unto them, Do ye not therefore err, because ye know not the scriptures, neither the power of God? 25 For when they shall rise from the dead, they neither marry, nor are given in marriage; but are as *the* angels which are in heaven. 26 And as touching the dead, that they rise: have ye not read in the book of Moses, how in the bush God spake unto him, saying, I *am* the God of Abraham, and the God of Isaac, and the God of Jacob? 27 He is not the God of the dead, but the God of the living: ye therefore do greatly err.

The great commandment

28 And one of the scribes came, and having heard them reasoning together, and perceiving that he had answered them well, asked him, Which is the first commandment of all? 29 And Jesus answered him, The first of all the commandments *is,* Hear, O Israel; The Lord our God is one Lord: 30 And thou shalt love the Lord thy God with all thy heart, and with all thy soul, and with all thy mind, and with all thy strength: this *is* the first commandment. 31 And the second *is* like, *namely* this, Thou shalt love thy neighbour as thyself. There is none other commandment greater than these. 32 And the scribe said unto him, Well, Master, thou hast said the truth: for there is one God; and there is none other but he: 33 And to love him with all the heart, and with all the understanding, and with all the soul, and with all the strength, and to love *his* neighbour as himself, is more than all whole burnt offerings and sacrifices. 34 And when Jesus saw that he answered discreetly, he said unto him, Thou art not far from the kingdom of God. And no *man* after that durst ask him *any question.* [Mat. 22:46]

The question about David's son

35 And Jesus answered and said, while he taught in the temple, How say the scribes that Christ is the Son of David? 36 For David himself said by the Holy Ghost, The LORD said to my Lord, Sit thou on my right hand, till I make thine enemies thy footstool. 37 David therefore himself calleth him Lord; and whence is he *then*

his son? And the common people heard him gladly.

38 And he said unto them in his doctrine, Beware of the scribes, which love to go in long clothing, and *love* salutations in the market-places, 39And the chief seats in the synagogues, and the uppermost rooms at feasts: 40Which devour widows' houses, and for a pretence make long prayers: these shall receive greater damnation. [Mat. 23:14]

The widow's mite

41 And Jesus sat over against the treasury, and beheld how the people cast money into the treasury: and many *that were* rich cast in much. 42And there came a certain poor widow, and she threw in two mites, which make a farthing. 43And he called unto *him* his disciples, and saith unto them, Verily I say unto you, That this poor widow hath cast more in, than all they which have cast into the treasury: 44For all *they* did cast in of their abundance; but she of her want did cast in all that she had, *even* all her living. [Deut. 24:6; 1 John 3:17]

Signs of the end of this age

13 And as he went out of the temple, one of his disciples saith unto him, Master, see what manner of stones and what buildings *are here.* 2And Jesus answering said unto him, Seest thou these great buildings? there shall not be left one stone upon another, that shall not be thrown down. 3And as he sat upon the mount of Olives over against the temple, Peter and James and John and Andrew asked him privately, 4Tell us,

when shall these *things* be? and what *shall be* the sign when all these *things* shall be fulfilled? 5And Jesus answering them began to say, Take heed lest any *man* deceive you: 6For many shall come in my name, saying, I am *Christ;* and shall deceive many. 7And when ye shall hear of wars and rumours of wars, be ye not troubled: for *such things* must needs be; but the end *shall* not *be* yet. 8For nation shall rise against nation, and kingdom against kingdom: and there shall be earthquakes in divers places, and there shall be famines and troubles: these *are* the beginnings of sorrows. [Mat. 24:8]

9 But take heed to yourselves: for they shall deliver you up to councils; and in the synagogues ye shall be beaten: and ye shall be brought before rulers and kings for my sake, for a testimony against them. 10And the gospel must first be published among all nations. 11But when they shall lead *you,* and deliver you up, take no thought beforehand what ye shall speak, neither do ye premeditate: but whatsoever shall be given you in that hour, that speak ye: for it is not ye that speak, but the Holy Ghost. 12Now the brother shall betray the brother to death, and the father the son; and children shall rise up against *their* parents, and shall cause them to be put to death. 13And ye shall be hated of all *men* for my name's sake: but he that shall endure unto the end, the same shall be saved. [Mat. 24:9; Luke 21:17; Dan. 12:12; Mat. 10:22; 24:13; Rev. 2:10]

14 But when ye shall see the abomination of desolation, spoken of by Daniel the prophet, standing where it ought not, (let him that readeth understand,) then let them that be in Judea flee to the mountains: **15**And let him that is on the housetop not go down into the house, neither enter *therein,* to take any *thing* out of his house: **16**And let him that is in the field not turn back again for to take up his garment. **17**But woe to them that are with child, and to them that give suck in those days. **18**And pray ye that your flight be not in the winter. **19**For *in* those days shall be affliction, such as was not from the beginning of the creation which God created unto this time, neither shall be. **20**And except that the Lord had shortened *those* days, no flesh should be saved: but for the elect's sake, whom he hath chosen, he hath shortened the days. **21**And then if any *man* shall say to you, Lo, here *is* Christ; or lo, *he is* there; believe *him* not: **22**For false Christs and false prophets shall rise, and shall shew signs and wonders, to seduce, if *it were* possible, even the elect. **23**But take ye heed: behold, I have foretold you all *things.* [2 Pet. 3:17]

24 But in those days, after that tribulation, the sun shall be darkened, and the moon shall not give her light, **25**And the stars of heaven shall fall, and the powers that are in heaven shall be shaken. **26**And then shall they see the Son of man coming in *the* clouds with great power and glory. **27**And then shall he send his angels, and shall gather together his elect from the four winds, from the uttermost part of the earth to the uttermost part of heaven. **28**Now learn a parable of the fig tree; When her branch is yet tender, and putteth forth leaves, ye know that summer is near: **29**So ye in like manner, when ye shall see these *things* come to pass, know that it is nigh, *even* at the doors. **30**Verily I say unto you, that this generation shall not pass, till all these *things* be done. **31**Heaven and earth shall pass away: but my words shall not pass away. [Is. 40:8]

32 But of that day and *that* hour knoweth no *man,* no, not the angels which are in heaven, neither the Son, but the Father. **33**Take ye heed, watch and pray: for ye know not when the time is. **34***For the Son of man is* as a man taking a far journey, who left his house, and gave authority to his servants, and to every man his work, and commanded the porter to watch. **35**Watch ye therefore: for ye know not when the master of the house cometh, at even, or at midnight, or at the cockcrowing, or in the morning: **36**Lest coming suddenly he find you sleeping. **37**And what I say unto you I say unto all, Watch.

Anointing of Jesus at Bethany

14 After two days was *the feast of* the passover, and *of* unleavened bread: and the chief priests and the scribes sought how they might take him by craft, and put *him* to death. **2**But they said, Not on the feast *day,* lest there be an uproar of the people.

3 And being in Bethany in the house of Simon the leper, as he sat at meat, there came a woman having an alabaster box of ointment of spikenard very precious; and she brake the box, and poured *it* on his head. 4 And there were some that had indignation within themselves, and said, Why was this waste of the ointment made? 5 For it might have been sold for more than three hundred pence, and have been given to the poor. And they murmured against her. 6 And Jesus said, Let her alone; why trouble you her? she hath wrought a good work on me. 7 For ye have the poor with you always, and whensoever ye will ye may do them good: but me ye have not always. 8 She hath done what she could: she is come aforehand to anoint my body to the burying. 9 Verily I say unto you, Wheresoever this gospel shall be preached throughout the whole world, *this* also that she hath done shall be spoken of for a memorial of her.

10 And Judas Iscariot, one of the twelve, went unto the chief priests, to betray him unto them. 11 And when they heard *it*, they were glad, and promised to give him money. And he sought how he might conveniently betray him.

The last supper

12 And the first day of unleavened bread, when they killed the passover, his disciples said unto him, Where wilt thou *that* we go and prepare that thou mayest eat the passover? 13 And he sendeth forth two of his disciples, and saith unto them, Go ye into the city, and there shall meet you a man bearing a pitcher of water: follow him. 14 And wheresoever he shall go in, say ye to the goodman of the house, The Master saith, Where is the guestchamber, where I shall eat the passover with my disciples? 15 And he will shew you a large upper room furnished *and* prepared: there make ready for us. 16 And his disciples went forth, and came into the city, and found as he had said unto them: and they made ready the passover.

17 And in the evening he cometh with the twelve. 18 And as they sat and did eat, Jesus said, Verily I say unto you, One of you which eateth with me shall betray me. 19 And they began to be sorrowful, and to say unto him one by one, *Is* it I? and another *said, Is* it I? 20 And he answered and said unto them, *It is* one of the twelve, that dippeth with me in the dish. 21 The Son of man indeed goeth, as it is written of him: but woe to that man by whom the Son of man is betrayed: good were it for that man if he had never been born. [Mat. 26:24; Luke 22:22]

22 And as they did eat, Jesus took bread, and blessed, and brake *it,* and gave to them, and said, Take, eat: this is my body. 23 And he took the cup, and when he had given thanks, he gave *it* to them: and they all drank of it. 24 And he said unto them, This is my blood of the new testament, which is shed for many. 25 Verily I say unto you, I will drink no more of the fruit of

the vine, until that day that I drink it new in the kingdom of God.

Peter's denial foretold

26 And when they had sung a hymn, they went out into the mount of Olives. 27And Jesus saith unto them, All ye shall be offended because of me this night: for it is written, I will smite the shepherd, and the sheep shall be scattered. 28But after that I am risen, I will go before you into Galilee. 29But Peter said unto him, Although all shall be offended, yet *will* not I. 30And Jesus saith unto him, Verily I say unto thee, That this day, *even* in this night, before *the* cock crow twice, thou shalt deny me thrice. 31But he spake the more vehemently, If I should die with thee, I will not deny thee in any wise. Likewise also said they all.

Jesus' agony in Gethsemane

32 And they came to a place which was named Gethsemane: and he saith to his disciples, Sit ye here, while I shall pray. 33And he taketh with him Peter and James and John, and began to be sore amazed, and to be very heavy; 34And saith unto them, My soul is exceeding sorrowful unto death: tarry ye here, and watch. 35And he went forward a little, and fell on the ground, and prayed that, if it were possible, the hour might pass from him. 36And he said, Abba, Father, all *things are* possible unto thee; take away this cup from me: nevertheless not that I will, but what thou *wilt.* 37And he cometh, and findeth them sleeping, and saith unto Peter, Simon, sleepest

thou? couldest not thou watch one hour? 38Watch ye and pray, lest ye enter into temptation. The spirit truly *is* ready, but the flesh *is* weak. 39And again he went away, and prayed, and spake the same words. 40And when he returned, he found them asleep again, (for their eyes were heavy,) neither wist they what to answer him. 41And he cometh the third time, and saith unto them, Sleep on now, and take your rest: it is enough, the hour is come; behold, the Son of man is betrayed into the hands of sinners. 42Rise up, let us go; lo, he that betrayeth me is at hand. [Mat. 26:46; John 18:1,2]

Jesus' betrayal and arrest

43 And immediately, while he yet spake, cometh Judas, one of the twelve, and with him a great multitude with swords and staves, from the chief priests and the scribes and the elders. 44And he that betrayed him had given them a token, saying, Whomsoever I shall kiss, *that* same is he; take him, and lead *him* away safely. 45And as soon as he was come, he goeth straightway to him, and saith, Master, master; and kissed him. 46And they laid their hands on him, and took him. 47And one of them that stood by drew a sword, and smote a servant of the high priest, and cut off his ear. 48And Jesus answered and said unto them, Are ye come out, as against a thief, with swords and *with* staves to take me? 49I was daily with you in the temple teaching, and ye took me not: but the

scriptures must be fulfilled. ⁵⁰And they all forsook him, and fled. ⁵¹And there followed him a certain young man, having a linen cloth cast about *his* naked *body;* and the young men laid hold on him: ⁵²And he left the linen cloth, and fled from them naked.

Jesus before Caiaphas

53 And they led Jesus away to the high priest: and with him were assembled all the chief priests and the elders and the scribes. ⁵⁴And Peter followed him afar off, even into the palace of the high priest: and he sat with the servants, and warmed himself at the fire. ⁵⁵And the chief priests and all the council sought for witness against Jesus to put him to death; and found none. ⁵⁶For many bare false witness against him, but *their* witness agreed not together. ⁵⁷And there arose certain, and bare false witness against him, saying, ⁵⁸We heard him say, I will destroy this temple that is made with hands, and within three days I will build another made without hands. ⁵⁹But neither so did their witness agree together. ⁶⁰And the high priest stood up in the midst, and asked Jesus, saying, Answerest thou nothing? what *is it which* these witness against thee? ⁶¹But he held his peace, and answered nothing. Again the high priest asked him, and said unto him, Art thou the Christ, the Son of the Blessed? ⁶²And Jesus said, I am: and ye shall see the Son of man sitting on the right hand of power, and coming in the clouds of heav-en. ⁶³Then the high priest rent his clothes, and saith, What need we any further witnesses? ⁶⁴Ye have heard the blasphemy: what think ye? And they all condemned him to be guilty of death. ⁶⁵And some began to spit on him, and to cover his face, and to buffet him, and to say unto him, Prophesy: and the servants did strike him with the palms of their hands.

Peter's denial of Jesus

66 And as Peter was beneath in the palace, there cometh one of the maids of the high priest: ⁶⁷And when she saw Peter warming himself, she looked upon him, and said, *And* thou also wast with Jesus of Nazareth. ⁶⁸But he denied, saying, I know not, neither understand I what thou sayest. And he went out into the porch; and *the* cock crew. ⁶⁹And a maid saw him again, and began to say to them that stood by, This is *one* of them. ⁷⁰And he denied *it* again. And a little after, they that stood by said again to Peter, Surely thou art *one* of them: for thou art a Galilean, and thy speech agreeth *thereto.* ⁷¹But he began to curse and to swear, *saying,* I know not this man of whom ye speak. ⁷²And the second time *the* cock crew. And Peter called to mind the word that Jesus said unto him, Before *the* cock crow twice, thou shalt deny me thrice. And when he thought thereon, he wept. [Mat. 26:75]

Jesus before Pontius Pilate

15 And straightway in the morning the chief priests held a consultation with the elders and scribes and the whole council, and bound Jesus, and carried *him* away, and delivered *him* to Pilate. ²And Pilate asked him, Art thou the King of the Jews? And he answering said unto him, Thou sayest *it.* ³And the chief priests accused him of many *things:* but he answered nothing. ⁴And Pilate asked him again, saying, Answerest thou nothing? behold how many *things* they witness against thee. ⁵But Jesus yet answered nothing; so that Pilate marvelled. [Is. 53:7; John 19:9]

6 Now at *that* feast he released unto them one prisoner, whomsoever they desired. ⁷And there was *one* named Barabbas, *which lay* bound with them that had made insurrection with *him,* who had committed murder in the insurrection. ⁸And the multitude crying aloud began to desire *him to do* as he had ever done unto them. ⁹But Pilate answered them, saying, Will ye *that* I release unto you the King of the Jews? ¹⁰For he knew that the chief priests had delivered him for envy. ¹¹But the chief priests moved the people, that he should rather release Barabbas unto them. ¹²And Pilate answered and said again unto them, What will ye then *that* I shall do *unto him* whom ye call the King of the Jews? ¹³And they cried out again, Crucify him. ¹⁴Then Pilate said unto them, Why, what evil hath he done? And they cried out the more exceedingly, Crucify him. ¹⁵And *so* Pilate, willing to content the people, released Barabbas unto them, and delivered Jesus, when he had scourged *him,* to be crucified. [Mat. 27:26; John 19:1,16]

Jesus crowned with thorns

16 And the soldiers led him away into the hall, called Pretorium; and they call together the whole band. ¹⁷And they clothed him with purple, and platted a crown of thorns, and put *it* about his *head,* ¹⁸And began to salute him, Hail, King of the Jews. ¹⁹And they smote him on the head with a reed, and did spit upon him, and bowing *their* knees worshipped him. ²⁰And when they had mocked him, they took off the purple from him, and put his own clothes on him, and led him out to crucify him. ²¹And they compel one Simon a Cyrenian, who passed by, coming out of the country, the father of Alexander and Rufus, to bear his cross. [Mat. 27:32; Luke 23:26]

Jesus crucified

22 And they bring him unto the place Golgotha, which is, being interpreted, The place of a skull. ²³And they gave him to drink wine mingled with myrrh: but he received *it* not. ²⁴And when they had crucified him, they parted his garments, casting lots upon them, what every *man* should take. ²⁵And it was the third hour, and they crucified him. ²⁶And the superscription of his accusation was written over, THE KING OF THE JEWS. ²⁷And with him they crucify two thieves; the one on *his* right hand, and the other on his left. ²⁸And the scripture was fulfilled, which saith, And he was num-

bered with the transgressors. [Is. 53:12; Luke 22:37]

29 And they that passed by railed on him, wagging their heads, and saying, Ah, *thou* that destroyest the temple, and buildest *it* in three days, **30**Save thyself, and come down from the cross. **31**Likewise also the chief priests mocking said among themselves with the scribes, He saved others; himself he cannot save. **32**Let Christ the King of Israel descend now from the cross, that we may see and believe. And they that were crucified with him reviled him. [Mat. 27:44; Luke 23:39]

The death of Jesus

33 And when the sixth hour was come, there was darkness over the whole land until the ninth hour. **34**And at the ninth hour Jesus cried with a loud voice, saying, ELOI, ELOI, LAMA SABACHTHANI? which is, being interpreted, My God, my God, why hast thou forsaken me? **35**And some of them that stood by, when they heard *it*, said, Behold, he calleth Elias. **36**And one ran and filled a spunge *full* of vinegar, and put *it* on a reed, and gave him to drink, saying, Let alone; let us see whether Elias will come to take him down. [Mat. 27:48; John 19:29; Ps. 69:21]

37 And Jesus cried with a loud voice, and gave up the ghost. **38**And the vail of the temple was rent in twain from the top to the bottom. **39**And when the centurion, which stood over against him, saw that he so cried out, and gave up the ghost, he said, Truly this man was the Son of God. **40**There were also women looking on afar off: among whom was Mary Magdalene, and Mary the mother of James the less and of Joses, and Salome; **41**(Who also, when he was in Galilee, followed him, and ministered unto him;) and many other *women* which came up with him unto Jerusalem. [Luke 8:2,3]

Jesus laid in the tomb

42 And now when the even was come, because it was the preparation, that is, the day before the sabbath, **43**Joseph of Arimathea, an honourable counseller, which also waited for the kingdom of God, came, and went in boldly unto Pilate, and craved the body of Jesus. **44**And Pilate marvelled if he were already dead: and calling unto *him* the centurion, he asked him whether he had been any while dead. **45**And when he knew *it* of the centurion, he gave the body to Joseph. **46**And he bought fine linen, and took him down, and wrapped *him* in the linen, and laid him in a sepulchre which was hewn out of a rock, and rolled a stone unto the door of the sepulchre. **47**And Mary Magdalene and Mary *the mother* of Joses beheld where he was laid.

The resurrection of Jesus

16 And when the sabbath was past, Mary Magdalene, and Mary *the mother* of James, and Salome, had bought *sweet* spices, that they might come and anoint him. **2**And very early in the morning the first *day* of the week, they came unto the sepulchre at the rising of the sun. 3And they said among themselves, Who shall roll us away the stone from the door of the sepulchre? 4And when they looked, they saw that the stone was rolled away: for it was very great. 5And entering into the sepulchre, they saw a young man sitting on the right side, clothed in a long white garment; and they were affrighted. 6And he saith unto them, Be not affrighted: Ye seek Jesus of Nazareth, which was crucified: he is risen; he is not here: behold the place where they laid him. 7But go your way, tell his disciples and Peter that he goeth before you into Galilee: there shall ye see him, as he said unto you. 8And they went out quickly, and fled from the sepulchre; for they trembled and were amazed: neither said they any *thing* to any *man;* for they were afraid. [Mat. 28:8; Luke 24:9]

9 Now when *Jesus* was risen early the first *day* of the week, he appeared first to Mary Magdalene, out of whom he had cast seven devils. 10*And* she went and told them that had been with him, as they mourned and wept. 11And they, when they had heard that he was alive, and had been seen of her, believed not. [Luke 24:11]

12 After that he appeared in another form unto two of them, as they walked, and went into the country. 13And they went and told *it* unto the residue: neither believed they them.

14 Afterward he appeared unto the eleven as they sat at meat, and upbraided them with their unbelief and hardness of heart, because they believed not them which had seen him after he was risen. 15And he said unto them, Go ye into all the world, and preach the gospel to every creature. 16He that believeth and is baptized shall be saved; but he that believeth not shall be damned. 17And these signs shall follow them that believe; In my name shall they cast out devils; they shall speak with new tongues; 18They shall take up serpents; and if they drink any deadly *thing,* it shall not hurt them; they shall lay hands on the sick, and they shall recover. [Luke 10:19; Acts 28:5; 5:15; Jas. 5:14]

19 So then after the Lord had spoken unto them, he was received up into heaven, and sat on the right hand of God. 20And they went forth, and preached every where, the Lord working with *them,* and confirming the word with signs following. Amen.

The Gospel According to
S. Luke

Preface

1 Forasmuch as many have taken in hand to set forth in order a declaration of those things which are most surely believed among us, ²Even as they delivered *them* unto us, which from the beginning were eyewitnesses, and ministers of the word; ³It seemed good to me also, having had perfect understanding of all *things* from the very first, to write unto thee in order, most excellent Theophilus, ⁴That thou mightest know the certainty of *those* things, wherein thou hast been instructed. [John 20:31]

Birth of John foretold

5 There was in the days of Herod, the king of Judea, a certain priest named Zacharias, of the course of Abia: and his wife *was* of the daughters of Aaron, and her name *was* Elisabeth. ⁶And they were both righteous before God, walking in all the commandments and ordinances of the Lord blameless. ⁷And they had no child, because that Elisabeth was barren, and they both were *now* well stricken in years. ⁸And it came to pass, *that* while he executed the priest's office before God in the order of his course, ⁹According to the custom of the priest's office, his lot was to burn incense when he went into the temple of the Lord. ¹⁰And the whole multitude of the people were praying without at the time of incense. ¹¹And there appeared unto him an angel of the Lord standing on the right side of the altar of incense. ¹²And when Zacharias saw *him,* he was troubled, and fear fell upon him. ¹³But the angel said unto him, Fear not, Zacharias: for thy prayer is heard; and thy wife Elisabeth shall bear thee a son, and thou shalt call his name John. ¹⁴And thou shalt have joy and gladness; and many shall rejoice at his birth. ¹⁵For he shall be great in the sight of the Lord, and shall drink neither wine nor strong drink; and he shall be filled with the Holy Ghost, even from his mother's womb. ¹⁶And many of the children of Israel shall he turn to the Lord their God. ¹⁷And he shall go before him in the spirit and power of Elias, to turn the hearts of the fathers to the children, and the disobedient to the wisdom of the just; to make ready a people prepared for the Lord. ¹⁸And Zacharias said unto the angel, Whereby shall I know this? for I am an old man, and my wife well stricken in years. ¹⁹And the angel answering said unto him, I am Gabriel, that stand in the presence of God; and am sent to speak unto thee, and to shew thee these glad tidings. ²⁰And behold, thou shalt be dumb, and not able to speak, until the day that these *things* shall be performed, because thou believest not my words, which shall be fulfilled in their season. ²¹And the people waited for Zacharias, and marvelled that he tarried *so* long in the temple.

22 And when he came out, he could not speak unto them: and they perceived that he had seen a vision in the temple: for he beckoned unto them, and remained speechless. 23 And it came to pass *that,* as soon as the days of his ministration were accomplished, he departed to his own house. 24 And after those days his wife Elisabeth conceived, and hid herself five months, saying, 25 Thus hath the Lord dealt with me in the days wherein he looked on *me,* to take away my reproach among men. [Gen. 30:23; Is. 4:1; 54:1,4]

The birth of Jesus foretold

26 And in the sixth month the angel Gabriel was sent from God unto a city of Galilee, named Nazareth, 27 To a virgin espoused to a man whose name was Joseph, of the house of David; and the virgin's name *was* Mary. 28 And the angel came in unto her, and said, Hail, *thou that art* highly favoured, the Lord *is* with thee: blessed *art* thou among women. 29 And when she saw *him,* she was troubled at his saying, and cast in her mind what manner of salutation this should be. 30 And the angel said unto her, Fear not, Mary: for thou hast found favour with God. 31 And behold, thou shalt conceive in *thy* womb, and bring forth a son, and shalt call his name JESUS. 32 He shall be great, and shall be called the Son of the Highest: and the Lord God shall give unto him the throne of his father David: 33 And he shall reign over the house of Jacob for ever; and of his kingdom there shall be no end. 34 Then said Mary unto the angel, How shall this be, seeing I know not a man? 35 And the angel answered and said unto her, The Holy Ghost shall come upon thee, and the power of the Highest shall overshadow thee: therefore also *that* holy thing which shall be born of thee shall be called the Son of God. 36 And behold, thy cousin Elisabeth, she hath also conceived a son in her old age: and this is the sixth month with her, who was called barren. 37 For with God nothing shall be impossible. 38 And Mary said, Behold the handmaid of the Lord; be it unto me according to thy word. And the angel departed from her.

Mary visits Elisabeth

39 And Mary arose in those days, and went into the hill country with haste, into a city of Juda; 40 And entered into the house of Zacharias, and saluted Elisabeth. 41 And it came to pass *that,* when Elisabeth heard the salutation of Mary, the babe leaped in her womb; and Elisabeth was filled with the Holy Ghost: 42 And she spake out with a loud voice, and said, Blessed *art* thou among women, and blessed *is* the fruit of thy womb. 43 And whence *is* this to me, that the mother of my Lord should come to me? 44 For lo, as soon as the voice of thy salutation sounded in mine ears, the babe leaped in my womb for joy. 45 And blessed *is* she that believed: for there shall be a performance of those *things* which were told her from the Lord.

The song of Mary

46 And Mary said, My soul doth magnify the Lord, 47 And my spirit hath rejoiced in God my Saviour. 48 For he hath regarded the low estate of his handmaiden: for behold, from henceforth all generations shall call me blessed. 49 For he *that is* mighty hath done to me great things; and holy *is* his name. 50 And his mercy *is* on them that fear him from generation to generation. 51 He hath shewed strength with his arm; he hath scattered the proud in the imagination of their hearts. 52 He hath put down the mighty from *their* seats, and exalted them of low degree. 53 He hath filled the hungry with good *things;* and the rich he hath sent empty away. 54 He hath holpen his servant Israel, in remembrance of *his* mercy, 55 (As he spake to our fathers), to Abraham, and to his seed for ever. 56 And Mary abode with her about three months, and returned to her own house.

The birth of John the Baptist

57 Now Elisabeth's full time came that she should be delivered; and she brought forth a son. 58 And *her* neighbours and her cousins heard how the Lord had shewed great mercy upon her; and they rejoiced with her. 59 And it came to pass, *that* on the eighth day they came to circumcise the child; and they called him Zacharias, after the name of his father. 60 And his mother answered and said, Not *so;* but he shall be called John. 61 And they said unto her, There is none of thy kindred that is called by this name. 62 And they made signs to his father, how he would have him called. 63 And he asked for a writing table, and wrote, saying, His name is John. And they marvelled all. 64 And his mouth was opened immediately, and his tongue *loosed,* and he spake, and praised God. 65 And fear came on all that dwelt round about them: and all these sayings were noised abroad throughout all the hill country of Judea. 66 And all they that heard *them* laid *them* up in their hearts, saying, What *manner of* child shall this be! And the hand of the Lord was with him. 67 And his father Zacharias was filled with the Holy Ghost, and prophesied, saying, [Joel 2:28]

The song of Zacharias

68 Blessed *be* the Lord God of Israel; for he hath visited and redeemed his people, 69 And hath raised up a horn of salvation for us in the house of his servant David; 70 (As he spake by the mouth of his holy prophets, which have been since the world began:) 71 That *we* should be saved from our enemies, and from the hand of all that hate us; 72 To perform the mercy *promised* to our fathers, and to remember his holy covenant; 73 The oath which he sware to our father Abraham, 74 That *he* would grant unto us, that *we* being delivered out of the hand of our enemies might serve him without fear, 75 In holiness and righteousness before him, all the days of our life. 76 And thou, child, shalt be called the prophet of the Highest: for thou shalt go be-

fore the face of the Lord to prepare his ways; 77To give knowledge of salvation unto his people by the remission of their sins, 78Through the tender mercy of our God; whereby the dayspring from on high hath visited us, 79To give light to them that sit in darkness and *in* the shadow of death, to guide our feet into the way of peace. 80And the child grew, and waxed strong in spirit, and was in the deserts till the day of his shewing unto Israel. [ch. 2:40; Mat. 3:1]

The birth of Jesus

2 And it came to pass in those days, *that* there went out a decree from Cesar Augustus, that all the world should be taxed. 2(*And* this taxing was first made when Cyrenius was governor of Syria.) 3And all went to be taxed, every one into his own city. 4And Joseph also went up from Galilee, out of the city of Nazareth, into Judea, unto the city of David, which is called Bethlehem; (because he was of the house and lineage of David:) 5To be taxed with Mary his espoused wife, being great with child. 6And so it was *that,* while they were there, the days were accomplished that she should be delivered. 7And she brought forth her firstborn son, and wrapped him in swaddling clothes, and laid him in a manger; because there was no room for them in the inn. 8And there were in the same country shepherds abiding in the field, keeping watch over their flock by night. 9And lo, *the* angel of the Lord came upon

them, and the glory of the Lord shone round about them: and they were sore afraid. 10And the angel said unto them, Fear not: for behold, I bring you good tidings of great joy, which shall be to all people. 11For unto you is born this day in the city of David a Saviour, which is Christ the Lord. 12And this *shall be* a sign unto you; Ye shall find *the* babe wrapped in swaddling clothes, lying in a manger. 13And suddenly there was with the angel a multitude of the heavenly host praising God, and saying, 14Glory to God in the highest, and on earth peace, good will towards men. [ch. 19:38; Eph. 1:6; Is. 57:19; Rom. 5:1; Eph. 2:17; Col. 1:20; John 3:16; Eph. 2:4,7; 2 Thes. 2:16; 1 John 4:9]

15 And it came to pass, as the angels were gone away from them into heaven, the shepherds said one to another, Let us now go *even* unto Bethlehem, and see this thing which is come to pass, which the Lord hath made known unto us. 16And they came with haste, and found Mary, and Joseph, and the babe lying in a manger. 17And when they had seen *it,* they made known abroad the saying which was told them concerning this child. 18And all they that heard *it* wondered at those *things* which were told them by the shepherds. 19But Mary kept all these things, and pondered *them* in her heart. 20And the shepherds returned, glorifying and praising God for all *the things* that they had heard and seen, as it was told unto them.

Jesus presented in the temple

21 And when eight days were accomplished for the circumcising of the child, his name was called JESUS, which was *so* named of the angel before he was conceived in the womb. [Gen. 17:12; Lev. 12:3; ch. 1:59; Mat. 1:21,25; ch. 1:31]

22 And when the days of her purification according to the law of Moses were accomplished, they brought him to Jerusalem, to present *him* to the Lord; **23**(As it is written in the law of the Lord, Every male that openeth the womb shall be called holy to the Lord;) **24**And to offer a sacrifice according to that which is said in the law of the Lord, A pair of turtledoves, or two young pigeons. [Lev. 12:2]

25 And behold, there was a man in Jerusalem, whose name *was* Simeon; and the same man *was* just and devout, waiting for the consolation of Israel: and the Holy Ghost was upon him. **26**And it was revealed unto him by the Holy Ghost, that *he* should not see death, before he had seen the Lord's Christ. **27**And he came by the Spirit into the temple: and when the parents brought in the child Jesus, to do for him after the custom of the law, **28**Then took he him *up* in his arms, and blessed God, and said, **29**Lord, now lettest thou thy servant depart in peace, according to thy word: **30**For mine eyes have seen thy salvation, **31**Which thou hast prepared before the face of all people; **32**A light to lighten the Gentiles, and the glory of thy people Israel. [Is. 9:2; 42:6; 49:6; 60:1-3; Mat. 4:16; Acts 13:47; 28:28]

33 And Joseph and his mother marvelled at those *things* which were spoken of him. **34**And Simeon blessed them, and said unto Mary his mother, Behold, this *child* is set for the fall and rising again of many in Israel; and for a sign which shall be spoken against; **35**(Yea, a sword shall pierce through thy own soul also,) that the thoughts of many hearts may be revealed. [Ps. 42:10; John 19:25]

36 And there was *one* Anna, a prophetess, the daughter of Phanuel, of the tribe of Aser: she was of a great age, and had lived with a husband seven years from her virginity; **37**And she *was* a widow of about fourscore and four years, which departed not from the temple, but served *God* with fastings and prayers night and day. **38**And she coming in that instant gave thanks *likewise* unto the Lord, and spake of him to all them that looked for redemption in Jerusalem. **39**And when they had performed all *things* according to the law of the Lord, they returned into Galilee, to their own city Nazareth. **40**And the child grew, and waxed strong in spirit, filled with wisdom: and the grace of God was upon him. [ver. 52; ch. 1:80]

The boy Jesus in the temple

41 Now his parents went to Jerusalem every year at the feast of the passover. **42**And when he was twelve years old, they went up to Jerusalem after the custom of the feast. **43**And when they had fulfilled the days, as they returned, the child Jesus tarried behind in

Jerusalem; and Joseph and his mother knew not *of it.* 44But they, supposing him to have been in the company, went a day's journey; and they sought him among *their* kinsfolk and acquaintance. 45And when they found him not, they turned back again to Jerusalem, seeking him. 46And it came to pass, *that* after three days they found him in the temple, sitting in the midst of the doctors, both hearing them, and asking them *questions.* 47And all that heard him were astonished at his understanding and answers. 48And when they saw him, they were amazed: and his mother said unto him, Son, why hast thou thus dealt with us? behold, thy father and I have sought thee sorrowing. 49And he said unto them, How *is it* that ye sought me? wist ye not that I must be about my Father's *business?* 50And they understood not the saying which he spake unto them. 51And he went down with them, and came to Nazareth, and was subject unto them: but his mother kept all these sayings in her heart. 52And Jesus increased in wisdom and stature, and in favour with God and man. [ver. 40; 1 Sam. 2:26].

John the Baptist

3 Now in the fifteenth year of the reign of Tiberius Cesar, Pontius Pilate being governor of Judea, and Herod being tetrarch of Galilee, and his brother Philip tetrarch of Iturea and of the region of Trachonitis, and Lysanias the tetrarch of Abilene, 2Annas and Caiaphas being the high priests, the word of God came unto John the son of Zacharias in the wilderness. 3And he came into all the country about Jordan, preaching the baptism of repentance for the remission of sins; 4As it is written in the book of the words of Esaias the prophet, saying, The voice of one crying in the wilderness, Prepare ye the way of the Lord, make his paths straight. 5Every valley shall be filled, and every mountain and hill shall be brought low; and the crooked shall be made straight, and the rough ways *shall be* made smooth; 6And all flesh shall see the salvation of God. 7Then said he to the multitude that came forth to be baptized of him, O generation of vipers, who hath warned you to flee from the wrath to come? 8Bring forth therefore fruits worthy of repentance, and begin not to say within yourselves, We have Abraham to *our* father: for I say unto you, That God is able of these stones to raise up children unto Abraham. 9And now also the axe is laid unto the root of the trees: every tree therefore which bringeth not forth good fruit is hewn down, and cast into the fire. [Mat. 7:19]

10 And the people asked him, saying, What shall we do then? 11He answereth and saith unto them, He that hath two coats, let him impart to him that hath none; and he that hath meat, let him do likewise. 12Then came also publicans to be baptized, and said unto him, Master, what shall we do? 13And he said unto them, Exact no more than that which is appointed

you. 14And *the* soldiers likewise demanded of him, saying, And what shall we do? And he said unto them, Do violence to no man, neither accuse *any* falsely; and be content with your wages. [Ex. 23:1; Lev. 19:11]

15 And as the people were in expectation, and all *men* mused in their hearts of John, whether he were the Christ, or not; 16John answered, saying unto *them* all, I indeed baptize you with water; but one mightier than I cometh, the latchet of whose shoes I am not worthy to unloose: he shall baptize you with the Holy Ghost and *with* fire: 17Whose fan *is* in his hand, and he will throughly purge his floor, and will gather the wheat into his garner; but the chaff he will burn with fire unquenchable. 18And many other *things* in his exhortation preached he unto the people. 19But Herod the tetrarch, being reproved by him for Herodias his brother Philip's wife, and for all the evils which Herod had done, 20Added yet this above all, that he shut up John in prison.

The baptism of Jesus

21 Now when all the people were baptized, it came to pass, *that* Jesus also being baptized, and praying, the heaven was opened, 22And the Holy Ghost descended in a bodily shape like a dove upon him, and a voice came from heaven, which said, Thou art my beloved Son; in thee I am well pleased.

The genealogy of Jesus

23 And Jesus himself began *to be* about thirty years of age, being (as was supposed) the son of Joseph, which was *the son* of Heli, 24Which was *the son* of Matthat, which was *the son* of Levi, which was *the son* of Melchi, which was *the son* of Janna, which was *the son* of Joseph, 25Which was *the son* of Mattathias, which was *the son* of Amos, which was *the son* of Naum, which was *the son* of Esli, which was *the son* of Nagge, 26Which was *the son* of Maath, which was *the son* of Mattathias, which was *the son* of Semei, which was *the son* of Joseph, which was *the son* of Juda, 27Which was *the son* of Joanna, which was *the son* of Rhesa, which was *the son* of Zorobabel, which was *the son* of Salathiel, which was *the son* of Neri, 28Which was *the son* of Melchi, which was *the son* of Addi, which was *the son* of Cosam, which was *the son* of Elmodam, which was *the son* of Er, 29Which was *the son* of Jose, which was *the son* of Eliezer, which was *the son* of Jorim, which was *the son* of Matthat, which was *the son* of Levi, 30Which was *the son* of Simeon, which was *the son* of Juda, which was *the son* of Joseph, which was *the son* of Jonan, which was *the son* of Eliakim, 31Which was *the son* of Melea, which was *the son* of Menan, which was *the son* of Mattatha, which was *the son* of Nathan, which was *the son* of David, 32Which was *the son* of Jesse, which was *the son* of Obed, which was *the son* of Booz, which was *the son* of Salmon, which was *the son* of Naasson, 33Which was *the son* of Aminadab, which was *the son* of Aram, which

was *the son* of Esrom, which was *the son* of Phares, which was *the son* of Juda, 34Which was *the son* of Jacob, which was *the son* of Isaac, which was *the son* of Abraham, which was *the son* of Thara, which was *the son* of Nachor, 35Which was *the son* of Saruch, which was *the son* of Ragau, which was *the son* of Phalec, which was *the son* of Heber, which was *the son* of Sala, 36Which was *the son* of Cainan, which was *the son* of Arphaxad, which was *the son* of Sem, which was *the son* of Noe, which was *the son* of Lamech, 37Which was *the son* of Mathusala, which was *the son* of Enoch, which was *the son* of Jared, which was *the son* of Maleleel, which was *the son* of Cainan, 38Which was *the son* of Enos, which was *the son* of Seth, which was *the son* of Adam, which was *the son* of God. [Gen. 5:12]

The temptation in the wilderness

4 And Jesus being full of the Holy Ghost returned from Jordan, and was led by the Spirit into the wilderness, 2Being forty days tempted of the devil. And in those days he did eat nothing: and when they were ended, he afterward hungered. 3And the devil said unto him, If thou be the Son of God, command this stone that it be made bread. 4And Jesus answered him, saying, It is written, That man shall not live by bread alone, but by every word of God. 5And the devil, taking him up into a high mountain, shewed unto him all the kingdoms of the world in a moment of time. 6And the devil said

unto him, All this power will I give thee, and the glory of them: for *that* is delivered unto me; and to whomsoever I will I give it. 7If thou therefore wilt worship me, all shall be thine. 8And Jesus answered and said unto him, Get thee behind me, Satan: for it is written, Thou shalt worship the Lord thy God, and him only shalt thou serve. 9And he brought him to Jerusalem, and set him on a pinnacle of the temple, and said unto him, If thou be the Son of God, cast thyself down from hence: 10For it is written, He shall give his angels charge over thee, to keep thee: 11And in *their* hands they shall bear thee up, lest at any time thou dash thy foot against a stone. 12And Jesus answering said unto him, It is said, Thou shalt not tempt the Lord thy God. 13And when the devil had ended all the temptation, he departed from him for a season. [John 14:30; Heb. 4:15]

Jesus rejected at Nazareth

14 And Jesus returned in the power of the Spirit into Galilee: and there went out a fame of him through all the region round about. 15And he taught in their synagogues, being glorified of all. 16And he came to Nazareth, where he had been brought up: and, as his custom was, he went into the synagogue on the sabbath day, and stood up for to read. 17And there was delivered unto him the book of the prophet Esaias. And when he had opened the book, he found the place where it was written, 18The Spirit of the Lord *is* upon me, be-

cause he hath anointed me to preach the gospel to the poor; he hath sent me to heal the broken-hearted, to preach deliverance to the captives, and recovering of sight to the blind, to set at liberty *them that are* bruised, 19To preach the acceptable year of the Lord. 20And he closed the book, and he gave *it* again to the minister, and sat down. And the eyes of all *them that were* in the synagogue were fastened on him. 21And he began to say unto them, This day is this scripture fulfilled in your ears. 22And all bare him witness, and wondered at the gracious words which proceeded out of his mouth. And they said, Is not this Joseph's son? 23And he said unto them, Ye will surely say unto me this proverb, Physician, heal thyself: whatsoever we have heard done in Capernaum, do also here in thy country. 24And he said, Verily I say unto you, No prophet is accepted in his own country. 25But I tell you of a truth, many widows were in Israel in the days of Elias, when the heaven was shut up three years and six months, when great famine was throughout all the land; 26But unto none of them was Elias sent, save unto Sarepta, *a city* of Sidon, unto a woman *that was* a widow. 27And many lepers were in Israel in the time of Eliseus the prophet; and none of them was cleansed, saving Naaman the Syrian. 28And all *they* in the synagogue, when they heard these *things,* were filled with wrath, 29And rose up, and thrust him out of the city, and led him unto the brow of the hill whereon their city was built, that *they* might cast him down headlong. 30But he passing through the midst of them went *his way,* 31And came down to Capernaum, a city of Galilee, and taught them on the sabbath days. 32And they were astonished at his doctrine: for his word was with power. [Mat. 7:28,29]

The unclean spirit cast out

33 And in the synagogue there was a man, which had a spirit of an unclean devil, and cried out with a loud voice, 34Saying, Let *us* alone; what have we to do with thee, *thou* Jesus of Nazareth? art thou come to destroy us? I know thee who thou art, the Holy One of God. 35And Jesus rebuked him, saying, Hold thy peace, and come out of him. And when the devil had thrown him in the midst, he came out of him, and hurt him not. 36And they were all amazed, and spake among themselves, saying, What a word *is* this! for with authority and power he commandeth the unclean spirits, and they come out. 37And the fame of him went out into every place of the country round about.

The sick healed; devils cast out

38 And he arose out of the synagogue, and entered into Simon's house. And Simon's wife's mother was taken with a great fever; and they besought him for her. 39And he stood over her, and rebuked the fever; and it left her: and immediately she arose and ministered unto them. 40Now when the sun was setting, all they that had *any* sick with divers diseases

brought them unto him; and he laid *his* hands on every one of them, and healed them. 41And devils also came out of many, crying out, and saying, Thou art Christ the Son of God. And he rebuking *them* suffered them not to speak: for they knew that he was Christ. [Mark 1:34; 3:11; ver. 34,35; Mark 1:25,34]

42 And when it was day, he departed and went into a desert place: and the people sought him, and came unto him, and stayed him, that *he* should not depart from them. 43And he said unto them, I must preach the kingdom of God to other cities also: for therefore am I sent. 44And he preached in the synagogues of Galilee. [Mark 1:39]

The call of the first disciples

5 And it came to pass that, as the people pressed upon him to hear the word of God, he stood by the lake of Gennesaret, 2And saw two ships standing by the lake: but the fishermen were gone out of them, and were washing *their* nets. 3And he entered into one of the ships, which was Simon's, and prayed him that *he* would thrust out a little from the land. And he sat down, and taught the people out of the ship. 4Now when he had left speaking, he said unto Simon, Launch out into the deep, and let down your nets for a draught. 5And Simon answering said unto him, Master, we have toiled all the night, and have taken nothing: nevertheless at thy word I will let down the net. 6And when they had

this done, they inclosed a great multitude of fishes: and their net brake. 7And they beckoned unto *their* partners, which were in the other ship, that *they* should come and help them. And they came, and filled both the ships, so that they began to sink. 8When Simon Peter saw *it*, he fell down at Jesus' knees, saying, Depart from me; for I am a sinful man, O Lord. 9For he was astonished, and all that were with him, at the draught of the fishes which they had taken: 10And so *was* also James, and John, *the* sons of Zebedee, which were partners with Simon. And Jesus said unto Simon, Fear not; from henceforth thou shalt catch men. 11And when they had brought *their* ships to land, they forsook all, and followed him. [Mat. 4:20; 19:27; Mark 1:18; ch. 18:28]

The leper cleansed

12 And it came to pass, when he was in a certain city, behold a man full of leprosy: who seeing Jesus fell on *his* face, and besought him, saying, Lord, if thou wilt, thou canst make me clean. 13And he put forth *his* hand, and touched him, saying, I will: be thou clean. And immediately the leprosy departed from him. 14And he charged him to tell no *man:* but go, and shew thyself to the priest, and offer for thy cleansing, according as Moses commanded, for a testimony unto them. 15But *so much* the more went there a fame abroad of him: and great multitudes came together to hear, and to be healed by him of their infirmities. 16And he withdrew himself into the wilderness, and prayed. [Mat. 14:23; Mark 6:46]

A man with palsy healed

17 And it came to pass on a certain day, as he was teaching, that there were Pharisees and doctors of the law sitting *by,* which were come out of every town of Galilee, and Judea, and Jerusalem: and the power of the Lord was *present* to heal them. 18 And behold, men brought in a bed a man which was taken with a palsy: and they sought *means* to bring him in, and to lay *him* before him. 19 And when they could not find by what *way* they might bring him in because of the multitude, they went upon the housetop, and let him down through the tiling with *his* couch into the midst before Jesus. 20 And when he saw their faith, he said unto him, Man, thy sins are forgiven thee. 21 And the scribes and the Pharisees began to reason, saying, Who is this which speaketh blasphemies? Who can forgive sins, but God alone? 22 But when Jesus perceived their thoughts, he answering said unto them, What reason ye in your hearts? 23 Whether is easier, to say, Thy sins be forgiven thee; or to say, Rise up and walk? 24 But that ye may know that the Son of man hath power upon earth to forgive sins, (he said unto the sick of the palsy,) I say unto thee, Arise, and take up thy couch, and go into thine house. 25 And immediately he rose up before them, and took up *that* whereon he lay, and departed to his own house,

glorifying God. 26 And they were all amazed, and they glorified God, and were filled with fear, saying, We have seen strange *things* to day.

The call of Levi

27 And after these *things* he went forth, and saw a publican, named Levi, sitting at the receipt of custom: and he said unto him, Follow me. 28 And he left all, rose up, and followed him. 29 And Levi made him a great feast in his own house: and there was a great company of publicans and of others that sat down with them. 30 But their scribes and Pharisees murmured against his disciples, saying, Why do ye eat and drink with publicans and sinners? 31 And Jesus answering said unto them, They that are whole need not a physician; but they that are sick. 32 I came not to call *the* righteous, but sinners to repentance. [Mat. 9:13; 1 Tim. 1:15]

The question about fasting

33 And they said unto him, Why do the disciples of John fast often, and make prayers, and likewise the *disciples* of the Pharisees; but thine eat and drink? 34 And he said unto them, Can ye make the children of the bridechamber fast, while the bridegroom is with them? 35 But the days will come, when the bridegroom shall be taken away from them, and then shall they fast in those days. 36 And he spake also a parable unto them; No *man* putteth a piece of a new garment upon an old; if otherwise, *then* both the new maketh a rent, and the piece that was *taken* out of

the new agreeth not with the old.
37And no *man* putteth new wine
into old bottles; else the new wine
will burst the bottles, and be
spilled, and the bottles shall perish.
38But new wine must be put into
new bottles; and both are preserved. 39No *man* also having
drunk old *wine* straightway desireth new: for he saith, The old is
better.

Jesus the Lord of the sabbath

6 And it came to pass on the
second sabbath after the first,
that he went through the corn
fields; and his disciples plucked the
ears of corn, and did eat, rubbing
them in *their* hands. 2And certain
of the Pharisees said unto them,
Why do ye *that* which is not lawful
to do on the sabbath days? 3And
Jesus answering them said, Have
ye not read so much as this, what
David did, when himself was a
hungred, and they which were
with him; 4How he went into the
house of God, and did take and eat
the shewbread, and gave also to
them that were with him; which it
is not lawful to eat but for the
priests alone? 5And he said unto
them, That the Son of man is Lord
also of the sabbath.

6 And it came to pass also on
another sabbath, that he entered
into the synagogue and taught: and
there was a man whose right hand
was withered. 7And the scribes
and Pharisees watched him,
whether he would heal on the sabbath day; that they might find an
accusation against him. 8But he
knew their thoughts, and said to
the man which had the withered
hand, Rise up, and stand *forth* in
the midst. And he arose and stood
forth. 9Then said Jesus unto them,
I will ask you one *thing;* Is it lawful
on the sabbath days to do good, or
to do evil? to save life, or to destroy
it? 10And looking round about
upon them all, he said unto the
man, Stretch forth thy hand. And
he did so: and his hand was restored whole as the other. 11And
they were filled with madness; and
communed one with another what
they might do to Jesus.

The choosing of the twelve

12 And it came to pass in those
days, *that* he went out into a
mountain to pray, and continued
all night in prayer to God. 13And
when it was day, he called unto
him his disciples: and of them he
chose twelve, whom also he
named apostles; 14Simon, (whom
he also named Peter,) and Andrew
his brother, James and John, Philip
and Bartholomew, 15Matthew and
Thomas, James the *son* of Alpheus,
and Simon called Zelotes, 16And
Judas *the brother* of James, and
Judas Iscariot, which also was the
traitor. [Jude 1]

Beatitudes and woes

17 And he came down with
them, and stood in the plain, and
the company of his disciples, and a
great multitude of people out of all
Judea and Jerusalem, and *from* the
sea coast of Tyre and Sidon, which
came to hear him, and to be healed
of their diseases; 18And they that
were vexed with unclean spirits:
and they were healed. 19And the

whole multitude sought to touch him: for there went virtue out of him, and healed *them* all. [Mat. 14:36; Mark 5:30; ch. 8:46]

20 And he lifted up his eyes on his disciples, and said, Blessed *be* ye poor: for yours is the kingdom of God. [Mat. 5:3; 11:5; Jas. 2:5]

21 Blessed *are ye* that hunger now: for ye shall be filled. Blessed *are ye* that weep now: for ye shall laugh. [Is. 55:1; 65:13; Mat. 5:6; Is. 61:3; Mat. 5:4]

22 Blessed are ye, when men shall hate you, and when they shall separate you *from their company,* and shall reproach *you,* and cast out your name as evil, for the Son of man's sake. **23**Rejoice ye in that day, and leap *for joy:* for behold, your reward *is* great in heaven: for in the like manner did their fathers unto the prophets. [Mat. 5:12; Acts 5:41; Col. 1:24; Jas. 1:2; Acts 7:51]

24 But woe unto you that are rich: for ye have received your consolation. [Amos 6:1; Jas. 5:1; ch. 12:21; Mat. 6:2,5,16; ch. 16:25]

25 Woe unto you that are full: for ye shall hunger. Woe unto you that laugh now: for ye shall mourn and weep. [Is. 65:13; Prov. 14:13]

26 Woe unto you, when all men shall speak well of you: for so did their fathers to the false prophets. [John 15:19; 1 John 4:5]

The law of love

27 But I say unto you which hear, Love your enemies, do good to them which hate you, **28**Bless them that curse you, and pray for them which despitefully use you. **29***And* unto him that smiteth thee on the *one* cheek offer also the other; and him that taketh away thy cloke forbid not *to take thy* coat also. **30**Give to every man that asketh of thee; and of him that taketh away thy *goods* ask *them* not again. **31**And as ye would that men should do to you, do ye also to them likewise. **32**For if ye love them which love you, what thank have ye? for sinners also love those that love them. **33**And if ye do good to them which do good to you, what thank have ye? for sinners also do *even* the same. **34**And if ye lend *to them* of whom ye hope to receive, what thank have ye? for sinners also lend to sinners, to receive as much again. **35**But love ye your enemies, and do good, and lend, hoping for nothing again; and your reward shall be great, and ye shall be the children of the Highest: for he is kind unto the unthankful and *to the* evil. **36**Be ye therefore merciful, as your Father also is merciful. **37**Judge not, and ye shall not be judged: condemn not, and ye shall not be condemned: forgive, and ye shall be forgiven: **38**Give, and it shall be given unto you; good measure, pressed down, and shaken *together,* and running over, shall *men* give into your bosom. For with the same measure that ye mete withal it shall be measured to you again. [Prov. 19:17; Ps. 79:12; Mat. 7:2; Mark 4:24; Jas. 2:13]

39 And he spake a parable unto them, Can the blind lead the blind? shall they not both fall into the ditch? **40**The disciple is not above his master: but every one *that is* perfect shall be as his master. ⁴¹And why beholdest thou the mote that is in thy brother's eye, but perceivest not the beam that is in thine own eye? ⁴²Either how canst thou say to thy brother, Brother, let me pull out the mote that is in thine eye, when thou thyself beholdest not the beam that is in thine own eye? *Thou* hypocrite, cast out first the beam out of thine own eye, and then shalt thou see clearly to pull out the mote that is in thy brother's eye. ⁴³For a good tree bringeth not forth corrupt fruit; neither doth a corrupt tree bring forth good fruit. ⁴⁴For every tree is known by his own fruit. For of thorns *men* do not gather figs, nor of a bramble bush gather they grapes. ⁴⁵A good man out of the good treasure of his heart bringeth forth that which is good; and an evil man out of the evil treasure of his heart bringeth forth that which is evil: for of the abundance of the heart his mouth speaketh. [Mat. 12:35; Mat. 12:34]

The wise and foolish builders

46 And why call ye me, Lord, Lord, and do not *the things* which I say? ⁴⁷Whosoever cometh to me, and heareth my sayings, and doeth them, I will shew you to whom he is like: ⁴⁸He is like a man which built a house, and digged deep, and laid the foundation on a rock: and when the flood arose, the stream beat vehemently upon that house, and could not shake it: for it was founded upon a rock. ⁴⁹But he that heareth, and doeth not, is like a man that without a foundation

built a house upon the earth; against which the stream did beat vehemently, and immediately it fell; and the ruin of that house was great.

The centurion's servant healed

7 Now when he had ended all his sayings in the audience of the people, he entered into Capernaum. ²And a certain centurion's servant, who was dear unto him, was sick, and ready to die. ³And when he heard of Jesus, he sent unto him *the* elders of the Jews, beseeching him that he would come and heal his servant. ⁴And when they came to Jesus, they besought him instantly, saying, That he was worthy for whom he should do this: ⁵For he loveth our nation, and he hath built us a synagogue. ⁶Then Jesus went with them. And when he was now not far from the house, the centurion sent friends to him, saying unto him, Lord, trouble not thyself: for I am not worthy that thou shouldest enter under my roof: ⁷Wherefore neither thought I myself worthy to come unto thee: but say in a word, and my servant shall be healed. ⁸For I also am a man set under authority, having under me soldiers, and I say unto one, Go, and he goeth; and to another, Come, and he cometh; and to my servant, Do this, and he doeth *it.* ⁹When Jesus heard these *things,* he marvelled at him, and turned him *about,* and said unto the people that followed him, I say unto you, I have not found so great faith, no, not in Israel. ¹⁰And they that were sent, returning to the house, found the servant whole that had been sick.

The raising of the widow's son

11 And it came to pass the *day* after, *that* he went into a city called Nain; and many of his disciples went with him, and much people. 12Now when he came nigh to the gate of the city, behold, there was a dead man carried out, the only son of his mother, and she was a widow: and much people of the city was with her. 13And when the Lord saw her, he had compassion on her, and said unto her, Weep not. 14And he came and touched the bier: and they that bare *him* stood still. And he said, Young man, I say unto thee, Arise. 15And he that was dead sat up, and began to speak. And he delivered him to his mother. 16And there came a fear on all: and they glorified God, saying, That a great prophet is risen up among us; and, That God hath visited his people. 17And this rumour of him went forth throughout all Judea, and throughout all the region round about.

Tribute to John the Baptist

18 And the disciples of John shewed him of all these *things*. 19And John calling unto *him* two of his disciples sent *them* to Jesus, saying, Art thou he that should come? or look we for another? 20When the men were come unto him, they said, John Baptist hath sent us unto thee, saying, Art thou he that should come? or look we for another? 21And in that *same* hour he cured many of *their* infirmities and plagues, and of evil spir-

its; and unto many *that were* blind he gave sight. 22Then Jesus answering said unto them, Go *your way,* and tell John what *things* ye have seen and heard; how that the blind see, the lame walk, the lepers are cleansed, the deaf hear, the dead are raised, to the poor the gospel is preached. 23And blessed is *he,* whosoever shall not be offended in me. 24And when the messengers of John were departed, he began to speak unto the people concerning John, What went ye out into the wilderness for to see? A reed shaken with the wind? 25But what went ye out for to see? A man clothed in soft raiment? Behold, they which are gorgeously apparelled, and live delicately, are in kings' courts. 26But what went ye out for to see? A prophet? Yea, I say unto you, and much more than a prophet. 27This is *he,* of whom it is written, Behold, I send my messenger before thy face, which shall prepare thy way before thee. 28For I say unto you, Among *those that are* born of women there is not a greater prophet than John the Baptist: but he that is least in the kingdom of God is greater than he. 29And all the people that heard *him,* and the publicans, justified God, being baptized *with* the baptism of John. 30But the Pharisees and lawyers rejected the counsel of God against themselves, being not baptized of him. [Acts 20:27]

31 And the Lord said, Whereunto then shall I liken the men of this generation? and to what are they like? 32They are like unto children sitting in the marketplace, and call-

ing one to another, and saying, We have piped unto you, and ye have not danced; we have mourned to you, and ye have not wept. 33For John the Baptist came neither eating bread nor drinking wine; and ye say, He hath a devil. 34The Son of man is come eating and drinking; and ye say, Behold a gluttonous man, and a winebibber, a friend of publicans and sinners. 35But wisdom is justified of all her children. [Mat. 11:19]

Jesus forgives a sinful woman

36 And one of the Pharisees desired him that he would eat with him. And he went into the Pharisee's house, and sat down to meat. 37And behold, a woman in the city, which was a sinner, when she knew that *Jesus* sat at meat in the Pharisee's house, brought an alabaster box of ointment, 38And stood at his feet behind *him* weeping, and began to wash his feet with tears, and did wipe *them* with the hairs of her head, and kissed his feet, and anointed *them* with the ointment. 39Now when the Pharisee which had bidden him saw *it,* he spake within himself, saying, This *man,* if he were a prophet, would have known who and what manner of woman *this is* that toucheth him: for she is a sinner. 40And Jesus answering said unto him, Simon, I have somewhat to say unto thee. And he saith, Master, say *on.* 41There was a certain creditor which had two debtors: the one ought five hundred pence, and the other fifty. 42And when they had nothing to

pay, he frankly forgave *them* both. Tell me therefore, which of them will love him most? 43Simon answered and said, I suppose that *he,* to whom he forgave most. And he said unto him, Thou hast rightly judged. 44And he turned to the woman, and said unto Simon, Seest thou this woman? I entered into thine house, thou gavest me no water for my feet: but she hath washed my feet with tears, and wiped *them* with the hairs of her head. 45Thou gavest me no kiss: but this *woman* since the time I came in hath not ceased to kiss my feet. 46Mine head with oil thou didst not anoint: but this *woman* hath anointed my feet with ointment. 47Wherefore I say unto thee, Her sins, which are many, are forgiven; for she loved much: but to whom little is forgiven, *the same* loveth little. 48And he said unto her, Thy sins are forgiven. 49And they that sat at meat with *him* began to say within themselves, Who is this that forgiveth sins also? 50And he said to the woman, Thy faith hath saved thee; go in peace. [Mat. 9:22; Mark 5:34; 10:52; ch. 8:48; 18:42]

The parable of the sower

8 And it came to pass afterward, that he went throughout every city and village, preaching and shewing the glad tidings of the kingdom of God: and the twelve *were* with him, 2And certain women, which had been healed of evil spirits and infirmities, Mary called Magdalene, out of whom went seven devils, 3And Joanna the wife of Chuza Herod's steward,

and Susanna, and many others, which ministered unto him of their substance.

4 And when much people were gathered together, and were come to him out of every city, he spake by a parable: 5A sower went out to sow his seed: and as he sowed, some fell by the way side; and it was trodden down, and the fowls of the air devoured it. 6And some fell upon a rock; and as soon as it was sprung up, it withered away, because it lacked moisture. 7And some fell among thorns; and the thorns sprang up with it, and choked it. 8And other fell on good ground, and sprang up, and bare fruit an hundredfold. And when he said these things, he cried, He that hath ears to hear, let him hear.

9 And his disciples asked him, saying, What might this parable be? 10And he said, Unto you it is given to know the mysteries of the kingdom of God: but to others in parables; that seeing they might not see, and hearing they might not understand. 11Now the parable is this: The seed is the word of God. 12Those by the way side are they that hear; then cometh the devil, and taketh away the word out of their hearts, lest they should believe and be saved. 13They on the rock are they, which, when they hear, receive the word with joy; and these have no root, which for a while believe, and in time of temptation fall away. 14And that which fell among thorns are they, which, when they have heard, go forth, and are choked with cares and riches and pleasures of this life, and bring no fruit to perfection. 15But that on the good ground are they, which in an honest and good heart, having heard the word, keep it, and bring forth fruit with patience.

16 No man, when he hath lighted a candle, covereth it with a vessel, or putteth it under a bed; but setteth it on a candlestick, that they which enter in may see the light. 17For nothing is secret, that shall not be made manifest; neither any thing hid, that shall not be known and come abroad. 18Take heed therefore how ye hear: for whosoever hath, to him shall be given; and whosoever hath not, from him shall be taken even that which he seemeth to have. [Mat. 13:12; 25:29; ch. 19:26]

Jesus' true family

19 Then came to him his mother and his brethren, and could not come at him for the press. 20And it was told him by certain which said, Thy mother and thy brethren stand without, desiring to see thee. 21And he answered and said unto them, My mother and my brethren are these which hear the word of God, and do it.

The storm stilled

22 Now it came to pass on a certain day, that he went into a ship with his disciples: and he said unto them, Let us go over unto the other side of the lake. And they launched forth. 23But as they sailed he fell asleep: and there came down a storm of wind on the lake; and they were filled with water, and were in jeopardy. 24And they came

to *him,* and awoke him, saying, Master, master, we perish. Then he rose, and rebuked the wind and the raging of the water: and they ceased, and there was a calm. 25 And he said unto them, Where is your faith? And they being afraid wondered, saying one to another, What *manner of man* is this? for he commandeth even the winds and water, and they obey him.

Devils cast out

26 And they arrived at the country of the Gadarenes, which is over against Galilee. 27 And when he went forth to land, there met him out of the city a certain man, which had devils long time, and ware no clothes, neither abode in *any* house, but in the tombs. 28 When he saw Jesus, he cried out, and fell down before him, and with a loud voice said, What have I to do with thee, Jesus, *thou* Son of God most high? I beseech thee, torment me not. 29 (For he had commanded the unclean spirit to come out of the man. For oftentimes it had caught him: and he was kept bound with chains and in fetters; and he brake the bands, and was driven of the devil into the wilderness.) 30 And Jesus asked him, saying, What is thy name? And he said, Legion: because many devils were entered into him. 31 And they besought him that he would not command them to go out into the deep. 32 And there was there a herd of many swine feeding on the mountain: and they besought him that he would suffer them to enter into them. And he suffered them.

33 Then went the devils out of the man, and entered into the swine: and the herd ran violently down a steep place into the lake, and were choked. 34 When they that fed *them* saw what was done, they fled, and went and told *it* in the city and in the country. 35 Then they went out to see what was done; and came to Jesus, and found the man, out of whom the devils were departed, sitting at the feet of Jesus, clothed, and in his right mind: and they were afraid. 36 They also which saw *it* told them by what means he that was possessed of the devils was healed. 37 Then the whole multitude of the country of the Gadarenes round about besought him to depart from them; for they were taken with great fear: and he went *up* into the ship, and returned *back again.* 38 Now the man out of whom the devils were departed besought him that *he* might be with him: but Jesus sent him away, saying, 39 Return to thine own house, and shew how great *things* God hath done unto thee. And he went his way, and published throughout the whole city how great *things* Jesus had done unto him.

A ruler's daughter raised

40 And it came to pass, that, when Jesus was returned, the people gladly received him: for they were all waiting for him. 41 And behold, there came a man named Jairus, and he was a ruler of the synagogue: and he fell down at Jesus' feet, and besought him that *he* would come into his house: 42 For

he had one only daughter, about twelve years of age, and she lay a dying. (But as he went the people thronged him. 43And a woman having an issue of blood twelve years, which had spent all *her* living upon physicians, neither could be healed of any, 44Came behind *him,* and touched the border of his garment: and immediately her issue of blood stanched. 45And Jesus said, Who touched me? When all denied, Peter and they that were with him said, Master, the multitude throng thee and press *thee,* and sayest thou, Who touched me? 46And Jesus said, Somebody hath touched me: for I perceive that virtue is gone out of me. 47And when the woman saw that she was not hid, she came trembling, and falling down before him, she declared unto him before all the people for what cause she had touched him, and how she was healed immediately. 48And he said unto her, Daughter, be of good comfort: thy faith hath made thee whole; go in peace.) 49While he yet spake, there cometh one from the ruler of the synagogue's *house,* saying to him, Thy daughter is dead; trouble not the Master. 50But when Jesus heard *it,* he answered him, saying, Fear not: believe only, and she shall be made whole. 51And when he came into the house, he suffered no *man* to go in, save Peter, and James, and John, and the father and the mother of the maiden. 52And all wept, and bewailed her: but he said, Weep not; she is not dead, but sleepeth. 53And they laughed him to scorn,

knowing that she was dead. 54And he put *them* all out, and took her by the hand, and called, saying, Maid, arise. 55And her spirit came again, and she arose straightway: and he commanded to give her meat. 56And her parents were astonished: but he charged them that they should tell no *man* what was done. [Mat. 8:4; 9:30; Mark 5:43]

The mission of the twelve

9 Then he called his twelve disciples together, and gave them power and authority over all devils, and to cure diseases. 2And he sent them to preach the kingdom of God, and to heal the sick. 3And he said unto them, Take nothing for *your* journey, neither staves, nor scrip, neither bread, neither money; neither have two coats apiece. 4And whatsoever house ye enter into, there abide, and thence depart. 5And whosoever will not receive you, when ye go out of that city, shake off the very dust from your feet for a testimony against them. 6And they departed, and went through the towns, preaching the gospel, and healing every where. [Mark 6:12]

7 Now Herod the tetrarch heard of all that was done by him: and he was perplexed, because that it was said of some, that John was risen from the dead; 8And of some, that Elias had appeared; and *of* others, that one of the old prophets was risen again. 9And Herod said, John have I beheaded: but who is this, of whom I hear such *things?* And he desired to see him. [ch. 23:8]

The five thousand fed

10 And the apostles, when they were returned, told him all that they had done. And he took them, and went aside privately into a desert place belonging to the city called Bethsaida. 11 And the people, when they knew *it,* followed him: and he received them, and spake unto them of the kingdom of God, and healed them that had need of healing. 12 And *when* the day began to wear away, then came the twelve, and said unto him, Send the multitude away, that they may go into the towns and country round about, and lodge, and get victuals: for we are here in a desert place. 13 But he said unto them, Give ye them to eat. And they said, We have no more but five loaves and two fishes; except we should go and buy meat for all this people. 14 For they were about five thousand men. And he said to his disciples, Make them sit down by fifties in a company. 15 And they did so, and made *them* all sit down. 16 Then he took the five loaves and the two fishes, and looking up to heaven, he blessed them, and brake, and gave to the disciples to set before the multitude. 17 And they did eat, and were all filled: and there was taken up of fragments that remained to them twelve baskets.

Peter's confession of faith

18 And it came to pass, as he was alone praying, *his* disciples were with him: and he asked them, saying, Whom say the people that I am? 19 They answering said, John the Baptist; but some *say,* Elias; and others *say,* that one of the old prophets is risen again. 20 He said unto them, But whom say ye that I am? Peter answering said, The Christ of God. 21 And he straitly charged them, and commanded *them* to tell no *man* that *thing;* 22 Saying, The Son of man must suffer many *things,* and be rejected of the elders and chief priests and scribes, and be slain, and be raised the third day. 23 And he said to *them* all, If any *man* will come after me, let him deny himself, and take up his cross daily, and follow me. 24 For whosoever will save his life shall lose it: but whosoever will lose his life for my sake, the same shall save it. 25 For what is a man advantaged, if he gain the whole world, and lose himself, or be cast away? 26 For whosoever shall be ashamed of me and of my words, of him shall the Son of man be ashamed, when he shall come in his own glory, and *in his* Father's, and of the holy angels. 27 But I tell you of a truth, there be some standing here, which shall not taste of death, till they see the kingdom of God. [Mat. 16:28; Mark 9:1]

The transfiguration

28 And it came to pass about an eight days after these sayings, he took Peter and John and James, and went up into a mountain to pray. 29 And as he prayed, the fashion of his countenance was altered, and his raiment *was* white *and* glistering. 30 And behold, there talked with him two men, which were Moses and Elias: 31 Who appeared

in glory, and spake of his decease which he should accomplish at Jerusalem. 32But Peter and they that were with him were heavy with sleep: and when they were awake, they saw his glory, and the two men that stood with him. 33And it came to pass, as they departed from him, Peter said unto Jesus, Master, it is good for us to be here: and let us make three tabernacles; one for thee, and one for Moses, and one for Elias: not knowing what he said. 34While he thus spake, there came a cloud, and overshadowed them: and they feared as they entered into the cloud. 35And there came a voice out of the cloud, saying, This is my beloved Son: hear him. 36And when the voice was past, Jesus was found alone. And they kept *it* close, and told no *man* in those days any of *those things* which they had seen. [Mat. 17:9]

A demoniac boy healed

37 And it came to pass, *that* on the next day, when they were come down from the hill, much people met him. 38And behold, a man of the company cried out, saying, Master, I beseech thee, look upon my son: for he is mine only child. 39And lo, a spirit taketh him, and he suddenly crieth out; and it teareth him that he foameth again, and bruising him hardly departeth from him. 40And I besought thy disciples to cast him out; and they could not. 41And Jesus answering said, O faithless and perverse generation, how long shall I be with you, and suffer you? Bring thy son

hither. 42And as he was yet a coming, the devil threw him down, and tare *him*. And Jesus rebuked the unclean spirit, and healed the child, and delivered him again to his father.

43 And they were all amazed at the mighty power of God. But while they wondered every one at all *things* which Jesus did, he said unto his disciples, 44Let these sayings sink down into your ears: for the Son of man shall be delivered into the hands of men. 45But they understood not this saying, and it was hid from them, that they perceived it not: and they feared to ask him of that saying. [Mark 9:32; ch. 2:50; 18:34]

True discipleship

46 Then there arose a reasoning among them, which of them should be greatest. 47And Jesus, perceiving the thought of their heart, took a child, and set him by him, 48And said unto them, Whosoever shall receive this child in my name receiveth me: and whosoever shall receive me receiveth him that sent me: for he that is least among you all, the same shall be great. [Mat. 10:40; 18:5; Mark 9:37; John 12:44; 13:20; Mat. 23:11,12]

49 And John answered and said, Master, we saw one casting out devils in thy name; and we forbad him, because he followeth not with us. 50And Jesus said unto him, Forbid *him* not: for he that is not against us is for us. [See Mat. 12:30; ch. 11:23]

James and John rebuked

51 And it came to pass, when

the time was come that he should be received up, he stedfastly set his face to go to Jerusalem, ⁵²And sent messengers before his face: and they went, and entered into a village of the Samaritans, to make ready for him. ⁵³And they did not receive him, because his face was *as though he* would go to Jerusalem. ⁵⁴And when his disciples James and John saw *this,* they said, Lord, wilt thou *that* we command fire to come down from heaven, and consume them, even as Elias did? ⁵⁵But he turned, and rebuked them, and said, Ye know not what manner of spirit ye are of. ⁵⁶For the Son of man is not come to destroy men's lives, but to save *them.* And they went to another village. [John 3:17; 12:47]

The teaching about discipleship

57 And it came to pass *that,* as they went in the way, a certain *man* said unto him, Lord, I will follow thee whithersoever thou goest. ⁵⁸And Jesus said unto him, Foxes have holes, and birds of the air *have* nests; but the Son of man hath not where to lay *his* head. ⁵⁹And he said unto another, Follow me. But he said, Lord, suffer me first to go and bury my father. ⁶⁰Jesus said unto him, Let the dead bury their dead: but go thou and preach the kingdom of God. ⁶¹And another also said, Lord, I will follow thee; but let me first go bid them farewell, which are *at home* in my house. ⁶²And Jesus said unto him, No *man* having put his hand to the plough, and looking back, is fit for the kingdom of God.

The mission of the seventy

10 After these *things* the Lord appointed other seventy also, and sent them two and two before his face into every city and place, whither he himself would come. ²Therefore said he unto them, The harvest truly *is* great, but the labourers *are* few: pray ye therefore the Lord of the harvest, that he would send forth labourers into his harvest. ³Go your ways: behold, I send you forth as lambs among wolves. ⁴Carry neither purse, nor scrip, nor shoes: and salute no *man* by the way. ⁵And into whatsoever house ye enter, first say, Peace *be* to this house. ⁶And if the son of peace be there, your peace shall rest upon it: if not, it shall turn to you again. ⁷And in the same house remain, eating and drinking such *things* as they give: for the labourer is worthy of his hire. Go not from house to house. ⁸And into whatsoever city ye enter, and they receive you, eat such *things* as are set before you: ⁹And heal the sick that are therein, and say unto them, The kingdom of God is come nigh unto you. ¹⁰But into whatsoever city ye enter, and they receive you not, go *your ways* out into the streets of the same, and say, ¹¹Even the *very* dust of your city, which cleaveth on us, we do wipe off against you: notwithstanding be ye sure of this, that the kingdom of God is come nigh unto you. ¹²But I say unto you, that it shall be more tolerable in that day for Sodom, than for that city. [Mat. 10:15; Mark 6:11]

13 Woe unto thee, Chorazin,

woe unto thee, Bethsaida: for if the mighty works had been done in Tyre and Sidon, which have been done in you, they had a great while ago repented, sitting in sackcloth and ashes. 14But it shall be more tolerable for Tyre and Sidon at the judgment, than for you. 15And thou, Capernaum, which art exalted to heaven, shalt be thrust down to hell. 16He that heareth you heareth me; and he that despiseth you despiseth me; and he that despiseth me despiseth him that sent me. [Mat. 10:40; Mark 9:37; John 13:20; 1 Thes. 4:8; John 5:23]

17 And the seventy returned *again* with joy, saying, Lord, even the devils are subject unto us through thy name. 18And he said unto them, I beheld Satan as lightning fall from heaven. 19Behold, I give unto you power to tread on serpents and scorpions, and over all the power of the enemy: and nothing shall by any means hurt you. 20Notwithstanding in this rejoice not, that the spirits are subject unto you; but rather rejoice, because your names are written in heaven. [Ex. 32:32; Ps. 69:28; Is. 4:3; Dan. 12:1; Phil. 4:3; Heb. 12:23; Rev. 13:8; 20:12]

21 In that hour Jesus rejoiced in spirit, and said, I thank thee, O Father, Lord of heaven and earth, that thou hast hid these *things* from the wise and prudent, and hast revealed them unto babes: even so, Father; for so it seemed good in thy sight. 22All *things* are delivered to me of my Father: and no *man* knoweth who the Son is, but the Father; and who the Father is, but the Son, and *he* to whom the Son

will reveal *him*. 23And he turned him unto *his* disciples, and said privately, Blessed *are* the eyes which see *the things* that ye see: 24For I tell you, that many prophets and kings have desired to see *those things* which ye see, and have not seen *them;* and to hear *those things* which ye hear, and have not heard *them*. [1 Pet. 1:10]

The good Samaritan

25 And behold, a certain lawyer stood up, and tempted him, saying, Master, what shall I do to inherit eternal life? 26He said unto him, What is written in the law? how readest thou? 27And he answering said, Thou shalt love the Lord thy God with all thy heart, and with all thy soul, and with all thy strength, and with all thy mind; and thy neighbour as thyself. 28And he said unto him, Thou hast answered right: this do, and thou shalt live. 29But he, willing to justify himself, said unto Jesus, And who is my neighbour? 30And Jesus answering said, A certain man went down from Jerusalem to Jericho, and fell among thieves, which stripped him of his raiment, and wounded *him,* and departed, leaving *him* half dead. 31And by chance there came down a certain priest that way: and when he saw him, he passed by on the other side. 32And likewise a Levite, when he was at the place, came and looked *on him,* and passed by on the other side. 33But a certain Samaritan, as he journeyed, came where he was: and when he saw him, he had compassion *on him,* 34And went to *him,*

and bound up his wounds, pouring in oil and wine, and set him on his own beast, and brought him to an inn, and took care of him. ³⁵And on the morrow when he departed, he took out two pence, and gave *them* to the host, and said unto him, Take care of him; and whatsoever thou spendest more, when I come again, I will repay thee. ³⁶Which now of these three, thinkest thou, was neighbour unto him that fell among the thieves? ³⁷And he said, He that shewed mercy on him. Then said Jesus unto him, Go, and do thou likewise.

Jesus visits Mary and Martha

38 Now it came to pass, as they went, that he entered into a certain village: and a certain woman named Martha received him into her house. ³⁹And she had a sister called Mary, which also sat at Jesus' feet, and heard his word. ⁴⁰But Martha was cumbered about much serving, and came to *him,* and said, Lord, dost thou not care that my sister hath left me to serve alone? bid her therefore that she help me. ⁴¹And Jesus answered and said unto her, Martha, Martha, thou art careful and troubled about many *things:* ⁴²But one *thing* is needful: and Mary hath chosen *that* good part, which shall not be taken away from her. [Ps. 27:4]

Jesus' teaching on prayer

11 And it came to pass *that,* as he was praying in a certain place, when he ceased, one of his disciples said unto him, Lord, teach us to pray, as John also taught his disciples. ²And he said unto them, When ye pray, say, Our Father which art in heaven, Hallowed be thy name. Thy kingdom come. Thy will be done, as in heaven, so in earth. ³Give us day by day our daily bread. ⁴And forgive us our sins; for we also forgive every one *that is* indebted to us. And lead us not into temptation; but deliver us from evil.

5 And he said unto them, Which of you shall have a friend, and shall go unto him at midnight, and say unto him, Friend, lend me three loaves; ⁶For a friend of mine in *his* journey is come to me, and I have nothing to set before him: ⁷And he from within shall answer and say, Trouble me not: the door is now shut, and my children are with me in bed; I cannot rise and give thee? ⁸I say unto you, Though he will not rise and give him, because *he* is his friend, yet because of his importunity he will rise and give him as many as he needeth. ⁹And I say unto you, Ask, and it shall be given you; seek, and ye shall find; knock, and it shall be opened unto you. ¹⁰For every one that asketh receiveth; and he that seeketh findeth; and to him that knocketh it shall be opened. ¹¹*If* a son shall ask bread of any of you that is a father, will he give him a stone? or if *he ask* a fish, will he for a fish give him a serpent? ¹²Or if he shall ask an egg, will he offer him a scorpion? ¹³If ye then, being evil, know how to give good gifts unto your children: how much more shall *your* heavenly Father give the Holy Spirit to them that ask him?

The Pharisees' slander

14 And he was casting out a devil, and it was dumb. And it came to pass, when the devil was gone out, the dumb spake; and the people wondered. 15But some of them said, He casteth out devils through Beelzebub the chief of the devils. 16And other, tempting *him*, sought of him a sign from heaven. 17But he, knowing their thoughts, said unto them, Every kingdom divided against itself is brought to desolation; and a house *divided* against a house falleth. 18If Satan also be divided against himself, how shall his kingdom stand? because ye say that I cast out devils through Beelzebub. 19And if I by Beelzebub cast out devils, by whom do your sons cast *them* out? therefore shall they be your judges. 20But if I with the finger of God cast out devils, no doubt the kingdom of God is come upon you. 21When a strong *man* armed keepeth his palace, his goods are in peace: 22But when a stronger than he shall come upon *him*, and overcome him, he taketh *from him* all his armour wherein he trusted, and divideth his spoils. 23He that is not with me is against me: and he that gathereth not with me scattereth. 24When the unclean spirit is gone out of a man, he walketh through dry places, seeking rest; and finding none, he saith, I will return unto my house whence I came out. 25And when he cometh, he findeth *it* swept and garnished. 26Then goeth he, and taketh to *him* seven other spirits more wicked than himself; and they enter in,

and dwell there: and the last *state* of that man is worse than the first. [John 5:14; Heb. 6:4; 10:26; 2 Pet. 2:20]

27 And it came to pass, as he spake these *things,* a certain woman of the company lift up her voice, and said unto him, Blessed *is* the womb that bare thee, and the paps which thou hast sucked. 28But he said, Yea rather, blessed *are* they that hear the word of God, and keep it. [Mat. 7:21; ch. 8:21; Jas. 1:25]

Warning against seeking signs

29 And when the people were gathered thick together, he began to say, This is an evil generation: they seek a sign; and there shall no sign be given it, but the sign of Jonas the prophet. 30For as Jonas was a sign unto the Ninevites, so shall also the Son of man be to this generation. 31*The* queen of the south shall rise up in the judgment with the men of this generation, and condemn them: for she came from the utmost parts of the earth to hear the wisdom of Solomon; and behold, a greater than Solomon *is* here. 32*The* men of Nineveh shall rise up in the judgment with this generation, and shall condemn it: for they repented at the preaching of Jonas; and behold, a greater than Jonas *is* here. [Jonah 3:5]

The parable of the lighted candle

33 No *man,* when he hath lighted a candle, putteth *it* in a secret place, neither under a bushel, but on a candlestick, that they which come in may see the light. 34The light of the body is the eye: there-

fore when thine eye is single, thy whole body also is full of light; but when *thine eye* is evil, thy body also *is* full of darkness. 35 Take heed therefore that the light which is in thee be not darkness. 36 If thy whole body therefore *be* full of light, having no part dark, the whole shall be full of light, as when the bright shining of a candle doth give thee light.

The warning against Pharisaism

37 And as *he* spake, a certain Pharisee besought him to dine with him: and he went in, and sat down to meat. 38 And when the Pharisee saw *it,* he marvelled that he had not first washed before dinner. 39 And the Lord said unto him, Now do ye Pharisees make clean the outside of the cup and the platter; but your inward part is full of ravening and wickedness. 40 *Ye* fools, did not he that made that *which is* without make that *which is* within also? 41 But rather give alms *of* such *things* as *you* have; and behold, all *things* are clean unto you. 42 But woe unto you, Pharisees! for ye tithe mint and rue and all *manner of* herbs, and pass over judgment and the love of God: these ought *ye* to have done, and not to leave the other undone. [Mat. 23:23]

43 Woe unto you, Pharisees! for ye love the uppermost seats in the synagogues, and greetings in the markets. [Mat. 23:6; Mark 12:38,39]

44 Woe unto you, scribes and Pharisees, hypocrites! for ye are as graves which appear not, and the men that walk over *them* are not aware *of them.* [Mat. 23:27; Ps. 5:9]

45 Then answered one of the lawyers, and said unto him, Master, thus saying thou reproachest us also. 46 And he said, Woe unto you also, *ye* lawyers! for ye lade men *with* burdens grievous to be borne, and ye yourselves touch not the burdens with one of your fingers. [Mat. 23:4]

47 Woe unto you! for ye build the sepulchres of the prophets, and your fathers killed them. 48 Truly ye bear witness that ye allow the deeds of your fathers: for they indeed killed them, and ye build their sepulchres. 49 Therefore also said the wisdom of God, I will send them prophets and apostles, and *some* of them they shall slay and persecute: 50 That the blood of all the prophets, which was shed from the foundation of the world, may be required of this generation; 51 From the blood of Abel unto the blood of Zacharias, which perished between the altar and the temple: verily I say unto you, It shall be required of this generation. [Gen. 4:8; 2 Chr. 24:20,21]

52 Woe unto you, lawyers! for ye have taken away the key of knowledge: ye entered not in yourselves, and them that were entering in ye hindered. [Mat. 23:13]

53 And as he said these *things* unto them, the scribes and the Pharisees began to urge *him* vehemently, and to provoke him to speak of many *things:* 54 Laying wait for him, and seeking to catch something out of his mouth, that they might accuse him. [Mark 12:13]

The value of life

12 In the mean time, when there were gathered together an innumerable multitude of people, insomuch that *they* trode one upon another, he began to say unto his disciples first *of all,* Beware ye of the leaven of the Pharisees, which is hypocrisy. ²For there is nothing covered, that shall not be revealed; neither hid, that shall not be known. ³Therefore whatsoever ye have spoken in darkness shall be heard in the light; and *that* which ye have spoken in the ear in closets shall be proclaimed upon the housetops. ⁴And I say unto you my friends, Be not afraid of them that kill the body, and after that have no more that *they* can do. ⁵But I will *fore*-warn you whom you shall fear: Fear him, which after *he* hath killed hath power to cast into hell; yea, I say unto you, Fear him. ⁶Are not five sparrows sold for two farthings, and not one of them is forgotten before God? ⁷But even the *very* hairs of your head are all numbered. Fear not therefore: ye are of more value than many sparrows. ⁸Also I say unto you, Whosoever shall confess me before men, him shall the Son of man also confess before the angels of God: ⁹But he that denieth me before men shall be denied before the angels of God. ¹⁰And whosoever shall speak a word against the Son of man, it shall be forgiven him: but unto him that blasphemeth against the Holy Ghost it shall not be forgiven. ¹¹And when they bring you unto the synagogues, and *unto* magistrates, and powers, take ye no thought how or what *thing* ye shall answer, or what ye shall say: ¹²For the Holy Ghost shall teach you in the same hour what ye ought to say.

The parable of the rich fool

13 And one of the company said unto him, Master, speak to my brother, that *he* divide the inheritance with me. ¹⁴And he said unto him, Man, who made me a judge or a divider over you? ¹⁵And he said unto them, Take heed, and beware of covetousness: for a man's life consisteth not in the abundance of the *things* which he possesseth. ¹⁶And he spake a parable unto them, saying, The ground of a certain rich man brought forth plentifully: ¹⁷And he thought within himself, saying, What shall I do, because I have no room where to bestow my fruits? ¹⁸And he said, This will I do: I will pull down my barns, and build greater; and there will I bestow all my fruits and my goods. ¹⁹And I will say to my soul, Soul, thou hast much goods laid up for many years; take thine ease, eat, drink, *and* be merry. ²⁰But God said unto him, *Thou* fool, this night thy soul shall be required of thee: then whose shall *those things* be, which thou hast provided? ²¹So *is* he that layeth up treasure for himself, and is not rich towards God. [ver. 33; Mat. 6:20; 1 Tim. 6:18,19; Jas. 2:5]

The teaching about anxiety

22 And he said unto his disciples, Therefore I say unto you, Take no thought for your life, what

ye shall eat; neither for the body, what ye shall put on. ²³The life is more than meat, and the body *is more* than raiment. ²⁴Consider the ravens: for they neither sow nor reap; which neither have storehouse nor barn; and God feedeth them: how much more are ye better than the fowls? ²⁵And which of you with taking thought can add to his stature one cubit? ²⁶If ye then be not able *to do that thing which is* least, why take ye thought for the rest? ²⁷Consider the lilies how they grow: they toil not, they spin not; and yet I say unto you, *that* Solomon in all his glory was not arrayed like one of these. ²⁸If then God so clothe the grass, which is to day in the field, and to morrow is cast into the oven; how much more *will he clothe* you, O ye of little faith? ²⁹And seek not ye what ye shall eat, or what ye shall drink, neither be ye of doubtful mind. ³⁰For all these *things* do the nations of the world seek after: and your Father knoweth that ye have need of these *things.* ³¹But rather seek ye the kingdom of God; and all these *things* shall be added unto you. ³²Fear not, little flock; for it is your Father's good pleasure to give you the kingdom. ³³Sell that ye have, and give alms; provide yourselves bags which wax not old, a treasure in the heavens that faileth not, where no thief approacheth, neither moth corrupteth. ³⁴For where your treasure is, there will your heart be also.

Parable of the watching servants
³⁵ Let your loins be girded

about, and *your* lights burning; ³⁶And ye yourselves like unto men that wait for their lord, when he will return from the wedding; that when *he* cometh and knocketh, they may open unto him immediately. ³⁷Blessed *are* those servants, whom the lord when he cometh shall find watching: verily I say unto you, that he shall gird himself, and make them to sit down to meat, and will come forth and serve them. ³⁸And if he shall come in the second watch, or come in the third watch, and find *them* so, blessed are those servants. ³⁹And this know, that if the goodman of the house had known what hour the thief would come, he would have watched, and not have suffered his house to be broken through. ⁴⁰Be ye therefore ready also: for the Son of man cometh at an hour when ye think not. [Mat. 24:44; 25:13; Mark 13:33; ch. 21:34,36; 1 Thes. 5:6; 2 Pet. 3:12]

41 Then Peter said unto him, Lord, speakest thou this parable unto us, or even to all? ⁴²And the Lord said, Who then is *that* faithful and wise steward, whom *his* lord shall make ruler over his household, to give *them their* portion of meat in due season? ⁴³Blessed *is* that servant, whom his lord when he cometh shall find so doing. ⁴⁴Of a truth I say unto you, that he will make him ruler over all that he hath. ⁴⁵But and if that servant say in his heart, My lord delayeth his coming; and shall begin to beat the menservants and maidens, and to eat and drink, and to be drunken; ⁴⁶The lord of that servant will

come in a day when he looketh not for *him,* and at an hour when he is not ware, and will cut him in sunder, and will appoint *him* his portion with the unbelievers. ⁴⁷And that servant, which knew his lord's will, and prepared not *himself,* neither did according to his will, shall be beaten with many *stripes.* ⁴⁸But he that knew not, and did commit *things* worthy of stripes, shall be beaten with few *stripes.* For unto whomsoever much is given, of him shall be much required: and to whom *men* have committed much, of him they will ask the more. [Lev. 5:17; 1 Tim. 1:13]

Jesus the divider

49 I am come to send fire on the earth; and what will I, if it be already kindled! ⁵⁰But I have a baptism to be baptized *with;* and how am I straitened till it be accomplished! ⁵¹Suppose ye that I am come to give peace on earth? I tell you, Nay; but rather division: ⁵²For from henceforth there shall be five in one house divided, three against two, and two against three. ⁵³The father shall be divided against the son, and the son against the father; the mother against the daughter, and the daughter against the mother; the mother in law against her daughter in law, and the daughter in law against her mother in law.

Interpreting the present time

54 And he said also to the people, When ye see a cloud rise out of the west, straightway ye say, There cometh a shower; and so it is. ⁵⁵And when *ye see* the south wind blow, ye say, There will be heat; and it cometh to pass. ⁵⁶Ye hypocrites, ye can discern the face of the sky and of the earth; but how *is it that* ye do not discern this time? ⁵⁷Yea, and why even of yourselves judge ye not what *is* right? ⁵⁸When thou goest with thine adversary to the magistrate, *as thou art* in the way, give diligence that *thou* mayest be delivered from him; lest he hale thee to the judge, and the judge deliver thee to the officer, and the officer cast thee into prison. ⁵⁹I tell thee, thou shalt not depart thence, till thou hast paid the very last mite.

Jesus' call to repentance

13 There were present at that season some that told him of the Galileans, whose blood Pilate had mingled with their sacrifices. ²And Jesus answering said unto them, Suppose ye that these Galileans were sinners above all the Galileans, because they suffered such *things?* ³I tell you, Nay: but, except ye repent, ye shall all likewise perish. ⁴Or those eighteen, upon whom the tower in Siloam fell, and slew them, think ye that they were sinners above all men that dwelt in Jerusalem? ⁵I tell you, Nay: but except ye repent, ye shall all likewise perish. ⁶He spake also this parable; A certain *man* had a fig tree planted in his vineyard; and he came and sought fruit thereon, and found none. ⁷Then said he unto the dresser of his vineyard, Behold, *these* three years I come seeking fruit on this fig tree, and find none: cut it down; why cumbereth it the ground? ⁸And he answering said unto him, Lord, let it alone this year also, till I shall dig about it, and dung *it:* 9And if it bear fruit, *well:* and if not, *then* after that thou shalt cut it down.

A woman healed on the sabbath

10 And he was teaching in one of the synagogues on the sabbath. 11And behold, there was a woman which had a spirit of infirmity eighteen years, and was bowed together, and could in no wise lift up *herself.* 12And when Jesus saw her, he called *her* to *him,* and said unto her, Woman, thou art loosed from thy infirmity. 13And he laid *his* hands on her: and immediately she was made straight, and glorified God. 14And the ruler of the synagogue answered with indignation, because that Jesus had healed on the sabbath day, and said unto the people, There are six days in which *men* ought to work: in them therefore come and be healed, and not on the sabbath day. 15The Lord then answered him, and said, *Thou* hypocrite, doth not each one of you on the sabbath loose his ox or *his* ass from the stall, and lead *him* away to watering? 16And ought not this *woman,* being a daughter of Abraham, whom Satan hath bound, lo *these* eighteen years, be loosed from this bond on the sabbath day? 17And when he had said these *things,* all his adversaries were ashamed: and all the people rejoiced for all the glorious *things* that were done by him.

Parables about the kingdom

18 Then said he, Unto what is the kingdom of God like? and whereunto shall I resemble it? 19It is like a grain of mustard seed, which a man took, and cast into his garden; and it grew, and waxed a great tree; and the fowls of the air lodged in the branches of it. 20And again he said, Whereunto shall I liken the kingdom of God? 21It is like leaven, which a woman took and hid in three measures of meal, till the whole was leavened.

The strait gate

22 And he went through the cities and villages, teaching, and journeying towards Jerusalem. 23Then said one unto him, Lord, are there few that be saved? And he said unto them, 24Strive to enter in at the strait gate: for many, I say unto you, will seek to enter in, and shall not be able. 25When once the master of the house is risen up, and hath shut to the door, and ye begin to stand without, and to knock at the door, saying, Lord, Lord, open unto us; and he shall answer and say unto you, I know you not whence you are: 26Then shall ye begin to say, We have eaten and drunk in thy presence, and thou hast taught in our streets. 27But he shall say, I tell you, I know you not whence you are; depart from me, all *ye* workers of iniquity. 28There shall be weeping and gnashing of teeth, when ye shall see Abraham, and Isaac, and Jacob, and all the prophets, in the kingdom of God, and you yourselves thrust out. 29And they shall come from the east, and *from* the west, and from the north, and *from* the south, and shall sit down in the kingdom of

God. ³⁰And behold, there are last which shall be first, and there are first which shall be last. [Mat. 19:30; 20:16; Mark 10:31]

The lament over Jerusalem

31 The same day there came certain *of the* Pharisees, saying unto him, Get *thee* out, and depart hence: for Herod will kill thee. ³²And he said unto them, Go ye, and tell that fox, Behold, I cast out devils, and I do cures to day and to morrow, and the third *day* I shall be perfected. ³³Nevertheless I must walk to day, and to morrow, and the *day* following: for it cannot be that a prophet perish out of Jerusalem. ³⁴O Jerusalem, Jerusalem, which killest the prophets, and stonest them that are sent unto thee; how often would I have gathered thy children together, as a hen *doth gather* her brood under *her* wings, and ye would not? ³⁵Behold, your house is left unto you desolate: and verily I say unto you, Ye shall not see me, until *the time* come when ye shall say, Blessed *is* he that cometh in the name of the Lord. [Lev. 26:31,32; Ps. 69:25; Is. 1:7; Dan. 9:27; Mic. 3:12; Ps. 118:26; Mat. 21:9; Mark 11:10; ch. 19:38; John 12:13].

Jesus heals on the sabbath

14 And it came to pass, as he went into the house of one of the chief Pharisees to eat bread on the sabbath day, that they watched him. ²And behold, there was a certain man before him, which had the dropsy. ³And Jesus answering spake unto the lawyers and Pharisees, saying, Is it lawful to heal on the sabbath day? ⁴And they held their peace. And he took *him,* and healed him, and let *him* go; ⁵And answered them, saying, Which of you shall have an ass or an ox fallen into a pit, and will not straightway pull him out on the sabbath day? ⁶And they could not answer him again to these *things.*

The honoured place

7 And he put forth a parable to those which were bidden, when he marked how they chose out the chief rooms; saying unto them, ⁸When thou art bidden of any *man* to a wedding, sit not down in the highest room; lest a more honourable *man* than thou be bidden of him; ⁹And he that bade thee and him come and say to thee, Give this *man* place; and thou begin with shame to take the lowest room. ¹⁰But when thou art bidden, go and sit down in the lowest room; that when he that bade thee cometh, he may say unto thee, Friend, go up higher: then shalt thou have worship in the presence of them that sit at meat with thee. ¹¹For whosoever exalteth himself shall be abased; and he that humbleth himself shall be exalted. [Job 22:29; Ps. 18:27; Prov. 29:23; Mat. 23:12; ch. 18:14; Jas. 4:6; 1 Pet. 5:5]

12 Then said he also to him that bade him, When thou makest a dinner or a supper, call not thy friends, nor thy brethren, neither thy kinsmen, nor *thy* rich neighbours; lest they also bid thee again, and a recompence be made thee. ¹³But when thou makest a feast, call the poor, the maimed, the lame, the blind: ¹⁴And thou shalt be blessed;

for they cannot recompense thee: for thou shalt be recompensed at the resurrection of the just.

The parable of the great supper

15 And when one of them that sat at meat with *him* heard these *things*, he said unto him, Blessed *is he* that shall eat bread in the kingdom of God. 16Then said he unto him, A certain man made a great supper, and bade many: 17And sent his servant at supper time to say to them that were bidden, Come; for all *things* are now ready. 18And they all with one *consent* began to make excuse. The first said unto him, I have bought a piece of ground, and I must needs go and see it: I pray thee have me excused. 19And another said, I have bought five yoke of oxen, and I go to prove them: I pray thee have me excused. 20And another said, I have married a wife, and therefore I cannot come. 21So that servant came, and shewed his lord these *things.* Then the master of the house being angry said to his servant, Go out quickly into the streets and lanes of the city, and bring in hither the poor, and the maimed, and the halt, and the blind. 22And the servant said, Lord, it is done as thou hast commanded, and yet there is room. 23And the lord said unto the servant, Go out into the *high*ways and hedges, and compel *them* to come in, that my house may be filled. 24For I say unto you, That none of those men which were bidden shall taste of my supper. [Mat. 21:43; 22:8; Acts 13:46]

The cost of discipleship

25 And there went great multitudes with him: and he turned, and said unto them, 26If any *man* come to me, and hate not his father, and mother, and wife, and children, and brethren, and sisters, yea, and his own life also, he cannot be my disciple. 27And whosoever doth not bear his cross, and come after me, cannot be my disciple. 28For which of you, intending to build a tower, sitteth not down first, and counteth the cost, whether he have sufficient to finish it? 29Lest haply, after he hath laid the foundation, and is not able to finish *it,* all that behold *it* begin to mock him, 30Saying, This man began to build, and was not able to finish. 31Or what king, going to make war against another king, sitteth not down first, and consulteth whether he be able with ten thousand to meet him that cometh against him with twenty thousand? 32Or else, while the other is yet a great way off, he sendeth an ambassage, and desireth conditions of peace. 33So likewise, whosoever *he be* of you that forsaketh not all that he hath, he cannot be my disciple. 34Salt *is* good: but if the salt have lost his savour, wherewith shall it be seasoned? 35It is neither fit for the land, nor yet for the dunghill; *but men* cast it out. He that hath ears to hear, let him hear.

The parable of the lost sheep

15 Then drew near unto him all the publicans and sinners for to hear him. 2And the Pharisees and scribes murmured,

saying, This *man* receiveth sinners, and eateth with them. 3And he spake this parable unto them, saying, 4What man of you, having a hundred sheep, if he lose one of them, doth not leave the ninety and nine in the wilderness, and go after that which is lost, until he find it? 5And when he hath found *it,* he layeth *it* on his shoulders, rejoicing. 6And when he cometh home, he calleth together *his* friends and neighbours, saying unto them, Rejoice with me; for I have found my sheep which was lost. 7I say unto you, that likewise joy shall be in heaven over one sinner that repenteth, *more* than over ninety and nine just *persons* which need no repentance. [ch. 5:32]

The lost piece of silver

8 Either what woman having ten pieces of silver, if she lose one piece, doth not light a candle, and sweep the house, and seek diligently till she find *it?* 9And when she hath found *it,* she calleth *her* friends and *her* neighbours together, saying, Rejoice with me; for I have found the piece which I had lost. 10Likewise, I say unto you, there is joy in the presence of the angels of God over one sinner that repenteth.

The parable of the lost son

11 And he said, A certain man had two sons: 12And the younger of them said to *his* father, Father, give me the portion of goods that falleth to *me.* And he divided unto them *his* living. 13And not many days after the younger son gathered all together, and took his jour-ney into a far country, and there wasted his substance with riotous living. 14And when he had spent all, there arose a mighty famine in that land; and he began to be in want. 15And he went and joined himself to a citizen of that country; and he sent him into his fields to feed swine. 16And he would fain have filled his belly with the husks that the swine did eat: and no *man* gave unto him. 17And when he came to himself, he said, How many hired *servants* of my father's have bread enough and to spare, and I perish with hunger? 18I will arise and go to my father, and will say unto him, Father, I have sinned against heaven, and before thee, 19And am no more worthy to be called thy son: make me as one of thy hired *servants.* 20And he arose, and came to his father. But when he was yet a great way off, his father saw him, and had compassion, and ran, and fell on his neck, and kissed him. 21And the son said unto him, Father, I have sinned against heaven, and in thy sight, and am no more worthy to be called thy son. 22But the father said to his servants, Bring forth the best robe, and put *it* on him; and put a ring on his hand, and shoes on *his* feet: 23And bring hither the fatted calf, and kill *it;* and let us eat, and be merry: 24For this my son was dead, and is alive again; he was lost, and is found. And they began to be merry. 25Now his elder son was in the field: and as he came and drew nigh to the house, he heard musick and dancing. 26And he called one of the servants, and

asked what these *things* meant. 27 And he said unto him, Thy brother is come; and thy father hath killed the fatted calf, because he hath received him *safe and* sound. 28 And he was angry, and would not go in: therefore came his father out and intreated him. 29 And he answering said to *his* father, Lo, these many years do I serve thee, neither transgressed I at any time thy commandment: and yet thou never gavest me a kid, that I might make merry with my friends: 30 But as soon as this thy son was come, which hath devoured thy living with harlots, thou hast killed for him the fatted calf. 31 And he said unto him, Son, thou art ever with me, and all that I have is thine. 32 It was meet that *we* should make merry, and be glad: for this thy brother was dead, and is alive again; and was lost, and is found. [ver. 24]

The unrighteous steward

16 And he said also unto his disciples, There was a certain rich man, which had a steward; and the same was accused unto him that he had wasted his goods. 2 And he called him, and said unto him, How *is* it *that* I hear this of thee? give an account of thy stewardship; for thou mayest be no longer steward. 3 Then the steward said within himself, What shall I do? for my lord taketh away from me the stewardship: I cannot dig; to beg I am ashamed. 4 I am resolved what to do, that, when I am put out of the stewardship, they may receive me into their houses.

5 So he called every one of his lord's debtors unto *him,* and said unto the first, How much owest thou unto my lord? 6 And he said, An hundred measures of oil. And he said unto him, Take thy bill, and sit down quickly, and write fifty. 7 Then said he to another, And how much owest thou? And he said, An hundred measures of wheat. And he said unto him, Take thy bill, and write fourscore. 8 And the lord commended the unjust steward, because he had done wisely: for the children of this world are in their generation wiser than the children of light. 9 And I say unto you, Make to yourselves friends of the mammon of unrighteousness; that, when ye fail, they may receive you into everlasting habitations. 10 He that is faithful in *that which is* least is faithful also in much: and he that is unjust in the least is unjust also in much. 11 If therefore ye have not been faithful in the unrighteous mammon, who will commit to your trust the true *riches?* 12 And if ye have not been faithful in that which is another *man's,* who shall give you that which is your own? 13 No servant can serve two masters: for either he will hate the one, and love the other; or else he will hold to the one, and despise the other. Ye cannot serve God and mammon. [Mat. 6:24]

14 And the Pharisees also, who were covetous, heard all these *things:* and they derided him. 15 And he said unto them, Ye are they which justify yourselves before men; but God knoweth your

hearts: for that which is highly esteemed amongst men is abomination in the sight of God. 16The law and the prophets *were* until John: since that time the kingdom of God is preached, and every *man* presseth into it. 17And it is easier for heaven and earth to pass, than one tittle of the law to fail. 18Whosoever putteth away his wife, and marrieth another, committeth adultery: and whosoever marrieth her that is put away from *her* husband committeth adultery. [Mat. 5:32; 19:9; Mark 10:11; 1 Cor. 7:10,11]

The rich man and Lazarus

19 There was a certain rich man, which was clothed in purple and fine linen, and fared sumptuously every day: 20And there was a certain beggar named Lazarus, which was laid at his gate, full of sores, 21And desiring to be fed with the crumbs which fell from the rich *man's* table: moreover the dogs came and licked his sores. 22And it came to pass that the beggar died, and was carried by the angels into Abraham's bosom: the rich *man* also died, and was buried; 23And in hell he lift up his eyes, being in torments, and seeth Abraham afar off, and Lazarus in his bosom. 24And he cried and said, Father Abraham, have mercy on me, and send Lazarus, that he may dip the tip of his finger in water, and cool my tongue; for I am tormented in this flame. 25But Abraham said, Son, remember that thou in thy lifetime receivedst thy good *things,* and likewise Lazarus evil *things:* but now he is comfort-

ed, and thou art tormented. 26And besides all this, between us and you there is a great gulf fixed: so that they which would pass from hence to you cannot; neither can they pass to us, that *would come* from thence. 27Then he said, I pray thee therefore, father, that thou wouldest send him to my father's house: 28For I have five brethren; that he may testify unto them, lest they also come into this place of torment. 29Abraham saith unto him, They have Moses and the prophets; let them hear them. 30And he said, Nay, father Abraham: but if one went unto them from the dead, they will repent. 31And he said unto him, If they hear not Moses and the prophets, neither will they be persuaded, though one rose from the dead. [John 12:10,11]

Faith and forgiveness

17 Then said he unto the disciples, It is impossible but that offences will come: but woe *unto him,* through whom they come. 2It were better for him that a millstone were hanged about his neck, and he cast into the sea, than that he should offend one of these little ones. 3Take heed to yourselves: If thy brother trespass against thee, rebuke him; and if he repent, forgive him. 4And if he trespass against thee seven times in a day, and seven times in a day turn again to thee, saying, I repent; thou shalt forgive him.

5 And the apostles said unto the Lord, Increase our faith. 6And the Lord said, If ye had faith as a grain

of mustard seed, ye might say unto this sycamine tree, Be thou plucked up by the root, and be thou planted in the sea; and it should obey you. 7But which of you, having a servant plowing or feeding cattle, will say *unto him* by and by, when he is come from the field, Go and sit down to meat? 8And will not *rather* say unto him, Make ready wherewith I may sup, and gird thyself, and serve me, till I have eaten and drunken; and afterward thou shalt eat and drink? 9Doth he thank that servant because he did the *things* that were commanded him? I trow not. 10So likewise ye, when ye shall have done all those *things* which are commanded you, say, We are unprofitable servants: we have done *that* which was our duty to do. [Job 22:3; 35:7; Ps. 16:2; Mat. 25:30; Rom. 3:12; 11:35; 1 Cor. 9:16,17; Philem. 11]

The healing of the ten lepers

11 And it came to pass, as he went to Jerusalem, that he passed through the midst of Samaria and Galilee. 12And as he entered into a certain village, there met him ten men *that were* lepers, which stood afar off: 13And they lifted up *their* voices, and said, Jesus, Master, have mercy on us. 14And when he saw *them,* he said unto them, Go shew yourselves unto the priests. And it came to pass *that,* as they went, they were cleansed. 15And one of them, when he saw that he was healed, turned back, and with a loud voice glorified God, 16And fell down on *his* face at his feet, giving him thanks: and he was a

Samaritan. 17And Jesus answering said, Were there not ten cleansed? but where *are* the nine? 18There are not found that returned to give glory to God, save this stranger. 19And he said unto him, Arise, go *thy way:* thy faith hath made thee whole. [Mat. 9:22; Mark 5:34; 10:52; ch. 7:50; 8:48; 18:42]

The coming of the kingdom

20 And when he was demanded of the Pharisees, when the kingdom of God should come, he answered them and said, The kingdom of God cometh not with observation: 21Neither shall they say, Lo here: or, lo there: for behold, the kingdom of God is within you. 22And he said unto the disciples, The days will come, when ye shall desire to see one of the days of the Son of man, and ye shall not see *it.* 23And they shall say to you, See here; or, see there: go not after *them,* nor follow *them.* 24For as the lightning, that lighteneth out of the one *part* under heaven, shineth unto the other *part* under heaven; so shall also the Son of man be in his day. 25But first must he suffer many *things,* and be rejected of this generation. 26And as it was in the days of Noe, so shall it be also in the days of the Son of man. 27They did eat, they drank, they married *wives,* they were given in marriage, until the day that Noe entered into the ark, and the flood came, and destroyed *them* all. 28Likewise also as it was in the days of Lot; they did eat, they drank, they bought, they sold, they planted, they builded; 29But the

same day that Lot went out of Sodom it rained fire and brimstone from heaven, and destroyed *them* all. ³⁰Even thus shall it be in the day when the Son of man is revealed. ³¹In that day, he which shall be upon the housetop, and his stuff in the house, let him not come down to take it away: and he that is in the field, let him likewise not return back. ³²Remember Lot's wife. ³³Whosoever shall seek to save his life shall lose it; and whosoever shall lose *his life* shall preserve it. ³⁴I tell you, in that night there shall be two *men* in one bed; the one shall be taken, and the other shall be left. ³⁵Two *women* shall be grinding together; the one shall be taken, and the other left. ³⁶Two *men* shall be in the field; the one shall be taken, and the other shall be left. ³⁷And they answered and said unto him, Where, Lord? And he said unto them, Wheresoever the body *is,* thither will the eagles be gathered together. [Job 39:30; Mat. 24:28]

The widow and the judge

18 And he spake a parable unto them *to this end,* that *men* ought always to pray, and not to faint; ²Saying, There was in a city a judge, which feared not God, neither regarded man: ³And there was a widow in that city; and she came unto him, saying, Avenge me of mine adversary. ⁴And he would not for a while: but afterward he said within himself, Though I fear not God, nor regard man; ⁵Yet because this widow troubleth me, I will avenge her, lest by her contin-

ual coming she weary me. ⁶And the Lord said, Hear what the unjust judge saith. ⁷And shall not God avenge his own elect, which cry day and night unto him, though he bear long with them? ⁸I tell you that he will avenge them speedily. Nevertheless when the Son of man cometh, shall he find faith on the earth? [Heb. 10:37; 2 Pet. 3:8,9]

The Pharisee and the publican

9 And he spake this parable unto certain which trusted in themselves that they were righteous, and despised other: ¹⁰Two men went up into the temple to pray; the one a Pharisee, and the other a publican. ¹¹The Pharisee stood and prayed thus with himself, God, I thank thee, that I am not as other men *are,* extortioners, unjust, adulterers, or even as this publican. ¹²I fast twice in the week, I give tithes of all that I possess. ¹³And the publican, standing afar off, would not lift up so much as *his* eyes unto heaven, but smote upon his breast, saying, God be merciful to me a sinner. ¹⁴I tell you, this man went down to his house justified *rather* than the other: for every one that exalteth himself shall be abased; and he that humbleth himself shall be exalted. [Job 22:29; Mat. 23:12; ch. 14:11; Jas. 4:6; 1 Pet. 5:5]

Jesus and the little children

15 And they brought unto him also infants, that he would touch them: but when *his* disciples saw *it,* they rebuked them. ¹⁶But Jesus called them unto *him,* and said, Suffer little children to come unto

me, and forbid them not: for of such is the kingdom of God. ¹⁷Verily I say unto you, Whosoever shall not receive the kingdom of God as a little child shall in no wise enter therein. [Mark 10:15]

The rich young ruler

18 And a certain ruler asked him, saying, Good Master, what shall I do to inherit eternal life? ¹⁹And Jesus said unto him, Why callest thou me good? none *is* good, save one, *that is,* God. ²⁰Thou knowest the commandments, Do not commit adultery, Do not kill, Do not steal, Do not bear false witness, Honour thy father and thy mother. ²¹And he said, All these have I kept from my youth up. ²²Now when Jesus heard these *things,* he said unto him, Yet lackest thou one *thing:* sell all that thou hast, and distribute unto the poor, and thou shalt have treasure in heaven: and come, follow me. ²³And when he heard this, he was very sorrowful: for he was very rich. ²⁴And when Jesus saw that he was very sorrowful, he said, How hardly shall they that have riches enter into the kingdom of God! ²⁵For it is easier for a camel to go through a needle's eye, than for a rich *man* to enter into the kingdom of God. ²⁶And they that heard *it* said, Who then can be saved? ²⁷And he said, The *things which are* impossible with men are possible with God. [Jer. 32:17; Zech. 8:6; Mat. 19:26; ch. 1:37]

28 Then Peter said, Lo, we have left all, and followed thee. ²⁹And he said unto them, Verily I say unto you, There is no *man* that hath left house, or parents, or brethren, or wife, or children, for the kingdom of God's sake, ³⁰Who shall not receive manifold more in this *present* time, and in the world to come life everlasting. [Job 42:10]

Jesus again foretells his death

31 Then he took unto *him* the twelve, and said unto them, Behold, we go up to Jerusalem, and all *things* that are written by the prophets concerning the Son of man shall be accomplished. ³²For he shall be delivered unto the Gentiles, and shall be mocked, and spitefully entreated, and spitted on: ³³And they shall scourge *him,* and put him to death: and the third day he shall rise again. ³⁴And they understood none of these *things:* and this saying was hid from them, neither knew they the *things* which were spoken. [Mark 9:32; ch. 2:50; 9:45; John 10:6; 12:16]

A blind man healed

35 And it came to pass, *that* as he was come nigh unto Jericho, a certain blind man sat by the way side begging: ³⁶And hearing the multitude pass by, he asked what it meant. ³⁷And they told him, that Jesus of Nazareth passeth by. ³⁸And he cried, saying, Jesus, *thou* Son of David, have mercy on me. ³⁹And they which went before rebuked him, that he should hold his peace: but he cried *so* much the more, *Thou* Son of David, have mercy on me. ⁴⁰And Jesus stood, and commanded him to be brought unto him: and when he was come near, he asked him, ⁴¹Saying, What wilt

thou *that* I shall do unto thee? And he said, Lord, that I may receive my sight. ⁴²And Jesus said unto him, Receive thy sight: thy faith hath saved thee. ⁴³And immediately he received his sight, and followed him, glorifying God: and all the people, when they saw *it*, gave praise unto God. [ch. 5:26; Acts 4:21; 11:18]

The conversion of Zaccheus

19 And *Jesus* entered and passed through Jericho. ²And behold, *there was* a man named Zaccheus, which was *the* chief among the publicans, and he was rich. ³And he sought to see Jesus who he was; and could not for the press, because he was little of stature. ⁴And he ran before, and climbed up into a sycomore tree to see him: for he was to pass that *way*. ⁵And when Jesus came to the place, he looked up, and saw him, and said unto him, Zaccheus, make haste, and come down; for to day I must abide at thy house. ⁶And he made haste, and came down, and received him joyfully. ⁷And when they saw *it*, they all murmured, saying, That he was gone to be guest with a man *that is* a sinner. ⁸And Zaccheus stood, and said unto the Lord; Behold, Lord, the half of my goods I give to the poor; and if I have taken any *thing* from any *man* by false accusation, I restore *him* fourfold. ⁹And Jesus said unto him, This day is salvation come to this house, forsomuch as he also is a son of Abraham. ¹⁰For the Son of man is come to seek and to save that which was lost. [Mat. 18:11; See Mat. 10:6; 15:24]

The parable of the pounds

11 And as they heard these *things*, he added and spake a parable, because he was nigh to Jerusalem, and *because* they thought that the kingdom of God should immediately appear. ¹²He said therefore, A certain nobleman went into a far country to receive for himself a kingdom, and to return. ¹³And he called his ten servants, and delivered them ten pounds, and said unto them, Occupy till I come. ¹⁴But his citizens hated him, and sent a message after him, saying, We will not have this *man* to reign over us. ¹⁵And it came to pass, that when he was returned, having received the kingdom, then he commanded these servants to be called unto him, to whom he had given the money, that he might know how much every *man* had gained by trading. ¹⁶Then came the first, saying, Lord, thy pound hath gained ten pounds. ¹⁷And he said unto him, Well, *thou* good servant: because thou hast been faithful in a very little, have thou authority over ten cities. ¹⁸And the second came, saying, Lord, thy pound hath gained five pounds. ¹⁹And he said likewise to him, Be thou also over five cities. ²⁰And another came, saying, Lord, behold, *here is* thy pound, which I have kept laid up in a napkin: ²¹For I feared thee, because thou art an austere man: thou takest up that thou layedst not down, and reapest that thou didst not sow. ²²And he saith unto him, Out of thine own mouth will I judge thee, *thou* wicked servant. Thou knewest that I was an austere

man, taking up that I laid not down, and reaping that I did not sow: 23Wherefore then gavest not thou my money into the bank, that at my coming I might have required *mine own* with usury? 24And he said unto them that stood by, Take from him the pound, and give *it* to him that hath ten pounds. 25(And they said unto him, Lord, he hath ten pounds.) 26For I say unto you, That unto every one which hath shall be given; and from him that hath not, even that he hath shall be taken away from him. 27But those mine enemies, which would not that I should reign over them, bring hither, and slay *them* before me.

The triumphal entry

28 And when he had thus spoken, he went before, ascending up to Jerusalem. 29And it came to pass, when he was come nigh to Bethphage and Bethany, at the mount called *the mount* of Olives, he sent two of his disciples, 30Saying, Go ye into the village over against *you;* in the which at your entering ye shall find a colt tied, whereon yet never man sat: loose him, and bring *him hither.* 31And if any *man* ask you, Why do ye loose *him?* thus shall ye say unto him, Because the Lord hath need of him. 32And they that were sent went their way, and found even as he had said unto them. 33And as they were loosing the colt, the owners thereof said unto them, Why loose ye the colt? 34And they said, The Lord hath need of him. 35And they brought him to Jesus: and they cast their garments upon the colt, and they set Jesus thereon. 36And as he went, they spread their clothes in the way. 37And when he was come nigh, *even* now at the descent of the mount of Olives, the whole multitude of the disciples began to rejoice and praise God with a loud voice for all the mighty works that they had seen; 38Saying, Blessed *be* the King that cometh in the name of the Lord: peace in heaven, and glory in the highest. 39And some of the Pharisees from among the multitude said unto him, Master, rebuke thy disciples. 40And he answered and said unto them, I tell you that, if these should hold their peace, the stones would immediately cry out. [Hab. 2:11]

41 And when he was come near, he beheld the city, and wept over it, 42Saying, If thou hadst known, even thou, at least in this thy day, the *things* which belong unto thy peace! but now they are hid from thine eyes. 43For the days shall come upon thee, that thine enemies shall cast a trench about thee, and compass thee round, and keep thee in on every side, 44And shall lay thee even with the ground, and thy children within thee: and they shall not leave in thee one stone upon another; because thou knewest not the time of thy visitation. [1 Ki. 9:7,8; Mic. 3:12; Mat. 24:2; Mark 13:2; ch. 21:6; Dan. 9:24; ch. 1:68,78; 1 Pet. 2:12]

The cleansing of the temple

45 And he went into the temple, and began to cast out them that sold therein, and *them that*

bought; 46Saying unto them, It is written, My house is the house of prayer: but ye have made it a den of thieves. 47And he taught daily in the temple. But the chief priests and the scribes and the chief of the people sought to destroy him, 48And could not find what they might do: for all the people were very attentive to hear him.

Jesus' authority challenged

20 And it came to pass, *that* on one of those days, as he taught the people in the temple, and preached the gospel, the chief priests and the scribes came upon *him* with the elders, 2And spake unto him, saying, Tell us, by what authority doest thou these *things?* or who is he that gave thee this authority? 3And he answered and said unto them, I will also ask you one thing; and answer me: 4The baptism of John, was it from heaven, or of men? 5And they reasoned with themselves, saying, If we shall say, From heaven; he will say, Why then believed ye him not? 6But *and* if we say, Of men; all the people will stone us: for they be persuaded that John was a prophet. 7And they answered, that *they* could not tell whence *it was.* 8And Jesus said unto them, Neither tell I you by what authority I do these *things.*

The parable of the husbandmen

9 Then began he to speak to the people this parable; A certain man planted a vineyard, and let it forth to husbandmen, and went into a far country for a long time. 10And at the season he sent a servant to the husbandmen, that they should give him of the fruit of the vineyard: but the husbandmen beat him, and sent *him* away empty. 11And again he sent another servant: and they beat him also, and entreated *him* shamefully, and sent *him* away empty. 12And again he sent a third: and they wounded him also, and cast *him* out. 13Then said the lord of the vineyard, What shall I do? I will send my beloved son: it may be they will reverence *him* when they see him. 14But when the husbandmen saw him, they reasoned among themselves, saying, This is the heir: come, let us kill him, that the inheritance may be ours. 15So they cast him out of the vineyard, and killed *him.* What therefore shall the lord of the vineyard do unto them? 16He shall come and destroy these husbandmen, and shall give the vineyard to others. And when they heard *it,* they said, God forbid. 17And he beheld them, and said, What is this then that is written, The stone which the builders rejected, the same is become the head of the corner? 18Whosoever shall fall upon that stone shall be broken; but on whomsoever it shall fall, it will grind him to powder. 19And the chief priests and the scribes the same hour sought to lay hands on him; and they feared the people: for they perceived that he had spoken this parable against them.

Tribute to Cesar

20 And they watched *him,* and sent forth spies, which *should* feign themselves just *men,* that

they might take hold of his words, that *so they* might deliver him unto the power and authority of the governor. 21And they asked him, saying, Master, we know that thou sayest and teachest rightly, neither acceptest thou the person *of any,* but teachest the way of God truly: 22Is it lawful for us to give tribute unto Cesar, or no? 23But he perceived their craftiness, and said unto them, Why tempt ye me? 24Shew me a penny. Whose image and superscription hath it? They answered and said, Cesar's. 25And he said unto them, Render therefore unto Cesar the *things* which be Cesar's, and unto God the *things* which be God's. 26And they could not take hold of his words before the people: and they marvelled at his answer, and held their peace.

Sadducees and the resurrection

27 Then came to *him* certain of the Sadducees, which deny that there is any resurrection; and they asked him, 28Saying, Master, Moses wrote unto us, If any *man's* brother die, having a wife, and he die without children, that his brother should take *his* wife, and raise up seed unto his brother. 29There were therefore seven brethren: and the first took a wife, and died without children. 30And the second took her to wife, and he died childless. 31And the third took her; and in like manner the seven also: and they left no children, and died. 32Last of all the woman died also. 33Therefore in the resurrection whose wife of them is she? for

seven had her to wife. 34And Jesus answering said unto them, The children of this world marry, and are given in marriage: 35But they which shall be accounted worthy to obtain that world, and the resurrection from the dead, neither marry, nor are given in marriage: 36Neither can they die any more: for they are equal unto *the* angels; and are the children of God, being the children of the resurrection. 37Now that the dead are raised, even Moses shewed at the bush, when he calleth the Lord the God of Abraham, and the God of Isaac, and the God of Jacob. 38For he is not a God of the dead, but of the living: for all live unto him. [Rom. 6:10,11]

The question about David's son

39 Then certain of the scribes answering said, Master, thou hast well said. 40And after that they durst not ask him any *question at all.* 41And he said unto them, How say they that Christ is David's son? 42And David himself saith in the book of Psalms, The Lord said unto my Lord, Sit thou on my right hand, 43Till I make thine enemies thy footstool. 44David therefore calleth him Lord, how is he then his son?

45 Then in the audience of all the people he said unto his disciples, 46Beware of the scribes, which desire to walk in long robes, and love greetings in the markets, and the highest seats in the synagogues, and the chief rooms at feasts; 47Which devour widows' houses, and for a shew make long

prayers: the same shall receive greater damnation. [Mat. 23:14]

The widow's offering

21 And he looked up, and saw the rich *men* casting their gifts into the treasury. ²And he saw also a certain poor widow casting in thither two mites. ³And he said, Of a truth I say unto you, that this poor widow hath cast in more than *they* all: ⁴For all these have of their abundance cast in unto the offerings of God: but she of her penury hath cast in all the living that she had.

Signs of the end of this age

5 And as some spake of the temple, how it was adorned with goodly stones and gifts, he said, ⁶As for these *things* which ye behold, the days will come, in the which there shall not be left one stone upon another, that shall not be thrown down. ⁷And they asked him, saying, Master, but when shall these *things* be? and what sign *will there be* when these *things* shall come to pass?

8 And he said, Take heed that ye be not deceived: for many shall come in my name, saying, I am *Christ;* and the time draweth near: go ye not therefore after them. ⁹But when ye shall hear of wars and commotions, be not terrified: for these *things* must first come to pass; but the end *is* not by and by.

10 Then said he unto them, Nation shall rise against nation, and kingdom against kingdom: ¹¹And great earthquakes shall be in divers places, and famines, and pestilences; and fearful sights and great signs shall there be from heaven. ¹²But before all these, they shall lay their hands on you, and persecute *you,* delivering *you* up to *the* synagogues, and into prisons, being brought before kings and rulers for my name's sake. ¹³And it shall turn to you for a testimony. ¹⁴Settle *it* therefore in your hearts, not to meditate before *what ye* shall answer: ¹⁵For I will give you a mouth and wisdom, which all your adversaries shall not be able to gainsay nor resist. ¹⁶And ye shall be betrayed both by parents, and brethren, and kinsfolks, and friends; and *some* of you shall they cause to be put to death. ¹⁷And ye shall be hated of all *men* for my name's sake. ¹⁸But there shall not a hair of your head perish. ¹⁹In your patience possess ye your souls.

20 And when ye shall see Jerusalem compassed with armies, then know that the desolation thereof is nigh. ²¹Then let them which are in Judea flee to the mountains; and let them which are in the midst of it depart out; and let not them that are in the countries enter thereinto. ²²For these be *the* days of vengeance, that all *things* which are written may be fulfilled. ²³But woe unto them that are with child, and to them that give suck, in those days! for there shall be great distress in the land, and wrath upon this people. ²⁴And they shall fall by the edge of the sword, and shall be led away captive into all nations: and Jerusalem shall be trodden down of the Gentiles, until the times of the Gentiles be fulfilled. ²⁵And there shall be

signs in the sun, and in the moon, and in the stars; and upon the earth distress of nations, with perplexity; the sea and the waves roaring; 26Men's hearts failing them for fear, and *for* looking after those *things* which are coming on the earth: for the powers of heaven shall be shaken. 27And then shall they see the Son of man coming in a cloud with power and great glory. 28And when these *things* begin to come to pass, *then* look up, and lift up your heads; for your redemption draweth nigh. [Rom. 8:19,23]

29 And he spake to them a parable; Behold the fig tree, and all the trees; 30When they now shoot forth, ye see and know of your own selves that summer is now nigh at hand. 31So likewise ye, when ye see these *things* come to pass, know ye that the kingdom of God is nigh at hand. 32Verily I say unto you, This generation shall not pass away, till all be fulfilled. 33Heaven and earth shall pass away: but my words shall not pass away. [Mat. 24:35]

34 And take heed to yourselves, lest at any time your hearts be overcharged with surfeiting, and drunkenness, and cares of *this* life, and *so* that day come upon you unawares. 35For as a snare shall it come on all them that dwell on the face of the whole earth. 36Watch ye therefore, and pray always, that ye may be accounted worthy to escape all these *things* that shall come to pass, and to stand before the Son of man. [Mat. 24:42; 25:13; Mark 13:33; ch. 18:1; Ps. 1:5; Eph. 6:13]

37 And in the day time he was teaching in the temple; and at night he went out, and abode in the mount that is called *the mount* of Olives. 38And all the people came early in the morning to him in the temple, for to hear him.

The plot to kill Jesus

22 Now the feast of unleavened bread drew nigh, which is called the Passover. 2And the chief priests and scribes sought how they might kill him; for they feared the people. [Ps. 2:2; John 11:47; Acts 4:27]

3 Then entered Satan into Judas surnamed Iscariot, being of the number of the twelve. 4And he went his way, and communed with the chief priests and captains, how he might betray him unto them. 5And they were glad, and covenanted to give him money. 6And he promised, and sought opportunity to betray him unto them in the absence of the multitude.

The last supper

7 Then came the day of unleavened bread, when the passover must be killed. 8And he sent Peter and John, saying, Go and prepare us the passover, that we may eat. 9And they said unto him, Where wilt thou *that* we prepare? 10And he said unto them, Behold, when ye are entered into the city, there shall a man meet you, bearing a pitcher of water; follow him into the house where he entereth in. 11And ye shall say unto the goodman of the house, The Master saith unto thee, Where is the guestchamber, where I shall eat the passover with my disciples? 12And

he shall shew you a large upper room furnished: there make ready. 13And they went, and found as he had said unto them: and they made ready the passover.

14 And when the hour was come, he sat down, and the twelve apostles with him. 15And he said unto them, With desire I have desired to eat this passover with you before I suffer: 16For I say unto you, I will not any more eat thereof, until it be fulfilled in the kingdom of God. 17And he took *the* cup, and gave thanks, and said, Take this, and divide *it* among yourselves: 18For I say unto you, I will not drink of the fruit of the vine, until the kingdom of God shall come. [Mat. 26:29; Mark 14:25]

19 And he took bread, and gave thanks, and brake *it,* and gave unto them, saying, This is my body which is given for you: this do in remembrance of me. 20Likewise also the cup after supper, saying, This cup *is* the new testament in my blood, which is shed for you. [1 Cor. 10:16]

21 But behold, the hand of him that betrayeth me *is* with me on the table. 22And truly the Son of man goeth, as it was determined: but woe unto that man by whom he is betrayed. 23And they began to inquire among themselves, which of them it was that should do this *thing.* [Mat. 26:22; John 13:22,25]

24 And there was also a strife among them, which of them should be accounted the greatest. 25And he said unto them, The kings of the Gentiles exercise lordship over them; and they that exercise authority upon them are called benefactors. 26But ye *shall* not *be* so: but he that is greatest among you, let him be as the younger; and he that is chief, as he that doth serve. 27For whether *is* greater, he that sitteth at meat, or he that serveth? *is* not he that sitteth at meat? but I am among you as he that serveth. 28Ye are they which have continued with me in my temptations. 29And I appoint unto you a kingdom, as my Father hath appointed unto me; 30That ye may eat and drink at my table in my kingdom, and sit on thrones judging the twelve tribes of Israel. [Mat. 8:11; ch. 14:15; Rev. 19:9; Ps. 49:14; Mat. 19:28; 1 Cor. 6:2; Rev. 3:21]

31 And the Lord said, Simon, Simon, behold, Satan hath desired *to have* you, that *he* may sift *you* as wheat: 32But I have prayed for thee, that thy faith fail not: and when thou art converted, strengthen thy brethren. 33And he said unto him, Lord, I am ready to go with thee, both into prison, and to death. 34And he said, I tell thee, Peter, *the* cock shall not crow this day, before that thou shalt thrice deny that *thou* knowest me. 35And he said unto them, When I sent you without purse, and scrip, and shoes, lacked ye any *thing?* And they said, Nothing. 36Then said he unto them, But now, he that hath a purse, let him take *it,* and likewise *his* scrip: and he that hath no sword, let him sell his garment, and buy one. 37For I say unto you, that this that is written must yet be accomplished in me, And he was reckoned among the transgressors:

for the *things* concerning me have an end. 38And they said, Lord, behold, here *are* two swords. And he said unto them, It is enough.

Jesus' agony in Gethsemane

39 And he came out, and went, as he was wont, to the mount of Olives; and his disciples also followed him. 40And when he was at the place, he said unto them, Pray that *ye* enter not into temptation. 41And he was withdrawn from them about a stone's cast, and kneeled down, and prayed, 42Saying, Father, if thou be willing, remove this cup from me: nevertheless not my will, but thine, be done. 43And there appeared an angel unto him from heaven, strengthening him. 44And being in an agony he prayed more earnestly: and his sweat was as it were great drops of blood falling down to the ground. 45And when he rose up from prayer, and was come to his disciples, he found them sleeping for sorrow, 46And said unto them, Why sleep ye? rise and pray, lest ye enter into temptation. [ver. 40]

Jesus' betrayal and arrest

47 And while he yet spake, behold a multitude, and he that was called Judas, one of the twelve, went before them, and drew near unto Jesus to kiss him. 48But Jesus said unto him, Judas, betrayest thou the Son of man with a kiss? 49When they which were about him saw what would follow, they said unto him, Lord, shall we smite with the sword? 50And one of them smote the servant of the high priest, and cut off his right ear. 51And Jesus answered and said, Suffer ye thus far. And he touched his ear, and healed him. 52Then Jesus said unto the chief priests, and captains of the temple, and the elders, which were come to him, Be ye come out, as against a thief, with swords and staves? 53When I was daily with you in the temple, ye stretched forth no hands against me: but this is your hour, and the power of darkness. [John 12:27]

Peter's denial of Jesus

54 Then took they him, and led *him,* and brought him into the high priest's house. And Peter followed afar off. 55And when they had kindled a fire in the midst of the hall, and were set down together, Peter sat down among them. 56But a certain maid beheld him as he sat by the fire, and earnestly looked upon him, and said, This *man* was also with him. 57And he denied him, saying, Woman, I know him not. 58And after a little while another saw him, and said, Thou art also of them. And Peter said, Man, I am not. 59And about the space of one hour after another confidently affirmed, saying, Of a truth this *fellow* also was with him: for he is a Galilean. 60And Peter said, Man, I know not what thou sayest. And immediately, while he yet spake, the cock crew. 61And the Lord turned, and looked upon Peter. And Peter remembered the word of the Lord, how he had said unto him, Before *the* cock crow, thou shalt deny me thrice. 62And Peter went out, and wept bitterly.

63 And the men that held Jesus mocked him, and smote *him.* 64And when they had blindfolded him, they stroke him on the face, and asked him, saying, Prophesy, who is it that smote thee? 65And many other *things* blasphemously spake they against him. 66And as soon as it was day, the elders of the people and the chief priests and the scribes came together, and led him into their council, saying, 67Art thou the Christ? tell us. And he said unto them, If I tell you, you will not believe: 68And if I also ask *you,* you will not answer me, nor let *me* go. 69Hereafter shall the Son of man sit on the right hand of the power of God. 70Then said they all, Art thou then the Son of God? And he said unto them, Ye say that I am. 71And they said, What need we any further witness? for we ourselves have heard of his own mouth. [Mat. 26:65; Mark 14:63]

Jesus before Pontius Pilate

23 And the whole multitude of them arose, and led him unto Pilate. 2And they began to accuse him, saying, We found this *fellow* perverting the nation, and forbidding to give tribute to Cesar, saying that he himself is Christ a King. 3And Pilate asked him, saying, Art thou the King of the Jews? And he answered him and said, Thou sayest *it.* 4Then said Pilate to the chief priests and *to* the people, I find no fault in this man. 5And they were the more fierce, saying, He stirreth up the people, teaching throughout all Jewry, beginning from Galilee to this place. 6When Pilate heard of Galilee, he asked whether the man were a Galilean. 7And as soon as he knew that he belonged unto Herod's jurisdiction, he sent him to Herod, who himself also was at Jerusalem at that time. 8And when Herod saw Jesus, he was exceeding glad: for he was desirous to see him of a long *season,* because *he* had heard many *things* of him; and he hoped to have seen some miracle done by him. 9Then he questioned *with* him in many words; but he answered him nothing. 10And the chief priests and scribes stood and vehemently accused him. 11And Herod with his men of war set him at nought, and mocked *him,* and arrayed him in a gorgeous robe, and sent him again to Pilate. 12And the same day Pilate and Herod were made friends together: for before they were at enmity between themselves. [Acts 4:27]

13 And Pilate, when he had called together the chief priests and the rulers and the people, 14Said unto them, Ye have brought this man unto me, as one that perverteth the people: and behold, I, having examined *him* before you, have found no fault in this man *touching those things* whereof ye accuse him: 15No, nor yet Herod: for I sent you to him; and lo, nothing worthy of death is done unto him. 16I will therefore chastise him, and release *him.* 17(For of necessity he must release one unto them at the feast.) 18And they cried out all at once, saying, Away with this *man,* and release unto us Barabbas: 19(Who for a certain sedition made in the city, and *for*

murder, was cast into prison.) 20Pilate therefore, willing to release Jesus, spake again to *them*. 21But they cried, saying, Crucify *him*, crucify him. 22And he said unto them the third time, Why, what evil hath he done? I have found no cause of death in him: I will therefore chastise him, and let *him* go. 23And they were instant with loud voices, requiring that he might be crucified. And the voices of them and of the chief priests prevailed. 24And Pilate gave sentence that it should be as they required. 25And he released unto them him that for sedition and murder was cast into prison, whom they had desired; but he delivered Jesus to their will.

Jesus crucified

26 And as they led him away, they laid hold upon one Simon, a Cyrenian, coming out of the country, and on him they laid the cross, that *he* might bear *it* after Jesus. 27And there followed him a great company of people, and of women, which also bewailed and lamented him. 28But Jesus turning unto them, said, Daughters of Jerusalem, weep not for me, but weep for yourselves, and for your children. 29For behold, the days are coming, in the which they shall say, Blessed *are* the barren, and the wombs that never bare, and the paps which never gave suck. 30Then shall they begin to say to the mountains, Fall on us; and to the hills, Cover us. 31For if they do these *things* in a green tree, what shall be done in the dry? 32And there were also two other, malefac-

tors, led with him to be put to death. [Is. 53:12; Mat. 27:38]

33 And when they were come to the place, which is called Calvary, there they crucified him, and the malefactors, one on the right hand, and the other on the left. 34Then said Jesus, Father, forgive them; for they know not what they do. And they parted his raiment, and cast lots. 35And the people stood beholding. And the rulers also with them derided *him*, saying, He saved others; let him save himself, if he be Christ, the chosen of God. 36And the soldiers also mocked him, coming to *him*, and offering him vinegar, 37And saying, If thou be the King of the Jews, save thyself. 38And a superscription also was written over him in letters of Greek, and Latin, and Hebrew, THIS IS THE KING OF THE JEWS. [Mat. 27:37; Mark 15:26; John 19:19]

39 And one of the malefactors which were hanged railed on him, saying, If thou be Christ, save thyself and us. 40But the other answering rebuked him, saying, Dost not thou fear God, seeing thou art in the same condemnation? 41And we indeed justly; for we receive the due reward of our deeds: but this *man* hath done nothing amiss. 42And he said unto Jesus, Lord, remember me when thou comest into thy kingdom. 43And Jesus said unto him, Verily I say unto thee, To day shalt thou be with me in paradise.

The death of Jesus

44 And it was about the sixth hour, and there was a darkness

over all the earth until the ninth hour. 45 And the sun was darkened, and the vail of the temple was rent in the midst. 46 And when Jesus had cried with a loud voice, he said, Father, into thy hands I commend my spirit: and having said thus, he gave up the ghost. [Ps. 31:5; 1 Pet. 2:23; Mat. 27:50; Mark 15:37; John 19:30]

47 Now when the centurion saw what was done, he glorified God, saying, Certainly this was a righteous man. 48 And all the people that came together to that sight, beholding the *things* which were done, smote their breasts, and returned. 49 And all his acquaintance, and the women that followed him from Galilee, stood afar off, beholding these *things*. [Ps. 38:11; Mat. 27:55; Mark 15:40; See John 19:25]

Jesus laid in the sepulchre

50 And behold, *there was* a man named Joseph, a counseller; *and he was* a good man, and a just: 51 (The same had not consented to the counsel and deed of them;) *he was* of Arimathea, a city of the Jews: who also himself waited for the kingdom of God. 52 This *man* went unto Pilate, and begged the body of Jesus. 53 And he took it down, and wrapped it in linen, and laid it in a sepulchre *that was* hewn in stone, wherein never man before was laid. 54 And *that* day was the preparation, and the sabbath drew on. [Mat. 27:62]

The resurrection of Jesus

55 And the women also, which came with him from Galilee, followed after, and beheld the sepulchre, and how his body was laid.

56 And they returned, and prepared spices and ointments; and rested the sabbath day according to the commandment. [Mark 16:1; Ex. 20:10]

24 Now upon the first *day* of the week, very early in the morning, they came unto the sepulchre, bringing the spices which they had prepared, and certain *others* with them. 2 And they found the stone rolled away from the sepulchre. 3 And they entered in, and found not the body of the Lord Jesus. 4 And it came to pass, as they were *much* perplexed thereabout, behold, two men stood by them in shining garments: 5 And as they were afraid, and bowed down *their* faces to the earth, they said unto them, Why seek ye the living among the dead? 6 He is not here, but is risen: remember how he spake unto you when he was yet in Galilee, 7 Saying, The Son of man must be delivered into the hands of sinful men, and be crucified, and the third day rise again. 8 And they remembered his words, 9 And returned from the sepulchre, and told all these *things* unto the eleven, and *to* all the rest. 10 It was Mary Magdalene, and Joanna, and Mary *the mother* of James, and other *women that were* with them, which told these *things* unto the apostles. 11 And their words seemed to them as idle tales, and they believed them not. 12 Then arose Peter, and ran unto the sepulchre; and stooping down, he beheld the linen clothes laid by themselves, and departed, wondering in himself at that which was come to pass. [John 20:3]

The walk to Emmaus

13 And behold, two of them went *that* same day to a village called Emmaus, which was from Jerusalem *about* threescore furlongs. 14And they talked together of all these *things* which had happened. 15And it came to pass, that while they communed *together* and reasoned, Jesus himself drew near, and went with them. 16But their eyes were holden that *they* should not know him. 17And he said unto them, What *manner of* communications *are* these that ye have one to another, as ye walk, and are sad? 18And the one *of them,* whose name *was* Cleopas, answering said unto him, Art thou only a stranger in Jerusalem, and hast not known the *things* which are come to pass there in these days? 19And he said unto them, What *things?* And they said unto him, Concerning Jesus of Nazareth, which was a prophet mighty in deed and word before God and all the people: 20And how the chief priests and our rulers delivered him to be condemned to death, and have crucified him. 21But we trusted that it had been he which should have redeemed Israel: and beside all this, to day is the third day since these *things* were done. 22Yea, and certain women *also* of our company made us astonished, which were early at the sepulchre; 23And when they found not his body, they came, saying, that *they* had also seen a vision of angels, which said that he was alive. 24And certain of them which were with us went to the sepulchre, and found *it* even so as the women had said: but him they saw not. 25Then he said unto them, O fools, and slow of heart to believe all that the prophets have spoken: 26Ought not Christ to have suffered these *things,* and to enter into his glory? 27And beginning at Moses and all the prophets, he expounded unto them in all the scriptures the *things* concerning himself. 28And they drew nigh unto the village, whither they went: and he made as though *he* would have gone further. 29But they constrained him, saying, Abide with us: for it is towards evening, and the day is far spent. And he went in to tarry with them. 30And it came to pass, as he sat at meat with them, he took bread, and blessed *it,* and brake, and gave to them. 31And their eyes were opened, and they knew him; and he vanished out of their sight. 32And they said one to another, Did not our heart burn within us, while he talked with us by the way, and while he opened to us the scriptures? 33And they rose up the same hour, and returned to Jerusalem, and found the eleven gathered together, and them that were with them, 34Saying, The Lord is risen indeed, and hath appeared to Simon. 35And they told what *things were done* in the way, and how he was known of them in breaking of bread.

Jesus appears to the ten

36 And as they thus spake, Jesus himself stood in the midst of them, and saith unto them, Peace *be* unto you. 37But they were terri-

fied and affrighted, and supposed that *they* had seen a spirit. 38And he said unto them, Why are ye troubled? and why do thoughts arise in your hearts? 39Behold my hands and my feet, that it is I myself: handle me, and see; for a spirit hath not flesh and bones, as ye see me have. 40And when he had thus spoken, he shewed them *his* hands and *his* feet. 41And while they yet believed not for joy, and wondered, he said unto them, Have ye here any meat? 42And they gave him a piece of a broiled fish, and of a honeycomb. 43And he took *it*, and did eat before them. 44And he said unto them, These *are* the words which I spake unto you, while I was yet with you, that all *things* must be fulfilled, which were written in the law of Moses, and *in* the prophets, and *in* the psalms, concerning me. 45Then opened he their understanding, that *they* might understand the scriptures, 46And said unto them, Thus it is written, and thus it behoved Christ to suffer, and to rise from the dead the third day: 47And that repentance and remission of sins should be preached in his name among all nations, beginning at Jerusalem. 48And ye are witnesses of these *things*. 49And behold, I send the promise of my Father upon you: but tarry ye in the city of Jerusalem, until ye be endued with power from on high. [Is. 44:3; Joel 2:28]

Jesus' ascension

50 And he led them out as far as to Bethany, and he lift up his hands, and blessed them. 51And it came to pass, while he blessed them, he was parted from them, and carried up into heaven. 52And they worshipped him, and returned to Jerusalem with great joy: 53And were continually in the temple, praising and blessing God. Amen.

S. John

The Word became flesh

1 In the beginning was the Word, and the Word was with God, and the Word was God. ²The same was in the beginning with God. ³All *things* were made by him; and without him was not any *thing* made that was made. ⁴In him was life; and the life was the light of men. ⁵And the light shineth in darkness; and the darkness comprehended it not. [ch. 3:19]

6 There was a man sent from God, whose name *was* John. ⁷The same came for a witness, to bear witness of the Light, that all *men* through him might believe. ⁸He was not *that* Light, but *was sent* to bear witness of *that* Light. ⁹*That* was the true Light, which lighteth every man *that* cometh into the world. ¹⁰He was in the world, and the world was made by him, and the world knew him not. ¹¹He came unto his own, and his own received him not. ¹²But as many as received him, to them gave he power to become the sons of God, *even* to them that believe on his name: ¹³Which were born, not of blood, nor of the will of the flesh, nor of the will of man, but of God. ¹⁴And the Word was made flesh, and dwelt among us, (and we beheld his glory, the glory as of the only begotten of the Father,) full of grace and truth. ¹⁵John bare witness of him, and cried, saying, This was he of whom I spake, He that cometh after me is preferred before me: for he was before me.

¹⁶And of his fulness have all we received, and grace for grace. ¹⁷For the law was given by Moses, *but* grace and truth came by Jesus Christ. ¹⁸No *man* hath seen God at any time; the only begotten Son, which is in the bosom of the Father, he hath declared *him*. [Ex. 33:20; Mat. 11:27; 1 Tim. 6:16; 1 John 4:9]

John's witness to himself

19 And this is the record of John, when the Jews sent priests and Levites from Jerusalem to ask him, Who art thou? ²⁰And he confessed, and denied not; but confessed, I am not the Christ. ²¹And they asked him, What then? Art thou Elias? And he saith, I am not. Art thou *that* prophet? And he answered, No. ²²Then said they unto him, Who art thou? that we may give an answer to them that sent us. What sayest thou of thyself? ²³He said, I *am* the voice of one crying in the wilderness, Make straight the way of the Lord, as said the prophet Esaias. ²⁴And they which were sent were of the Pharisees. ²⁵And they asked him, and said unto him, Why baptizest thou then, if thou be not *that* Christ, nor Elias, neither *that* prophet? ²⁶John answered them, saying, I baptize with water: but there standeth one among you, whom ye know not; ²⁷He it is, who coming after me is preferred before me, whose shoe's latchet I am not worthy to unloose. ²⁸These *things* were done in Bethabara be-

yond Jordan, where John was baptizing. [Judg. 7:24; ch. 10:40]

John's witness to Jesus

29 The next day John seeth Jesus coming unto him, and saith, Behold the Lamb of God, which taketh away the sin of the world. 30This is he of whom I said, After me cometh a man which is preferred before me: for he was before me. 31And I knew him not: but that he should be made manifest to Israel, therefore am I come baptizing with water. 32And John bare record, saying, I saw the Spirit descending from heaven like a dove, and it abode upon him. 33And I knew him not: but he that sent me to baptize with water, the same said unto me, Upon whom thou shalt see the Spirit descending, and remaining on him, the same is he which baptizeth with the Holy Ghost. 34And I saw, and bare record that this is the Son of God.

Andrew and Peter follow Jesus

35 Again the next day *after* John stood, and two of his disciples; 36And looking upon Jesus as he walked, he saith, Behold the Lamb of God. 37And the two disciples heard him speak, and they followed Jesus. 38Then Jesus turned, and saw them following, and saith unto them, What seek ye? They said unto him, Rabbi, (which is to say, being interpreted, Master,) where dwellest thou? 39He saith unto them, Come and see. They came and saw where he dwelt, and abode with him that day: for it was about the tenth hour. 40One of the two which heard John speak, and followed him, was Andrew, Simon Peter's brother. 41He first findeth his own brother Simon, and saith unto him, We have found the Messias, which is, being interpreted, the Christ. 42And he brought him to Jesus. And when Jesus beheld him, he said, Thou art Simon the son of Jona: thou shalt be called Cephas, which is by interpretation, A stone. [Mat. 16:18]

Philip and Nathanael follow Jesus

43 The day following Jesus would go forth into Galilee, and findeth Philip, and saith unto him, Follow me. 44Now Philip was of Bethsaida, the city of Andrew and Peter. 45Philip findeth Nathanael, and saith unto him, We have found him, of whom Moses in the law, and the prophets, did write, Jesus of Nazareth, the son of Joseph. 46And Nathanael said unto him, Can there any good *thing* come out of Nazareth? Philip saith unto him, Come and see. 47Jesus saw Nathanael coming to him, and saith of him, Behold an Israelite indeed, in whom is no guile. 48Nathanael saith unto him, Whence knowest thou me? Jesus answered and said unto him, Before that Philip called thee, when thou wast under the fig tree, I saw thee. 49Nathanael answered and saith unto him, Rabbi, thou art the Son of God; thou art the King of Israel. 50Jesus answered and said unto him, Because I said unto thee, I saw thee under the fig tree, believest thou? thou shalt see greater *things* than these. 51And he saith

unto him, Verily, verily, I say unto you, Hereafter ye shall see heaven open, and the angels of God ascending and descending upon the Son of man. [Gen. 28:12; Mat. 4:11; Luke 2:9,13; 22:43; Acts 1:10]

Water made into wine

2 And the third day there was a marriage in Cana of Galilee; and the mother of Jesus was there: 2And both Jesus was called, and his disciples, to the marriage. 3And when they wanted wine, the mother of Jesus saith unto him, They have no wine. 4Jesus saith unto her, Woman, what have I to do with thee? mine hour is not yet come. 5His mother saith unto the servants, Whatsoever he saith unto you, do *it.* 6And there were set there six waterpots of stone, after the manner of the purifying of the Jews, containing two or three firkins apiece. 7Jesus saith unto them, Fill the waterpots with water. And they filled them up to the brim. 8And he saith unto them, Draw out now, and bear unto the governor of the feast. And they bare *it.* 9When the ruler of the feast had tasted the water *that was* made wine, and knew not whence it was: (but the servants which drew the water knew;) the governor of the feast called the bridegroom, 10And saith unto him, Every man at the beginning doth set forth good wine; and when *men* have well drunk, then that which is worse: *but* thou hast kept the good wine until now. 11This beginning of miracles did Jesus in Cana of Galilee, and manifested

forth his glory; and his disciples believed on him. [ch. 1:14]

The cleansing of the temple

12 After this he went down to Capernaum, he, and his mother, and his brethren, and his disciples: and they continued there not many days. 13And the Jews' passover was at hand, and Jesus went up to Jerusalem, 14And found in the temple those that sold oxen and sheep and doves, and the changers of money sitting: 15And when he had made a scourge of small cords, he drove *them* all out of the temple, and the sheep and the oxen; and poured out the changers' money, and overthrew the tables; 16And said unto them that sold doves, Take these *things* hence; make not my Father's house a house of merchandise. 17And his disciples remembered that it was written, The zeal of thine house hath eaten me up. [Ps. 69:9]

18 Then answered the Jews and said unto him, What sign shewest thou unto us, seeing that thou doest these *things?* 19Jesus answered and said unto them, Destroy this temple, and in three days I will raise it up. 20Then said the Jews, Forty and six years was this temple in building, and wilt thou rear it up in three days? 21But he spake of the temple of his body. 22When therefore he was risen from the dead, his disciples remembered that he had said this unto them; and they believed the scripture, and the word which Jesus had said. 23Now when he was in Jerusalem at the passover,

in the feast *day,* many believed in his name, when they saw the miracles which he did. ²⁴But Jesus did not commit himself unto them, because he knew all *men,* ²⁵And needed not that any should testify of man: for he knew what was in man. [1 Sam. 16:7; 1 Chr. 28:9; Mat. 9:4; Mark 2:8; ch. 6:64; 16:30; Acts 1:24; Rev. 2:23]

Nicodemus visits Jesus

3 There was a man of the Pharisees, named Nicodemus, a ruler of the Jews: ²The same came to Jesus by night, and said unto him, Rabbi, we know that thou art a teacher come from God: for no *man* can do these miracles that thou doest, except God be with him. ³Jesus answered and said unto him, Verily, verily, I say unto thee, Except a man be born again, he cannot see the kingdom of God. ⁴Nicodemus saith unto him, How can a man be born when he is old? can he enter the second time into his mother's womb, and be born? ⁵Jesus answered, Verily, verily, I say unto thee, Except a man be born of water and *of* the Spirit, he cannot enter into the kingdom of God. ⁶That which is born of the flesh is flesh; and that which is born of the Spirit is spirit. ⁷Marvel not that I said unto thee, Ye must be born again. ⁸The wind bloweth where it listeth, and thou hearest the sound thereof, but canst not tell whence it cometh, and whither it goeth: so is every one that is born of the Spirit. ⁹Nicodemus answered and said unto him, How can these *things* be? ¹⁰Jesus answered and said unto him, Art thou a master of Israel, and knowest not these *things?* ¹¹Verily, verily, I say unto thee, We speak that we do know, and testify that we have seen; and ye receive not our witness. ¹²If I have told you earthly *things,* and ye believe not, how shall ye believe, if I tell you *of* heavenly *things?* ¹³And no *man* hath ascended up to heaven, but he that came down from heaven, *even* the Son of man which is in heaven. ¹⁴And as Moses lifted up the serpent in the wilderness, *even* so must the Son of man be lifted up: ¹⁵That whosoever believeth in him should not perish, but have eternal life. ¹⁶For God so loved the world, that he gave his only begotten Son, that whosoever believeth in him should not perish, but have everlasting life. ¹⁷For God sent not his Son into the world to condemn the world; but that the world through him might be saved. ¹⁸He that believeth on him is not condemned: but he that believeth not is condemned already, because he hath not believed in the name of the only begotten Son of God. ¹⁹And this is the condemnation, that light is come into the world, and men loved darkness rather than light, because their deeds were evil. ²⁰For every one that doeth evil hateth the light, neither cometh to the light, lest his deeds should be reproved. ²¹But he that doeth truth cometh to the light, that his deeds may be made manifest, that they are wrought in God.

John's testimony to Jesus

22 After these *things* came Jesus and his disciples into the land of Judea; and there he tarried with them, and baptized. **23** And John also was baptizing in Aenon near to Salim, because there was much water there: and they came, and were baptized. **24** For John was not yet cast into prison. **25** Then there arose a question between *some* of John's disciples and the Jews about purifying. **26** And they came unto John, and said unto him, Rabbi, *he* that was with thee beyond Jordan, to whom thou barest witness, behold, the same baptizeth, and all *men* come to him. **27** John answered and said, A man can receive nothing, except it be given him from heaven. **28** Ye yourselves bear me witness, that I said, I am not the Christ, but that I am sent before him. **29** He that hath the bride is the bridegroom: but the friend of the bridegroom, which standeth and heareth him, rejoiceth greatly because of the bridegroom's voice: this my joy therefore is fulfilled. **30** He must increase, but I *must* decrease. **31** He that cometh from above is above all: he that is of the earth is earthly, and speaketh of the earth: he that cometh from heaven is above all. **32** And what he hath seen and heard, that he testifieth; and no *man* receiveth his testimony. **33** He that hath received his testimony hath set to *his* seal that God is true. **34** For he whom God hath sent speaketh the words of God: for God giveth not the Spirit by measure *unto him.* **35** The Father loveth the Son, and hath given all *things* into his hand. **36** He that believeth on the Son hath everlasting life: and he that believeth not the Son shall not see life; but the wrath of God abideth on him. [ver. 15,16; ch. 1:12; 6:47; Rom. 1:17; 1 John 5:10]

The woman of Samaria

4 When therefore the Lord knew how the Pharisees had heard that Jesus made and baptized more disciples than John, **2** (Though Jesus himself baptized not, but his disciples,) **3** He left Judea, and departed again into Galilee. **4** And he must needs go through Samaria. **5** Then cometh he to a city of Samaria, which is called Sychar, near to the parcel of ground that Jacob gave to his son Joseph. **6** Now Jacob's well was there. Jesus therefore, being wearied with *his* journey, sat thus on the well: *and* it was about the sixth hour. **7** There cometh a woman of Samaria to draw water: Jesus saith unto her, Give me to drink. **8** (For his disciples were gone away unto the city to buy meat.) **9** Then saith the woman of Samaria unto him, How *is it that* thou, being a Jew, askest drink of me, which am a woman of Samaria? For the Jews have no dealings with the Samaritans. **10** Jesus answered and said unto her, If thou knewest the gift of God, and who it is that saith to thee, Give me to drink; thou wouldest have asked of him, and he would have given thee living water. **11** The woman saith unto him, Sir, thou hast nothing to draw with, and the well is deep: from whence then hast thou *that* living water? 12Art thou greater than our father Jacob, which gave us the well, and drank thereof himself, and his children, and his cattle? 13Jesus answered and said unto her, Whosoever drinketh of this water shall thirst again: 14But whosoever drinketh of the water that I shall give him shall never thirst; but the water that I shall give him shall be in him a well of water springing up into everlasting life. 15The woman saith unto him, Sir, give me this water, that I thirst not, neither come hither to draw. 16Jesus saith unto her, Go, call thy husband, and come hither. 17The woman answered and said, I have no husband. Jesus said unto her, Thou hast well said, I have no husband: 18For thou hast had five husbands; and he whom thou now hast is not thy husband: *in* that saidst thou truly. 19The woman saith unto him, Sir, I perceive that thou art a prophet. 20Our fathers worshipped in this mountain; and ye say, that in Jerusalem is the place where *men* ought to worship. 21Jesus saith unto her, Woman, believe me, the hour cometh, when ye shall neither in this mountain, nor *yet* at Jerusalem, worship the Father. 22Ye worship ye know not what: we know what we worship: for salvation is of the Jews. 23But the hour cometh, and now is, when the true worshippers shall worship the Father in spirit and *in* truth: for the Father seeketh such to worship him. 24God *is* a Spirit: and they that worship him must worship *him* in spirit and *in* truth. 25The woman saith unto him, I know that Messias cometh, which is called Christ: when he is come, he will tell us all *things*. 26Jesus saith unto her, I that speak unto thee am *he*. [Mat. 26:63,64; Mark 14:61,62]

27 And upon this came his disciples, and marvelled that he talked with *the* woman: yet no *man* said, What seekest thou? or, Why talkest thou with her? 28The woman then left her waterpot, and went her way into the city, and saith to the men, 29Come, see a man, which told me all *things* that ever I did: is not this the Christ? 30Then they went out of the city, and came unto him.

The conversion of Samaritans

31 In the mean while *his* disciples prayed him, saying, Master, eat. 32But he said unto them, I have meat to eat that ye know not of. 33Therefore said the disciples one to another, Hath any *man* brought him *ought* to eat? 34Jesus saith unto them, My meat is to do the will of him that sent me, and to finish his work. 35Say not ye, There are yet four months, and *then* cometh harvest? behold, I say unto you, Lift up your eyes, and look on the fields; for they are white already to harvest. 36And he that reapeth receiveth wages, and gathereth fruit unto life eternal: that both he that soweth and he that reapeth may rejoice together. 37And herein is *that* saying true, One soweth, and another reapeth. 38I sent you to reap *that* whereon ye bestowed no labour: other *men*

laboured, and ye are entered into their labours. 39And many of the Samaritans of that city believed on him for the saying of the woman, which testified, He told me all that ever I did. 40So when the Samaritans were come unto him, they besought him that he would tarry with them: and he abode there two days. 41And many more believed because of his own word; 42And said unto the woman, Now we believe, not because of thy saying: for we have heard him ourselves, and know that this is indeed the Christ, the Saviour of the world. [ch. 17:8; 1 John 4:14]

The healing of the nobleman's son

43 Now after two days he departed thence, and went into Galilee. 44For Jesus himself testified, that a prophet hath no honour in his own country. 45Then when he was come into Galilee, the Galileans received him, having seen all *the things* that he did at Jerusalem at the feast: for they also went unto the feast. 46So Jesus came again into Cana of Galilee, where he made the water wine. And there was a certain nobleman, whose son was sick at Capernaum. 47When he heard that Jesus was come out of Judea into Galilee, he went unto him, and besought him that he would come down, and heal his son: for he was at the point of death. 48Then said Jesus unto him, Except ye see signs and wonders, ye will not believe. 49The nobleman saith unto him, Sir, come down ere my child die.

50Jesus saith unto him, Go *thy way; thy son liveth.* And the man believed the word that Jesus had spoken unto him, and he went *his way.* 51And as he was now going down, his servants met him, and told *him,* saying, Thy son liveth. 52Then inquired he of them the hour when he began to amend. And they said unto him, Yesterday at the seventh hour the fever left him. 53So the father knew that *it was* at the same hour, in the which Jesus said unto him, Thy son liveth: and himself believed, and his whole house. 54This *is* again the second miracle *that* Jesus did, when he was come out of Judea into Galilee.

Jesus heals on the sabbath

5 After this there was a feast of the Jews; and Jesus went up to Jerusalem. 2Now there is at Jerusalem by the sheep *market* a pool, which is called in the Hebrew tongue Bethesda, having five porches. 3In these lay a great multitude of impotent *folk,* of blind, halt, withered, waiting for the moving of the water. 4For an angel went down at a *certain* season into the pool, and troubled the water: whosoever then first after the troubling of the water stepped in, was made whole of whatsoever disease he had. 5And a certain man was there, which had an infirmity thirty *and* eight years. 6When Jesus saw him lie, and knew that he had been now a long time *in that case,* he saith unto him, Wilt thou be made whole? 7The impotent *man* answered him, Sir, I have no man,

when the water is troubled, to put me into the pool: but while I am coming, another steppeth down before me. ⁸Jesus saith unto him, Rise, take up thy bed, and walk. ⁹And immediately the man was made whole, and took up his bed, and walked: and on the same day was the sabbath. ¹⁰The Jews therefore said unto him that was cured, It is the sabbath day: it is not lawful for thee to carry *thy* bed. ¹¹He answered them, He that made me whole, the same said unto me, Take up thy bed, and walk. ¹²Then asked they him, What man is that which said unto thee, Take up thy bed, and walk? ¹³And he that was healed wist not who it was: for Jesus had conveyed himself away, a multitude being in *that* place. ¹⁴Afterward Jesus findeth him in the temple, and said unto him, Behold, thou art made whole: sin no more, lest a worse *thing* come unto thee. ¹⁵The man departed, and told the Jews that it was Jesus, which had made him whole.

The Son's witness to the Father

16 And therefore did the Jews persecute Jesus, and sought to slay him, because he had done these *things* on the sabbath day. ¹⁷But Jesus answered them, My Father worketh hitherto, and I work. ¹⁸Therefore the Jews sought the more to kill him, because he not only had broken the sabbath, but said also that God was his Father, making himself equal with God. ¹⁹Then answered Jesus and said unto them, Verily, verily, I say unto you, The Son can do nothing of himself, but what he seeth the Father do: for what *things* soever he doeth, these also doeth the Son likewise. ²⁰For the Father loveth the Son, and sheweth him all *things* that himself doeth: and he will shew him greater works than these, that ye may marvel. ²¹For as the Father raiseth up the dead, and quickeneth *them;* even so the Son quickeneth whom he will. ²²For the Father judgeth no *man,* but hath committed all judgment unto the Son: ²³That all *men* should honour the Son, even as they honour the Father. He that honoureth not the Son honoureth not the Father which hath sent him. ²⁴Verily, verily, I say unto you, He that heareth my word, and believeth on him that sent me, hath everlasting life, and shall not come into condemnation; but is passed from death unto life. ²⁵Verily, verily, I say unto you, The hour is coming, and now is, when the dead shall hear the voice of the Son of God: and they that hear shall live. ²⁶For as the Father hath life in himself; so hath he given to the Son to have life in himself; ²⁷And hath given him authority to execute judgment also, because he is the Son of man. ²⁸Marvel not at this: for the hour is coming, in the which all that are in the graves shall hear his voice, ²⁹And shall come forth; they that have done good, unto the resurrection of life; and they that have done evil, unto the resurrection of damnation. [Is. 26:19; 1 Cor. 15:52; Dan. 12:2; Mat. 25:32,33,46]

The Father's witness to the Son

30 I can of mine own self do nothing: as I hear, I judge: and my judgment is just; because I seek not mine own will, but the will of the Father which hath sent me. 31 If I bear witness of myself, my witness is not true. 32 There is another that beareth witness of me; and I know that the witness which he witnesseth of me is true. 33 Ye sent unto John, and he bare witness unto the truth. 34 But I receive not testimony from man: but these *things* I say, that ye might be saved. 35 He was a burning and a shining light: and ye were willing for a season to rejoice in his light. 36 But I have greater witness than *that of* John: for the works which the Father hath given me to finish, the same works that I do, bear witness of me, that the Father hath sent me. 37 And the Father himself, which hath sent me, hath borne witness of me. Ye have neither heard his voice at any time, nor seen his shape. 38 And ye have not his word abiding in you: for whom he hath sent, him ye believe not. 39 Search the Scriptures; for in them ye think ye have eternal life: and they are they which testify of me. 40 And ye will not come to me, that ye might have life. 41 I receive not honour from men. 42 But I know you, that ye have not the love of God in you. 43 I am come in my Father's name, and ye receive me not: if another shall come in his own name, him ye will receive. 44 How can ye believe, which receive honour one of another, and seek not the honour that *cometh* from God only? 45 Do

not think that I will accuse you to the Father: there is *one* that accuseth you, *even* Moses, in whom ye trust. 46 For had ye believed Moses, ye would have believed me: for he wrote of me. 47 But if ye believe not his writings, how shall ye believe my words?

The five thousand fed

6 After these *things* Jesus went over the sea of Galilee, *which is* the *sea* of Tiberias. 2 And a great multitude followed him, because they saw his miracles which he did on them that were diseased. 3 And Jesus went up into a mountain, and there he sat with his disciples. 4 And the passover, a feast of the Jews, was nigh. 5 When Jesus then lift up *his* eyes, and saw a great company come unto him, he saith unto Philip, Whence shall we buy bread, that these may eat? 6 And this he said to prove him: for he himself knew what he would do. 7 Philip answered him, Two hundred pennyworth of bread is not sufficient for them, that every one of them may take a little. 8 One of his disciples, Andrew, Simon Peter's brother, saith unto him, 9 There is a lad here, which hath five barley loaves, and two small fishes: but what are they among so many? 10 And Jesus said, Make the men sit down. Now there was much grass in the place. So the men sat down, *in* number about five thousand. 11 And Jesus took the loaves; and when he had given thanks, he distributed to the disciples, and the disciples to them that were set down; and likewise of the

fishes as much as they would.
12When they were filled, he said
unto his disciples, Gather up the
fragments that remain, that nothing be lost. 13Therefore they gathered *them* together, and filled
twelve baskets with the fragments
of the five barley loaves, which remained over and above unto them
that had eaten. 14Then *those* men,
when they had seen the miracle
that Jesus did, said, This is of a
truth *that* prophet that should
come into the world. [Gen. 49:10; Deut.
18:15,18; Mat. 11:3; ch. 1:21; 4:19,25; 7:40]

Jesus walks on the sea

15 When Jesus therefore perceived that they would come and
take him by force, to make him a
king, he departed again into a
mountain himself alone. 16And
when even was *now* come, his disciples went down unto the sea,
17And entered into a ship, and
went over the sea towards Capernaum. And it was now dark, and
Jesus was not come to them. 18And
the sea arose by reason of a great
wind that blew. 19So when they
had rowed about five and twenty
or thirty furlongs, they see Jesus
walking on the sea, and drawing
nigh unto the ship: and they were
afraid. 20But he saith unto them, It
is I; be not afraid. 21Then they willingly received him into the ship:
and immediately the ship was at
the land whither they went.

Jesus the bread of life

22 The day following, when the
people which stood on the other
side of the sea saw that there was
none other boat there, save that
one whereinto his disciples were
entered, and that Jesus went not
with his disciples into the boat, but
that his disciples were gone away
alone; 23(Howbeit there came
other boats from Tiberias nigh unto
the place where they did eat bread,
after that the Lord had given
thanks:) 24When the people therefore saw that Jesus was not there,
neither his disciples, they also took
shipping, and came to Capernaum,
seeking for Jesus. 25And when they
had found him on the other side of
the sea, they said unto him, Rabbi,
when camest thou hither? 26Jesus
answered them and said, Verily,
verily, I say unto you, Ye seek me,
not because ye saw *the* miracles,
but because ye did eat of the
loaves, and were filled. 27Labour
not for the meat which perisheth,
but for *that* meat which endureth
unto everlasting life, which the
Son of man shall give unto you: for
him hath God the Father sealed.
28Then said they unto him, What
shall we do, that we might work
the works of God? 29Jesus answered and said unto them, This is
the work of God, that ye believe on
him whom he hath sent. 30They
said therefore unto him, What sign
shewest thou then, that we may
see, and believe thee? what dost
thou work? 31Our fathers did eat
manna in the desert; as it is written, He gave them bread from
heaven to eat. 32Then Jesus said
unto them, Verily, verily, I say unto
you, Moses gave you not *that* bread
from heaven; but my Father giveth
you the true bread from heaven.
33For the bread of God is he which

cometh down from heaven, and giveth life unto the world. ³⁴Then said they unto him, Lord, evermore give us this bread. ³⁵And Jesus said unto them, I am the bread of life: he that cometh to me shall never hunger; and he that believeth on me shall never thirst. ³⁶But I said unto you, That ye also have seen me, and believe not. ³⁷All that the Father giveth me shall come to me; and him that cometh to me I will in no wise cast out. ³⁸For I came down from heaven, not to do mine own will, but the will of him that sent me. ³⁹And this is the Father's will which hath sent me, that of all which he hath given me I should lose nothing, but should raise it up *again* at the last day. ⁴⁰And this is the will of him that sent me, that every one which seeth the Son, and believeth on him, may have everlasting life: and I will raise him up *at* the last day.

[ver. 27,47,54; ch. 3:15,16; 4:14]

41 The Jews then murmured at him, because he said, I am the bread which came down from heaven. ⁴²And they said, Is not this Jesus, the son of Joseph, whose father and mother we know? how *is it* then *that* he saith, I came down from heaven? ⁴³Jesus therefore answered and said unto them, Murmur not among yourselves. ⁴⁴No *man* can come to me, except the Father which hath sent me draw him: and I will raise him up *at* the last day. ⁴⁵It is written in the prophets, And they shall be all taught of God. Every *man* therefore that hath heard, and hath learned of the Father, cometh unto me. ⁴⁶Not that any *man* hath seen the Father, save he which is of God, he hath seen the Father. ⁴⁷Verily, verily, I say unto you, He that believeth on me hath everlasting life. ⁴⁸I am *that* bread of life. ⁴⁹Your fathers did eat manna in the wilderness, and are dead. ⁵⁰This is the bread which cometh down from heaven, that a man may eat thereof, and not die. ⁵¹I am the living bread which came down from heaven: if any *man* eat of this bread, he shall live for ever: and the bread that I will give is my flesh, which I will give for the life of the world. ⁵²The Jews therefore strove amongst themselves, saying, How can this *man* give us *his* flesh to eat? ⁵³Then Jesus said unto them, Verily, verily, I say unto you, Except ye eat the flesh of the Son of man, and drink his blood, ye have no life in you. ⁵⁴Whoso eateth my flesh, and drinketh my blood, hath eternal life; and I will raise him up *at* the last day. ⁵⁵For my flesh is meat indeed, and my blood is drink indeed. ⁵⁶He that eateth my flesh, and drinketh my blood, dwelleth in me, and I in him. ⁵⁷As the living Father hath sent me, and I live by the Father: so he that eateth me, even he shall live by me. ⁵⁸This is *that* bread which came down from heaven: not as your fathers did eat manna, and are dead: he that eateth *of* this bread shall live for ever. ⁵⁹These *things* said he in the synagogue, as he taught in Capernaum.

The questioning disciples

60 Many therefore of his disciples, when they had heard *this,*

said, This is a hard saying; who can hear it? 61When Jesus knew in himself that his disciples murmured at it, he said unto them, Doth this offend you? 62*What and if ye shall see the Son of man ascend up where he was before? 63It is the spirit that quickeneth; the flesh profiteth nothing: the words that I speak unto you, *they* are spirit, and *they* are life. 64But there are some of you that believe not. For Jesus knew from the beginning who they were that believed not, and who should betray him. 65And he said, Therefore said I unto you, that no *man* can come unto me, except it were given unto him of my Father. [ver. 44,45]

66 From that *time* many of his disciples went back, and walked no more with him. 67Then said Jesus unto the twelve, Will ye also go away? 68Then Simon Peter answered him, Lord, to whom shall we go? thou hast the words of eternal life. 69And we believe and are sure that thou art *that* Christ, the Son of the living God. 70Jesus answered them, Have not I chosen you twelve, and one of you is a devil? 71He spake of Judas Iscariot *the son* of Simon: for he *it was that* should betray him, being one of the twelve.

Jesus at the feast of tabernacles

7 After these *things* Jesus walked in Galilee: for he would not walk in Jewry, because the Jews sought to kill him. 2Now the Jews' feast of tabernacles was at hand. 3His brethren therefore said unto him, Depart hence, and go into Judea, that thy disciples also may see the works that thou doest. 4For *there is* no *man that* doeth any *thing* in secret, and he himself seeketh to be known openly. If thou do these *things*, shew thyself to the world. 5For neither did his brethren believe in him. 6Then Jesus said unto them, My time is not yet come: but your time is alway ready. 7The world cannot hate you; but me it hateth, because I testify of it, that the works thereof are evil. 8Go ye up unto this feast: I go not up yet unto this feast; for my time is not yet full come. 9When he had said these *words* unto them, he abode *still* in Galilee.

10 But when his brethren were gone up, then went he also up unto the feast, not openly, but as it were in secret. 11Then the Jews sought him at the feast, and said, Where is he? 12And there was much murmuring among the people concerning him: *for* some said, He is a good *man*: others said, Nay; but he deceiveth the people. 13Howbeit no *man* spake openly of him for fear of the Jews. [ch. 9:22; 12:42; 19:38]

Jesus teaches in the temple

14 Now about the midst of the feast Jesus went up into the temple, and taught. 15And the Jews marvelled, saying, How knoweth this *man* letters, having never learned? 16Jesus answered them, and said, My doctrine is not mine, but his that sent me. 17If any *man* will do his will, he shall know of the doctrine, whether it be of God, or *whether* I speak of myself. 18He

that speaketh of himself seeketh his own glory: but he that seeketh his glory that sent him, the same is true, and no unrighteousness is in him. ¹⁹Did not Moses give you the law, and *yet* none of you keepeth the law? Why go ye about to kill me? ²⁰The people answered and said, Thou hast a devil: who goeth about to kill thee? ²¹Jesus answered and said unto them, I have done one work, and ye all marvel. ²²Moses therefore gave unto you circumcision, not because it is of Moses, but of the fathers; and ye on the sabbath day circumcise a man. ²³If a man on the sabbath day receive circumcision, that the law of Moses should not be broken; are ye angry at me, because I have made a man every whit whole on the sabbath day? ²⁴Judge not according to the appearance, but judge righteous judgment. ²⁵Then said some of them of Jerusalem, Is not this he, whom they seek to kill? ²⁶But lo, he speaketh boldly, and they say nothing unto him. Do the rulers know indeed that this is the very Christ? ²⁷Howbeit we know this *man* whence he is: but when Christ cometh, no *man* knoweth whence he is. ²⁸Then cried Jesus in the temple as he taught, saying, Ye both know me, and ye know whence I am: and I am not come of myself, but he that sent me is true, whom ye know not. ²⁹But I know him: for I am from him, and he hath sent me. ³⁰Then they sought to take him: but no *man* laid hands on him, because his hour was not yet come. ³¹And many of the people believed

on him, and said, When Christ cometh, will he do more miracles than these which this *man* hath done? ³²The Pharisees heard that the people murmured such *things* concerning him; and the Pharisees and the chief priests sent officers to take him. ³³Then said Jesus unto them, Yet a little while am I with you, and *then* I go unto him that sent me. ³⁴Ye shall seek me, and shall not find *me:* and where I am, *thither* ye cannot come. ³⁵Then said the Jews among themselves, Whither will he go, that we shall not find him? will he go unto the dispersed among the Gentiles, and teach the Gentiles? ³⁶What *manner of* saying is this that he said, Ye shall seek me, and shall not find *me:* and where I am, *thither* ye cannot come?

The last day of the feast

37 In the last day, *that* great *day* of the feast, Jesus stood and cried, saying, If any *man* thirst, let him come unto me, and drink. ³⁸He that believeth on me, as the scripture hath said, out of his belly shall flow rivers of living water. ³⁹(But this spake he of the Spirit, which they that believe on him should receive: for the Holy Ghost was not yet *given;* because that Jesus was not yet glorified.) ⁴⁰Many of the people therefore, when they heard *this* saying, said, Of a truth this is the Prophet. ⁴¹Others said, This is the Christ. But some said, Shall Christ come out of Galilee? ⁴²Hath not the scripture said, That Christ cometh of the seed of David, and out of the town of Bethlehem,

where David was? 43So there was a division among the people because of him. 44And some of them would have taken him; but no *man* laid hands on him. [ver. 30]

45 Then came the officers to the chief priests and Pharisees; and they said unto them, Why have ye not brought him? 46The officers answered, Never man spake like this man. 47Then answered them the Pharisees, Are ye also deceived? 48Have any of the rulers or of the Pharisees believed on him? 49But this people who knoweth not the law are cursed. 50Nicodemus saith unto them, (he that came to *Jesus* by night, being one of them,) 51Doth our law judge any man, before it hear him, and know what he doeth? 52They answered and said unto him, Art thou also of Galilee? Search, and look: for out of Galilee ariseth no prophet. [ver. 41; Is. 9:1,2; Mat. 4:15; ch. 1:46]

The woman caught in adultery

53 And every man went unto his own house.

8 Jesus went unto the mount of Olives. 2And early in the morning he came again into the temple, and all the people came unto him; and he sat down, and taught them. 3And the scribes and Pharisees brought unto him a woman taken in adultery; and when they had set her in the midst, 4They say unto him, Master, this woman was taken in adultery, in the very act. 5Now Moses in the law commanded us, that such should be stoned: but what sayest thou? 6This they said, tempting

him, that they might have to accuse him. But Jesus stooped down, and with *his* finger wrote on the ground, *as though he heard them not.* 7So when they continued asking him, he lift up *himself,* and said unto them, He that is without sin among you, let him first cast a stone at her. 8And again he stooped down, and wrote on the ground. 9And they which heard *it,* being convicted by *their own* conscience, went out one by one, beginning at the eldest, *even* unto the last: and Jesus was left alone, and the woman standing in the midst. 10When Jesus had lift up *himself,* and saw none but the woman, he said unto her, Woman, where are those thine accusers? hath no *man* condemned thee? 11She said, No *man,* Lord. And Jesus said unto her, Neither do I condemn thee: go, and sin no more. [Luke 9:56; 12:14; ch. 3:17; ch. 5:14]

Jesus the light of the world

12 Then spake Jesus again unto them, saying, I am the light of the world: he that followeth me shall not walk in darkness, but shall have the light of life. 13The Pharisees therefore said unto him, Thou bearest record of thyself; thy record is not true. 14Jesus answered and said unto them, Though I bear record of myself, *yet* my record is true: for I know whence I came, and whither I go; but ye cannot tell whence I come, and whither I go. 15Ye judge after the flesh; I judge no *man.* 16And yet if I judge, my judgment is true: for I am not alone, but I and the Fa-

ther that sent me. [17]It is also written in your law, that the testimony of two men is true. [18]I am *one* that bear witness of myself, and the Father that sent me beareth witness of me. [19]Then said they unto him, Where is thy Father? Jesus answered, Ye neither know me, nor my Father: if ye had known me, ye should have known my Father also. [20]These words spake Jesus in the treasury, as he taught in the temple: and no *man* laid hands on him; for his hour was not yet come. [Mark 12:41; ch. 7:30; ch. 7:8]

Jesus warns against unbelief

[21] Then said Jesus again unto them, I go my way, and ye shall seek me, and shall die in your sins: whither I go, ye cannot come. [22]Then said the Jews, Will he kill himself? because he saith, Whither I go, ye cannot come. [23]And he said unto them, Ye are from beneath; I am from above: ye are of this world; I am not of this world. [24]I said therefore unto you, that ye shall die in your sins: for if ye believe not that I am *he,* ye shall die in your sins. [25]Then said they unto him, Who art thou? And Jesus saith unto them, Even the same that I said unto you *from* the beginning. [26]I have many *things* to say and to judge of you: but he that sent me is true; and I speak to the world those *things* which I have heard of him. [27]They understood not that he spake to them of the Father. [28]Then said Jesus unto them, When ye have lift up the Son of man, then shall ye know that I am *he,* and *that* I do nothing of myself;

but as my Father hath taught me, I speak these *things.* [29]And he that sent me is with me: the Father hath not left me alone; for I do always those *things* that please him. [30]As he spake these *words,* many believed on him. [ch. 7:31; 10:42; 11:45]

The true children of Abraham

[31] Then said Jesus to those Jews which believed on him, If ye continue in my word, *then* are ye my disciples indeed; [32]And ye shall know the truth, and the truth shall make you free. [33]They answered him, We be Abraham's seed, and were never in bondage to any *man:* how sayest thou, Ye shall be made free? [34]Jesus answered them, Verily, verily, I say unto you, Whosoever committeth sin is the servant of sin. [35]And the servant abideth not in the house for ever: *but* the son abideth ever. [36]If the Son therefore shall make you free, ye shall be free indeed. [37]I know that ye are Abraham's seed; but ye seek to kill me, because my word hath no place in you. [38]I speak *that* which I have seen with my Father: and ye do *that* which ye have seen with your father. [39]They answered and said unto him, Abraham is our father. Jesus saith unto them, If ye were Abraham's children, ye would do the works of Abraham. [40]But now ye seek to kill me, a man that hath told you the truth, which I have heard of God: this did not Abraham. [41]Ye do the deeds of your father. Then said they unto him, We be not born of fornication; we have one Father, *even* God. [42]Jesus said unto them, If God were your

Father, ye would love me: for I proceeded forth and came from God; neither came I of myself, but he sent me. 43Why do ye not understand my speech? *even* because ye cannot hear my word. 44Ye are of *your* father the devil, and the lusts of your father ye will do. He was a murderer from the beginning, and abode not in the truth, because there is no truth in him. When he speaketh a lie, he speaketh of his own: for he is a liar, and the father of it. 45And because I tell *you* the truth, ye believe me not. 46Which of you convinceth me of sin? And if I say the truth, why do ye not believe me? 47He that is of God heareth God's words: ye therefore hear *them* not, because ye are not of God. [ch. 10:26; 1 John 4:6]

Controversy with the Jews

48 Then answered the Jews, and said unto him, Say we not well that thou art a Samaritan, and hast a devil? 49Jesus answered, I have not a devil; but I honour my Father, and ye do dishonour me. 50And I seek not mine own glory: there is *one* that seeketh and judgeth. 51Verily, verily, I say unto you, If a man keep my saying, he shall never see death. 52Then said the Jews unto him, Now we know that thou hast a devil. Abraham is dead, and the prophets; and thou sayest, If a man keep my saying, he shall never taste of death. 53Art thou greater than our father Abraham, which is dead? and the prophets are dead: whom makest thou thyself? 54Jesus answered, If I honour myself, my honour is nothing: it is my Father that honoureth me; of whom ye say, that he is your God: 55Yet ye have not known him; but I know him: and if I should say, I know him not, I shall be a liar like unto you: but I know him, and keep his saying. 56Your father Abraham rejoiced to see my day: and he saw *it,* and was glad. 57Then said the Jews unto him, Thou art not yet fifty years old, and hast thou seen Abraham? 58Jesus said unto them, Verily, verily, I say unto you, Before Abraham was, I am. 59Then took they up stones to cast at him: but Jesus hid himself, and went out of the temple, going through the midst of them, and so passed by. [ch. 10:31,39; 11:8; Luke 4:30]

Jesus heals the man born blind

9 And as *Jesus* passed by, he saw a man *which was* blind from *his* birth. 2And his disciples asked him, saying, Master, who did sin, this *man,* or his parents, that he was born blind? 3Jesus answered, Neither hath this *man* sinned, nor his parents: but that the works of God should be made manifest in him. 4I must work the works of him that sent me, while it is day: the night cometh, when no *man* can work. 5As long as I am in the world, I am the light of the world. 6When he had thus spoken, he spat on the ground, and made clay of the spittle, and he anointed the eyes of the blind man with the clay, 7And said unto him, Go, wash in the pool of Siloam, (which is by interpretation, Sent.) He went his way therefore, and washed, and came seeing. [Neh. 3:15; See 2 Ki. 5:14]

8 The neighbours therefore, and they which before had seen him that he was blind, said, Is not this he that sat and begged? 9Some said, This is he: others *said*, He is like him: *but* he said, I am *he*. 10Therefore said they unto him, How were thine eyes opened? 11He answered and said, A man *that is* called Jesus made clay, and anointed mine eyes, and said unto me, Go to the pool of Siloam, and wash: and I went and washed, and I received sight. 12Then said they unto him, Where is he? He said, I know not.

Pharisees question the healed man

13 They brought to the Pharisees him that aforetime was blind. 14And it was the sabbath day when Jesus made the clay, and opened his eyes. 15Then again the Pharisees also asked him how he had received his sight. He said unto them, He put clay upon mine eyes, and I washed, and do see. 16Therefore said some of the Pharisees, This man is not of God, because he keepeth not the sabbath day. Others said, How can a man *that is* a sinner do such miracles? And there was a division among them. 17They say unto the blind man again, What sayest thou of him, that he hath opened thine eyes? He said, He is a prophet. 18But the Jews did not believe concerning him, that he had been blind, and received his sight, until they called the parents of him that had received his sight. 19And they asked them, saying, Is this your son, who

ye say was born blind? how then doth he now see? 20His parents answered them and said, We know that this is our son, and that he was born blind: 21But by what means he now seeth, we know not; or who hath opened his eyes, we know not: he is of age; ask him: he shall speak for himself. 22These *words* spake his parents, because they feared the Jews: for the Jews had agreed already, that if any *man* did confess that he *was* Christ, he should be put out of the synagogue. 23Therefore said his parents, He is of age; ask him. 24Then again called they the man that was blind, and said unto him, Give God the praise: we know that this man is a sinner. 25He answered and said, Whether he be a sinner *or no*, I know not: one *thing* I know, that, whereas I was blind, now I see. 26Then said they to him again, What did he to thee? how opened he thine eyes? 27He answered them, I have told you already, and ye did not hear: wherefore would you hear *it* again? will ye also be his disciples? 28Then they reviled him, and said, Thou art his disciple; but we are Moses' disciples. 29We know that God spake unto Moses: *as for* this *fellow*, we know not from whence he is. 30The man answered and said unto them, Why herein is a marvellous *thing*, that ye know not from whence he is, and *yet* he hath opened mine eyes. 31Now we know that God heareth not sinners: but if any *man* be a worshipper of God, and doeth his will, him he heareth. 32Since the world began was it not heard that any *man* opened the eyes of one that was born blind. ³³If this *man* were not of God, he could do nothing. ³⁴They answered and said unto him, Thou wast altogether born in sins, and dost thou teach us? And they cast him out. [ver. 2]

Jesus talks to the healed man

35 Jesus heard that they had cast him out; and when he had found him, he said unto him, Dost thou believe on the Son of God? ³⁶He answered and said, Who is he, Lord, that I might believe on him? ³⁷And Jesus said unto him, Thou hast both seen him, and it is he that talketh with thee. ³⁸And he said, Lord, I believe. And he worshipped him.

39 And Jesus said, For judgment I am come into this world, that they which see not might see; and that they which see might be made blind. ⁴⁰And *some* of the Pharisees which were with him heard these *words,* and said unto him, Are we blind also? ⁴¹Jesus said unto them, If ye were blind, ye should have no sin: but now ye say, We see; therefore your sin remaineth. [ch. 15:22,24]

Jesus the good shepherd

10 Verily, verily, I say unto you, He that entereth not by the door into the sheepfold, but climbeth up some other way, the same is a thief and a robber. ²But he that entereth in by the door is the shepherd of the sheep. ³To him the porter openeth; and the sheep hear his voice: and he calleth his own sheep by name, and leadeth them out. ⁴And when he putteth forth his own sheep, he goeth before them, and the sheep follow him: for they know his voice. ⁵And a stranger will they not follow, but will flee from him: for they know not the voice of strangers. ⁶This parable spake Jesus unto them: but they understood not what *things* they were which he spake unto them.

7 Then said Jesus unto them again, Verily, verily, I say unto you, I am the door of the sheep. ⁸All that ever came before me are thieves and robbers: but the sheep did not hear them. ⁹I am the door: by me if any *man* enter in, he shall be saved, and shall go in and out, and find pasture. ¹⁰The thief cometh not, but for to steal, and to kill, and to destroy: I am come that they might have life, and that they might have *it* more abundantly. ¹¹I am the good shepherd: the good shepherd giveth his life for the sheep. ¹²But *he that is* a hireling, and not the shepherd, whose own the sheep are not, seeth the wolf coming, and leaveth the sheep, and fleeth: and the wolf catcheth them, and scattereth the sheep. ¹³The hireling fleeth, because he is a hireling, and careth not for the sheep. ¹⁴I am the good shepherd, and know my *sheep,* and am known of mine. ¹⁵As the Father knoweth me, *even* so know I the Father: and I lay down my life for the sheep. ¹⁶And other sheep I have, which are not of this fold: them also I must bring, and they shall hear my voice; and there shall be one fold, *and* one shepherd. ¹⁷Therefore doth *my* Father love

me, because I lay down my life, that I might take it again. ¹⁸No *man* taketh it from me, but I lay it down of myself. I have power to lay it down, and I have power to take it again. This commandment have I received of my Father. ¹⁹There was a division therefore again among the Jews for these sayings. ²⁰And many of them said, He hath a devil, and is mad; why hear ye him? ²¹Others said, These are not the words of him that hath a devil. Can a devil open the eyes of the blind? [Ex. 4:11; Ps. 94:9; 146:8; ch. 9:6,7,32,33]

The Jews try to arrest Jesus

22 And it was at Jerusalem *the feast of* the dedication, and it was winter. ²³And Jesus walked in the temple in Solomon's porch. ²⁴Then came the Jews round about him, and said unto him, How long dost thou make us to doubt? If thou be the Christ, tell us plainly. ²⁵Jesus answered them, I told you, and ye believe not: the works that I do in my Father's name, they bear witness of me. ²⁶But ye believe not, because ye are not of my sheep, as I said unto you. ²⁷My sheep hear my voice, and I know them, and they follow me: ²⁸And I give unto them eternal life; and they shall never perish, neither shall any *man* pluck them out of my hand. ²⁹My Father, which gave *them* me, is greater than all; and no *man* is able to pluck *them* out of my Father's hand. ³⁰I and *my* Father are one. ³¹Then the Jews took up stones again to stone him. ³²Jesus answered them, Many good works

have I shewed you from my Father; for which of those works do ye stone me? ³³The Jews answered him, saying, For a good work we stone thee not; but for blasphemy; and because that thou, being a man, makest thyself God. ³⁴Jesus answered them, Is it not written in your law, I said, Ye are gods? ³⁵If he called them gods, unto whom the word of God came, and the scripture cannot be broken; ³⁶Say ye *of him,* whom the Father hath sanctified, and sent into the world, Thou blasphemest; because I said, I am the Son of God? ³⁷If I do not the works of my Father, believe me not. ³⁸But if I do, though ye believe not me, believe the works: that ye may know, and believe, that the Father *is* in me, and I in him. ³⁹Therefore they sought again to take him: but he escaped out of their hand, ⁴⁰And went away again beyond Jordan into the place where John at first baptized; and there he abode. ⁴¹And many resorted unto him, and said, John did no miracle: but all *things* that John spake of this *man* were true. ⁴²And many believed on him there. [ch. 8:30; 11:45]

Jesus hears of Lazarus's death

11 Now a certain *man* was sick, *named* Lazarus, of Bethany, the town of Mary and her sister Martha. ²(It was *that* Mary which anointed the Lord with ointment, and wiped his feet with her hair, whose brother Lazarus was sick.) ³Therefore *his* sisters sent unto him, saying, Lord, behold, he whom thou lovest is sick. ⁴When

Jesus heard *that,* he said, This sickness is not unto death, but for the glory of God, that the Son of God might be glorified thereby. 5Now Jesus loved Martha, and her sister, and Lazarus. 6When he had heard therefore that he was sick, he abode two days *still* in the *same* place where he was. 7Then after that saith he to *his* disciples, Let us go into Judea again. 8*His* disciples say unto him, Master, the Jews of late sought to stone thee; and goest thou thither again? 9Jesus answered, Are there not twelve hours in the day? If any *man* walk in the day, he stumbleth not, because he seeth the light of this world. 10But if a man walk in the night, he stumbleth, because there is no light in him. 11These *things* said he: and after that he saith unto them, Our friend Lazarus sleepeth; but I go, that I may awake him out of sleep. 12Then said his disciples, Lord, if he sleep, he shall do well. 13Howbeit Jesus spake of his death: but they thought that he had spoken of taking of rest in sleep. 14Then said Jesus unto them plainly, Lazarus is dead. 15And I am glad for your sakes that I was not there, to the intent ye may believe; nevertheless let us go unto him. 16Then said Thomas, which is called Didymus, unto *his* fellow-disciples, Let us also go, that we may die with him.

Jesus the resurrection and the life

17 Then when Jesus came, he found that he had *lien* in the grave four days already. 18Now Bethany was nigh unto Jerusalem, about fifteen furlongs off: 19And many of the Jews came to Martha and Mary, to comfort them concerning their brother. 20Then Martha, as soon as she heard that Jesus was coming, went and met him: but Mary sat *still* in the house. 21Then said Martha unto Jesus, Lord, if thou hadst been here, my brother had not died. 22But I know, that even now, whatsoever thou wilt ask of God, God will give *it* thee. 23Jesus saith unto her, Thy brother shall rise again. 24Martha saith unto him, I know that he shall rise again in the resurrection at the last day. 25Jesus said unto her, I am the resurrection, and the life: he that believeth in me, though he were dead, *yet* shall he live: 26And whosoever liveth and believeth in me shall never die. Believest thou this? 27She saith unto him, Yea, Lord: I believe that thou art the Christ, the Son of God, which should come into the world. 28And when she had so said, she went her way, and called Mary her sister secretly, saying, The Master is come, and calleth for thee. 29As soon as she heard *that,* she arose quickly, and came unto him. 30Now Jesus was not yet come into the town, but was in *that* place where Martha met him. 31The Jews then which were with her in the house, and comforted her, when they saw Mary, that she rose up hastily and went out, followed her, saying, She goeth unto the grave to weep there. 32Then when Mary was come where Jesus was, and saw him, she fell down at his feet, say-

ing unto him, Lord, if thou hadst been here, my brother had not died. 33When Jesus therefore saw her weeping, and the Jews also weeping which came with her, he groaned in the spirit, and was troubled, 34And said, Where have ye laid him? They say unto him, Lord, come and see. 35Jesus wept. 36Then said the Jews, Behold, how he loved him. 37And some of them said, Could not this *man,* which opened the eyes of the blind, have caused that even this *man* should not have died? [ch. 9:6]

Jesus raises Lazarus

38 Jesus therefore again groaning in himself cometh to the grave. It was a cave, and a stone lay upon it. 39Jesus said, Take ye away the stone. Martha, the sister of him that was dead, saith unto him, Lord, by this time he stinketh: for he hath been *dead* four days. 40Jesus saith unto her, Said I not unto thee, that, if thou wouldest believe, thou shouldest see the glory of God? 41Then they took away the stone *from the place* where the dead was laid. And Jesus lift up *his* eyes, and said, Father, I thank thee that thou hast heard me. 42And I knew that thou hearest me always: but because of the people which stand by I said *it,* that they may believe that thou hast sent me. 43And when he thus had spoken, he cried with a loud voice, Lazarus, come forth. 44And he that was dead came forth, bound hand and foot with graveclothes: and his face was bound about with a napkin. Jesus saith

unto them, Loose him, and let *him* go. [ch. 20:7]

Pharisees plot to kill Jesus

45 Then many of the Jews which came to Mary, and had seen *the things* which Jesus did, believed on him. 46But some of them went their ways to the Pharisees, and told them what *things* Jesus had done. 47Then gathered the chief priests and the Pharisees a council, and said, What do we? for this man doeth many miracles. 48If we let him thus alone, all *men* will believe on him: and the Romans shall come and take away both our place and nation. 49And one of them, *named* Caiaphas, being the high priest that *same* year, said unto them, Ye know nothing at all, 50Nor consider that it is expedient for us, that one man should die for the people, and *that* the whole nation perish not. 51And this spake he not of himself: but being high priest that year, he prophesied that Jesus should die for *that* nation; 52And not for *that* nation only, but that also he should gather together in one the children of God that were scattered abroad. 53Then from that day forth they took counsel together for to put him to death. 54Jesus therefore walked no more openly among the Jews; but went thence unto a country near to the wilderness, into a city called Ephraim, and there continued with his disciples. 55And the Jews' passover was nigh at hand: and many went out of the country up to Jerusalem before the passover, to purify themselves. 56Then sought

they for Jesus, and spake among themselves, as they stood in the temple, What think ye, that he will not come to the feast? ⁵⁷Now both the chief priests and the Pharisees had given a commandment, that, if any *man* knew where he were, he should shew *it*, that they might take him.

Jesus anointed at Bethany

12 Then Jesus six days before the passover came to Bethany, where Lazarus was which had been dead, whom he raised from the dead. ²There they made him a supper; and Martha served: but Lazarus was one of them that sat at the table with him. ³Then took Mary a pound of ointment of spikenard, very costly, and anointed the feet of Jesus, and wiped his feet with her hair: and the house was filled with the odour of the ointment. ⁴Then saith one of his disciples, Judas Iscariot, Simon's *son*, which should betray him, ⁵Why was not this ointment sold for three hundred pence, and given to the poor? ⁶This he said, not that he cared for the poor; but because he was a thief, and had the bag, and bare what was put *therein*. ⁷Then said Jesus, Let her alone: against the day of my burying hath she kept this. ⁸For the poor always ye have with you; but me ye have not always. [Mat. 26:11; Mark 14:7]

9 Much people of the Jews therefore knew that he was there: and they came not for Jesus' sake only, but that they might see Lazarus also, whom he had raised from the dead. ¹⁰But the chief priests consulted that they might put Lazarus also to death; ¹¹Because that by reason of him many of the Jews went away, and believed on Jesus. [ver. 18; ch. 11:45]

The triumphal entry

12 On the next day much people that were come to the feast, when they heard that Jesus was coming to Jerusalem, ¹³Took branches of palm trees, and went forth to meet him, and cried, Hosanna: Blessed *is* the King of Israel that cometh in the name of the Lord. ¹⁴And Jesus, when he had found a young ass, sat thereon; as it is written, ¹⁵Fear not, daughter of Sion: behold, thy King cometh, sitting on an ass's colt. ¹⁶These *things* understood not his disciples at the first: but when Jesus was glorified, then remembered they that these *things* were written of him, and *that* they had done these *things* unto him. ¹⁷The people therefore that was with him when he called Lazarus out of *his* grave, and raised him from the dead, bare record. ¹⁸For this cause the people also met him, for that they heard that he had done this miracle. ¹⁹The Pharisees therefore said among themselves, Perceive ye how ye prevail nothing? behold, the world is gone after him. [ch. 11:47,48]

Jesus sought by the Gentiles

20 And there were certain Greeks among them that came up to worship at the feast: ²¹The same came therefore to Philip, which was of Bethsaida of Galilee, and desired him, saying, Sir, we would

see Jesus. 22Philip cometh and telleth Andrew: and again Andrew and Philip tell Jesus. 23And Jesus answered them, saying, The hour is come, that the Son of man should be glorified. 24Verily, verily, I say unto you, Except a corn of wheat fall into the ground and die, it abideth alone: but if it die, it bringeth forth much fruit. 25He that loveth his life shall lose it; and he that hateth his life in this world shall keep it unto life eternal. 26If any *man* serve me, let him follow me; and where I am, there shall also my servant be: if any *man* serve me, him will *my* Father honour. 27Now is my soul troubled; and what shall I say? Father, save me from this hour: but for this cause came I unto this hour. 28Father, glorify thy name. Then came there a voice from heaven, *saying,* I have both glorified *it,* and will glorify *it* again. 29The people therefore, that stood *by,* and heard *it,* said that it thundered: others said, An angel spake to him. 30Jesus answered and said, This voice came not because of me, but for your sakes. 31Now is the judgment of this world: now shall the prince of this world be cast out. 32And I, if I be lifted up from the earth, will draw all *men* unto me. 33This he said, signifying what death he should die. 34The people answered him, We have heard out of the law that Christ abideth for ever: and how sayest thou, The Son of man must be lift up? who is this Son of man? 35Then Jesus said unto them, Yet a little while is the light with you. Walk while ye have the light,

lest darkness come upon you: for he that walketh in darkness knoweth not whither he goeth. 36While ye have light, believe in the light, that ye may be the children of light. These *things* spake Jesus, and departed, and did hide himself from them. [Luke 16:8; Eph. 5:8; 1 Thes. 5:5; 1 John 2:9-11; ch. 8:59; 11:54]

The cause of unbelief

37 But though he had done so many miracles before them, *yet* they believed not on him: 38That the saying of Esaias the prophet might be fulfilled, which he spake, Lord, who hath believed our report? and to whom hath the arm of the Lord been revealed? 39Therefore they could not believe, because that Esaias said again, 40He hath blinded their eyes, and hardened their heart; that they should not see with *their* eyes, nor understand with *their* heart, and be converted, and I should heal them. 41These *things* said Esaias, when he saw his glory, and spake of him. 42Nevertheless among the *chief* rulers also many believed on him; but because of the Pharisees they did not confess *him,* lest they should be put out of the synagogue: 43For they loved the praise of men more than the praise of God. [ch. 5:44]

A summary of Jesus' claims

44 Jesus cried and said, He that believeth on me, believeth not on me, but on him that sent me. 45And he that seeth me seeth him that sent me. 46I am come a light into the world, that whosoever be-

lieveth on me should not abide in darkness. ⁴⁷And if any *man* hear my words, and believe not, I judge him not: for I came not to judge the world, but to save the world. ⁴⁸He that rejecteth me, and receiveth not my words, hath *one* that judgeth him: the word that I have spoken, the same shall judge him in the last day. ⁴⁹For I have not spoken of myself; but the Father which sent me, he gave me a commandment, what I should say, and what I should speak. ⁵⁰And I know that his commandment is life everlasting: whatsoever I speak therefore, even as the Father said unto me, so I speak.

Washing the disciples' feet

13 Now before the feast of the passover, when Jesus knew that his hour was come that he should depart out of this world unto the Father, having loved his own which were in the world, he loved them unto the end. ²And supper being ended, the devil having now put into the heart of Judas Iscariot, Simon's *son,* to betray him; ³Jesus knowing that the Father had given all *things* into his hands, and that he was come from God, and went to God; ⁴He riseth from supper, and laid aside *his* garments; and took a towel, and girded himself. ⁵After that, he poureth water into a bason, and began to wash the disciples' feet, and to wipe *them* with the towel wherewith he was girded. ⁶Then cometh he to Simon Peter: and *Peter* saith unto him, Lord, dost thou wash my feet? ⁷Jesus answered and said

unto him, What I do thou knowest not now; but thou shalt know hereafter. ⁸Peter saith unto him, Thou shalt never wash my feet. Jesus answered him, If I wash thee not, thou hast no part with me. ⁹Simon Peter saith unto him, Lord, not *my* feet only, but also *my* hands and *my* head. ¹⁰Jesus saith to him, He that is washed needeth not save to wash *his* feet, but is clean every whit: and ye are clean, but not all. ¹¹For he knew who should betray him; therefore said he, Ye are not all clean. [ch. 6:64]

12 So after he had washed their feet, and had taken his garments, and was set down again, he said unto them, Know ye what I have done to you? ¹³Ye call me Master and Lord: and ye say well; for *so* I am. ¹⁴If I then, *your* Lord and Master, have washed your feet; ye also ought to wash one another's feet. ¹⁵For I have given you an example, that ye should do as I have done to you. ¹⁶Verily, verily, I say unto you, The servant is not greater than his lord; neither he that is sent greater than he that sent him. ¹⁷If ye know these *things,* happy are ye if ye do them. ¹⁸I speak not of you all: I know whom I have chosen: but that the scripture may be fulfilled, He that eateth bread with me hath lift up his heel against me. ¹⁹Now I tell you before it come, that, when it is come to pass, ye may believe that I am *he.* ²⁰Verily, verily, I say unto you, He that receiveth whomsoever I send receiveth me; and he that receiveth me receiveth him that sent me. [Mat. 10:40; 25:40; Luke 10:16]

Jesus dismisses Judas

21 When Jesus had thus said, he was troubled in spirit, and testified, and said, Verily, verily, I say unto you, that one of you shall betray me. 22Then the disciples looked one on another, doubting of whom he spake. 23Now there was leaning on Jesus' bosom one of his disciples, whom Jesus loved. 24Simon Peter therefore beckoned to him, that *he* should ask who it should be of whom he spake. 25He then lying on Jesus' breast saith unto him, Lord, who is it? 26Jesus answered, He it is, to whom I shall give a sop, when I have dipped *it.* And when he had dipped the sop, he gave *it* to Judas Iscariot, *the son* of Simon. 27And after the sop Satan entered into him. Then said Jesus unto him, That thou doest, do quickly. 28Now no *man* at the table knew for what intent he spake this unto him. 29For some *of them* thought, because Judas had the bag, that Jesus had said unto him, Buy *those things* that we have need of against the feast; or that he should give something to the poor. 30He then having received the sop went immediately out: and it was night.

31 Therefore, when he was gone out, Jesus said, Now is the Son of man glorified, and God is glorified in him. 32If God be glorified in him, God shall also glorify him in himself, and shall straightway glorify him. 33Little children, yet a little while I am with you. Ye shall seek me: and as I said unto the Jews, Whither I go, ye cannot come; so now I say to you. 34A new commandment I give unto you, That ye love one another; as I have loved you, that ye also love one another. 35By this shall all *men* know that ye are my disciples, if ye have love one to another. [1 John 2:5; 4:20]

Peter's denial foretold

36 Simon Peter said unto him, Lord, whither goest thou? Jesus answered him, Whither I go, thou canst not follow me now; but thou shalt follow me afterwards. 37Peter said unto him, Lord, why cannot I follow thee now? I will lay down my life for thy sake. 38Jesus answered him, Wilt thou lay down thy life for my sake? Verily, verily, I say unto thee, The cock shall not crow, till thou hast denied me thrice.

The way, the truth, and the life

14 Let not your heart be troubled: ye believe in God, believe also in me. 2In my Father's house are many mansions: if *it were* not *so,* I would have told you. I go to prepare a place for you. 3And if I go and prepare a place for you, I will come again, and receive you unto myself; that where I am, *there* ye may be also. 4And whither I go ye know, and the way ye know. 5Thomas saith unto him, Lord, we know not whither thou goest; and how can we know the way? 6Jesus saith unto him, I am the way, the truth, and the life: no *man* cometh unto the Father, but by me. 7If ye had known me, ye should have known my Father also: and from henceforth ye know him, and have seen him. 8Philip saith unto him, Lord, shew us the Father, and it sufficeth us. ⁹Jesus saith unto him, Have I been so long time with you, and *yet* hast thou not known me, Philip? he that hath seen me hath seen the Father; and how sayest thou *then,* Shew us the Father? ¹⁰Believest thou not that I am in the Father, and the Father in me? the words that I speak unto you, I speak not of myself: but the Father that dwelleth in me, he doeth the works. ¹¹Believe me that I *am* in the Father, and the Father in me: or else believe me for the very works' sake. ¹²Verily, verily, I say unto you, He that believeth on me, the works that I do shall he do also; and greater *works* than these shall he do; because I go unto my Father. ¹³And whatsoever ye shall ask in my name, that will I do, that the Father may be glorified in the Son. ¹⁴If ye shall ask any *thing* in my name, I will do *it.*

The promise of the Spirit

15 If ye love me, keep my commandments. ¹⁶And I will pray the Father, and he shall give you another Comforter, that he may abide with you for ever; ¹⁷*Even* the Spirit of truth; whom the world cannot receive, because it seeth him not, neither knoweth him: but ye know him; for he dwelleth with you, and shall be in you. ¹⁸I will not leave you comfortless: I will come to you. ¹⁹Yet a little while, and the world seeth me no more; but ye see me: because I live, ye shall live also. ²⁰At that day ye shall know that I *am* in my Father, and you in me, and I in you. ²¹He that hath my commandments, and keepeth

them, he it is that loveth me: and he that loveth me shall be loved of my Father, and I will love him, and will manifest myself to him. ²²Judas saith unto him, not Iscariot, Lord, how is it that thou wilt manifest thyself unto us, and not unto the world? ²³Jesus answered and said unto him, If a man love me, he will keep my words: and my Father will love him, and we will come unto him, and make *our* abode with him. ²⁴He that loveth me not keepeth not my sayings: and the word which you hear is not mine, but the Father's which sent me. [ch. 5:19]

25 These *things* have I spoken unto you, being *yet* present with you. ²⁶But the Comforter, *which is* the Holy Ghost, whom the Father will send in my name, he shall teach you all *things,* and bring all *things* to your remembrance, whatsoever I have said unto you. ²⁷Peace I leave with you, my peace I give unto you: not as the world giveth, give I unto you. Let not your heart be troubled, neither let it be afraid. ²⁸Ye have heard how I said unto you, I go away, and come *again* unto you. If ye loved me, ye would rejoice, because I said, I go unto the Father: for my Father is greater than I. ²⁹And now I have told you before it come to pass, that, when it is come to pass, ye might believe. ³⁰Hereafter I will not talk much with you: for the prince of this world cometh, and hath nothing in me. ³¹But that the world may know that I love the Father; and as the Father gave me commandment, *even* so I do. Arise, let us go hence. [ch. 10:18; Phil. 2:8; Heb. 5:8]

Jesus the true vine

15 I am the true vine, and my Father is the husbandman. ²Every branch in me that beareth not fruit he taketh away: and every *branch* that beareth fruit, he purgeth it, that it may bring forth more fruit. ³Now ye are clean through the word which I have spoken unto you. ⁴Abide in me, and I in you. As the branch cannot bear fruit of itself, except it abide in the vine; no more can ye, except ye abide in me. ⁵I am the vine, ye *are* the branches: He that abideth in me, and I in him, the same bringeth forth much fruit: for without me ye can do nothing. ⁶If a man abide not in me, he is cast forth as a branch, and is withered; and *men* gather them, and cast *them* into the fire, and they are burned. ⁷If ye abide in me, and my words abide in you, ye shall ask what ye will, and it shall be done unto you. ⁸Herein is my Father glorified, that ye bear much fruit; so shall ye be my disciples. ⁹As the Father hath loved me, so have I loved you: continue ye in my love. ¹⁰If ye keep my commandments, ye shall abide in my love; even as I have kept my Father's commandments, and abide in his love. [ch. 14:15]

The hatred of the world

11 These *things* have I spoken unto you, that my joy might remain in you, and *that* your joy might be full. ¹²This is my commandment, That ye love one another, as I have loved you. ¹³Greater love hath no *man* than this, that a man lay down his life for his friends. ¹⁴Ye are my friends, if ye do whatsoever I command you. ¹⁵Henceforth I call you not servants; for the servant knoweth not what his lord doeth: but I have called you friends; for all *things* that I have heard of my Father I have made known unto you. ¹⁶Ye have not chosen me, but I have chosen you, and ordained you, that you should go and bring forth fruit, and *that* your fruit should remain: that whatsoever ye shall ask of the Father in my name, he may give it you. ¹⁷These *things* I command you, that ye love one another. ¹⁸If the world hate you, ye know that it hated me before *it hated* you. ¹⁹If ye were of the world, the world would love his own: but because ye are not of the world, but I have chosen you out of the world, therefore the world hateth you. ²⁰Remember the word that I said unto you, The servant is not greater than his lord. If they have persecuted me, they will also persecute you; if they have kept my saying, they will keep yours also. ²¹But all these *things* will they do unto you for my name's sake, because they know not him that sent me. ²²If I had not come and spoken unto them, they had not had sin: but now they have no cloke for their sin. ²³He that hateth me hateth my Father also. ²⁴If I had not done among them the works which none other *man* did, they had not had sin: but now have they both seen and hated both me and my Father. ²⁵But *this cometh to pass,* that the word might be fulfilled that is written in their law,

They hated me without a cause.
²⁶But when the Comforter is
come, whom I will send unto you
from the Father, *even* the Spirit of
truth, which proceedeth from the
Father, he shall testify of me:
²⁷And ye also shall bear witness,
because ye have been with me
from the beginning. [Luke 24:48; Acts
1:21; 2:32; 3:15; 4:20,33; 5:32; 10:39; 13:31;
1 Pet. 5:1; 2 Pet. 1:16; Luke 1:2; 1 John 1:1]

The coming of the Spirit

16 These *things* have I spoken unto you, that ye
should not be offended. ²They
shall put you out of the synagogues: yea, the time cometh, that
whosoever killeth you will think
that he doeth God service. ³And
these *things* will they do unto you,
because they have not known the
Father, nor me. ⁴But these *things*
have I told you, that when the time
shall come, ye may remember that
I told you of them. And these
things I said not unto you at the beginning, because I was with you.
⁵But now I go my way to him that
sent me; and none of you asketh
me, Whither goest thou? ⁶But because I have said these *things* unto
you, sorrow hath filled your heart.
⁷Nevertheless I tell you the truth;
It is expedient for you that I go
away: for if I go not away, the Comforter will not come unto you; but
if I depart, I will send him unto
you. ⁸And when he is come, he
will reprove the world of sin, and
of righteousness, and of judgment:
⁹Of sin, because they believe not
on me; ¹⁰Of righteousness, because I go to my Father, and ye see

me no more; ¹¹Of judgment, because the prince of this world is
judged. [Acts 26:18; Luke 10:18; Eph. 2:2;
Col. 2:15; Heb. 2:14].

12 I have yet many *things* to say
unto you, but ye cannot bear *them*
now. ¹³Howbeit when he, the Spirit of truth, is come, he will guide
you into all truth: for he shall not
speak of himself; but whatsoever
he shall hear, *that* shall he speak:
and he will shew you *things* to
come. ¹⁴He shall glorify me: for he
shall receive of mine, and shall
shew *it* unto you. ¹⁵All *things* that
the Father hath are mine: therefore
said I, that he shall take of mine,
and shall shew *it* unto you. ¹⁶A little while, and ye shall not see me:
and again, a little while, and ye
shall see me, because I go to the
Father. [ch. 13:3]

Jesus' farewell to his disciples

17 Then said *some* of his disciples among themselves, What is
this that he saith unto us, A little
while, and ye shall not see me: and
again, a little while, and ye shall
see me: and, Because I go to the Father? ¹⁸They said therefore, What
is this that he saith, A little while?
we cannot tell what he saith.
¹⁹Now Jesus knew that they were
desirous to ask him, and said unto
them, Do ye inquire among yourselves of that I said, A little while,
and ye shall not see me: and again,
a little while, and ye shall see me?
²⁰Verily, verily, I say unto you, That
ye shall weep and lament, but the
world shall rejoice: and ye shall be
sorrowful, but your sorrow shall be
turned into joy. ²¹A woman when

she is in travail hath sorrow, because her hour is come: but as soon as she is delivered of the child, she remembereth no more the anguish, for joy that a man is born into the world. 22And ye now therefore have sorrow: but I will see you again, and your heart shall rejoice, and your joy no *man* taketh from you. 23And in that day ye shall ask me nothing. Verily, verily, I say unto you, Whatsoever ye shall ask the Father in my name, he will give *it* you. 24Hitherto have ye asked nothing in my name: ask, and ye shall receive, that your joy may be full. 25These *things* have I spoken unto you in proverbs: but the time cometh, when I shall no more speak unto you in proverbs, but I shall shew you plainly of the Father. 26At that day ye shall ask in my name: and I say not unto you, that I will pray the Father for you: 27For the Father himself loveth you, because ye have loved me, and have believed that I came out from God. 28I came forth from the Father, and am come into the world: again, I leave the world, and go to the Father. [ch. 13:3]

29 His disciples said unto him, Lo, now speakest thou plainly, and speakest no proverb. 30Now are we sure that thou knowest all *things,* and needest not that any *man* should ask thee: by this we believe that thou camest forth from God. 31Jesus answered them, Do ye now believe? 32Behold, the hour cometh, yea, is now come, that ye shall be scattered, every man to his own, and shall leave me alone: and *yet* I am not alone, because the Father is with me. 33These *things* I have spoken unto you, that in me ye might have peace. In the world ye shall have tribulation: but be of good cheer; I have overcome the world. [Is. 9:6; Rom. 5:1; Eph. 2:14; 2 Tim. 3:12; Rom. 8:37; 1 John 4:4]

The prayer to be glorified

17 These *words* spake Jesus, and lift up his eyes to heaven, and said, Father, the hour is come; glorify thy Son, that thy Son also may glorify thee: 2As thou hast given him power over all flesh, that he should give eternal life to as many as thou hast given him. 3And this is life eternal, that they might know thee the only true God, and Jesus Christ, whom thou hast sent. 4I have glorified thee on the earth: I have finished the work which thou gavest me to do. 5And now, O Father, glorify thou me with thine own self with the glory which I had with thee before the world was. [Phil. 2:6; Col. 1:15; Heb. 1:3]

The prayer for the disciples

6 I have manifested thy name unto the men which thou gavest me out of the world: thine they were, and thou gavest them me; and they have kept thy word. 7Now they have known that all *things* whatsoever thou hast given me are of thee. 8For I have given unto them the words which thou gavest me; and they have received *them,* and have known surely that I came out from thee, and they have believed that thou didst send me. 9I pray for them: I pray not for

the world, but for *them* which thou hast given me; for they are thine. ¹⁰And all mine are thine, and thine are mine; and I am glorified in them. ¹¹And *now* I am no more in the world, but these are in the world, and I come to thee. Holy Father, keep through thine own name those whom thou hast given me, that they may be one, as we *are.* ¹²While I was with them in the world, I kept them in thy name: *those* that thou gavest me I have kept, and none of them is lost, but the son of perdition; that the scripture might be fulfilled. ¹³And now come I to thee; and these *things* I speak in the world, that they might have my joy fulfilled in themselves. ¹⁴I have given them thy word; and the world hath hated them, because they are not of the world, even as I am not of the world. ¹⁵I pray not that thou shouldest take them out of the world, but that thou shouldest keep them from the evil. ¹⁶They are not of the world, even as I am not of the world. ¹⁷Sanctify them through thy truth: thy word is truth. ¹⁸As thou hast sent me into the world, even *so* have I also sent them into the world. ¹⁹And for their sakes I sanctify myself, that they also might be sanctified through the truth. [1 Cor. 1:2; 1 Thes. 4:7; Heb. 10:10]

The prayer for the church

20 Neither pray I for these alone, but for them also which shall believe on me through their word; ²¹That they all may be one; as thou, Father, *art* in me, and I in thee, that they also may be one in us: that the world may believe that thou hast sent me. ²²And the glory which thou gavest me I have given them; that they may be one, even as we are one: ²³I in them, and thou in me, that they may be made perfect in one; and that the world may know that thou hast sent me, and hast loved them, as thou hast loved me. ²⁴Father, I will that they also, whom thou hast given me, be with me where I am; that they may behold my glory, which thou hast given me: for thou lovedst me before the foundation of the world. ²⁵O righteous Father, the world hath not known thee: but I have known thee, and these have known that thou hast sent me. ²⁶And I have declared unto them thy name, and will declare *it:* that the love where*with* thou hast loved me may be in them, and I in them. [ver. 6; ch. 15:15; ch. 15:9]

Jesus' betrayal and arrest

18 When Jesus had spoken these *words,* he went forth with his disciples over the brook Cedron, where was a garden, into the which he entered, and his disciples. ²And Judas also, which betrayed him, knew the place: for Jesus ofttimes resorted thither with his disciples. ³Judas then, having received a band *of men,* and officers from the chief priests and Pharisees, cometh thither with lanterns and torches and weapons. ⁴Jesus therefore, knowing all *things* that should come upon him, went forth, and said unto them, Whom seek ye? ⁵They answered

him, Jesus of Nazareth. Jesus saith unto them, I am *he*. And Judas also, which betrayed him, stood with them. ⁶As soon then as he had said unto them, I am *he*, they went backward, and fell to the ground. ⁷Then asked he them again, Whom seek ye? And they said, Jesus of Nazareth. ⁸Jesus answered, I have told you that I am *he*: if therefore ye seek me, let these go their way: ⁹That the saying might be fulfilled, which he spake, Of them which thou gavest me have I lost none. ¹⁰Then Simon Peter having a sword drew it, and smote the high priest's servant, and cut off his right ear. The servant's name was Malchus. ¹¹Then said Jesus unto Peter, Put up thy sword into the sheath: the cup which my Father hath given me, shall I not drink it? [Mat. 20:22; 26:39,42]

Jesus before Jewish authorities

12 Then the band and the captain and officers of the Jews took Jesus, and bound him, ¹³And led him away to Annas first; for he was father in law to Caiaphas, which was the high priest that *same* year. ¹⁴Now Caiaphas was he, which gave counsel to the Jews, that it was expedient that one man should die for the people. [ch. 11:50]

15 And Simon Peter followed Jesus, and *so did* another disciple: that disciple was known unto the high priest, and went in with Jesus into the palace of the high priest. ¹⁶But Peter stood at the door without. Then went out *that* other disciple, which was known unto the

high priest, and spake unto her that kept the door, and brought in Peter. ¹⁷Then saith the damsel that kept the door unto Peter, Art not thou also *one* of this man's disciples? He saith, I am not. ¹⁸And the servants and officers stood *there*, who had made a fire of coals; for it was cold: and they warmed themselves: and Peter stood with them, and warmed himself.

19 The high priest then asked Jesus of his disciples, and of his doctrine. ²⁰Jesus answered him, I spake openly to the world; I ever taught in the synagogue, and in the temple, whither the Jews always resort; and in secret have I said nothing. ²¹Why askest thou me? ask them which heard *me*, what I have said unto them: behold, they know what I said. ²²And when he had thus spoken, one of the officers which stood by stroke Jesus with the palm of his hand, saying, Answerest thou the high priest so? ²³Jesus answered him, If I have spoken evil, bear witness of the evil: but if well, why smitest thou me? ²⁴Now Annas had sent him bound unto Caiaphas the high priest. [Mat. 26:57]

25 And Simon Peter stood and warmed himself. They said therefore unto him, Art not thou also *one* of his disciples? He denied *it*, and said, I am not. ²⁶One of the servants of the high priest, being *his* kinsman whose ear Peter cut off, saith, Did not I see thee in the garden with him? ²⁷Peter then denied again: and immediately *the* cock crew. [Mat. 26:74; Mark 14:72; Luke 22:60; ch. 13:38]

Jesus before Pontius Pilate

28 Then led they Jesus from Caiaphas unto the hall of judgment: and it was early; and they themselves went not into the judgment hall, lest they should be defiled; but that they might eat the passover. 29 Pilate then went out unto them, and said, What accusation bring you against this man? 30 They answered and said unto him, If he were not a malefactor, we would not have delivered him up unto thee. 31 Then said Pilate unto them, Take ye him, and judge him according to your law. The Jews therefore said unto him, It is not lawful for us to put any *man* to death: 32 That the saying of Jesus might be fulfilled, which he spake, signifying what death he should die. 33 Then Pilate entered into the judgment hall again, and called Jesus, and said unto him, Art thou the King of the Jews? 34 Jesus answered him, Sayest thou this *thing* of thyself, or did others tell *it* thee of me? 35 Pilate answered, Am I a Jew? Thine own nation and the chief priests have delivered thee unto me: what hast thou done? 36 Jesus answered, My kingdom is not of this world: if my kingdom were of this world, then would my servants fight, that I should not be delivered to the Jews: but now is my kingdom not from hence. 37 Pilate therefore said unto him, Art thou a king then? Jesus answered, Thou sayest that I am a king. To this end was I born, and for this cause came I into the world, that I should bear witness unto the truth. Every one that is of the truth heareth my voice. 38 Pilate saith unto him, What is truth? And when he had said this, he went out again unto the Jews, and saith unto them, I find in him no fault *at all*. 39 But ye have a custom, that I should release unto you one at the passover: will ye therefore *that* I release unto you the King of the Jews? 40 Then cried they all again, saying, Not this *man*, but Barabbas. Now Barabbas was a robber. [Acts 3:14; Luke 23:19]

Jesus crowned with thorns

19 Then Pilate therefore took Jesus, and scourged *him*. 2 And the soldiers platted a crown of thorns, and put *it* on his head, and they put on him a purple robe, 3 And said, Hail, King of the Jews: and they smote him with their hands. 4 Pilate therefore went forth again, and saith unto them, Behold, I bring him forth to you, that ye may know that I find no fault in him. 5 Then came Jesus forth, wearing the crown of thorns, and the purple robe. And *Pilate* saith unto them, Behold the man. 6 When the chief priests therefore and officers saw him, they cried out, saying, Crucify *him*, crucify *him*. Pilate saith unto them, Take ye him, and crucify *him*: for I find no fault in him. 7 The Jews answered him, We have a law, and by our law he ought to die, because he made himself the Son of God. [Lev. 24:16; Mat. 26:65; ch. 5:18; 10:33].

8 When Pilate therefore heard that saying, he was the more afraid; 9 And went again into the judgment hall, and saith unto

Jesus, Whence art thou? But Jesus gave him no answer. 10Then saith Pilate unto him, Speakest thou not unto me? knowest thou not that I have power to crucify thee, and have power to release thee? 11Jesus answered, Thou couldest have no power *at all* against me, except it were given thee from above: therefore he that delivered me unto thee hath the greater sin. 12*And* from thenceforth Pilate sought to release him: but the Jews cried out, saying, If thou let this *man* go, thou art not Cesar's friend: whosoever maketh himself a king speaketh against Cesar. 13When Pilate therefore heard that saying, he brought Jesus forth, and sat down in the judgment seat in a place *that is* called the Pavement, but in the Hebrew, Gabbatha. 14And it was the preparation of the passover, and about the sixth hour: and he saith unto the Jews, Behold your King. 15But they cried out, Away with *him,* away with *him,* crucify him. Pilate saith unto them, Shall I crucify your King? The chief priests answered, We have no king but Cesar. 16Then delivered he him therefore unto them to be crucified. And they took Jesus, and led *him* away. [Mat. 27:26,31; Mark 15:15; Luke 23:24]

Jesus crucified

17 And he bearing his cross went forth into a place called *the place* of a skull, which is called in the Hebrew Golgotha: 18Where they crucified him, and two other with him, on either side one, and Jesus in the midst. 19And Pilate wrote a title, and put *it* on the cross. And the writing was, JESUS OF NAZARETH THE KING OF THE JEWS. 20This title then read many of the Jews: for the place where Jesus was crucified was nigh to the city: and it was written in Hebrew, *and* Greek, *and* Latin. 21Then said the chief priests of the Jews to Pilate, Write not, The King of the Jews; but that he said, I am King of the Jews. 22Pilate answered, What I have written I have written. 23Then the soldiers, when they had crucified Jesus, took his garments, and made four parts, to every soldier a part; and *also his* coat: now the coat was without seam, woven from the top throughout. 24They said therefore among themselves, Let us not rent it, but cast lots for it, whose it shall be: that the scripture might be fulfilled, which saith, They parted my raiment among them, and for my vesture they did cast lots. These *things* therefore the soldiers did. [Ps. 22:18]

25 Now there stood by the cross of Jesus his mother, and his mother's sister, Mary the *wife* of Cleophas, and Mary Magdalene. 26When Jesus therefore saw *his* mother, and the disciple standing by, whom he loved, he saith unto his mother, Woman, behold thy son. 27Then saith he to the disciple, Behold thy mother. And from that hour *that* disciple took her unto his own *home.* [ch. 1:11; 16:32]

The death of Jesus

28 After this, Jesus knowing that all *things* were now accom-

plished, that the scripture might be fulfilled, saith, I thirst. ²⁹Now there was set a vessel full of vinegar: and they filled a spunge with vinegar, and put *it* upon hyssop, and put *it* to his mouth. ³⁰When Jesus therefore had received the vinegar, he said, It is finished: and he bowed *his* head, and gave up the ghost. [ch. 17:4]

31 The Jews therefore, because it was the preparation, that the bodies should not remain upon the cross on the sabbath day, (for that sabbath day was a high day,) besought Pilate that their legs might be broken, and *that* they might be taken away. ³²Then came the soldiers, and brake the legs of the first, and of the other which was crucified with him. ³³But when they came to Jesus, and saw that he was dead already, they brake not his legs: ³⁴But one of the soldiers with a spear pierced his side, and forthwith came there out blood and water. ³⁵And he that saw *it* bare record, and his record is true: and he knoweth that he saith true, that ye might believe. ³⁶For these *things* were done, that the scripture should be fulfilled, A bone of him shall not be broken. ³⁷And again another scripture saith, They shall look on *him* whom they pierced. [Ps. 22:16,17; Zech. 12:10; Rev. 1:7]

Jesus laid in the sepulchre

38 And after this Joseph of Arimathea, being a disciple of Jesus, but secretly for fear of the Jews, besought Pilate that he might take away the body of Jesus: and Pilate gave *him* leave. He came therefore, and took the body of Jesus. ³⁹And there came also Nicodemus, which at the first came to Jesus by night, and brought a mixture of myrrh and aloes, about an hundred pound *weight.* ⁴⁰Then took they the body of Jesus, and wound it in linen clothes with the spices, as the manner of the Jews is to bury. ⁴¹Now in the place where he was crucified there was a garden; and in the garden a new sepulchre, wherein was never man yet laid. ⁴²There laid they Jesus therefore because of the Jews' preparation *day;* for the sepulchre was nigh at hand. [Is. 53:9; ver. 31]

The resurrection of Jesus

20 The first *day* of the week cometh Mary Magdalene early, when it was yet dark, unto the sepulchre, and seeth the stone taken away from the sepulchre. ²Then she runneth, and cometh to Simon Peter, and to the other disciple, whom Jesus loved, and saith unto them, They have taken away the Lord out of the sepulchre, and we know not where they have laid him. ³Peter therefore went forth, and *that* other disciple, and came to the sepulchre. ⁴So they ran both together: and the other disciple did outrun Peter, and came first to the sepulchre. ⁵And he stooping down, and looking in, saw the linen clothes lying; yet went he not in. ⁶Then cometh Simon Peter following him, and went into the sepulchre, and seeth the linen clothes lie, ⁷And the napkin, that was about his head, not lying with the linen clothes, but wrapped together in a place by itself. [8]Then went in also *that* other disciple, which came first to the sepulchre, and he saw, and believed. [9]For as yet they knew not the scripture, that he must rise again from the dead. [10]Then the disciples went away again unto their own home.

Jesus appears to the disciples

[11] But Mary stood without at the sepulchre weeping: and as she wept, she stooped down, and looked into the sepulchre, [12]And seeth two angels in white sitting, the one at the head, and the other at the feet, where the body of Jesus had lain. [13]And they say unto her, Woman, why weepest thou? She saith unto them, Because they have taken away my Lord, and I know not where they have laid him. [14]And when she had thus said, she turned herself back, and saw Jesus standing, and knew not that it was Jesus. [15]Jesus saith unto her, Woman, why weepest thou? whom seekest thou? She, supposing him to be the gardener, saith unto him, Sir, if thou have borne him *hence,* tell me where thou hast laid him, and I will take him away. [16]Jesus saith unto her, Mary. She turned herself, and saith unto him, Rabboni; which is to say, Master. [17]Jesus saith unto her, Touch me not; for I am not yet ascended to my Father: but go to my brethren, and say unto them, I ascend unto my Father, and your Father; and *to* my God, and your God. [18]Mary Magdalene came and told the disciples that she had seen the Lord, and *that* he had spoken

these *things* unto her. [Mat. 28:10; Luke 24:10]

[19] Then the same day at evening, being the first *day* of the week, when the doors were shut where the disciples were assembled for fear of the Jews, came Jesus and stood in the midst, and saith unto them, Peace *be* unto you. [20]And when he had so said, he shewed unto them *his* hands and his side. Then were the disciples glad, when they saw the Lord. [21]Then said Jesus to them again, Peace *be* unto you: as *my* Father hath sent me, even *so* send I you. [22]And when he had said this, he breathed on *them,* and saith unto them, Receive ye the Holy Ghost: [23]Whose soever sins ye remit, they are remitted unto them; *and* whose soever *sins* ye retain, they are retained. [Mat. 16:10; 18:18]

Thomas' doubt and belief

[24] But Thomas, one of the twelve, called Didymus, was not with them when Jesus came. [25]The other disciples therefore said unto him, We have seen the Lord. But he said unto them, Except I shall see in his hands the print of the nails, and put my finger into the print of the nails, and thrust my hand into his side, I will not believe. [26]And after eight days again his disciples were within, and Thomas with them: *then* came Jesus, the doors being shut, and stood in the midst, and said, Peace *be* unto you. [27]Then saith he to Thomas, Reach hither thy finger, and behold my hands; and reach *hither* thy hand, and thrust *it* into

my side: and be not faithless, but believing. 28 And Thomas answered and said unto him, My Lord and my God. 29 Jesus saith unto him, Thomas, because thou hast seen me, thou hast believed: blessed *are* they that have not seen, and *yet* have believed. [2 Cor. 5:7; 1 Pet 1:8]

30 And many other signs truly did Jesus in the presence of his disciples, which are not written in this book: 31 But these are written, that ye might believe that Jesus is the Christ, the Son of God; and that believing ye might have life through his name. [Luke 1:4; ch. 3:15,16; 5:24; 1 Pet. 1:8,9]

The appearance beside the sea

21 After these *things* Jesus shewed himself again to the disciples at the sea of Tiberias; and on this wise shewed he him-*self.* 2 There were together Simon Peter, and Thomas called Didymus, and Nathanael of Cana in Galilee, and the *sons* of Zebedee, and two other of his disciples. 3 Simon Peter saith unto them, I go a fishing. They say unto him, We also go with thee. They went forth, and entered into a ship immediately; and that night they caught nothing. 4 But when the morning was now come, Jesus stood on the shore: but the disciples knew not that it was Jesus. 5 Then Jesus saith unto them, Children, have ye any meat? They answered him, No. 6 And he said unto them, Cast the net on the right side of the ship, and ye shall find. They cast therefore, and now they were not able to draw it for the multitude of fishes. 7 Therefore

that disciple whom Jesus loved saith unto Peter, It is the Lord. Now when Simon Peter heard that it was the Lord, he girt *his* fisher's coat unto him, (for he was naked,) and did cast himself into the sea. 8 And the other disciples came in a little ship; (for they were not far from land, but as it were two hundred cubits,) dragging the net with fishes. 9 As soon then as they were come to land, they saw a fire of coals there, and fish laid thereon, and bread. 10 Jesus saith unto them, Bring of the fish which ye have now caught. 11 Simon Peter went up, and drew the net to land full of great fishes, an hundred and fifty *and* three: and for all there were so many, *yet* was not the net broken. 12 Jesus saith unto them, Come *and* dine. And none of the disciples durst ask him, Who art thou? knowing that it was the Lord. 13 Jesus then cometh, and taketh bread, and giveth them, and fish likewise. 14 This *is* now the third time *that* Jesus shewed himself to his disciples, after that he was risen from the dead. [See ch. 20:19,26]

Jesus questions Peter

15 So when they had dined, Jesus saith to Simon Peter, Simon, *son* of Jonas, lovest thou me more than these? He saith unto him, Yea, Lord; thou knowest that I love thee. He saith unto him, Feed my lambs. 16 He saith to him again the second time, Simon, *son* of Jonas, lovest thou me? He saith unto him, Yea, Lord; thou knowest that I love thee. He saith unto him, Feed my sheep. 17 He saith unto him the

third time, Simon, *son* of Jonas, lovest thou me? Peter was grieved because he said unto him the third time, Lovest thou me? And he said unto him, Lord, thou knowest all *things;* thou knowest that I love thee. Jesus saith unto him, Feed my sheep. [18]Verily, verily, I say unto thee, When thou wast young, thou girdedst thyself, and walkedst whither thou wouldest: but when thou shalt be old, thou shalt stretch forth thy hands, and another shall gird thee, and carry *thee* whither thou wouldest not. [19]This spake he, signifying by what death he should glorify God. And when he had spoken this, he saith unto him, Follow me. [20]Then Peter, turning about, seeth the disciple whom Jesus loved following; which also leaned on his breast at supper, and said, Lord, which is he that betrayeth thee? [21]Peter seeing him saith to Jesus, Lord, and what *shall* this *man do?* [22]Jesus saith unto him, If I will that he tarry till I come, what *is that* to thee? follow thou me. [23]Then went this saying abroad among the brethren, that that disciple should not die: yet Jesus said not unto him, He shall not die; but, If I will that he tarry till I come, what *is that* to thee?

[24] This is the disciple which testifieth of these *things,* and wrote these *things:* and we know that his testimony is true. [25]And there are also many other *things* which Jesus did, the which, if they should be written every one, I suppose that even the world itself could not contain the books that should be written. Amen.

The Acts
of the Apostles

The ascension

1 The former treatise have I made, O Theophilus, of all that Jesus began both to do and teach, ²Until the day *in* which he was taken up, after that he through the Holy Ghost had given commandments unto the Apostles whom he had chosen: ³To whom also he shewed himself alive after his passion by many infallible proofs, being seen of them forty days, and speaking of the *things* pertaining to the kingdom of God: ⁴And, being assembled together with them, commanded them that *they* should not depart from Jerusalem, but wait for the promise of the Father, which, *saith he,* ye have heard of me. ⁵For John truly baptized with water; but ye shall be baptized with the Holy Ghost not many days hence. ⁶When they therefore were come together, they asked of him, saying, Lord, wilt thou at this time restore again the kingdom to Israel? ⁷And he said unto them, It is not for you to know *the* times or *the* seasons, which the Father hath put in his own power. ⁸But ye shall receive power, after that the Holy Ghost is come upon you: and ye shall be witnesses unto me both in Jerusalem, and in all Judea, and in Samaria, and unto the uttermost part of the earth. ⁹And when he had spoken these *things,* while they beheld, he was taken up; and a cloud received him out of their sight. ¹⁰And while they looked stedfastly toward heaven as he went *up,* behold, two men stood by them in white apparel; ¹¹Which also said, Ye men of Galilee, why stand ye gazing up into heaven? this *same* Jesus, which is taken up from you into heaven, shall so come *in* like manner as ye have seen him go into heaven. ¹²Then returned they unto Jerusalem from the mount called Olivet, which is from Jerusalem a sabbath day's journey. ¹³And when they were come in, they went up into an upper room, where abode both Peter, and James, and John, and Andrew, Philip, and Thomas, Bartholomew, and Matthew, James *the son* of Alpheus, and Simon Zelotes, and Judas *the brother* of James. ¹⁴These all continued with one accord in prayer and supplication, with the women, and Mary the mother of Jesus, and with his brethren. [ch. 2:1,46; Luke 23:49,55; Mat. 13:55]

Matthias chosen to replace Judas

15 And in those days Peter stood up in the midst of the disciples, and said, (the number of names together were about an hundred *and* twenty,) ¹⁶Men *and* brethren, this scripture must needs have been fulfilled, which the Holy Ghost by the mouth of David spake before concerning Judas, which was guide to them that took Jesus. ¹⁷For he was numbered with us, and had obtained part of this ministry. ¹⁸Now this *man* purchased a field with the reward of iniquity; and falling headlong, he burst

asunder in the midst, and all his bowels gushed out. ¹⁹And it was known unto all the dwellers at Jerusalem; insomuch as that field is called in their proper tongue, Aceldama, that is to say, The field of blood. ²⁰For it is written in the book of Psalms, Let his habitation be desolate, and let no man dwell therein: and his bishoprick let another take. ²¹Wherefore of these men which have companied with us all the time that the Lord Jesus went in and out among us, ²²Beginning from the baptism of John, unto *that same* day that he was taken up from us, must one be ordained *to be* a witness with us of his resurrection. ²³And they appointed two, Joseph called Barsabas, who was surnamed Justus, and Matthias. ²⁴And they prayed, and said, Thou, Lord, which knowest the hearts of all *men,* shew whether of these two thou hast chosen, ²⁵That *he* may take part of this ministry and apostleship, from which Judas by transgression fell, that *he* might go to his own place. ²⁶And they gave forth their lots; and the lot fell upon Matthias; and he was numbered with the eleven apostles.

The gift of the Holy Spirit

2 And when the day of Pentecost was fully come, they were all with one accord in one place. ²And suddenly there came a sound from heaven as of a rushing mighty wind, and it filled all the house where they were sitting. ³And there appeared unto them cloven tongues like as of fire, and it sat upon each of them. ⁴And they were all filled with the Holy Ghost, and began to speak with other tongues, as the Spirit gave them utterance. ⁵And there were dwelling at Jerusalem Jews, devout men, out of every nation under heaven. ⁶Now when this was noised abroad, the multitude came together, and were confounded, because that every man heard them speak in his own language. ⁷And they were all amazed and marvelled, saying one to another, Behold, are not all these which speak Galileans? ⁸And how hear we every man in our own tongue, wherein we were born? ⁹Parthians, and Medes, and Elamites, and the dwellers in Mesopotamia, and in Judea, and Cappadocia, in Pontus, and Asia, ¹⁰Phrygia, and Pamphylia, in Egypt, and in the parts of Libya about Cyrene, and strangers of Rome, Jews and proselytes, ¹¹Cretes and Arabians, we do hear them speak in our tongues the wonderful works of God. ¹²And they were all amazed, and were in doubt, saying one to another, What meaneth this? ¹³Others mocking said, *These men* are full of new wine.

Peter's Pentecostal sermon

14 But Peter, standing up with the eleven, lift up his voice, and said unto them, Ye men of Judea, and all *ye* that dwell at Jerusalem, be this known unto you, and hearken to my words: ¹⁵For these are not drunken, as ye suppose, seeing it is *but* the third hour of the day. ¹⁶But this is that which was spoken by the prophet Joel;

[17]And it shall come to pass in the last days, saith God, I will pour out of my Spirit upon all flesh: and your sons and your daughters shall prophesy, and your young men shall see visions, and your old men shall dream dreams: [18]And on my servants and on my handmaidens I will pour out in those days of my Spirit; and they shall prophesy: [19]And I will shew wonders in heaven above, and signs in the earth beneath; blood, and fire, and vapour of smoke: [20]The sun shall be turned into darkness, and the moon into blood, before *that* great and notable day of the Lord come: [21]And it shall come to pass, *that* whosoever shall call on the name of the Lord shall be saved. [22]Ye men of Israel, hear these words; Jesus of Nazareth, a man approved of God among you by miracles and wonders and signs, which God did by him in the midst of you, as ye yourselves also know: [23]Him, being delivered by the determinate counsel and foreknowledge of God, ye have taken, and by wicked hands have crucified and slain: [24]Whom God hath raised up, having loosed the pains of death: because it was not possible that he should be holden of it. [25]For David speaketh concerning him, I foresaw the Lord always before my face, for he is on my right hand, that I should not be moved: [26]Therefore did my heart rejoice, and my tongue was glad; moreover also my flesh shall rest in hope: [27]Because thou wilt not leave my soul in hell, neither wilt thou suffer thine Holy One to see corrup-

tion. [28]Thou hast made known to me the ways of life; thou shalt make me full of joy with thy countenance. [29]Men *and* brethren, let *me* freely speak unto you of the patriarch David, that he is both dead and buried, and his sepulchre is with us unto this day. [30]Therefore being a prophet, and knowing that God had sworn with an oath to him, that of the fruit of his loins, according to the flesh, *he* would raise up Christ to sit on his throne; [31]He seeing *this* before, spake of the resurrection of Christ, that his soul was not left in hell, neither his flesh did see corruption. [32]This Jesus hath God raised up, whereof we all are witnesses. [33]Therefore being by the right hand of God exalted, and having received of the Father the promise of the Holy Ghost, he hath shed forth this, which ye now see and hear. [34]For David is not ascended into the heavens: but he saith himself, The Lord said unto my Lord, Sit thou on my right hand, [35]Until I make thy foes thy footstool. [36]Therefore let all the house of Israel know assuredly, that God hath made that same Jesus, whom ye have crucified, both Lord and Christ.

The community of the believers

[37] Now when they heard *this,* they were pricked in *their* heart, and said unto Peter and *to* the rest of the apostles, Men *and* brethren, what shall we do? [38]Then Peter said unto them, Repent, and be baptized every one of you in the name of Jesus Christ for the remission of sins, and ye shall receive

the gift of the Holy Ghost. 39For the promise is unto you, and to your children, and to all that are afar off, *even* as many as the Lord our God shall call. 40And with many other words did he testify and exhort, saying, Save yourselves from this untoward generation.

41 Then they that gladly received his word were baptized: and the same day there were added *unto them* about three thousand souls. 42And they continued stedfastly in the apostles' doctrine and fellowship, and in breaking of bread, and in prayers. 43And fear came upon every soul: and many wonders and signs were done by the apostles. 44And all that believed were together, and had all *things* common; 45And sold their possessions and goods, and parted them to all *men,* as every *man* had need. 46And they, continuing daily with one accord in the temple, and breaking bread from house to house, did eat *their* meat with gladness and singleness of heart, 47Praising God, and having favour with all the people. And the Lord added to the church daily such as should be saved. [ch. 4:33; Rom. 14:18; ch. 5:14]

The healing of the lame man

3 Now Peter and John went up together into the temple at the hour of prayer, *being* the ninth hour. 2And a certain man lame from his mother's womb was carried, whom they laid daily at the gate of the temple which is called Beautiful, to ask alms of them that entered into the temple; 3Who seeing Peter and John about to go into the temple, asked an alms. 4And Peter, fastening his eyes upon him with John, said, Look on us. 5And he gave heed unto them, expecting to receive something of them. 6Then Peter said, Silver and gold have I none; but such as I have give I thee: In the name of Jesus Christ of Nazareth rise up and walk. 7And he took him by the right hand, and lift *him* up: and immediately his feet and ankle bones received strength, 8And he leaping up stood, and walked, and entered with them into the temple, walking, and leaping, and praising God. 9And all the people saw him walking and praising God: 10And they knew that it was he which sat for alms at the Beautiful gate of the temple: and they were filled with wonder and amazement at that which had happened unto him. [John 9:8]

Peter's sermon

11 And as the lame *man* which was healed held Peter and John, all the people ran together unto them in the porch that is called Solomon's, greatly wondering. 12And when Peter saw *it,* he answered unto the people, Ye men of Israel, why marvel ye at this? or why look ye *so* earnestly on us, as though by our own power or holiness we had made this *man* to walk? 13The God of Abraham, and of Isaac, and of Jacob, the God of our fathers, hath glorified his Son Jesus; whom ye delivered up, and denied him in the presence of Pilate, when he was determined to let *him* go. 14But ye denied the

Holy One and the Just, and desired a murderer to be granted unto you; [15]And killed the Prince of life, whom God hath raised from the dead; whereof we are witnesses. [16]And his name through faith in his name hath made this *man* strong, whom ye see and know: yea, the faith which is by him hath given him this perfect soundness in the presence of you all. [17]And now, brethren, I wot that through ignorance ye did *it,* as *did* also your rulers. [18]But *those things,* which God before had shewed by the mouth of all his prophets, that Christ should suffer, he hath so fulfilled. [19]Repent ye therefore, and be converted, that your sins may be blotted out, when *the* times of refreshing shall come from the presence of the Lord; [20]And he shall send Jesus Christ, which before was preached unto you: [21]Whom the heaven must receive until the times of restitution of all *things,* which God hath spoken by the mouth of all his holy prophets since the world began. [22]For Moses truly said unto the fathers, A prophet shall the Lord your God raise up unto you of your brethren, like unto me; him shall ye hear in all *things* whatsoever he shall say unto you. [23]And it shall come to pass, *that* every soul, which will not hear that prophet, shall be destroyed from among the people. [24]Yea, and all the prophets from Samuel and those that follow after, as many as have spoken, have likewise foretold of these days. [25]Ye are the children of the prophets, and of the covenant which God made with our fathers, saying unto Abraham, And in thy seed shall all the kindreds of the earth be blessed. [26]Unto you first God, having raised up his Son Jesus, sent him to bless you, in turning away every one of you from *his* iniquities. [Mat. 10:5; 15:24; Luke 24:47; ch. 13:32,33,46; ver. 22; Mat. 1:21]

Peter and John arrested

4 And as they spake unto the people, the priests, and the captain of the temple, and the Sadducees, came upon them, [2]Being grieved that they taught the people, and preached through Jesus the resurrection from the dead. [3]And they laid hands on them, and put *them* in hold unto the next day: for it was now eventide. [4]Howbeit many of them which heard the word believed; and the number of the men was about five thousand. [5]And it came to pass on the morrow, that their rulers, and elders, and scribes, [6]And Annas the high priest, and Caiaphas, and John, and Alexander, and as many as were of the kindred of the high priest, were gathered together at Jerusalem. [7]And when they had set them in the midst, they asked, By what power, or by what name, have ye done this? [8]Then Peter, filled with the Holy Ghost, said unto them, Ye rulers of the people, and elders of Israel, [9]If we this day be examined of the good deed done to the impotent man, by what *means* he is made whole; [10]Be it known unto you all, and to all the people of Israel, that by the name of Jesus Christ of Nazareth, whom

ye crucified, whom God raised from the dead, *even* by him doth this *man* stand here before you whole. 11This is the stone which was set at nought of you builders, which is become the head of the corner. 12Neither is there salvation in any other: for there is none other name under heaven given among men, whereby we must be saved. [Mat. 1:21; ch. 10:43; 1 Tim. 2:5,6]

13 Now when they saw the boldness of Peter and John, and perceived that they were unlearned and ignorant men, they marvelled; and they took knowledge of them, that they had been with Jesus. 14And beholding the man which was healed standing with them, they could say nothing against *it.* 15But when they had commanded them to go aside out of the council, they conferred among themselves, 16Saying, What shall we do to these men? for that indeed a notable miracle hath been done by them *is* manifest to all them that dwell in Jerusalem; and we cannot deny *it.* 17But that it spread no further among the people, let us straitly threaten them, that *they* speak henceforth to no man in this name. 18And they called them, and commanded them not to speak at all nor teach in the name of Jesus. 19But Peter and John answered and said unto them, Whether it be right in the sight of God to hearken unto you more than unto God, judge ye. 20For we cannot but speak *the things* which we have seen and heard. 21So when they had further threatened *them,* they let them go, finding nothing how they might

punish them, because of the people: for all *men* glorified God for that which was done. 22For the man was above forty years old, on whom this miracle of healing was shewed.

The report to the believers

23 And being let go, they went to their own *company,* and reported all that the chief priests and elders had said unto them. 24And when they heard *that,* they lift up their voice to God with one accord, and said, Lord, thou *art* God, which hast made heaven, and earth, and the sea, and all that in them is: 25Who by the mouth of thy servant David hast said, Why did the heathen rage, and the people imagine vain *things?* 26The kings of the earth stood up, and the rulers were gathered together against the Lord, and against his Christ. 27For of a truth against thy holy child Jesus, whom thou hast anointed, both Herod, and Pontius Pilate, with the Gentiles, and the people of Israel, were gathered together, 28For to do whatsoever thy hand and thy counsel determined before to be done. 29And now, Lord, behold their threatenings: and grant unto thy servants, that with all boldness *they* may speak thy word, 30By stretching forth thine hand to heal; and that signs and wonders may be done by the name of thy holy child Jesus. 31And when they had prayed, the place was shaken where they were assembled together; and they were all filled with the Holy Ghost, and they spake the word of God with boldness. [ch. 2:2,4; 16:26; ver. 29]

The community of possessions

32 And the multitude of them that believed were of one heart and of one soul: neither said any *of them* that ought of the *things* which he possessed was his own; but they had all *things* common. 33And with great power gave the apostles witness of the resurrection of the Lord Jesus: and great grace was upon them all. 34Neither was there any among them that lacked: for as many as were possessors of lands or houses sold them, and brought the prices of the *things* that were sold, 35And laid *them down* at the apostles' feet: and distribution was made unto every man according as he had need. 36And Joses, who by the apostles was surnamed Barnabas, (which is, being interpreted, The son of consolation,) a Levite, *and* of the country of Cyprus, 37Having land, sold *it,* and brought the money, and laid *it* at the apostles' feet. [ver. 34,35; ch. 5:1,2]

Ananias and Sapphira punished

5 But a certain man named Ananias, with Sapphira his wife, sold a possession, 2And kept back *part* of the price, his wife also being privy *to it,* and brought a certain part, and laid *it* at the apostles' feet. 3But Peter said, Ananias, why hath Satan filled thine heart to lie to the Holy Ghost, and to keep back *part* of the price of the land? 4Whiles it remained, was it not thine own? and after it was sold, was it not in thine own power? why hast thou conceived this thing in thine heart? thou hast not lied unto men, but

unto God. 5And Ananias hearing these words fell down, and gave up the ghost: and great fear came on all them that heard these *things.* 6And the young men arose, wound him up, and carried *him* out, and buried *him.* 7And it was about the space of three hours after, when his wife, not knowing what was done, came in. 8And Peter answered unto her, Tell me whether ye sold the land for so much? And she said, Yea, for so much. 9Then Peter said unto her, How *is it* that ye have agreed together to tempt the Spirit of the Lord? behold, the feet of them which have buried thy husband *are* at the door, and shall carry thee out. 10Then fell she down straightway at his feet, and yielded up the ghost: and the young men came in, and found her dead, and, carrying *her* forth, buried *her* by her husband. 11And great fear came upon all the church, and upon as many as heard these *things.* [ver. 5; ch. 2:43; 19:17]

12 And by the hands of the apostles were many signs and wonders wrought among the people; (and they were all with one accord in Solomon's porch. 13And of the rest durst no *man* join himself to them: but the people magnified them. 14And believers were the more added to the Lord, multitudes both of men and women.) 15Insomuch that *they* brought forth the sick into the streets, and laid *them* on beds and couches, that at the least the shadow of Peter passing by might overshadow some of them. 16There came also a multitude *out* of the cities round about unto Jerusalem,

bringing sick *folks,* and *them which were* vexed with unclean spirits: and they were healed every one. [Mark 16:17,18; John 14:12]

The apostles imprisoned

17 Then the high priest rose up, and all they that were with him, (which is the sect of the Sadducees,) and were filled with indignation, 18And laid their hands on the apostles, and put them in the common prison. 19But *the* angel of the Lord by night opened the prison doors, and brought them forth, and said, 20Go, stand and speak in the temple to the people all the words of this life. 21And when they heard *that,* they entered into the temple early in the morning, and taught. But the high priest came, and they that were with him, and called the council together, and all the senate of the children of Israel, and sent to the prison to have them brought. 22But when the officers came, and found them not in the prison, they returned, and told, 23Saying, The prison truly found we shut with all safety, and the keepers standing without before the doors: but when we had opened, we found no *man* within. 24Now when the *high* priest and the captain of the temple and the chief priests heard these things, they doubted of them whereunto this would grow. 25Then came one and told them, saying, Behold, the men whom ye put in prison are standing in the temple, and teaching the people. 26Then went the captain with the officers, and brought them without violence: for they feared the people, lest they should have been stoned. 27And when they had brought them, they set *them* before the council: and the high priest asked them, 28Saying, Did not we straitly command you that *you* should not teach in this name? and behold, ye have filled Jerusalem with your doctrine, and intend to bring this man's blood upon us. 29Then Peter and the *other* apostles answered and said, We ought to obey God rather than men. 30The God of our fathers raised up Jesus, whom ye slew and hanged on a tree. 31Him hath God exalted with his right hand *to be* a Prince and a Saviour, for to give repentance to Israel, and forgiveness of sins. 32And we are his witnesses of these things; and *so is* also the Holy Ghost, whom God hath given to them that obey him. [John 15:26,27; ch. 2:4; 10:44]

The counsel of Gamaliel

33 When they heard *that,* they were cut *to the heart,* and took counsel to slay them. 34Then stood there up one in the council, a Pharisee, named Gamaliel, a doctor of law, had in reputation among all the people, and commanded to put the apostles forth a little space; 35And said unto them, Ye men of Israel, take heed to yourselves what ye intend to do as touching these men. 36For before these days rose up Theudas, boasting himself to be somebody; to whom a number of men, about four hundred, joined themselves: who was slain; and all, as many as obeyed him,

were scattered, and brought to nought. ³⁷After this *man* rose up Judas of Galilee in the days of the taxing, and drew away much people after him: he also perished; and all, *even* as many as obeyed him, were dispersed. ³⁸And now I say unto you, Refrain from these men, and let them alone: for if this counsel or this work be of men, it will come to nought: ³⁹But if it be of God, ye cannot overthrow it; lest haply ye be found even to fight against God. ⁴⁰And to him they agreed: and when they had called the apostles, and beaten *them,* they commanded that *they* should not speak in the name of Jesus, and let them go. ⁴¹And they departed from the presence of the council, rejoicing that they were counted worthy to suffer shame for his name. ⁴²And daily in the temple, and in every house, they ceased not to teach and preach Jesus Christ. [ch. 2:46; ch. 4:20,29]

The appointment of the seven

6 And in those days, when the number of the disciples was multiplied, there arose a murmuring of the Grecians against the Hebrews, because their widows were neglected in the daily ministration. ²Then the twelve called the multitude of the disciples unto *them,* and said, It is not reason that we should leave the word of God, and serve tables. ³Wherefore, brethren, look ye out among you seven men of honest report, full of the Holy Ghost and wisdom, whom we may appoint over this business. ⁴But we will give ourselves contin-

ually to prayer, and to the ministry of the word. ⁵And the saying pleased the whole multitude: and they chose Stephen, a man full of faith and of the Holy Ghost, and Philip, and Prochorus, and Nicanor, and Timon, and Parmenas, and Nicolas a proselyte of Antioch: ⁶Whom they set before the apostles: and when they had prayed, they laid *their* hands on them. ⁷And the word of God increased; and the number of the disciples multiplied in Jerusalem greatly; and a great company of the priests were obedient to the faith. [ch. 12:24; 19:20; Col. 1:6; John 12:42]

The arrest of Stephen

8 And Stephen, full of faith and power, did great wonders and miracles among the people. ⁹Then there arose certain of the synagogue, which is called *the synagogue* of the Libertines, and Cyrenians, and Alexandrians, and of them of Cilicia and of Asia, disputing with Stephen. ¹⁰And they were not able to resist the wisdom and the spirit by which he spake. ¹¹Then they suborned men, which said, We have heard him speak blasphemous words against Moses, and *against* God. ¹²And they stirred up the people, and the elders, and the scribes, and came upon *him,* and caught him, and brought *him* to the council, ¹³And set up false witnesses, which said, This man ceaseth not to speak blasphemous words against this holy place, and the law: ¹⁴For we have heard him say, that this Jesus of Nazareth shall destroy this place,

and shall change the customs which Moses delivered us. 15 And all that sat in the council, looking stedfastly on him, saw his face as it had been the face of an angel.

The defence of Stephen

7 Then said the high priest, Are these *things* so? 2 And he said, Men, brethren, and fathers, hearken; The God of glory appeared unto our father Abraham, when he was in Mesopotamia, before he dwelt in Charran, 3 And said unto him, Get thee out of thy country, and from thy kindred, and come into the land which I shall shew thee. 4 Then came he out of the land of the Chaldeans, and dwelt in Charran: and from thence, when his father was dead, he removed him into this land, wherein ye now dwell. 5 And he gave him none inheritance in it, no, not so much as to set his foot on: yet he promised that *he* would give it to him for a possession, and to his seed after him, when *as yet* he had no child. 6 And God spake on this wise, That his seed should sojourn in a strange land; and that they should bring them into bondage, and entreat *them* evil four hundred years. 7 And the nation to whom they shall be in bondage will I judge, said God: and after that shall they come forth, and serve me in this place. 8 And he gave him the covenant of circumcision: and so *Abraham* begat Isaac, and circumcised him the eighth day; and Isaac *begat* Jacob; and Jacob *begat* the twelve patriarchs. 9 And the patriarchs, moved with envy, sold Joseph into Egypt: but God was with him, 10 And delivered him out of all his afflictions, and gave him favour and wisdom in the sight of Pharaoh king of Egypt; and he made him governor over Egypt and all his house. 11 Now there came a dearth over all the land of Egypt and Canaan, and great affliction: and our fathers found no sustenance. 12 But when Jacob heard that there was corn in Egypt, he sent out our fathers first. 13 And at the second time Joseph was made known to his brethren; and Joseph's kindred was made known unto Pharaoh. 14 Then sent Joseph, and called his father Jacob to *him,* and all his kindred, threescore and fifteen souls. 15 So Jacob went down into Egypt, and died, he, and our fathers, 16 And were carried over into Sychem, and laid in the sepulchre that Abraham bought for a sum of money of the sons of Emmor the *father* of Sychem. 17 But when the time of the promise drew nigh, which God had sworn to Abraham, the people grew and multiplied in Egypt, 18 Till another king arose, which knew not Joseph. 19 The same dealt subtilly with our kindred, and evil entreated our fathers, so that *they* cast out their young children, to the end *they* might not live. 20 In which time Moses was born, and was exceeding fair, and nourished up in his father's house three months: 21 And when he was cast out, Pharaoh's daughter took him up, and nourished him for her own son. 22 And Moses was learned in all the wisdom of the Egyptians, and was mighty in words and in deeds.

23 And when he was full forty years old, it came into his heart to visit his brethren the children of Israel. 24 And seeing one *of them* suffer wrong, he defended *him,* and avenged him that was oppressed, and smote the Egyptian: 25 For he supposed his brethren would have understood how that God by his hand would deliver them: but they understood not. 26 And the next day he shewed himself unto them as they strove, and would have set them at one *again,* saying, Sirs, ye are brethren; why do ye wrong one to another? 27 But he that did his neighbour wrong thrust him away, saying, Who made thee a ruler and a judge over us? 28 Wilt thou kill me, as thou didst the Egyptian yesterday? 29 Then fled Moses at this saying, and was a stranger in the land of Madian, where he begat two sons. 30 And when forty years were expired, there appeared to him in the wilderness of mount Sina an angel of the Lord in a flame of fire in a bush. 31 When Moses saw *it,* he wondered at the sight: and as he drew near to behold *it,* the voice of the Lord came unto him, 32 Saying, I *am* the God of thy fathers, the God of Abraham, and the God of Isaac, and the God of Jacob. Then Moses trembled, and durst not behold. 33 Then said the Lord to him, Put off *thy* shoes from thy feet: for the place where thou standest is holy ground. 34 I have seen, I have seen the affliction of my people which is in Egypt, and I have heard their groaning, and am come down to deliver them. And now come, I will send thee into Egypt. 35 This Moses whom they refused, saying, Who made thee a ruler and a judge? the same did God send *to be* a ruler and a deliverer by the hand of the angel which appeared to him in the bush. 36 He brought them out, after that he had shewed wonders and signs in the land of Egypt, and in the Red sea, and in the wilderness forty years. 37 This is *that* Moses, which said unto the children of Israel, A prophet shall the Lord your God raise up unto you of your brethren, like unto me; him shall ye hear. 38 This is he, that was in the church in the wilderness with the angel which spake to him in the mount Sina, and *with* our fathers: who received *the* lively oracles to give unto us: 39 To whom our fathers would not obey, but thrust *him* from *them,* and in their hearts turned *back again* into Egypt, 40 Saying unto Aaron, Make us gods to go before us: for *as for* this Moses, which brought us out of the land of Egypt, we wot not what is become of him. 41 And they made a calf in those days, and offered sacrifice unto the idol, and rejoiced in the works of their own hands. 42 Then God turned, and gave them up to worship the host of heaven; as it is written in the book of the prophets, O *ye* house of Israel, have ye offered to me slain beasts and sacrifices *by the space of* forty years in the wilderness? 43 Yea, ye took up the tabernacle of Moloch, and the star of your god Remphan, figures which ye made to worship them: and I will carry you away beyond Babylon. 44 Our fathers had

the tabernacle of Witness in the wilderness, as he had appointed, speaking unto Moses, that *he* should make it according to the fashion that he had seen. 45Which also our fathers that came after brought in with Jesus into the possession of the Gentiles, whom God drave out before the face of our fathers, unto the days of David; 46Who found favour before God, and desired to find a tabernacle for the God of Jacob. 47But Solomon built him a house. 48Howbeit the most High dwelleth not in temples made with hands; as saith the prophet, 49Heaven *is* my throne, and earth *is* my footstool: what house will ye build me? saith the Lord: or what *is* the place of my rest? 50Hath not my hand made all these *things?*

51 Ye stiffnecked and uncircumcised in heart and ears, ye do always resist the Holy Ghost: as your fathers *did,* so *do* ye. 52Which of the prophets have not your fathers persecuted? and they have slain them which shewed before of the coming of the Just One; of whom ye have been now the betrayers and murderers: 53Who have received the law by the disposition of angels, and have not kept *it.* [Ex. 20:1; Gal. 3:19]

The stoning of Stephen

54 When they heard these *things,* they were cut to the heart, and they gnashed on him *with their* teeth. 55But he, being full of the Holy Ghost, looked up stedfastly into heaven, and saw the glory of God, and Jesus standing on the

right hand of God, 56And said, Behold, I see the heavens opened, and the Son of man standing on the right hand of God. 57Then they cried out with a loud voice, and stopped their ears, and ran upon him with one accord, 58And cast *him* out of the city, and stoned *him:* and the witnesses laid down their clothes at a young man's feet, whose name was Saul. 59And they stoned Stephen, calling upon *God,* and saying, Lord Jesus, receive my spirit. 60And he kneeled down, and cried with a loud voice, Lord, lay not this sin to their charge. And when he had said this, he fell asleep. [ch. 9:40; Mat. 5:44; Luke 6:28]

The persecution of the church

8 And Saul was consenting unto his death. And at that time there was a great persecution against the church which was at Jerusalem; and they were all scattered abroad throughout the regions of Judea and Samaria, except the apostles. 2And devout men carried Stephen *to his burial,* and made great lamentation over him. 3As for Saul, he made havock of the church, entering into every house, and haling men and women committed *them* to prison. 4Therefore they that were scattered abroad went every where preaching the word. [Mat. 10:23]

Philip at Samaria

5 Then Philip went down to the city of Samaria, and preached Christ unto them. 6And the people with one accord gave heed unto those *things* which Philip spake, hearing and seeing the miracles

which he did. 7For unclean spirits, crying with loud voice, came out of many that were possessed *with them:* and many taken with palsies, and *that were* lame, were healed. 8And there was great joy in that city.

Conversion of Simon the sorcerer

9 But there was a certain man, called Simon, which beforetime in the *same* city used sorcery, and bewitched the people of Samaria, giving out that himself was some great one: 10To whom they all gave heed, from the least to the greatest, saying, This *man* is the great power of God. 11And to him they had regard, because that of long time *he* had bewitched them with sorceries. 12But when they believed Philip preaching the *things* concerning the kingdom of God, and the name of Jesus Christ, they were baptized, both men and women. 13Then Simon himself believed also: and when he was baptized, he continued with Philip, and wondered, beholding *the* miracles and signs *which were* done.

14 Now when the apostles which were at Jerusalem heard that Samaria had received the word of God, they sent unto them Peter and John: 15Who, when they were come down, prayed for them, that they might receive the Holy Ghost: 16(For as yet he was fallen upon none of them: only they were baptized in the name of the Lord Jesus.) 17Then laid they *their* hands on them, and they received the Holy Ghost. 18And when Simon

saw that through laying on of the apostles' hands the Holy Ghost was given, he offered them money, 19Saying, Give me also this power, that on whomsoever I lay hands, he may receive the Holy Ghost. 20But Peter said unto him, Thy money perish with thee, because thou hast thought that the gift of God may be purchased with money. 21Thou hast neither part nor lot in this matter: for thy heart is not right in the sight of God. 22Repent therefore of this thy wickedness, and pray God, if perhaps the thought of thine heart may be forgiven thee. 23For I perceive that thou art in the gall of bitterness, and *in* the bond of iniquity. 24Then answered Simon, and said, Pray ye to the Lord for me, that none of *these things* which ye have spoken come upon me. 25And they, when they had testified and preached the word of the Lord, returned to Jerusalem, and preached the gospel in many villages of the Samaritans.

Conversion of the Ethiopian

26 And *the* angel of the Lord spake unto Philip, saying, Arise, and go toward the south unto the way that goeth down from Jerusalem unto Gaza, which is desert. 27And he arose and went: and behold, a man of Ethiopia, an eunuch of great authority under Candace queen of the Ethiopians, who had the charge of all her treasure, and had come to Jerusalem for to worship, 28Was returning, and sitting in his chariot read Esaias the prophet. 29Then the Spirit said unto Philip, Go near, and

join thyself to this chariot. 30And Philip ran *thither* to *him,* and heard him read the prophet Esaias, and said, Understandest thou what thou readest? 31And he said, How can I, except some *man* should guide me? And he desired Philip that *he* would come up and sit with him. 32The place of the scripture which he read was this, He was led as a sheep to the slaughter; and like a lamb dumb before his shearer, so opened he not his mouth: 33In his humiliation his judgment was taken away: and who shall declare his generation? for his life is taken from the earth. 34And the eunuch answered Philip, and said, I pray thee, of whom speaketh the prophet this? of himself, or of some other *man?* 35Then Philip opened his mouth, and began at the same scripture, and preached unto him Jesus. 36And as they went on *their* way, they came unto a certain water: and the eunuch said, See, *here is* water; what doth hinder me to be baptized? 37And Philip said, If thou believest with all *thine* heart, *thou* mayest. And he answered and said, I believe that Jesus Christ is the Son of God. 38And he commanded the chariot to stand still: and they went down both into the water, both Philip and the eunuch; and he baptized him. 39And when they were come up out of the water, the Spirit of the Lord caught away Philip, that the eunuch saw him no more: and he went *on* his way rejoicing. 40But Philip was found at Azotus: and passing through he preached in all the cities, till he came to Cesarea.

Conversion of Saul

9 And Saul, yet breathing out threatenings and slaughter against the disciples of the Lord, went unto the high priest, 2And desired of him letters to Damascus to the synagogues, that if he found any of *this* way, whether they were men or women, he might bring *them* bound unto Jerusalem. 3And as *he* journeyed, he came near Damascus: and suddenly there shined round about him a light from heaven: 4And he fell to the earth, and heard a voice saying unto him, Saul, Saul, why persecutest thou me? 5And he said, Who art thou, Lord? And the Lord said, I am Jesus whom thou persecutest: *it is* hard for thee to kick against the pricks. 6And he trembling and astonished said, Lord, what wilt thou have me to do? And the Lord *said* unto him, Arise, and go into the city, and it shall be told thee what thou must do. 7And the men which journeyed with him stood speechless, hearing a voice, but seeing no *man.* 8And Saul arose from the earth; and when his eyes were opened, he saw no *man:* but they led him by the hand, and brought *him* into Damascus. 9And he was three days without sight, and neither did eat nor drink.

10 And there was a certain disciple at Damascus, named Ananias; and to him said the Lord in a vision, Ananias. And he said, Behold, I *am here,* Lord. 11And the Lord *said* unto him, Arise, and go into the street which is called Straight, and inquire in the house of Judas for *one* called Saul, of Tarsus: for

behold, he prayeth, 12And hath seen in a vision a man named Ananias coming in, and putting *his* hand on him, that he might receive his sight. 13Then Ananias answered, Lord, I have heard by many of this man, how much evil he hath done to thy saints at Jerusalem: 14And here he hath authority from the chief priests to bind all that call on thy name. 15But the Lord said unto him, Go *thy way:* for he is a chosen vessel unto me, to bear my name before the Gentiles, and kings, and the children of Israel: 16For I will shew him how great *things* he must suffer for my name's sake. 17And Ananias went his way, and entered into the house; and putting his hands on him said, Brother Saul, the Lord, *even* Jesus, that appeared unto thee in the way as thou camest, hath sent me, that thou mightest receive thy sight, and be filled with the Holy Ghost. 18And immediately there fell from his eyes as it had been scales: and he received sight forthwith, and arose, and was baptized, 19And when he had received meat, he was strengthened. Then was Saul certain days with the disciples which were at Damascus. [ch. 26:20]

Paul preaches at Damascus

20 And straightway he preached Christ in the synagogues, that he is the Son of God. 21But all that heard *him* were amazed, and said; Is not this he that destroyed them which called on this name in Jerusalem, and came hither for that *intent,* that he might bring them bound unto the chief priests? 22But Saul increased the more in strength, and confounded the Jews which dwelt at Damascus, proving that this is *very* Christ. [ch. 18:28]

Paul escapes to Jerusalem

23 And after that many days were fulfilled, the Jews took counsel to kill him: 24But their laying await was known of Saul. And they watched the gates day and night to kill him. 25Then the disciples took him by night, and let *him* down by the wall in a basket. 26And when Saul was come to Jerusalem, he assayed to join himself to the disciples: but they were all afraid of him, and believed not that he was a disciple. 27But Barnabas took him, and brought *him* to the apostles, and declared unto them how he had seen the Lord in the way, and that he had spoken to him, and how he had preached boldly at Damascus in the name of Jesus. 28And he was with them coming in and going out at Jerusalem. 29And he spake boldly in the name of the Lord Jesus, and disputed against the Grecians: but they went about to slay him. 30Which when the brethren knew, they brought him down to Cesarea, and sent him forth to Tarsus. 31Then had the churches rest throughout all Judea and Galilee and Samaria, and were edified; and walking in the fear of the Lord, and in the comfort of the Holy Ghost, were multiplied. [See ch. 8:1]

Aeneas and Tabitha

32 And it came to pass, as Peter passed throughout all *quarters,* he

came down also to the saints which dwelt at Lydda. 33 And there he found a certain man named Aeneas, which had kept his bed eight years, and was sick of the palsy. 34 And Peter said unto him, Aeneas, Jesus Christ maketh thee whole: arise, and make thy bed. And he arose immediately. 35 And all that dwelt at Lydda and Saron saw him, and turned to the Lord. [1 Chr. 5:16; ch. 11:21]

36 Now there was at Joppa a certain disciple named Tabitha, which by interpretation is called Dorcas: this *woman* was full of good works and almsdeeds which she did. 37 And it came to pass in those days, that she was sick, and died: whom when they had washed, they laid *her* in an upper chamber. 38 And forasmuch as Lydda was nigh to Joppa, and the disciples had heard that Peter was there, they sent unto him two men, desiring *him* that *he* would not delay to come to them. 39 Then Peter arose and went with them. When he was come, they brought him into the upper chamber: and all the widows stood by him weeping, and shewing the coats and garments which Dorcas made, while she was with them. 40 But Peter put *them* all forth, and kneeled down, and prayed; and turning *him* to the body said, Tabitha, arise. And she opened her eyes: and when she saw Peter, she sat up. 41 And he gave her *his* hand, and lift her up, and when he had called the saints and widows, presented her alive. 42 And it was known throughout all Joppa; and many believed in the Lord. 43 And it came to pass, that he tarried many days in Joppa with one Simon a tanner. [ch. 10:6]

Cornelius' vision

10 There was a certain man in Cesarea called Cornelius, a centurion of the band called the Italian *band*, 2 A devout *man*, and one that feared God with all his house, which gave much alms to the people, and prayed to God alway. 3 He saw in a vision evidently, about the ninth hour of the day, an angel of God coming in to him, and saying unto him, Cornelius. 4 And when he looked on him, he was afraid, and said, What is it, Lord? And he said unto him, Thy prayers and thine alms are come up for a memorial before God. 5 And now send men to Joppa, and call for *one* Simon, whose surname is Peter: 6 He lodgeth with one Simon a tanner, whose house is by the sea side: he shall tell thee what thou oughtest to do. 7 And when the angel which spake unto Cornelius was departed, he called two of his household servants, and a devout soldier of them that waited on him continually; 8 And when he had declared all *these things* unto them, he sent them to Joppa.

Peter's vision

9 On the morrow, as they went on their journey, and drew nigh unto the city, Peter went up upon the house to pray about the sixth hour: 10 And he became very hungry, and would have eaten: but while they made ready, he fell into a trance, 11 And saw heaven opened, and a certain vessel de-

scending unto him, as *it had been* a great sheet knit at the four corners, and let down to the earth: 12Wherein were all *manner of* fourfooted beasts of the earth, and wild beasts, and creeping things, and fowls of the air. 13And there came a voice to him, Rise, Peter; kill, and eat. 14But Peter said, Not so, Lord; for I have never eaten any *thing that is* common or unclean. 15And *the* voice *spake* unto him again the second time, What God hath cleansed, *that* call not thou common. 16This was done thrice: and the vessel was received up again into heaven.

Peter's visit to Cornelius

17 Now while Peter doubted in himself what *this* vision which he had seen should mean, behold, the men which were sent from Cornelius had made inquiry for Simon's house, and stood before the gate, 18And called, and asked whether Simon, which was surnamed Peter, were lodged there. 19While Peter thought on the vision, the Spirit said unto him, Behold, three men seek thee: 20Arise therefore, and get *thee* down, and go with them, doubting nothing: for I have sent them. 21Then Peter went down to the men which were sent unto him from Cornelius; and said, Behold, I am he whom ye seek: what *is* the cause wherefore ye are come? 22And they said, Cornelius the centurion, a just man, and one that feareth God, and of good report among all the nation of the Jews, was warned from God by a holy angel to send for thee into his

house, and to hear words of thee. 23Then called he them in, and lodged *them.* And on the morrow Peter went away with them, and certain brethren from Joppa accompanied him. 24And the morrow *after* they entered into Cesarea. And Cornelius waited for them, and had called together his kinsmen and near friends.

25 And as Peter was coming in, Cornelius met him, and fell down at *his* feet, and worshipped *him.* 26But Peter took him up, saying, Stand up; I myself also am a man. 27And as he talked with him, he went in, and found many *that were* come together. 28And he said unto them, Ye know how that it is an unlawful *thing* for a man *that is* a Jew to keep company, or come unto one of another nation; but God hath shewed me that *I* should not call any man common or unclean. 29Therefore came I *unto you* without gainsaying, as soon as I was sent for: I ask therefore for what intent ye have sent for me? 30And Cornelius said, Four days ago I was fasting until this hour; and at the ninth hour I prayed in my house, and behold, a man stood before me in bright clothing, 31And said, Cornelius, thy prayer is heard, and thine alms are had in remembrance in the sight of God. 32Send therefore to Joppa, and call hither Simon, whose surname is Peter; he is lodged in the house of *one* Simon a tanner by the sea side: who, when he cometh, shall speak unto thee. 33Immediately therefore I sent to thee; and thou hast well done that thou art come. Now

therefore are we all here present before God, to hear all *things* that are commanded thee of God.

34 Then Peter opened *his* mouth, and said, Of a truth I perceive that God is no respecter of persons: 35 But in every nation he that feareth him, and worketh righteousness, is accepted with him. 36 The word which *God* sent unto the children of Israel, preaching peace by Jesus Christ: (he is Lord of all:) 37 *That* word, *I say,* you know, which was published throughout all Judea, and began from Galilee, after the baptism which John preached; 38 How God anointed Jesus of Nazareth with the Holy Ghost and with power: who went about doing good, and healing all that were oppressed of the devil; for God was with him. 39 And we are witnesses of all *things* which he did both in the land of the Jews, and in Jerusalem; whom they slew and hanged on a tree: 40 Him God raised up the third day, and shewed him openly; 41 Not to all the people, but unto witnesses chosen before of God, *even* to us, who did eat and drink with him after he rose from the dead. 42 And he commanded us to preach unto the people, and to testify that it is he which was ordained of God *to be* the Judge of quick and dead. 43 To him give all the prophets witness, that through his name whosoever believeth in him shall receive remission of sins. [Is. 53:11; Jer. 31:34; Dan. 9:24; Mic. 7:18; Zech. 13:1; Mal. 4:2; ch. 26:18; Rom. 10:11; Gal. 3:22]

Gentiles receive the Holy Ghost

44 While Peter yet spake these words, the Holy Ghost fell on all them which heard the word. 45 And they of the circumcision which believed were astonished, as many as came with Peter, because that on the Gentiles also was poured out the gift of the Holy Ghost. 46 For they heard them speak with tongues, and magnify God. Then answered Peter, 47 Can any *man* forbid water, that these should not be baptized, which have received the Holy Ghost as well as we? 48 And he commanded them to be baptized in the name of the Lord. Then prayed they him to tarry certain days. [1 Cor. 1:17; ch. 2:38; 8:16]

11 And the apostles and brethren that were in Judea heard that the Gentiles had also received the word of God. 2 And when Peter was come up to Jerusalem, they that were of the circumcision contended with him, 3 Saying, Thou wentest in to men uncircumcised, and didst eat with them. 4 But Peter *rehearsed the matter* from the beginning, *and* expounded *it* by order unto them, saying, 5 I was in the city of Joppa praying: and in a trance I saw a vision, A certain vessel descend, as *it had been* a great sheet, let down from heaven by four corners; and it came *even* to me: 6 Upon the which when I had fastened mine eyes, I considered, and saw fourfooted beasts of the earth, and wild beasts, and creeping things, and fowls of the air. 7 And I heard a voice saying unto me, Arise, Peter; slay and eat. 8 But I said, Not so, Lord: for noth-

ing common or unclean hath at any time entered into my mouth. 9But *the* voice answered me again from heaven, What God hath cleansed, *that* call not thou common. 10And this was done three times: and all were drawn up again into heaven. 11And behold, immediately there were three men already come unto the house where I was, sent from Cesarea unto me. 12And the Spirit bade me go with them, nothing doubting. Moreover these six brethren accompanied me, and we entered into the man's house: 13And he shewed us how he had seen an angel in his house, which stood and said unto him, Send men to Joppa, and call for Simon, whose surname is Peter; 14Who shall tell thee words, whereby thou and all thy house shall be saved. 15And as I began to speak, the Holy Ghost fell on them, as on us at the beginning. 16Then remembered I the word of the Lord, how that he said, John indeed baptized with water; but ye shall be baptized with the Holy Ghost. 17Forasmuch then as God gave them the like gift as *he did* unto us, who believed on the Lord Jesus Christ; what was I, that I could withstand God? 18When they heard these *things,* they held their peace, and glorified God, saying, Then hath God also to the Gentiles granted repentance unto life. [Rom. 10:12,13; 15:9,16]

The church at Antioch

19 Now they which were scattered abroad upon the persecution that arose about Stephen travelled as far as Phenice, and Cyprus, and Antioch, preaching the word to none but unto *the* Jews only. 20And some of them were men of Cyprus and Cyrene, which, when they were come to Antioch, spake unto the Grecians, preaching the Lord Jesus. 21And the hand of the Lord was with them: and a great number believed, and turned unto the Lord. 22Then tidings of these *things* came unto the ears of the church which was in Jerusalem: and they sent forth Barnabas, that *he* should go as far as Antioch. 23Who, when he came, and had seen the grace of God, was glad, and exhorted *them* all, that with purpose of heart *they* would cleave unto the Lord. 24For he was a good man, and full of the Holy Ghost and of faith: and much people was added unto the Lord. 25Then departed Barnabas to Tarsus, for to seek Saul: 26And when he had found him, he brought him unto Antioch. And it came to pass, that a whole year they assembled themselves with the church, and taught much people, and the disciples were called Christians first in Antioch.

27 And in these days came prophets from Jerusalem unto Antioch. 28And there stood up one of them named Agabus, and signified by the Spirit that there should be great dearth throughout all the world: which came to pass in the days of Claudius Cesar. 29Then the disciples, every man according to his ability, determined to send relief unto the brethren which dwelt in Judea: 30Which also they did, and sent it to the elders by the hands of Barnabas and Saul. [ch. 12:25]

Peter delivered from prison

12 Now about that time Herod the king stretched forth *his* hands to vex certain of the church. ²And he killed James the brother of John with the sword. ³And because he saw it pleased the Jews, he proceeded further to take Peter also. (Then were the days of unleavened bread.) ⁴And when he had apprehended him, he put *him* in prison, and delivered *him* to four quaternions of soldiers to keep him; intending after Easter to bring him forth to the people. ⁵Peter therefore was kept in prison: but prayer was made without ceasing of the church unto God for him. ⁶And when Herod would have brought him forth, the same night Peter was sleeping between two soldiers, bound with two chains: and *the* keepers before the door kept the prison. ⁷And behold, *the* angel of the Lord came upon *him,* and a light shined in the prison: and he smote Peter on the side, and raised him up, saying, Arise up quickly. And his chains fell off from *his* hands. ⁸And the angel said unto him, Gird thyself, and bind on thy sandals. And so he did. And he saith unto him, Cast thy garment about thee, and follow me. ⁹And he went out, and followed him; and wist not that it was true which was done by the angel; but thought he saw a vision. ¹⁰When they were past the first and the second ward, they came unto the iron gate that leadeth unto the city; which opened to them of his own accord: and they went out, and passed on through one street; and forthwith the angel departed from him. ¹¹And when Peter was come to himself, he said, Now I know of a surety, that the Lord hath sent his angel, and hath delivered me out of the hand of Herod, and *from* all the expectation of the people of the Jews. ¹²And when he had considered *the thing,* he came to the house of Mary the mother of John, whose surname was Mark; where many were gathered together praying. [ch. 4:23; ch. 15:37; ver. 5]

13 And as Peter knocked at the door of the gate, a damsel came to hearken, named Rhoda. ¹⁴And when she knew Peter's voice, she opened not the gate for gladness, but ran in, and told how Peter stood before the gate. ¹⁵And they said unto her, Thou art mad. But she constantly affirmed that it was *even* so. Then said they, It is his angel. ¹⁶But Peter continued knocking: and when they had opened *the door,* and saw him, they were astonished. ¹⁷But he, beckoning unto them with the hand to hold their peace, declared unto them how the Lord had brought him out of the prison. And he said, *Go* shew these *things* unto James, and to the brethren. And he departed, and went into another place. ¹⁸Now as soon as it was day, there was no small stir among the soldiers, what was become of Peter. ¹⁹And when Herod had sought for him, and found *him* not, he examined the keepers, and commanded that *they* should be put to death. And he went down

from Judea to Cesarea, and *there* abode.

The death of Herod

20 And Herod was highly displeased with them of Tyre and Sidon: but they came with one accord to him, and, having made Blastus the king's chamberlain their friend, desired peace; because their country was nourished by the king's *country.* 21 And upon a set day Herod, arrayed in royal apparel, sat upon his throne, and made an oration unto them. 22 And the people gave a shout, *saying, It is* the voice of a god, and not of a man. 23 And immediately *the* angel of the Lord smote him, because he gave not God the glory: and he was eaten of worms, and gave up the ghost. 24 But the word of God grew and multiplied. 25 And Barnabas and Saul returned from Jerusalem, when they had fulfilled *their* ministry, and took with *them* John, whose surname was Mark. [ch. 13:5,13; 15:37; ver. 12]

Paul and Barnabas on Cyprus

13 Now there were in the church that was at Antioch certain prophets and teachers; as Barnabas, and Simeon that was called Niger, and Lucius of Cyrene, and Manaen, which had been brought up with Herod the tetrarch, and Saul. 2 As they ministered to the Lord, and fasted, the Holy Ghost said, Separate me Barnabas and Saul for the work whereunto I have called them. 3 And when they had fasted and prayed, and laid *their* hands on them, they sent *them* away. 4 So they, being

sent forth by the Holy Ghost, departed unto Seleucia; and from thence they sailed to Cyprus. 5 And when they were at Salamis, they preached the word of God in the synagogues of the Jews: and they had also John to *their* minister. 6 And when they had gone through the isle unto Paphos, they found a certain sorcerer, a false prophet, a Jew, whose name *was* Bar-jesus: 7 Which was with the deputy *of the country,* Sergius Paulus, a prudent man; who called for Barnabas and Saul, and desired to hear the word of God. 8 But Elymas the sorcerer (for so is his name by interpretation) withstood them, seeking to turn away the deputy from the faith. 9 Then Saul, (who also *is called* Paul,) filled with the Holy Ghost, set his eyes on him, 10 And said, O full of all subtilty and all mischief, *thou* child of the devil, *thou* enemy of all righteousness, wilt thou not cease to pervert the right ways of the Lord? 11 And now behold, the hand of the Lord *is* upon thee, and thou shalt be blind, not seeing the sun for a season. And immediately there fell on him a mist and a darkness; and he went about seeking *some* to lead him by the hand. 12 Then the deputy, when he saw what was done, believed, being astonished at the doctrine of the Lord.

Preaching in Perga and Antioch

13 Now when Paul and his company loosed from Paphos, they came to Perga in Pamphylia: and John departing from them returned to Jerusalem. 14 But when they de-

parted from Perga, they came to Antioch in Pisidia, and went into the synagogue on the sabbath day, and sat down. 15 And after the reading of the law and the prophets the rulers of the synagogue sent unto them, saying, Ye men *and* brethren, if ye have *any* word of exhortation for the people, say *on.* 16 Then Paul stood up, and beckoning with *his* hand said, Men of Israel, and ye that fear God, give audience. 17 The God of this people of Israel chose our fathers, and exalted the people when *they* dwelt as strangers in the land of Egypt, and with a high arm brought he them out of it. 18 And about the time of forty years suffered he their manners in the wilderness. 19 And when he had destroyed seven nations in the land of Canaan, he divided their land to them by lot. 20 And after that he gave *unto* them judges about *the space of* four hundred and fifty years, until Samuel the prophet. 21 And afterward they desired a king: and God gave unto them Saul the son of Cis, a man of the tribe of Benjamin, *by the space of* forty years. 22 And when he had removed him, he raised up unto them David to be their king; to whom also he gave testimony, and said, I have found David the *son* of Jesse, a man after mine own heart, which shall fulfil all my will. 23 Of this *man's* seed hath God according to *his* promise raised unto Israel a Saviour, Jesus: 24 When John had first preached before his coming the baptism of repentance to all the people of Israel. 25 And as John fulfilled *his* course, he said, Whom

think ye that I am? I am not *he.* But behold, there cometh *one* after me, whose shoes of *his* feet I am not worthy to loose. 26 Men *and* brethren, children of the stock of Abraham, and whosoever among you feareth God, to you is the word of this salvation sent. 27 For they that dwell at Jerusalem, and their rulers, because they knew him not, nor *yet* the voices of the prophets which are read every sabbath day, they have fulfilled *them* in condemning *him.* 28 And though they found no cause of death *in him, yet* desired they Pilate that he should be slain. 29 And when they had fulfilled all that was written of him, they took *him* down from the tree, and laid *him* in a sepulchre. 30 But God raised him from the dead: 31 And he was seen many days of them which came up with him from Galilee to Jerusalem, who are his witnesses unto the people. 32 And we declare unto you glad tidings, how that the promise which was made unto the fathers, 33 God hath fulfilled the same unto us their children, in that he hath raised up Jesus again; as it is also written in the second psalm, Thou art my Son, this day have I begotten thee. 34 And as concerning that he raised him up from the dead, *now* no more to return to corruption, he said on this wise, I will give you the sure mercies of David. 35 Wherefore he saith also in another *psalm,* Thou shalt not suffer thine Holy One to see corruption. 36 For David, after he had served his own generation by the will of God, fell on sleep, and was laid unto his fathers, and saw corruption: ³⁷But he, whom God raised *again,* saw no corruption. ³⁸Be it known unto you therefore, men *and* brethren, that through this *man* is preached unto you the forgiveness of sins: ³⁹And by him all that believe are justified from all *things, from* which ye could not be justified by the law of Moses. ⁴⁰Beware therefore, lest that come upon you, which is spoken of in the prophets; ⁴¹Behold *ye* despisers, and wonder, and perish: for I work a work in your days, a work which you shall in no wise believe, though a man declare it unto you.

42 And when the Jews were gone out of the synagogue, the Gentiles besought that these words might be preached to them the next sabbath. ⁴³Now when the congregation was broken up, many of the Jews and religious proselytes followed Paul and Barnabas: who, speaking to them, persuaded them to continue in the grace of God. ⁴⁴And the next sabbath day came almost the whole city together to hear the word of God. ⁴⁵But when the Jews saw the multitudes, they were filled with envy, and spake against those *things* which were spoken by Paul, contradicting and blaspheming. ⁴⁶Then Paul and Barnabas waxed bold, and said, It was necessary that the word of God should first have been spoken to you: but seeing ye put it from *you,* and judge yourselves unworthy of everlasting life, lo, we turn to the Gentiles. ⁴⁷For so hath the Lord commanded us, *saying,* I have set thee to be a light of the Gentiles,

that thou shouldest be for salvation unto the ends of the earth. ⁴⁸And when the Gentiles heard *this,* they were glad, and glorified the word of the Lord: and as many as were ordained to eternal life believed. ⁴⁹And the word of the Lord was published throughout all the region. ⁵⁰But the Jews stirred up the devout and honourable women, and the chief *men* of the city, and raised persecution against Paul and Barnabas, and expelled them out of their coasts. ⁵¹But they shook off the dust of their feet against them, and came unto Iconium. ⁵²And the disciples were filled with joy, and with the Holy Ghost. [Mat. 5:12; John 16:22; ch. 2:46]

Preaching at Iconium

14 And it came to pass in Iconium, that they went *both* together into the synagogue of the Jews, and so spake, that a great multitude both of the Jews and *also* of the Greeks believed. ²But the unbelieving Jews stirred up the Gentiles, and made their minds evil affected against the brethren. ³Long time therefore abode they speaking boldly in the Lord, which gave testimony unto the word of his grace, and granted signs and wonders to be done by their hands. ⁴But the multitude of the city was divided: and part held with the Jews, and part with the apostles. ⁵And when there was an assault made both of the Gentiles, and *also* of the Jews with their rulers, to use *them* despitefully, and to stone them, ⁶They were ware of *it,* and fled unto Lystra and Derbe, cities

of Lycaonia, and *unto* the region that lieth round about: 7And there they preached the gospel.

Preaching at Lystra

8 And there sat a certain man at Lystra, impotent in *his* feet, being a cripple from his mother's womb, who never had walked: 9The same heard Paul speak: who stedfastly beholding him, and perceiving that he had faith to be healed, 10Said with a loud voice, Stand upright on thy feet. And he leaped and walked. 11And when the people saw what Paul had done, they lift up their voices, saying in the speech of Lycaonia, The gods are come down to us in the likeness of men. 12And they called Barnabas, Jupiter; and Paul, Mercurius, because he was the chief speaker. 13Then the priest of Jupiter, which was before their city, brought oxen and garlands unto the gates, and would have done sacrifice with the people. 14Which when the apostles, Barnabas and Paul, heard *of,* they rent their clothes, and ran in among the people, crying out, 15And saying, Sirs, why do ye these *things?* We also are men of like passions with you, and preach unto you that *ye* should turn from these vanities unto the living God, which made heaven, and earth, and the sea, and all *things* that are therein: 16Who in times past suffered all nations to walk in their own ways. 17Nevertheless he left not himself without witness, in that he did good, and gave us rain from heaven, and fruitful seasons, filling our hearts with food and gladness.

18And with these sayings scarce restrained they the people, that *they* had not done sacrifice unto them.

The return to Antioch

19 And there came thither *certain* Jews from Antioch and Iconium, who persuaded the people, and, having stoned Paul, drew *him* out of the city, supposing he had been dead. 20Howbeit, as the disciples stood round about him, he rose up, and came into the city: and the next day he departed with Barnabas to Derbe. 21And when they had preached the gospel to that city, and had taught many, they returned *again* to Lystra, and *to* Iconium, and Antioch, 22Confirming the souls of the disciples, *and* exhorting *them* to continue in the faith, and that we must through much tribulation enter into the kingdom of God. 23And when they had ordained them elders in every church, and had prayed with fasting, they commended them to the Lord, on whom they believed. 24And after they had passed throughout Pisidia, they came to Pamphylia. 25And when they had preached the word in Perga, they went down into Attalia: 26And thence sailed to Antioch, from whence they had been recommended to the grace of God for the work which they fulfilled. 27And when they were come, and had gathered the church together, they rehearsed all that God had done with them, and how he had opened *the* door of faith unto the Gentiles. 28And there they abode long time with the disciples.

The council at Jerusalem

15 And certain *men* which came down from Judea taught the brethren, *and said,* Except ye be circumcised after the manner of Moses, ye cannot be saved. ²When therefore Paul and Barnabas had no small dissension and disputation with them, they determined that Paul and Barnabas, and certain other of them, should go up to Jerusalem unto the apostles and elders about this question. ³And being brought on their way by the church, they passed through Phenice and Samaria, declaring the conversion of the Gentiles: and they caused great joy unto all the brethren. ⁴And when they were come to Jerusalem, they were received of the church, and *of* the apostles and elders, and they declared all *things* that God had done with them. ⁵But there rose up certain of the sect of the Pharisees which believed, saying, That it was needful to circumcise them, and to command *them* to keep the law of Moses. [ver. 1]

6 And the apostles and elders came together for to consider of this matter. ⁷And when there had been much disputing, Peter rose up, and said unto them, Men *and* brethren, ye know how that a good while ago God made choice among us, that the Gentiles by my mouth should hear the word of the gospel, and believe. ⁸And God, which knoweth the hearts, bare them witness, giving them the Holy Ghost, even as *he did* unto us; ⁹And put no difference between us and them, purifying their hearts by faith. ¹⁰Now therefore why tempt ye God, to put a yoke upon the neck of the disciples, which neither our fathers nor we were able to bear? ¹¹But we believe that through the grace of the Lord Jesus Christ *we* shall be saved, even as they. ¹²Then all the multitude kept silence, and gave audience to Barnabas and Paul, declaring what miracles and wonders God had wrought among the Gentiles by them. [ch. 14:27]

13 And after they had held their peace, James answered, saying, Men *and* brethren, hearken unto me: ¹⁴Simeon hath declared how God at the first did visit the Gentiles, to take out of them a people for his name. ¹⁵And to this agree the words of the prophets; as it is written, ¹⁶After this I will return, and will build again the tabernacle of David, which is fallen down; and I will build again the ruins thereof, and I will set it up: ¹⁷That the residue of men might seek after the Lord, and all the Gentiles, upon whom my name is called, saith the Lord, who doeth all these *things.* ¹⁸Known unto God are all his works from the beginning of the world. ¹⁹Wherefore my sentence is, that *we* trouble not them, which from among the Gentiles are turned to God: ²⁰But that *we* write unto them, that *they* abstain from pollutions of idols, and *from* fornication, and *from* things strangled, and *from* blood. ²¹For Moses of old time hath in every city them that preach him, being read in the synagogues every sabbath day. [ch. 13:15,27]

Letters sent to the Gentiles

22 Then pleased it the apostles and elders, with the whole church, to send chosen men of their own company to Antioch with Paul and Barnabas; *namely,* Judas surnamed Barsabas, and Silas, chief *men* among the brethren: **23** And they wrote *letters* by them after this manner; The apostles and elders and brethren *send* greeting unto the brethren which are of the Gentiles in Antioch and Syria and Cilicia: **24** Forasmuch as we have heard, that certain which went out from us have troubled you with words, subverting your souls, saying, *Ye must* be circumcised, and keep the law: to whom we gave no *such* commandment: **25** It seemed good unto us, being assembled with one accord, to send chosen men unto you with our beloved Barnabas and Paul, **26** Men that have hazarded their lives for the name of our Lord Jesus Christ. **27** We have sent therefore Judas and Silas, who shall also tell *you* the same *things* by mouth. **28** For it seemed good to the Holy Ghost, and to us, to lay upon you no greater burden than these necessary *things;* **29** That *ye* abstain from meats offered to idols, and from blood, and from things strangled, and from fornication: from which if ye keep yourselves, ye shall do well. Fare ye well. [ver. 20; ch. 21:25; Rev. 2:14,20; Lev. 17:14]

30 So when they were dismissed, they came to Antioch: and when they had gathered the multitude together, they delivered the epistle: **31** *Which* when they had read, they rejoiced for the consolation. **32** And Judas and Silas, being prophets also themselves, exhorted the brethren with many words, and confirmed *them.* **33** And after they had tarried *there* a space, they were let go in peace from the brethren unto the apostles. **34** Notwithstanding it pleased Silas to abide there *still.* **35** Paul also and Barnabas continued in Antioch, teaching and preaching the word of the Lord, with many others also. [ch. 13:1]

Separation of Paul and Barnabas

36 And some days after Paul said unto Barnabas, Let us go again and visit our brethren in every city where we have preached the word of the Lord, *and see* how they do. **37** And Barnabas determined to take with *them* John, whose surname was Mark. **38** But Paul thought not good to take him with *them,* who departed from them from Pamphylia, and went not with them to the work. **39** And the contention was so sharp *between them,* that they departed asunder one from the other: and *so* Barnabas took Mark, and sailed unto Cyprus; **40** And Paul chose Silas, and departed, being recommended by the brethren unto the grace of God. **41** And he went through Syria and Cilicia, confirming the churches. [ch. 16:5]

The selection of Timothy

16 Then came he to Derbe and Lystra: and behold, a certain disciple was there, named Timotheus, the son of a certain woman, *which was* a Jewess, and believed; but his father *was* a Greek: 2Which was well reported of by the brethren that were at Lystra and Iconium. 3Him would Paul have to go forth with him; and took and circumcised him because of the Jews which were in those quarters: for they knew all that his father was a Greek. 4And as they went through the cities, they delivered them the decrees for to keep, that were ordained of the apostles and elders which were at Jerusalem. 5And so were the churches established in the faith, and increased in number daily. [ch. 15:41]

The Macedonian call

6 Now when they had gone throughout Phrygia and the region of Galatia, and were forbidden of the Holy Ghost to preach the word in Asia, 7After they were come to Mysia, they assayed to go into Bithynia: but the Spirit suffered them not. 8And they passing by Mysia came down to Troas. 9And a vision appeared to Paul in the night; There stood a man of Macedonia, and prayed him, saying, Come over into Macedonia, and help us. 10And after he had seen the vision, immediately we endeavoured to go into Macedonia, assuredly gathering that the Lord had called us for to preach the gospel unto them. 11Therefore loosing from Troas, we came with a straight course to Samothracia, and the next *day* to Neapolis; 12And from thence to Philippi, which is the chief city of *that* part of Macedonia, *and* a colony: and we were in that city abiding certain days. [Phil. 1:1]

The conversion of Lydia

13 And on the sabbath we went out of the city by a river side, where prayer was wont to be made; and we sat down, and spake unto the women which resorted *thither.* 14And a certain woman named Lydia, a seller of purple, of the city of Thyatira, which worshipped God, heard *us:* whose heart the Lord opened, that *she* attended unto the *things* which were spoken of Paul. 15And when she was baptized, and her household, she besought *us,* saying, If ye have judged me to be faithful to the Lord, come into my house, and abide *there.* And she constrained us. [Gen. 19:3; 33:11; Judg. 19:21; Luke 24:29; Heb. 13:2]

Paul and Silas imprisoned

16 And it came to pass, as we went to prayer, a certain damsel possessed with a spirit of divination met us, which brought her masters much gain by soothsaying: 17The same followed Paul and us, and cried, saying, These men are the servants of the most high God, which shew unto us the way of salvation. 18And this did she many days. But Paul, being grieved, turned and said to the spirit, I command thee in the name of Jesus Christ to come out of her. And he came out the same hour. 19And when her masters saw that the hope of their gains was gone, they caught Paul and Silas, and drew *them* into the market-place unto the rulers, 20And brought them to the magistrates, saying, These men, being Jews, do exceedingly

trouble our city, 21 And teach customs, which are not lawful for us to receive, neither to observe, being Romans. 22 And the multitude rose up together against them: and the magistrates rent off their clothes, and commanded to beat *them*. 23 And when they had laid many stripes upon them, they cast *them* into prison, charging the jailor to keep them safely: 24 Who, having received such a charge, thrust them into the inner prison, and made their feet fast in the stocks.

25 And at midnight Paul and Silas prayed, and sang praises unto God: and the prisoners heard them. 26 And suddenly there was a great earthquake, so that the foundations of the prison were shaken: and immediately all the doors were opened, and every one's bands were loosed. 27 And the keeper of the prison awaking out of his sleep, and seeing the prison doors open, he drew out his sword, and would have killed himself, supposing that the prisoners had been fled. 28 But Paul cried with a loud voice, saying, Do thyself no harm: for we are all here. 29 Then he called for a light, and sprang in, and came trembling, and fell down before Paul and Silas, 30 And brought them out, and said, Sirs, what must I do to be saved? 31 And they said, Believe on the Lord Jesus Christ, and thou shalt be saved, and thy house. 32 And they spake unto him the word of the Lord, and to all that were in his house. 33 And he took them the same hour of the night, and washed *their* stripes; and was

baptized, he and all his, straightway. 34 And when he had brought them into his house, he set meat before *them,* and rejoiced, believing in God with all his house. [Luke 5:29; 19:6]

35 And when it was day, the magistrates sent the sergeants, saying, Let those men go. 36 And the keeper of the prison told this saying to Paul, The magistrates have sent to let you go: now therefore depart, and go in peace. 37 But Paul said unto them, They have beaten us openly uncondemned, being Romans, and have cast *us* into prison; and now do they thrust us out privily? nay verily; but let them come themselves and fetch us out. 38 And the sergeants told these words unto the magistrates: and they feared, when they heard that they were Romans, 39 And they came and besought them, and brought *them* out, and desired *them* to depart out of the city. 40 And they went out of the prison, and entered into *the house of* Lydia: and when they had seen the brethren, they comforted them, and departed. [ver. 14]

Paul at Thessalonica

17 Now when they had passed through Amphipolis and Apollonia, they came to Thessalonica, where was a synagogue of the Jews: 2 And Paul, as his manner was, went in unto them, and three sabbath days reasoned with them out of the scriptures, 3 Opening and alleging, that Christ must needs have suffered, and risen again from the dead; and

that this Jesus, whom I preach unto you, is Christ. 4And some of them believed, and consorted with Paul and Silas; and of the devout Greeks a great multitude, and of the chief women not a few. 5But the Jews which believed not, moved with envy, took unto *them* certain lewd fellows of the baser sort, and gathered a company, and set all the city on an uproar, and assaulted the house of Jason, and sought to bring them out to the people. 6And when they found them not, they drew Jason and certain brethren unto the rulers of the city, crying, These that have turned the world upside down are come hither also; 7Whom Jason hath received: and these all do contrary to the decrees of Cesar, saying that there is another king, *one* Jesus. 8And they troubled the people and the rulers of the city, when they heard these *things.* 9And when they had taken security of Jason, and *of* the other, they let them go.

Paul at Berea

10 And the brethren immediately sent away Paul and Silas by night unto Berea: who coming *thither* went into the synagogue of the Jews. 11These were more noble than those in Thessalonica, in that they received the word with all readiness of mind, and searched the scriptures daily, whether those *things* were so. 12Therefore many of them believed; also of honourable women which were Greeks, and of men, not a few. 13But when the Jews of Thessalonica had knowledge that the word of God was preached of Paul at Berea, they came thither also, and stirred up the people. 14And then immediately the brethren sent away Paul to go as *it were* to the sea: but Silas and Timotheus abode there still. 15And they that conducted Paul brought him unto Athens: and receiving a commandment unto Silas and Timotheus for to come to him with all speed, they departed. [ch. 18:5]

Paul at Athens

16 Now while Paul waited for them at Athens, his spirit was stirred in him, when he saw the city wholly given to idolatry. 17Therefore disputed he in the synagogue with the Jews, and with the devout *persons,* and in the market daily with them that met with *him.* 18Then certain philosophers of the Epicureans, and of the Stoicks, encountered him. And some said, What will this babbler say? other *some,* He seemeth to be a setter forth of strange gods: because he preached unto them Jesus, and the resurrection. 19And they took him, and brought him unto Areopagus, saying, May we know what this new doctrine, whereof thou speakest, *is?* 20For thou bringest certain strange *things* to our ears: we would know therefore what these *things* mean. 21(For all the Athenians and strangers which were there spent their time in nothing else, but *either* to tell, or to hear some new *thing.*) 22Then Paul stood in the midst of Mars' hill, and said, *Ye* men of Athens, I perceive that in all *things* ye are too

superstitious. 23For as I passed by, and beheld your devotions, I found an altar with this inscription, TO *THE* UNKNOWN GOD. Whom therefore ye ignorantly worship, him declare I unto you. 24God that made the world and all *things* therein, seeing that he is Lord of heaven and earth, dwelleth not in temples made with hands; 25Neither is worshipped with men's hands, as though he needed any *thing,* seeing he giveth to all life, and breath, and all *things;* 26And hath made of one blood all nations of men for to dwell on all the face of the earth, and hath determined the times before appointed, and the bounds of their habitation; 27That *they* should seek the Lord, if haply they might feel after him, and find *him,* though he be not far from every one of us: 28For in him we live, and move, and have our being; as certain also of your own poets have said, For we are also his offspring. 29Forasmuch then as we are the offspring of God, we ought not to think that the Godhead is like unto gold, or silver, or stone, graven by art and man's device. 30And the times of *this* ignorance God winked at; but now commandeth all men every where to repent: 31Because he hath appointed a day, in the which he will judge the world in righteousness by *that* man whom he hath ordained; *whereof* he hath given assurance unto all *men,* in that he hath raised him from the dead. [ch. 10:42; Rom. 2:16; 14:10; ch. 2:24]

32 And when they heard of the resurrection of the dead, some mocked: and others said, We will hear thee again of this *matter.* 33So Paul departed from among them. 34Howbeit certain men clave unto him, and believed: among which *was* Dionysius the Areopagite, and a woman named Damaris, and others with them.

Paul at Corinth

18 After these *things* Paul departed from Athens, and came to Corinth; 2And found a certain Jew named Aquila, born in Pontus, lately come from Italy, with his wife Priscilla; (because that Claudius had commanded all Jews to depart from Rome:) and came unto them. 3And because *he* was of the same craft, he abode with them, and wrought: for *by* their occupation they were tentmakers. 4And he reasoned in the synagogue every sabbath, and persuaded *the* Jews and *the* Greeks. 5And when Silas and Timotheus were come from Macedonia, Paul was pressed in spirit, and testified to the Jews *that* Jesus *was* Christ. 6And when they opposed themselves, and blasphemed, he shook *his* raiment, and said unto them, Your blood *be* upon your own heads; I *am* clean: from henceforth I will go unto the Gentiles. 7And he departed thence, and entered into a certain *man's* house, named Justus, one that worshipped God, whose house joined hard to the synagogue. 8And Crispus, the *chief* ruler of the synagogue, believed on the Lord with all his house; and many of the Corinthians hearing believed, and were baptized. 9Then spake the

Lord to Paul in the night by a vision, Be not afraid, but speak, and hold not thy peace: [10]For I am with thee, and no *man* shall set on thee to hurt thee: for I have much people in this city. [11]And he continued *there* a year and six months, teaching the word of God among them.

12 And when Gallio was the deputy of Achaia, the Jews made insurrection with one accord against Paul, and brought him to the judgment seat, [13]Saying, This *fellow* persuadeth men to worship God contrary to the law. [14]And when Paul was *now* about to open *his* mouth, Gallio said unto the Jews, If it were a matter of wrong or wicked lewdness, O *ye* Jews, reason would that I should bear with you: [15]But if it be a question of words and names, and *of* your law, look ye *to it;* for I will be no judge of such *matters.* [16]And he drave them from the judgment seat. [17]Then all the Greeks took Sosthenes, the *chief* ruler of the synagogue, and beat *him* before the judgment seat. And Gallio cared for none of those *things.* [1 Cor. 1:1]

Paul returns to Antioch

18 And Paul *after this* tarried *there* yet a good while, and then took his leave of the brethren, and sailed thence into Syria, and with him Priscilla and Aquila; having shorn *his* head in Cenchrea: for he had a vow. [19]And he came to Ephesus, and left them there: but he himself entered into the synagogue, and reasoned with the Jews. [20]When they desired *him* to tarry longer time with them, he consented not; [21]But bade them farewell, saying, I must by all means keep *this* feast that cometh in Jerusalem: but I will return again unto you, if God will. And he sailed from Ephesus. [22]And when he had landed at Cesarea, and gone up, and saluted the church, he went down to Antioch. [23]And after he had spent some time *there,* he departed, and went over *all* the country of Galatia and Phrygia in order, strengthening all the disciples. [Gal. 1:2; 4:14; ch. 14:22; 15:32,41]

Apollos' preaching at Ephesus

24 And a certain Jew named Apollos, born at Alexandria, an eloquent man, *and* mighty in the scriptures, came to Ephesus. [25]This *man* was instructed in the way of the Lord; and being fervent in the spirit, he spake and taught diligently the *things* of the Lord, knowing only the baptism of John. [26]And he began to speak boldly in the synagogue: whom when Aquila and Priscilla had heard, they took him unto *them,* and expounded unto him the way of God more perfectly. [27]And when he was disposed to pass into Achaia, the brethren wrote, exhorting the disciples to receive him: who, when he was come, helped them much which had believed through grace: [28]For he mightily convinced the Jews, *and that* publickly, shewing by the scriptures that Jesus was Christ. [ver. 5; ch. 9:22; 17:3]

Paul's work in Ephesus

19 And it came to pass that, while Apollos was at Corinth, Paul having passed through the upper coasts came to Ephesus: and finding certain disciples, ²He said unto them, Have ye received the Holy Ghost since ye believed? And they said unto him, We have not so much as heard whether there be *any* Holy Ghost. ³And he said unto them, Unto what then were ye baptized? And they said, Unto John's baptism. ⁴Then said Paul, John verily baptized *with* the baptism of repentance, saying unto the people, that they should believe on him which should come after him, that is, on Christ Jesus. ⁵When they heard *this,* they were baptized in the name of the Lord Jesus. ⁶And when Paul had laid *his* hands upon them, the Holy Ghost came on them; and they spake with tongues, and prophesied. ⁷And all the men were about twelve. ⁸And he went into the synagogue, and spake boldly for the space of three months, disputing and persuading the *things* concerning the kingdom of God. ⁹But when divers were hardened, and believed not, but spake evil of *that* way before the multitude, he departed from them, and separated the disciples, disputing daily in the school of one Tyrannus. ¹⁰And this continued by the space of two years; so that all they which dwelt in Asia heard the word of the Lord Jesus, both Jews and Greeks. ¹¹And God wrought special miracles by the hands of Paul: ¹²So that from his body were brought unto the sick handkerchiefs or aprons, and the diseases departed from them, and the evil spirits went out of them. [See 2 Ki. 4:29; ch. 5:15]

¹³ Then certain of the vagabond Jews, exorcists, took upon them to call over them which had evil spirits the name of the Lord Jesus, saying, We adjure you by Jesus whom Paul preacheth. ¹⁴And there were seven sons of *one* Sceva, a Jew, *and* chief of the priests, which did so. ¹⁵And the evil spirit answered and said, Jesus I know, and Paul I know; but who are ye? ¹⁶And the man in whom the evil spirit was leapt on them, and overcame them, and prevailed against them, so that *they* fled out of that house naked and wounded. ¹⁷And this was known to all the Jews and Greeks also dwelling at Ephesus; and fear fell on them all, and the name of the Lord Jesus was magnified. ¹⁸And many that believed came, and confessed, and shewed their deeds. ¹⁹Many also of them which used curious arts brought their books together, and burned *them* before all *men:* and they counted the price of them, and found *it* fifty thousand *pieces* of silver. ²⁰So mightily grew the word of God and prevailed. [ch. 6:7; 12:24]

The riot at Ephesus

21 After these *things* were ended, Paul purposed in the spirit, when he had passed through Macedonia and Achaia, to go to Jerusalem, saying, After I have been there, I must also see Rome. ²²So he sent into Macedonia two of them that ministered unto him, Timotheus and Erastus; but he himself stayed in Asia for a season. ²³And the same time there arose no small stir about *that* way. ²⁴For

a certain *man* named Demetrius, a silversmith, which made silver shrines for Diana, brought no small gain unto the craftsmen; 25Whom he called together with the workmen of like occupation, and said, Sirs, ye know that by this craft we have our wealth. 26Moreover ye see and hear, that not alone at Ephesus, but almost throughout all Asia, this Paul hath persuaded and turned away much people, saying that they be no gods, which are made with hands: 27So *that* not only this our craft is in danger to be set at nought; but also that the temple of the great goddess Diana should be despised, and her magnificence should be destroyed, whom all Asia and the world worshippeth. 28And when they heard *these sayings,* they were full of wrath, and cried out, saying, Great *is* Diana of the Ephesians. 29And the whole city was filled with confusion: and having caught Gaius and Aristarchus, men of Macedonia, Paul's companions in travel, they rushed with one accord into the theatre. 30And when Paul would have entered in unto the people, the disciples suffered him not. 31And certain of the chief of Asia, which were his friends, sent unto him, desiring *him* that *he* would not adventure himself into the theatre. 32Some therefore cried one *thing,* and some another: for the assembly was confused; and the more part knew not wherefore they were come together. 33And they drew Alexander out of the multitude, the Jews putting him forward. And Alexander beckoned with the hand, and would have made *his* defence unto the people. 34But when *they* knew that he was a Jew, all with one voice about the space of two hours cried out, Great *is* Diana of the Ephesians. 35And when the townclerk had appeased the people, he said, *Ye* men of Ephesus, what man is there that knoweth not how that the city of the Ephesians is a worshipper of the great goddess Diana, and of the *image* which fell down from Jupiter? 36Seeing then that these *things* cannot be spoken against, ye ought to be quiet, and to do nothing rashly. 37For ye have brought *hither* these men, *which are* neither robbers of churches, nor yet blasphemers of your goddess. 38Wherefore if Demetrius, and the craftsmen which are with him, have a matter against any *man,* the law is open, and there are deputies: let them implead one another. 39But if ye inquire any *thing* concerning other *matters,* it shall be determined in a lawful assembly. 40For we are in danger to be called in question for this day's uproar, there being no cause whereby we may give an account of this concourse. 41And when he had thus spoken, he dismissed the assembly.

Macedonia and Greece

20 And after the uproar was ceased, Paul called unto *him* the disciples, and embraced *them,* and departed for to go into Macedonia. 2And when he had gone over those parts, and had given them much exhortation, he came into Greece, ³And *there* abode three months: and when the Jews laid wait for him, as he was about to sail into Syria, he purposed to return through Macedonia. ⁴And there accompanied him into Asia Sopater of Berea; and of the Thessalonians, Aristarchus and Secundus; and Gaius of Derbe, and Timotheus; and of Asia, Tychicus and Trophimus. [ch. 19:29; 27:2; Col. 4:10; ch. 19:29; ch. 16:1; Eph. 6:21; Col. 4:7; 2 Tim. 4:12; Tit. 3:12; ch. 21:29; 2 Tim. 4:20]

From Philippi to Miletus

5 These going before tarried for us at Troas. ⁶And we sailed away from Philippi after the days of unleavened bread, and came unto them to Troas in five days; where we abode seven days. ⁷And upon the first *day* of the week, when the disciples came together to break bread, Paul preached unto them, ready to depart on the morrow; and continued *his* speech until midnight. ⁸And there were many lights in the upper chamber, where they were gathered together. ⁹And there sat in a window a certain young man named Eutychus, being fallen into a deep sleep: and as Paul was long preaching, he sunk down with sleep, and fell down from the third loft, and was taken up dead. ¹⁰And Paul went down, and fell on him, and embracing *him* said, Trouble not yourselves; for his life is in him. ¹¹When he therefore was come up *again,* and had broken bread, and eaten, and talked a long while, *even* till break of day, so he departed. ¹²And they

brought the young man alive, and were not a little comforted.

13 And we went before to ship, and sailed unto Assos, there intending to take in Paul: for so had he appointed, minding himself to go afoot. ¹⁴And when he met with us at Assos, we took him in, and came to Mitylene. ¹⁵And we sailed thence, and came the next *day* over against Chios; and the next *day* we arrived at Samos, and tarried at Trogyllium; and the next *day* we came to Miletus. ¹⁶For Paul had determined to sail by Ephesus, because he would not spend the time in Asia: for he hasted, if it were possible for him, to be at Jerusalem the day of Pentecost. [ch. 18:21; 19:21; 21:4,12; ch. 24:17; ch. 2:1; 1 Cor. 16:8]

Paul and the Ephesian elders

17 And from Miletus he sent to Ephesus, and called the elders of the church. ¹⁸And when they were come to him, he said unto them, Ye know, from the first day that I came into Asia, after what manner I have been with you at all seasons, ¹⁹Serving the Lord with all humility of mind, and *with* many tears, and temptations, which befell me by the lying in wait of the Jews: ²⁰*And* how I kept back nothing that was profitable *unto you,* but have shewed you, and have taught you publickly, and from house to house, ²¹Testifying both to the Jews, and *also* to the Greeks, repentance toward God, and faith toward our Lord Jesus Christ. ²²And now behold, I go bound in the spirit unto Jerusalem, not knowing the

things that shall befall me there: 23Save that the Holy Ghost witnesseth in every city, saying that bonds and afflictions abide me. 24But none of these *things* move me, neither count I my life dear unto myself, so that *I* might finish my course with joy, and the ministry, which I have received of the Lord Jesus, to testify the gospel of the grace of God. 25And now behold, I know that ye all, among whom I have gone preaching the kingdom of God, shall see my face no more. 26Wherefore I take you to record this day, that I *am* pure from the blood of all *men.* 27For I have not shunned to declare unto you all the counsel of God. 28Take heed therefore unto yourselves, and to all the flock, over the which the Holy Ghost hath made you overseers, to feed the church of God, which he hath purchased with his own blood. 29For I know this, that after my departing shall grievous wolves enter in among you, not sparing the flock. 30Also of your own selves shall men arise, speaking perverse *things,* to draw away disciples after them. 31Therefore watch, and remember, that *by the space of* three years I ceased not to warn every one night and day with tears. 32And now, brethren, I commend you to God, and to the word of his grace, which is able to build *you* up, and to give you an inheritance among all them which are sanctified. 33I have coveted no *man's* silver, or gold, or apparel. 34Yea, ye yourselves know, that these hands have ministered unto my necessities, and to them that

were with me. 35I have shewed you all *things,* how that so labouring *ye* ought to support the weak, and to remember the words of the Lord Jesus, how he said, It is more blessed to give than to receive. [Rom. 15:1; 1 Cor. 9:12; 2 Cor. 11:9,12; 12:13; Eph. 4:28; 1 Thes. 4:11; 5:14; 2 Thes. 3:8]

36 And when he had thus spoken, he kneeled down, and prayed with them all. 37And *they* all wept sore, and fell on Paul's neck, and kissed him, 38Sorrowing most *of all* for the words which he spake, that they should see his face no more. And they accompanied him unto the ship. [ver. 25]

Paul travels to Cesarea

21 And it came to pass, that after we were gotten from them, and had launched, we came with a straight course unto Cos, and the *day* following unto Rhodes, and from thence unto Patara: 2And finding a ship sailing over unto Phenicia, we went aboard, and set forth. 3Now when we had discovered Cyprus, we left it on the left hand, and sailed into Syria, and landed at Tyre: for there the ship was to unlade *her* burden. 4And finding disciples, we tarried there seven days: who said to Paul through the Spirit, that *he* should not go up to Jerusalem. 5And when we had accomplished *those* days, we departed and went *our way;* and *they* all brought us on our way, with wives and children, till *we were* out of the city: and we kneeled down on the shore, and prayed. 6And when we had taken our leave one of another, we took

ship; and they returned home *again.* 7And when we had finished *our* course from Tyre, we came to Ptolemais, and saluted the brethren, and abode with them one day. 8And the next day we that were of Paul's company departed, and came unto Cesarea: and we entered into the house of Philip the evangelist, which was *one* of the seven; and abode with him. 9And the same *man* had four daughters, virgins, which did prophesy. 10And as we tarried *there* many days, there came down from Judea a certain prophet, named Agabus. 11And when he was come unto us, he took Paul's girdle, and bound his *own* hands and feet, and said, Thus saith the Holy Ghost, So shall the Jews at Jerusalem bind the man that oweth this girdle, and shall deliver *him* into the hands of the Gentiles. 12And when we heard these *things,* both we, and they of that place, besought him not to go up to Jerusalem. 13Then Paul answered, What mean ye to weep and to break mine heart? for I am ready not to be bound only, but also to die at Jerusalem for the name of the Lord Jesus. 14And when he would not be persuaded, we ceased, saying, The will of the Lord be done. 15And after those days we took up our carriages, and went up to Jerusalem. 16There went with us also *certain* of the disciples of Cesarea, and brought *with them* one Mnason of Cyprus, an old disciple, with whom we should lodge.

Paul in Jerusalem

17 And when we were come to Jerusalem, the brethren received us gladly. 18And the *day* following Paul went in with us unto James; and all the elders were present. 19And when he had saluted them, he declared particularly what *things* God had wrought among the Gentiles by his ministry. 20And when they heard *it,* they glorified the Lord, and said unto him, Thou seest, brother, how many thousands of Jews there are which believe; and they are all zealous of the law: 21And they are informed of thee, that thou teachest all the Jews which are among the Gentiles to forsake Moses, saying that they *ought* not to circumcise *their* children, neither to walk after the customs. 22What is it therefore? the multitude must needs come together: for they will hear that thou art come. 23Do therefore this that we say to thee: We have four men which have a vow on them; 24Them take, and purify thyself with them, and be at charges with them, that they may shave *their* heads: and all may know that *those things,* whereof they were informed concerning thee, are nothing; but *that* thou thyself also walkest orderly, and keepest the law. 25As touching the Gentiles which believe, we have written and concluded that they observe no such *thing,* save only that they keep themselves from things offered to idols, and from blood, and from strangled, and from fornication. 26Then Paul took the men, and the next day purifying himself with

them entered into the temple, to signify the accomplishment of the days of purification, until that an offering should be offered for every one of them. [ch. 24:18; Num. 6:13]

Paul's arrest

27 And when the seven days were almost ended, the Jews which were of Asia, when they saw him in the temple, stirred up all the people, and laid hands on him, 28Crying out, Men of Israel, help: This is the man, that teacheth all *men* every where against the people, and the law, and this place: and further brought Greeks also into the temple, and hath polluted this holy place. 29(For they had seen before with him in the city Trophimus an Ephesian, whom they supposed that Paul had brought into the temple.) 30And all the city was moved, and the people ran together: and they took Paul, and drew him out of the temple: and forthwith the doors were shut. 31And as *they* went about to kill him, tidings came unto the chief captain of the band, that all Jerusalem was in an uproar. 32Who immediately took soldiers and centurions, and ran down unto them: and when they saw the chief captain and the soldiers, they left beating of Paul. 33Then the chief captain came near, and took him, and commanded *him* to be bound with two chains; and demanded who he was, and what he had done. 34And some cried one *thing,* some another, among the multitude: and when he could not know the certainty for the tumult, he commanded him to

be carried into the castle. 35And when he came upon the stairs, so it was, that he was borne of the soldiers for the violence of the people. 36For the multitude of the people followed *after,* crying, Away with him. [Luke 23:18; John 19:15; ch. 22:22]

Paul's defence

37 And as Paul was to be led into the castle, he said unto the chief captain, May I speak unto thee? Who said, Canst thou speak Greek? 38Art not thou *that* Egyptian, which before these days madest an uproar, and leddest out into the wilderness four thousand men that were murderers? 39But Paul said, I am a man *which am* a Jew of Tarsus, *a city* in Cilicia, a citizen of no mean city: and, I beseech thee, suffer me to speak unto the people. 40And when he had given *him* licence, Paul stood on the stairs, and beckoned with the hand unto the people. And when there was made a great silence, he spake unto *them* in the Hebrew tongue, saying, [ch. 12:17]

22 Men, brethren, and fathers, hear ye my defence *which I make* now unto you. 2(And when they heard that he spake in the Hebrew tongue to them, they kept the more silence: and he saith,) 3I am verily a man *which am* a Jew, born in Tarsus, *a city* in Cilicia, yet brought up in this city at the feet of Gamaliel, *and* taught according to the perfect manner of the law of the fathers, and was zealous towards God, as ye all are this day. 4And I persecuted this way unto the death, binding and deliv-

ering into prisons both men and women. 5As also the high priest doth bear me witness, and all the estate of the elders: from whom also I received letters unto the brethren, and went to Damascus, to bring them which were there, bound unto Jerusalem, for to be punished. 6And it came to pass that, as I made my journey, and was come nigh unto Damascus about noon, suddenly there shone from heaven a great light round about me. 7And I fell unto the ground, and heard a voice saying unto me, Saul, Saul, why persecutest thou me? 8And I answered, Who art thou, Lord? And he said unto me, I am Jesus of Nazareth, whom thou persecutest. 9And they that were with me saw indeed the light, and were afraid; but they heard not the voice of him that spake to me. 10And I said, What shall I do, Lord? And the Lord said unto me, Arise, and go into Damascus; and there it shall be told thee of all *things* which are appointed for thee to do. 11And when I could not see for the glory of that light, being led by the hand of them that were with me, I came into Damascus. 12And one Ananias, a devout man according to the law, having a good report of all the Jews which dwelt *there,* 13Came unto me, and stood, and said unto me, Brother Saul, receive thy sight. And the same hour I looked up upon him. 14And he said, The God of our fathers hath chosen thee, that *thou* shouldest know his will, and see *that* Just One, and shouldest hear the voice of his mouth. 15For thou shalt be his wit-

ness unto all men of what thou hast seen and heard. 16And now why tarriest thou? arise, and be baptized, and wash away thy sins, calling on the name of the Lord. 17And it came to pass that, when I was come again to Jerusalem, even while I prayed in the temple, I was in a trance; 18And saw him saying unto me, Make haste, and get *thee* quickly out of Jerusalem: for they will not receive thy testimony concerning me. 19And I said, Lord, they know that I imprisoned and beat in every synagogue them that believed on thee: 20And when the blood of thy martyr Stephen was shed, I also was standing by, and consenting unto his death, and kept the raiment of them that slew him. 21And he said unto me, Depart: for I will send thee far hence unto the Gentiles. [ch. 9:15; 13:2,46,47; 18:6; 26:17; Rom. 1:5; 11:13; 15:16; Gal. 1:15,16; 2:7,8; Eph. 3:7,8; 1 Tim. 2:7; 2 Tim. 1:11]

22 And they gave him audience unto this word, and *then* lift up their voices, and said, Away with such *a fellow* from the earth: for it is not fit that he should live. 23And as they cried out, and cast *off their* clothes, and threw dust into the air, 24The chief captain commanded him to be brought into the castle, and bade that he should be examined by scourging; that he might know wherefore they cried so against him. 25And as they bound him with thongs, Paul said unto the centurion that stood *by,* Is it lawful for you to scourge a man *that is* a Roman, and uncondemned? 26When the centurion heard *that,* he went and told the

chief captain, saying, Take heed what thou doest: for this man is a Roman. 27Then the chief captain came, and said unto him, Tell me, art thou a Roman? He said, Yea. 28And the chief captain answered, With a great sum obtained I this freedom. And Paul said, But I was *free* born. 29Then straightway they departed from him which should have examined him: and the chief captain also was afraid, after he knew that he was a Roman, and because he had bound him.

Before the Sanhedrin

30 On the morrow, because he would have known the certainty wherefore he was accused of the Jews, he loosed him from *his* bands, and commanded the chief priests and all their council to appear, and brought Paul down, and set *him* before them.

23 And Paul, earnestly beholding the council, said, Men *and* brethren, I have lived in all good conscience before God until this day. 2And the high priest Ananias commanded them that stood by him to smite him on the mouth. 3Then said Paul unto him, God shall smite thee, *thou* whited wall: for sittest thou to judge me after the law, and commandest me to be smitten contrary to the law? 4And they that stood by said, Revilest thou God's high priest? 5Then said Paul, I wist not, brethren, that he was the high priest: for it is written, Thou shalt not speak evil of the ruler of thy people. 6But when Paul perceived that the one part were Sadducees,

and the other Pharisees, he cried out in the council, Men *and* brethren, I am a Pharisee, the son of a Pharisee: of the hope and resurrection of the dead I am called in question. 7And when he had so said, there arose a dissension between the Pharisees and the Sadducees: and the multitude was divided. 8For the Sadducees say that there is no resurrection, neither angel nor spirit: but the Pharisees confess both. 9And there arose a great cry: and the scribes *that were* of the Pharisees' part arose, and strove, saying, We find no evil in this man: but if a spirit or an angel hath spoken to him, let us not fight against God. 10And when there arose a great dissension, the chief captain, fearing lest Paul should have been pulled in pieces of them, commanded the soldiers to go down, and to take him by force from among them, and to bring *him* into the castle.

The plot to kill Paul

11 And the night following the Lord stood by him, and said, Be of good cheer, Paul: for as thou hast testified of me in Jerusalem, so must thou bear witness also at Rome. 12And when it was day, certain of the Jews banded together, and bound themselves under a curse, saying that *they* would neither eat nor drink till they had killed Paul. 13And they were more *than* forty which had made this conspiracy. 14And they came to the chief priests and elders, and said, We have bound ourselves under a great curse, that *we* will eat noth-

ing until we have slain Paul.
15 Now therefore ye with the council signify to the chief captain that he bring him down unto you to morrow, as though ye would inquire something more perfectly concerning him: and we, or ever he come near, are ready to kill him.
16 And when Paul's sister's son heard of *their* lying in wait, he went and entered into the castle, and told Paul. 17 Then Paul called one of the centurions unto *him*, and said, Bring this young man unto the chief captain: for he hath a certain *thing* to tell him. 18 So he took him, and brought *him* to the chief captain, and said, Paul the prisoner called me unto *him*, and prayed *me* to bring this young man unto thee, who hath something to say unto thee. 19 Then the chief captain took him by the hand, and went *with him* aside privately, and asked *him*, What is that thou hast to tell me? 20 And he said, The Jews have agreed to desire thee that thou wouldest bring down Paul to morrow into the council, as though they would inquire somewhat of him more perfectly. 21 But do not thou yield unto them: for there lie in wait for him of them more *than* forty men, which have bound themselves with an oath, that *they* will neither eat nor drink till they have killed him: and now are they ready, looking for a promise from thee. 22 So the chief captain then let the young man depart, and charged *him, See thou* tell no *man* that thou hast shewed these *things* to me. 23 And he called unto *him* two centurions, saying, Make

ready two hundred soldiers to go to Cesarea, and horsemen threescore *and* ten, and spearmen two hundred, at the third hour of the night; 24 And provide *them* beasts, that they may set Paul on, and bring *him* safe unto Felix the governor. 25 And he wrote a letter after this manner:

26 Claudius Lysias unto the most excellent governor Felix *sendeth* greeting. 27 This man was taken of the Jews, and should have been killed of them: then came I with an army, and rescued him, having understood that he was a Roman. 28 And when I would have known the cause wherefore they accused him, I brought him forth into their council: 29 Whom I perceived to be accused of questions of their law, but to have nothing laid to his charge worthy of death or of bonds. 30 And when it was told me how that the Jews laid wait for the man, I sent straightway to thee, and gave commandment to *his* accusers also to say before thee what *they had* against him. Farewell. [ver. 20; ch. 24:8; 25:6]

Paul taken to Cesarea

31 Then the soldiers, as it was commanded them, took Paul, and brought *him* by night to Antipatris. 32 On the morrow they left the horsemen to go with him, and returned to the castle: 33 Who, when they came to Cesarea, and delivered the epistle to the governor, presented Paul also before him. 34 And when the governor had read *the letter,* he asked of what province he was: and when he under-

stood that *he was* of Cilicia; 35I will hear thee, said he, when thine accusers are also come. And he commanded him to be kept in Herod's judgment hall. [ch. 24:1,10; 25:16; Mat. 27:27]

Paul tried before Felix

24 And after five days Ananias the high priest descended with the elders, and *with* a certain orator *named* Tertullus, who informed the governor against Paul. 2And when he was called *forth*, Tertullus began to accuse *him*, saying, Seeing that by thee we enjoy great quietness, and that very worthy deeds are done unto this nation by thy providence, 3We accept *it* always, and in all places, most noble Felix, with all thankfulness. 4Notwithstanding, that I be not further tedious unto thee, I pray *thee* that thou wouldest hear us of thy clemency a few words. 5For we have found this man a pestilent *fellow*, and a mover of sedition among all the Jews throughout the world, and a ringleader of the sect of the Nazarenes: 6Who also hath gone about to profane the temple: whom we took, and would have judged according to our law. 7But the chief captain Lysias came *upon us*, and with great violence took *him* away out of our hands, 8Commanding his accusers to come unto thee: by examining of whom thyself mayest take knowledge of all these *things*, whereof we accuse him. 9And the Jews also assented, saying that these *things* were so.

10 Then Paul, after that the governor had beckoned unto him to speak, answered, Forasmuch as I know that thou hast been of many years a judge unto this nation, I do the more cheerfully answer for myself: 11Because that thou mayest understand, that there are *yet* but twelve days since I went up to Jerusalem for to worship. 12And they neither found me in the temple disputing with any *man*, neither raising up the people, neither in the synagogues, nor in the city: 13Neither can they prove *the things* whereof they now accuse me. 14But this I confess unto thee, that after the way which they call heresy, so worship I the God of my fathers, believing all *things* which are written in the law and the prophets: 15And have hope towards God, which they themselves also allow, that there shall be a resurrection of the dead, both of the just and unjust. 16And herein do I exercise myself, to have always a conscience void of offence toward God, and *toward* men. 17Now after many years I came to bring alms to my nation, and offerings. 18Whereupon certain Jews from Asia found me purified in the temple, neither with multitude, nor with tumult. 19Who ought to have been here before thee, and object, if they had ought against me. 20Or else let these same *here* say, if they have found any evil doing in me, while I stood before the council, 21Except *it be* for this one voice, that I cried standing among them, Touching the resurrection of the dead I am called in question by you this day. [ch. 23:6; 28:20]

22 And when Felix heard these *things,* having more perfect knowledge of *that* way, he deferred them, and said, When Lysias the chief captain shall come down, I will know the uttermost of your matter. **23** And he commanded a centurion to keep Paul, and to let *him* have liberty, and that *he* should forbid none of his acquaintance to minister or come unto him. **24** And after certain days, when Felix came with his wife Drusilla, which was a Jewess, he sent for Paul, and heard him concerning the faith in Christ. **25** And as he reasoned of righteousness, temperance, and judgment to come, Felix trembled, and answered, Go *thy way* for *this* time; when I have a convenient season, I will call for thee. **26** He hoped also that money should have been given him of Paul, that he might loose him: wherefore he sent for him the oftener, and communed with him. **27** But after two years Porcius Festus came into Felix' room: and Felix, willing to shew the Jews a pleasure, left Paul bound. [Ex. 23:2; ch. 12:3; 25:9,14]

Paul tried before Festus

25 Now when Festus was come into the province, after three days he ascended from Cesarea to Jerusalem. **2** Then the high priest and the chief of the Jews informed him against Paul, and besought him, **3** And desired favour against him, that he would send for him to Jerusalem, laying wait in the way to kill him. **4** But Festus answered, that Paul should be kept at Cesarea, and that he himself would depart shortly *thither.* **5** Let them therefore, said he, which among you are able, go down with *me,* and accuse this man, if there be any *wickedness* in him. **6** And when he had tarried among them more than ten days, he went down unto Cesarea; and the next day sitting in the judgment seat, commanded Paul to be brought. **7** And when he was come, the Jews which came down from Jerusalem stood round about, and laid many and grievous complaints against Paul, which they could not prove. **8** While he answered for himself, Neither against the law of the Jews, neither against the temple, nor *yet* against Cesar, have I offended any *thing at all.* **9** But Festus, willing to do the Jews a pleasure, answered Paul, and said, Wilt thou go up to Jerusalem, and there be judged of these *things* before me? **10** Then said Paul, I stand at Cesar's judgment seat, where I ought to be judged: to the Jews have I done no wrong, as thou very well knowest. **11** For if I be an offender, or have committed any *thing* worthy of death, I refuse not to die: but if there be none *of these things* whereof these accuse me, no *man* may deliver me unto them. I appeal unto Cesar. **12** Then Festus, when he had conferred with the council, answered, Hast thou appealed unto Cesar? unto Cesar shalt thou go.

Paul's case discussed

13 And after certain days king Agrippa and Bernice came unto Cesarea to salute Festus. **14** And when they had been there many days, Festus declared Paul's cause unto the king, saying, There is a certain man left in bonds by Felix: 15 About whom, when I was at Jerusalem, the chief priests and the elders of the Jews informed *me,* desiring *to have* judgment against him. 16 To whom I answered, It is not the manner of the Romans to deliver any man to die, before that he which is accused have the accusers face to face, and have licence to answer for himself concerning the crime laid *against him.* 17 Therefore, when they were come hither, without any delay, on the morrow I sat on the judgment seat, and commanded the man to be brought *forth.* 18 Against whom when the accusers stood *up,* they brought none accusation of *such things* as I supposed: 19 But had certain questions against him of their own superstition, and of one Jesus, *which was* dead, whom Paul affirmed to be alive. 20 And because I doubted of such *manner of* questions, I asked *him* whether he would go to Jerusalem, and there be judged of these *matters.* 21 But when Paul had appealed to be reserved unto the hearing of Augustus, I commanded him to be kept till I might send him to Cesar. 22 Then Agrippa said unto Festus, I would also hear the man myself. To morrow, said he, thou shalt hear him. [See ch. 9:15]

23 And on the morrow, when Agrippa was come, and Bernice, with great pomp, and were entered into the place of hearing, with the chief captains, and principal men of the city, at Festus' commandment Paul was brought *forth.* 24 And Festus said, King Agrippa, and all men which are here present with us, ye see this *man,* about whom all the multitude of the Jews have dealt with me, both at Jerusalem, and *also* here, crying that he ought not to live any longer. 25 But when I found that he had committed nothing worthy of death, and *that* he himself hath appealed to Augustus, I have determined to send him. 26 Of whom I have no certain *thing* to write unto *my* lord. Wherefore I have brought him forth before you, and specially before thee, O king Agrippa, that, after examination had, I might have somewhat to write. 27 For it seemeth to me unreasonable to send a prisoner, and not withal to signify the crimes *laid* against him.

26 Then Agrippa said unto Paul, Thou art permitted to speak for thyself. Then Paul stretched forth the hand, and answered for himself:

Paul tried before Agrippa

2 I think myself happy, king Agrippa, because I shall answer for myself this day before thee touching all *the things* whereof I am accused of the Jews: 3 Especially *because I know* thee to be expert in all customs and questions which are among the Jews: wherefore I beseech thee to hear me patiently. 4 My manner of life from *my* youth, which was at the first among mine own nation at Jerusalem, know all the Jews; 5 Which knew me from the beginning, if they would testi-

fy, that after the most straitest sect of our religion I lived a Pharisee. 6And now I stand and am judged for the hope of the promise made of God unto *our* fathers: 7Unto which *promise* our twelve tribes, instantly serving *God* day and night, hope to come. For which hope's sake, king Agrippa, I am accused of the Jews. 8Why should it be thought *a thing* incredible with you, that God should raise the dead? 9I verily thought with myself, that *I* ought to do many *things* contrary to the name of Jesus of Nazareth. 10Which *thing* I also did in Jerusalem: and many of the saints did I shut up in prison, having received authority from the chief priests; and when they were put to death, I gave my voice against *them.* 11And I punished them oft in every synagogue, and compelled *them* to blaspheme; and being exceedingly mad against them, I persecuted *them* even unto strange cities. 12Whereupon as I went to Damascus with authority and commission from the chief priests, 13At midday, O king, I saw in the way a light from heaven, above the brightness of the sun, shining round about me and them which journeyed with me. 14And when we were all fallen to the earth, I heard a voice speaking unto me, and saying in the Hebrew tongue, Saul, Saul, why persecutest thou me? *it is* hard for thee to kick against the pricks. 15And I said, Who art thou, Lord? And he said, I am Jesus whom thou persecutest. 16But rise, and stand upon thy feet: for I have appeared unto thee for

this *purpose,* to make thee a minister and a witness both of *these things* which thou hast seen, and *of those things* in the which I will appear unto thee; 17Delivering thee from the people, and *from* the Gentiles, unto whom now I send thee, 18To open their eyes, *and* to turn *them* from darkness to light, and *from* the power of Satan unto God, that they may receive forgiveness of sins, and inheritance among them which are sanctified by faith that is in me. 19Whereupon, O king Agrippa, I was not disobedient unto the heavenly vision: 20But shewed first unto them of Damascus, and at Jerusalem, and throughout all the coasts of Judea, and *then* to the Gentiles, that *they* should repent and turn to God, and do works meet for repentance. 21For these causes the Jews caught me in the temple, and went about to kill *me.* 22Having therefore obtained help of God, I continue unto this day, witnessing both to small and great, saying none other *things* than those which the prophets and Moses did say should come: 23That Christ should suffer, *and* that he *should be* the first *that* should rise from the dead, and should shew light unto the people, and to the Gentiles. [Luke 24:26; 1 Cor. 15:20; Col. 1:18; Rev. 1:5; Luke 2:32]

24 And as he thus spake for himself, Festus said with a loud voice, Paul, thou art beside thyself; much learning doth make thee mad. 25But he said, I am not mad, most noble Festus; but speak forth *the* words of truth and soberness. 26For the king knoweth of these *things,*

before whom also I speak freely: for I am persuaded that none of these *things* are hidden from him; for this *thing* was not done in a corner. 27King Agrippa, believest thou the prophets? I know that thou believest. 28Then Agrippa said unto Paul, Almost thou persuadest me to be a Christian. 29And Paul said, I would to God, that not only thou, but also all that hear me this day, were both almost, and altogether such as I am, except these bonds. 30And when he had thus spoken, the king rose up, and the governor, and Bernice, and they that sat with them: 31And when they were gone aside, they talked between themselves, saying, This man doeth nothing worthy of death or of bonds. 32Then said Agrippa unto Festus, This man might have been set at liberty, if he had not appealed unto Cesar. [ch. 25:11]

Paul sent to Rome

27 And when it was determined that we should sail into Italy, they delivered Paul and certain other prisoners unto *one* named Julius, a centurion of Augustus' band. 2And entering into a ship of Adramyttium, we launched, meaning to sail by the coasts of Asia; *one* Aristarchus, a Macedonian of Thessalonica, being with us. 3And the next *day* we touched at Sidon. And Julius courteously entreated Paul, and gave *him* liberty to go unto *his* friends to refresh himself. 4And when we had launched from thence, we sailed under Cyprus, because the winds were contrary. 5And when we had

sailed over the sea of Cilicia and Pamphylia, we came to Myra, *a city* of Lycia. 6And there the centurion found a ship of Alexandria sailing into Italy; and he put us therein. 7And when we had sailed slowly many days, and scarce were come over against Cnidus, the wind not suffering us, we sailed under Crete, over against Salmone; 8And hardly passing it, came unto a place *which is* called The fair havens; nigh whereunto was the city *of* Lasea. 9Now when much time was spent, and when sailing was now dangerous, because the fast was now already past, Paul admonished *them,* 10And said unto them, Sirs, I perceive that *this* voyage will be with hurt and much damage, not only of the lading and ship, but also of our lives. 11Nevertheless the centurion believed the master and the owner of the ship, more than those *things* which were spoken by Paul. 12And because the haven was not commodious to winter in, the more part advised to depart thence also, if by any means they might attain to Phenice, *and there* to winter; *which is* a haven of Crete, and lieth toward the south west and north west.

The storm at sea

13 And when the south wind blew softly, supposing that *they* had obtained *their* purpose, loosing *thence,* they sailed close by Crete. 14But not long after there arose against it a tempestuous wind, called Euroclydon. 15And when the ship was caught, and could not

bear up into the wind, we let *her* drive. 16And running under a certain island *which is* called Clauda, we had much work to come by the boat: 17Which when they had taken up, they used helps, undergirding the ship; and fearing lest they should fall into the quicksands, strake sail, and so were driven. 18And we being exceedingly tossed with a tempest, the next *day* they lightened the ship; 19And the third *day* we cast *out* with our own hands the tackling of the ship. 20And when neither sun nor stars in many days appeared, and no small tempest lay on *us,* all hope that we should be saved was then taken away. 21But after long abstinence Paul stood *forth* in the midst of them, and said, Sirs, *ye* should have hearkened unto me, and not have loosed from Crete, and to have gained this harm and loss. 22And now I exhort you to be of good cheer: for there shall be no loss of *any man's* life among you, but of the ship. 23For there stood by me this night *the* angel of God, whose I am, and whom I serve, 24Saying, Fear not, Paul; thou must be brought before Cesar: and lo, God hath given thee all them that sail with thee. 25Wherefore, sirs, be of good cheer: for I believe God, that it shall be even as it was told me. 26Howbeit we must be cast upon a certain island. [ch. 28:1]

The shipwreck

27 But when the fourteenth night was come, as we were driven up and down in Adria, about midnight the shipmen deemed that they drew near to some country; 28And sounded, and found *it* twenty fathoms: and when they had gone a little further, they sounded again, and found *it* fifteen fathoms. 29Then fearing lest we should have fallen upon rocks, they cast four anchors out of the stern, and wished for the day. 30And as the shipmen were about to flee out of the ship, when they had let down the boat into the sea, under colour as though they would have cast anchors out of the foreship, 31Paul said to the centurion and to the soldiers, Except these abide in the ship, ye cannot be saved. 32Then the soldiers cut off the ropes of the boat, and let her fall off. 33And while the day was coming on, Paul besought *them* all to take meat, saying, This day is the fourteenth day that ye have tarried and continued fasting, having taken nothing. 34Wherefore I pray you to take *some* meat: for this is for your health: for there shall not a hair fall from the head of any of you. 35And when he had thus spoken, he took bread, and gave thanks to God in presence of *them* all: and when he had broken *it,* he began to eat. 36Then were they all of good cheer, and they also took *some* meat. 37And we were in all in the ship two hundred threescore *and* sixteen souls. 38And when they had eaten enough, they lightened the ship, and cast out the wheat into the sea. 39And when it was day, they knew not the land: but they discovered a certain creek with a shore, into the which they were minded, if it were possible, to

thrust in the ship. 40 And when they had taken up the anchors, they committed *themselves* unto the sea, and loosed the rudder bands, and hoised up the mainsail to the wind, and made toward shore. 41 And falling into a place where two seas met, they ran the ship aground; and the forepart stuck fast, and remained unmoveable, but the hinder part was broken with the violence of the waves. 42 And the soldiers' counsel was to kill the prisoners, lest any *of them* should swim out, and escape. 43 But the centurion, willing to save Paul, kept them from *their* purpose; and commanded that they which could swim should cast *themselves* first into *the sea,* and get to land: 44 And the rest, some on boards, and some on broken pieces of the ship. And so it came to pass, that *they* escaped all safe to land. [ver. 22]

The stopover at Melita

28 And when they were escaped, then they knew that the island was called Melita. 2 And the barbarous people shewed us no little kindness: for they kindled a fire, and received us every one, because of the present rain, and because of the cold. 3 And when Paul had gathered a bundle of sticks, and laid *them* on the fire, there came a viper out of the heat, and fastened on his hand. 4 And when the barbarians saw the *venomous* beast hang on his hand, they said among themselves, No doubt this man is a murderer, whom, though he hath escaped the sea, yet Vengeance suffereth not to live. 5 And he shook off the beast into the fire, and felt no harm. 6 Howbeit they looked when he should have swollen, or fallen down dead suddenly: but after they had looked a great while, and saw no harm come to him, they changed *their minds,* and said that he was a god. 7 In the same quarters were possessions of the chief *man* of the island, whose name was Publius; who received us, and lodged *us* three days courteously. 8 And it came to pass, that the father of Publius lay sick of a fever and of a bloody flixe: to whom Paul entered in, and prayed, and laid *his* hands on him, and healed him. 9 So when this was done, others also, which had diseases in the island, came, and were healed: 10 Who also honoured us with many honours; and when we departed, they laded *us* with such *things* as were necessary. [Mat. 15:6; 1 Tim. 5:17]

11 And after three months we departed in a ship of Alexandria, which had wintered in the isle, *whose* sign *was* Castor and Pollux. 12 And landing at Syracuse, we tarried *there* three days. 13 And from thence we fet a compass, and came to Rhegium: and after one day the south wind blew, and we came the next day to Puteoli: 14 Where we found brethren, and were desired to tarry with them seven days: and so we went toward Rome. 15 And from thence, when the brethren heard of us, they came to meet us as far as Appii forum, and The three taverns: whom when Paul saw, he thanked God, and took

courage. [16]And when we came to Rome, the centurion delivered the prisoners to the captain of the guard: but Paul was suffered to dwell by himself with a soldier that kept him. [ch. 24:25; 27:3]

The arrival at Rome

[17] And it came to pass, that after three days Paul called the chief of the Jews together: and when they were come together, he said unto them, Men *and* brethren, though I have committed nothing against the people, or customs of our fathers, *yet* was I delivered prisoner from Jerusalem into the hands of the Romans. [18]Who, when they had examined me, would have let *me* go, because there was no cause of death in me. [19]But when the Jews spake against *it,* I was constrained to appeal unto Cesar; not that I had ought to accuse my nation of. [20]For this cause therefore have I called for you, to see *you,* and to speak with *you:* because that for the hope of Israel I am bound with this chain. [21]And they said unto him, We neither received letters out of Judea concerning thee, neither any of the brethren that came shewed or spake any harm of thee. [22]But we desire to hear of thee what thou thinkest: for as concerning this sect, we know that every where it is spoken against. [23]And when they had appointed him a day, there came many to him into *his* lodging; to whom he expounded and testified the kingdom of God, persuading them concerning Jesus, both out of the law of Moses, and *out of* the prophets, from morning till evening. [24]And some believed the *things* which were spoken, and some believed not. [25]And when they agreed not among themselves, they departed, after that Paul had spoken one word, Well spake the Holy Ghost by Esaias the prophet unto our fathers, [26]Saying, Go unto this people, and say, Hearing ye shall hear, and shall not understand; and seeing ye shall see, and not perceive: [27]For the heart of this people is waxed gross, and *their* ears are dull of hearing, and their eyes have they closed; lest they should see with *their* eyes, and hear with *their* ears, and understand with *their* heart, and should be converted, and I should heal them. [28]Be it known therefore unto you, that the salvation of God is sent unto the Gentiles, and *that* they will hear it. [29]And when he had said these *words,* the Jews departed, and had great reasoning among themselves.

[30] And Paul dwelt two whole years in his own hired house, and received all that came in unto him, [31]Preaching the kingdom of God, and teaching those *things* which concern the Lord Jesus Christ, with all confidence, no man forbidding him.

Romans

1 Paul, a servant of Jesus Christ, called *to be* an apostle, separated unto the gospel of God, ²(Which he had promised afore by his prophets in the holy scriptures,) ³Concerning his Son Jesus Christ our Lord, which was made of the seed of David according to the flesh; ⁴*And* declared *to be* the Son of God with power, according to the Spirit of holiness, by the resurrection from the dead: ⁵By whom we have received grace and apostleship, for obedience to the faith among all nations, for his name: ⁶Among whom are ye also *the* called of Jesus Christ: ⁷To all that be in Rome, beloved of God, called *to be* saints: Grace to you and peace from God our Father, and the Lord Jesus Christ. [1 Cor. 1:2; 1 Cor. 1:3]

Thanksgiving and prayers

8 First, I thank my God through Jesus Christ for you all, that your faith is spoken of throughout the whole world. ⁹For God is my witness, whom I serve with my spirit in the gospel of his Son, that without ceasing I make mention of you, always in my prayers, ¹⁰Making request, if by any means now at length I might have a prosperous journey by the will of God to come unto you. ¹¹For I long to see you, that I may impart unto you some spiritual gift, to the end you may be established; ¹²That is, that *I* may be comforted together with you by the mutual faith both of you and me. ¹³Now I would not have you ignorant, brethren, that oftentimes I purposed to come unto you, (but was let hitherto,) that I might have some fruit among you also, even as among other Gentiles. ¹⁴I am debtor both to the Greeks, and to the barbarians; both to the wise, and to the unwise. ¹⁵So, as much as in me is, I am ready to preach the gospel to you that are at Rome also. ¹⁶For I am not ashamed of the gospel of Christ: for it is the power of God unto salvation to every one that believeth; to the Jew first, and *also* to the Greek. ¹⁷For therein is the righteousness of God revealed from faith to faith: as it is written, The just shall live by faith. [ch. 3:21; Hab. 2:4; John 3:36; Gal. 3:11]

The Gentiles: guilty before God

18 For the wrath of God is revealed from heaven against all ungodliness and unrighteousness of men, who hold the truth in unrighteousness; ¹⁹Because that which may be known of God is manifest in them; for God hath shewed *it* unto them. ²⁰For the invisible *things* of him from the creation of the world are clearly seen, being understood by the things that are made, *even* his eternal power and Godhead; so that they are without excuse: ²¹Because that, when they knew God, they glorified *him* not as God, neither were thankful; but became vain in their imaginations, and their foolish heart was darkened. ²²Profess-

ing *themselves* to be wise, they became fools, 23And changed the glory of the uncorruptible God into an image made like to corruptible man, and to birds, and fourfooted beasts, and creeping things. 24Wherefore God also gave them up to uncleanness through the lusts of their own hearts, to dishonour their own bodies between themselves: 25Who changed the truth of God into a lie, and worshipped and served the creature more than the Creator, who is blessed for ever. Amen. [1 Thes. 1:9; 1 John 5:20; Is. 44:20; Jer. 10:14]

26 For this cause God gave them up unto vile affections: for even their women did change the natural use into that which is against nature: 27And likewise also the men, leaving the natural use of the woman, burned in their lust one towards another; men with men working that which is unseemly, and receiving in themselves *that* recompence of their error which was meet. 28And even as they did not like to retain God in *their* knowledge, God gave them over to a reprobate mind, to do those *things* which are not convenient; 29Being filled with all unrighteousness, fornication, wickedness, covetousness, maliciousness; full of envy, murder, debate, deceit, malignity; whisperers, 30Backbiters, haters of God, despiteful, proud, boasters, inventors of evil *things,* disobedient to parents, 31Without understanding, covenant-breakers, without natural affection, implacable, unmerciful: 32Who knowing the judgment of

God, that they which commit such *things* are worthy of death, not only do the same, but have pleasure in them that do *them.* [ch. 2:2; ch. 6:21; Ps. 50:18; Hos. 7:3]

God's principles of judgment

2 Therefore thou art inexcusable, O man, whosoever thou art that judgest: for wherein thou judgest another, thou condemnest thyself; for thou that judgest doest the same *things.* 2But we are sure that the judgment of God is according to truth against them which commit such *things.* 3And thinkest thou this, O man, that judgest them which do such *things,* and doest the same, that thou shalt escape the judgment of God? 4Or despisest thou the riches of his goodness and forbearance and longsuffering; not knowing that the goodness of God leadeth thee to repentance? 5But after thy hardness and impenitent heart treasurest up unto thyself wrath against the day of wrath and revelation of the righteous judgment of God; 6Who will render to every *man* according to his deeds: 7To them who by patient continuance in well doing seek for glory and honour and immortality, eternal life: 8But unto them that are contentious, and do not obey the truth, but obey unrighteousness, indignation and wrath, 9Tribulation and anguish, upon every soul of man that doeth evil, of the Jew first, and *also* of the Gentile; 10But glory, honour, and peace, to every *man* that worketh good, to the Jew first, and *also* to the Gentile: 11For there is no respect of persons with God.

¹²For as many as have sinned without law shall also perish without law: and as many as have sinned in the law shall be judged by the law; ¹³(For not the hearers of the law *are* just before God, but the doers of the law shall be justified. ¹⁴For when *the* Gentiles, which have not the law, do by nature the *things* contained in the law, these, having not the law, are a law unto themselves: ¹⁵Which shew the work of the law written in their hearts, their conscience also bearing witness, and *their* thoughts the mean while accusing or else excusing one another;) ¹⁶In the day when God shall judge the secrets of men by Jesus Christ according to my gospel. [Eccl. 12:14; Mat. 25:31; Rev. 20:12; John 5:22; Acts 10:42; 1 Tim. 1:11]

The Jews: guilty before God

17 Behold, thou art called a Jew, and restest in the law, and makest thy boast of God, ¹⁸And knowest *his* will, and approvest the *things* that are more excellent, being instructed out of the law; ¹⁹And art confident that thou thyself art a guide of the blind, a light of them which are in darkness, ²⁰An instructor of the foolish, a teacher of babes, which hast the form of knowledge and of the truth in the law. ²¹Thou therefore which teachest another, teachest thou not thyself? thou that preachest *a man* should not steal, dost thou steal? ²²Thou that sayest *a man* should not commit adultery, dost thou commit adultery? thou that abhorrest idols, dost thou commit sacrilege? ²³Thou that

makest thy boast of the law, through breaking the law dishonourest thou God? ²⁴For the name of God is blasphemed among the Gentiles through you, as it is written. ²⁵For circumcision verily profiteth, if thou keep the law: but if thou be a breaker of the law, thy circumcision is made uncircumcision. ²⁶Therefore if the uncircumcision keep the righteousness of the law, shall not his uncircumcision be counted for circumcision? ²⁷And shall not uncircumcision which is by nature, if it fulfil the law, judge thee, who by the letter and circumcision dost transgress the law? ²⁸For he is not a Jew, which is one outwardly; neither *is that* circumcision, which is outward in the flesh: ²⁹But he *is* a Jew, which is one inwardly; and circumcision *is that* of the heart, in the spirit, *and* not *in* the letter; whose praise *is* not of men, but of God. [1 Pet. 3:4; Phil. 3:3; ch. 7:6; 1 Cor. 4:5; 2 Cor. 10:18; 1 Thes. 2:4]

3 What advantage then hath the Jew? or what profit *is there* of circumcision? ²Much every way: chiefly, because that unto them were committed the oracles of God. ³For what if some did not believe? shall their unbelief make the faith of God without effect? ⁴God forbid: yea, let God be true, but every man a liar; as it is written, That thou mightest be justified in thy sayings, and mightest overcome when thou art judged. ⁵But if our unrighteousness commend the righteousness of God, what shall we say? *Is* God unrighteous who taketh vengeance? (I speak as a

man) ⁶God forbid: for then how shall God judge the world? ⁷For if the truth of God hath *more* abounded through my lie unto his glory; why yet am I also judged as a sinner? ⁸And not *rather*, (as we be slanderously reported, and as some affirm that we say,) Let us do evil, that good may come? whose damnation is just. [ch. 5:20]

The world: guilty before God

9 What then? are we better *than they*? No, in no wise: for we have before proved both Jews and Gentiles, that *they* are all under sin; ¹⁰As it is written, There is none righteous, no, not one: ¹¹There is none that understandeth, there is none that seeketh after God. ¹²They are all gone out of the way, they are together become unprofitable; there is none that doeth good, no, not one. ¹³Their throat *is* an open sepulchre; with their tongues they have used deceit; the poison of asps *is* under their lips: ¹⁴Whose mouth is full of cursing and bitterness: ¹⁵Their feet *are* swift to shed blood: ¹⁶Destruction and misery *are* in their ways: ¹⁷And the way of peace have they not known: ¹⁸There is no fear of God before their eyes. ¹⁹Now we know that what *things* soever the law saith, it saith to them who are under the law: that every mouth may be stopped, and all the world may become guilty before God. ²⁰Therefore by the deeds of the law there shall no flesh be justified in his sight: for by the law *is* the knowledge of sin. [Ps. 143:2; Acts 13:39; Gal. 2:16; ch. 7:7]

Faith: the means of salvation

21 But now the righteousness of God without the law is manifested, being witnessed by the law and the prophets; ²²Even the righteousness of God *which is* by faith of Jesus Christ unto all and upon all them that believe: for there is no difference: ²³For all have sinned, and come short of the glory of God; ²⁴Being justified freely by his grace through the redemption that is in Christ Jesus: ²⁵Whom God hath set forth *to be* a propitiation through faith in his blood, to declare his righteousness for the remission of sins that are past, through the forbearance of God; ²⁶To declare, *I say*, at this time his righteousness: that he might be just, and the justifier of him which believeth in Jesus. ²⁷Where *is* boasting then? It is excluded. By what law? of works? Nay: but by the law of faith. ²⁸Therefore we conclude that a man is justified by faith without the deeds of the law. ²⁹*Is he* the God of the Jews only? *is he* not also of the Gentiles? Yes, of the Gentiles also: ³⁰Seeing *it is* one God, which shall justify the circumcision by faith, and uncircumcision through faith. ³¹Do we then make void the law through faith? God forbid: yea, we establish the law.

Abraham saved by faith

4 What shall we say then that Abraham our father, as pertaining to the flesh, hath found? ²For if Abraham were justified by works, he hath whereof to glory;

but not before God. ³For what saith the scripture? Abraham believed God, and it was counted unto him for righteousness. ⁴Now to him that worketh is the reward not reckoned of grace, but of debt. ⁵But to him that worketh not, but believeth on him that justifieth the ungodly, his faith is counted for righteousness. ⁶Even as David also describeth the blessedness of the man, unto whom God imputeth righteousness without works, ⁷*Saying,* Blessed *are they* whose iniquities are forgiven, and whose sins are covered. ⁸Blessed *is* the man to whom the Lord will not impute sin. ⁹*Cometh* this blessedness then upon the circumcision *only,* or upon the uncircumcision also? for we say that faith was reckoned to Abraham for righteousness. ¹⁰How was it then reckoned? when he was in circumcision, or in uncircumcision? Not in circumcision, but in uncircumcision. ¹¹And he received the sign of circumcision, a seal of the righteousness of the faith which he had *yet* being uncircumcised: that he might be the father of all them that believe, though they be not circumcised; that righteousness might be imputed unto them also: ¹²And the father of circumcision to them who are not of the circumcision only, but who also walk in the steps of *that* faith of our father Abraham, which he had being *yet* uncircumcised. ¹³For the promise, that he should be the heir of the world, *was* not to Abraham, or to his seed, through the law, but through the righteousness of faith. ¹⁴For if they

which are of the law *be* heirs, faith is made void, and the promise made of none effect: ¹⁵Because the law worketh wrath: for where no law is, *there is* no transgression. ¹⁶Therefore *it is* of faith, that *it might be* by grace; to the end the promise might be sure to all the seed; not to that only which is of the law, but to that also which is of the faith of Abraham; who is the father of us all, ¹⁷(As it is written, I have made thee a father of many nations,) before *him* whom he believed, *even* God, who quickeneth the dead, and calleth those *things* which be not as though they were. ¹⁸Who against hope believed in hope, that he might become the father of many nations; according to that which was spoken, So shall thy seed be. ¹⁹And being not weak in faith, he considered not his own body now dead, when he was about an hundred year old, neither *yet* the deadness of Sara's womb: ²⁰He staggered not at the promise of God through unbelief; but was strong in faith, giving glory to God; ²¹And being fully persuaded that, what he had promised, he was able also to perform. ²²And therefore it was imputed to him for righteousness. ²³Now it was not written for his sake alone, that it was imputed to him; ²⁴But for us also, to whom it shall be imputed, if we believe on him that raised up Jesus our Lord from the dead; ²⁵Who was delivered for our offences, and was raised *again* for our justification.

[Is. 53:5,6; ch. 3:25; Gal. 1:4; Heb. 9:28; 1 Cor. 15:17; 1 Pet. 1:21]

Results of justification by faith

5 Therefore being justified by faith, we have peace with God through our Lord Jesus Christ: ²By whom also we have access by faith into this grace wherein we stand, and rejoice in hope of the glory of God. ³And not only *so,* but we glory in tribulations also: knowing that tribulation worketh patience; ⁴And patience, experience; and experience, hope: ⁵And hope maketh not ashamed; because the love of God is shed abroad in our hearts by the Holy Ghost which is given unto us. ⁶For when we were yet without strength, in due time Christ died for the ungodly. ⁷For scarcely for a righteous *man* will one die: yet peradventure for a good *man* some would even dare to die. ⁸But God commendeth his love toward us, in that, while we were yet sinners, Christ died for us. ⁹Much more then, being now justified by his blood, we shall be saved from wrath through him. ¹⁰For if, when we were enemies, we were reconciled to God by the death of his Son, much more, being reconciled, we shall be saved by his life. ¹¹And not only *so,* but we also joy in God through our Lord Jesus Christ, by whom we have now received the atonement. [Gal. 4:9]

Christ the basis of our salvation

12 Wherefore, as by one man sin entered into the world, and death by sin; and so death passed upon all men, for that all have sinned: ¹³For until the law sin was in the world: but sin is not imputed when there is no law. ¹⁴Nevertheless death reigned from Adam to Moses, even over them that had not sinned after the similitude of Adam's transgression, who is the figure of *him* that was to come. ¹⁵But not as the offence, so also *is* the free gift. For if through the offence of one be dead, much more the grace of God, and the gift by grace, which is by one man, Jesus Christ, hath abounded unto many. ¹⁶And not as *it was* by one that sinned, *so is* the gift: for the judgment *was* by one to condemnation, but the free gift *is* of many offences unto justification. ¹⁷For if by one man's offence death reigned by one; much more they which receive abundance of grace and of the gift of righteousness shall reign in life by one, Jesus Christ. ¹⁸Therefore as by the offence of one *judgment came* upon all men to condemnation; even so by the righteousness of one *the free gift came* upon all men unto justification of life. ¹⁹For as by one man's disobedience many were made sinners, so by the obedience of one shall many be made righteous. ²⁰Moreover the law entered, that the offence might abound. But where sin abounded, grace did much more abound: ²¹That as sin hath reigned unto death, even so might grace reign through righteousness unto eternal life by Jesus Christ our Lord.

Believers dead to sin

6 What shall we say then? Shall we continue in sin, that grace may abound? ²God forbid. How shall we, that are dead to sin, live

any longer therein? ³Know ye not, that so many of us as were baptized into Jesus Christ were baptized into his death? ⁴Therefore we are buried with him by baptism into death: that like as Christ was raised up from the dead by the glory of the Father, *even* so we also should walk in newness of life. ⁵For if we have been planted together in the likeness of his death, we shall be also *in the likeness* of *his* resurrection: ⁶Knowing this, that our old man is crucified with *him,* that the body of sin might be destroyed, that henceforth we should not serve sin. ⁷For he that is dead is freed from sin. ⁸Now if we be dead with Christ, we believe that we shall also live with him: ⁹Knowing that Christ being raised from the dead dieth no more; death hath no more dominion over him. ¹⁰For in that he died, he died unto sin once: but in that he liveth, he liveth unto God. ¹¹Likewise reckon ye also yourselves to be dead indeed unto sin, but alive unto God through Jesus Christ our Lord. ¹²Let not sin therefore reign in your mortal body, that *ye* should obey it in the lusts thereof. ¹³Neither yield ye your members *as* instruments of unrighteousness unto sin: but yield yourselves unto God, as *those that are* alive from the dead, and your members *as* instruments of righteousness unto God. ¹⁴For sin shall not have dominion over you: for ye are not under the law, but under grace. [ch. 7:4,6; 8:2; Gal. 5:18]

Slaves to righteousness

15 What then? shall we sin, because we are not under the law, but under grace? God forbid. ¹⁶Know ye not, that to whom ye yield yourselves servants to obey, *his* servants ye are to whom ye obey; whether of sin unto death, or of obedience unto righteousness? ¹⁷But God be thanked, that ye were the servants of sin, but ye have obeyed from the heart *that* form of doctrine which was delivered you. ¹⁸Being then made free from sin, ye became the servants of righteousness. ¹⁹I speak after the manner of men because of the infirmity of your flesh: for as ye have yielded your members servants to uncleanness and to iniquity unto iniquity; *even* so now yield your members servants to righteousness unto holiness. ²⁰For when ye were the servants of sin, ye were free from righteousness. ²¹What fruit had ye then *in those things* whereof ye are now ashamed? for the end of those *things is* death. ²²But now being made free from sin, and become servants to God, ye have your fruit unto holiness, and the end everlasting life. ²³For the wages of sin *is* death; but the gift of God *is* eternal life through Jesus Christ our Lord. [Gen. 2:17; ch. 5:12; Jas. 1:15; ch. 2:7; 1 Pet. 1:4]

Married to Christ

7 Know ye not, brethren, (for I speak to them that know the law,) how that the law hath dominion over a man, as long as he liveth? ²For the woman which hath a husband is bound by the law

to *her* husband so long as he liveth; but if the husband be dead, she is loosed from the law of the husband. ³So then if, while *her* husband liveth, she be married to another man, she shall be called an adulteress: but if *her* husband be dead, she is free from *that* law; so that she is no adulteress, though she be married to another man. ⁴Wherefore, my brethren, ye also are become dead to the law by the body of Christ; that ye should be married to another, *even* to him who is raised from the dead, that we should bring forth fruit unto God. ⁵For when we were in the flesh, the motions of sins, which were by the law, did work in our members to bring forth fruit unto death. ⁶But now we are delivered from the law, *that* being dead wherein we were held; that we should serve in newness of spirit, and not *in* the oldness of the letter.

[ch. 2:29; 2 Cor. 3:6]

The Christian struggle

7 What shall we say then? *Is* the law sin? God forbid. Nay, I had not known sin, but by the law: for I had not known lust, except the law had said, Thou shalt not covet. ⁸But sin, taking occasion by the commandment, wrought in me all *manner of* concupiscence. For without the law sin *was* dead. ⁹For I was alive without the law once: but when the commandment came, sin revived, and I died. ¹⁰And the commandment, which was *ordained* to life, I found *to be* unto death. ¹¹For sin, taking occasion by the commandment, deceived me, and by it slew *me.* ¹²Wherefore the law *is* holy, and the commandment holy, and just, and good. ¹³Was then that which is good made death unto me? God forbid. But sin, that it might appear sin, working death in me by that which is good; that sin by the commandment might become exceeding sinful.

14 For we know that the law is spiritual: but I am carnal, sold under sin. ¹⁵For *that* which I do I allow not: for what I would, that do I not; but what I hate, that do I. ¹⁶If then I do that which I would not, I consent unto the law that *it is* good. ¹⁷Now then it is no more I that do it, but sin that dwelleth in me. ¹⁸For I know that in me (that is, in my flesh,) dwelleth no good *thing:* for to will is present with me; but *how* to perform that which is good I find not. ¹⁹For the good that I would I do not: but the evil which I would not, that I do. ²⁰Now if I do that I would not, it is no more I that do it, but sin that dwelleth in me. ²¹I find then a law, that, when I would do good, evil is present with me. ²²For I delight in the law of God after the inward man: ²³But I see another law in my members, warring against the law of my mind, and bringing me into captivity to the law of sin which is in my members. ²⁴O wretched man that I am! who shall deliver me from the body of this death? ²⁵I thank God through Jesus Christ our Lord. So then with the mind I myself serve the law of God; but with the flesh the law of sin. [1 Cor. 15:57]

Life in the Spirit

8 *There is* therefore now no condemnation to them *which are* in Christ Jesus who walk not after the flesh, but after the Spirit. ²For the law of the Spirit of life in Christ Jesus hath made me free from the law of sin and death. ³For what the law could not do, in that it was weak through the flesh, God sending his own Son in the likeness of sinful flesh, and for sin, condemned sin in the flesh: ⁴That the righteousness of the law might be fulfilled in us, who walk not after the flesh, but after the Spirit. ⁵For they that are after the flesh do mind the *things* of the flesh; but they *that are* after the Spirit the *things* of the Spirit. ⁶For to be carnally minded *is* death; but to be spiritually minded *is* life and peace. ⁷Because the carnal mind *is* enmity against God: for it is not subject to the law of God, neither indeed can be. ⁸So then they that are in the flesh cannot please God. ⁹But ye are not in the flesh, but in the Spirit, if so be that the Spirit of God dwell in you. Now if any *man* have not the Spirit of Christ, he is none of his. ¹⁰And if Christ *be* in you, the body *is* dead because of sin; but the Spirit *is* life because of righteousness. ¹¹But if the Spirit of him that raised up Jesus from the dead dwell in you, he that raised up Christ from the dead shall also quicken your mortal bodies by his Spirit that dwelleth in you. [Acts 2:24; 1 Cor. 6:14; 2 Cor. 4:14]

¹² Therefore, brethren, we are debtors, not to the flesh, to live after the flesh. ¹³For if ye live after the flesh, ye shall die: but if ye through the Spirit do mortify the deeds of the body, ye shall live. ¹⁴For as many as are led by the Spirit of God, they are the sons of God. ¹⁵For ye have not received the spirit of bondage again to fear; but ye have received the Spirit of adoption, whereby we cry, Abba, Father. ¹⁶The Spirit itself beareth witness with our spirit, that we are the children of God: ¹⁷And if children, then heirs; heirs of God, and joint-heirs with Christ; if so be that we suffer with *him,* that we may be also glorified together. [Acts 26:18; Phil. 1:29]

The future glory

18 For I reckon that the sufferings of *this* present time *are* not worthy to be compared with the glory which shall be revealed in us. ¹⁹For the earnest expectation of the creature waiteth for the manifestation of the sons of God. ²⁰For the creature was made subject to vanity, not willingly, but by reason of him who hath subjected *the same,* in hope, ²¹Because the creature itself also shall be delivered from the bondage of corruption into the glorious liberty of the children of God. ²²For we know that the whole creation groaneth and travaileth in pain together until now. ²³And not only *they,* but ourselves also, which have the firstfruits of the Spirit, even we ourselves groan within ourselves, waiting for the adoption, *to wit,* the redemption of our body. ²⁴For we are saved by hope: but hope that is seen is not hope: for what a

man seeth, why doth he yet hope for? 25But if we hope for that we see not, *then* do we with patience wait for *it.* 26Likewise the Spirit also helpeth our infirmities: for we know not what we should pray for as we ought: but the Spirit itself maketh intercession for us with groanings which cannot be uttered. 27And he that searcheth the hearts knoweth what *is* the mind of the Spirit, because he maketh intercession for the saints according to *the will of* God. 28And we know that all *things* work together for good to them that love God, to them who are *the* called according to *his* purpose. 29For whom he did foreknow, he also did predestinate *to be* conformed to the image of his Son, that he might be the firstborn amongst many brethren. 30Moreover whom he did predestinate, them he also called: and whom he called, them he also justified: and whom he justified, them he also glorified. 31What shall we then say to these *things?* If God *be* for us, who *can be* against us? 32He that spared not his own Son, but delivered him up for us all, how shall he not with him also freely give us all *things?* 33Who shall lay any thing to the charge of God's elect? *It is* God that justifieth? 34Who *is* he that condemneth? *It is* Christ that died, yea rather, that is risen *again,* who is even at the right hand of God, who also maketh intercession for us. 35Who shall separate us from the love of Christ? *shall* tribulation, or distress, or persecution, or famine, or nakedness, or peril, or sword? 36As it is written, For

thy sake we are killed all the day long; we are accounted as sheep for the slaughter. 37Nay, in all these *things* we are more than conquerors through him that loved us. 38For I am persuaded, that neither death, nor life, nor angels, nor principalities, nor powers, nor *things* present, nor *things* to come, 39Nor height, nor depth, nor any other creature, shall be able to separate us from the love of God, which is in Christ Jesus our Lord.

God's righteousness and mercy

9 I say the truth in Christ, I lie not, my conscience also bearing me witness in the Holy Ghost, 2That I have great heaviness and continual sorrow in my heart. 3For I could wish that myself were accursed from Christ for my brethren, my kinsmen according to the flesh: 4Who are Israelites; to whom pertaineth the adoption, and the glory, and the covenants, and the giving of the law, and the service *of God,* and the promises; 5Whose *are* the fathers, and of whom as concerning the flesh Christ *came,* who is over all, God blessed for ever. Amen. 6Not as though the word of God hath taken none effect. For they *are* not all Israel, which are of Israel: 7Neither, because they are the seed of Abraham, *are they* all children: but, In Isaac shall thy seed be called. 8That is, *They which are* the children of the flesh, these *are* not the children of God: but the children of the promise are counted for the seed. 9For this *is* the word of promise, At this time will I come, and

Sara shall have a son. 10And not only *this;* but when Rebecca also had conceived by one, *even* by our father Isaac; 11(For *the children* being not yet born, neither having done any good or evil, that the purpose of God according to election might stand, not of works, but of him that calleth;) 12It was said unto her, The elder shall serve the younger. 13As it is written, Jacob have I loved, but Esau have I hated. [Mal. 1:2,3; Mat. 10:37]

14 What shall we say then? *Is there* unrighteousness with God? God forbid. 15For he saith to Moses, I will have mercy on whom I will have mercy, and I will have compassion on whom I will have compassion. 16So then *it is* not of him that willeth, nor of him that runneth, but of God that sheweth mercy. 17For the scripture saith unto Pharaoh, Even for this same *purpose* have I raised thee up, that I might shew my power in thee, and that my name might be declared throughout all the earth. 18Therefore hath he mercy on whom he will *have mercy,* and whom he will he hardeneth.

19Thou wilt say then unto me, Why doth he yet find fault? For who hath resisted his will? 20Nay but, O man, who art thou that repliest against God? Shall the thing formed say to him that formed *it,* Why hast thou made me thus? 21Hath not the potter power over the clay, of the same lump to make one vessel unto honour, and another unto dishonour? 22What if God, willing to shew *his* wrath, and to make his power known, endured with much longsuffering *the* vessels of wrath fitted to destruction: 23And that he might make known the riches of his glory on the vessels of mercy, which he had afore prepared unto glory, 24Even us, whom he hath called, not of the Jews only, but also of the Gentiles? 25As he saith also in Osee, I will call *them* my people, which were not my people; and her beloved, which was not beloved. 26And it shall come to pass, *that* in the place where it was said unto them, Ye *are* not my people; there shall they be called the children of the living God. 27Esaias also crieth concerning Israel, Though the number of the children of Israel be as the sand of the sea, a remnant shall be saved: 28For he will finish the work, and cut *it* short in righteousness: because a short work will the Lord make upon the earth. 29And as Esaias said before, Except the Lord of sabaoth had left us a seed, we had been as Sodoma, and been made like unto Gomorrha. [Is. 1:9; Lam. 3:22; Is. 13:19; Jer. 50:40]

The gospel offered to the Jews

30 What shall we say then? That the Gentiles, which followed not *after* righteousness, have attained to righteousness, even the righteousness which is of faith. 31But Israel, which followed *after* the law of righteousness, hath not attained to the law of righteousness. 32Wherefore? Because *they sought it* not by faith, but as *it were* by the works of the law. For they stumbled at *that* stumblingstone; 33As it is written, Behold, I lay in

Sion a stumblingstone and rock of offence: and whosoever believeth on him shall not be ashamed. [Ps. 118:22; Is. 8:14; 28:16; Mat. 21:42; 1 Pet. 2:6-8; ch. 10:11]

10 Brethren, my heart's desire and prayer to God for Israel is, that *they* might be saved. ²For I bear them record that they have a zeal of God, but not according to knowledge. ³For they being ignorant of God's righteousness, and going about to establish their own righteousness, have not submitted themselves unto the righteousness of God. ⁴For Christ *is* the end of the law for righteousness to every one that believeth. ⁵For Moses describeth the righteousness which is of the law, That the man which doeth those *things* shall live by them. ⁶But the righteousness which is of faith speaketh on this wise, Say not in thine heart, Who shall ascend into heaven? (that is, to bring Christ down *from above*:) ⁷Or, Who shall descend into the deep? (that is, to bring up Christ again from the dead.) ⁸But what saith it? The word is nigh thee, *even* in thy mouth, and in thy heart: that is, the word of faith, which we preach; ⁹That if thou shalt confess with thy mouth the Lord Jesus, and shalt believe in thine heart that God hath raised him from the dead, thou shalt be saved. ¹⁰For with the heart *man* believeth unto righteousness; and with the mouth confession is made unto salvation. ¹¹For the scripture saith, Whosoever believeth on him shall not be ashamed. ¹²For there is no differ-

ence between the Jew and the Greek: for the same Lord over all *is* rich unto all that call upon him. ¹³For whosoever shall call upon the name of the Lord shall be saved. ¹⁴How then shall they call on *him* in whom they have not believed? and how shall they believe *in him* of whom they have not heard? and how shall they hear without a preacher? ¹⁵And how shall they preach, except they be sent? as it is written, How beautiful *are* the feet of them that preach the gospel of peace, and bring glad tidings of good *things!* ¹⁶But they have not all obeyed the gospel. For Esaias saith, Lord, who hath believed our report? ¹⁷So then faith *cometh* by hearing, and hearing by the word of God. ¹⁸But I say, Have they not heard? Yes verily, their sound went into all the earth, and their words unto the ends of the world. ¹⁹But I say, Did not Israel know? First Moses saith, I will provoke you to jealousy by *them that are* no people, *and* by a foolish nation I will anger you. ²⁰But Esaias is very bold, and saith, I was found of them that sought me not; I was made manifest unto them that asked not after me. ²¹But to Israel he saith, All day long have I stretched forth my hands unto a disobedient and gainsaying people. [Is. 65:2]

The remnant of Israel

11 I say then, Hath God cast away his people? God forbid. For I also am an Israelite, of the seed of Abraham, *of* the tribe of Benjamin. ²God hath not cast away his people which he foreknew. Wot ye not what the scripture saith of Elias? how he maketh intercession to God against Israel, saying, 3 Lord, they have killed thy prophets, and digged down thine altars; and I am left alone, and they seek my life. 4 But what saith the answer of God unto him? I have reserved to myself seven thousand men, who have not bowed the knee to *the image of* Baal. 5 *Even* so then at *this* present time also there is a remnant according to the election of grace. 6 And if by grace, *then is it* no more of works: otherwise grace is no more grace. But if *it be* of works, *then* is it no more grace: otherwise work is no more work. 7 What then? Israel hath not obtained that which he seeketh for; but the election hath obtained *it,* and the rest were blinded, 8 (According as it is written, God hath given them the spirit of slumber, eyes that *they* should not see, and ears that *they* should not hear;) unto this day. 9 And David saith, Let their table be made a snare, and a trap, and a stumblingblock, and a recompence unto them: 10 Let their eyes be darkened, that *they* may not see, and bow down their back alway.

[Ps. 69:23]

Israel's future salvation

11 I say then, Have they stumbled that they should fall? God forbid: but *rather* through their fall salvation *is* come unto the Gentiles, for to provoke them to jealousy. 12 Now if the fall of them *be* the riches of the world, and the diminishing of them the riches of the Gentiles; how much more their fulness? 13 For I speak to you Gentiles, inasmuch as I am the apostle of the Gentiles, I magnify mine office: 14 If by any means I may provoke to emulation *them which are* my flesh, and might save some of them. 15 For if the casting away of them *be* the reconciling of the world, what *shall* the receiving *of them be,* but life from the dead? 16 For if the firstfruit *be* holy, the lump *is* also *holy:* and if the root *be* holy, so *are* the branches. 17 And if some of the branches be broken off, and thou, being a wild olive tree, wert graffed in amongst them, and with *them* partakest of the root and fatness of the olive tree; 18 Boast not against the branches: but if thou boast, thou bearest not the root, but the root thee. 19 Thou wilt say then, The branches were broken off, that I might be graffed in. 20 Well; because of unbelief they were broken off, and thou standest by faith. Be not high-minded, but fear: 21 For if God spared not the natural branches, *take heed* lest he also spare not thee. 22 Behold therefore the goodness and severity of God: on them which fell, severity; but toward thee, goodness, if thou continue in *his* goodness: otherwise thou also shalt be cut off. 23 And they also, if they bide not still in unbelief, shall be graffed in: for God is able to graff them in again. 24 For if thou wert cut out of the olive tree which is wild by nature, and wert graffed contrary to nature into a good olive tree: how much

more shall these, which be the natural *branches,* be graffed into their own olive tree?

25 For I would not, brethren, that ye should be ignorant of this mystery, lest ye should be wise in your own conceits; that blindness in part is happened to Israel, until the fulness of the Gentiles be come in. 26 And so all Israel shall be saved: as it is written, There shall come out of Sion the Deliverer, and shall turn away ungodliness from Jacob: 27 For this *is* my covenant unto them, when I shall take away their sins. 28 As concerning the gospel, *they are* enemies for your sakes: but as touching the election, *they are* beloved for the fathers' sakes. 29 For the gifts and calling of God *are* without repentance. 30 For as ye in times past have not believed God, yet have now obtained mercy through their unbelief: 31 *Even* so have these also now not believed, that through your mercy they also may obtain mercy. 32 For God hath concluded *them* all in unbelief, that he might have mercy upon all. [ch. 3:9]

33 O the depth of the riches both of the wisdom and knowledge of God! how unsearchable *are* his judgments, and his ways past finding out! 34 For who hath known the mind of the Lord? or who hath been his counseller? 35 Or who hath first given to him, and it shall be recompensed unto him *again?* 36 For of him, and through him, and to him, *are* all *things:* to whom *be* glory for ever. Amen. [Col. 1:16; Heb. 13:21; Rev. 1:6]

Christian conduct

12 I beseech you therefore, brethren, by the mercies of God, that *ye* present your bodies a living sacrifice, holy, acceptable unto God, *which is* your reasonable service. 2 And be not conformed to this world: but be ye transformed by the renewing of your mind, that ye may prove what *is that* good, and acceptable, and perfect, will of God. 3 For I say, through the grace given unto me, to every *man* that is among you, not to think *of himself* more highly than he ought to think; but to think soberly, according as God hath dealt to every man the measure of faith. 4 For as we have many members in one body, and all members have not the same office: 5 So we, being many, are one body in Christ, and every one members one of another. 6 Having then gifts differing according to the grace that is given to us, whether prophecy, *let us prophesy* according to the proportion of faith; 7 Or ministry, *let us wait* on *our* ministering: or he that teacheth, on teaching; 8 Or he that exhorteth, on exhortation: he that giveth, *let him do it* with simplicity; he that ruleth, with diligence; he that sheweth mercy, with cheerfulness. [Acts 15:32; Mat. 6:1-3; Acts 20:28; 2 Cor. 9:7]

9 *Let* love *be* without dissimulation. Abhor *that which is* evil; cleave to *that which is* good. 10 *Be* kindly affectioned one to another with brotherly love; in honour preferring one another; 11 Not slothful in business; fervent in spirit; serving the Lord; 12 Rejoicing in hope;

patient in tribulation; continuing instant in prayer; 13Distributing to the necessity of saints; given to hospitality. 14Bless them which persecute you: bless, and curse not. 15Rejoice with them that do rejoice, and weep with them that weep. 16Be of the same mind one towards another. Mind not high things, but condescend to men of low estate. Be not wise in your own conceits. 17Recompense to no man evil for evil. Provide things honest in the sight of all men. 18If it be possible, as much as lieth in you, live peaceably with all men. 19Dearly beloved, avenge not yourselves, but rather give place unto wrath: for it is written, Vengeance is mine; I will repay, saith the Lord. 20Therefore if thine enemy hunger, feed him; if he thirst, give him drink: for in so doing thou shalt heap coals of fire on his head. 21Be not overcome of evil, but overcome evil with good.

13 Let every soul be subject unto the higher powers. For there is no power but of God: the powers that be are ordained of God. 2Whosoever therefore resisteth the power, resisteth the ordinance of God: and they that resist shall receive to themselves damnation. 3For rulers are not a terror to good works, but to the evil. Wilt thou then not be afraid of the power? do that which is good, and thou shalt have praise of the same: 4For he is the minister of God to thee for good. But if thou do that which is evil, be afraid; for he beareth not the sword in vain: for he is the minister of God, a re-

venger to execute wrath upon him that doeth evil. 5Wherefore ye must needs be subject, not only for wrath, but also for conscience sake. 6For for this cause pay you tribute also: for they are God's ministers, attending continually upon this very thing. 7Render therefore to all their dues: tribute to whom tribute is due; custom to whom custom; fear to whom fear; honour to whom honour. 8Owe no man any thing, but to love one another: for he that loveth another hath fulfilled the law. 9For this, Thou shalt not commit adultery, Thou shalt not kill, Thou shalt not steal, Thou shalt not bear false witness, Thou shalt not covet; and if there be any other commandment, it is briefly comprehended in this saying, namely, Thou shalt love thy neighbour as thyself. 10Love worketh no ill to his neighbour: therefore love is the fulfilling of the law. [Mat. 22:40]

11 And that, knowing the time, that now it is high time to awake out of sleep: for now is our salvation nearer than when we believed. 12The night is far spent, the day is at hand: let us therefore cast off the works of darkness, and let us put on the armour of light. 13Let us walk honestly, as in the day; not in rioting and drunkenness, not in chambering and wantonness, not in strife and envying. 14But put ye on the Lord Jesus Christ, and make not provision for the flesh, to fulfil the lusts thereof. [Gal. 3:27; Eph. 4:24; Gal. 5:16]

The weak and the strong

14 Him that is weak in the faith receive you, *but* not to doubtful disputations. ²For one believeth that *he* may eat all *things:* another, who is weak, eateth herbs. ³Let not him that eateth despise him that eateth not; and let not him which eateth not judge him that eateth: for God hath received him. ⁴Who art thou that judgest another *man's* servant? to his own master he standeth or falleth. Yea, he shall be holden up: for God is able to make him stand. ⁵One man esteemeth one day above another: another esteemeth every day *alike.* Let every man be fully persuaded in his own mind. ⁶He that regardeth the day, regardeth *it* unto the Lord; and he that regardeth not the day, to the Lord he doth not regard *it.* He that eateth, eateth to the Lord, for he giveth God thanks; and he that eateth not, to the Lord he eateth not, and giveth God thanks. ⁷For none of us liveth to himself, and no *man* dieth to himself. ⁸For whether we live, we live unto the Lord; and whether we die, we die unto the Lord: whether we live therefore, or die, we are the Lord's. ⁹For to this end Christ both died, and rose, and revived, that he might be Lord both of the dead and living. [2 Cor. 5:15; Acts 10:36]

10 But why dost thou judge thy brother? or why dost thou set at nought thy brother? for we shall all stand before the judgment seat of Christ. ¹¹For it is written, *As* I live, saith the Lord, every knee shall bow to me, and every tongue shall confess to God. ¹²So then every one of us shall give account of himself to God. ¹³Let us not therefore judge one another any more: but judge this rather, that no *man* put a stumblingblock or an occasion to fall in *his* brother's way. ¹⁴I know, and am persuaded by the Lord Jesus, that *there is* nothing unclean of itself: but to him that esteemeth any *thing* to be unclean, to him *it is* unclean. ¹⁵But if thy brother be grieved with *thy* meat, now walkest thou not charitably. Destroy not him with thy meat, for whom Christ died. ¹⁶Let not then your good be evil spoken of: ¹⁷For the kingdom of God is not meat and drink; but righteousness, and peace, and joy in the Holy Ghost. ¹⁸For he that in these *things* serveth Christ *is* acceptable to God, and approved of men. ¹⁹Let us therefore follow *after* the *things* which make for peace, and *things* wherewith one may edify another. ²⁰For meat destroy not the work of God. All *things* indeed *are* pure; but *it is* evil for *that* man who eateth with offence. ²¹*It is* good neither to eat flesh, nor to drink wine, nor *any thing* whereby thy brother stumbleth, or is offended, or is *made* weak. ²²Hast thou faith? have *it* to thyself before God. Happy *is* he that condemneth not himself in *that thing* which he alloweth. ²³And he that doubteth is damned if he eat, because *he eateth* not of faith: for whatsoever *is* not of faith is sin. [Tit. 1:15]

15 We then that are strong ought to bear the infirmities of the weak, and not to please ourselves. ²Let every one of us please *his* neighbour for *his* good to edification. ³For even Christ pleased not himself; but, as it is written, The reproaches of them that reproached thee fell on me. ⁴For whatsoever *things* were written aforetime were written for our learning, that we through patience and comfort of the scriptures might have hope. ⁵Now the God of patience and consolation grant you to be likeminded one towards another according to Christ Jesus: ⁶That ye may with one mind *and* one mouth glorify God, even the Father of our Lord Jesus Christ. ⁷Wherefore receive ye one another, as Christ also received us, to the glory of God. ⁸Now I say that Jesus Christ was a minister of the circumcision for the truth of God, to confirm the promises made unto the fathers: ⁹And that the Gentiles might glorify God for *his* mercy; as it is written, For this cause I will confess to thee among the Gentiles, and sing unto thy name. ¹⁰And again *he* saith, Rejoice, *ye* Gentiles, with his people. ¹¹And again, Praise the Lord, all ye Gentiles; and laud him, all ye people. ¹²And again Esaias saith, There shall be a root of Jesse, and he that *shall* rise to reign over the Gentiles; in him shall the Gentiles trust. ¹³Now the God of hope fill you with all joy and peace in believing, that ye may abound in hope, through the power of the Holy Ghost. [ch. 12:12]

Paul's reason for writing

14 And I myself also am persuaded of you, my brethren, that ye also are full of goodness, filled with all knowledge, able also to admonish one another. ¹⁵Nevertheless, brethren, I have written the more boldly unto you in some sort, as putting you in mind, because of the grace that is given to me of God, ¹⁶That I should be the minister of Jesus Christ to the Gentiles, ministering the gospel of God, that the offering up of the Gentiles might be acceptable, being sanctified by the Holy Ghost. ¹⁷I have therefore whereof *I* may glory through Jesus Christ *in those things* which pertain to God. ¹⁸For I will not dare to speak of any of *those things* which Christ hath not wrought by me, to make the Gentiles obedient, by word and deed, ¹⁹Through mighty signs and wonders, by the power of the Spirit of God; so that from Jerusalem, and round about unto Illyricum, I have fully preached the gospel of Christ. ²⁰Yea, so have I strived to preach the gospel, not where Christ was named, lest I should build upon another *man's* foundation: ²¹But as it is written, To whom he was not spoken of, they shall see: and they that have not heard shall understand. [Is. 52:15]

Paul's future plans

22 For which cause also I have been much hindered from coming to you. ²³But now having no more place in these parts, and having a great desire these many years to come unto you; ²⁴Whensoever I take my journey into Spain, I will come to you: for I trust to see you in my journey, and to be brought on my way thitherward by you, if first I be somewhat filled with your *company.* 25But now I go unto Jerusalem to minister unto the saints. 26For it hath pleased *them of* Macedonia and Achaia to make a certain contribution for the poor saints which are at Jerusalem. 27It hath pleased them verily; and their debtors they are. For if the Gentiles have been made partakers of their spiritual *things,* their duty is also to minister unto them in carnal *things.* 28When therefore I have performed this, and have sealed to them this fruit, I will come by you into Spain. 29And I am sure that, when I come unto you, I shall come in the fulness of the blessing of the gospel of Christ. 30Now I beseech you, brethren, for the Lord Jesus Christ's sake, and for the love of the Spirit, that *ye* strive together with me in *your* prayers to God for me; 31That I may be delivered from them that do not believe in Judea; and that my service which I have for Jerusalem may be accepted of the saints; 32That I may come unto you with joy by the will of God, and may with you be refreshed. 33Now the God of peace *be* with you all. Amen. [ch. 16:20; 1 Cor. 14:33; 2 Cor. 13:11; Phil. 4:9; 1 Thes. 5:23; 2 Thes. 3:16; Heb. 13:20]

Commendations and greetings

16 I commend unto you Phebe our sister, which is a servant of the church which is at Cenchrea: 2That ye receive her in the Lord, as becometh saints, and *that* ye assist her in whatsoever

business she hath need of you: for she hath been a succourer of many, and of myself *also.* 3Greet Priscilla and Aquila my helpers in Christ Jesus: 4Who have for my life laid down their own necks: unto whom not only I give thanks, but also all the churches of the Gentiles. 5Likewise *greet* the church that is in their house. Salute my well-beloved Epenetus, who is the first-fruits of Achaia unto Christ. 6Greet Mary, who bestowed much labour on us. 7Salute Andronicus and Junia, my kinsmen, and my fellow-prisoners, who are of note among the apostles, who also were in Christ before me. 8Greet Amplias my beloved in the Lord. 9Salute Urban our helper in Christ, and Stachys my beloved. 10Salute Apelles approved in Christ. Salute them which are of Aristobulus' *household.* 11Salute Herodion my kinsman. Greet them that be of the *household* of Narcissus, which are in the Lord. 12Salute Tryphena and Tryphosa, who labour in the Lord. Salute the beloved Persis, which laboured much in the Lord. 13Salute Rufus chosen in the Lord, and his mother and mine. 14Salute Asyncritus, Phlegon, Hermas, Patrobas, Hermes, and the brethren which are with them. 15Salute Philologus, and Julia, Nereus, and his sister, and Olympas, and all the saints which are with them. 16Salute one another with a holy kiss. The churches of Christ salute you. [1 Cor. 16:20; 2 Cor. 13:12]

17 Now I beseech you, brethren, mark them which cause divisions and offences contrary to the

doctrine which ye have learned; and avoid them. 18For *they that are* such serve not our Lord Jesus Christ, but their own belly; and by good words and fair speeches deceive the hearts of the simple. 19For your obedience is come abroad unto all *men.* I am glad therefore on your behalf: but *yet* I would have you wise unto *that which is* good, and simple concerning evil. 20And the God of peace shall bruise Satan under your feet shortly. The grace of our Lord Jesus Christ *be* with you. Amen. [ch. 15:33; Gen. 3:15; 1 Cor. 16:23]

21 Timotheus my workfellow, and Lucius, and Jason, and Sosipater, my kinsmen, salute you. 22I Tertius, who wrote *this* epistle, salute you in the Lord. 23Gaius mine host, and of the whole church, saluteth you. Erastus the chamberlain of the city saluteth you, and Quartus a brother. 24The grace of our Lord Jesus Christ *be* with you all. Amen. [1 Thes. 5:28]

25 Now to him that is of power to stablish you according to my gospel, and the preaching of Jesus Christ, according to the revelation of the mystery, which was kept secret since the world began, 26But now is made manifest, and by the scriptures of the prophets, according to the commandment of the everlasting God, made known to all nations for the obedience of faith: 27To God only wise, *be* glory through Jesus Christ for ever. Amen. [Jude 25]

¶ Written to the Romans from Corinthus, *and sent* by Phebe servant of the church at Cenchrea.

The First Epistle of Paul the Apostle to the

Corinthians

Paul's thanksgiving

1 Paul, called *to be* an apostle of Jesus Christ through the will of God, and Sosthenes *our* brother, 2Unto the church of God which is at Corinth, to them that are sanctified in Christ Jesus, called *to be* saints, with all that in every place call upon the name of Jesus Christ our Lord, both theirs and ours: 3Grace *be* unto you, and peace, from God our Father, and *from* the Lord Jesus Christ. [Rom. 1:7; 2 Cor. 1:2]

4 I thank my God always on your behalf, for the grace of God which is given you by Jesus Christ; 5That in every *thing* ye are enriched by him, in all utterance, and *in* all knowledge; 6Even as the testimony of Christ was confirmed in you: 7So that ye come behind in no gift; waiting for the coming of our Lord Jesus Christ: 8Who shall also confirm you unto the end, *that ye may be* blameless in the day of our Lord Jesus Christ. 9God *is* faithful, by whom ye were called unto the fellowship of his Son Jesus Christ our Lord. [Is. 49:7; 1 Thes. 5:24; John 15:4]

An appeal for unity

10 Now I beseech you, brethren, by the name of our Lord Jesus Christ, that ye all speak the same *thing*, and *that* there be no divisions among you; but *that* ye be perfectly joined together in the same mind and in the same judgment. 11For it hath been declared unto me of you, my brethren, by them which are of the *house* of Chloe, that there are contentions among you. 12Now this I say, that every one of you saith, I am of Paul; and I of Apollos; and I of Cephas; and I of Christ. 13Is Christ divided? was Paul crucified for you? or were ye baptized in the name of Paul? 14I thank God that I baptized none of you, but Crispus and Gaius; 15Lest any should say that I had baptized in mine own name. 16And I baptized also the household of Stephanas: besides, I know not whether I baptized any other. [ch. 16:15]

Christ, God's power and wisdom

17 For Christ sent me not to baptize, but to preach the gospel: not with wisdom of words, lest the cross of Christ should be made of none effect. 18For the preaching of the cross is to them that perish foolishness; but unto us which are saved it is the power of God. 19For it is written, I will destroy the wisdom of the wise, and will bring to nothing the understanding of the prudent. 20Where *is* the wise? where *is* the scribe? where *is* the disputer of this world? hath not God made foolish the wisdom of this world? 21For after that in the wisdom of God the world by wisdom knew not God, it pleased God by the foolishness of preaching to save them that believe. 22For the Jews require a sign, and the Greeks seek after wisdom: 23But we preach Christ crucified, unto the Jews a stumblingblock, and unto the Greeks foolishness; 24But unto them which are called, both Jews

and Greeks, Christ the power of God, and the wisdom of God. 25Because the foolishness of God is wiser than men; and the weakness of God is stronger than men. 26For ye see your calling, brethren, how that not many wise *men* after the flesh, not many mighty, not many noble, *are called:* 27But God hath chosen the foolish *things* of the world to confound the wise; and God hath chosen the weak *things* of the world to confound the *things which are* mighty; 28And base *things* of the world, and *things* which are despised, hath God chosen, *yea,* and *things* which are not, to bring to nought *things* that are: 29That no flesh should glory in his presence. 30But of him are ye in Christ Jesus, who of God is made unto us wisdom, and righteousness, and sanctification, and redemption: 31That, according as it is written, He that glorieth, let him glory in the Lord. [Jer. 9:23]

2 And I, brethren, when I came to you, came not with excellency of speech or of wisdom, declaring unto you the testimony of God. 2For I determined not to know any *thing* among you, save Jesus Christ, and him crucified. 3And I was with you in weakness, and in fear, and in much trembling. 4And my speech and my preaching *was* not with enticing words of man's wisdom, but in demonstration of the Spirit and of power: 5That your faith should not stand in the wisdom of men, but in the power of God. [2 Cor. 4:7]

True wisdom the gift of God
6 Howbeit we speak wisdom among *them that are* perfect: yet not the wisdom of this world, nor of the princes of this world, that come to nought: 7But we speak the wisdom of God in a mystery, *even* the hidden *wisdom,* which God ordained before the world unto our glory: 8Which none of the princes of this world knew: for had they known *it,* they would not have crucified the Lord of glory. 9But as it is written, Eye hath not seen, nor ear heard, neither have entered into the heart of man, *the things* which God hath prepared for them that love him. 10But God hath revealed *them* unto us by his Spirit: for the Spirit searcheth all *things,* yea, the deep things of God. 11For what man knoweth the *things* of a man, save the spirit of man which is in him? even so the *things* of God knoweth no *man,* but the Spirit of God. 12Now we have received, not the spirit of the world, but the Spirit which is of God; that we might know the *things* that are freely given to us of God. 13Which *things* also we speak, not in the words which man's wisdom teacheth, but which the Holy Ghost teacheth; comparing spiritual *things* with spiritual. 14But the natural man receiveth not the *things* of the Spirit of God: for they are foolishness unto him: neither can he know *them,* because they are spiritually discerned. 15But he that is spiritual judgeth all *things,* yet he himself is judged of no *man.* 16For who hath known the mind of the Lord, that he may instruct him? But we have the mind of Christ. [Job 15:8; John 15:15]

Fellow labourers for God

3 And I, brethren, could not speak unto you as unto spiritual, but as unto carnal, *even* as unto babes in Christ. ²I have fed you with milk, and not with meat: for hitherto ye were not able *to bear it,* neither yet now are ye able. ³For ye are yet carnal: for whereas *there is* among you envying, and strife, and divisions, are ye not carnal, and walk as men? ⁴For while one saith, I am of Paul; and another, I *am* of Apollos; are ye not carnal?

5 Who then is Paul, and who *is* Apollos, but ministers by whom ye believed, even as the Lord gave to every man? ⁶I have planted, Apollos watered; but God gave the increase. ⁷So then neither is he that planteth any *thing,* neither he that watereth; but God that giveth the increase. ⁸Now he that planteth and he that watereth are one: and every man shall receive his own reward according to his own labour. ⁹For we are labourers together with God: ye are God's husbandry, *ye are* God's building. ¹⁰According to the grace of God which is given unto me, as a wise masterbuilder, I have laid the foundation, and another buildeth thereon. But let every man take heed how he buildeth thereupon. ¹¹For other foundation can no *man* lay than that is laid, which is Jesus Christ. ¹²Now if any *man* build upon this foundation gold, silver, precious stones, wood, hay, stubble; ¹³Every man's work shall be made manifest: for the day shall declare *it,* because it shall be revealed by fire; and the fire shall try

every man's work of what sort it is. ¹⁴If any *man's* work abide which he hath built thereupon, he shall receive a reward. ¹⁵If any *man's* work shall be burnt, he shall suffer loss: but he himself shall be saved; yet so as by fire. ¹⁶Know ye not that ye are the temple of God, and *that* the Spirit of God dwelleth in you? ¹⁷If any *man* defile the temple of God, him shall God destroy; for the temple of God is holy, which *temple* ye are. ¹⁸Let no *man* deceive himself. If any *man* among you seemeth to be wise in this world, let him become a fool, that he may be wise. ¹⁹For the wisdom of this world is foolishness with God. For it is written, He taketh the wise in their own craftiness. ²⁰And again, The Lord knoweth the thoughts of the wise, that they are vain. ²¹Therefore let no *man* glory in men. For all *things* are yours; ²²Whether Paul, or Apollos, or Cephas, or the world, or life, or death, or *things* present, or *things* to come; all are yours; ²³And ye *are* Christ's; and Christ *is* God's. [Rom. 14:8; 2 Cor. 10:7; Gal. 3:29]

Apostles of Christ

4 Let a man so account of us, as of the ministers of Christ, and stewards of the mysteries of God. ²Moreover it is required in stewards, that a man be found faithful. ³But with me it is a very small *thing* that I should be judged of you, or of man's judgment: yea, I judge not mine own self. ⁴For I know nothing by myself; yet am I not hereby justified: but he that judgeth me is the Lord. ⁵Therefore judge nothing before the time, until the Lord come, who both will bring to light the hidden *things* of darkness, and will make manifest the counsels of the hearts: and then shall every man have praise of God. [Mat. 7:1; Rom. 2:1; Rev. 20:12; Rom. 2:29; 2 Cor. 5:10]

6 And these *things,* brethren, I have in a figure transferred to myself and *to* Apollos for your sakes; that ye might learn in us not to think *of men* above *that* which is written, that no one of you be puffed up for one against another. ⁷For who maketh thee to differ *from another?* and what hast thou that thou didst not receive? now if thou didst receive *it,* why dost thou glory, as if thou hadst not received *it?* ⁸Now ye are full, now ye are rich, ye have reigned as kings without us: and I would *to God* ye did reign, that we also might reign with you. ⁹For I think that God hath set forth us the apostles last, as *it were* appointed to death: for we are made a spectacle unto the world, and to angels, and to men. ¹⁰We *are* fools for Christ's sake, but ye *are* wise in Christ; we *are* weak, but ye *are* strong; ye *are* honourable, but we *are* despised. ¹¹Even unto this present hour we both hunger, and thirst, and are naked, and are buffeted, and have no certain dwelling place; ¹²And labour, working with our own hands: being reviled, we bless; being persecuted, we suffer *it:* ¹³Being defamed, we intreat: we are made as the filth of the world, *and are* the offscouring of all *things* unto this day. ¹⁴I write not these *things* to shame you, but as my beloved sons I warn *you.* ¹⁵For

though you have ten thousand instructors in Christ, yet *have ye* not many fathers: for in Christ Jesus I have begotten you through the gospel. ¹⁶Wherefore I beseech you, be ye followers of me. ¹⁷For this cause have I sent unto you Timotheus, who is my beloved son, and faithful in the Lord, who shall bring you into remembrance of my ways which be in Christ, as I teach every where in every church. ¹⁸Now some are puffed up, as though I would not come to you. ¹⁹But I will come to you shortly, if the Lord will, and will know, not the speech of them which are puffed up, but the power. ²⁰For the kingdom of God *is* not in word, but in power. ²¹What will ye? shall I come unto you with a rod, or in love, and *in* the spirit of meekness? [2 Cor. 10:2]

Judgment of the immoral

5 It is reported commonly *that there is* fornication among you, and such fornication as is not so much as named amongst the Gentiles, that one should have *his* father's wife. ²And ye are puffed up, and have not rather mourned, that he that hath done this deed might be taken away from among you. ³For I verily, as absent in body, but present in spirit, have judged already, as though I were present, *concerning* him that hath so done this *deed,* ⁴In the name of our Lord Jesus Christ, when ye are gathered together, and my spirit, with the power of our Lord Jesus Christ, ⁵To deliver such a one unto Satan for the destruction of the flesh, that the spirit may be saved

in the day of the Lord Jesus. 6Your glorying *is* not good. Know ye not that a little leaven leaveneth the whole lump? 7Purge out therefore the old leaven, that ye may be a new lump, as ye are unleavened. For even Christ our passover is sacrificed for us: 8Therefore let us keep the feast, not with old leaven, neither with the leaven of malice and wickedness; but with the unleavened bread of sincerity and truth. [Ex. 12:15; Deut. 16:3; Mat. 16:6; Mark 8:15; Luke 12:1]

9 I wrote unto you in an epistle not to company with fornicators: 10Yet not altogether with the fornicators of this world, or with the covetous, or extortioners, or with idolaters; for then must ye needs go out of the world. 11But now I have written unto you not to keep company, if any *man that is* called a brother be a fornicator, or covetous, or an idolater, or a railer, or a drunkard, or an extortioner; with such a one no not to eat. 12For what have I to do to judge them also that are without? do not ye judge them that are within? 13But them that are without God judgeth. Therefore put away from among yourselves *that* wicked *person.* [Deut. 13:5]

Lawsuits among brethren

6 Dare any of you, having a matter against another, go to law before the unjust, and not before the saints? 2Do ye not know that the saints shall judge the world? and if the world shall be judged by you, are ye unworthy to judge the smallest matters? 3Know ye not

that we shall judge angels? how much more *things* that pertain to *this* life? 4If then ye have judgments *of things* pertaining to *this* life, set them to judge who are least esteemed in the church. 5I speak to your shame. Is it so, that there is not a wise *man* amongst you? no, not one that shall be able to judge between his brethren? 6But brother goeth to law with brother, and that before the unbelievers. 7Now therefore there is utterly a fault among you, because ye go to law one with another. Why do ye not rather take wrong? why do ye not rather *suffer yourselves to* be defrauded? 8Nay, you do wrong, and defraud, and that *your* brethren. 9Know ye not that the unrighteous shall not inherit the kingdom of God? Be not deceived: neither fornicators, nor idolaters, nor adulterers, nor effeminate, nor abusers of themselves with mankind, 10Nor thieves, nor covetous, nor drunkards, nor revilers, nor extortioners, shall inherit the kingdom of God. 11And such were some of you: but ye are washed, but ye are sanctified, but ye are justified in the name of the Lord Jesus, and by the Spirit of our God. [ch. 12:2; Heb. 10:22]

God to be glorified in the body

12 All *things* are lawful unto me, but all *things* are not expedient: all *things* are lawful for me, but I will not be brought under the power of any. 13Meats for the belly, and the belly for meats: but God shall destroy both it and them. Now the body *is* not for fornica-

tion, but for the Lord; and the Lord for the body. ¹⁴And God hath both raised up the Lord, and will *also* raise up us by his own power. ¹⁵Know ye not that your bodies are the members of Christ? shall I then take the members of Christ, and make *them* the members of a harlot? God forbid. ¹⁶What? know ye not that he which is joined to a harlot is one body? for two, saith *he,* shall be one flesh. ¹⁷But he that is joined unto the Lord is one spirit. ¹⁸Flee fornication. Every sin that a man doeth is without the body; but he that committeth fornication sinneth against his own body. ¹⁹What? know ye not that your body is the temple of the Holy Ghost which is in you, which ye have of God, and ye are not your own? ²⁰For ye are bought with a price: therefore glorify God in your body, and in your spirit, which are God's. [Acts 20:28; Gal. 3:13; Heb. 9:12; 1 Pet. 1:18; 2 Pet. 2:1; Rev. 5:9]

Marriage

7 Now concerning *the things* whereof ye wrote unto me: *It is* good for a man not to touch a woman. ²Nevertheless, to avoid fornication, let every man have his own wife, and let every woman have her own husband. ³Let the husband render unto the wife due benevolence: and likewise also the wife unto the husband. ⁴The wife hath not power of her own body, but the husband: and likewise also the husband hath not power of his own body, but the wife. ⁵Defraud you not one the other, except *it be* with consent for a time, that ye may give yourselves to fasting and prayer, and come together again, that Satan tempt you not for your incontinency. ⁶But I speak this by permission, *and* not of commandment. ⁷For I would that all men were even as I myself. But every man hath his proper gift of God, one after this manner, and another after that. [Acts 26:29; ch. 9:5; ch. 12:11]

8 I say therefore to the unmarried and widows, It is good for them if they abide even as I. ⁹But if they cannot contain, let them marry: for it is better to marry than to burn. ¹⁰And unto the married I command, *yet* not I, but the Lord, Let not the wife depart from *her* husband: ¹¹But and if she depart, let her remain unmarried, or be reconciled to *her* husband: and let not the husband put away *his* wife. ¹²But to the rest speak I, not the Lord: If any brother hath a wife that believeth not, and she be pleased to dwell with him, let him not put her away. ¹³And the woman which hath a husband that believeth not, and *if* he be pleased to dwell with her, let her not leave him. ¹⁴For the unbelieving husband is sanctified by the wife, and the unbelieving wife is sanctified by the husband: else were your children unclean; but now are they holy. ¹⁵But if the unbelieving depart, let him depart. A brother or a sister is not under bondage in such *cases:* but God hath called us to peace. ¹⁶For what knowest thou, O wife, whether thou shalt save *thy* husband? or how knowest thou, O man, whether thou shalt save *thy* wife? ¹⁷But as God hath

distributed to every man, as the Lord hath called every one, so let him walk. And so ordain I in all churches. ¹⁸Is any *man* called being circumcised? let him not become uncircumcised. Is any called in uncircumcision? let him not be circumcised. ¹⁹Circumcision is nothing, and uncircumcision is nothing, but the keeping of the commandments of God. ²⁰Let every man abide in the same calling wherein he was called. ²¹Art thou called *being* a servant? care not for it: but if thou mayest be made free, use *it* rather. ²²For he that is called in the Lord, *being* a servant, is the Lord's freeman: likewise also he that is called, *being* free, is Christ's servant. ²³Ye are bought with a price; be not ye the servants of men. ²⁴Brethren, let every man, wherein he is called, therein abide with God.

25 Now concerning virgins I have no commandment of the Lord: yet I give *my* judgment, as one that hath obtained mercy of the Lord to be faithful. ²⁶I suppose therefore that this is good for the present distress, *I say,* that *it is* good for a man so to be. ²⁷Art thou bound unto a wife? seek not to be loosed. Art thou loosed from a wife? seek not a wife. ²⁸But and if thou marry, thou hast not sinned; and if a virgin marry, she hath not sinned. Nevertheless such shall have trouble in the flesh: but I spare you. ²⁹But this I say, brethren, the time *is* short: it remaineth, that both they that have wives be as though they had none; ³⁰And they that weep, as though they wept not; and they that re-

joice, as though they rejoiced not; and they that buy, as though they possessed not; ³¹And they that use this world, as not abusing *it:* for the fashion of this world passeth away. ³²But I would have you without carefulness. He *that is* unmarried careth for the *things* that belong to the Lord, how he may please the Lord: ³³But he that is married careth for the *things that are* of the world, how he may please *his* wife. ³⁴There is difference *also* between a wife and a virgin. The unmarried *woman* careth for the *things* of the Lord, that she may be holy both in body and in spirit: but she that is married careth for the *things* of the world, how she may please *her* husband. ³⁵And this I speak for your own profit; not that I may cast a snare upon you, but for *that which is* comely, and that you may attend upon the Lord without distraction. ³⁶But if any *man* think that he behaveth himself uncomely toward his virgin, if she pass the flower of *her* age, and need so require, let him do what he will, he sinneth not: let them marry. ³⁷Nevertheless he that standeth stedfast in *his* heart, having no necessity, but hath power over his own will, and hath so decreed in his heart that *he* will keep his virgin, doeth well. ³⁸So then he that giveth *her* in marriage doeth well; but he that giveth *her* not in marriage doeth better. [Heb. 13:4]

39 The wife is bound by the law as long as her husband liveth; but if her husband be dead, she is at liberty to be married to whom she will; only in the Lord. ⁴⁰But she is

happier if she so abide, after my judgment: and I think also that *I* have the Spirit of God. [ver. 25; 1 Thes. 4:8]

Food offered to idols

8 Now as touching things offered unto idols, we know that we all have knowledge. Knowledge puffeth up, but charity edifieth. ²And if any *man* think that *he* knoweth any *thing,* he knoweth nothing yet as he ought to know. ³But if any *man* love God, the same is known of him. ⁴As concerning therefore the eating of those things that are offered in sacrifice unto idols, we know that an idol *is* nothing in the world, and that *there is* none other God but one. ⁵For though there be that are called gods, whether in heaven or in earth, (as there be gods many, and lords many,) ⁶But to us *there is but* one God, the Father, of whom *are* all *things,* and we in him; and one Lord Jesus Christ, by whom *are* all *things,* and we by him. ⁷Howbeit *there is* not in every *man that* knowledge: for some with conscience of the idol unto this hour, eat *it* as a thing offered unto an idol; and their conscience being weak is defiled. ⁸But meat commendeth us not to God: for neither, if we eat, are we the better; neither, if we eat not, are we the worse. ⁹But take heed lest by any means this liberty of yours become a stumblingblock to them that are weak. ¹⁰For if any *man* see thee which hast knowledge sit at meat in the idol's temple, shall not the conscience of him which is weak

be emboldened to eat those things which are offered to idols; ¹¹And through thy knowledge shall the weak brother perish, for whom Christ died? ¹²But when ye sin so against the brethren, and wound their weak conscience, ye sin against Christ. ¹³Wherefore, if meat make my brother to offend, I will eat no flesh while the world standeth, lest I make my brother to offend. [Rom. 14:21; 2 Cor. 11:29]

Christian rights

9 Am I not an apostle? am I not free? have I not seen Jesus Christ our Lord? are not you my work in the Lord? ²If I be not an apostle unto others, yet doubtless I am to you: for the seal of mine apostleship are ye in the Lord. ³Mine answer to them that do examine me is this: ⁴Have we not power to eat and to drink? ⁵Have we not power to lead about a sister, a wife, as well as other apostles, and *as* the brethren of the Lord, and Cephas? ⁶Or I only and Barnabas, have not we power to forbear working? ⁷Who goeth a warfare any time at his own charges? who planteth a vineyard, and eateth not of the fruit thereof? or who feedeth a flock, and eateth not of the milk of the flock? ⁸Say I these *things* as a man? or saith not the law the same also? ⁹For it is written in the law of Moses, Thou shalt not muzzle the mouth of the ox that treadeth out the corn. Doth God take care for oxen? ¹⁰Or saith he *it* altogether for our sakes? For our sakes, no doubt, *this* is written: that he that ploweth should plow in hope; and that he

that thresheth in hope should be partaker of his hope. 11If we have sown unto you spiritual *things, is it* a great *thing* if we shall reap your carnal *things?* 12If others be partakers of *this* power over you, *are* not we rather? Nevertheless we have not used this power; but suffer all *things,* lest we should hinder the gospel of Christ. 13Do ye not know that they which minister about holy *things* live of *the things of* the temple? *and* they which wait at the altar are partakers with the altar? 14Even so hath the Lord ordained that they which preach the gospel should live of the gospel. 15But I have used none of these *things:* neither have I written these *things,* that it should be so done unto me: for *it were* better for me to die, than that any *man* should make my glorying void. 16For though I preach the gospel, I have nothing to glory of: for necessity is laid upon me; yea, woe is unto me, if I preach not the gospel! 17For if I do this *thing* willingly, I have a reward: but if against my will, a dispensation *of the gospel* is committed unto me. 18What is my reward then? *Verily* that, when I preach the gospel, I may make the gospel of Christ without charge, that *I* abuse not my power in the gospel. 19For though I be free from all *men,* yet have I made myself servant unto all, that I might gain the more. 20And unto the Jews I became as a Jew, that I might gain *the* Jews; to them that are under the law, as under the law, that I might gain them that are under the law; 21To them *that are* without law, as without law, (being

not without law to God, but under the law to Christ,) that I might gain them *that are* without law. 22To the weak became I as weak, that I might gain the weak: I am made all *things* to all *men,* that I might by all means save some. 23And this I do for the gospel's sake, that I might be partaker thereof with *you.*

24 Know ye not that they which run in a race run all, but one receiveth the prize? So run, that ye may obtain. 25And every *man* that striveth for the mastery is temperate in all *things.* Now they *do it* to obtain a corruptible crown; but we an incorruptible. 26I therefore so run, not as uncertainly; so fight I, not as one that beateth the air: 27But I keep under my body, and bring *it* into subjection: lest that by any means, when I have preached to others, I myself should be a castaway. [Rom. 8:13; Col. 3:5; Rom. 6:18; Jer. 6:30; 2 Cor. 13:5]

The idolatry in the wilderness

10 Moreover, brethren, I would not that ye should be ignorant, how that all our fathers were under the cloud, and all passed through the sea; 2And were all baptized unto Moses in the cloud and in the sea; 3And did all eat the same spiritual meat; 4And did all drink the same spiritual drink: for they drank of *that* spiritual Rock that followed *them:* and *that* Rock was Christ. 5But with many of them God was not well pleased: for they were overthrown in the wilderness. 6Now these *things* were our examples, to the intent we should not lust after evil *things,* as they also lusted. ⁷Neither be ye idolaters, as *were* some of them; as it is written, The people sat down to eat and drink, and rose up to play. ⁸Neither let us commit fornication, as some of them committed, and fell in one day three and twenty thousand. ⁹Neither let us tempt Christ, as some of them also tempted, and were destroyed of serpents. ¹⁰Neither murmur ye, as some of them also murmured, and were destroyed of the destroyer. ¹¹Now all these *things* happened unto them for ensamples: and they are written for our admonition, upon whom the ends of the world are come. ¹²Wherefore let him that thinketh he standeth take heed lest he fall. ¹³There hath no temptation taken you but such as is common to man: but God *is* faithful, who will not suffer you to be tempted above that ye are able; but will with the temptation also make a way to escape, that ye may be able to bear *it.* ¹⁴Wherefore, my dearly beloved, flee from idolatry. ¹⁵I speak as to wise *men;* judge ye what I say. [ch. 8:1]

Prohibition of idol feasts

16 The cup of blessing which we bless, is it not the communion of the blood of Christ? The bread which we break, is it not the communion of the body of Christ? ¹⁷For we being many are one bread, *and* one body: for we are all partakers of *that* one bread. ¹⁸Behold Israel after the flesh: are not they which eat *of* the sacrifices partakers of the altar? ¹⁹What say I then? that the idol is any *thing,* or that which is offered in sacrifice to idols is any *thing?* ²⁰But *I say,* that *the things* which the Gentiles sacrifice, they sacrifice to devils, and not to God: and I would not that ye should have fellowship with devils. ²¹Ye cannot drink the cup of the Lord, and the cup of devils: ye cannot be partakers of the Lord's table, and of the table of devils. ²²Do we provoke the Lord to jealousy? are we stronger than he? [Deut. 32:21; Ezek. 22:14]

Do all to the glory of God

23 All *things* are lawful for me, but all *things* are not expedient: all *things* are lawful for me, but all *things* edify not. ²⁴Let no *man* seek his own, but every man another's *wealth.* ²⁵Whatsoever is sold in the shambles, *that* eat, asking no question for conscience sake: ²⁶For the earth *is* the Lord's, and the fulness thereof. ²⁷If any of them that believe not bid you *to a feast,* and ye be disposed to go; whatsoever is set before you, eat, asking no question for conscience sake. ²⁸But if any *man* say unto you, This is offered in sacrifice unto idols, eat not for his sake that shewed *it,* and *for* conscience *sake:* for the earth *is* the Lord's, and the fulness thereof: ²⁹Conscience, I say, not thine own, but of the other's: for why is my liberty judged of another *man's* conscience? ³⁰For if I by grace be a partaker, why am I evil spoken of for *that for* which I give thanks? ³¹Whether therefore ye eat, or drink, or whatsoever ye do, do all to the glory of God. ³²Give none offence, neither to the Jews, nor to

the Gentiles, nor to the church of God: 33Even as I please all *men* in all *things,* not seeking mine own profit, but the *profit* of many, that they may be saved. [Rom. 15:2; ver. 24]

11
Be ye followers of me, even as I also *am* of Christ. [Eph. 5:1; Phil. 3:17]

The covering of women's heads

2 Now I praise you, brethren, that you remember me in all *things,* and keep the ordinances, as I delivered *them* to you. 3But I would have you know, that the head of every man is Christ; and the head of the woman *is* the man; and the head of Christ *is* God. 4Every man praying or prophesying, having *his* head covered, dishonoureth his head. 5But every woman that prayeth or prophesieth with *her* head uncovered dishonoureth her head: for *that* is even all one as if she were shaven. 6For if the woman be not covered, let her also be shorn: but *if it* be a shame for a woman to be shorn or shaven, let her be covered. 7For a man indeed ought not to cover *his* head, forasmuch as he is the image and glory of God: but the woman is the glory of the man. 8For the man is not of the woman; but the woman of the man. 9Neither was the man created for the woman; but the woman for the man. 10For this cause ought the woman to have power on *her* head because of the angels. 11Nevertheless neither *is* the man without the woman, neither the woman without the man, in the Lord. 12For as the woman *is* of the man, *even* so *is*

the man also by the woman; but all *things* of God. 13Judge in yourselves: is it comely that a woman pray unto God uncovered? 14Doth not even nature itself teach you, that, if a man have long hair, it is a shame unto him? 15But if a woman have long hair, it is a glory to her: for *her* hair is given her for a covering. 16But if any *man* seem to be contentious, we have no such custom, neither the churches of God. [1 Tim. 6:4; ch. 7:17]

The Lord's supper

17 Now in this that I declare *unto you* I praise *you* not, that you come together not for the better, but for the worse. 18For first of all, when ye come together in the church, I hear that there be divisions among you; and I partly believe *it.* 19For there must be also heresies among you, that they *which are* approved may be made manifest among you. 20When ye come together therefore into one place, *this* is not to eat the Lord's supper. 21For in eating every one taketh before *other* his own supper: and one is hungry, and another is drunken. 22What? have ye not houses to eat and to drink *in?* or despise ye the church of God, and shame them that have not? What shall I say to you? shall I praise you in this? I praise *you* not. 23For I have received of the Lord *that* which also I delivered unto you, That the Lord Jesus the *same* night in which he was betrayed took bread: 24And when he had given thanks, he brake *it,* and said, Take, eat: this is my body, which is bro-

ken for you: this do in remembrance of me. 25After the same manner also *he took* the cup, when *he* had supped, saying, This cup is the new testament in my blood: this do ye, as oft as ye drink *it,* in remembrance of me. 26For as often as ye eat this bread, and drink this cup, ye do shew the Lord's death till he come. 27Wherefore whosoever shall eat this bread, and drink *this* cup of the Lord unworthily, shall be guilty of the body and blood of the Lord. 28But let a man examine himself, and so let him eat of *that* bread, and drink of *that* cup. 29For he that eateth and drinketh unworthily, eateth and drinketh damnation to himself, not discerning the Lord's body. 30For this cause many *are* weak and sickly among you, and many sleep. 31For if we would judge ourselves, we should not be judged. 32But when we are judged, we are chastened of the Lord, that we should not be condemned with the world. 33Wherefore, my brethren, when ye come together to eat, tarry one for another. 34And if any *man* hunger, let him eat at home; that ye come not together unto condemnation. And the rest will I set in order when I come. [Tit. 1:5; ch. 4:19]

The diversities of gifts

12 Now concerning spiritual *gifts,* brethren, I would not have you ignorant. 2Ye know that ye were Gentiles, carried away unto *these* dumb idols, *even* as ye were led. 3Wherefore I give you to understand, that no *man* speaking by the Spirit of God calleth Jesus accursed: and *that* no *man* can say that Jesus is the Lord, but by the Holy Ghost. 4Now there are diversities of gifts, but the same Spirit. 5And there are differences of administrations, but the same Lord. 6And there are diversities of operations, but it is the same God which worketh all in all. 7But the manifestation of the Spirit is given to every man to profit withal. 8For to one is given by the Spirit the word of wisdom; to another the word of knowledge by the same Spirit; 9To another faith by the same Spirit; to another the gifts of healing by the same Spirit; 10To another the working of miracles; to another prophecy; to another discerning of spirits; to another *divers* kinds of tongues; to another the interpretation of tongues: 11But all these worketh *that* one and the selfsame Spirit, dividing to every man severally as he will. [Rom. 12:6; 2 Cor. 10:13; John 3:8]

12 For as the body is one, and hath many members, and all the members of *that* one body, being many, are one body: so also *is* Christ. 13For by one Spirit are we all baptized into one body, whether *we be* Jews or Gentiles, whether *we be* bond or free; and have been all made to drink into one Spirit. 14For the body is not one member, but many. 15If the foot shall say, Because I am not the hand, I am not of the body; is it therefore not of the body? 16And if the ear shall say, Because I am not the eye, I am not of the body; is it therefore not of the body? 17If the whole body *were* an eye, where *were* the hear-

ing? If the whole *were* hearing, where *were* the smelling? 18But now hath God set the members every one of them in the body, as it hath pleased him. 19And if they were all one member, where *were* the body? 20But now *are they* many members, yet *but* one body. 21And the eye cannot say unto the hand, I have no need of thee: nor again the head to the feet, I have no need of you. 22Nay, much more those members of the body, which seem to be more feeble, are necessary: 23And those *members* of the body, which we think to be less honourable, upon these we bestow more abundant honour; and our uncomely *parts* have more abundant comeliness. 24For our comely *parts* have no need: but God hath tempered the body together, having given more abundant honour to that *part* which lacked: 25That there should be no schism in the body; but *that* the members should have the same care one for another. 26And whether one member suffer, all the members suffer with *it;* or one member be honoured, all the members rejoice with *it.* 27Now ye are the body of Christ, and members in particular. [Rom. 12:5; Eph. 1:23; 4:12; 5:23,30; Col. 1:24; Eph. 5:30]

28 And God hath set some in the church, first apostles, secondarily prophets, thirdly teachers, after that miracles, then gifts of healings, helps, governments, diversities of tongues. 29*Are* all apostles? *are* all prophets? *are* all teachers? *are* all workers of miracles? 30Have all the gifts of healing? do all speak with tongues? do all interpret? 31But covet earnestly the best gifts: and yet shew I unto you a more excellent way. [ch. 14:1,39]

The way of love

13 Though I speak with the tongues of men and of angels, and have not charity, I am become *as* sounding brass, or a tinkling cymbal. 2And though I have *the gift of* prophecy, and understand all mysteries, and all knowledge; and though I have all faith, so that *I* could remove mountains, and have no charity, I am nothing. 3And though I bestow all my goods to feed *the poor,* and though I give my body to be burned, and have not charity, it profiteth me nothing. 4Charity suffereth long, *and* is kind; charity envieth not; charity vaunteth not itself, is not puffed up, 5Doth not behave itself unseemly, seeketh not her own, is not easily provoked, thinketh no evil; 6Rejoiceth not in iniquity, but rejoiceth in the truth; 7Beareth all *things,* believeth all *things,* hopeth all *things,* endureth all *things.* 8Charity never faileth: but whether *there be* prophecies, they shall fail; whether *there be* tongues, they shall cease; whether *there be* knowledge, it shall vanish away. 9For we know in part, and we prophesy in part. 10But when *that which is* perfect is come, then that which is in part shall be done away. 11When I was a child, I spake as a child, I understood as a child, I thought as a child: but when I became a man, I put away childish *things.* 12For now we see through a glass, darkly; but then face to face: now I know in part; but then shall I know even as also I am known. 13And now abideth faith, hope, charity, these three; but the greatest of these *is* charity.

Prophecy and tongues

14 Follow after charity, and desire spiritual *gifts*, but rather that ye may prophesy. 2For he that speaketh in an *unknown* tongue speaketh not unto men, but unto God: for no *man* understandeth *him;* howbeit in the spirit he speaketh mysteries. 3But he that prophesieth speaketh unto men *to* edification, and exhortation, and comfort. 4He that speaketh in an *unknown* tongue edifieth himself; but he that prophesieth edifieth *the* church. 5I would that ye all spake with tongues, but rather that ye prophesied: for greater *is* he that prophesieth than he that speaketh with tongues, except he interpret, that the church may receive edifying. 6Now, brethren, if I come unto you speaking with tongues, what shall I profit you, except I shall speak to you either by revelation, or by knowledge, or by prophesying, or by doctrine? 7*And* even *things* without life giving sound, whether pipe or harp, except they give a distinction in the sounds, how shall it be known what is piped or harped? 8For if the trumpet give an uncertain sound, who shall prepare himself to the battle? 9So likewise you, except ye utter by the tongue words easy to be understood, how shall it be known what is spoken? for ye shall speak into

the air. 10There are, it may be, so many kinds of voices in the world, and none of them *is* without signification. 11Therefore if I know not the meaning of the voice, I shall be unto him that speaketh a barbarian, and he that speaketh *shall be* a barbarian unto me. 12Even so ye, forasmuch as ye are zealous of spiritual *gifts,* seek that ye may excel to the edifying of the church. 13Wherefore let him that speaketh in an *unknown* tongue pray that he may interpret. 14For if I pray in an *unknown* tongue, my spirit prayeth, but my understanding is unfruitful. 15What is it then? I will pray with the spirit, and will pray with the understanding also: I will sing with the spirit, and I will sing with the understanding also. 16Else when thou shalt bless with the spirit, how shall he that occupieth the room of the unlearned say Amen at thy giving of thanks, seeing he understandeth not what thou sayest? 17For thou verily givest thanks well, but the other is not edified. 18I thank my God, I speak with tongues more than you all: 19Yet in the church I had rather speak five words with my understanding, that *by my voice* I might teach others also, than ten thousand words in an *unknown* tongue. 20Brethren, be not children in understanding: howbeit in malice be ye children, but in understanding be men. 21In the law it is written, With *men* of other tongues and other lips will I speak unto this people; and yet for all that will they not hear me, saith the Lord. 22Wherefore tongues are for a sign, not to them that believe, but to them that believe not: but prophesying *serveth* not for them that believe not, but for them which believe. ²³If therefore the whole church be come together into one place, and all speak with tongues, and there come in *those that are* unlearned, or unbelievers, will they not say that ye are mad? ²⁴But if all prophesy, and there come in one that believeth not, or *one* unlearned, he is convinced of all, he is judged of all: ²⁵And thus are the secrets of his heart made manifest; and so falling down on *his* face he will worship God, and report that God is in you of a truth. [Is. 45:14; Zech. 8:23]

The use of spiritual gifts

26 How is it then, brethren? when ye come together, every one of you hath a psalm, hath a doctrine, hath a tongue, hath a revelation, hath an interpretation. Let all *things* be done unto edifying. ²⁷If any *man* speak in an *unknown* tongue, *let it be* by two, or at the most *by* three, and *that* by course; and let one interpret. ²⁸But if there be no interpreter, let him keep silence in the church; and let him speak to himself, and to God. ²⁹Let the prophets speak two or three, and let the other judge. ³⁰If *any thing* be revealed to another that sitteth *by,* let the first hold his peace. ³¹For ye may all prophesy one by one, that all may learn, and all may be comforted. ³²And the spirits of the prophets are subject to the prophets: ³³For God is not *the author* of confusion, but of peace, as in all churches of the saints. [ch. 11:16]

34 Let your women keep silence in the churches: for it is not permitted unto them to speak; but *they are commanded* to be under obedience, as also saith the law. ³⁵And if they will learn any *thing,* let them ask their husbands at home: for it is a shame for women to speak in the church. ³⁶What? came the word of God out from you? or came it unto you only? ³⁷If any *man* think himself to be a prophet, or spiritual, let him acknowledge that *the things* that I write unto you are the commandments of the Lord. ³⁸But if any *man* be ignorant, let him be ignorant. ³⁹Wherefore, brethren, covet to prophesy, and forbid not to speak with tongues. ⁴⁰Let all *things* be done decently and in order. [ver. 33]

The resurrection

15 Moreover, brethren, I declare unto you the gospel which I preached unto you, which also you have received, and wherein ye stand; ²By which also ye are saved, if ye keep in memory what I preached unto you, unless ye have believed in vain. ³For I delivered unto you first *of all* that which I also received, how that Christ died for our sins according to the scriptures; ⁴And that he was buried, and that he rose *again* the third day according to the scriptures: ⁵And that he was seen of Cephas, then of the twelve: ⁶After that, he was seen of above five hundred brethren at once; of whom the greater part remain unto this pres-

ent, but some are fallen asleep. 7After that, he was seen of James; then of all the apostles. 8And last of all he was seen of me also, as of one born out of due time. 9For I am the least of the apostles, that am not meet to be called an apostle, because I persecuted the church of God. 10But by the grace of God I am what I am: and his grace which was *bestowed* upon me was not in vain; but I laboured more abundantly than they all: yet not I, but the grace of God which was with me. 11Therefore whether *it were* I or they, so we preach, and so ye believed.

12 Now if Christ be preached that he rose from the dead, how say some among you that there is no resurrection of the dead? 13But if there be no resurrection of the dead, then is Christ not risen: 14And if Christ be not risen, then *is* our preaching vain, and your faith *is* also vain. 15Yea, and we are found false witnesses of God; because we have testified of God that he raised up Christ: whom he raised not up, if so be that the dead rise not. 16For if the dead rise not, then is not Christ raised: 17And if Christ be not raised, your faith *is* vain; ye are yet in your sins. 18Then they also which are fallen asleep in Christ are perished. 19If in this life only we have hope in Christ, we are of all men most miserable. 20But now is Christ risen from the dead, *and* become the firstfruits of them that slept. 21For since by man *came* death, by man *came* also the resurrection of the dead. 22For as in Adam all die,

even so in Christ shall all be made alive. 23But every man in his own order: Christ the firstfruits; afterward they that are Christ's at his coming. 24Then *cometh* the end, when he shall have delivered up the kingdom to God, even the Father; when he shall have put down all rule and all authority and power. 25For he must reign, till he hath put all enemies under his feet. 26The last enemy *that* shall be destroyed *is* death. 27For he hath put all *things* under his feet. But when *he* saith, all *things* are put under *him, it is* manifest that he is excepted, which did put all *things* under him. 28And when all *things* shall be subdued unto him, then shall the Son also himself be subject unto him that put all *things* under him, that God may be all in all. 29Else what shall they do which are baptized for the dead, if the dead rise not at all? why are they then baptized for the dead? 30And why stand we in jeopardy every hour? 31I protest by your rejoicing which I have in Christ Jesus our Lord, I die daily. 32If after the manner of men I have fought with beasts at Ephesus, what advantageth it me, if the dead rise not? let us eat and drink; for to morrow we die. 33Be not deceived: evil communications corrupt good manners. 34Awake to righteousness, and sin not: for some have not the knowledge of God: I speak *this* to your shame. [Rom. 13:11; Eph. 5:14; 1 Thes. 4:5; ch. 6:5]

35 But some *man* will say, How are the dead raised up? and with what body do they come? 36*Thou*

fool, *that* which thou sowest is not quickened, except it die: 37And *that* which thou sowest, thou sowest not that body that shall be, but bare grain, it may chance of wheat, or of some other *grain:* 38But God giveth it a body as it hath pleased him, and to every seed his own body. 39All flesh *is* not the same flesh: but *there is* one *kind of* flesh of men, another flesh of beasts, another of fishes, *and* another of birds. 40*There are* also celestial bodies, and bodies terrestrial: but the glory of the celestial *is* one, and the *glory* of the terrestrial *is* another. 41*There is* one glory of the sun, and another glory of the moon, and another glory of the stars: for *one* star differeth from *another* star in glory. 42So also *is* the resurrection of the dead. It is sown in corruption; it is raised in incorruption: 43It is sown in dishonour; it is raised in glory: it is sown in weakness; it is raised in power: 44It is sown a natural body; it is raised a spiritual body. There is a natural body, and there is a spiritual body. 45And so it is written, The first man Adam was made a living soul; the last Adam *was made* a quickening spirit. 46Howbeit *that was* not first *which is* spiritual, but *that which is* natural; *and* afterward *that which is* spiritual. 47The first man *is* of the earth, earthy: the second man *is* the Lord from heaven. 48As *is* the earthy, such *are they* also *that are* earthy: and as *is* the heavenly, such *are they* also *that are* heavenly. 49And as we have borne the image of the earthy, we shall also bear the image of the heavenly. [Gen. 5:3; Rom. 8:29; 2 Cor. 3:18; Phil. 3:21; 1 John 3:2]

50 Now this I say, brethren, that flesh and blood cannot inherit the kingdom of God; neither doth corruption inherit incorruption. 51Behold, I shew you a mystery; We shall not all sleep, but we shall all be changed, 52In a moment, in the twinkling of an eye, at the last trump: for the trumpet shall sound, and the dead shall be raised incorruptible, and we shall be changed. 53For this corruptible must put on incorruption, and this mortal *must* put on immortality. 54So when this corruptible shall have put on incorruption, and this mortal shall have put on immortality, then shall be brought to pass the saying that is written, Death is swallowed up in victory. 55O death, where *is* thy sting? O grave, where *is* thy victory? 56The sting of death *is* sin; and the strength of sin *is* the law. 57But thanks *be* to God, which giveth us the victory through our Lord Jesus Christ. 58Therefore, my beloved brethren, be ye stedfast, unmoveable, always abounding in the work of the Lord, forasmuch as you know that your labour is not in vain in the Lord. [2 Pet. 3:14; ch. 3:8]

The collection for the poor

16 Now concerning the collection for the saints, as I have given order to the churches of Galatia, even so do ye. 2Upon the first *day* of the week let every one of you lay by him in store, as *God* hath prospered him, that there be no gatherings when I come. 3And when I come, whomsoever you shall approve by *your* letters, them will I send to bring your liberality unto Jerusalem. 4And if it be meet that I go also, they shall go with me. [2 Cor. 8:19]

Paul's itinerary

5 Now I will come unto you, when I shall pass through Macedonia: for I do pass through Macedonia. 6And it may be that I will abide, yea, and winter with you, that ye may bring me on my journey whithersoever I go. 7For I will not see you now by the way; but I trust to tarry a while with you, if the Lord permit. 8But I will tarry at Ephesus until Pentecost. 9For a great door and effectual is opened unto me, and *there are* many adversaries. 10Now if Timotheus come, see that he may be with you without fear: for he worketh the work of the Lord, as I also *do*. 11Let no *man* therefore despise him: but conduct him forth in peace, that he may come unto me: for I look for him with the brethren. 12As touching *our* brother Apollos, I greatly desired him to come unto you with the brethren: but *his* will was not at all to come at this time; but he will come when he shall have convenient time. [ch. 1:12]

Concluding message

13 Watch ye, stand fast in the faith, quit you like men, be strong. 14Let all your *things* be done with charity. [1 Pet. 4:8]

15 I beseech you, brethren, (ye know the house of Stephanas, that it is the firstfruits of Achaia, and *that* they have addicted themselves to the ministry of the saints,) 16That ye submit yourselves unto such, and to every one that helpeth with *us,* and laboureth. 17I am glad of the coming of Stephanas and Fortunatus and Achaicus: for that which was lacking on your part they have supplied. 18For they have refreshed my spirit and yours: therefore acknowledge ye *them that are* such. 19The churches of Asia salute you. Aquila and Priscilla salute you much in the Lord, with the church that is in their house. 20All the brethren greet you. Greet ye one another with a holy kiss. [Rom. 16:16]

21 The salutation of *me* Paul with mine own hand. 22If any *man* love not the Lord Jesus Christ, let him be anathema, Maran-atha. 23The grace of *our* Lord Jesus Christ *be* with you. 24My love *be* with you all in Christ Jesus. Amen.

¶ The first *epistle* to the Corinthians was written from Philippi by Stephanas, and Fortunatus, and Achaicus, and Timotheus.

The Second Epistle of Paul the Apostle to the

Corinthians

The God of all comfort

1 Paul, an apostle of Jesus Christ by the will of God, and Timothy *our* brother, unto the church of God which is at Corinth, with all the saints which are in all Achaia: ²Grace *be* to you and peace from God our Father, and *from* the Lord Jesus Christ. [Rom. 1:7; 1 Cor. 1:3; Gal. 1:3; Phil. 1:2; Col. 1:2; 1 Thes. 1:1; 2 Thes. 1:2]

3 Blessed *be* God, even the Father of our Lord Jesus Christ, the Father of mercies, and the God of all comfort; ⁴Who comforteth us in all our tribulation, that we may be able to comfort them which are in any trouble, by the comfort wherewith we ourselves are comforted of God. ⁵For as the sufferings of Christ abound in us, so our consolation also aboundeth by Christ. ⁶And whether we be afflicted, *it is* for your consolation and salvation, which is effectual in the enduring of the same sufferings which we also suffer: or whether we be comforted, *it is* for your consolation and salvation. ⁷And our hope of you *is* stedfast, knowing, that as you are partakers of the sufferings, so *shall ye be* also of the consolation. ⁸For we would not, brethren, have you ignorant of our trouble which came to us in Asia, that we were pressed out of measure, above strength, insomuch that we despaired even of life: ⁹But we had the sentence of death in ourselves, that we should not trust in ourselves, but in God which raiseth the dead: ¹⁰Who delivered us from so great a death, and doth deliver: in whom we trust that he will yet deliver *us;* ¹¹You also helping together by prayer for us, that for the gift *bestowed* upon us by the means of many persons thanks may be given by many on our behalf. [Rom. 15:30; Phil. 1:19; Philem. 22; ch. 4:15]

Paul's change of plans

12 For our rejoicing is this, that the testimony of our conscience, that in simplicity and godly sincerity, not with fleshly wisdom, but by the grace of God, we have had our conversation in the world, and more abundantly to you-wards. ¹³For we write none other *things* unto you, than what you read or acknowledge; and I trust you shall acknowledge even to the end; ¹⁴As also you have acknowledged us in part, that we are your rejoicing, even as ye also *are* ours in the day of the Lord Jesus. ¹⁵And in this confidence I was minded to come unto you before, that you might have a second benefit; ¹⁶And to pass by you into Macedonia, and to come again out of Macedonia unto you, and of you to be brought on *my* way toward Judea. ¹⁷When I therefore was thus minded, did I use lightness? or *the things* that I purpose, do I purpose according to the flesh, that with me there should be yea yea, and nay nay? ¹⁸But *as* God *is* true, our word toward you was not yea and nay. ¹⁹For the Son of God, Jesus Christ, who was preached among you by

us, *even* by me and Silvanus and Timotheus, was not yea and nay, but in him was yea. 20For all the promises of God in him *are* yea, and in him Amen, unto the glory of God by us. 21Now he which stablisheth us with you in Christ, and hath anointed us, *is* God; 22Who hath also sealed us, and given the earnest of the Spirit in our hearts. [Eph. 4:30; 2 Tim. 2:19; Rev. 2:17; ch. 5:5; Eph. 1:14]

23 Moreover I call God for a record upon my soul, that to spare you I came not as yet unto Corinth. 24Not for that we have dominion over your faith, but are helpers of your joy: for by faith ye stand. [1 Cor. 3:5; 1 Pet. 5:3; Rom. 11:20; 1 Cor. 15:1]

2 But I determined this with myself, that *I* would not come again to you in heaviness. 2For if I make you sorry, who is he then that maketh me glad, but *the same* which is made sorry by me? 3And I wrote this same unto you, lest, when I came, I should have sorrow from *them of* whom I ought to rejoice; having confidence in you all, that my joy is *the joy of* you all. 4For out of much affliction and anguish of heart I wrote unto you with many tears; not that you should be grieved, but that ye might know the love which I have more abundantly unto you. [ch. 7:8,9]

Forgiveness of an offender
5 But if any have caused grief, he hath not grieved me, but in part: that I may not overcharge you all. 6Sufficient to such a man *is* this punishment, which *was inflicted* of many. 7So that contrariwise ye

ought rather to forgive *him*, and comfort *him*, lest perhaps such a one should be swallowed up with overmuch sorrow. 8Wherefore I beseech you that *you* would confirm *your* love towards him. 9For to this end also did I write, that I might know the proof of you, whether ye be obedient in all *things*. 10To whom ye forgive any thing, I *forgive* also: for if I forgave any *thing*, to whom I forgave *it*, for your sakes *forgave I it* in the person of Christ; 11Lest Satan should get an advantage of us: for we are not ignorant of his devices.

Ministers of the new testament
12 Furthermore, when I came to Troas to *preach* Christ's gospel, and a door was opened unto me of the Lord, 13I had no rest in my spirit, because I found not Titus my brother: but taking my leave of them, I went from *thence* into Macedonia. 14Now thanks *be* unto God, which always causeth us to triumph in Christ, and maketh manifest the savour of his knowledge by us in every place. 15For we are unto God a sweet savour of Christ, in them that are saved, and in them that perish: 16To the one *we are* the savour of death unto death; and to the other the savour of life unto life. And who *is* sufficient for these *things*? 17For we are not as many, which corrupt the word of God: but as of sincerity, but as of God, in the sight of God speak we in Christ. [2 Pet. 2:3; ch. 1:12]

3 Do we begin again to commend ourselves? or need we, as some *others*, epistles of com-

mendation to you, or *letters* of commendation from you? ²Ye are our epistle written in our hearts, known and read of all men: ³Forasmuch as ye are manifestly declared to be the epistle of Christ ministered by us, written not with ink, but with the Spirit of the living God; not in tables of stone, but in fleshy tables of the heart. ⁴And such trust have we through Christ to God-ward: ⁵Not that we are sufficient of ourselves to think any *thing* as of ourselves; but our sufficiency *is* of God; ⁶Who also hath made us able ministers of the new testament; not of the letter, but of the spirit: for the letter killeth, but the spirit giveth life. [1 Cor. 3:5; Eph. 3:7; Col. 1:25; Jer. 31:31; Mat. 26:28; Heb. 8:6,8; Rom. 2:27; Rom. 3:20; Gal. 3:10; John 6:63; Rom. 8:2]

A ministry of glory

7 But if the ministration of death, written *and* engraven in stones, was glorious, so that the children of Israel could not stedfastly behold the face of Moses for the glory of his countenance; which *glory* was to be done away: ⁸How shall not the ministration of the spirit be rather glorious? ⁹For if the ministration of condemnation *be* glory, much more doth the ministration of righteousness exceed in glory. ¹⁰For even that which was made glorious had no glory in this respect, by reason of the glory that excelleth. ¹¹For if that which is done away *was* glorious, much more that which remaineth *is* glorious. ¹²Seeing then that we have such hope, we use great plainness of speech: ¹³And not as Moses, *which* put a vail over his face, that the children of Israel could not stedfastly look to the end of that which is abolished: ¹⁴But their minds were blinded: for until this day remaineth the same vail untaken away in the reading of the old testament; which *vail* is done away in Christ. ¹⁵But *even* unto this day, when Moses is read, the vail is upon their heart. ¹⁶Nevertheless when *it* shall turn to the Lord, the vail shall be taken away. ¹⁷Now the Lord is *that* Spirit: and where the Spirit of the Lord *is,* there *is* liberty. ¹⁸But we all, with open face beholding as in a glass the glory of the Lord, are changed *into* the same image from glory to glory, even as by the Spirit of the Lord. [1 Cor. 13:12; ch. 4:4,6; Rom. 8:29]

An honest and tried ministry

4 Therefore seeing we have this ministry, as we have received mercy, we faint not; ²But have renounced the hidden *things* of dishonesty, not walking in craftiness, nor handling the word of God deceitfully; but by manifestation of the truth commending ourselves to every man's conscience in the sight of God. ³But if our gospel be hid, it is hid to them that are lost: ⁴In whom the god of this world hath blinded the minds of them which believe not, lest the light of the glorious gospel of Christ, who is the image of God, should shine unto them. ⁵For we preach not ourselves, but Christ Jesus the Lord; and ourselves your servants for Jesus' sake. ⁶For God, who

commanded the light to shine out of darkness, hath shined in our hearts, to give the light of the knowledge of the glory of God in the face of Jesus Christ. [Gen. 1:3; 2 Pet. 1:19; 1 Pet. 2:9]

7 But we have this treasure in earthen vessels, that the excellency of the power may be of God, and not of us. **8** *We are* troubled on every *side,* yet not distressed; *we are* perplexed, but not in despair; **9** Persecuted, but not forsaken; cast down, but not destroyed; **10** Always bearing about in the body the dying of the Lord Jesus, that the life also of Jesus might be made manifest in our body. **11** For we which live are alway delivered unto death for Jesus' sake, that the life also of Jesus might be made manifest in our mortal flesh. **12** So then death worketh in us, but life in you. **13** We having the same spirit of faith, according as it is written, I believed, *and* therefore have I spoken; we also believe, and therefore speak; **14** Knowing that he which raised up the Lord Jesus shall raise up us also by Jesus, and shall present *us* with you. **15** For all *things are* for your sakes, that the abundant grace might through the thanksgiving of many redound to the glory of God. **16** For which cause we faint not; but though our outward man perish, yet the inward *man* is renewed day by day. **17** For our light affliction, which is but for a moment, worketh for us a far more exceeding *and* eternal weight of glory; **18** While we look not at the *things* which are seen, but at the *things* which are not

seen: for the *things* which are seen *are* temporal; but the *things* which are not seen *are* eternal. [Rom. 8:24; Heb. 11:1]

A confident ministry

5 For we know that if our earthly house of *this* tabernacle were dissolved, we have a building of God, a house not made with hand, eternal in the heavens. **2** For in this we groan, earnestly desiring to be clothed upon with our house which is from heaven: **3** If so be that being clothed we shall not be found naked. **4** For we that are in *this* tabernacle do groan, being burdened: not for that we would be unclothed, but clothed upon, that mortality might be swallowed up of life. **5** Now he that hath wrought us for the selfsame *thing is* God, who also hath given unto us the earnest of the Spirit. **6** Therefore *we are* always confident, knowing that, whilst we are at home in the body, we are absent from the Lord: **7** (For we walk by faith, not by sight:) **8** We are confident, I say, and willing rather to be absent from the body, and to be present with the Lord. [Phil. 1:23]

A reconciling ministry

9 Wherefore we labour, that, whether present or absent, we may be accepted of him. **10** For we must all appear before the judgment seat of Christ; that every one may receive the *things done* in *his* body, according to that he hath done, whether *it be* good or bad. **11** Knowing therefore the terror of the Lord, we persuade men; but we are made manifest unto God;

and I trust also are made manifest in your consciences. 12For we commend not ourselves again unto you, but give you occasion to glory on our behalf, that you may have *somewhat* to *answer* them which glory in appearance, and not in heart. 13For whether we be besides ourselves, *it is* to God: or whether we be sober, *it is* for your cause. 14For the love of Christ constraineth us; because we thus judge, that if one died for all, then were all dead: 15And *that* he died for all, that they which live should not henceforth live unto themselves, but unto him which died for them, and rose *again.* 16Wherefore henceforth know we no *man* after the flesh: yea, though we have known Christ after the flesh, yet now henceforth know we *him* no more. 17Therefore if any *man* be in Christ, *he is* a new creature: old *things* are past away; behold, all *things* are become new. 18And all *things are* of God, who hath reconciled us to himself by Jesus Christ, and hath given to us the ministry of reconciliation. 19To wit, that God was in Christ reconciling the world unto himself, not imputing their trespasses unto them; and hath committed unto us the word of reconciliation. 20*Now* then we are ambassadors for Christ, as though God did beseech *you* by us: we pray *you* in Christ's stead, be ye reconciled to God. 21For he hath made him *to be* sin for us, who knew no sin; that we might be made the righteousness of God in him. [Is. 53:6,9; Gal. 3:13; 1 Pet. 2:22; 1 John 3:5; Rom. 1:17; 10:3]

A suffering ministry

6 We then, *as* workers together *with him,* beseech *you* also that ye receive not the grace of God in vain. 2(For he saith, I have heard thee in a time accepted, and in the day of salvation have I succoured thee: behold, now *is* the accepted time; behold, now *is* the day of salvation.) 3Giving no offence in any *thing,* that the ministry be not blamed: 4But in all *things* approving ourselves as the ministers of God, in much patience, in afflictions, in necessities, in distresses, 5In stripes, in imprisonments, in tumults, in labours, in watchings, in fastings; 6By pureness, by knowledge, by longsuffering, by kindness, by the Holy Ghost, by love unfeigned, 7By the word of truth, by the power of God, by the armour of righteousness on the right hand and on the left, 8By honour and dishonour, by evil report and good report: as deceivers, and *yet* true; 9As unknown, and *yet* well known; as dying, and behold, we live; as chastened, and not killed; 10As sorrowful, yet alway rejoicing; as poor, yet making many rich; as having nothing, and *yet* possessing all *things.*

Believers are the temple of God

11 O *ye* Corinthians, our mouth is open unto you, our heart is enlarged. 12Ye are not straitened in us, but ye are straitened in your own bowels. 13Now for a recompence in the same, (I speak as unto *my* children,) be ye also enlarged. 14Be ye not unequally yoked together with unbelievers: for what

fellowship hath righteousness with unrighteousness? and what communion hath light with darkness? 15And what concord hath Christ with Belial? or what part hath he that believeth with an infidel? 16And what agreement hath the temple of God with idols? for ye are the temple of the living God; as God hath said, I will dwell in them, and walk in *them;* and I will be their God, and they shall be my people. 17Wherefore come out from among them, and be ye separate, saith the Lord, and touch not the unclean *thing;* and I will receive you, 18And will be a Father unto you, and ye shall be my sons and daughters, saith the Lord Almighty. [Jer. 31:1,9; Rev. 21:7]

7 Having therefore these promises, dearly beloved, let us cleanse ourselves from all filthiness of the flesh and spirit, perfecting holiness in the fear of God. [1 John 3:3]

The joy of good news

2 Receive us; we have wronged no *man,* we have corrupted no *man,* we have defrauded no *man.* 3I speak not *this* to condemn *you:* for I have said before, that you are in our hearts to die and live with *you.* 4Great *is* my boldness of speech toward you, great *is* my glorying of you: I am filled with comfort, I am exceeding joyful in all our tribulation. 5For, when we were come into Macedonia, our flesh had no rest, but *we were* troubled on every *side;* without *were* fightings, within *were* fears. 6Nevertheless God, that comforteth *those that are* cast down, comfort-

ed us by the coming of Titus; 7And not by his coming only, but by the consolation wherewith he was comforted in you, when he told us your earnest desire, your mourning, your fervent mind toward me; so that I rejoiced the more. 8For though I made you sorry with a letter, I do not repent, though I did repent: for I perceive that the same epistle hath made you sorry, though *it were* but for a season. 9Now I rejoice, not that ye were made sorry, but that ye sorrowed to repentance: for ye were made sorry after a godly manner, that ye might receive damage by us in nothing. 10For godly sorrow worketh repentance to salvation not to be repented of: but the sorrow of the world worketh death. 11For behold this selfsame *thing,* that ye sorrowed after a godly sort, what carefulness it wrought in you, yea, *what* clearing of yourselves, yea, *what* indignation, yea, *what* fear, yea, *what* vehement desire, yea, *what* zeal, yea, *what* revenge! In all *things* ye have approved yourselves to be clear in *this* matter. 12Wherefore, though I wrote unto you, *I did it* not for his cause that had done the wrong, nor for his cause that suffered wrong, but that our care for you in the sight of God might appear unto you. 13Therefore we were comforted in your comfort: *yea,* and exceedingly the more joyed we for the joy of Titus, because his spirit was refreshed by you all. 14For if I have boasted any *thing* to him of you, I am not ashamed; but as we spake all *things* to you in truth, even so our boasting, which *I made* before Titus, is found a truth. 15And his inward affection is more abundant toward you, whilst he remembereth the obedience of you all, how with fear and trembling you received him. 16I rejoice therefore that I have confidence in you in all *things.* [2 Thes. 3:4; Philem. 8,21]

The giving of the Macedonians

8 Moreover, brethren, we do you to wit of the grace of God bestowed on the churches of Macedonia; 2How that in a great trial of affliction the abundance of their joy and their deep poverty abounded unto the riches of their liberality. 3For to *their* power, I bear record, *yea,* and beyond *their* power *they were* willing of themselves; 4Praying us with much intreaty that we would receive the gift, and *take upon us* the fellowship of the ministering to the saints. 5And *this they did,* not as we hoped, but first gave their own selves to the Lord, and unto us by the will of God. 6Insomuch that we desired Titus, that as he had begun, so he would also finish in you the same grace also. 7Therefore, as ye abound in every *thing, in* faith, and utterance, and knowledge, and *in* all diligence, and *in* your love to us, *see* that ye abound in this grace also. [1 Cor. 1:5; 12:13; ch. 9:8]

The example of Jesus

8 I speak not by commandment, but by occasion of the forwardness of others, and to prove the sincerity of your love. 9For ye know the grace of our Lord Jesus Christ, that, though he was rich, *yet* for your

sakes he became poor, that ye through his poverty might be rich. 10And herein I give *my* advice: for this is expedient for you, who have begun before, not only to do, but also to be forward a year ago. 11Now therefore perform the doing of *it; that* as *there was* a readiness to will, so *there may be* a performance also out of that which *you* have. 12For if there be first a willing mind, *it is* accepted according to that a man hath, *and* not according to that he hath not. 13For *I mean* not that other *men* be eased, and *you* burdened; 14But by an equality, *that* now at *this* time your abundance *may be a supply* for their want, that their abundance also may be *a supply* for your want: that there may be equality: 15As it is written, He that *had gathered* much had nothing over; and he that *had gathered* little had no lack. [Ex. 16:18]

Coming of Titus

16 But thanks be to God, which put the same earnest care into the heart of Titus for you. 17For indeed he accepted the exhortation; but being more forward, of his own accord he went unto you. 18And we have sent with him the brother, whose praise *is* in the gospel throughout all the churches; 19And not *that* only, but who was also chosen of the churches to travel with us with this grace, which is administered by us to the glory of the same Lord, and *declaration of* your ready mind: 20Avoiding this, that no *man* should blame us in this abundance which is adminis-

tered by us: [21]Providing *for* honest *things,* not only in the sight of the Lord, but also in the sight of men. [22]And we have sent with them our brother, whom we have oftentimes proved diligent in many *things,* but now much more diligent, upon the great confidence which *I have* in you. [23]Whether *any do inquire* of Titus, *he is* my partner and fellowhelper concerning you: or our brethren *be inquired of, they are* the messengers of the churches, *and* the glory of Christ. [24]Wherefore shew ye to them, and before the churches, the proof of your love, and of our boasting on your behalf. [ch. 7:14; 9:2]

God loveth a cheerful giver

9 For as touching the ministering to the saints, it is superfluous for me to write to you: [2]For I know the forwardness of your mind, for which I boast of you to them of Macedonia, that Achaia was ready a year ago; and your zeal hath provoked very many. [3]Yet have I sent the brethren, lest our boasting of you should be in vain in this behalf; that, as I said, ye may be ready: [4]Lest haply if they of Macedonia come with me, and find you unprepared, we (that we say not, you) should be ashamed in this *same* confident boasting. [5]Therefore I thought it necessary to exhort the brethren, that they would go before unto you, and make up beforehand your bounty, whereof *ye* had notice before, that the same might be ready, as *a matter of* bounty, and not as *of* covetousness. [6]But this *I say,* He

which soweth sparingly shall reap also sparingly; and he which soweth bountifully shall reap also bountifully. [7]Every man according as he purposeth in *his* heart, *so let him give;* not grudgingly, or of necessity: for God loveth a cheerful giver. [8]And God *is* able to make all grace abound towards you; that ye, always having all sufficiency in all *things,* may abound to every good work: [9](As it is written, He hath dispersed abroad; he hath given to the poor: his righteousness remaineth for ever. [10]Now he that ministereth seed to the sower both minister bread for *your* food, and multiply your seed sown, and increase the fruits of your righteousness;) [11]Being enriched in every *thing* to all bountifulness, which causeth through us thanksgiving to God. [12]For the administration of this service not only supplieth the want of the saints, but is abundant also by many thanksgivings unto God; [13]Whiles by the experiment of this ministration they glorify God for your professed subjection unto the gospel of Christ, and *for your* liberal distribution unto them, and unto all *men;* [14]And by their prayer for you, which long after you for the exceeding grace of God in you. [15]Thanks *be* unto God for his unspeakable gift. [Jas. 1:17]

Paul defends his ministry

10 Now I Paul myself beseech you by the meekness and gentleness of Christ, who in presence *am* base among you, but being absent am bold toward you: [2]But I beseech *you,* that I may not be bold when I am present with *that* confidence, wherewith I think to be bold against some, which think of us as if we walked according to the flesh. ³For though we walk in the flesh, we do not war after the flesh: ⁴(For the weapons of our warfare *are* not carnal, but mighty through God to the pulling down of strong holds;) ⁵Casting down imaginations, and every high thing that exalteth itself against the knowledge of God, and bringing into captivity every thought to the obedience of Christ; ⁶And having in a readiness to revenge all disobedience, when your obedience is fulfilled. [ch. 13:2,10; ch. 7:15]

7 Do ye look on *things* after the outward appearance? If any *man* trust to himself that *he* is Christ's, let him of himself think this again, that, as he *is* Christ's, even so *are* we Christ's. ⁸For though I should boast somewhat more of our authority, which the Lord hath given us for edification, and not for your destruction, I should not be ashamed: ⁹That I may not seem as if *I* would terrify you by letters. ¹⁰For *his* letters, say they, *are* weighty and powerful; but *his* bodily presence *is* weak, and *his* speech contemptible. ¹¹Let such a one think this, that, such as we are in word by letters when we are absent, such *will we be* also in deed when we are present.

12 For we dare not make *ourselves* of the number, or compare ourselves with some that commend themselves: but they measuring themselves by themselves, and comparing themselves amongst themselves, are not wise. ¹³But we will not boast of *things* without *our* measure, but according to the measure of the rule which God hath distributed to us, a measure to reach even unto you. ¹⁴For we stretch not ourselves beyond *our measure,* as though we reached not unto you: for we are come as far as to you also in *preaching* the gospel of Christ: ¹⁵Not boasting of *things* without *our* measure, *that is,* of other *men's* labours; but having hope, when your faith is increased, that *we* shall be enlarged by you according to our rule abundantly, ¹⁶To preach the gospel in the *regions* beyond you, *and* not to boast in another *man's* line of *things* made ready to our hand. ¹⁷But he that glorieth, let him glory in the Lord. ¹⁸For not he that commendeth himself is approved, but whom the Lord commendeth. [Prov. 27:2; Rom. 2:29; 1 Cor. 4:5]

Paul's fear of false teachers

11 Would *to God* you could bear with me a little in *my* folly: and indeed bear with me. ²For I am jealous over you with godly jealousy: for I have espoused you to one husband, that *I* may present *you as* a chaste virgin to Christ. ³But I fear, lest by any means, as the serpent beguiled Eve through his subtilty, so your minds should be corrupted from the simplicity that is in Christ. ⁴For if he that cometh preacheth another Jesus, whom we have not preached, or *if* ye receive another spirit, which ye have not received, or another gospel, which ye have not accepted, ye might well bear with *him.* 5For I suppose *I* was not a whit behind the very chiefest apostles. 6But though *I* be rude in speech, yet not in knowledge; but we *have been* throughly made manifest among you in all *things.* 7Have I committed an offence in abasing myself that you might be exalted, because I have preached to you the gospel of God freely? 8I robbed other churches, taking wages *of them,* to do you service. 9And when I was present with you, and wanted, I was chargeable to no *man:* for that which was lacking to me the brethren which came from Macedonia supplied: and in all *things* I have kept myself from being burdensome to you, and *so* will I keep *myself.* 10As the truth of Christ is in me, no *man* shall stop me of this boasting in the regions of Achaia. 11Wherefore? because I love you not? God knoweth. 12But what I do, that I will do, that I may cut off occasion from them which desire occasion; that wherein they glory, they may be found even as we. 13For such *are* false apostles, deceitful workers, transforming themselves into the apostles of Christ. 14And no marvel; for Satan himself is transformed into an angel of light. 15Therefore *it is* no great *thing* if his ministers also be transformed as the ministers of righteousness; whose end shall be according to their works. [Phil. 3:19]

Paul's rightful boasting

16 I say again, Let no *man* think me a fool; if otherwise, yet as a fool receive me, that I may boast myself a little. 17*That* which I speak, I speak *it* not after the Lord, but as *it were* foolishly, in this confidence of boasting. 18Seeing that many glory after the flesh, I will glory also. 19For ye suffer fools gladly, seeing ye *yourselves* are wise. 20For ye suffer, if a man bring you into bondage, if a man devour *you,* if a man take *of you,* if a man exalt himself, if a man smite you on the face. 21I speak as concerning reproach, as though we had been weak. Howbeit whereinsoever any is bold, (I speak foolishly,) I am bold also. 22Are they Hebrews? so *am* I. Are they Israelites? so *am* I. Are they the seed of Abraham? so *am* I. 23Are they ministers of Christ? (I speak as a fool) I *am* more; in labours more abundant, in stripes above measure, in prisons more frequent, in deaths oft. 24Of the Jews five times received I forty *stripes* save one. 25Thrice was I beaten with rods, once was I stoned, thrice I suffered shipwrack, a night and a day I have been in the deep; 26*In* journeyings often, *in* perils of waters, *in* perils of robbers, *in* perils by *my own* countrymen, *in* perils by the heathen, *in* perils in the city, *in* perils in the wilderness, *in* perils in the sea, *in* perils among false brethren; 27In weariness and painfulness, in watchings often, in hunger and thirst, in fastings often, in cold and nakedness. 28Besides those *things* that are without, that which cometh upon me daily, the care of all the churches. 29Who is weak, and I am not weak? who is offend-

ed, and I burn not? 30If I must needs glory, I will glory of the *things* which concern mine infirmities. 31The God and Father of our Lord Jesus Christ, which is blessed for evermore, knoweth that I lie not. 32In Damascus the governor under Aretas the king kept the city of the Damascenes *with a garrison,* desirous to apprehend me: 33And through a window in a basket was I let down by the wall, and escaped his hands.

Paul's visions of the Lord

12 It is not expedient for me doubtless to glory. I will come to visions and revelations of the Lord. 2I knew a man in Christ above fourteen years ago, (whether in the body, I cannot tell; or whether out of the body, I cannot tell: God knoweth;) such a one caught up to the third heaven. 3And I knew such a man, (whether in the body, or out of the body, I cannot tell: God knoweth;) 4How that he was caught up into paradise, and heard unspeakable words, which *it is* not lawful for a man to utter. 5Of such a one will I glory: yet of myself I will not glory, but in mine infirmities. 6For though I would desire to glory, I shall not be a fool; for I will say the truth: but *now* I forbear, lest any *man* should think of me above *that* which he seeth me *to be,* or that he heareth of me. 7And lest I should be exalted above measure through the abundance of the revelations, there was given to me a thorn in the flesh, the messenger of Satan to buffet me, lest I should

be exalted above measure. 8For this *thing* I besought the Lord thrice, that it might depart from me. 9And he said unto me, My grace is sufficient for thee: for my strength is made perfect in weakness. Most gladly therefore will I rather glory in my infirmities, that the power of Christ may rest upon me. 10Therefore I take pleasure in infirmities, in reproaches, in necessities, in persecutions, in distresses for Christ's sake: for when I am weak, then am I strong. [Rom. 5:3; ch. 7:4; ch. 13:4]

The signs of a true apostle

11 I am become a fool in glorying; ye have compelled me: for I ought to have been commended of you: for *in* nothing am I behind the very chiefest apostles, though I be nothing. 12Truly the signs of an apostle were wrought among you in all patience, in signs, and wonders, and mighty deeds. 13For what is it wherein ye were inferior to other churches, except *it be* that I myself was not burdensome to you? forgive me this wrong. [1 Cor. 1:7; 1 Cor. 9:12; ch. 11:9; ch. 11:7]

14 Behold, the third *time* I am ready to come to you; and I will not be burdensome to you: for I seek not yours, but you: for the children ought not to lay up for the parents, but the parents for the children. 15And I will very gladly spend and be spent for you; though the more abundantly I love you, the less I be loved. 16But be it so, I did not burden you: nevertheless, being crafty, I caught you with guile. 17Did I make a gain of you by any of them

whom I sent unto you? ¹⁸I desired Titus, and with *him* I sent a brother. Did Titus make a gain of you? walked we not in the same spirit? *walked we* not in the same steps? [ch. 8:6,18]

The appeal for repentance
19 Again, think you that we excuse ourselves unto you? we speak before God in Christ: but *we do* all *things,* dearly beloved, for your edifying. ²⁰For I fear, lest, when I come, I shall not find you such as I would, and *that* I shall be found unto you such as ye would not: lest *there be* debates, envyings, wraths, strifes, backbitings, whisperings, swellings, tumults: ²¹*And* lest, when I come again, my God will humble *me* among you, and *that* I shall bewail many which have sinned already, and have not repented of the uncleanness and fornication and lasciviousness which they have committed. [ch. 2:1,4; ch. 13:2; 1 Cor. 5:1]

13 This *is* the third *time* I am coming to you. In the mouth of two or three witnesses shall every word be established. ²I told *you* before, and foretell *you,* as if I were present the second *time;* and being absent now I write to them which heretofore have sinned, and to all other, that, if I come again, I will not spare: ³Since ye seek a proof of Christ speaking in me, which to you-ward is not weak, but is mighty in you. ⁴For though he was crucified through weakness, yet he liveth by the power of God. For we also are weak in him, but we shall live with him by the power of God toward you. ⁵Examine yourselves, whether ye be in the faith; prove your own selves. Know ye not your own selves, how that Jesus Christ is in you, except ye be reprobates? ⁶But I trust that ye shall know that we are not reprobates. ⁷Now I pray to God that ye do no evil; not that we should appear approved, but that ye should do *that which is* honest, though we be as reprobates. ⁸For we can do nothing against the truth, but for the truth. ⁹For we are glad, when we are weak, and ye are strong: and this also we wish, *even* your perfection. ¹⁰Therefore I write these *things* being absent, lest being present I should use sharpness, according to the power which the Lord hath given me to edification, and not to destruction. [1 Cor. 4:21; ch. 12:20,21]

Farewell and benediction
11 Finally, brethren, farewell. Be perfect, be of good comfort, be of one mind, live in peace; and the God of love and peace shall be with you. ¹²Greet one another with a holy kiss. ¹³All the saints salute you. ¹⁴The grace of the Lord Jesus Christ, and the love of God, and the communion of the Holy Ghost, *be* with you all. Amen. [Rom. 16:24; Phil. 2:1]

¶ The second *epistle* to the Corinthians was written from Philippi, *a city* of Macedonia, by Titus and Lucas.

No other gospel

1 Paul, an apostle, (not of men, neither by man, but by Jesus Christ, and God the Father, who raised him from the dead;) ²And all the brethren which are with me, unto the churches of Galatia: ³Grace *be* to you and peace from God the Father, and *from* our Lord Jesus Christ, ⁴Who gave himself for our sins, that he might deliver us from *this* present evil world, according to the will of God and our Father: ⁵To whom *be* glory for ever and ever. Amen.

6 I marvel that you are so soon removed from him that called you into the grace of Christ unto another gospel: ⁷Which is not another; but there be some that trouble you, and would pervert the gospel of Christ. ⁸But though we, or an angel from heaven, preach any other gospel unto you than *that* which we have preached unto you, let him be accursed. ⁹As we said before, so say I now again, If any *man* preach any other gospel unto you than that ye have received, let him be accursed. ¹⁰For do I now persuade men, or God? or do I seek to please men? for if I yet pleased men, I should not be the servant of Christ. [1 Thes. 2:4; 1 Sam. 24:7; Mat. 28:14; 1 Thes. 2:4; Jas. 4:4]

Paul's authority of divine origin

11 But I certify you, brethren, that the gospel which was preached of me is not after man. ¹²For I neither received it of man, neither was I taught *it,* but by the revelation of Jesus Christ. ¹³For ye have heard of my conversation in time past in the Jews' religion, how that beyond measure I persecuted the church of God, and wasted it: ¹⁴And profited in the Jews' religion above many *my* equals in mine own nation, being more exceedingly zealous of the traditions of my fathers. ¹⁵But when it pleased God, who separated me from my mother's womb, and called *me* by his grace, ¹⁶To reveal his Son in me, that I might preach him among the heathen; immediately I conferred not with flesh and blood: ¹⁷Neither went I up to Jerusalem to them which were apostles before me: but I went into Arabia, and returned again unto Damascus. ¹⁸Then after three years I went up to Jerusalem to see Peter, and abode with him fifteen days. ¹⁹But other of the apostles saw I none, save James the Lord's brother. ²⁰Now *the things* which I write unto you, behold, before God, I lie not. ²¹Afterwards I came into the regions of Syria and Cilicia; ²²And was unknown by face unto the churches of Judea which were in Christ: ²³But they had heard only, That he which persecuted us in times past now preacheth the faith which once he destroyed. ²⁴And they glorified God in me.

Paul accepted by the church

2 Then fourteen years after I went up again to Jerusalem with Barnabas, and took Titus with *me* also. ²And I went up by revelation, and communicated unto them *that* gospel which I preach among the Gentiles, but privately to them which were of reputation, lest by any means I should run, or had run, in vain. ³But neither Titus, who was with me, being a Greek, was compelled to be circumcised: ⁴And *that* because of false brethren unawares brought in, who came in privily to spy out our liberty which we have in Christ Jesus, that they might bring us into bondage: ⁵To whom we gave place by subjection, no, not for an hour; that the truth of the gospel might continue with you. ⁶But of these who seemed to be somewhat, (whatsoever they were, it maketh no matter to me: God accepteth no man's person:) for they who seemed *to be somewhat* in conference added nothing to me: ⁷But contrariwise, when they saw that the gospel of the uncircumcision was committed unto me, as *the gospel* of the circumcision *was* unto Peter; ⁸(For he that wrought effectually in Peter to the apostleship of the circumcision, *the same* was mighty in me towards the Gentiles:) ⁹And when James, Cephas, and John, who seemed to be pillars, perceived the grace that was given unto me, they gave to me and Barnabas the right hands of fellowship; that we *should go* unto the heathen, and they unto the circumcision. ¹⁰Only *they would* that we should remember the poor; the same which I also was forward to do. [Acts 11:30; Rom. 15:25]

Paul's opposition to Peter

11 But when Peter was come to Antioch, I withstood him to the face, because he was *to be* blamed.

¹²For before that certain came from James, he did eat with the Gentiles: but when they were come, he withdrew and separated himself, fearing them which were of the circumcision. ¹³And the other Jews dissembled likewise with him; insomuch that Barnabas also was carried away with their dissimulation. ¹⁴But when I saw that they walked not uprightly according to the truth of the gospel, I said unto Peter before *them* all, If thou, being a Jew, livest after the manner of Gentiles, and not as do the Jews, why compellest thou the Gentiles to live as do the Jews? ¹⁵We *who are* Jews by nature, and not sinners of the Gentiles, ¹⁶Knowing that a man is not justified by the works of the law, but by the faith of Jesus Christ, even we have believed in Jesus Christ, that we might be justified by the faith of Christ, and not by the works of the law: for by the works of the law shall no flesh be justified. ¹⁷But if, while we seek to be justified by Christ, we ourselves also are found sinners, *is* therefore Christ the minister of sin? God forbid. ¹⁸For if I build again the *things* which I destroyed, I make myself a transgressor. ¹⁹For I through the law am dead to the law, that I might live unto God. ²⁰I am crucified with Christ: nevertheless I live; yet not I, but Christ liveth in me: and *the life* which I now live in the flesh I live by the faith of the Son of God, who loved me, and gave himself for me. ²¹I do not frustrate the grace of God: for if righteousness *come* by the law, then Christ is dead in vain. [Heb. 7:11; Rom. 11:6]

Receiving the Spirit by faith

3 O foolish Galatians, who hath bewitched you, that *you* should not obey the truth, before whose eyes Jesus Christ hath been evidently set forth, crucified among you? **2**This only would I learn of you, Received ye the Spirit by the works of the law, or by the hearing of faith? **3**Are ye so foolish? having begun in the Spirit, are ye now made perfect by the flesh? **4**Have ye suffered so many *things* in vain? if *it* be yet in vain. **5**He therefore that ministereth to you the Spirit, and worketh miracles among you, *doeth he it* by the works of the law, or by the hearing of faith? **6**Even as Abraham believed God, and it was accounted to him for righteousness. **7**Know ye therefore that they which are of faith, the same are the children of Abraham. **8**And the scripture, foreseeing that God would justify the heathen through faith, preached before the gospel unto Abraham, *saying,* In thee shall all nations be blessed. **9**So then they which be of faith are blessed with faithful Abraham. **10**For as many as are of the works of the law are under the curse: for it is written, Cursed *is* every one that continueth not in all *things* which are written in the book of the law to do them. **11**But that no *man* is justified by the law in the sight of God, *it is* evident: for, The just shall live by faith. **12**And the law is not of faith: but, The man that doeth them shall live in them. **13**Christ hath redeemed us from the curse of the law, being made a curse for us: for it is written, Cursed *is* every one that hangeth on

a tree: **14**That the blessing of Abraham might come on the Gentiles through Jesus Christ; that we might receive the promise of the Spirit through faith. **15**Brethren, I speak after the manner of men; Though *it* be but a man's covenant, *yet if it be* confirmed, no *man* disannulleth, or added thereto. **16**Now to Abraham and his seed were the promises made. *He* saith not, And to seeds, as of many; but as of one, And to thy seed, which is Christ. **17**And this I say, *that* the covenant, that was confirmed before of God in Christ, the law, which was four hundred and thirty years after, cannot disannul, that *it* should make the promise of none effect. **18**For if the inheritance *be* of the law, *it is* no more of promise: but God gave *it* to Abraham by promise. [Rom. 8:17; Rom. 4:14]

The function of the law

19 Wherefore then *serveth* the law? It was added because of transgressions, till the seed should come to whom the promise was made; *and it was* ordained by angels in the hand of a mediator. **20**Now a mediator is not *a mediator* of one, but God is one. **21***Is* the law then against the promises of God? God forbid: for if there had been a law given which could have given life, verily righteousness should have been by the law. **22**But the scripture hath concluded all under sin, that the promise by faith of Jesus Christ might be given to them that believe. **23**But before faith came, we were kept under the law, shut up unto the faith which should afterwards be revealed. **24**Wherefore the law was our schoolmaster *to bring us* unto Christ, that we might be justified by faith. 25But after that faith is come, we are no longer under a schoolmaster. 26For ye are all the children of God by faith in Christ Jesus. 27For as many of you as have been baptized into Christ have put on Christ. 28There is neither Jew nor Greek, there is neither bond nor free, there is neither male nor female: for ye are all one in Christ Jesus. 29And if ye *be* Christ's, then are ye Abraham's seed, and heirs according to the promise. [Gen. 21:10; Heb. 11:18; Rom. 8:17]

Do not return to bondage

4 Now I say, *That* the heir, as long as he is a child, differeth nothing from a servant, though he be lord of all; 2But is under tutors and governors until the time appointed of the father. 3Even so we, when we were children, were in bondage under the elements of the world: 4But when the fulness of the time was come, God sent forth his Son, made of a woman, made under the law, 5To redeem them that were under the law, that we might receive the adoption of sons. 6And because ye are sons, God hath sent forth the Spirit of his Son into your hearts, crying, Abba, Father. 7Wherefore thou art no more a servant, but a son; and if a son, then an heir of God through Christ. 8Howbeit then, when ye knew not God, ye did service unto them which by nature are no gods. 9But now, after that ye have known God, or rather are known of God, how turn ye again to the weak and beggarly elements, whereunto ye desire again to be in bondage? 10Ye observe days, and months, and times, and years. 11I am afraid of you, lest I have bestowed upon you labour in vain. [1 Thes. 3:5]

Paul's concern for the Galatians

12 Brethren, I beseech you, be as I *am;* for I *am* as ye *are:* ye have not injured me at all. 13Ye know how through infirmity of the flesh I preached the gospel unto you at the first. 14And my temptation which was in my flesh ye despised not, nor rejected; but received me as an angel of God, *even* as Christ Jesus. 15Where is then the blessedness ye spake of? for I bear you record, that if *it had been* possible, ye would have plucked out your own eyes, and have given *them* to me. 16Am I therefore become your enemy, because I tell you the truth? 17They zealously affect you, *but* not well; yea, they would exclude you, that you might affect them. 18But *it is* good to be zealously affected always in a good *thing,* and not only when I am present with you. 19My little children, of whom I travail in birth again until Christ be formed in you, 20I desire to be present with you now, and to change my voice; for I stand in doubt of you.

The allegory of Abraham

21 Tell me, ye that desire to be under the law, do ye not hear the law? 22For it is written, that Abraham had two sons, the one by a bondmaid, the other by a freewoman. 23But he who was of the bondwoman was born after the

flesh; but he of the freewoman *was* by promise. 24Which *things* are an allegory: for these are the two covenants; the one from the mount Sinai, which gendereth to bondage, which is Agar. 25For *this* Agar is mount Sinai in Arabia, and answereth to Jerusalem which now is, and is in bondage with her children. 26But Jerusalem which is above is free, which is the mother of us all. 27For it is written, Rejoice, *thou* barren that bearest not; break forth and cry, thou that travailest not: for the desolate hath many more children than she which hath a husband. 28Now we, brethren, as Isaac was, are the children of promise. 29But as then he that was born after the flesh persecuted him that was *born* after the Spirit, even so *it is* now. 30Nevertheless what saith the scripture? Cast out the bondwoman and her son: for the son of the bondwoman shall not be heir with the son of the freewoman. 31So then, brethren, we are not children of *the* bondwoman, but of the free. [John 8:36]

Liberty threatened by legalism

5 Stand fast therefore in the liberty wherewith Christ hath made us free, and be not entangled again with the yoke of bondage. 2Behold, I Paul say unto you, that if ye be circumcised, Christ shall profit you nothing. 3For I testify again to every man that is circumcised, that he is a debtor to do the whole law. 4Christ is become of no effect unto you, whosoever of you are justified by the law; ye are fallen from

grace. 5For we through the Spirit wait for the hope of righteousness by faith. 6For in Jesus Christ neither circumcision availeth any *thing,* nor uncircumcision; but faith which worketh by love. 7Ye did run well; who did hinder you that ye should not obey the truth? 8*This* persuasion *cometh* not of him that calleth you. 9A little leaven leaveneth the whole lump. 10I have confidence in you through the Lord, that ye will be none otherwise minded: but he that troubleth you shall bear *his* judgment, whosoever he be. 11And I, brethren, if I yet preach circumcision, why do I yet suffer persecution? then is the offence of the cross ceased. 12I would they were even cut off which trouble you. [Josh. 7:25; Acts 15:1,2]

Liberty defined

13 For, brethren, ye have been called unto liberty; only *use* not liberty for an occasion to the flesh, but by love serve one another. 14For all the law is fulfilled in one word, *even* in *this;* Thou shalt love thy neighbour as thyself. 15But if ye bite and devour one another, take heed ye be not consumed one of another. 16*This* I say then, Walk in the Spirit, and ye shall not fulfil the lust of the flesh. 17For the flesh lusteth against the Spirit, and the Spirit against the flesh: and these are contrary the one to the other: so that ye cannot do the *things* that ye would. 18But if ye be led of the Spirit, ye are not under the law. 19Now the works of the flesh are manifest, which are *these;* Adul-

tery, fornication, uncleanness, lasciviousness, 20Idolatry, witchcraft, hatred, variance, emulations, wrath, strife, seditions, heresies, 21Envyings, murders, drunkenness, revellings, and such like: of the which I tell you before, as I have also told *you* in time past, that they which do such *things* shall not inherit the kingdom of God. 22But the fruit of the Spirit is love, joy, peace, longsuffering, gentleness, goodness, faith, 23Meekness, temperance: against such there is no law. 24And they that are Christ's have crucified the flesh with the affections and lusts. 25If we live in the Spirit, let us also walk in the Spirit. 26Let us not be desirous of vain glory, provoking one another, envying one another. [Phil. 2:3]

Fulfilling the law of Christ

6 Brethren, if a man be overtaken in a fault, ye which are spiritual, restore such a one in the spirit of meekness; considering thyself, lest thou also be tempted. 2Bear ye one another's burdens, and so fulfil the law of Christ. 3For if a man think himself to be something, when he is nothing, he deceiveth himself. 4But let every man prove his own work, and then shall he have rejoicing in himself alone, and not in another. 5For every man shall bear his own burden. 6Let him that is taught in the word communicate unto him that teacheth in all good *things*. 7Be not deceived; God is not mocked: for whatsoever a man soweth, that shall he also reap. 8For he that

soweth to his flesh shall of the flesh reap corruption; but he that soweth to the Spirit shall of the Spirit reap life everlasting. 9And let us not be weary in well doing: for in due season we shall reap, if we faint not. 10As we have therefore opportunity, let us do good unto all *men,* especially unto them who are of the household of faith. [John 9:4; Tit. 3:8; Eph. 2:19]

Paul's personal benediction

11 Ye see how large a letter I have written unto you with mine own hand. 12As many as desire to make a fair shew in the flesh, they constrain you to be circumcised; only lest they should suffer persecution for the cross of Christ. 13For neither they themselves who are circumcised keep the law; but desire to have you circumcised, that they may glory in your flesh. 14But God forbid that I should glory, save in the cross of our Lord Jesus Christ, by whom the world is crucified unto me, and I unto the world. 15For in Christ Jesus neither circumcision availeth any *thing,* nor uncircumcision, but a new creature. 16And as many as walk according to this rule, peace *be* on them, and mercy, and upon the Israel of God. 17From henceforth let no *man* trouble me: for I bear in my body the marks of the Lord Jesus. 18Brethren, the grace of our Lord Jesus Christ *be* with your spirit. Amen. [2 Tim. 4:22]

¶ Unto the Galatians written from Rome.

Ephesians

1 Paul, an apostle of Jesus Christ by the will of God, to the saints which are at Ephesus, and to the faithful in Christ Jesus: ²Grace *be* to you, and peace, from God our Father, and *from* the Lord Jesus Christ. [Gal. 1:3]

Spiritual blessings in Christ

3 Blessed *be* the God and Father of our Lord Jesus Christ, who hath blessed us with all spiritual blessings in heavenly *places* in Christ: ⁴According as he hath chosen us in him before the foundation of the world, that we should be holy and without blame before him in love: ⁵Having predestinated us unto the adoption of children by Jesus Christ to himself, according to the good pleasure of his will, ⁶To the praise of the glory of his grace, wherein he hath made us accepted in the beloved: ⁷In whom we have redemption through his blood, the forgiveness of sins, according to the riches of his grace; ⁸Wherein he hath abounded toward us in all wisdom and prudence; ⁹Having made known unto us the mystery of his will, according to his good pleasure which he had purposed in himself: ¹⁰That in the dispensation of the fulness of times *he* might gather together in one all *things* in Christ, both which are in heaven, and which are on earth; *even* in him: ¹¹In whom also we have obtained an inheritance, being predestinated according to the purpose of him who worketh all *things* after the counsel of his own will:

¹²That we should be to the praise of his glory, who first trusted in Christ: ¹³In whom ye also *trusted,* after that ye heard the word of truth, the gospel of your salvation: in whom also after that ye believed, ye were sealed with *that* holy Spirit of promise, ¹⁴Which is the earnest of our inheritance, until the redemption of the purchased possession, unto the praise of his glory. [2 Cor. 5:5; Rom. 8:23; Acts 20:28; 1 Pet. 2:9]

Prayer for wisdom and knowledge

15 Wherefore I also, after I heard of your faith in the Lord Jesus, and love unto all the saints, ¹⁶Cease not to give thanks for you, making mention of you in my prayers; ¹⁷That the God of our Lord Jesus Christ, the Father of glory, may give unto you the spirit of wisdom and revelation in the knowledge of him: ¹⁸The eyes of your understanding being enlightened; that ye may know what is the hope of his calling, and what the riches of the glory of his inheritance in the saints, ¹⁹And what *is* the exceeding greatness of his power to us-ward who believe, according to the working of his mighty power, ²⁰Which he wrought in Christ, when he raised him from the dead, and set *him* at his own right hand in the heavenly *places,* ²¹Far above all principality, and power, and might, and dominion, and every name that is named, not only in this world, but also in that which is

to come: 22And hath put all *things* under his feet, and gave him *to be* the head over all *things* to the church, 23Which is his body, the fulness of him that filleth all in all. [Rom. 12:5; Col. 2:9; 1 Cor. 12:6]

New life with Christ

2 And you *hath he quickened,* who were dead in trespasses and sins; 2Wherein in time past ye walked according to the course of this world, according to the prince of the power of the air, the spirit that now worketh in the children of disobedience: 3Among whom also we all had our conversation in times past in the lusts of our flesh, fulfilling the desires of the flesh and of the mind; and were by nature the children of wrath, even as others. 4But God, who is rich in mercy, for his great love wherewith he loved us, 5Even when we were dead in sins, hath quickened *us* together with Christ, (by grace ye are saved;) 6And hath raised *us* up together, and made *us* sit together in heavenly *places* in Christ Jesus: 7That in the ages to come he might shew the exceeding riches of his grace in *his* kindness towards us through Christ Jesus. 8For by grace are ye saved through faith; and that not of yourselves: *it is* the gift of God: 9Not of works, lest any *man* should boast. 10For we are his workmanship, created in Christ Jesus unto good works, which God hath before ordained that we should walk in them. [Is. 19:25]

The household of God

11 Wherefore remember, that ye *being* in time passed Gentiles in the flesh, who are called Uncircumcision by that which is called the Circumcision in the flesh made by hands; 12That at that time ye were without Christ, being aliens from the commonwealth of Israel, and strangers from the covenants of promise, having no hope, and without God in the world: 13But now in Christ Jesus ye who sometimes were far off are made nigh by the blood of Christ. 14For he is our peace, who hath made both one, and hath broken down the middle wall of partition *between us;* 15Having abolished in his flesh the enmity, *even* the law of commandments *contained* in ordinances; for to make in himself of twain one new man, *so* making peace; 16And *that* he might reconcile both unto God in one body by the cross, having slain the enmity thereby: 17And came and preached peace to you which were afar off, and to them that were nigh; 18For through him we both have access by one Spirit unto the Father. 19Now therefore ye are no more strangers and foreigners, but fellowcitizens with the saints, and of the household of God; 20And are built upon the foundation of the apostles and prophets, Jesus Christ himself being the chief corner *stone;* 21In whom all the building fitly framed together groweth unto a holy temple in the Lord: 22In whom you also are builded together for a habitation of God through the Spirit. [1 Pet. 2:5]

Paul, apostle to the Gentiles

3 For this cause I Paul, the prisoner of Jesus Christ for you Gentiles, 2If ye have heard of the

dispensation of the grace of God which is given me to you-ward: ³How that by revelation he made known unto me the mystery; (as I wrote afore in few *words,* ⁴Whereby, when ye read, ye may understand my knowledge in the mystery of Christ) ⁵Which in other ages was not made known unto the sons of men, as it is now revealed unto his holy apostles and prophets by the Spirit; ⁶That the Gentiles should be fellowheirs, and of the same body, and partakers of his promise in Christ by the gospel: ⁷Whereof I was made a minister, according to the gift of the grace of God given unto me by the effectual working of his power. ⁸Unto me, *who am* less than the least of all saints, is this grace given, that *I* should preach among the Gentiles the unsearchable riches of Christ; ⁹And to make all *men* see what *is* the fellowship of the mystery, which from the beginning of the world hath been hid in God, who created all *things* by Jesus Christ: ¹⁰To the intent that now unto the principalities and powers in heavenly *places* might be known by the church the manifold wisdom of God, ¹¹According to the eternal purpose which he purposed in Christ Jesus our Lord: ¹²In whom we have boldness and access with confidence by the faith of him. ¹³Wherefore I desire that *ye* faint not at my tribulations for you, which is your glory. [Phil. 1:14; 2 Cor. 1:6]

Strength through the Spirit

14 For this cause I bow my knees unto the Father of our Lord Jesus Christ, ¹⁵Of whom the whole family in heaven and earth is named, ¹⁶That he would grant you, according to the riches of his glory, to be strengthened with might by his Spirit in the inner man; ¹⁷That Christ may dwell in your hearts by faith; that ye, being rooted and grounded in love, ¹⁸May be able to comprehend with all saints what *is* the breadth, and length, and depth, and height; ¹⁹And to know the love of Christ, which passeth knowledge, that ye might be filled with all the fulness of God. ²⁰Now unto him that is able to do exceeding abundantly above all that we ask or think, according to the power that worketh in us, ²¹Unto him *be* glory in the church by Christ Jesus throughout all ages, world without end. Amen. [Rom. 11:36]

The unity of the Spirit

4 I therefore, the prisoner of the Lord, beseech you that *ye* walk worthy of the vocation wherewith ye are called, ²With all lowliness and meekness, with longsuffering, forbearing one another in love; ³Endeavouring to keep the unity of the Spirit in the bond of peace. ⁴*There is* one body, and one Spirit, even as ye are called in one hope of your calling; ⁵One Lord, one faith, one baptism, ⁶One God and Father of all, who *is* above all, and through all, and in you all. ⁷But unto every one of us is given grace according to the measure of the gift of Christ. ⁸Wherefore *he* saith, When he ascended up on high, he led captivity captive, and gave gifts unto men. ⁹(Now that he ascended, what is it but that he also descended first into

the lower parts of the earth? ¹⁰He that descended is the same also that ascended up far above all heavens, that he might fill all *things*.) ¹¹And he gave some, apostles; and some, prophets; and some, evangelists; and some, pastors and teachers; ¹²For the perfecting of the saints for the work of the ministry, for the edifying of the body of Christ: ¹³Till we all come in the unity of the faith, and of the knowledge of the Son of God, unto a perfect man, unto the measure of the stature of the fulness of Christ: ¹⁴That we *henceforth* be no more children, tossed to and fro, and carried about with every wind of doctrine, by the sleight of men, and cunning craftiness, whereby they lie in wait to deceive; ¹⁵But speaking the truth in love, may grow *up* into him *in* all *things*, which is the head, *even* Christ: ¹⁶From whom the whole body fitly joined together and compacted by that which every joint supplieth, according to the effectual working in the measure of every part, maketh increase of the body unto the edifying of itself in love. [Col. 2:19]

The old life and the new

17 This I say therefore, and testify in the Lord, that ye henceforth walk not as other Gentiles walk, in the vanity of their mind, ¹⁸Having the understanding darkened, being alienated from the life of God through the ignorance that is in them, because of the blindness of their heart: ¹⁹Who being past feeling have given themselves over unto lasciviousness, to work all uncleanness with greediness. ²⁰But ye have not so learned Christ; ²¹If so be that ye have heard him, and have been taught by him, as the truth is in Jesus: ²²That ye put off concerning the former conversation the old man, which is corrupt according to the deceitful lusts; ²³And be renewed in the spirit of your mind; ²⁴And that *ye* put on the new man, which after God is created in righteousness and true holiness. [Rom. 6:4]

25 Wherefore putting away lying, speak every man truth with his neighbour: for we are members one of another. ²⁶Be ye angry, and sin not: let not the sun go down upon your wrath: ²⁷Neither give place to the devil. ²⁸Let him that stole steal no more: but rather let him labour, working with *his* hands the *thing which is* good, that he may have to give to him that needeth. ²⁹Let no corrupt communication proceed out of your mouth, but that which *is* good to the use of edifying, that it may minister grace unto the hearers. ³⁰And grieve not the holy Spirit of God, whereby ye are sealed unto the day of redemption. ³¹Let all bitterness, and wrath, and anger, and clamour, and evil speaking, be put away from you, with all malice: ³²And be ye kind one to another, tenderhearted, forgiving one another, even as God for Christ's sake hath forgiven you. [2 Cor. 2:10; Mark 11:25]

The works of light and darkness

5 Be ye therefore followers of God, as dear children; ²And walk in love, as Christ also hath loved us, and hath given himself for

us an offering and a sacrifice to God for a sweetsmelling savour. 3 But fornication, and all uncleanness, or covetousness, let it not be once named amongst you, as becometh saints; 4 Neither filthiness, nor foolish talking, nor jesting, which are not convenient: but rather giving of thanks. 5 For this ye know, that no whoremonger, nor unclean *person*, nor covetous man who is an idolater, hath *any* inheritance in the kingdom of Christ and of God. 6 Let no *man* deceive you with vain words: for because of these *things* cometh the wrath of God upon the children of disobedience. 7 Be not ye therefore partakers with them. 8 For ye were sometimes darkness, but now *are ye* light in the Lord: walk as children of light: 9 (For the fruit of the Spirit *is* in all goodness and righteousness and truth;) 10 Proving what is acceptable unto the Lord. 11 And have no fellowship with the unfruitful works of darkness, but rather reprove *them.* 12 For it is a shame even to speak of those *things* which are done of them in secret. 13 But all *things* that are reproved are made manifest by the light: for whatsoever doth make manifest is light. 14 Wherefore *he* saith, Awake thou that sleepest, and arise from the dead, and Christ shall give thee light. 15 See then that ye walk circumspectly, not as fools, but as wise, 16 Redeeming the time, because the days are evil. 17 Wherefore be ye not unwise, but understanding what the will of the Lord *is.* 18 And be not drunk with wine, wherein is excess; but be filled with the Spirit; 19 Speaking to yourselves in psalms and hymns and spiritual songs,

singing and making melody in your heart to the Lord; 20 Giving thanks always for all *things* unto God and the Father in the name of our Lord Jesus Christ; 21 Submitting yourselves one to another in the fear of God. [Phil. 2:3]

Analogy of family and church

22 Wives, submit yourselves unto your own husbands, as unto the Lord. 23 For the husband is the head of the wife, even as Christ *is* the head of the church: and he is the saviour of the body. 24 Therefore as the church is subject unto Christ, so *let* the wives *be* to their own husbands in every *thing.* 25 Husbands, love your wives, even as Christ also loved the church, and gave himself for it; 26 That he might sanctify and cleanse *it* with the washing of water by the word, 27 That he might present it to himself a glorious church, not having spot, or wrinkle, or any such *thing;* but that it should be holy and without blemish. 28 So ought men to love their wives as their own bodies. He that loveth his wife loveth himself. 29 For no *man* ever yet hated his own flesh; but nourisheth and cherisheth it, even as the Lord the church: 30 For we are members of his body, of his flesh, and of his bones. 31 For this cause shall a man leave his father and mother, and shall be joined unto his wife, and they two shall be one flesh. 32 This is a great mystery: but I speak concerning Christ and the church. 33 Nevertheless let every one of you in particular so love his wife even as himself; and the wife

see that she reverence *her* husband. [Col. 3:19; 1 Pet. 3:6]

6 Children, obey your parents in the Lord: for this is right. [2]Honour thy father and mother; (which is the first commandment with promise;) [3]That it may be well with thee, and thou mayest live long on the earth. [4]And, ye fathers, provoke not your children to wrath: but bring them up in the nurture and admonition of the Lord. [Col. 3:21; Gen. 18:19]

5 Servants, be obedient to *them that are your* masters according to the flesh, with fear and trembling, in singleness of your heart, as unto Christ; [6]Not with eyeservice, as menpleasers; but as the servants of Christ, doing the will of God from the heart; [7]With good will doing service, as to the Lord, and not to men: [8]Knowing that whatsoever good *thing* any man doeth, the same shall he receive of the Lord, whether *he be* bond or free. [9]And, ye masters, do the same *things* unto them, forbearing threatening: knowing that your Master also is in heaven; neither is there respect of persons with him. [Col. 4:1; Rom. 2:11]

The whole armour of God

10 Finally, my brethren, be strong in the Lord, and in the power of his might. [11]Put on the whole armour of God, that ye may be able to stand against the wiles of the devil. [12]For we wrestle not against flesh and blood, but against principalities, against powers, against the rulers of the darkness of this world, against spiritual wickedness in high *places*. [13]Wherefore take unto *you* the whole armour of God, that ye may be able to withstand in the evil day, and having done all, to stand. [14]Stand therefore, having your loins girt about with truth, and having on the breastplate of righteousness; [15]And *your* feet shod with the preparation of the gospel of peace; [16]Above all, taking the shield of faith, wherewith ye shall be able to quench all the fiery darts of the wicked. [17]And take the helmet of salvation, and the sword of the Spirit, which is the word of God: [18]Praying always with all prayer and supplication in the Spirit, and watching thereunto with all perseverance and supplication for all saints; [19]And for me, that utterance may be given unto me, that *I* may open my mouth boldly, to make known the mystery of the gospel, [20]For which I am an ambassador in bonds: that therein I may speak boldly, as I ought to speak. [2 Cor. 5:20; Phil. 1:20]

Concluding benediction

21 But that ye also may know my affairs, *and* how I do, Tychicus, a beloved brother and faithful minister in the Lord, shall make known to you all *things*: [22]Whom I have sent unto you for the same purpose, that ye might know our affairs, and *that* he might comfort your hearts. [23]Peace *be* to the brethren, and love with faith, from God the Father and the Lord Jesus Christ. [24]Grace *be* with all them that love our Lord Jesus Christ in sincerity. Amen.

¶ Written from Rome unto the Ephesians by Tychicus.

The Epistle of Paul the Apostle to the

Philippians

1 Paul and Timotheus, the servants of Jesus Christ, to all the saints in Christ Jesus which are at Philippi, with the bishops and deacons: ²Grace *be* unto you, and peace, from God our Father, and *from* the Lord Jesus Christ. [1 Pet. 1:2]

Prayer of thankfulness

3 I thank my God upon every remembrance of you, ⁴Always in every prayer of mine for you all making request with joy, ⁵For your fellowship in the gospel from the first day until now; ⁶Being confident of this very *thing,* that he which hath begun a good work in you will perform *it* until the day of Jesus Christ: ⁷Even as it is meet for me to think this of you all, because I have you in *my* heart; inasmuch as both in my bonds, and *in* the defence and confirmation of the gospel, ye all be partakers of my grace. ⁸For God is my record, how *greatly* I long after you all in the bowels of Jesus Christ. ⁹And this I pray, that your love may abound yet more and more in knowledge and *in* all judgment; ¹⁰That ye may approve *things* that are excellent; that ye may be sincere and without offence till the day of Christ; ¹¹Being filled with the fruits of righteousness, which are by Jesus Christ unto the glory and praise of God. [Eph. 2:10; Col. 1:6; John 15:8]

Paul's boldness in prison

12 But I would ye should understand, brethren, that the *things which happened* unto me have fallen out rather unto the furtherance of the gospel; ¹³So that my bonds in Christ are manifest in all the palace, and *in* all other *places;* ¹⁴And many of the brethren in the Lord, waxing confident by my bonds, are much more bold to speak the word without fear. ¹⁵Some indeed preach Christ even of envy and strife; and some also of good will: ¹⁶The one preach Christ of contention, not sincerely, supposing to add affliction to my bonds: ¹⁷But the other of love, knowing that I am set for the defence of the gospel. ¹⁸What then? notwithstanding, every way, whether in pretence, or in truth, Christ is preached; and I therein do rejoice, yea, and will rejoice. ¹⁹For I know that this shall turn to my salvation through your prayer, and the supply of the Spirit of Jesus Christ, ²⁰According to my earnest expectation and *my* hope, that in nothing I shall be ashamed, but *that* with all boldness, as always, *so* now also Christ shall be magnified in my body, whether *it be* by life, or by death. ²¹For to me to live *is* Christ, and to die *is* gain. ²²But if *I* live in the flesh, this *is* the fruit of my labour: yet what I shall choose I wot not. ²³For I am in a strait betwixt two, having a desire to depart, and to be with Christ; *which is* far better: ²⁴Nevertheless to abide in the flesh *is* more needful for you. ²⁵And having this confidence, I know that I shall abide and continue with you all for your

furtherance and joy of faith; 26That your rejoicing may be *more* abundant in Jesus Christ for me by my coming to you again. [2 Cor. 1:14]

The example of Christ

27 Only let your conversation be as it becometh the gospel of Christ: that whether I come and see you, or *else* be absent, I may hear of your affairs, that ye stand fast in one spirit, with one mind striving together for the faith of the gospel; 28And in nothing terrified by *your* adversaries: which is to them an evident token of perdition, but to you of salvation, and that of God. 29For unto you it is given in the behalf of Christ, not only to believe on him, but also to suffer for his sake; 30Having the same conflict which ye saw in me, and now hear *to be* in me. [Col. 2:1; Acts 16:19; 1 Thes. 2:2]

2 If *there* be therefore any consolation in Christ, if any comfort of love, if any fellowship of the Spirit, if any bowels and mercies, 2Fulfil ye my joy, that ye be likeminded, having the same love, *being* of one accord, of one mind. 3*Let* nothing *be done* through strife or vainglory; but in lowliness of mind *let* each esteem other better than themselves. 4Look not every man on his own *things,* but every man also on the *things* of others. 5Let this mind be in you, which *was* also in Christ Jesus: 6Who, being in the form of God, thought it not robbery to be equal with God: 7But made himself of no reputation, and took *upon him* the form of a servant, and was made in

the likeness of men: 8And being found in fashion as a man, he humbled himself, and became obedient unto death, even the death of the cross. 9Wherefore God also hath highly exalted him, and given him a name which is above every name: 10That at the name of Jesus every knee should bow, of *things* in heaven, and *things* in earth, and *things* under the earth; 11And *that* every tongue should confess that Jesus Christ *is* Lord, to the glory of God the Father. [John 13:13; Acts 2:36]

Obligations of Christians

12 Wherefore, my beloved, as ye have always obeyed, not as in my presence only, but now much more in my absence, work out your own salvation with fear and trembling. 13For it is God which worketh in you both to will and to do of *his* good pleasure. 14Do all *things* without murmurings and disputings: 15That ye may be blameless and harmless, the sons of God without rebuke, in the midst of a crooked and perverse nation, among whom ye shine as lights in the world; 16Holding forth the word of life; that I may rejoice in the day of Christ, that I have not run in vain, neither laboured in vain. 17Yea, and if I be offered upon the sacrifice and service of your faith, I joy, and rejoice with you all. 18*For* the same *cause* also do ye joy, and rejoice with me.

Timotheus and Epaphroditus

19 But I trust in the Lord Jesus to send Timotheus shortly unto you, that I also may be of good comfort, when I know your state.

20For I have no *man* likeminded, who will naturally care for your state. 21For all seek their own, not the *things which are* Jesus Christ's. 22But ye know the proof of him, that, as a son *with the* father, he hath served with me in the gospel. 23Him therefore I hope to send presently, so soon as I shall see how it will go with me. 24But I trust in the Lord that I also myself shall come shortly. 25Yet I supposed it necessary to send to you Epaphroditus, my brother, and companion in labour, and fellow-soldier, but your messenger, and he that ministered to my wants. 26For he longed after you all, and *was* full of heaviness, because that ye had heard that he had been sick. 27For indeed he was sick nigh unto death: but God had mercy on him; and not on him only, but on me also, lest I should have sorrow upon sorrow. 28I sent him therefore the more carefully, that, when ye see him again, ye may rejoice, and *that* I may be the less sorrowful. 29Receive him therefore in the Lord with all gladness; and hold such in reputation: 30Because for the work of Christ he was nigh unto death, not regarding *his* life, to supply your lack of service toward me. [1 Cor. 16:17]

The example of Paul

3 Finally, my brethren, rejoice in the Lord. To write the same *things* to you, to me indeed *is* not grievous, but for you *it is* safe. 2Beware of dogs, beware of evil workers, beware of the concision. 3For we are the circumcision, which worship God in the spirit, and rejoice in Christ Jesus, and have no confidence in the flesh. 4Though I *might* also have confidence in the flesh. If any other *man* thinketh that *he hath whereof he* might trust in the flesh, I more: 5Circumcised the eighth day, of the stock of Israel, of the tribe of Benjamin, a Hebrew of the Hebrews; as touching the law, a Pharisee; 6Concerning zeal, persecuting the church; touching the righteousness which is in the law, blameless. 7But what *things* were gain to me, those I counted loss for Christ. 8Yea doubtless, and I count all *things but* loss for the excellency of the knowledge of Christ Jesus my Lord: for whom I have suffered the loss of all *things,* and do count *them but* dung, that I may win Christ, 9And be found in him, not having mine own righteousness, which is of the law, but that which is through the faith of Christ, the righteousness which is of God by faith: 10That *I* may know him, and the power of his resurrection, and the fellowship of his sufferings, being made conformable unto his death; 11If by any means I might attain unto the resurrection of the dead. [Acts 26:7]

The high calling of God

12 Not as though I had already attained, either were already perfect: but I follow *after,* if that I may apprehend *that* for which also I am apprehended of Christ Jesus. 13Brethren, I count not myself to have apprehended: but *this* one thing I do, forgetting those *things which are* behind, and reaching

forth unto those *things which are* before, [14]I press toward the mark for the prize of the high calling of God in Christ Jesus. [15]Let us therefore, as many as *be* perfect, be thus minded: and if in any *thing* ye be otherwise minded, God shall reveal even this unto you. [16]Nevertheless, whereto we have *already* attained, *let us* walk by the same rule, *let us* mind the same *thing.* [Rom. 12:16; 15:6; Gal. 6:16]

17 Brethren, be followers together of me, and mark them which walk so as ye have us for an ensample. [18](For many walk, of whom I have told you often, and now tell *you* even weeping, *that they are* the enemies of the cross of Christ: [19]Whose end *is* destruction, whose God *is their* belly, and *whose* glory *is* in their shame, who mind earthly *things.*) [20]For our conversation is in heaven; from whence also we look for the Saviour, the Lord Jesus Christ: [21]Who shall change our vile body, that it may be fashioned like unto his glorious body, according to the working whereby he is able even to subdue all *things* unto himself. [1 Cor. 15:43; Col. 3:4; Eph. 1:19; 1 Cor. 15:26]

Appeal to rejoice in the Lord

4 Therefore, my brethren dearly beloved and longed for, my joy and crown, so stand fast in the Lord, *my* dearly beloved. [2]I beseech Euodias, and beseech Syntyche, that *they* be of the same mind in the Lord. [3]And I intreat thee also, true yokefellow, help those *women* which laboured with me in the gospel, with Clement also, and

with other my fellowlabourers, whose names *are* in the book of life. [Rom. 16:3; Ex. 32:32; Ps. 69:28; Dan. 12:1]

4 Rejoice in the Lord alway: *and* again I say, Rejoice. [5]Let your moderation be known unto all men. The Lord *is* at hand. [6]Be careful for nothing; but in every *thing* by prayer and supplication with thanksgiving let your requests be made known unto God. [7]And the peace of God, which passeth all understanding, shall keep your hearts and minds through Christ Jesus. [8]Finally, brethren, whatsoever *things* are true, whatsoever *things* are honest, whatsoever *things are* just, whatsoever *things are* pure, whatsoever *things are* lovely, whatsoever *things are* of good report; if *there be* any virtue, and if *there be* any praise, think on these *things.* [9]Those *things,* which ye have both learned, and received, and heard, and seen in me, do: and the God of peace shall be with you. [ch. 3:17; Rom. 15:33]

The Philippian gifts

10 But I rejoiced in the Lord greatly, that now at the last your care of me hath flourished again; wherein ye were also careful, but ye lacked opportunity. [11]Not that I speak in respect of want: for I have learned, in whatsoever *state* I am, *therewith* to be content. [12]I know both *how* to be abased, and I know *how* to abound: every where and in all *things* I am instructed both to be full and to be hungry, both to abound and to suffer need. [13]I can do all *things* through Christ which

strengtheneth me. [14]Notwithstanding ye have well done, that ye did communicate with my affliction. [15]Now ye Philippians know also, that in the beginning of the gospel, when I departed from Macedonia, no church communicated with me as concerning giving and receiving, but ye only. [16]For even in Thessalonica ye sent once and again unto my necessity. [17]Not because I desire a gift: but I desire fruit that *may* abound to your account. [18]But I have all, and abound: I am full, having received of Epaphroditus the *things which were sent* from you, an odour of a sweet smell, a sacrifice acceptable, well pleasing to God. [19]But my God shall supply all your need according to his riches in glory by Christ Jesus. [20]Now unto God and our Father *be* glory for ever and ever. Amen. [Rom. 16:27]

Concluding benediction

21 Salute every saint in Christ Jesus. The brethren which are with me greet you. [22]All the saints salute you, chiefly they that are of Cesar's household. [23]The grace of our Lord Jesus Christ *be* with you all. Amen. [Rom. 16:24]

¶ It was written to the Philippians from Rome by Epaphroditus.

Colossians

Salutation and thanksgiving

1 Paul, an apostle of Jesus Christ by the will of God, and Timotheus *our* brother, ²To the saints and faithful brethren in Christ which are at Colosse: Grace *be* unto you, and peace, from God our Father and the Lord Jesus Christ. [1 Cor. 4:17; Gal. 1:3]

3 We give thanks to God and the Father of our Lord Jesus Christ, praying always for you, ⁴Since we heard of your faith in Christ Jesus, and of the love which *ye have* to all the saints, ⁵For the hope which is laid up for you in heaven, whereof ye heard before in the word of the truth of the gospel; ⁶Which is come unto you, as *it is* in all the world; and bringeth forth fruit, as *it doth* also in you, since the day ye heard of *it,* and knew the grace of God in truth: ⁷As ye also learned of Epaphras our dear fellowservant, who is for you a faithful minister of Christ; ⁸Who also declared unto us your love in the Spirit. [Rom. 15:30]

Paul's prayer for the Colossians

9 For this cause we also, since the day we heard *it,* do not cease to pray for you, and to desire that ye might be filled *with* the knowledge of his will in all wisdom and spiritual understanding; ¹⁰That ye might walk worthy of the Lord unto all pleasing, being fruitful in every good work, and increasing in the knowledge of God; ¹¹Strengthened with all might, according to his glorious power, unto all patience and longsuffering with joyfulness; ¹²Giving thanks unto the Father, which hath made us meet to be partakers of the inheritance of the saints in light: ¹³Who hath delivered us from the power of darkness, and hath translated *us* into the kingdom of his dear Son: ¹⁴In whom we have redemption through his blood, *even* the forgiveness of sins: [Eph. 1:7]

Christ's preeminence

15 Who is the image of the invisible God, the firstborn of every creature: ¹⁶For by him were all *things* created, that are in heaven, and that are in earth, visible and invisible, whether *they be* thrones, or dominions, or principalities, or powers: all *things* were created by him, and for him: ¹⁷And he is before all *things,* and by him all *things* consist. ¹⁸And he is the head of the body, the church: who is the beginning, the firstborn from the dead; that in all *things* he might have the preeminence. ¹⁹For it pleased the *Father* that in him should all fulness dwell; ²⁰And, having made peace through the blood of his cross, by him to reconcile all *things* unto himself; by him, *I say,* whether *they be things* in earth, or *things* in heaven. [Eph. 2:14; 2 Cor. 5:18; Eph. 1:10]

The ministry of Paul

21 And you, that were sometimes alienated and enemies in *your* mind by wicked works, yet now hath he reconciled ²²In the body of his flesh through death, to present you holy and unblameable and unreproveable in his sight: ²³If ye continue in the faith grounded and settled, and *be* not moved away from the hope of the gospel, which ye have heard, *and* which was preached to every creature which is under heaven; whereof I Paul am made a minister; 24Who now rejoice in my sufferings for you, and fill up that which is behind of the afflictions of Christ in my flesh for his body's sake, which is the church: 25Whereof I am made a minister, according to the dispensation of God which is given to me for you, to fulfil the word of God; 26*Even* the mystery which hath been hid from ages and from generations, but now is made manifest to his saints: 27To whom God would make known what *is* the riches of the glory of this mystery among the Gentiles; which is Christ in you, the hope of glory: 28Whom we preach, warning every man, and teaching every man in all wisdom; that we may present every man perfect in Christ Jesus: 29Whereunto I also labour, striving according to his working, which worketh in me mightily. [1 Cor. 15:10; ch. 2:1; Eph. 1:19]

2 For I would that ye knew what great conflict I have for you, and *for* them at Laodicea, and *for* as many as have not seen my face in the flesh; 2That their hearts might be comforted, being knit together in love, and unto all riches of the full assurance of understanding, to the acknowledgement of the mystery of God and of the Father, and of Christ; 3In whom are hid all the treasures of wisdom and knowledge. 4And this I say, lest any *man* should beguile you with enticing words. 5For though I be absent in the flesh, yet am I with you in the spirit, joying and beholding your order, and the stedfastness of your faith in Christ. 6As ye have therefore received Christ Jesus the Lord, *so* walk ye in him: 7Rooted and built up in him, and stablished in the faith, as ye have been taught, abounding therein with thanksgiving. [Eph. 2:21]

The sufficiency of Christ

8 Beware lest any *man* spoil you through philosophy and vain deceit, after the tradition of men, after the rudiments of the world, and not after Christ. 9For in him dwelleth all the fulness of the Godhead bodily. 10And ye are complete in him, which is the head of all principality and power: 11In whom also ye are circumcised with the circumcision made without hands, in putting off the body of the sins of the flesh, by the circumcision of Christ: 12Buried with him in baptism, wherein also you are risen with *him* through the faith of the operation of God, who hath raised him from the dead. 13And you, being dead in *your* sins and the uncircumcision of your flesh, hath he quickened together with him, having forgiven you all trespasses; 14Blotting out the handwriting of ordinances that was against us, which was contrary to us, and took it out of the way, nailing it to *his* cross; 15And having spoiled principalities and powers, he made a shew of *them* openly, triumphing over them in it. [Is. 53:12; Eph. 6:12]

16 Let no *man* therefore judge you in meat, or in drink, or in respect of a holyday, or of the new moon, or of the sabbath days:

17Which are a shadow of *things* to come; but the body *is* of Christ. 18Let no *man* beguile you of your reward in a voluntary humility and worshipping of angels, intruding into *those things* which he hath not seen, vainly puft up by his fleshly mind, 19And not holding the head, from which all the body by joints and bands having nourishment ministered, and knit together, increaseth *with* the increase of God. 20Wherefore if ye dead with Christ from the rudiments of the world, why, as though living in the world, are ye subject to ordinances, 21(Touch not; taste not; handle not; 22Which all are to perish with the using;) after the commandments and doctrines of men? 23Which *things* have indeed a shew of wisdom in will worship, and humility, and neglecting of the body, not in any honour to the satisfying of the flesh. [1 Tim. 4:8]

The true center of Christian life

3 If ye then be risen with Christ, seek those *things* which are above, where Christ sitteth on the right hand of God. 2Set your affection on *things* above, not on *things* on the earth. 3For ye are dead, and your life is hid with Christ in God. 4When Christ, *who is* our life, shall appear, then shall ye also appear with him in glory. [1 John 3:2; John 14:6; 1 Cor. 15:43]

5 Mortify therefore your members which are upon the earth; fornication, uncleanness, inordinate affection, evil concupiscence, and covetousness, which is idolatry: 6For which *things'* sake the wrath of God cometh on the children of disobedience: 7In the which ye also walked sometime, when ye lived in them. 8But now you also put off all *these;* anger, wrath, malice, blasphemy, filthy communication out of your mouth. 9Lie not one to another, seeing that ye have put off the old man with his deeds; 10And have put on the new *man,* which is renewed in knowledge after the image of him that created him: 11Where there is neither Greek nor Jew, circumcision nor uncircumcision, barbarian, Scythian, bond *nor* free: but Christ *is* all, and in all. 12Put on therefore, as the elect of God, holy and beloved, bowels of mercies, kindness, humbleness of mind, meekness, longsuffering; 13Forbearing one another, and forgiving one another, if any *man* have a quarrel against any: even as Christ forgave you, so also *do* ye. 14And above all these *things put on* charity, which is the bond of perfectness. 15And let the peace of God rule in your hearts, to the which also ye are called in one body; and be ye thankful. 16Let the word of Christ dwell in you richly in all wisdom; teaching and admonishing one another in psalms and hymns and spiritual songs, singing with grace in your hearts to the Lord. 17And whatsoever ye do in word or deed, *do* all in the name of the Lord Jesus, giving thanks to God and the Father by him. [1 Cor. 10:31]

The Christian family

18 Wives, submit yourselves unto your own husbands, as it is fit in the Lord. 19Husbands, love *your* wives, and be not bitter against

them. 20Children, obey *your* parents in all *things:* for this is well pleasing unto the Lord. 21Fathers, provoke not your children *to anger,* lest they be discouraged. 22Servants, obey in all *things your* masters according to the flesh; not with eyeservice, as menpleasers; but in singleness of heart, fearing God: 23And whatsoever ye do, do *it* heartily, as to the Lord, and not unto men; 24Knowing that of the Lord ye shall receive the reward of the inheritance: for ye serve the Lord Christ. 25But he that doeth wrong shall receive *for* the wrong which he hath done: and there is no respect of persons. [Rom. 2:11; Eph. 6:9; 1 Pet. 1:17; Deut. 10:17]

4 Masters, give unto *your* servants that which is just and equal; knowing that ye also have a Master in heaven. [Eph. 6:9]

2 Continue in prayer, and watch in the same with thanksgiving; 3Withal praying also for us, that God would open unto us a door of utterance, to speak the mystery of Christ, for which I am also in bonds: 4That I may make it manifest, as I ought to speak. 5Walk in wisdom toward them that are without, redeeming the time. 6Let your speech *be* alway with grace, seasoned with salt, that *you* may know how ye ought to answer every man. [Eccl. 10:12; Mark 9:50; 1 Pet. 3:15]

Tychicus and Onesimus

7 All my state shall Tychicus declare unto you, *who is* a beloved brother, and a faithful minister and fellowservant in the Lord: 8Whom I have sent unto you for the same purpose, that he might know your estate, and comfort your hearts; 9With Onesimus, a faithful and beloved brother, who is *one* of you. They shall make known unto you all *things* which *are done* here. [Philem. 10]

Greetings and final instructions

10 Aristarchus my fellowprisoner saluteth you, and Marcus, sister's son to Barnabas, (touching whom ye received commandments: if he come unto you, receive him;) 11And Jesus, which is called Justus, who are of the circumcision. These only *are my* fellowworkers unto the kingdom of God, which have been a comfort unto me. 12Epaphras, who is *one* of you, a servant of Christ, saluteth you, always labouring fervently for you in prayers, that ye may stand perfect and complete in all the will of God. 13For I bear him record, that he hath a great zeal for you, and them that are in Laodicea, and them in Hierapolis. 14Luke, the beloved physician, and Demas, greet you. 15Salute the brethren which are in Laodicea, and Nymphas, and the church which is in his house. 16And when *this* epistle is read amongst you, cause that it be read also in the church of the Laodiceans; and that ye likewise read the *epistle* from Laodicea. 17And say to Archippus, Take heed to the ministry which thou hast received in the Lord, that thou fulfil it. 18The salutation by the hand of me Paul. Remember my bonds. Grace *be* with you. Amen. [1 Cor. 16:21; 2 Thes. 3:17; Heb. 13:3; Heb. 13:25]

¶ Written from Rome to the Colossians by Tychicus and Onesimus.

Thessalonians

Salutation and thanksgiving

1 Paul, and Silvanus, and Timotheus, unto the church of the Thessalonians *which is* in God the Father and *in* the Lord Jesus Christ: Grace *be* unto you, and peace, from God our Father, and the Lord Jesus Christ. [1 Pet. 5:12; Eph. 1:2]

2 We give thanks to God always for you all, making mention of you in our prayers; 3 Remembering without ceasing your work of faith, and labour of love, and patience of hope in our Lord Jesus Christ, in the sight of God and our Father; 4 Knowing, brethren beloved, your election of God. 5 For our gospel came not unto you in word only, but also in power, and in the Holy Ghost, and in much assurance; as ye know what manner of *men* we were among you for your sake. 6 And ye became followers of us, and of the Lord, having received the word in much affliction, with joy of the Holy Ghost: 7 So that ye were ensamples to all that believe in Macedonia and Achaia. 8 For from you sounded out the word of the Lord not only in Macedonia and Achaia, but also in every place your faith to God-ward is spread abroad; so that we need not to speak any *thing*. 9 For they themselves shew of us what manner of entering in we had unto you, and how ye turned to God from idols to serve the living and true God, 10 And to wait for his Son from heaven, whom he raised from the dead, *even* Jesus, which delivered us from the wrath to come. [Rom. 2:7; 2 Pet. 3:12; Acts 1:11; Acts 2:24; Rom. 5:9]

Paul's work in Thessalonica

2 For yourselves, brethren, know our entrance in unto you, that it was not in vain: 2 But even after that we had suffered before, and were shamefully entreated, as ye know, at Philippi, we were bold in our God to speak unto you the gospel of God with much contention. 3 For our exhortation *was* not of deceit, nor of uncleanness, nor in guile: 4 But as we were allowed of God to be put in trust with the gospel, *even* so we speak; not as pleasing men, but God, which trieth our hearts. 5 For neither at any time used we flattering words, as ye know, nor a cloke of covetousness; God *is* witness: 6 Nor of men sought we glory, neither of you, nor *yet* of others, when we might have been burdensome, as *the* apostles of Christ. 7 But we were gentle among you, *even* as a nurse cherisheth her children: 8 So being affectionately desirous of you, we were willing to have imparted unto you, not the gospel of God only, but also our own souls, because ye were dear unto us. 9 For ye remember, brethren, our labour and travail: for labouring night and day, because *we* would not be chargeable unto any of you, we preached unto you the gospel of God. 10 Ye *are* witnesses, and God

also, how holily and justly and un-blameably we behaved ourselves among you that believe: ¹¹As you know how we exhorted and comforted and charged every one of you, as a father *doth* his children, ¹²That ye would walk worthy of God, who hath called you unto his kingdom and glory. [Col. 1:10; 1 Cor. 1:9; 2 Thes. 2:14]

Paul's reception in Thessalonica

13 For this cause also thank we God without ceasing, because, when ye received the word of God which *ye* heard of us, ye received *it* not as the word of men, but as it is in truth, the word of God, which effectually worketh also in you that believe. ¹⁴For ye, brethren, became followers of the churches of God which in Judea are in Christ Jesus: for ye also have suffered like *things* of your own countrymen, even as they *have* of the Jews: ¹⁵Who both killed the Lord Jesus, and their own prophets, and have persecuted us; and they please not God, and are contrary to all men: ¹⁶Forbidding us to speak to the Gentiles that they might be saved, to fill up their sins alway: for the wrath is come upon them to the uttermost. [Luke 11:52; Acts 13:50; Gen. 15:16; Mat. 23:32; Mat. 24:6]

17 But we, brethren, being taken from you for a short time in presence, not in heart, endeavoured the more abundantly to see your face with great desire. ¹⁸Wherefore we would have come unto you, even I Paul, once and again; but Satan hindered us. ¹⁹For what *is* our hope, or joy, or crown of rejoicing? *Are* not even ye in the presence of our Lord Jesus Christ at his coming? ²⁰For ye are our glory and joy.

Timotheus's visit and report

3 Wherefore when we could no longer forbear, we thought it good to be left at Athens alone; ²And sent Timotheus, our brother, and minister of God, and our fellowlabourer in the gospel of Christ, to establish you, and to comfort you concerning your faith: ³That no *man* should be moved by these afflictions: for yourselves know that we are appointed thereunto. ⁴For verily, when we were with you, we told you before that we should suffer tribulation; even as it came to pass, and ye know. ⁵For this cause, when I could no longer forbear, I sent to know your faith, lest by some means the tempter have tempted you, and our labour be in vain. ⁶But now when Timotheus came from you unto us, and brought us good tidings of your faith and charity, and that ye have good remembrance of us always, desiring greatly to see us, as we also *to see* you: ⁷Therefore, brethren, we were comforted over you in all our affliction and distress, by your faith: ⁸For now we live, if ye stand fast in the Lord. ⁹For what thanks can we render to God again for you, for all the joy wherewith we joy for your sakes before our God; ¹⁰Night and day praying exceedingly that *we* might see your face, and might perfect that which is lacking in your faith? ¹¹Now God himself and our Father,

and our Lord Jesus Christ, direct our way unto you. 12And the Lord make you to increase and abound in love one towards another, and towards all *men,* even as we *do* towards you: 13To the end *he* may stablish your hearts unblameable in holiness before God, even our Father, at the coming of our Lord Jesus Christ with all his saints. [1 Cor. 1:8; Phil. 1:10; Zech. 14:5]

Living to please God

4 Furthermore then we beseech you, brethren, and exhort *you* by the Lord Jesus, that as ye have received of us how ye ought to walk and to please God, *so* ye would abound more *and more.* 2For ye know what commandments we gave you by the Lord Jesus. 3For this is the will of God, *even* your sanctification, that ye should abstain from fornication: 4That every one of you should know how to possess his vessel in sanctification and honour; 5Not in the lust of concupiscence, even as the Gentiles which know not God: 6That no *man* go beyond and defraud his brother in *any* matter: because that the Lord *is* the avenger of all such, as we also have forewarned you and testified. 7For God hath not called us unto uncleanness, but unto holiness. 8He therefore that despiseth, despiseth not man, but God, who hath also given unto us his holy Spirit. [Luke 10:16; 1 Cor. 2:10]

9 But as touching brotherly love ye need not that *I* write unto you: for ye yourselves are taught of God to love one another. 10And indeed

ye do it towards all the brethren which are in all Macedonia: but we beseech you, brethren, that *ye* increase more *and more;* 11And that *ye* study to be quiet, and to do your own *business,* and to work with your own hands, as we commanded you; 12That ye may walk honestly toward them that are without, and *that* ye may have lack of no*thing.* [Rom. 13:13]

The sudden coming of the Lord

13 But I would not have you to be ignorant, brethren, concerning them which are asleep, that ye sorrow not, even as others which have no hope. 14For if we believe that Jesus died and rose again, *even* so them also which sleep in Jesus will God bring with him. 15For this we say unto you by the word of the Lord, that we which are alive *and* remain unto the coming of the Lord shall not prevent them which are asleep. 16For the Lord himself shall descend from heaven with a shout, with the voice of the archangel, and with the trump of God: and the dead in Christ shall rise first: 17Then we which are alive *and* remain shall be caught up together with them in the clouds, to meet the Lord in the air: and so shall we ever be with the Lord. 18Wherefore comfort one another with these words. [ch. 5:11]

5 But of the times and the seasons, brethren, ye have no need that *I* write unto you. 2For yourselves know perfectly that the day of the Lord so cometh as a thief in the night. 3For when they shall say, Peace and safety; then sudden

destruction cometh upon them, as travail upon a *woman* with child; and they shall not escape. 4But ye, brethren, are not in darkness, that *that* day should overtake you as a thief. 5Ye are all the children of light, and the children of the day: we are not of the night, nor of darkness. 6Therefore let us not sleep, as *do* others; but let us watch and be sober. 7For they that sleep sleep in the night; and they that be drunken are drunken in the night. 8But let us, who are of the day, be sober, putting on the breastplate of faith and love; and for a helmet, the hope of salvation. 9For God hath not appointed us to wrath, but to obtain salvation by our Lord Jesus Christ, 10Who died for us, that, whether we wake or sleep, we should live together with him. 11Wherefore comfort yourselves together, and edify one another, even as also ye do. [ch. 4:18]

12 And we beseech you, brethren, to know them which labour among you, and are over you in the Lord, and admonish you; 13And to esteem them very highly in love for their work's sake. *And* be at peace among yourselves. 14Now we exhort you, brethren, warn

them that are unruly, comfort the feebleminded, support the weak, be patient toward all *men.* 15See that none render evil for evil unto any *man;* but ever follow *that which is* good, both among yourselves, and to all *men.* 16Rejoice evermore. 17Pray without ceasing. 18In every *thing* give thanks: for this *is* the will of God in Christ Jesus concerning you. 19Quench not the Spirit. 20Despise not prophesyings. 21Prove all *things;* hold fast *that which is* good. 22Abstain from all appearance of evil. 23And the very God of peace sanctify you wholly; and *I pray God* your whole spirit and soul and body be preserved blameless unto the coming of our Lord Jesus Christ. 24Faithful *is* he that calleth you, who also will do *it.* [1 Cor. 1:9]

Conclusion

25 Brethren, pray for us. 26Greet all the brethren with a holy kiss. 27I charge you by the Lord that *this* epistle be read unto all the holy brethren. 28The grace of our Lord Jesus Christ *be* with you. Amen. [Rom. 16:20]

¶ The first *epistle* unto the Thessalonians was written from Athens.

Thessalonians

Thanksgiving and prayer

1 Paul, and Silvanus, and Timotheus, unto the church of the Thessalonians in God our Father and the Lord Jesus Christ: 2Grace unto you, and peace, from God our Father and the Lord Jesus Christ. [1 Cor. 1:3]

3 We are bound to thank God always for you, brethren, as it is meet, because that your faith groweth exceedingly, and the charity of every one of you all towards each other aboundeth; 4So that we ourselves glory in you in the churches of God for your patience and faith in all your persecutions and tribulations that ye endure: 5*Which is* a manifest token of the righteous judgment of God, that ye may be counted worthy of the kingdom of God, for which ye also suffer: 6Seeing *it is* a righteous *thing* with God to recompense tribulation to them that trouble you; 7And to you who are troubled rest with us, when the Lord Jesus shall be revealed from heaven with his mighty angels, 8In flaming fire, taking vengeance on them that know not God, and that obey not the gospel of our Lord Jesus Christ: 9Who shall be punished *with* everlasting destruction from the presence of the Lord, and from the glory of his power; 10When he shall come to be glorified in his saints, and to be admired in all them that believe (because our testimony among you was believed) in that day. 11Wherefore also we pray always for you, that our God would count you worthy of *this* calling, and fulfil all the good pleasure of *his* goodness, and the work of faith with power: 12That the name of our Lord Jesus Christ may be glorified in you, and ye in him, according to the grace of our God and the Lord Jesus Christ. [1 Pet. 1:7]

The man of sin

2 Now we beseech you, brethren, by the coming of our Lord Jesus Christ, and *by* our gathering together unto him, 2That ye be not soon shaken in mind, or be troubled, neither by spirit, nor by word, nor by letter as from us, as that the day of Christ is at hand. 3Let no *man* deceive you by any means: for *that day shall not come,* except there come a falling away first, and *that* man of sin be revealed, the son of perdition; 4Who opposeth and exalteth himself above all that is called God, or that is worshipped; so that he as God sitteth in the temple of God, shewing himself that he is God. 5Remember ye not, that, when I was yet with you, I told you these *things?* 6And now ye know what withholdeth that he might be revealed in his time. 7For the mystery of iniquity doth already work: only he who now letteth *will let,* until he be taken out of the way. 8And then shall *that* Wicked be revealed, whom the Lord shall consume with the spirit of his mouth, and shall destroy with the bright-

ness of his coming: ⁹*Even him,* whose coming is after the working of Satan with all power and signs and lying wonders, ¹⁰And with all deceivableness of unrighteousness in them that perish; because they received not the love of the truth, that they might be saved. ¹¹And for this cause God shall send them strong delusion, that they should believe a lie: ¹²That they all might be damned who believed not the truth, but had pleasure in unrighteousness. [Rom. 1:32]

Thanksgiving and appeal

13 But we are bound to give thanks alway to God for you, brethren beloved of the Lord, because God hath from the beginning chosen you to salvation through sanctification of the Spirit and belief of the truth: ¹⁴Whereunto he called you by our gospel, to the obtaining of the glory of our Lord Jesus Christ. ¹⁵Therefore, brethren, stand fast, and hold the traditions which ye have been taught, whether by word, or by our epistle. ¹⁶Now our Lord Jesus Christ himself, and God, even our Father, which hath loved us, and hath given *us* everlasting consolation and good hope through grace, ¹⁷Comfort your hearts, and stablish you in every good word and work. [1 Cor. 1:8]

Appeals for prayer and labour

3 Finally, brethren, pray for us, that the word of the Lord may have *free* course, and be glorified, even as *it is* with you: ²And that we may be delivered from unreasonable and wicked men: for all

men have not faith. ³But the Lord is faithful, who shall stablish you, and keep *you* from evil. ⁴And we have confidence in the Lord touching you, that ye both do and will do *the things* which we command you. ⁵And the Lord direct your hearts into the love of God, and into the patient waiting for Christ. [1 Chr. 29:18]

6 Now we command you, brethren, in the name of our Lord Jesus Christ, that ye withdraw yourselves from every brother that walketh disorderly, and not after the tradition which he received of us. ⁷For yourselves know how *ye* ought to follow us: for we behaved not ourselves disorderly among you; ⁸Neither did we eat any *man's* bread for nought; but wrought with labour and travail night and day, that *we* might not be chargeable to any of you: ⁹Not because we have not power, but to make ourselves an ensample unto you to follow us. ¹⁰For even when we were with you, this we commanded you, that if any would not work, neither should he eat. ¹¹For we hear that *there are* some which walk among you disorderly, working not at all, but are busybodies. ¹²Now *them that are* such we command and exhort by our Lord Jesus Christ, that with quietness they work, and eat their own bread. ¹³But ye, brethren, be not weary in well doing. ¹⁴And if any *man* obey not our word by *this* epistle, note that *man,* and have no company with him, that he may be ashamed. ¹⁵Yet count *him* not as an enemy,

but admonish *him* as a brother. [Lev. 19:17; Tit. 3:10]

Benediction

16 Now the Lord of peace himself give you peace always by all means. The Lord *be* with you all. [Rom. 15:33]

17 The salutation of Paul with mine own hand, which is the token in every epistle: so I write. 18 The grace of our Lord Jesus Christ *be* with you all. Amen. [Rom. 16:24]

¶ The second *epistle* to the Thessalonians was written from Athens.

Timothy

1 Paul, an apostle of Jesus Christ by the commandment of God our Saviour, and Lord Jesus Christ, *which is* our hope; ²Unto Timothy, *my* own son in the faith: Grace, mercy, *and* peace, from God our Father and Jesus Christ our Lord. [Acts 16:1; Tit. 1:4; Gal. 1:3]

The problem of unsound doctrine

3 As I besought thee to abide *still* at Ephesus, when I went into Macedonia, that thou mightest charge some that *they* teach no other doctrine, ⁴Neither give heed to fables and endless genealogies, which minister questions, rather than godly edifying which is in faith: *so do.* ⁵Now the end of the commandment is charity out of a pure heart, and *of* a good conscience, and *of* faith unfeigned: ⁶From which some having swerved have turned aside unto vain jangling; ⁷Desiring to be teachers of the law; understanding neither what they say, nor whereof they affirm. ⁸But we know that the law *is* good, if a man use it lawfully; ⁹Knowing this, that the law is not made for a righteous *man,* but for the lawless and disobedient, for the ungodly and for sinners, for unholy and profane, for murderers of fathers and murderers of mothers, for manslayers, ¹⁰For whoremongers, for them that defile themselves with mankind, for menstealers, for liars, for perjured *persons,* and if *there be* any other *thing that* is contrary to sound doctrine; ¹¹According to the glorious gospel of the blessed God, which was committed to my trust. [1 Cor. 9:17; Gal. 2:7; Col. 1:25]

The testimony of Paul

12 And I thank Christ Jesus our Lord, who hath enabled me, for that he counted me faithful, putting *me* into the ministry; ¹³Who was before a blasphemer, and a persecutor, and injurious: but I obtained mercy, because I did *it* ignorantly in unbelief. ¹⁴And the grace of our Lord was exceeding abundant with faith and love which is in Christ Jesus. ¹⁵*This is* a faithful saying, and worthy of all acceptation, that Christ Jesus came into the world to save sinners; of whom I am chief. ¹⁶Howbeit for this cause I obtained mercy, that in me first Jesus Christ might shew forth all longsuffering, for a pattern to them which should hereafter believe on him to life everlasting. ¹⁷Now unto the King eternal, immortal, invisible, the only wise God, *be* honour and glory for ever and ever. Amen. ¹⁸This charge I commit unto thee, son Timothy, according to the prophecies which went before on thee, that thou by them mightest war a good warfare; ¹⁹Holding faith, and a good conscience; which some having put away, concerning faith have made shipwrack: ²⁰Of whom is Hymeneus and Alexander; whom I have delivered unto Satan, that they may

learn not to blaspheme. [2 Tim. 2:17; 4:14; 1 Cor. 5:5; Acts 13:45]

Prayer and sobriety

2 I exhort therefore that, first of all, supplications, prayers, intercessions, *and* giving of thanks, be made for all men; ²For kings, and *for* all that are in authority; that we may lead a quiet and peaceable life in all godliness and honesty. ³For this *is* good and acceptable in the sight of God our Saviour; ⁴Who will have all men to be saved, and to come unto the knowledge of the truth. ⁵For *there is* one God, and one mediator between God and men, *the* man Christ Jesus; ⁶Who gave himself a ransom for all, to be testified in due time. ⁷Whereunto I am ordained a preacher, and an apostle, (I speak the truth in Christ, *and* lie not;) a teacher of the Gentiles in faith and verity. ⁸I will therefore that men pray every where, lifting up holy hands, without wrath and doubting. ⁹In like manner also, that women adorn themselves in modest apparel, with shamefastness and sobriety; not with broided hair, or gold, or pearls, or costly array; ¹⁰But (which becometh women professing godliness) with good works. ¹¹Let the woman learn in silence with all subjection. ¹²But I suffer not a woman to teach, nor to usurp authority over the man, but to be in silence. ¹³For Adam was first formed, then Eve. ¹⁴And Adam was not deceived, but the woman being deceived was in the transgression. ¹⁵Notwithstanding she shall be saved in childbearing, if they continue in faith and charity and holiness with sobriety.

Bishops and deacons

3 *This is* a true saying, If a man desire the office of a bishop, he desireth a good work. ²A bishop then must be blameless, the husband of one wife, vigilant, sober, of good behaviour, given to hospitality, apt to teach; ³Not given to wine, no striker, not greedy of filthy lucre; but patient, not a brawler, not covetous; ⁴One that ruleth well his own house, having *his* children in subjection with all gravity; ⁵(For if a man know not how to rule his own house, how shall he take care of the church of God?) ⁶Not a novice, lest being lifted up with pride he fall into the condemnation of the devil. ⁷Moreover he must have a good report of them which are without; lest he fall into reproach and the snare of the devil. ⁸Likewise *must* the deacons *be* grave, not doubletongued, not given to much wine, not greedy of filthy lucre; ⁹Holding the mystery of the faith in a pure conscience. ¹⁰And let these also first be proved; then let them use the office of a deacon, being *found* blameless. ¹¹Even so *must their* wives *be* grave, not slanderers, sober, faithful in all *things*. ¹²Let the deacons be the husbands of one wife, ruling *their* children and their own houses well. ¹³For they that have used the office of a deacon well purchase to themselves a good degree, and great boldness in the faith which is in Christ Jesus. [Mat. 25:21]

14 These *things* write I unto thee, hoping to come unto thee shortly: 15 But if I tarry long, that thou mayest know how *thou* oughtest to behave thyself in the house of God, which is the church of the living God, the pillar and ground of the truth. 16 And without controversy great is the mystery of godliness: God was manifest in the flesh, justified in the Spirit, seen of angels, preached unto the Gentiles, believed on in the world, received up into glory. [John 1:14; 1 John 1:2; Mat. 3:16; Rom. 1:4; Mat. 28:2; Mark 16:5; Acts 10:34; Rom. 10:18; Col. 1:6,23; Luke 24:51]

Instructions for godly living

4 Now the Spirit speaketh expressly, that in the latter times some shall depart from the faith, giving heed to seducing spirits, and doctrines of devils; 2 Speaking lies in hypocrisy, having their conscience seared with a hot iron; 3 Forbidding to marry, *and commanding* to abstain from meats, which God hath created to be received with thanksgiving of them which believe and know the truth. 4 For every creature of God *is* good, and nothing to be refused, if it be received with thanksgiving: 5 For it is sanctified by the word of God and prayer. 6 If thou put the brethren in remembrance of these *things,* thou shalt be a good minister of Jesus Christ, nourished up in the words of faith and of good doctrine, whereunto thou hast attained. 7 But refuse profane and old wives' fables, and exercise thyself *rather* unto godliness. 8 For bodily

exercise profiteth little: but godliness is profitable unto all *things,* having promise of the life that now is, and of that which is to come. 9 *This is* a faithful saying and worthy of all acceptation. 10 For therefore we both labour and suffer reproach, because we trust in the living God, who is the Saviour of all men, specially of those that believe. 11 These *things* command and teach.

12 Let no *man* despise thy youth; but be thou an example of the believers, in word, in conversation, in charity, in spirit, in faith, in purity. 13 Till I come, give attendance to reading, to exhortation, to doctrine. 14 Neglect not the gift that is in thee, which was given thee by prophecy, with the laying on of the hands of the presbytery. 15 Meditate upon these *things;* give thyself wholly to them; that thy profiting may appear to all. 16 Take heed unto thyself, and unto the doctrine; continue in them: for in doing this thou shalt both save thyself, and them that hear thee. [Acts 20:28; Ezek. 33:9]

Pastoral duties

5 Rebuke not an elder, but intreat *him* as a father; *and* the younger *men* as brethren; 2 The elder *women* as mothers; the younger as sisters, with all purity. 3 Honour widows that are widows indeed. 4 But if any widow have children or nephews, let them learn first to shew piety at home, and to requite *their* parents: for that is good and acceptable before God. 5 Now she that is a widow in-

deed, and desolate, trusteth in God, and continueth in supplications and prayers night and day. 6But she that liveth in pleasure is dead while she liveth. 7And these *things* give in charge, that they may be blameless. 8But if any provide not for his own, and specially for those of his own house, he hath denied the faith, and is worse than an infidel. 9Let not a widow be taken into the number under threescore years old, having been the wife of one man, 10Well reported of for good works; if she have brought up children, if she have lodged strangers, if she have washed the saints' feet, if she have relieved the afflicted, if she have diligently followed every good work. 11But the younger widows refuse: for when they have *begun to* wax wanton against Christ, they will marry; 12Having damnation, because they have cast off *their* first faith. 13And withal they learn *to be* idle, wandering about from house to house; and not only idle, but tattlers also and busybodies, speaking *things* which they ought not. 14I will therefore that the younger *women* marry, bear children, guide the house, give none occasion to the adversary to speak reproachfully. 15For some are already turned aside after Satan. 16If any man or woman that believeth have widows, let them relieve them, and let not the church be charged; that it may relieve them that are widows indeed. [ver. 3,5]

17 Let the elders that rule well be counted worthy of double honour, especially they who labour in the word and doctrine. 18For the scripture saith, Thou shalt not muzzle the ox that treadeth out the corn. And, The labourer *is* worthy of his reward. 19Against an elder receive not an accusation, but before two or three witnesses. 20Them that sin rebuke before all, that others also may fear. 21I charge *thee* before God, and the Lord Jesus Christ, and the elect angels, that thou observe these *things* without preferring one *before another,* doing nothing by partiality. 22Lay hands suddenly on no *man,* neither be partaker of other *men's* sins: keep thyself pure. 23Drink no longer water, but use a little wine for thy stomach's sake and thine often infirmities. 24Some men's sins are open beforehand, going before to judgment; and some *men* they follow after. 25Likewise also the good works *of some* are manifest beforehand; and they that are otherwise cannot be hid.

6 Let as many servants as are under the yoke count their own masters worthy of all honour, that the name of God and *his* doctrine be not blasphemed. 2And they that have believing masters, let them not despise *them,* because they are brethren; but rather do *them* service, because they are faithful and beloved, partakers of the benefit. These *things* teach and exhort. [Col. 4:1]

The use of wealth

3 If any *man* teach otherwise, and consent not to wholesome words, *even* the *words* of our Lord Jesus Christ, and to the doctrine

which is according to godliness; [4]He is proud, knowing nothing, but doting about questions and strifes of words, whereof cometh envy, strife, railings, evil surmisings, [5]Perverse disputings of men of corrupt minds, and destitute of the truth, supposing that gain is godliness: from such withdraw thyself. [6]But godliness with contentment is great gain. [7]For we brought nothing into *this* world, *and it is* certain we can carry nothing out. [8]And having food and raiment let us be therewith content. [9]But they that will be rich fall into temptation and a snare, and *into* many foolish and hurtful lusts, which drown men in destruction and perdition. [10]For the love of money is the root of all evil: which while some coveted after, they have erred from the faith, and pierced themselves through with many sorrows. [Deut. 16:19]

The good fight of faith

[11] But thou, O man of God, flee these *things;* and follow *after* righteousness, godliness, faith, love, patience, meekness. [12]Fight the good fight of faith, lay hold on eternal life, whereunto thou art also called, and hast professed a good profession before many witnesses. [13]I give thee charge in the sight of God, who quickeneth all *things,* and *before* Christ Jesus, who before Pontius Pilate witnessed a good confession; [14]That thou keep *this* commandment without spot, unrebukeable, until the appearing of our Lord Jesus Christ: [15]Which in his times he shall shew, *who is* the blessed and only Potentate, the King of kings, and Lord of lords; [16]Who only hath immortality, dwelling in the light which no *man* can approach unto; whom no man hath seen, nor can see: to whom *be* honour and power everlasting. Amen. [John 6:46; Eph. 3:21]

Final charge and benediction

[17] Charge *them that are* rich in this world, that *they* be not highminded, nor trust in uncertain riches, but in the living God, who giveth us richly all *things* to enjoy; [18]That *they* do good, that *they* be rich in good works, ready to distribute, willing to communicate; [19]Laying up in store for themselves a good foundation against the time to come, that they may lay hold on eternal life. [20]O Timothy, keep that which is committed to *thy* trust, avoiding profane *and* vain babblings, and oppositions of science falsely so called: [21]Which some professing have erred concerning the faith. Grace *be* with thee. Amen. [2 Tim. 2:18]

¶ The first to Timothy was written from Laodicea, which is the chiefest city of Phrygia Pacatiana.

Timothy

1 Paul, an apostle of Jesus Christ by the will of God, according to the promise of life which is in Christ Jesus, ²To Timothy, *my* dearly beloved son: Grace, mercy, *and* peace, from God the Father and Christ Jesus our Lord. [1 Tim. 1:2]

Appeal for faithfulness

3 I thank God, whom I serve from *my* forefathers with pure conscience, that without ceasing I have remembrance of thee in my prayers night and day; ⁴Greatly desiring to see thee, being mindful of thy tears, that I may be filled with joy; ⁵When I call to remembrance the unfeigned faith that is in thee, which dwelt first in thy grandmother Lois, and thy mother Eunice; and I am persuaded that in thee also. ⁶Wherefore I put thee in remembrance that *thou* stir up the gift of God, which is in thee by the putting on of my hands. ⁷For God hath not given us the spirit of fear; but of power, and of love, and of a sound mind. ⁸Be not thou therefore ashamed of the testimony of our Lord, nor of me his prisoner: but be thou partaker of the afflictions of the gospel according to the power of God; ⁹Who hath saved us, and called *us* with a holy calling, not according to our works, but according to his own purpose and grace, which was given us in Christ Jesus before the world began, ¹⁰But is now made manifest by the appearing of our Saviour Jesus Christ, who hath abolished death, and hath brought life and immortality to light through the gospel: ¹¹Whereunto I am appointed a preacher, and an apostle, and a teacher of the Gentiles. ¹²For the which cause I also suffer these *things:* nevertheless I am not ashamed: for I know whom I have believed, and I am persuaded that he is able to keep that which I have committed unto *him* against that day. ¹³Hold fast the form of sound words, which thou hast heard of me, in faith and love which is in Christ Jesus. ¹⁴That good thing which was committed unto *thee* keep by the Holy Ghost which dwelleth in us. ¹⁵This thou knowest, that all they which are in Asia be turned away from me; of whom are Phygellus and Hermogenes. ¹⁶The Lord give mercy unto the house of Onesiphorus; for he oft refreshed me, and was not ashamed of my chain: ¹⁷But, when he was in Rome, he sought me out very diligently, and found *me*. ¹⁸The Lord grant unto him that *he* may find mercy of the Lord in that day: and in how many *things* he ministered *unto me* at Ephesus, thou knowest very well. [2 Thes. 1:10; Heb. 6:10]

2 Thou therefore, my son, be strong in the grace that is in Christ Jesus. ²And *the things* that thou hast heard of me among many witnesses, the same commit thou to faithful men, who shall be able to teach others also. ³Thou therefore endure hardness, as a good soldier of Jesus Christ. 4No *man* that warreth entangleth himself with the affairs of *this* life; that he may please him who hath chosen *him* to be a soldier. 5And if a man also strive for masteries, *yet* is he not crowned, except he strive lawfully. 6The husbandman that laboureth must be first partaker of the fruits. 7Consider what I say; and the Lord give thee understanding in all *things.* 8Remember that Jesus Christ of the seed of David *was* raised from the dead according to my gospel: 9Wherein I suffer trouble, as an evil doer, *even* unto bonds; but the word of God is not bound. 10Therefore I endure all *things* for the elects' sakes, that they may also obtain the salvation which is in Christ Jesus with eternal glory. 11*It is* a faithful saying: For if we be dead with *him,* we shall also live with *him:* 12If we suffer, we shall also reign with *him:* if we deny *him,* he also will deny us: 13If we believe not, *yet* he abideth faithful: he cannot deny himself.

[Rom. 3:3; Num. 23:19]

A workman approved unto God

14 Of these *things* put *them* in remembrance, charging *them* before the Lord that *they* strive not about words to no profit, *but* to the subverting of the hearers. 15Study to shew thyself approved unto God, a workman that needeth not to be ashamed, rightly dividing the word of truth. 16But shun profane *and* vain babblings: for they will increase unto more ungodliness. 17And their word will eat as *doth* a canker: of whom is Hymeneus and Philetus; 18Who concerning the truth have erred, saying that the resurrection is past already; and overthrow the faith of some. 19Nevertheless the foundation of God standeth sure, having this seal, The Lord knoweth them that are his. And, Let every one that nameth the name of Christ depart from iniquity. 20But in a great house there are not only vessels of gold and of silver, but also of wood and of earth; and some to honour, and some to dishonour. 21If a man therefore purge himself from these, he shall be a vessel unto honour, sanctified, and meet for the master's use, *and* prepared unto every good work. 22Flee also youthful lusts: but follow righteousness, faith, charity, peace, with them that call on the Lord out of a pure heart. 23But foolish and unlearned questions avoid, knowing that they do gender strifes. 24And the servant of the Lord must not strive; but be gentle unto all *men,* apt to teach, patient, 25In meekness instructing those that oppose themselves; if God peradventure will give them repentance to the acknowledging of the truth; 26And *that* they may recover themselves out of the snare of the devil, *who are* taken captive by him at his will. [1 Tim. 3:7]

The coming apostasy

3 This know also, that in the last days perilous times shall come. 2For men shall be lovers of their own selves, covetous, boasters, proud, blasphemers, disobedient to parents, unthankful, unholy,

³Without natural affection, truce-breakers, false accusers, incontinent, fierce, despisers of *those that are* good, ⁴Traitors, heady, high-minded, lovers of pleasures more than lovers of God; ⁵Having a form of godliness, but denying the power thereof: from such turn away. ⁶For of this sort are they which creep into houses, and lead captive silly women laden with sins, led away with divers lusts, ⁷Ever learning, and never able to come to the knowledge of the truth. ⁸Now as Jannes and Jambres withstood Moses, so do these also resist the truth: men of corrupt minds, reprobate concerning the faith. ⁹But they shall proceed no further: for their folly shall be manifest unto all *men*, as theirs also was. [Ex. 7:12]

The defence of the faith

10 But thou hast fully known my doctrine, manner of life, purpose, faith, longsuffering, charity, patience, ¹¹Persecutions, afflictions, which came unto me at Antioch, at Iconium, at Lystra; what persecutions I endured: but out of *them* all the Lord delivered me. ¹²Yea, and all that will live godly in Christ Jesus shall suffer persecution. ¹³But evil men and seducers shall wax worse and worse, deceiving, and being deceived. ¹⁴But continue thou in *the things* which thou hast learned and hast been assured of, knowing of whom thou hast learned *them;* ¹⁵And that from a child thou hast known the holy scriptures, which are able to make thee wise unto salvation through faith which is in Christ Jesus. ¹⁶All scripture *is* given by inspiration of God, and *is* profitable for doctrine, for reproof, for correction, for instruction in righteousness: ¹⁷That the man of God may be perfect, throughly furnished unto all good works. [1 Tim. 6:11; ch. 2:21]

4 I charge *thee* therefore before God, and the Lord Jesus Christ, who shall judge the quick and the dead at his appearing and his kingdom; ²Preach the word; be instant in season, out of season; reprove, rebuke, exhort with all longsuffering and doctrine. ³For the time will come when they will not endure sound doctrine; but after their own lusts shall they heap to themselves teachers, having itching ears; ⁴And they shall turn away *their* ears from the truth, and shall be turned unto fables. ⁵But watch thou in all *things,* endure afflictions, do the work of an evangelist, make full proof of thy ministry. ⁶For I am now ready to be offered, and the time of my departure is at hand. ⁷I have fought a good fight, I have finished *my* course, I have kept the faith: ⁸Henceforth there is laid up for me a crown of righteousness, which the Lord, the righteous judge, shall give me at that day: and not to me only, but unto all them also that love his appearing. [Jas. 1:12; ch. 1:12]

Greetings and benediction

9 Do thy diligence to come shortly unto me: ¹⁰For Demas hath forsaken me, having loved *this* present world, and is departed unto Thessalonica; Crescens to Ga-

latia, Titus unto Dalmatia. ¹¹Only Luke is with me. Take Mark, and bring *him* with thee: for he is profitable to me for the ministry. ¹²And Tychicus have I sent to Ephesus. ¹³The cloke that I left at Troas with Carpus, when thou comest, bring *with thee,* and the books, *but* especially the parchments. ¹⁴Alexander the coppersmith did me much evil: the Lord reward him according to his works: ¹⁵Of whom be thou ware also; for he hath greatly withstood our words. ¹⁶At my first answer no *man* stood with me, but all *men* forsook me: *I pray God* that it may not be laid to their charge. ¹⁷Notwithstanding the Lord stood with me, and strengthened me; that by me the preaching might be fully known, and *that* all the Gentiles might hear: and I was delivered out of the mouth of the lion.

¹⁸And the Lord shall deliver me from every evil work, and will preserve *me* unto his heavenly kingdom: to whom *be* glory for ever and ever. Amen. [Ps. 121:7; Rom. 11:36; Gal. 1:5; Heb. 13:21]

19 Salute Prisca and Aquila, and the household of Onesiphorus. ²⁰Erastus abode at Corinth: but Trophimus have I left at Miletum sick. ²¹Do thy diligence to come before winter. Eubulus greeteth thee, and Pudens, and Linus, and Claudia, and all the brethren. ²²The Lord Jesus Christ *be* with thy spirit. Grace *be* with you. Amen. [Gal. 6:18; Philem. 25]

¶ The second *epistle* unto Timotheus, ordained the first bishop of the church of the Ephesians, was written from Rome, when Paul was brought before Nero the second time.

Titus

1 Paul, a servant of God, and an apostle of Jesus Christ, according to the faith of God's elect, and the acknowledging of the truth which is after godliness, ²In hope of eternal life, which God, that cannot lie, promised before the world began; ³But hath in due times manifested his word through preaching, which is committed unto me according to the commandment of God our Saviour; ⁴To Titus, *mine* own son after the common faith: Grace, mercy, *and* peace, from God the Father and the Lord Jesus Christ our Saviour. [2 Cor. 2:13; Eph. 1:2]

Qualifications for elders

5 For this cause left I thee in Crete, that thou shouldest set in order the *things* that are wanting, and ordain elders in every city, as I had appointed thee: ⁶If any be blameless, the husband of one wife, having faithful children not accused of riot or unruly. ⁷For a bishop must be blameless, as the steward of God; not selfwilled, not soon angry, not given to wine, no striker, not given to filthy lucre; ⁸But a lover of hospitality, a lover of good *men*, sober, just, holy, temperate; ⁹Holding fast the faithful word as *he* hath been taught, that he may be able by sound doctrine both to exhort and to convince the gainsayers. [1 Tim. 1:10]

Dealing with false teachers

10 For there are many unruly and vain talkers and deceivers, specially they of the circumcision: ¹¹Whose mouths must be stopped, who subvert whole houses, teaching *things* which *they* ought not, for filthy lucre's sake. ¹²One of themselves, *even* a prophet of their own, said, The Cretians *are* alway liars, evil beasts, slow bellies. ¹³This witness is true. Wherefore rebuke them sharply, that they may be sound in the faith; ¹⁴Not giving heed to Jewish fables, and commandments of men, that turn from the truth. ¹⁵Unto the pure all *things are* pure: but unto them that are defiled and unbelieving *is* nothing pure; but even their mind and conscience is defiled. ¹⁶They profess that *they* know God; but in works they deny *him*, being abominable, and disobedient, and unto every good work reprobate. [2 Tim. 3:5; Rom. 1:28]

Christian doctrine and conduct

2 But speak thou *the things* which become sound doctrine: ²That the aged men be sober, grave, temperate, sound in faith, in charity, in patience. ³The aged women likewise, *that they be* in behaviour as becometh holiness, not false accusers, not given to much wine, teachers of good things; ⁴That they may teach the young *women* to be sober, to love their husbands, to love their children, ⁵*To be* discreet, chaste, keepers at home, good, obedient to their own husbands, that the word of God be not blasphemed. ⁶Young *men* likewise exhort to be sober minded. ⁷In all *things* shewing thyself a pattern of good works: in doctrine *shewing* uncorruptness, gravity, sincerity, 8Sound speech that cannot be condemned; that he that is of the contrary *part* may be ashamed, having no evil *thing* to say of you. 9*Exhort* servants to be obedient unto their own masters, *and* to please *them* well in all *things;* not answering again; 10Not purloining, but shewing all good fidelity; that they may adorn the doctrine of God our Saviour in all *things.* 11For the grace of God that bringeth salvation hath appeared to all men, 12Teaching us that denying ungodliness and worldly lusts we should live soberly, righteously, and godly, in *this* present world; 13Looking for *that* blessed hope, and the glorious appearing of the great God and our Saviour Jesus Christ; 14Who gave himself for us, that he might redeem us from all iniquity, and purify unto himself a peculiar people, zealous of good works. 15These *things* speak, and exhort, and rebuke with all authority. Let no *man* despise thee. [2 Tim. 4:2]

Faith and works

3 Put them in mind to be subject to principalities and powers, to obey magistrates, to be ready to every good work, 2To speak evil of no *man,* to be no brawlers, *but* gentle, shewing all meekness unto all men. 3For we ourselves also were sometimes foolish, disobedient, deceived, serving divers lusts and pleasures, living in malice and envy, hateful, *and* hating one another. 4But after that the kindness and love of God our Saviour toward man appeared,

5Not by works of righteousness which we have done, but according to his mercy he saved us, by the washing of regeneration, and renewing of the Holy Ghost; 6Which he shed on us abundantly through Jesus Christ our Saviour; 7That being justified by his grace, we should be made heirs according to the hope of eternal life. 8*This is* a faithful saying, and these *things* I will that thou affirm constantly, that they which have believed in God might be careful to maintain good works. These *things* are good and profitable unto men. 9But avoid foolish questions, and genealogies, and contentions, and strivings about the law; for they are unprofitable and vain. 10A man *that is* a heretick after the first and second admonition, reject; 11Knowing that *he that is* such is subverted, and sinneth, being condemned of himself. [Acts 13:46]

Closing instruction, benediction

12 When I shall send Artemas unto thee, or Tychicus, be diligent to come unto me to Nicopolis: for I have determined there to winter. 13Bring Zenas the lawyer and Apollos on their journey diligently, that nothing be wanting unto them. 14And let ours also learn to maintain good works for necessary uses, that they be not unfruitful. 15All that are with me salute thee. Greet them that love us in the faith. Grace *be* with you all. Amen.

¶ It was written to Titus, ordained the first bishop of the church of the Cretians, from Nicopolis of Macedonia.

The Epistle of Paul to

Philemon

1 Paul, a prisoner of Jesus Christ, and Timothy *our* brother, unto Philemon *our* dearly beloved, and fellowlabourer, 2And to *our* beloved Apphia, and Archippus our fellowsoldier, and to the church in thy house: 3Grace to you, and peace, from God our Father and the Lord Jesus Christ. [Eph. 1:2]

Thanksgiving and prayer

4 I thank my God, making mention of thee always in my prayers, 5Hearing of thy love and faith, which thou hast toward the Lord Jesus, and toward all saints; 6That the communication of thy faith may become effectual by the acknowledging of every good *thing* which is in you in Christ Jesus. 7For we have great joy and consolation in thy love, because the bowels of the saints are refreshed by thee, brother. [ver. 20; 2 Cor. 7:13; 2 Tim. 1:16]

Appeal for Onesimus

8 Wherefore, though I might be much bold in Christ to enjoin thee that which is convenient, 9Yet for love's sake I rather beseech *thee*, being such a one as Paul the aged, and now also a prisoner of Jesus Christ. 10I beseech thee for my son Onesimus, whom I have begotten in my bonds: 11Which in time past was to thee unprofitable, but now profitable to thee and to me: 12Whom I have sent again: thou therefore receive him, that is, mine own bowels: 13Whom I would have retained with me, that in thy stead he might have ministered unto me in the bonds of the gospel: 14But without thy mind would I do nothing; that thy benefit should not be as *it were* of necessity, but willingly. 15For perhaps he therefore departed for a season, that thou shouldest receive him for ever; 16Not now as a servant, but above a servant, a brother beloved, specially to me, but how much more unto thee, both in the flesh, and in the Lord? 17If thou count me therefore a partner, receive him as myself. 18If he hath wronged thee, or oweth *thee* ought, put that on mine account; 19I Paul have written *it* with mine own hand, I will repay *it:* albeit I do not say to thee how thou owest unto me even thine own self besides. 20Yea, brother, let me have joy of thee in the Lord: refresh my bowels in the Lord. 21Having confidence in thy obedience I wrote unto thee, knowing that thou wilt also do more than I say. 22But withal prepare me also a lodging: for I trust that through your prayers I shall be given unto you. 23There salute thee Epaphras, my fellowprisoner in Christ Jesus; 24Marcus, Aristarchus, Demas, Lucas, my fellowlabourers. 25The grace of our Lord Jesus Christ *be* with your spirit. Amen. [2 Tim. 4:22]

¶ Written from Rome to Philemon, by Onesimus a servant.

The Epistle of Paul the Apostle to the

Hebrews

The Son is God's revelation

1 God, who at sundry times and in divers manners spake in time past unto the fathers by the prophets, 2Hath in these last days spoken unto us by *his* Son, whom he hath appointed heir of all *things,* by whom also he made the worlds; 3Who being the brightness of *his* glory, and the express image of his person, and upholding all *things* by the word of his power, when he had by himself purged our sins, sat down on the right hand of the Majesty on high; 4Being made so much better than the angels, as he hath by inheritance obtained a more excellent name than they. 5For unto which of the angels said he at any time, Thou art my Son, this day have I begotten thee? And again, I will be to him a Father, and he shall be to me a Son? 6And again, when he bringeth in the firstbegotten into the world, he saith, And let all the angels of God worship him. 7And of the angels he saith, Who maketh his angels spirits, and his ministers a flame of fire. 8But unto the Son he saith, Thy throne, O God, *is* for ever and ever: a sceptre of righteousness *is* the sceptre of thy kingdom. 9Thou hast loved righteousness, and hated iniquity; therefore God, *even* thy God, hath anointed thee *with* the oil of gladness above thy fellows. 10And, Thou, Lord, in the beginning hast laid the foundation of the earth; and the heavens are the works of thine hands: 11They shall perish; but thou remainest; and they all shall wax old as *doth* a garment; 12And as a vesture shalt thou fold them up, and they shall be changed: but thou art the same, and thy years shall not fail. 13But to which of the angels said he at any time, Sit on my right hand, until I make thine enemies thy footstool? 14Are they not all ministering spirits, sent forth to minister for them who shall be heirs of salvation? [Ps. 103:20; Mat. 18:10; Rom. 8:17]

The role of Christ in salvation

2 Therefore we ought to give the more earnest heed to the *things* which we have heard, lest at any time we should let *them* slip. 2For if the word spoken by angels was stedfast, and every transgression and disobedience received a just recompence of reward; 3How shall we escape, if we neglect so great salvation; which at the first began to be spoken by the Lord, and was confirmed unto us by them that heard *him;* 4God also bearing *them* witness, both with signs and wonders, and with divers miracles, and gifts of the Holy Ghost, according to his own will? [Mark 16:20; Acts 2:22; 1 Cor. 12:4,7,11; Eph. 1:5,9]

Christ the high priest

5 For unto *the* angels hath he not put in subjection the world to come, whereof we speak: 6But one in a certain place testified, saying, What is man, that thou art mindful

of him? or the son of man, that thou visitest him? 7Thou madest him a little lower than the angels; thou crownedst him with glory and honour, and didst set him over the works of thy hands: 8Thou hast put all *things* in subjection under his feet. For in that *he* put all in subjection under him, he left nothing *that is* not put under him. But now we see not yet all *things* put under him. 9But we see Jesus, who was made a little lower than the angels, for the suffering of death, crowned with glory and honour; that he by the grace of God should taste death for every *man.* 10For it became him, for whom *are* all *things,* and by whom *are* all *things,* in bringing many sons unto glory, to make the captain of their salvation perfect through sufferings. 11For both he that sanctifieth and they who are sanctified *are* all of one: for which cause he is not ashamed to call them brethren, 12Saying, I will declare thy name unto my brethren, in the midst of the church will I sing praise unto thee. 13And again, I will put my trust in him. And again, Behold, I, and the children which God hath given me. 14Forasmuch then as the children are partakers of flesh and blood, he also himself likewise took part of the same; that through death he might destroy him that had the power of death, that is, the devil; 15And deliver them who through fear of death were all their lifetime subject to bondage. 16For verily he took not on *him the nature of* angels; but he took on *him* the seed of Abraham. 17Wherefore in all

things it behoved him to be made like unto *his* brethren, that he might be a merciful and faithful high priest *in things* pertaining to God, to make reconciliation for the sins of the people. 18For in that he himself hath suffered being tempted, he is able to succour them that are tempted. [ch. 4:15,16]

Christ superior to Moses

3 Wherefore, holy brethren, partakers of the heavenly calling, consider the Apostle and High Priest of our profession, Christ Jesus; 2Who was faithful to him that appointed him, as also Moses *was faithful* in all his house. 3For this *man* was counted worthy of more glory than Moses, inasmuch as he who hath builded the house hath more honour than the house. 4For every house is builded by some *man;* but he that built all *things is* God. 5And Moses verily *was* faithful in all his house, as a servant, for a testimony of those *things* which were to be spoken after; 6But Christ as a Son over his own house; whose house are we, if we hold fast the confidence and the rejoicing of the hope firm unto the end. 7Wherefore, as the Holy Ghost saith, To day if ye will hear his voice, 8Harden not your hearts, as in the provocation, in the day of temptation in the wilderness: 9When your fathers tempted me, proved me, and saw my works forty years. 10Wherefore I was grieved with that generation, and said, They do alway err in *their* heart; and they have not known my ways. 11So I sware in my

wrath, They shall not enter into my rest.

The disobedient generation

12 Take heed, brethren, lest there be in any of you an evil heart of unbelief, in departing from the living God. 13But exhort one another daily, while it is called To day; lest any of you be hardened through the deceitfulness of sin. 14For we are made partakers of Christ, if we hold the beginning of *our* confidence stedfast unto the end; 15Whilst it is said, To day if ye will hear his voice, harden not your hearts, as in the provocation. 16For some, when they had heard, did provoke: howbeit not all that came out of Egypt by Moses. 17But with whom was he grieved forty years? *was it* not with them that had sinned, whose carcases fell in the wilderness? 18And to whom sware he that *they* should not enter into his rest, but to them that believed not? 19So we see that they could not enter in because of unbelief.

The promise of rest

4 Let us therefore fear, lest, a promise being left *us* of entering into his rest, any of you should seem to come short *of it.* 2For unto us was the gospel preached, as well as unto them: but the word preached did not profit them, not being mixed with faith in them that heard *it.* 3For we which have believed do enter into rest, as *he* said, As I have sworn in my wrath, if they shall enter into my rest: although the works were finished from the foundation of the world.

4For *he* spake in a certain place of the seventh *day* on this wise, And God did rest the seventh day from all his works. 5And in this *place* again, If they shall enter into my rest. 6Seeing therefore it remaineth that some *must* enter therein, and they to whom it was first preached entered not in because of unbelief, 7Again he limiteth a certain day, saying in David, To day, after so long a time; as it is said, To day if ye will hear his voice, harden not your hearts. 8For if Jesus had given them rest, *then* would he not afterward have spoken of another day. 9There remaineth therefore a rest to the people of God. 10For he that is entered into his rest, he also hath ceased from his own works, as God *did* from his. 11Let us labour therefore to enter into that rest, lest any *man* fall after the same example of unbelief. 12For the word of God *is* quick, and powerful, and sharper than any twoedged sword, piercing even to the dividing asunder of soul and spirit, and of the joints and marrow, and *is* a discerner of the thoughts and intents of the heart. 13Neither is there any creature *that is* not manifest in his sight: but all *things are* naked and opened unto the eyes of him with whom we have to do. [Ps. 90:8; Job 26:6]

Christ the way to God

14 Seeing then that we have a great high priest, that is passed into the heavens, Jesus the Son of God, let us hold fast *our* profession. 15For we have not a high priest

which cannot be touched with the feeling of our infirmities; but was in all *points* tempted like as *we are, yet* without sin. 16Let us therefore come boldly unto the throne of grace, that we may obtain mercy, and find grace to help in time of need. [Eph. 2:18]

5 For every high priest taken from among men is ordained for men *in things* pertaining to God, that he may offer both gifts and sacrifices for sins: 2Who can have compassion on the ignorant, and on them that are out of the way; for that he himself also is compassed with infirmity. 3And by reason hereof he ought, as for the people, so also for himself, to offer for sins. 4And no *man* taketh *this* honour unto himself, but he that is called of God, as *was* Aaron. 5So also Christ glorified not himself to be made a high priest; but he that said unto him, Thou art my Son, to day have I begotten thee. 6As he saith also in another *place,* Thou *art* a priest for ever after the order of Melchisedec. 7Who in the days of his flesh, when he had offered up prayers and supplications with strong crying and tears unto him that was able to save him from death, and was heard in that *he* feared; 8Though he were a Son, *yet* learned he obedience by *the things* which he suffered; 9And being made perfect, he became the author of eternal salvation unto all them that obey him; 10Called of God a high priest after the order of Melchisedec.

Warning against apostasy

11 Of whom we have many things to say, and hard to be uttered, seeing ye are dull of hearing. 12For when for the time ye ought to be teachers, ye have need that *one* teach you again which *be* the first principles of the oracles of God; and are become such as have need of milk, and not of strong meat. 13For every one that useth milk *is* unskilful in the word of righteousness: for he is a babe. 14But strong meat belongeth to *them that are* of full age, *even* those who by reason of use have their senses exercised to discern both good and evil. [Is. 7:15; 1 Cor. 2:14]

6 Therefore leaving the principles of the doctrine of Christ, let us go on unto perfection; not laying again the foundation of repentance from dead works, and of faith towards God, 2Of the doctrine of baptisms, and of laying on of hands, and of resurrection of the dead, and of eternal judgment. 3And this will we do, if God permit. 4For *it is* impossible for those who were once enlightened, and have tasted of the heavenly gift, and were made partakers of the Holy Ghost, 5And have tasted the good word of God, and the powers of the world to come, 6If they shall fall away, to renew *them* again unto repentance; seeing they crucify to themselves the Son of God afresh, and put *him* to an open shame. 7For the earth which drinketh *in* the rain that cometh oft upon it, and bringeth forth herbs meet for them by whom it is

dressed, receiveth blessing from God: 8But that which beareth thorns and briers *is* rejected, and *is* nigh unto cursing; whose end *is* to be burned. [Is. 5:6]

God's oath unchanging

9 But, beloved, we are persuaded better *things* of you, and *things* that accompany salvation, though we thus speak. 10For God *is* not unrighteous to forget your work and labour of love, which ye have shewed toward his name, in that ye have ministered to the saints, and do minister. 11And we desire that every one of you do shew the same diligence to the full assurance of hope unto the end: 12That ye be not slothful, but followers of them who through faith and patience inherit the promises. 13For when God made promise to Abraham, because he could swear by no greater, he sware by himself, 14Saying, Surely blessing I will bless thee, and multiplying I will multiply thee. 15And so, after he had patiently endured, he obtained the promise. 16For men verily swear by the greater: and an oath for confirmation *is* to them an end of all strife. 17Wherein God, willing more abundantly to shew unto the heirs of promise the immutability of his counsel, confirmed *it* by an oath: 18That by two immutable things, in which *it was* impossible for God to lie, we might have a strong consolation, who have fled for refuge to lay hold upon the hope set before *us:* 19Which *hope* we have as an anchor of the soul, both sure and stedfast, and which

entereth into that within the vail; 20Whither the forerunner is for us entered, *even* Jesus, made a high priest for ever after the order of Melchisedec. [ch. 4:14; 8:1; 9:24; 3:1; 5:6,10; 7:17]

The priesthood of Melchisedec

7 For this Melchisedec, king of Salem, priest of the most high God, who met Abraham returning from the slaughter of the kings, and blessed him; 2To whom also Abraham gave a tenth *part* of all; first being by interpretation King of righteousness, and after that also King of Salem, which is, King of peace; 3Without father, without mother, without descent, having neither beginning of days, nor end of life; but made like unto the Son of God; abideth a priest continually. 4Now consider how great this *man was,* unto whom even the patriarch Abraham gave the tenth of the spoils. 5And verily they that are of the sons of Levi who receive the office of the priesthood have a commandment to take tithes of the people according to the law, that is, of their brethren, though they come out of the loins of Abraham: 6But he whose descent is not counted from them received tithes of Abraham, and blessed him that had the promises. 7And without all contradiction the less is blessed of the better. 8And here men that die receive tithes; but there he *receiveth them,* of whom it is witnessed that he liveth. 9And as *I* may so say, Levi also, who receiveth tithes, payed tithes in Abraham. 10For he was yet in the

loins of his father, when Melchisedec met him. 11If therefore perfection were by the Levitical priesthood, (for under it the people received the law,) what further need *was there* that another priest should rise after the order of Melchisedec, and not be called after the order of Aaron? 12For the priesthood being changed, there is made of necessity a change also of the law. 13For he of whom these *things* are spoken pertaineth to another tribe, of which no *man* gave attendance at the altar. 14For *it is* evident that our Lord sprang out of Juda; of which tribe Moses spake nothing concerning priesthood. 15And it is yet far more evident: for that after the similitude of Melchisedec there ariseth another priest, 16Who is made, not after the law of a carnal commandment, but after the power of an endless life. 17For *he* testifieth, Thou *art* a priest for ever after the order of Melchisedec. 18For there is verily a disannulling of the commandment going before for the weakness and unprofitableness thereof. 19For the law made nothing perfect, but the bringing in of a better hope *did;* by the which we draw nigh unto God. 20And inasmuch as not without an oath *he was made priest:* 21(For those priests were made without an oath; but this with an oath by him that said unto him, The Lord sware and will not repent, Thou *art* a priest for ever after the order of Melchisedec:) 22By so much was Jesus made a surety of a better testament. 23And they truly were many priests, because *they* were

not suffered to continue by reason of death: 24But this *man,* because he continueth ever, hath an unchangeable priesthood. 25Wherefore he is able also to save them to the uttermost that come unto God by him, seeing he ever liveth to make intercession for them. [Rom. 8:34; 1 Tim. 2:5; 1 John 2:1]

Christ's priesthood superior

26 For such a high priest became us, *who is* holy, harmless, undefiled, separate from sinners, and made higher than the heavens; 27Who needeth not daily, as *those* high priests, to offer up sacrifice, first for his own sins, *and* then for the people's: for this he did once, when he offered up himself. 28For the law maketh men high priests which have infirmity; but the word of the oath, which was since the law, *maketh* the Son, who is consecrated for evermore. [ch. 5:1,2; ch. 2:10; 5:9]

Superiority of the new covenant

8 Now of the *things* which we have spoken *this is* the sum: We have such a high priest, who is set on the right hand of the throne of the Majesty in the heavens; 2A minister of the sanctuary, and of the true tabernacle, which the Lord pitched, and not man. 3For every high priest is ordained to offer gifts and sacrifices: wherefore *it is* of necessity that this *man* have somewhat also to offer. 4For if he were on earth, he should not be a priest, seeing that there are priests that offer gifts according to the law: 5Who serve unto the example and shadow of heavenly *things,* as

Moses was admonished of God when he was about to make the tabernacle: for, See, saith *he, that* thou make all *things* according to the pattern shewed to thee in the mount. ⁶But now hath he obtained a more excellent ministry, by how much also he is the mediator of a better covenant, which was established upon better promises. [2 Cor. 3:6,8; ch. 7:22]

7 For if that first *covenant* had been faultless, *then* should no place have been sought for the second. ⁸For finding fault with them, *he* saith, Behold, the days come, saith the Lord, when I will make a new covenant with the house of Israel and with the house of Juda: ⁹Not according to the covenant that I made with their fathers in the day when I took them by the hand to lead them out of the land of Egypt; because they continued not in my covenant, and I regarded them not, saith the Lord. ¹⁰For this *is* the covenant that I will make with the house of Israel after those days, saith the Lord; I will put my laws into their mind, and write them in their hearts: and I will be to them a God, and they shall be to me a people: ¹¹And they shall not teach every man his neighbour, and every man his brother, saying, Know the Lord: for all shall know me, from the least to the greatest. ¹²For I will be merciful to their unrighteousness, and their sins and their iniquities will I remember no more. ¹³In that *he* saith, A new *covenant,* he hath made the first old. Now that which decayeth and

waxeth old *is* ready to vanish away. [2 Cor. 5:17]

Temporary sacrifices by Levites

9 Then verily the first *covenant* had also ordinances of divine service, and a worldly sanctuary. ²For there was a tabernacle made; the first, wherein *was* the candlestick, and the table, and the shewbread; which is called the sanctuary. ³And after the second vail, the tabernacle which is called the holiest of all; ⁴Which had the golden censer, and the ark of the covenant overlaid round about with gold, wherein *was* the golden pot that had manna, and Aaron's rod that budded, and the tables of the covenant; ⁵And over it the cherubims of glory shadowing the mercy seat; of which *we* cannot now speak particularly. ⁶Now when these *things* were thus ordained, the priests went always into the first tabernacle, accomplishing the service *of God.* ⁷But into the second *went* the high priest alone once every year, not without blood, which he offered for himself, and *for* the errors of the people: ⁸The Holy Ghost this signifying, that the way into the holiest *of all* was not yet made manifest, while as the first tabernacle was yet standing: ⁹Which *was* a figure for the time *then* present, in which were offered both gifts and sacrifices, that could not make him that did the service perfect, as pertaining to the conscience; ¹⁰*Which stood* only in meats and drinks, and divers washings, and carnal ordinances, imposed *on them* until the time of

reformation. [11]But Christ being come a high priest of good *things* to come, by a greater and more perfect tabernacle, not made with hands, that is to say, not of this building, [12]Neither by the blood of goats and calves, but by his own blood he entered in once into the holy *place,* having obtained eternal redemption *for us.* [13]For if the blood of bulls and of goats, and the ashes of a heifer sprinkling the unclean, sanctifieth to the purifying of the flesh: [14]How much more shall the blood of Christ, who through the eternal Spirit offered himself without spot to God, purge your conscience from dead works to serve the living God? [1 John 1:7; Rom. 1:4; ch. 10:22; ch. 6:1; Luke 1:74]

Christ's once-for-all sacrifice

15 And for this cause he is the mediator of the new testament, that by means of death, for the redemption of the transgressions that were under the first testament, they which are called might receive the promise of eternal inheritance. [16]For where a testament *is,* there must also of necessity be the death of the testator. [17]For a testament *is* of force after *men* are dead: otherwise it is of no strength at all whilst the testator liveth. [18]Whereupon neither the first *testament* was dedicated without blood. [19]For when Moses had spoken every precept to all the people according to the law, he took the blood of calves and of goats, with water, and scarlet wool, and hyssop, and sprinkled both the book, and all the people, [20]Saying, This *is* the blood of the testament which God hath enjoined unto you. [21]Moreover he sprinkled with blood both the tabernacle, and all the vessels of the ministry. [22]And almost all *things* are by the law purged with blood; and without shedding of blood is no remission. [23]*It was* therefore necessary that the patterns of *things* in the heavens should be purified with these; but the heavenly *things* themselves with better sacrifices than these. [24]For Christ is not entered into the holy *places* made with hands, *which are* the figures of the true; but into heaven itself, now to appear in the presence of God for us: [25]Nor yet that he should offer himself often, as the high priest entereth into the holy *place* every year with blood of others; [26]For then must he often have suffered since the foundation of the world: but now once in the end of the world hath he appeared to put away sin by the sacrifice of himself. [27]And as it is appointed unto men once to die, but after this the judgment: [28]So Christ was once offered to bear the sins of many; and unto them that look for him shall he appear the second time without sin unto salvation. [Rom. 6:10; 1 Pet. 3:18; 2:24; 1 John 3:5; Mat. 26:28; Rom. 5:15; Tit. 2:13]

10 For the law having a shadow of good *things* to come, *and* not the very image of the things, can never with those sacrifices which they offered year by year continually make the comers *thereunto* perfect. [2]For then would they not have ceased to be offered? because that the worshippers once purged should have had no more conscience of sins. ³But in those *sacrifices there is* a remembrance *again made* of sins every year. ⁴For *it is* not possible that the blood of bulls and of goats should take away sins. ⁵Wherefore when he cometh into the world, he saith, Sacrifice and offering thou wouldest not, but a body hast thou prepared me: ⁶In burnt offerings and *sacrifices* for sin thou hast had no pleasure. ⁷Then said I, Lo, I come (in the volume of the book it is written of me,) to do thy will, O God. ⁸Above when he said, Sacrifice and offering and burnt offerings and *offering* for sin thou wouldest not, neither hadst pleasure *therein:* which are offered by the law; ⁹Then said he, Lo, I come to do thy will, O God. He taketh away the first, that he may establish the second. ¹⁰By the which will we are sanctified through the offering of the body of Jesus Christ once for all. ¹¹And every priest standeth daily ministering and offering oftentimes the same sacrifices, which can never take away sins: ¹²But this *man,* after he had offered one sacrifice for sins for ever, sat down on the right hand of God; ¹³From henceforth expecting till his enemies be made his footstool. ¹⁴For by one offering he hath perfected for ever them that are sanctified. ¹⁵*Whereof* the Holy Ghost also is a witness to us: for after that *he* had said before, ¹⁶This *is* the covenant that I will make with them after those days, saith the Lord, I will put my laws into their hearts, and in their minds will I write them;

¹⁷And their sins and iniquities will I remember no more. ¹⁸Now where remission of these *is, there is* no more offering for sin.

The appeal to hold fast

19 Having therefore, brethren, boldness to enter into the holiest by the blood of Jesus, ²⁰*By* a new and living way, which he hath consecrated for us, through the vail, that is to say, his flesh; ²¹And *having* a high priest over the house of God; ²²Let us draw near with a true heart in full assurance of faith, having *our* hearts sprinkled from an evil conscience, and *our* bodies washed with pure water. ²³Let us hold fast the profession of *our* hope without wavering; (for he *is* faithful that promised;) ²⁴And let us consider one another to provoke unto love and to good works: ²⁵Not forsaking the assembling of ourselves together, as the manner of some *is;* but exhorting *one another:* and so much the more, as ye see the day approaching. [Acts 2:42; Rom. 13:11; Phil. 4:5; 2 Pet. 3:9]

26 For if we sin wilfully after that *we* have received the knowledge of the truth, there remaineth no more sacrifice for sins, ²⁷But a certain fearful looking for of judgment and fiery indignation, which shall devour the adversaries. ²⁸He that despised Moses' law died without mercy under two or three witnesses: ²⁹Of how much sorer punishment, suppose ye, shall he be thought worthy, who hath trodden under foot the Son of God, and hath counted the blood of the covenant, wherewith he was sancti-

fied, an unholy *thing,* and hath done despite unto the Spirit of grace? 30For we know him that hath said, Vengeance *belongeth* unto me, I will recompense, saith the Lord. And again, The Lord shall judge his people. 31*It is* a fearful *thing* to fall into the hands of the living God. 32But call to remembrance the former days, in which, after ye were illuminated, ye endured a great fight of afflictions; 33Partly, whilst ye were made a gazingstock both by reproaches and afflictions; and partly, whilst ye became companions of them that were so used. 34For ye had compassion *of me* in my bonds, and took joyfully the spoiling of your goods, knowing in yourselves that *ye* have in heaven a better and an enduring substance. 35Cast not away therefore your confidence, which hath great recompence of reward. 36For ye have need of patience, that, after ye have done the will of God, ye might receive the promise. 37For yet a little while, *and* he that shall come will come, and will not tarry. 38Now the just shall live by faith: but if *any man* draw back, my soul shall have no pleasure in him. 39But we are not of *them* who draw back unto perdition; but of *them* that believe to the saving of the soul. [2 Pet. 2:20; Acts 16:31; 1 Thes. 5:9; 2 Thes. 2:14]

Faith defined and exemplified

11 Now faith is the substance of *things* hoped for, the evidence of things not seen. 2For by it the elders obtained a good report. 3Through faith we understand that the worlds were framed by the word of God, so that *things* which are seen were not made of *things* which do appear. 4By faith Abel offered unto God a more excellent sacrifice than Cain, by which he obtained witness that he was righteous, God testifying of his gifts: and by it he being dead yet speaketh. 5By faith Enoch was translated that *he* should not see death; and was not found, because God had translated him: for before his translation he had this testimony, that *he* pleased God. 6But without faith *it is* impossible to please *him:* for he that cometh to God must believe that he is, and *that* he is a rewarder of them that diligently seek him. 7By faith Noah, being warned of God of *things* not seen as yet, moved with fear, prepared an ark to the saving of his house; by the which he condemned the world, and became heir of the righteousness which is by faith. 8By faith Abraham, when he was called to go out into a place which he should after receive for an inheritance, obeyed; and he went out, not knowing whither he went. 9By faith he sojourned in the land of promise, as *in* a strange *country,* dwelling in tabernacles with Isaac and Jacob, the heirs with *him* of the same promise: 10For he looked for a city which hath foundations, whose builder and maker *is* God. 11Through faith also Sara herself received strength to conceive seed, and was delivered of a child when *she* was past age, because she judged him faithful who had promised. 12Therefore sprang there even of one, and him as good as dead, *so many* as the stars of the sky in multitude, and as the sand which is by the sea shore innumerable. ¹³These all died in faith, not having received the promises, but having seen them afar off, and were persuaded of *them,* and embraced *them,* and confessed that they were strangers and pilgrims on the earth. ¹⁴For they that say such *things* declare plainly that they seek a country. ¹⁵And truly, if they had been mindful of that *country* from whence they came out, they might have had opportunity to have returned. ¹⁶But now they desire a better *country,* that is, a heavenly: wherefore God is not ashamed to be called their God: for he hath prepared for them a city. ¹⁷By faith Abraham, when he was tried, offered up Isaac: and he that had received the promises offered up *his* only begotten *son,* ¹⁸Of whom it was said, That in Isaac shall thy seed be called: ¹⁹Accounting that God *was* able to raise *him* up, even from the dead; from whence also he received him in a figure. ²⁰By faith Isaac blessed Jacob and Esau concerning *things* to come. ²¹By faith Jacob, when he was a dying, blessed both the sons of Joseph; and worshipped, *leaning* upon the top of his staff. ²²By faith Joseph, when he died, made mention of the departing of the children of Israel; and gave commandment concerning his bones. ²³By faith Moses, when he was born, was hid three months of his parents, because they saw *he was* a proper child; and they were not afraid of the king's commandment. ²⁴By faith Moses, when he was come to years, refused to be called the son of Pharaoh's daughter; ²⁵Choosing rather to suffer affliction with the people of God, than to enjoy the pleasures of sin for a season; ²⁶Esteeming the reproach of Christ greater riches than the treasures in Egypt: for he had respect unto the recompence of the reward. ²⁷By faith he forsook Egypt, not fearing the wrath of the king: for he endured, as seeing *him who is* invisible. ²⁸Through faith he kept the passover, and the sprinkling of blood, lest he that destroyed the firstborn should touch them. ²⁹By faith they passed through the Red sea as by dry *land:* which the Egyptians assaying to do were drowned. ³⁰By faith the walls of Jericho fell down, after they were compassed about seven days. ³¹By faith the harlot Rahab perished not with them that believed not, when she had received the spies with peace. [Josh. 6:23; Josh. 2:1]

32 And what shall I more say? for the time would fail me to tell of Gedeon, and *of* Barak, and *of* Samson, and *of* Jephthae; *of* David also, and Samuel, and *of* the prophets: ³³Who through faith subdued kingdoms, wrought righteousness, obtained promises, stopped the mouths of lions, ³⁴Quenched the violence of fire, escaped the edge of the sword, out of weakness were made strong, waxed valiant in fight, turned to flight the armies of the aliens. ³⁵Women received their dead raised to life again: and others were tortured, not accepting deliv-

erance; that they might obtain a better resurrection: 36And others had trial of *cruel* mockings and scourgings, yea, moreover of bonds and imprisonment: 37They were stoned, they were sawn asunder, were tempted, were slain with the sword: they wandered about in sheepskins and goatskins; being destitute, afflicted, tormented; 38(Of whom the world was not worthy:) they wandered in deserts, and *in* mountains, and *in* dens and caves of the earth. 39And these all, having obtained a good report through faith, received not the promise: 40God having provided some better *thing* for us, that they without us should not be made perfect. [ch. 5:9]

Christ our example

12 Wherefore seeing we also are compassed about with so great a cloud of witnesses, let us lay aside every weight, and the sin which doth so easily beset *us,* and let us run with patience the race that is set before us, 2Looking unto Jesus the author and finisher of *our* faith; who for the joy that was set before him endured the cross, despising the shame, and is set down at the right hand of the throne of God. 3For consider him that endured such contradiction of sinners against himself, lest ye be wearied and faint in your minds. [Mat. 10:24; John 15:20; Gal. 6:9]

An appeal for endurance

4 Ye have not yet resisted unto blood, striving against sin. 5And ye have forgotten the exhortation which speaketh unto you as unto children, My son, despise not thou the chastening of the Lord, nor faint when thou art rebuked of him: 6For whom the Lord loveth he chasteneth, and scourgeth every son whom he receiveth. 7If ye endure chastening, God dealeth with you as with sons; for what son is *he* whom the father chasteneth not? 8But if ye be without chastisement, whereof all are partakers, then are ye bastards, and not sons. 9Furthermore we have had fathers of our flesh which corrected *us,* and we gave *them* reverence: shall we not much rather be in subjection unto the Father of spirits, and live? 10For they verily for a few days chastened *us* after their own pleasure; but he for *our* profit, that *we* might be partakers of his holiness. 11Now no chastening for the present seemeth to be joyous, but grievous: nevertheless afterward it yieldeth the peaceable fruit of righteousness unto them which are exercised thereby. 12Wherefore lift up the hands which hang down, and the feeble knees; 13And make straight paths for your feet, lest *that which is* lame be turned out of the way; but let it rather be healed. 14Follow peace with all *men,* and holiness, without which no *man* shall see the Lord: 15Looking diligently lest any *man* fail of the grace of God; lest any root of bitterness springing up trouble *you,* and thereby many be defiled; 16Lest there *be* any fornicator, or profane *person,* as Esau, who for one morsel of meat sold his birthright. 17For ye know how that afterward, when he would have inherited the

blessing, he was rejected: for he found no place of repentance, though he sought it carefully with tears. [Gen. 27:34]

18 For ye are not come unto the mount that might be touched, and that burned with fire, nor unto blackness, and darkness, and tempest, ¹⁹And the sound of a trumpet, and the voice of words; which *voice* they that heard intreated that the word should not be spoken to them any more: ²⁰(For they could not endure that which was commanded, And if *so much as* a beast touch the mountain, it shall be stoned, or thrust through with a dart: ²¹And so terrible was the sight, *that* Moses said, I exceedingly fear and quake;) ²²But ye are come unto mount Sion, and unto the city of the living God, the heavenly Jerusalem, and to an innumerable company of angels, ²³To the general assembly, and church of the firstborn, which are written in heaven, and to God the Judge of all, and to the spirits of just *men* made perfect, ²⁴And to Jesus the mediator of the new covenant, and to the blood of sprinkling, that speaketh better *things* than *that of* Abel. ²⁵See *that* ye refuse not him that speaketh: for if they escaped not who refused him that spake on earth, much more *shall not* we *escape,* if we turn away from him that *speaketh* from heaven: ²⁶Whose voice then shook the earth: but now he hath promised, saying, Yet once *more* I shake not the earth only, but also heaven. ²⁷And this *word,* Yet once *more,* signifieth the removing of those

things that are shaken, as of *things* that are made, that those *things* which cannot be shaken may remain. ²⁸Wherefore we receiving a kingdom which cannot be moved, let us have grace, whereby we may serve God acceptably with reverence and godly fear: ²⁹For our God *is* a consuming fire. [Ex. 24:17; Deut. 4:24]

Warnings and requests

13 Let brotherly love continue. ²Be not forgetful to entertain strangers: for thereby some have entertained angels unawares. ³Remember *them that are* in bonds, as bound with *them; and* them which suffer adversity, as being yourselves also in the body. ⁴Marriage *is* honourable in all, and the bed undefiled: but whoremongers and adulterers God will judge. ⁵*Let your* conversation *be* without covetousness; *and be* content with such *things* as ye have: for he hath said, I will never leave thee, nor forsake thee. ⁶So that we may boldly say, The Lord *is* my helper, and I will not fear what man shall do unto me. ⁷Remember them which have the rule over you, who have spoken unto you the word of God: whose faith follow, considering the end of *their* conversation. ⁸Jesus Christ the same yesterday, and to day, and for ever. ⁹Be not carried about with divers and strange doctrines. For *it is* a good *thing* that the heart be established with grace; not with meats, which have not profited them that have been occupied therein. ¹⁰We have an altar, whereof they have no right to eat which serve the tabernacle. [11]For the bodies of those beasts, whose blood is brought into the sanctuary by the high priest for sin, are burnt without the camp. [12]Wherefore Jesus also, that he might sanctify the people with his own blood, suffered without the gate. [13]Let us go forth therefore unto him without the camp, bearing his reproach. [14]For here have we no continuing city, but we seek one to come. [15]By him therefore let us offer the sacrifice of praise to God continually, that is, the fruit of *our* lips giving thanks to his name. [16]But to do good and to communicate forget not: for with such sacrifices God is well pleased. [17]Obey them that have the rule over you, and submit yourselves: for they watch for your souls, as they that must give account, that they may do it with joy, and not with grief: for that *is* unprofitable for you. [18]Pray for us: for we trust we have a good conscience, in all *things*

willing to live honestly. [19]But I beseech *you* the rather to do this, that I may be restored to you the sooner.

20 Now the God of peace, that brought again from the dead our Lord Jesus, *that* great shepherd of the sheep, through the blood of the everlasting covenant, [21]Make you perfect in every good work to do his will, working in you *that which is* well pleasing in his sight, through Jesus Christ; to whom *be* glory for ever and ever. Amen. [22]And I beseech you, brethren, suffer the word of exhortation: for I have written a letter unto you in few *words.* [23]Know ye that *our* brother Timothy is set at liberty; with whom, if he come shortly, I will see you. [24]Salute all them that have the rule over you, and all the saints. They of Italy salute you. [25]Grace *be* with you all. Amen. [Tit. 3:15]

¶ Written to the Hebrews from Italy by Timothy.

The General Epistle of

James

1 James, a servant of God and of the Lord Jesus Christ, to the twelve tribes which are scattered abroad, greeting. [Acts 12:17; Tit. 1:1; Acts 26:7; Deut. 32:26; John 7:35; Acts 2:5; 1 Pet. 1:1]

Patience in temptation

2 My brethren, count *it* all joy when ye fall into divers temptations; 3Knowing *this,* that the trying of your faith worketh patience. 4But let patience have *her* perfect work, that ye may be perfect and entire, wanting nothing. 5If any of you lack wisdom, let him ask of God, that giveth to all *men* liberally, and upbraideth not; and it shall be given him. 6But let him ask in faith, nothing wavering: for he that wavereth is like a wave of the sea driven with the wind and tossed. 7For let not that man think that he shall receive any *thing* of the Lord. 8A double minded man *is* unstable in all his ways. 9Let the brother of low degree rejoice in that he is exalted: 10But the rich, in that he is made low: because as the flower of the grass he shall pass away. 11For the sun is no sooner risen with a burning heat, but it withereth the grass, and the flower thereof falleth, and the grace of the fashion of it perisheth: so also shall the rich *man* fade away in his ways. 12Blessed *is* the man that endureth temptation: for when he is tried, he shall receive the crown of life, which the Lord hath promised to them that love him. 13Let no *man*

say when he is tempted, I am tempted of God: for God cannot be tempted with evil, neither tempteth he any *man:* 14But every man is tempted, when he is drawn away of his own lust, and enticed. 15Then when lust hath conceived, it bringeth forth sin: and sin, when it is finished, bringeth forth death. 16Do not err, my beloved brethren. 17Every good gift and every perfect gift is from above, and cometh down from the Father of lights, with whom is no variableness, neither shadow of turning. 18Of his own will begat he us with the word of truth, that we should be a kind of firstfruits of his creatures. [John 1:13; 1 Cor. 4:15; Eph. 1:12; Rev. 14:4]

The conduct of true religion

19 Wherefore, my beloved brethren, let every man be swift to hear, slow to speak, slow to wrath: 20For the wrath of man worketh not the righteousness of God. 21Wherefore lay apart all filthiness and superfluity of naughtiness, and receive with meekness the engrafted word, which is able to save your souls. 22But be ye doers of the word, and not hearers only, deceiving your own selves. 23For if any be a hearer of the word, and not a doer, he is like unto a man beholding his natural face in a glass: 24For he beholdeth himself, and goeth his way, and straightway forgetteth what manner of *man* he was. 25But whoso looketh into the perfect law of liberty, and continueth *therein,*

he being not a forgetful hearer, but a doer of the work, this *man* shall be blessed in his deed. 26If any *man* among you seem to be religious, and bridleth not his tongue, but deceiveth his own heart, this *man's* religion *is* vain. 27Pure religion and undefiled before God and the Father is this, To visit the fatherless and widows in their affliction, *and* to keep himself unspotted from the world. [Is. 1:16; Mat. 25:36; Rom. 12:2; 1 John 5:18]

True faith impartial

2 My brethren, have not the faith of our Lord Jesus Christ, *the Lord* of glory, with respect of persons. 2For if there come unto your assembly a man with a gold ring, in goodly apparel, and there come in also a poor *man* in vile raiment; 3And ye have respect to him that weareth the gay clothing, and say unto him, Sit thou here in a good place; and say to the poor, Stand thou there, or sit here under my footstool: 4Are ye not then partial in yourselves, and are become judges of evil thoughts? 5Hearken, my beloved brethren, Hath not God chosen the poor of this world rich in faith, and heirs of the kingdom which he hath promised to them that love him? 6But ye have despised the poor. Do not rich *men* oppress you, and draw you before the judgment seats? 7Do not they blaspheme *that* worthy name by the which ye are called? 8If ye fulfil the royal law according to the scripture, Thou shalt love thy neighbour as thyself, ye do well: 9But if ye have respect to persons,

ye commit sin, and are convinced of the law as transgressors. 10For whosoever shall keep the whole law, and *yet* offend in one *point*, he is guilty of all. 11For he that said, Do not commit adultery, said also, Do not kill. Now if thou commit no adultery, yet *if* thou kill, thou art become a transgressor of the law. 12So speak ye, and so do, as they that shall be judged by the law of liberty. 13For he shall have judgment without mercy, that hath shewed no mercy; and mercy rejoiceth against judgment. [Job 22:6; 1 John 4:17]

True faith evidenced by works

14 What *doth it* profit, my brethren, though a man say *he* hath faith, and have not works? can faith save him? 15If a brother or sister be naked, and destitute of daily food, 16And one of you say unto them, Depart in peace, be you warmed and filled; notwithstanding ye give them not those *things which doth it* profit? 17Even so faith, if it hath not works, is dead, *being* alone. 18Yea, a man may say, Thou hast faith, and I have works: shew me thy faith without thy works, and I will shew thee my faith by my works. 19Thou believest that there is one God; thou doest well: the devils also believe, and tremble. 20But wilt thou know, O vain man, that faith without works is dead? 21Was not Abraham our father justified by works, when he had offered Isaac his son upon the altar? 22Seest thou how faith wrought with his works, and by

works was faith made perfect? 23 And the scripture was fulfilled which saith, Abraham believed God, and it was imputed unto him for righteousness: and he was called the Friend of God. 24 Ye see then how that by works a man is justified, and not by faith only. 25 Likewise also was not Rahab the harlot justified by works, when she had received the messengers, and had sent *them* out another way? 26 For as the body without the spirit is dead, so faith without works is dead also.

True faith evidenced by words

3 My brethren, be not many masters, knowing that we shall receive the greater condemnation. 2 For *in* many *things* we offend all. If any *man* offend not in word, the same *is* a perfect man, *and* able also to bridle the whole body. 3 Behold, we put bits in the horses' mouths, that they may obey us; and we turn about their whole body. 4 Behold also the ships, which though they be so great, and are driven of fierce winds, *yet* are they turned about with a very small helm, whithersoever the governor listeth. 5 Even so the tongue is a little member, and boasteth great things. Behold, how great a matter a little fire kindleth. 6 And the tongue *is* a fire, a world of iniquity: so *is* the tongue amongst our members, that it defileth the whole body, and setteth on fire the course of nature; and it is set on fire of hell. 7 For every kind of beasts, and of birds, and of serpents, and of *things* in the sea, is

tamed, and hath been tamed of mankind: 8 But the tongue can no man tame; *it is* an unruly evil, full of deadly poison. 9 Therewith bless we God, even the Father; and therewith curse we men, which are made after the similitude of God. 10 Out of the same mouth proceedeth blessing and cursing. My brethren, these *things* ought not so to be. 11 Doth a fountain send forth at the same place sweet *water* and bitter? 12 Can the fig tree, my brethren, bear olive berries? either a vine, figs? so *can* no fountain *both* yield salt water and fresh.

True and false wisdom

13 Who *is* a wise *man* and endued with knowledge amongst you? let him shew out of a good conversation his works with meekness of wisdom. 14 But if ye have bitter envying and strife in your hearts, glory not, and lie *not* against the truth. 15 This wisdom descendeth not from above, but *is* earthly, sensual, devilish. 16 For where envying and strife *is*, there *is* confusion and every evil work. 17 But the wisdom that is from above is first pure, then peaceable, gentle, *and* easy to be intreated, full of mercy and good fruits, without partiality, and without hypocrisy. 18 And the fruit of righteousness is sown in peace of them that make peace. [Prov. 11:18]

Friendship and humility

4 From whence *come* wars and fightings among you? *come they* not hence, *even* of your lusts that war in your members? 2 Ye lust, and have not: ye kill, and de-

sire *to have,* and cannot obtain: ye fight and war, yet ye have not, because ye ask not. ³Ye ask, and receive not, because ye ask amiss, that ye may consume *it* upon your lusts. ⁴Ye adulterers and adulteresses, know ye not that the friendship of the world is enmity with God? whosoever therefore will be a friend of the world is the enemy of God. ⁵Do ye think that the scripture saith in vain, the spirit that dwelleth in us lusteth to envy? ⁶But he giveth more grace. Wherefore *he* saith, God resisteth the proud, but giveth grace unto the humble. ⁷Submit yourselves therefore to God. Resist the devil, and he will flee from you. ⁸Draw nigh to God, and he will draw nigh to you. Cleanse *your* hands, *ye* sinners; and purify *your* hearts, *ye* double minded. ⁹Be afflicted, and mourn, and weep: let your laughter be turned to mourning, and *your* joy to heaviness. ¹⁰Humble yourselves in the sight of the Lord, and he shall lift you up. [Job 22:29]

Slander and false confidence

11 Speak not evil one of another, brethren. He that speaketh evil of *his* brother, and judgeth his brother, speaketh evil of the law, and judgeth the law: but if thou judge the law, thou art not a doer of the law, but a judge. ¹²There is one lawgiver, who is able to save and to destroy: who art thou that judgest another? [Mat. 10:28; Rom. 14:4]

13 Go to now, ye that say, To day or to morrow we will go into such a city, and continue there a year, and buy and sell, and get gain: ¹⁴Whereas ye know not what *shall be* on the morrow: for what *is* your life? It is even a vapour, that appeareth for a little *time,* and then vanisheth away. ¹⁵For that ye *ought* to say, If the Lord will, we shall live, and do this, or that. ¹⁶But now ye rejoice in your boastings: all such rejoicing is evil. ¹⁷Therefore to him that knoweth to do good, and doeth *it* not, to him it is sin. [Luke 12:47; John 9:41]

The miseries of the rich

5 Go to now, ye rich *men,* weep and howl for your miseries that shall come upon *you.* ²Your riches are corrupted, and your garments are motheaten. ³Your gold and silver is cankered; and the rust of them shall be a witness against you, and shall eat your flesh as *it were* fire: ye have heaped treasure together for the last days. ⁴Behold, the hire of the labourers which have reaped *down* your fields, which is of you kept back by fraud, crieth: and the cries of them which have reaped are entered into the ears of the Lord of sabaoth. ⁵Ye have lived in pleasure on the earth, and been wanton; ye have nourished your hearts, as in a day of slaughter. ⁶Ye have condemned *and* killed the just; *and* he doth not resist you. [ch. 2:6]

The patience of the saints

7 Be patient therefore, brethren, unto the coming of the Lord. Behold, the husbandman waiteth for the precious fruit of the earth, and hath long patience for it, until he receive the early and latter rain. ⁸Be ye also patient; stablish your

hearts: for the coming of the Lord draweth nigh. 9Grudge not one against another, brethren, lest ye be condemned: behold, the judge standeth before the door. 10Take, my brethren, the prophets, who have spoken in the name of the Lord, for an example of suffering affliction, and of patience. 11Behold, we count them happy which endure. Ye have heard of the patience of Job, and have seen the end of the Lord; that the Lord is very pitiful, and of tender mercy. 12But above all *things*, my brethren, swear not, neither by heaven, neither by the earth, neither by any other oath: but let your yea be yea; and *your* nay, nay; lest ye fall into condemnation. [Mat. 5:34]

Prayer and confession

13 Is any among you afflicted? let him pray. Is any merry? let him sing psalms. 14Is any sick among you? let him call for the elders of the church; and let them pray over him, anointing him with oil in the name of the Lord: 15And the prayer of faith shall save the sick, and the Lord shall raise him up; and if he have committed sins, they shall be forgiven him. 16Confess *your* faults one to another, and pray one for another, that ye may be healed. The effectual fervent prayer of a righteous *man* availeth much. 17Elias was a man subject to like passions as we are, and he prayed earnestly that it might not rain: and it rained not on the earth *by the space of* three years and six months. 18And he prayed again, and the heaven gave rain, and the earth brought forth her fruit. [1 Ki. 18:42,45]

19 Brethren, if any of you do err from the truth, and one convert him; 20Let him know, that he which converteth the sinner from the error of his way shall save a soul from death, and shall hide a multitude of sins.

Peter

1 Peter, an apostle of Jesus Christ, to the strangers scattered throughout Pontus, Galatia, Cappadocia, Asia, and Bithynia, 2 Elect according to the foreknowledge of God the Father, through sanctification of the Spirit, unto obedience and sprinkling of the blood of Jesus Christ: Grace unto you, and peace, be multiplied. [Eph. 1:4; Rom. 8:29; 2 Thes. 2:13; Heb. 12:24; Rom. 1:7]

The risen Christ

3 Blessed *be* the God and Father of our Lord Jesus Christ, which according to his abundant mercy hath begotten us again unto a lively hope by the resurrection of Jesus Christ from the dead, 4 To an inheritance incorruptible, and undefiled, and that fadeth not away, reserved in heaven for you, 5 Who are kept by the power of God through faith unto salvation ready to be revealed in the last time. 6 Wherein ye greatly rejoice, though now for a season, if need be, ye are in heaviness through manifold temptations: 7 That the trial of your faith, *being* much more precious than of gold that perisheth, though it be tried with fire, might be found unto praise and honour and glory at the appearing of Jesus Christ: 8 Whom having not seen, ye love; in whom, though now ye see *him* not, yet believing, ye rejoice with joy unspeakable and full of glory: 9 Receiving the end of your faith, *even* the salvation of *your* souls. 10 Of which salvation the prophets have in-

quired and searched diligently, who prophesied of the grace *that should come* unto you: 11 Searching what, or what manner of time the Spirit of Christ which was in them did signify, when it testified beforehand the sufferings of Christ, and the glory that should follow. 12 Unto whom it was revealed, that not unto themselves, but unto us they did minister the things, which are now reported unto you by them that have preached the gospel unto you with the Holy Ghost sent *down* from heaven; which *things the* angels desire to look into. [Dan. 9:24; Heb. 11:13; Acts 2:4; Dan. 8:13]

An appeal for a holy life

13 Wherefore gird up the loins of your mind, be sober, and hope to the end for the grace that is *to be* brought unto you at the revelation of Jesus Christ; 14 As obedient children, not fashioning yourselves according to the former lusts in your ignorance: 15 But as he which hath called you is holy, so be ye holy in all *manner of* conversation; 16 Because it is written, Be ye holy; for I am holy. 17 And if ye call on the Father, who without respect of persons judgeth according to every man's work, pass the time of your sojourning *here* in fear: 18 Forasmuch as ye know that ye were not redeemed with corruptible *things, as* silver and gold, from your vain conversation received by tradition from your fathers; 19 But with the precious blood of Christ, as of a

lamb without blemish and without spot: 20Who verily was foreordained before the foundation of the world, but was manifest in *these* last times for you, 21Who by him do believe in God, that raised him up from the dead, and gave him glory; that your faith and hope might be in God. 22Seeing ye have purified your souls in obeying the truth through the Spirit unto unfeigned love of the brethren, *see that ye* love one another with a pure heart fervently: 23Being born again, not of corruptible seed, but *of* incorruptible, by the word of God, which liveth and abideth for ever. 24For all flesh *is* as grass, and all the glory of man as the flower of grass. The grass withereth, and the flower thereof falleth away: 25But the word of the Lord endureth for ever. And this is the word which by the gospel is preached unto you. [Is. 40:8; John 1:1]

Christ our corner stone

2 Wherefore laying aside all malice, and all guile, and hypocrisies, and envies, and all evil speakings, 2As newborn babes, desire the sincere milk of the word, that ye may grow thereby: 3If so be ye have tasted that the Lord *is* gracious. 4To whom coming, *as unto* a living stone, disallowed indeed of men, but chosen of God, *and* precious, 5Ye also, as lively stones, are built *up* a spiritual house, a holy priesthood, to offer up spiritual sacrifices, acceptable to God by Jesus Christ. 6Wherefore also it is contained in the scripture, Behold, I lay in Sion a chief corner stone, elect, precious: and he that believeth on him shall not be confounded. 7Unto you therefore which believe *he is* precious: but unto them which be disobedient, the stone which the builders disallowed, the same is made the head of the corner, 8And a stone of stumbling, and a rock of offence, *even to them* which stumble at the word, being disobedient: whereunto also they were appointed. 9But ye *are* a chosen generation, a royal priesthood, a holy nation, a peculiar people; that ye should shew forth the praises of him who hath called you out of darkness into his marvellous light: 10Which in time past *were* not a people, but *are* now the people of God: which had not obtained mercy, but now have obtained mercy. [Hos. 1:9]

Christian submission

11 Dearly beloved, I beseech *you* as strangers and pilgrims, abstain from fleshly lusts, which war against the soul; 12Having your conversation honest among the Gentiles: that, whereas they speak against you as evildoers, they may by *your* good works, *which* they shall behold, glorify God in the day of visitation. 13Submit yourselves to every ordinance of man for the Lord's sake: whether *it be* to the king, as supreme; 14Or unto governors, as unto them that are sent by him for the punishment of evildoers, and *for* the praise of them that do well. 15For so is the will of God, that with well doing *ye* may put to silence the ignorance of foolish men: 16As free, and not using *your* liberty for a cloke of maliciousness,

but as the servants of God. ¹⁷Honour all *men.* Love the brotherhood. Fear God. Honour the king. ¹⁸Servants, *be* subject to *your* masters with all fear; not only to the good and gentle, but also to the froward. ¹⁹For this *is* thankworthy, if a man for conscience toward God endure grief, suffering wrongfully. ²⁰For what glory *is it,* if, when ye be buffeted for your faults, ye shall take it patiently? but if, when ye do well, and suffer *for it,* ye take it patiently, this *is* acceptable with God.

Christ our great example

21 For *even* hereunto were ye called: because Christ also suffered for us, leaving us an example, that ye should follow his steps: ²²Who did no sin, neither was guile found in his mouth: ²³Who, when he was reviled, reviled not again; when he suffered, he threatened not; but committed *himself* to him that judgeth righteously: ²⁴Who his own self bare our sins in his own body on the tree, that we, being dead to sins, should live unto righteousness: by whose stripes ye were healed. ²⁵For ye were as sheep going astray; but are now returned unto the Shepherd and Bishop of your souls.

[Is. 53:6; Ezek. 34:23; Heb. 13:20]

The husband and the wife

3 Likewise, ye wives, *be* in subjection to your own husbands; that, if any obey not the word, they also may without the word be won by the conversation of the wives; ²While they behold your chaste conversation *coupled* with fear. ³Whose adorning let it not be that outward *adorning* of plaiting of

hair, and of wearing of gold, or of putting on of apparel; ⁴But *let it be* the hidden man of the heart, in *that* which *is* not corruptible, *even the* ornament of a meek and quiet spirit, which is in the sight of God of great price. ⁵For after this manner in the old time the holy women also, who trusted in God, adorned themselves, being in subjection unto their own husbands: ⁶*Even* as Sara obeyed Abraham, calling him lord: whose daughters ye are, as long as ye do well, and are not afraid *with* any amazement. ⁷Likewise, ye husbands, dwell with *them* according to knowledge, giving honour unto the wife, as unto the weaker vessel, and as *being* heirs together of the grace of life; that your prayers be not hindered.

[1 Cor. 7:3; 12:23; Job 42:8; Mat. 18:19]

Christian conduct

8 Finally, *be ye* all of one mind, having compassion one of another, love as brethren, *be* pitiful, *be* courteous: ⁹Not rendering evil for evil, or railing for railing: but contrariwise blessing; knowing that ye are thereunto called, that ye should inherit a blessing. ¹⁰For he that will love life, and see good days, let him refrain his tongue from evil, and his lips that *they* speak no guile: ¹¹Let him eschew evil, and do good; let him seek peace, and ensue it. ¹²For the eyes of the Lord *are* over the righteous, and his ears *are open* unto their prayers: but the face of the Lord *is* against them that do evil. ¹³And who *is* he that will harm you, if ye be followers of *that which is* good? ¹⁴But and if ye

suffer for righteousness' sake, happy *are ye:* and be not afraid of their terror, neither be troubled; 15But sanctify the Lord God in your hearts: and *be* ready always to *give* an answer to every *man* that asketh you a reason of the hope that is in you with meekness and fear: 16Having a good conscience; that, whereas they speak evil of you, as of evildoers, they may be ashamed that falsely accuse your good conversation in Christ. 17For *it is* better, if the will of God be so, that *ye* suffer for well doing, than for evil doing. 18For Christ also hath once suffered for sins, the just for the unjust, that he might bring us to God, being put to death in the flesh, but quickened by the Spirit: 19By which also he went and preached unto the spirits in prison; 20Which sometime were disobedient, when once the longsuffering of God waited in the days of Noah, while the ark was a preparing, wherein few, that is, eight souls were saved by water. 21The like figure whereunto *even* baptism doth also now save us (not the putting away of the filth of the flesh, but the answer of a good conscience toward God,) by the resurrection of Jesus Christ: 22Who is gone into heaven, and is on the right hand of God; angels and authorities and powers being made subject unto him. [Ps. 110:1; Rom. 8:34; Rom. 8:38; 1 Cor. 15:24]

4 Forasmuch then as Christ hath suffered for us in the flesh, arm yourselves likewise with the same mind: for he that hath suffered in the flesh hath ceased from sin; 2That *he* no longer should live the rest of *his* time in the flesh to the lusts of men, but to the will of God. 3For the time past of *our* life may suffice us to have wrought the will of the Gentiles, when we walked in lasciviousness, lusts, excess of wine, revellings, banquetings, and abominable idolatries: 4Wherein they think it strange that you run not with *them* to the same excess of riot, speaking evil *of you:* 5Who shall give account to him that is ready to judge the quick and the dead. 6For for this cause was the gospel preached also to *them that are* dead, that they might be judged according to men in the flesh, but live according to God in the spirit. [ch. 3:19]

7 But the end of all *things* is at hand: be ye therefore sober, and watch unto prayer. 8And above all *things* have fervent charity among yourselves: for charity shall cover the multitude of sins. 9Use hospitality one to another without grudging. 10As every man hath received *the* gift, *even so* minister the same one to another, as good stewards of the manifold grace of God. 11If any *man* speak, *let him speak* as the oracles of God; if any *man* minister, *let him do it* as of the ability which God giveth: that God in all *things* may be glorified through Jesus Christ, to whom be praise and dominion for ever and ever. Amen. [Jer. 23:22; 1 Cor. 3:10; Eph. 5:20; 1 Tim. 6:16]

The Christian and suffering

12 Beloved, think it not strange concerning the fiery trial which is

to try you, as though *some* strange *thing* happened unto you: ¹³But rejoice, inasmuch as ye are partakers of Christ's sufferings; that, when his glory shall be revealed, ye may be glad also with exceeding joy. ¹⁴If ye be reproached for the name of Christ, happy *are ye;* for the spirit of glory and of God resteth upon you: on their part he is evil spoken of, but on your part he is glorified. ¹⁵But let none of you suffer as a murderer, or *as* a thief, or *as* an evildoer, or as a busybody in other men's matters. ¹⁶Yet if *any man* suffer as a Christian, let him not be ashamed; but let him glorify God on this behalf. ¹⁷For the time *is come* that judgment must begin at the house of God: and if *it* first *begin* at us, what *shall* the end *be* of them that obey not the gospel of God? ¹⁸And if the righteous scarcely be saved, where shall the ungodly and the sinner appear? ¹⁹Wherefore let them that suffer according to the will of God commit the keeping of their souls *to* him in well doing, as unto a faithful Creator. [2 Tim. 1:12]

Christian life in God's care

5 The elders which are among you I exhort, who am also an elder, and a witness of the sufferings of Christ, and also a partaker of the glory that shall be revealed: ²Feed the flock of God which is among you, taking the oversight *thereof,* not by constraint, but willingly; not for filthy lucre, but of a ready mind; ³Neither as being lords over *God's* heritage, but being ensamples to the flock. ⁴And when the chief Shepherd shall appear, ye shall receive a crown of glory that fadeth not away. ⁵Likewise, *ye* younger, submit yourselves unto the elder. Yea, all *of you* be subject one to another, and be clothed with humility: for God resisteth the proud, and giveth grace to the humble. ⁶Humble yourselves therefore under the mighty hand of God, that he may exalt you in due time: ⁷Casting all your care upon him; for he careth for you. ⁸Be sober, be vigilant; because your adversary the devil, as a roaring lion, walketh about, seeking whom he may devour: ⁹Whom resist stedfast in the faith, knowing that the same afflictions are accomplished in your brethren that are in the world. ¹⁰But the God of all grace, who hath called us into his eternal glory by Christ Jesus, after that ye have suffered a while, make you perfect, stablish, strengthen, settle *you.* ¹¹To him *be* glory and dominion for ever and ever. Amen. [Rev. 1:6]

Conclusion and benediction

¹² By Silvanus, a faithful brother unto you, as I suppose, I have written briefly, exhorting, and testifying that this is the true grace of God wherein ye stand. ¹³The *church that is* at Babylon, elected together with *you,* saluteth you; and *so doth* Marcus my son. ¹⁴Greet ye one another with a kiss of charity. Peace *be* with you all that are in Christ Jesus. Amen.

The Second Epistle General of

Peter

1 Simon Peter, a servant and an apostle of Jesus Christ, to them that have obtained like precious faith with us through the righteousness of God and our Saviour Jesus Christ: ²Grace and peace be multiplied unto you through the knowledge of God, and of Jesus our Lord. [Dan. 4:1]

The growth of true knowledge

3 According as his divine power hath given unto us all *things* that *pertain* unto life and godliness, through the knowledge of him that hath called us to glory and virtue: ⁴Whereby are given unto us exceeding great and precious promises: that by these you might be partakers of the divine nature, having escaped the corruption that is in the world through lust: ⁵And beside this, giving all diligence, add to your faith virtue; and to virtue knowledge; ⁶And to knowledge temperance; and to temperance patience; and to patience godliness; ⁷And to godliness brotherly kindness; and to brotherly kindness charity. ⁸For if these *things* be in you, and abound, they make *you that ye shall* neither *be* barren nor unfruitful in the knowledge of our Lord Jesus Christ. ⁹But he that lacketh these *things* is blind, and cannot see far off, and hath forgotten that *he* was purged from his old sins. ¹⁰Wherefore the rather, brethren, give diligence to make your calling and election sure: for if ye do these *things,* ye shall never fall: ¹¹For so an entrance shall be ministered unto you abundantly into the everlasting kingdom of our Lord and Saviour Jesus Christ.

The basis of true knowledge

12 Wherefore I will not be negligent to put you always in remembrance of these *things,* though ye know *them,* and be stablished in the present truth. ¹³Yea, I think it meet, as long as I am in this tabernacle, to stir you up by putting *you* in remembrance; ¹⁴Knowing that shortly *I* must put off *this* my tabernacle, even as our Lord Jesus Christ hath shewed me. ¹⁵Moreover I will endeavour that you may be able after my decease to have these *things* always in remembrance. ¹⁶For we have not followed cunningly devised fables, when we made known unto you the power and coming of our Lord Jesus Christ, but were eyewitnesses of his majesty. ¹⁷For he received from God the Father honour and glory, when there came such a voice to him from the excellent glory, This is my beloved Son, in whom I am well pleased. ¹⁸And this voice which came from heaven we heard, when we were with him in the holy mount. ¹⁹We have also a more sure word of prophecy; whereunto ye do well that ye take heed, as unto a light that shineth in a dark place, until the day dawn, and the day star arise in your hearts: ²⁰Knowing this first, that no prophecy of the scripture is of

any private interpretation. 21For the prophecy came not in old time by the will of man: but holy men of God spake *as they were* moved by the Holy Ghost. [2 Tim. 3:16; 1 Pet. 1:11; 2 Sam. 23:2; Acts 1:16]

False prophets and teachers

2 But there were false prophets also among the people, even as there shall be false teachers among you, who privily shall bring in damnable heresies, even denying the Lord that bought them, and bring upon themselves swift destruction. 2And many shall follow their pernicious ways; by reason of whom the way of truth shall be evil spoken of. 3And through covetousness shall they with feigned words make merchandise of you: whose judgment now of a long time lingereth not, and their damnation slumbereth not. 4For if God spared not the angels that sinned, but cast *them* down to hell, and delivered *them* into chains of darkness, *to be* reserved unto judgment; 5And spared not the old world, but saved Noah the eighth *person,* a preacher of righteousness, bringing in the flood upon the world of the ungodly; 6And turning the cities of Sodom and Gomorrha into ashes condemned *them* with an overthrow, making *them* an ensample unto those that after should live ungodly; 7And delivered just Lot, vexed with the filthy conversation of the wicked: 8(For *that* righteous *man* dwelling among them, in seeing and hearing, vexed *his* righteous soul from day to day with *their* unlawful deeds;) 9The Lord knoweth *how* to deliver the godly out of temptations, and to reserve the unjust unto the day of judgment *to be* punished: 10But chiefly them that walk after the flesh in the lust of uncleanness, and despise government. Presumptuous *are they,* selfwilled, they are not afraid to speak evil of dignities. 11Whereas angels, which are greater in power and might, bring not railing accusation against them before the Lord. 12But these, as natural brute beasts, made to be taken and destroyed, speak evil of *the things* that they understand not; and shall utterly perish in their own corruption; 13And shall receive the reward of unrighteousness, *as* they that count it pleasure to riot in the day time. Spots *they are* and blemishes, sporting themselves with their own deceivings while they feast with you; 14Having eyes full of adultery, and that cannot cease from sin; beguiling unstable souls: a heart they have exercised with covetous practices; cursed children: 15Which have forsaken the right way, and are gone astray, following the way of Balaam *the son* of Bosor, who loved the wages of unrighteousness; 16But was rebuked for his iniquity: the dumb ass speaking with man's voice forbad the madness of the prophet. 17These are wells without water, clouds that are carried with a tempest; to whom the mist of darkness is reserved for ever. 18For when they speak great swelling *words* of vanity, they allure through the lusts of the flesh, through much wantonness, those

that were clean escaped from them who live in error. 19While they promise them liberty, they themselves are the servants of corruption: for of whom a man is overcome, of the same is he brought in bondage. 20For if after they have escaped the pollutions of the world through the knowledge of the Lord and Saviour Jesus Christ, they are again entangled therein, and overcome, the latter *end* is worse with them than the beginning. 21For it had been better for them not to have known the way of righteousness, than, after they have known *it,* to turn from the holy commandment delivered unto them. 22But it is happened unto them according to the true proverb, The dog *is* turned to his own vomit again; and, The sow that was washed to *her* wallowing in the mire. [Prov. 26:11]

Christ's coming

3 This second epistle, beloved, I now write unto you; in both which I stir up your pure minds by way of remembrance: 2That *ye* may be mindful of the words which were spoken before by the holy prophets, and of the commandment of us the apostles of the Lord and Saviour: 3Knowing this first, that there shall come in the last days scoffers, walking after their own lusts, 4And saying, Where is the promise of his coming? for since the fathers fell asleep, all *things* continue as *they were* from the beginning of the creation. 5For this they willingly are ignorant of, that by the word of

God the heavens were of old, and the earth standing out of the water and in the water: 6Whereby the world that then was, being overflowed with water, perished: 7But the heavens and the earth, which are now, by the same word are kept in store, reserved unto fire against the day of judgment and perdition of ungodly men. 8But, beloved, be not ignorant of this one *thing,* that one day *is* with the Lord as a thousand years, and a thousand years as one day. [Ps. 90:4]

The concluding appeal

9 The Lord is not slack concerning *his* promise, as some *men* count slackness; but is longsuffering to us-ward, not willing that any should perish, but that all should come to repentance. 10But the day of the Lord will come as a thief in the night; in the which the heavens shall pass away with a great noise, and the elements shall melt with fervent heat, the earth also and the works that are therein shall be burnt up. 11Seeing then that all these *things shall* be dissolved, what manner *of persons* ought ye to be in all holy conversation and godliness, 12Looking for and hasting *unto* the coming of the day of God, wherein the heavens being on fire shall be dissolved, and the elements shall melt with fervent heat? 13Nevertheless we, according to his promise, look for new heavens and a new earth, wherein dwelleth righteousness. 14Wherefore, beloved, seeing that ye look for such *things,* be diligent that ye may be found of him in

peace, without spot, and blameless. 15And account *that* the longsuffering of our Lord *is* salvation; even as our beloved brother Paul also according to the wisdom given unto him hath written unto you; 16As also in all *his* epistles, speaking in them of these *things;* in which are some *things* hard to be understood, which *they that are* unlearned and unstable wrest, as *they do* also the other scriptures, unto their own destruction. 17Ye therefore, beloved, seeing ye know *these things* before, beware lest ye also, being led away with the error of the wicked, fall from your own stedfastness. 18But grow in grace, and *in* the knowledge of our Lord and Saviour Jesus Christ. To him *be* glory both now and for ever. Amen.

John

The Word of life

1 *That* which was from the beginning, which we have heard, which we have seen with our eyes, which we have looked upon, and our hands have handled, of the Word of life; ²(For the life was manifested, and we have seen *it,* and bear witness, and shew unto you *that* eternal life, which was with the Father, and was manifested unto us;) ³*That* which we have seen and heard declare we unto you, that ye also may have fellowship with us: and truly our fellowship *is* with the Father, and with his Son Jesus Christ. ⁴And these *things* write we unto you, that your joy may be full. [John 16:24]

The test of righteousness

5 This then is the message which we have heard of him, and declare unto you, that God is light, and in him is no darkness at all. ⁶If we say that we have fellowship with him, and walk in darkness, we lie, and do not the truth: ⁷But if we walk in the light, as he is in the light, we have fellowship one with another, and the blood of Jesus Christ his Son cleanseth us from all sin. ⁸If we say that we have no sin, we deceive ourselves, and the truth is not in us. ⁹If we confess our sins, he is faithful and just to forgive us *our* sins, and to cleanse us from all unrighteousness. ¹⁰If we say that we have not sinned, we make him a liar, and his word is not in us.

2 My little children, these *things* write I unto you, that ye sin not. And if any *man* sin, we have an advocate with the Father, Jesus Christ *the* righteous: ²And he is the propitiation for our sins: and not for ours only, but also for *the sins of* the whole world. ³And hereby we do know that we know him, if we keep his commandments. ⁴He that saith, I know him, and keepeth not his commandments, is a liar, and the truth is not in him. ⁵But whoso keepeth his word, in him verily is the love of God perfected: hereby know we that we are in him. ⁶He that saith *he* abideth in him ought himself also so to walk, even as he walked. ⁷Brethren, I write no new commandment unto you, but an old commandment which ye had from the beginning. The old commandment is the word which ye have heard from the beginning. ⁸Again, a new commandment I write unto you, which *thing* is true in him and in you: because the darkness is past, and the true light now shineth. ⁹He that saith *he* is in the light, and hateth his brother, is in darkness *even* until now. ¹⁰He that loveth his brother abideth in the light, and there is none occasion of stumbling in him. ¹¹But he that hateth his brother is in darkness, and walketh in darkness, and knoweth not whither he goeth, because that darkness hath blinded his eyes.

12 I write unto you, little chil-

dren, because *your* sins are forgiven you for his name's sake. 13I write unto you, fathers, because ye have known him that is from the beginning. I write unto you, young men, because you have overcome the wicked one. I write unto you, little children, because ye have known the Father. 14I have written unto you, fathers, because ye have known him that is from the beginning. I have written unto you, young men, because ye are strong, and the word of God abideth in you, and ye have overcome the wicked one. 15Love not the world, neither the *things* that are in the world. If any *man* love the world, the love of the Father is not in him. 16For all that is in the world, the lust of the flesh, and the lust of the eyes, and the pride of life, is not of the Father, but is of the world. 17And the world passeth away, and the lust thereof: but he that doeth the will of God abideth for ever. 18Little children, it is the last time: and as ye have heard that antichrist shall come, even now are there many antichrists; whereby we know that it is the last time. 19They went out from us, but they were not of us; for if they had been of us, they would *no doubt* have continued with us: but *they went out,* that they might be made manifest that they were not all of us. 20But ye have an unction from the Holy One, and ye know all *things.* 21I have not written unto you because ye know not the truth, but because ye know it, and that no lie is of the truth. 22Who is a liar but he that denieth that Jesus is the Christ? He is antichrist, that denieth the Father and the Son. 23Whosoever denieth the Son, the same hath not the Father: [*but*] *he that acknowledgeth the Son hath the Father also.* 24Let *that* therefore abide in you, which ye have heard from the beginning. If *that* which ye have heard from the beginning shall remain in you, ye also shall continue in the Son, and in the Father. 25And this is the promise that he hath promised us, *even* eternal life. 26These *things* have I written unto you concerning them that seduce you. 27But the anointing which ye have received of him abideth in you, and ye need not that any *man* teach you: but as the same anointing teacheth you of all *things,* and is truth, and is no lie, and even as it hath taught you, ye shall abide in him. 28And now, little children, abide in him; that, when he shall appear, we may have confidence, and not be ashamed before him at his coming. 29If ye know that he is righteous, ye know that every one which doeth righteousness is born of him. [Acts 22:14; ch. 3:7,10]

Obedience and love

3 Behold, what manner of love the Father hath bestowed upon us, that we should be called the sons of God: therefore the world knoweth us not, because it knew him not. 2Beloved, now are we the sons of God, and it doth not yet appear what we shall be: but we know that, when he shall appear, we shall be like him; for we shall see him as he is. 3And every

man that hath this hope in him purifieth himself, even as he is pure. 4Whosoever committeth sin transgresseth also the law: for sin is the transgression of the law. 5And ye know that he was manifested to take away our sins; and in him is no sin. 6Whosoever abideth in him sinneth not: whosoever sinneth hath not seen him, neither known him. 7Little children, let no _man_ deceive you: he that doeth righteousness is righteous, even as he is righteous. 8He that committeth sin is of the devil; for the devil sinneth from the beginning. For this purpose the Son of God was manifested, that he might destroy the works of the devil. 9Whosoever is born of God doth not commit sin; for his seed remaineth in him: and he cannot sin, because he is born of God. 10In this the children of God are manifest, and the children of the devil: whosoever doeth not righteousness is not of God, neither he that loveth not his brother.

[ch. 2:29; ch. 4:8]

Love in action

11 For this is the message that ye heard from the beginning, that we should love one another. 12Not as Cain, _who_ was of _that_ wicked one, and slew his brother. And wherefore slew he him? Because his own works were evil, and his brother's righteous. 13Marvel not, my brethren, if the world hate you. 14We know that we have passed from death unto life, because we love the brethren. He that loveth not _his_ brother abideth in death. 15Whosoever hateth his brother is a murderer: and ye know that no murderer hath eternal life abiding in him. 16Hereby perceive we the love _of God,_ because he laid down his life for us: and we ought to lay down _our_ lives for the brethren. 17But whoso hath _this_ world's good, and seeth his brother hath need, and shutteth up his bowels _of compassion_ from him, how dwelleth the love of God in him?

[Deut. 15:7; Luke 3:11; ch. 4:20]

The test of belief

18 My little children, let us not love in word, neither in tongue; but in deed and in truth. 19And hereby we know that we are of the truth, and shall assure our hearts before him. 20For if _our_ heart condemn us, God is greater than our heart, and knoweth all _things._ 21Beloved, if our heart condemn us not, _then_ have we confidence towards God. 22And whatsoever we ask, we receive of him, because we keep his commandments, and do those _things_ that are pleasing in his sight. 23And this is his commandment, That we should believe on the name of his Son Jesus Christ, and love one another, as he gave us commandment. 24And he that keepeth his commandments dwelleth in him, and he in him. And hereby we know that he abideth in us, by the Spirit which he hath given us.

[John 14:23; 17:21; Rom. 8:9]

4 Beloved, believe not every spirit, but try the spirits whether they are of God: because many false prophets are gone out into the world. 2Hereby know ye

the Spirit of God: Every spirit that confesseth that Jesus Christ is come in the flesh is of God: ³And every spirit that confesseth not that Jesus Christ is come in the flesh is not of God: and this is *that spirit* of antichrist, whereof you have heard that it should come; and *even* now already is it in the world. ⁴Ye are of God, little children, and have overcome them: because greater is he that is in you, than he that is in the world. ⁵They are of the world, therefore speak they of the world, and the world heareth them. ⁶We are of God: he that knoweth God heareth us; *he* that is not of God heareth not us. Hereby know we the spirit of truth, and the spirit of error. [John 8:47; Is. 8:20]

The source of love

7 Beloved, let us love one another: for love is of God; and every one that loveth is born of God, and knoweth God. ⁸He that loveth not, knoweth not God; for God is love. ⁹In this was manifested the love of God towards us, because that God sent his only begotten Son into the world, that we might live through him. ¹⁰Herein is love, not that we loved God, but that he loved us, and sent his Son *to be* the propitiation for our sins. ¹¹Beloved, if God so loved us, we ought also to love one another. ¹²No *man* hath seen God at any time. If we love one another, God dwelleth in us, and his love is perfected in us. ¹³Hereby know we that we dwell in him, and he in us, because he hath given us of his Spirit. [John 14:20]

14 And we have seen and do testify that the Father sent the Son *to be* the Saviour of the world. ¹⁵Whosoever shall confess that Jesus is the Son of God, God dwelleth in him, and he in God. ¹⁶And we have known and believed the love that God hath to us. God is love; and he that dwelleth in love dwelleth in God, and God in him. ¹⁷Herein is our love made perfect, that we may have boldness in the day of judgment: because as he is, so are we in this world. ¹⁸There is no fear in love; but perfect love casteth out fear: because fear hath torment. He that feareth is not made perfect in love. ¹⁹We love him, because he first loved us. ²⁰If a man say, I love God, and hateth his brother, he is a liar: for he that loveth not his brother whom he hath seen, how can he love God whom he hath not seen? ²¹And this commandment have we from him, That he who loveth God love his brother also. [Mat. 22:37; John 13:34]

Faith through the Son

5 Whosoever believeth that Jesus is the Christ is born of God: and every one that loveth him that begat loveth him also that is begotten of him. ²By this we know that we love the children of God, when we love God, and keep his commandments. ³For this is the love of God, that we keep his commandments: and his commandments are not grievous. ⁴For whatsoever is born of God overcometh the world: and this is the victory that overcometh the world,

even our faith. ⁵Who is he that overcometh the world, but he that believeth that Jesus is the Son of God? ⁶This is he that came by water and blood, *even* Jesus Christ; not by water only, but by water and blood. And it is the Spirit that beareth witness, because the Spirit is truth. ⁷For there are three that bear record in heaven, the Father, the Word, and the Holy Ghost: and these three are one. ⁸And there are three that bear witness in earth, the Spirit, and the water, and the blood: and *these* three agree in one. ⁹If we receive the witness of men, the witness of God is greater: for this is the witness of God which he hath testified of his Son. ¹⁰He that believeth on the Son of God hath the witness in himself: he that believeth not God hath made him a liar; because he believeth not the record that God gave of his Son. ¹¹And this is the record, that God hath given to us eternal life, and this life is in his Son. ¹²He that hath the Son hath life; *and* he that hath not the Son of God hath not life. [John 3:36]

The certainties of faith

13 These *things* have I written unto you that believe on the name of the Son of God; that ye may know that ye have eternal life, and that ye may believe on the name of the Son of God. ¹⁴And this is the confidence that we have in him, that, if we ask any *thing* according to his will, he heareth us: ¹⁵And if we know that he hear us, whatsoever we ask, we know that we have the petitions that we desired of him. ¹⁶If any *man* see his brother sin a sin *which is* not unto death, he shall ask, and he shall give him life for them that sin not unto death. There is a sin unto death: I do not say that he shall pray for it. ¹⁷All unrighteousness is sin: and there is a sin not unto death. ¹⁸We know that whosoever is born of God sinneth not; but he that is begotten of God keepeth himself, and *that* wicked one toucheth him not. ¹⁹*And* we know that we are of God, and the whole world lieth in wickedness. ²⁰And we know that the Son of God is come, and hath given us an understanding, that we may know him *that is* true, and we are in him *that is* true, *even* in his Son Jesus Christ. This is the true God, and eternal life. ²¹Little children, keep yourselves from idols. Amen.

The Second Epistle of
John

1 The elder unto the elect lady and her children, whom I love in the truth; and not I only, but also all they that have known the truth; 2For the truth's sake, which dwelleth in us, and shall be with us for ever. 3Grace be with you, mercy, *and* peace, from God the Father, and from the Lord Jesus Christ, the Son of the Father, in truth and love. [1 Tim. 1:2]

Counsel and warnings

4 I rejoiced greatly that I found of thy children walking in truth, as we have received a commandment from the Father. 5And now I beseech thee, lady, not as though I wrote a new commandment unto thee, but *that* which we had from the beginning, that we love one another. 6And this is love, that we walk after his commandments. This is the commandment, That, as ye have heard from the beginning, ye should walk in it. 7For many deceivers are entered into the world, who confess not that Jesus Christ is come in the flesh. This is a deceiver and an antichrist. 8Look to yourselves, that we lose not *those things* which we have wrought, but *that* we receive a full reward. 9Whosoever transgresseth, and abideth not in the doctrine of Christ, hath not God. He that abideth in the doctrine of Christ, he hath both the Father and the Son. 10If there come any unto you, and bring not this doctrine, receive him not into *your* house, neither bid him God speed: 11For he that biddeth him God speed is partaker of his evil deeds.

12 Having many *things* to write unto you, I would not *write* with paper and ink: but I trust to come unto you, and speak face to face, that our joy may be full. 13The children of thy elect sister greet thee. Amen.

The Third Epistle of

John

Encouragement and reproof

1 The elder unto the well-beloved Gaius, whom I love in the truth. 2 Beloved, I wish above all *things* that thou mayest prosper and be in health, even as thy soul prospereth. 3 For I rejoiced greatly, when *the* brethren came and testified of the truth *that is* in thee, even as thou walkest in the truth. 4 I have no greater joy than to hear that my children walk in truth. 5 Beloved, thou doest faithfully whatsoever thou doest to the brethren, and to strangers; 6 Which have borne witness of thy charity before the church: whom if thou bring forward on their journey after a godly sort, thou shalt do well: 7 Because that for his name's sake they went forth, taking nothing of the Gentiles. 8 We therefore ought to receive such, that we might be fellowhelpers to the truth.

9 I wrote unto the church: but Diotrephes, who loveth to have the preeminence among them, receiveth us not. 10 Wherefore, if I come, I will remember his deeds which he doeth, prating against us with malicious words: and not content therewith, neither doth he himself receive the brethren, and forbiddeth them that would, and casteth *them* out of the church. 11 Beloved, follow not *that which is* evil, but *that which is* good. He that doeth good is of God: but he that doeth evil hath not seen God. 12 Demetrius hath good report of all *men,* and of the truth itself: yea, and we also bear record; and ye know that our record is true. [1 Tim. 3:7; John 21:24]

13 I had many *things* to write, but I will not with ink and pen write unto thee: 14 But I trust *I* shall shortly see thee, and we shall speak face to face. Peace *be* to thee. *Our* friends salute thee. Greet the friends by name.

Jude

1 Jude, the servant of Jesus Christ, and brother of James, to them that are sanctified by God the Father, and preserved *in* Jesus Christ, *and* called: 2 Mercy unto you, and peace, and love, be multiplied. [1 Pet. 1:2; 2 Pet. 1:2]

The doom of false teachers

3 Beloved, when I gave all diligence to write unto you of the common salvation, it was needful for me to write unto you, and exhort *you* that *ye* should earnestly contend for the faith which was once delivered unto the saints. 4 For there are certain men crept in unawares, who were before of old ordained to this condemnation, ungodly *men,* turning the grace of our God into lasciviousness, and denying the only Lord God, and our Lord Jesus Christ. 5 I will therefore put you in remembrance, though ye once knew this, how that the Lord, having saved the people out of the land of Egypt, afterward destroyed them that believed not. 6 And the angels which kept not their first estate, but left their own habitation, he hath reserved in everlasting chains under darkness unto the judgment of the great day. 7 Even as Sodom and Gomorrha, and the cities about them, in like manner giving themselves over to fornication, and going after strange flesh, are set forth for an example, suffering the vengeance of eternal fire. 8 Likewise also these *filthy* dreamers defile the flesh, despise dominion, and speak evil of dignities. 9 Yet Michael the archangel, when contending about the body of Moses, durst not bring against *him* a railing accusation, but said, The Lord rebuke thee. 10 But these speak evil of those *things* which they know not: but what they know naturally, as brute beasts, in those *things* they corrupt themselves. 11 Woe unto them! for they have gone in the way of Cain, and ran greedily after the error of Balaam for reward, and perished in the gainsaying of Core. [1 John 3:12; 2 Pet. 2:15; Num. 16:1]

12 These are spots in your feasts of charity when they feast with *you,* feeding themselves without fear: clouds *they are* without water, carried about of winds; trees whose fruit withereth, without fruit, twice dead, plucked up by the roots; 13 Raging waves of the sea, foaming out their own shame; wandering stars, to whom is reserved the blackness of darkness for ever. 14 And Enoch also, the seventh from Adam, prophesied of these, saying, Behold, the Lord cometh with ten thousands of his saints, 15 To execute judgment upon all, and to convince all *that are* ungodly among them of all their ungodly deeds which they have ungodly committed, and of all *their* hard *speeches* which ungodly sinners have spoken against him. [1 Sam. 2:3; Ps. 31:18]

Hold to the true faith

16 These are murmurers, complainers, walking after their own lusts; and their mouth speaketh great swelling *words,* having *men's* persons in admiration because of advantage. 17But, beloved, remember ye the words which were spoken before of the apostles of our Lord Jesus Christ; 18How that they told you there should be mockers in the last time, who should walk after their own ungodly lusts. 19These be they who separate themselves, sensual, having not the Spirit. 20But ye, beloved, building up yourselves on your most holy faith, praying in the Holy Ghost, 21Keep yourselves in the love of God, looking for the mercy of our Lord Jesus Christ unto eternal life. 22And of some have compassion, making a difference: 23And others save with fear, pulling *them* out of the fire; hating even the garment spotted by the flesh. [Rom. 11:14; Amos 4:11; Zech. 3:2; Zech. 3:4,5]

Benediction

24 Now unto him that is able to keep you from falling, and to present *you* faultless before the presence of his glory with exceeding joy, 25To the only wise God our Saviour, *be* glory and majesty, dominion and power, both now and ever. Amen.

The Revelation
of S. John the Divine

The source of the revelation

1 The Revelation of Jesus Christ, which God gave unto him, to shew unto his servants *things* which must shortly come to pass; and he sent and signified *it* by his angel unto his servant John: 2Who bare record of the word of God, and of the testimony of Jesus Christ, and of all *things* that he saw. 3Blessed *is* he that readeth, and they that hear the words of *this* prophecy, and keep those *things* which are written therein: for the time *is* at hand. [Luke 11:28; Jas. 5:8]

The salutation

4 John to the seven churches which are in Asia: Grace *be* unto you, and peace, from him which is, and which was, and which is to come; and from the seven spirits which are before his throne; 5And from Jesus Christ, *who is* the faithful witness, *and* the first begotten of the dead, and the prince of the kings of the earth. Unto him that loved us, and washed us from our sins in his own blood, 6And hath made us kings and priests unto God and his Father; to him *be* glory and dominion for ever and ever. Amen. [1 Pet. 2:5; 1 Tim. 6:16]

7 Behold, he cometh with clouds; and every eye shall see him, and they *also* which pierced him: and all kindreds of the earth shall wail because of him. Even so, Amen. 8I am Alpha and Omega, the beginning and the ending, saith the Lord, which is, and which was, and which is to come, the Almighty. [Is. 41:4; ch. 4:8]

The voice and the vision

9 I John, who also am your brother, and companion in tribulation, and in the kingdom and patience of Jesus Christ, was in the isle that is called Patmos, for the word of God, and for the testimony of Jesus Christ. 10I was in the spirit on the Lord's day, and heard behind me a great voice, as of a trumpet, 11Saying, I am Alpha and Omega, the first and the last: and, What thou seest, write in a book, and send *it* unto the seven churches which are in Asia; unto Ephesus, and unto Smyrna, and unto Pergamos, and unto Thyatira, and unto Sardis, and unto Philadelphia, and unto Laodicea. 12And I turned to see the voice that spake with me. And being turned, I saw seven golden candlesticks; 13And in the midst of the seven candlesticks one like unto the Son of man, clothed with a garment down to the foot, and girt about the paps with a golden girdle. 14His head and *his* hairs *were* white like wool, *as* white as snow; and his eyes *were* as a flame of fire; 15And his feet like unto fine brass, as if they burned in a furnace; and his voice as the sound of many waters. 16And he had in his right hand seven stars: and out of his mouth went a sharp twoedged sword: and his countenance *was* as the sun shineth in his strength. 17And when I saw him, I fell at his

feet as dead. And he laid his right hand upon me, saying unto me, Fear not; I am the first and the last: [18]I am he that liveth, and was dead; and behold, I am alive for evermore, Amen; and have the keys of hell and of death. [19]Write *the things* which thou hast seen, and *the things* which are, and *the things* which shall be hereafter; [20]The mystery of the seven stars which thou sawest in my right hand, and the seven golden candlesticks. The seven stars are the angels of the seven churches: and the seven candlesticks which thou sawest are the seven churches. [Mal. 2:7; ch. 2:1; Zech. 4:2; Mat. 5:15; Phil. 2:15]

The message to Ephesus

2 Unto the angel of the church of Ephesus write; These *things* saith he that holdeth the seven stars in his right hand, who walketh in the midst of the seven golden candlesticks; [2]I know thy works, and thy labour, and thy patience, and how thou canst not bear *them which are* evil: and thou hast tried them which say *they* are apostles, and are not, and hast found them liars: [3]And hast borne, and hast patience, and for my name's sake hast laboured, and hast not fainted. [4]Nevertheless I have *somewhat* against thee, because thou hast left thy first love. [5]Remember therefore from whence thou art fallen, and repent, and do the first works; or else I *will* come unto thee quickly, and will remove thy candlestick out of his place, except thou repent. [6]But this thou hast, that thou hatest the deeds of the Nicolaitans, which I also hate. [7]He that hath an ear, let him hear what the Spirit saith unto the churches; To him that overcometh will I give to eat of the tree of life, which is in the midst of the paradise of God. [Mat. 11:15; 13:9,43; ch. 3:6,13; ch. 22:2,14; Gen. 2:9]

The message to Smyrna

8 And unto the angel of the church in Smyrna write; These *things* saith the first and the last, which was dead, and is alive; [9]I know thy works, and tribulation, and poverty, (but thou art rich) and *I know* the blasphemy of them which say they are Jews, and are not, but *are* the synagogue of Satan. [10]Fear none *of those things* which thou shalt suffer: behold, the devil shall cast *some* of you into prison, that ye may be tried; and ye shall have tribulation ten days: be thou faithful unto death, and I will give thee a crown of life. [11]He that hath an ear, let him hear what the Spirit saith unto the churches; He that overcometh shall not be hurt of the second death. [ch. 13:9; ch. 20:1; 21:8]

The message to Pergamos

12 And to the angel of the church in Pergamos write; These *things* saith he which hath the sharp sword with two edges; [13]I know thy works, and where thou dwellest, *even* where Satan's seat *is:* and thou holdest fast my name, and hast not denied my faith, even in *those* days wherein Antipas *was* my faithful martyr, who was slain among you, where Satan dwelleth. [14]But I have a few *things* against

thee, because thou hast there them that hold the doctrine of Balaam, who taught Balac to cast a stumblingblock before the children of Israel, to eat things sacrificed unto idols, and to commit fornication. 15So hast thou also them that hold the doctrine of the Nicolaitans, which *thing* I hate. 16Repent; or else I *will* come unto thee quickly, and will fight against them with the sword of my mouth. 17He that hath an ear, let him hear what the Spirit saith unto the churches; To him that overcometh will I give to eat of the hidden manna, and will give him a white stone, and in the stone a new name written, which no *man* knoweth saving he that receiveth *it.* [ch. 3:12; 19:12]

The message to Thyatira

18 And unto the angel of the church in Thyatira write; These *things* saith the Son of God, who hath his eyes like unto a flame of fire, and his feet *are* like fine brass; 19I know thy works, and charity, and service, and faith, and thy patience, and thy works; and the last *to be* more than the first. 20Notwithstanding I have a few *things* against thee, because thou sufferest *that* woman Jezebel, which calleth herself a prophetess, to teach and to seduce my servants to commit fornication, and to eat things sacrificed unto idols. 21And I gave her space to repent of her fornication; and she repented not. 22Behold, I *will* cast her into a bed, and them that commit adultery with her into great tribulation, except they repent of their deeds.

23And I will kill her children with death; and all the churches shall know that I am he which searcheth the reins and hearts: and I will give unto every one of you according to your works. 24But unto you I say, and unto the rest in Thyatira, as many as have not this doctrine, and which have not known the depths of Satan, as they speak; I will put upon you none other burden. 25But *that* which ye have *already* hold fast till I come. 26And he that overcometh, and keepeth my works unto the end, to him will I give power over the nations: 27And he shall rule them with a rod of iron; as the vessels of a potter *shall* they be broken to shivers: even as I received of my Father. 28And I will give him the morning star. 29He that hath an ear, let him hear what the Spirit saith unto the churches. [ver. 7]

The message to Sardis

3 And unto the angel of the church in Sardis write; These *things* saith he that hath the seven spirits of God, and the seven stars; I know thy works, that thou hast a name that thou livest, and art dead. 2Be watchful, and strengthen the *things* which remain, that are ready to die: for I have not found thy works perfect before God. 3Remember therefore how thou hast received and heard, and hold fast, and repent. If therefore thou shalt not watch, I will come on thee as a thief, and thou shalt not know what hour I will come upon thee. 4Thou hast a few names even in Sardis, which have not defiled their gar-

ments; and they shall walk with me in white: for they are worthy. ⁵He that overcometh, the same shall be clothed in white raiment; and I will not blot out his name out of the book of life, but I will confess his name before my Father, and before his angels. ⁶He that hath an ear, let him hear what the Spirit saith unto the churches. [ch. 2:7]

The message to Philadelphia

7 And to the angel of the church in Philadelphia write; These *things* saith he *that is* holy, he *that is* true, he that hath the key of David, he that openeth, and no *man* shutteth; and shutteth, and no *man* openeth; ⁸I know thy works: behold, I have set before thee an open door, and no *man* can shut it: for thou hast a little strength, and hast kept my word, and hast not denied my name. ⁹Behold, I *will* make *them* of the synagogue of Satan, which say they are Jews, and are not, but do lie; behold, I will make them to come and worship before thy feet, and to know that I have loved thee. ¹⁰Because thou hast kept the word of my patience, I also will keep thee from the hour of temptation, which shall come upon all the world, to try them that dwell upon the earth. ¹¹Behold, I come quickly: hold *that* fast which thou hast, that no *man* take thy crown. ¹²Him that overcometh will I make a pillar in the temple of my God, and he shall go no more out: and I will write upon him the name of my God, and the name of the city of my God, *which is* new Jerusalem, which cometh down out of heaven from my God: and *I will write upon him* my new name. ¹³He that hath an ear, let him hear what the Spirit saith unto the churches. [ch. 2:7]

The message to Laodicea

14 And unto the angel of the church of the Laodiceans write; These *things* saith the Amen, the faithful and true witness, the beginning of the creation of God; ¹⁵I know thy works, that thou art neither cold nor hot: I would thou wert cold or hot. ¹⁶So *then* because thou art lukewarm, and neither cold nor hot, I will spue thee out of my mouth. ¹⁷Because thou sayest, I am rich, and increased with goods, and have need of nothing; and knowest not that thou art wretched, and miserable, and poor, and blind, and naked: ¹⁸I counsel thee to buy of me gold tried in the fire, that thou mayest be rich; and white raiment, that thou mayest be clothed, and *that* the shame of thy nakedness do not appear; and anoint thine eyes *with* eyesalve, that thou mayest see. ¹⁹As many as I love, I rebuke and chasten: be zealous therefore, and repent. ²⁰Behold, I stand at the door, and knock: if any *man* hear my voice, and open the door, I will come in to him, and will sup with him, and he with me. ²¹To him that overcometh will I grant to sit with me in my throne, *even* as I also overcame, and am set down with my Father in his throne. ²²He that hath an ear, let him hear what the Spirit saith unto the churches. [ch. 2:7]

The heavenly worship

4 After this I looked, and behold, a door *was* opened in heaven: and the first voice which I heard *was* as *it were* of a trumpet talking with me; which said, Come up hither, and I will shew thee *things* which must be hereafter. 2And immediately I was in the spirit: and behold, a throne was set in heaven, and one sat on the throne. 3And he that sat was to look upon like a jasper and a sardine stone: and *there was* a rainbow round about the throne, in sight like unto an emerald. 4And round about the throne *were* four and twenty seats: and upon the seats I saw four and twenty elders sitting, clothed in white raiment; and they had on their heads crowns of gold. 5And out of the throne proceeded lightnings and thunderings and voices: and *there were* seven lamps of fire burning before the throne, which are the seven spirits of God. 6And before the throne *there was* a sea of glass like unto crystal: and in the midst of the throne, and round about the throne, *were* four beasts full of eyes before and behind. 7And the first beast *was* like a lion, and the second beast like a calf, and the third beast had a face as a man, and the fourth beast *was* like a flying eagle. 8And the four beasts had each of them six wings about *him;* and *they were* full of eyes within: and they rest not day and night, saying, Holy, holy, holy, Lord God Almighty, which was, and is, and is to come. 9And when *those* beasts give glory and honour and thanks to him that sat on the throne, who liveth for ever and ever, 10The four and twenty elders fall down before him that sat on the throne, and worship him that liveth for ever and ever, and cast their crowns before the throne, saying, 11Thou art worthy, O Lord, to receive glory and honour and power: for thou hast created all *things,* and for thy pleasure they are and were created. [ch. 5:12; Gen. 1:1; Acts 17:24; Eph. 3:9]

The book and the Lamb

5 And I saw in the right hand of him that sat on the throne a book written within and on the backside, sealed with seven seals. 2And I saw a strong angel proclaiming with a loud voice, Who is worthy to open the book, and to loose the seals thereof? 3And no *man* in heaven, nor in earth, neither under the earth, was able to open the book, neither to look thereon. 4And I wept much, because no *man* was found worthy to open and to read the book, neither to look thereon. 5And one of the elders saith unto me, Weep not: behold, the Lion of the tribe of Juda, the root of David, hath prevailed to open the book, and to loose the seven seals thereof. 6And I beheld, and lo, in the midst of the throne and of the four beasts, and in the midst of the elders, stood a Lamb as *it had been* slain, having seven horns and seven eyes, which are the seven spirits of God sent forth into all the earth. 7And he came and took the book out of the right hand of him that sat upon the throne. 8And when he had taken the book, the four beasts and four *and* twenty elders fell down before the Lamb, having every one *of them* harps, and golden vials full of odours, which are the prayers of saints. 9And they sung a new song, saying, Thou art worthy to take the book, and to open the seals thereof: for thou wast slain, and hast redeemed us to God by thy blood out of every kindred, and tongue, and people, and nation; 10And hast made us unto our God kings and priests: and we shall reign on the earth. [Ex. 19:6; 1 Pet. 2:5]

11 And I beheld, and I heard the voice of many angels round about the throne and the beasts and the elders: and the number of them was ten thousand times ten thousand, and thousands of thousands; 12Saying with a loud voice, Worthy is the Lamb that was slain to receive power, and riches, and wisdom, and strength, and honour, and glory, and blessing. 13And every creature which is in heaven, and on the earth, and under the earth, and such as are in the sea, and all that are in them, heard I saying, Blessing, and honour, and glory, and power, *be* unto him that sitteth upon the throne, and unto the Lamb for ever and ever. 14And the four beasts said, Amen. And the four *and* twenty elders fell down and worshipped him that liveth for ever and ever. [ch. 19:4; ch. 4:9,10]

Six of the seals opened

6 And I saw when the Lamb opened one of the seals, and I heard, as *it were* the noise of thunder, one of the four beasts saying, Come and see. 2And I saw, and behold a white horse: and he that sat on him had a bow; and a crown was given unto him: and he went forth conquering, and to conquer. [Zech. 6:3; ch. 19:11; Ps. 45:4,5 LXX; Zech. 6:11; ch. 14:14]

3 And when he had opened the second seal, I heard the second beast say, Come and see. 4And there went out another horse *that was* red: and *power* was given to him that sat thereon to take peace from the earth, and that they should kill one another: and there was given unto him a great sword. [Zech. 6:2]

5 And when he had opened the third seal, I heard the third beast say, Come and see. And I beheld, and lo a black horse; and he that sat on him had a pair of balances in his hand. 6And I heard a voice in the midst of the four beasts say, A measure of wheat for a penny, and three measures of barley for a penny; and *see* thou hurt not the oil and the wine. [ch. 9:4]

7 And when he had opened the fourth seal, I heard the voice of the fourth beast say, Come and see. 8And I looked, and behold a pale horse: and his name that sat on him *was* Death, and Hell followed with him. And power was given unto them over the fourth *part* of the earth, to kill with sword, and with hunger, and with death, and with the beasts of the earth. [Zech. 6:3; Ezek. 14:21; Lev. 26:22]

9 And when he had opened the fifth seal, I saw under the altar the souls of them that were slain for the word of God, and for the testimony which they held: 10And they cried with a loud voice, saying,

How long, O Lord, holy and true, dost thou not judge and avenge our blood on them that dwell on the earth? ¹¹And white robes were given unto every one of them; and it was said unto them, that they should rest yet for a little season, until their fellowservants also and their brethren, that should be killed as they *were,* should be fulfilled. [ch. 3:4,5; Heb. 11:40]

12 And I beheld when he had opened the sixth seal, and lo, there was a great earthquake; and the sun became black as sackcloth of hair, and the moon became as blood; ¹³And the stars of heaven fell unto the earth, *even* as a fig tree casteth her untimely figs, when she is shaken of a mighty wind. ¹⁴And the heaven departed as a scrole when it is rolled together; and every mountain and island were moved out of their places. ¹⁵And the kings of the earth, and the great men, and the rich *men,* and the chief captains, and the mighty *men,* and every bondman, and every free *man,* hid themselves in the dens and in the rocks of the mountains; ¹⁶And said to the mountains and rocks, Fall on us, and hide us from the face of him that sitteth on the throne, and from the wrath of the Lamb: ¹⁷For the great day of his wrath is come; and who shall be able to stand? [Is. 13:6; Zeph. 1:14; ch. 16:14; Ps. 76:7]

The sealing of God's servants

7 And after these *things* I saw four angels standing on the four corners of the earth, holding the four winds of the earth, that the wind should not blow on the earth, nor on the sea, nor on any tree. ²And I saw another angel ascending from the east, having the seal of the living God: and he cried with a loud voice to the four angels, to whom it was given to hurt the earth and the sea, ³Saying, Hurt not the earth, neither the sea, nor the trees, till we have sealed the servants of our God in their foreheads. ⁴And I heard the number of them which were sealed: *and there were* sealed an hundred *and* forty *and* four thousand of all the tribes of the children of Israel. ⁵Of the tribe of Juda *were* sealed twelve thousand. Of the tribe of Reuben *were* sealed twelve thousand. Of the tribe of Gad *were* sealed twelve thousand. ⁶Of the tribe of Aser *were* sealed twelve thousand. Of the tribe of Nephthalim *were* sealed twelve thousand. Of the tribe of Manasses *were* sealed twelve thousand. ⁷Of the tribe of Simeon *were* sealed twelve thousand. Of the tribe of Levi *were* sealed twelve thousand. Of the tribe of Isachar *were* sealed twelve thousand. ⁸Of the tribe of Zabulon *were* sealed twelve thousand. Of the tribe of Joseph *were* sealed twelve thousand. Of the tribe of Benjamin *were* sealed twelve thousand.

The saints in white robes

9 After this I beheld, and lo, a great multitude, which no *man* could number, of all nations, and kindreds, and people, and tongues, stood before the throne, and before the Lamb, clothed with white robes, and palms in their hands;

¹⁰And cried with a loud voice, saying, Salvation to our God which sitteth upon the throne, and unto the Lamb. ¹¹And all the angels stood round about the throne, and *about* the elders and the four beasts, and fell before the throne on their faces, and worshipped God, ¹²Saying, Amen: Blessing, and glory, and wisdom, and thanksgiving, and honour, and power, and might, *be* unto our God for ever and ever. Amen. ¹³And one of the elders answered, saying unto me, What are these which are arrayed in white robes? and whence came they? ¹⁴And I said unto him, Sir, thou knowest. And he said to me, These are they which came out of great tribulation, and have washed their robes, and made them white in the blood of the Lamb. ¹⁵Therefore are they before the throne of God, and serve him day and night in his temple: and he that sitteth on the throne shall dwell among them. ¹⁶They shall hunger no more, neither thirst any more; neither shall the sun light on them, nor any heat. ¹⁷For the Lamb which is in the midst of the throne shall feed them, and shall lead them unto living fountains of waters: and God shall wipe away all tears from their eyes. [Ps. 23:1; 36:8; John 10:11,14; Is. 25:8; ch. 21:4]

The seventh seal

8 And when he had opened the seventh seal, there was silence in heaven about the space of half an hour. [ch. 6:1]

2 And I saw the seven angels which stood before God; and to them were given seven trumpets.

³And another angel came and stood at the altar, having a golden censer; and there was given unto him much incense, that he should offer *it* with the prayers of all saints upon the golden altar which was before the throne. ⁴And the smoke of the incense, *which came* with the prayers of the saints, ascended up before God out of the angel's hand. ⁵And the angel took the censer, and filled it with fire of the altar, and cast *it* into the earth: and there were voices, and thunderings, and lightnings, and an earthquake. ⁶And the seven angels which had the seven trumpets prepared themselves to sound.

7 The first angel sounded, and there followed hail and fire mingled with blood, and they were cast upon the earth: and the third *part* of trees was burnt up, and all green grass was burnt up. [Ezek. 38:22; ch. 16:2; Is. 2:13; ch. 9:4]

8 And the second angel sounded, and as *it were* a great mountain burning with fire was cast into the sea: and the third *part* of the sea became blood; ⁹And the third *part* of the creatures which were in the sea, and had life, died; and the third *part* of the ships were destroyed. [ch. 16:3]

10 And the third angel sounded, and there fell a great star from heaven, burning as *it were* a lamp, and it fell upon the third *part* of the rivers, and upon the fountains of waters; ¹¹And the name of the star is called Wormwood: and the third *part* of the waters became wormwood; and many men died of the

waters, because they were made bitter. [Ruth 1:20; Ex. 15:23]

12 And the fourth angel sounded, and the third *part* of the sun was smitten, and the third *part* of the moon, and the third *part* of the stars; so as the third *part* of them was darkened, and the day shone not for a third *part* of it, and the night likewise. 13 And I beheld, and heard an angel flying through the midst of heaven, saying with a loud voice, Woe, woe, woe, to the inhabiters of the earth by reason of the other voices of the trumpet of the three angels, which are yet to sound. [ch. 14:6; 19:17; ch. 9:12; 11:14]

The plague of locusts

9 And the fifth angel sounded, and I saw a star fall from heaven unto the earth: and to him was given the key of the bottomless pit. 2 And he opened the bottomless pit; and there arose a smoke out of the pit, as the smoke of a great furnace; and the sun and the air were darkened by reason of the smoke of the pit. 3 And there came out of the smoke locusts upon the earth: and unto them was given power, as the scorpions of the earth have power. 4 And it was commanded them that they should not hurt the grass of the earth, neither any green *thing,* neither any tree; but only *those* men which have not the seal of God in their foreheads. 5 And to them it was given that they should not kill them, but that they should be tormented five months: and their torment *was* as the torment of a scorpion, when he striketh a man. 6 And in those days shall men

seek death, and shall not find it; and shall desire to die, and death shall flee from them. 7 And the shapes of the locusts *were* like unto horses prepared unto battle; and on their heads *were* as *it were* crowns like gold, and their faces *were* as the faces of men. 8 And they had hair as the hair of women, and their teeth were as *the teeth* of lions. 9 And they had breastplates, as *it were* breastplates of iron; and the sound of their wings *was* as the sound of chariots of many horses running to battle. 10 And they had tails like unto scorpions, and there were stings in their tails: and their power *was* to hurt men five months. 11 And they had a king over them, *which is* the angel of the bottomless *pit,* whose name in the Hebrew tongue *is* Abaddon, but in the Greek *tongue* hath *his* name Apollyon. 12 One woe is past; *and* behold, there come two woes more hereafter. [ch. 8:13]

13 And the sixth angel sounded, and I heard a voice from the four horns of the golden altar which is before God, 14 Saying to the sixth angel which had the trumpet, Loose the four angels which are bound in the great river Euphrates. 15 And the four angels were loosed, which were prepared for an hour, and a day, and a month, and a year, for to slay the third *part* of men. 16 And the number of the army of the horsemen *were* two hundred thousand thousand: and I heard the number of them. 17 And thus I saw the horses in the vision, and them that sat on them, having breastplates of fire,

and of jacinth, and brimstone: and the heads of the horses *were* as the heads of lions; and out of their mouths issued fire and smoke and brimstone. 18By these three was the third *part* of men killed, by the fire, and by the smoke, and by the brimstone, which issued out of their mouths. 19For their power is in their mouth, and in their tails: for their tails *were* like unto serpents, and had heads, and with them they do hurt. 20And the rest of the men which were not killed by these plagues *yet* repented not of the works of their hands, that they should not worship devils, and idols of gold, and silver, and brass, and stone, and of wood: which neither can see, nor hear, nor walk: 21Neither repented they of their murders, nor of their sorceries, nor of their fornication, nor of their thefts. [ch. 22:15]

John eats the book

10 And I saw another mighty angel come down from heaven, clothed with a cloud: and a rainbow *was* upon *his* head, and his face *was* as *it were* the sun, and his feet as pillars of fire: 2And he had in his hand a little book open: and he set his right foot upon the sea, and *his* left *foot* on the earth, 3And cried with a loud voice, as *when* a lion roareth: and when he had cried, seven thunders uttered their voices. 4And when the seven thunders had uttered their voices, I was about to write: and I heard a voice from heaven saying unto me, Seal *up those things* which the seven thunders uttered, and write

them not. 5And the angel which I saw stand upon the sea and upon the earth lifted up his hand to heaven, 6And sware by him that liveth for ever and ever, who created heaven, and the *things* that therein are, and the earth, and the *things* that therein are, and the sea, and the *things* which are therein, that there should be time no longer: 7But in the days of the voice of the seventh angel, when he shall begin to sound, the mystery of God should be finished, as he hath declared to his servants the prophets. [ch. 11:15]

8 And the voice which I heard from heaven spake unto me again, and said, Go *and* take the little book which is open in the hand of the angel which standeth upon the sea and upon the earth. 9And I went unto the angel, and said unto him, Give me the little book. And he said unto me, Take *it,* and eat it up; and it shall make thy belly bitter, but it shall be in thy mouth sweet as honey. 10And I took the little book out of the angel's hand, and ate it up; and it was in my mouth sweet as honey: and as soon as I had eaten it, my belly was bitter. 11And he said unto me, Thou must prophesy again before many peoples, and nations, and tongues, and kings.

The two witnesses

11 And there was given me a reed like unto a rod: and the angel stood, saying, Rise, and measure the temple of God, and the altar, and them that worship therein. 2But the court which is without the temple leave out, and measure it not; for it is given unto the Gentiles: and the holy city shall they tread under foot forty *and* two months. ³And I will give *power* unto my two witnesses, and they shall prophesy a thousand two hundred *and* threescore days, clothed *in* sackcloth. ⁴These are the two olive trees, and the two candlesticks standing before the God of the earth. ⁵And if any *man* will hurt them, fire proceedeth out of their mouth, and devoureth their enemies: and if any *man* will hurt them, he must in this manner be killed. ⁶These have power to shut heaven, that it rain not in the days of their prophecy: and have power over waters to turn them to blood, and to smite the earth with all plagues, as often as they will. ⁷And when they shall have finished their testimony, the beast that ascendeth out of the bottomless *pit* shall make war against them, and shall overcome them, and kill them. ⁸And their dead bodies *shall lie* in the street of the great city, which spiritually is called Sodom and Egypt, where also our Lord was crucified. ⁹And *they* of the people and kindreds and tongues and nations shall see their dead bodies three days and a half, and shall not suffer their dead bodies to be put in graves. ¹⁰And they that dwell upon the earth shall rejoice over them, and make merry, and shall send gifts one to another; because these two prophets tormented them that dwelt on the earth. ¹¹And after three days and a half the spirit of life from God entered into them, and they

stood upon their feet; and great fear fell upon them which saw them. ¹²And they heard a great voice from heaven saying unto them, Come up hither. And they ascended up to heaven in a cloud; and their enemies beheld them. ¹³And the same hour was there a great earthquake, and the tenth *part* of the city fell, and in the earthquake were slain of men seven thousand: and the remnant were affrighted, and gave glory to the God of heaven. ¹⁴The second woe is past; *and* behold, the third woe cometh quickly. [ch. 8:13]

The seventh trumpet

15 And the seventh angel sounded; and there were great voices in heaven, saying, The kingdoms of *this* world are become *the kingdoms* of our Lord, and of his Christ; and he shall reign for ever and ever. ¹⁶And the four and twenty elders, which sat before God on their seats, fell upon their faces, and worshipped God, ¹⁷Saying, We give thee thanks, O Lord God Almighty, which art, and wast, and art to come; because thou hast taken *to thee* thy great power, and hast reigned. ¹⁸And the nations were angry, and thy wrath is come, and the time of the dead, that *they* should be judged, and that *thou* shouldest give reward unto thy servants the prophets, and to the saints, and them that fear thy name, small and great; and shouldest destroy them which destroy the earth. [ver. 2,9; Dan. 7:9; ch. 19:5; ch. 13:10]

The woman and the dragon

19 And the temple of God was opened in heaven, and there was seen in his temple the ark of his testament: and there were lightnings, and voices, and thunderings, and an earthquake, and great hail. [ch. 15:5,8; ch. 8:5; ch. 16:21]

12 And there appeared a great wonder in heaven; a woman clothed with the sun, and the moon under her feet, and upon her head a crown of twelve stars: 2And she being with child cried, travailing in birth, and pained to be delivered. 3And there appeared another wonder in heaven; and behold a great red dragon, having seven heads and ten horns, and seven crowns upon his heads. 4And his tail drew the third *part* of the stars of heaven, and did cast them to the earth: and the dragon stood before the woman which was ready to be delivered, for to devour her child as soon as it was born. 5And she brought forth a man child, who was to rule all nations with a rod of iron: and her child was caught up unto God, and *to* his throne. 6And the woman fled into the wilderness, where she hath a place prepared of God, that they should feed her there a thousand two hundred *and* threescore days. [ver. 4; ch. 11:3]

7 And there was war in heaven: Michael and his angels fought against the dragon; and the dragon fought and his angels, 8And prevailed not; neither was their place found any more in heaven. 9And the great dragon was cast *out, that* old serpent, called the devil, and Satan, which deceiveth the whole world: he was cast *out* into the earth, and his angels were cast *out* with him. 10And I heard a loud voice saying in heaven, Now is come salvation, and strength, and the kingdom of our God, and the power of his Christ: for the accuser of our brethren is cast down, which accused them before our God day and night. 11And they overcame him by the blood of the Lamb, and by the word of their testimony; and they loved not their lives unto the death. 12Therefore rejoice, ye heavens, and ye that dwell in them. Woe to the inhabiters of the earth and of the sea! for the devil is come down unto you, having great wrath, because he knoweth that he hath *but* a short time. [Ps. 96:11; Is. 49:13; ch. 18:20; ch. 8:13; ch. 10:6]

13 And when the dragon saw that he was cast unto the earth, he persecuted the woman which brought forth the man *child.* 14And to the woman were given two wings of a great eagle, that she might fly into the wilderness, into her place, where she is nourished for a time, and times, and half a time, from the face of the serpent. 15And the serpent cast out of his mouth water as a flood after the woman, that he might cause her to be carried away of the flood. 16And the earth helped the woman, and the earth opened her mouth, and swallowed up the flood which the dragon cast out of his mouth. 17And the dragon was wroth with the woman, and went to make war with the remnant of her seed,

which keep the commandments of God, and have the testimony of Jesus Christ. [Gen. 3:15; ch. 11:7; ch. 14:12; 1 Cor. 2:1; 1 John 5:10]

The beast from the sea

13 And I stood upon the sand of the sea, and saw a beast rise up out of the sea, having seven heads and ten horns, and upon his horns ten crowns, and upon his heads the name of blasphemy. 2 And the beast which I saw was like unto a leopard, and his feet *were* as *the feet* of a bear, and his mouth as the mouth of a lion: and the dragon gave him his power, and his seat, and great authority. 3 And I saw one of his heads as *it were* wounded to death; and his deadly wound was healed: and all the world wondered after the beast. 4 And they worshipped the dragon which gave power unto the beast: and they worshipped the beast, saying, Who *is* like unto the beast? who is able to make war with him? 5 And there was given unto him a mouth speaking great *things* and blasphemies; and power was given unto him to continue forty *and* two months. 6 And he opened his mouth in blasphemy against God, to blaspheme his name, and his tabernacle, and them that dwell in heaven. 7 And it was given unto him to make war with the saints, and to overcome them: and power was given him over all kindreds, and tongues, and nations. 8 And all that dwell upon the earth shall worship him, whose names are not written in the book of life of the Lamb slain from the foundation of the world. 9 If any *man* have an ear, let him hear. 10 He that leadeth into captivity *shall* go into captivity: he that killeth with the sword must be killed with the sword. Here is the patience and the faith of the saints. [Is. 33:1; Gen. 9:6; Mat. 26:52; ch. 14:12]

The beast from the earth

11 And I beheld another beast coming up out of the earth; and he had two horns like a lamb, and he spake as a dragon. 12 And he exerciseth all the power of the first beast before him, and causeth the earth and them which dwell therein to worship the first beast, whose deadly wound was healed. 13 And he doeth great wonders, so that he maketh fire come down from heaven on the earth in the sight of men, 14 And deceiveth them that dwell on the earth by the means of *those* miracles which he had power to do in the sight of the beast; saying to them that dwell on the earth, that *they* should make an image to the beast, which had the wound by a sword, and did live. 15 And he had power to give life unto the image of the beast, that the image of the beast should both speak, and cause that as many as would not worship the image of the beast should be killed. 16 And he causeth all, *both* small and great, rich and poor, free and bond, to receive a mark in their right hand, or in their foreheads: 17 And that no *man* might buy or sell, save he that had the mark, or the name of the beast, or the number of his name. 18 Here is wisdom. Let him that hath under-

standing count the number of the beast: for it is the number of a man; and his number *is* Six hundred threescore *and* six. [ch. 17:9; ch. 15:2; ch. 21:17]

The Lamb on mount Zion

14 And I looked, and lo, a Lamb stood on the mount Sion, and with him an hundred forty *and* four thousand, having his Father's name written in their foreheads. ²And I heard a voice from heaven, as the voice of many waters, and as the voice of a great thunder: and I heard the voice of harpers harping with their harps: ³And they sung as *it were* a new song before the throne, and before the four beasts, and the elders: and no *man* could learn *that* song but the hundred *and* forty *and* four thousand, which were redeemed from the earth. ⁴These are they which were not defiled with women; for they are virgins. These are they which follow the Lamb whithersoever he goeth. These were redeemed from among men, *being* the firstfruits unto God and to the Lamb. ⁵And in their mouth was found no guile: for they are without fault before the throne of God. [Ps. 32:2; Zeph. 3:13; Eph. 5:27; Jude 24]

The angelic messages

6 And I saw another angel fly in the midst of heaven, having the everlasting gospel to preach unto them that dwell on the earth, and to every nation, and kindred, and tongue, and people, ⁷Saying with a loud voice, Fear God, and give glory to him; for the hour of his judgment is come: and worship him that made heaven, and earth, and the sea, and the fountains of waters. ⁸And there followed another angel, saying, Babylon is fallen, is fallen, *that* great city, because she made all nations drink of the wine of the wrath of her fornication. ⁹And *the* third angel followed them, saying with a loud voice, If any *man* worship the beast and his image, and receive *his* mark in his forehead, or in his hand, ¹⁰The same shall drink of the wine of the wrath of God, which is poured out without mixture into the cup of his indignation; and he shall be tormented with fire and brimstone in the presence of the holy angels, and in the presence of the Lamb: ¹¹And the smoke of their torment ascendeth up for ever and ever: and they have no rest day nor night, who worship the beast and his image, and whosoever receiveth the mark of his name. ¹²Here is the patience of the saints: here *are* they that keep the commandments of God, and the faith of Jesus. ¹³And I heard a voice from heaven saying unto me, Write, Blessed *are* the dead which die in the Lord from henceforth: Yea, saith the Spirit, that they may rest from their labours; and their works do follow them. [Eccl. 4:1,2; 1 Cor. 15:18; 1 Thes. 4:16; 2 Thes. 1:7; Heb. 4:9,10]

14 And I looked, and behold a white cloud, and upon the cloud one sat like unto the Son of man, having on his head a golden crown, and in his hand a sharp sickle. ¹⁵And another angel came out of the temple, crying with a loud voice to him that sat on the cloud,

Thrust in thy sickle, and reap: for the time is come for thee to reap; for the harvest of the earth is ripe. ¹⁶And he that sat on the cloud thrust in his sickle on the earth; and the earth was reaped.

17 And another angel came out of the temple which is in heaven, he also having a sharp sickle. ¹⁸And another angel came out from the altar, which had power over fire; and cried with a loud cry to him that had the sharp sickle, saying, Thrust in thy sharp sickle, and gather the clusters of the vine of the earth; for her grapes are fully ripe. ¹⁹And the angel thrust in his sickle into the earth, and gathered the vine of the earth, and cast *it* into the great winepress of the wrath of God. ²⁰And the winepress was trodden without the city, and blood came out of the winepress, *even* unto the horse bridles, by the space of a thousand *and* six hundred furlongs. [Is. 63:3; Lam. 1:15; Heb. 13:12; ch. 19:14]

The seven plagues

15 And I saw another sign in heaven, great and marvellous, seven angels having the seven last plagues; for in them is filled up the wrath of God. ²And I saw as *it were* a sea of glass mingled with fire: and them that had gotten the victory over the beast, and over his image, and over his mark, *and* over the number of his name, stand on the sea of glass, having *the* harps of God. ³And they sing the song of Moses the servant of God, and the song of the Lamb, saying, Great and marvellous *are* thy works, Lord God Almighty; just and true *are* thy ways, thou King of saints. ⁴Who shall not fear thee, O Lord, and glorify thy name? for *thou* only *art* holy: for all nations shall come and worship before thee; for thy judgments are made manifest. [Ex. 15:14; Jer. 10:7; Is. 66:23]

5 And after that I looked, and behold, the temple of the tabernacle of the testimony in heaven was opened: ⁶And the seven angels came out of the temple, having the seven plagues, clothed in pure and white linen, and having their breasts girded with golden girdles. ⁷And one of the four beasts gave unto the seven angels seven golden vials full of the wrath of God, who liveth for ever and ever. ⁸And the temple was filled with smoke from the glory of God, and from his power; and no *man* was able to enter into the temple, till the seven plagues of the seven angels were fulfilled. [Ex. 40:34; 2 Chr. 5:14; 2 Thes. 1:9]

The vials of God's wrath

16 And I heard a great voice out of the temple saying to the seven angels, Go your ways, and pour out the vials of the wrath of God upon the earth. ²And the first went, and poured out his vial upon the earth; and there fell a noisome and grievous sore upon the men which *had* the mark of the beast, and *upon* them which worshipped his image. [ch. 8:7; Ex. 9:9-11; ch. 13:16; ch. 13:14]

3 And the second angel poured out his vial upon the sea; and it became as the blood of a dead *man:* and every living soul died in the sea. [ch. 8:8; Ex. 7:17; ch. 8:9]

4 And the third angel poured out his vial upon the rivers and fountains of waters; and they became blood. **5** And I heard the angel of the waters say, Thou art righteous, O Lord, which art, and wast, and shalt be, because thou hast judged thus. **6** For they have shed the blood of saints and prophets, and thou hast given them blood to drink; for they are worthy. **7** And I heard another out of the altar say, Even so, Lord God Almighty, true and righteous *are* thy judgments. [ch. 15:3; ch. 13:10]

8 And the fourth angel poured out his vial upon the sun; and *power* was given unto him to scorch men with fire. **9** And men were scorched *with* great heat, and blasphemed the name of God, which hath power over these plagues: and they repented not to give him glory. [ver. 11,21; Dan. 5:22; ch. 11:13]

10 And the fifth angel poured out his vial upon the seat of the beast; and his kingdom was full of darkness; and they gnawed their tongues for pain, **11** And blasphemed the God of heaven because of their pains and their sores, and repented not of their deeds. [ver. 9,21; ver. 2; ver. 9]

12 And the sixth angel poured out his vial upon the great river Euphrates; and the water thereof was dried up, that the way of the kings of the east might be prepared. **13** And I saw three unclean spirits like frogs *come* out of the mouth of the dragon, and out of the mouth of the beast, and out of the mouth of the false prophet. **14** For they are the spirits of devils, working miracles, which go forth unto the kings of the earth and of the whole world, to gather them to the battle of that great day of God Almighty. **15** Behold, I come as a thief. Blessed *is* he that watcheth, and keepeth his garments, lest he walk naked, and they see his shame. **16** And he gathered them together into a place called in the Hebrew tongue Armageddon. [ch. 19:19]

17 And the seventh angel poured out his vial into the air; and there came a great voice out of the temple of heaven, from the throne, saying, It is done. **18** And there were voices, and thunders, and lightnings; and there was a great earthquake, such as was not since men were upon the earth, so mighty an earthquake, *and* so great. **19** And the great city was *divided* into three parts, and the cities of the nations fell: and great Babylon came in remembrance before God, to give unto her the cup of the wine of the fierceness of his wrath. **20** And every island fled *away,* and the mountains were not found. **21** And there fell upon men a great hail out of heaven, *every stone* about the weight of a talent: and men blasphemed God because of the plague of the hail; for the plague thereof was exceeding great. [ch. 11:19; ver. 9,11; Ex. 9:23]

The woman on the beast

17 And there came one of the seven angels which had the seven vials, and talked with me, saying unto me, *Come* hither; I will shew unto thee the judgment of the great whore that sitteth upon many waters: ²With whom the kings of the earth have committed fornication, and the inhabiters of the earth have been made drunk with the wine of her fornication. ³So he carried me away in the spirit into the wilderness: and I saw a woman sit upon a scarlet coloured beast, full of names of blasphemy, having seven heads and ten horns. ⁴And the woman was arrayed in purple and scarlet colour, and decked with gold and precious stone and pearls, having a golden cup in her hand full of abominations and filthiness of her fornication: ⁵And upon her forehead *was* a name written, MYSTERY, BABYLON THE GREAT, THE MOTHER OF HARLOTS AND ABOMINATIONS OF THE EARTH. ⁶And I saw the woman drunken with the blood of the saints, and with the blood of the martyrs of Jesus: and when I saw her, I wondered *with* great admiration. ⁷And the angel said unto me, Wherefore didst thou marvel? I will tell thee the mystery of the woman, and of the beast that carrieth her, which hath the seven heads and ten horns. ⁸The beast that thou sawest was, and is not; and shall ascend out of the bottomless *pit,* and go into perdition: and they that dwell on the earth shall wonder, whose names were not written in the book of life from the foundation of the world, when they behold the beast that was, and is not, and yet is. ⁹*And* here *is* the mind which hath wisdom. The seven heads are seven mountains, on which the woman sitteth. ¹⁰And there are

seven kings: five are fallen, and one is, *and* the other is not yet come; and when he cometh, he must continue a short *space.* ¹¹And the beast that was, and is not, even he is the eighth, and is of the seven, and goeth into perdition. ¹²And the ten horns which thou sawest are ten kings, which have received no kingdom as yet; but receive power as kings one hour with the beast. ¹³These have one mind, and shall give their power and strength unto the beast. ¹⁴These shall make war with the Lamb, and the Lamb shall overcome them: for he is Lord of lords, and King of kings: and they that are with him *are* called, and chosen, and faithful. ¹⁵And he saith unto me, The waters which thou sawest, where the whore sitteth, are peoples, and multitudes, and nations, and tongues. ¹⁶And the ten horns which thou sawest upon the beast, these shall hate the whore, and shall make her desolate and naked, and shall eat her flesh, and burn her with fire. ¹⁷For God hath put in their hearts to fulfil his will, and to agree, and give their kingdom unto the beast, until the words of God shall be fulfilled. ¹⁸And the woman which thou sawest is *that* great city, which reigneth over the kings of the earth. [ch. 16:19; ch. 12:4]

The desolation of Babylon

18 And after these *things* I saw another angel come down from heaven, having great power; and the earth was lightened with his glory. ²And he cried mightily with a strong voice, saying, Babylon the great is fallen, is fallen, and is become the habitation of devils, and the hold of every foul spirit, and a cage of every unclean and hateful bird. ³For all nations have drunk of the wine of the wrath of her fornication, and the kings of the earth have committed fornication with her, and the merchants of the earth are waxed rich through the abundance of her delicacies. [ch. 14:8; Is. 47:15]

4 And I heard another voice from heaven, saying, Come out of her, my people, that ye be not partakers of her sins, and that ye receive not of her plagues. ⁵For her sins have reached unto heaven, and God hath remembered her iniquities. ⁶Reward her even as she rewarded you, and double unto her double according to her works: in the cup which she hath filled fill to her double. ⁷How much she hath glorified herself, and lived deliciously, so much torment and sorrow give her: for she saith in her heart, I sit a queen, and am no widow, and shall see no sorrow. ⁸Therefore shall her plagues come in one day, death, and mourning, and famine; and she shall be utterly burnt with fire: for strong *is* the Lord God who judgeth her. ⁹And the kings of the earth, who have committed fornication and lived deliciously with her, shall bewail her, and lament for her, when they shall see the smoke of her burning, ¹⁰Standing afar off for the fear of her torment, saying, Alas, alas, *that* great city Babylon, *that* mighty city! for in one hour is thy judg-

ment come. ¹¹And the merchants of the earth *shall* weep and mourn over her; for no *man* buyeth their merchandise any more: ¹²The merchandise of gold, and silver, and precious stones, and of pearls, and fine linen, and purple, and silk, and scarlet, and all thyine wood, and all *manner* vessels of ivory, and all *manner* vessels of most precious wood, and of brass, and iron, and marble, ¹³And cinnamon, and odours, and ointments, and frankincense, and wine, and oil, and fine flour, and wheat, and beasts, and sheep, and horses, and chariots, and slaves, and souls of men. ¹⁴And the fruits that thy soul lusted after are departed from thee, and all *things which were* dainty and goodly are departed from thee, and thou shalt find them no more at all. ¹⁵The merchants of these *things,* which were made rich by her, shall stand afar off for the fear of her torment, weeping and wailing, ¹⁶And saying, Alas, alas, *that* great city, that was clothed in fine linen, and purple, and scarlet, and decked with gold, and precious stones, and pearls: ¹⁷For in one hour so great riches is come to nought. And every shipmaster, and all the company in ships, and sailers, and as many as trade by sea, stood afar off, ¹⁸And cried when they saw the smoke of her burning, saying, What *city is* like unto *this* great city? ¹⁹And they cast dust on their heads, and cried, weeping and wailing, saying, Alas, alas, *that* great city, wherein were made rich all that had ships in the sea by reason of her costliness: for in one hour is she made desolate. 20Rejoice over her, *thou* heaven, and ye holy apostles and prophets; for God hath avenged you on her. [Is. 44:23; 49:13; Jer. 51:48; Luke 11:49; ch. 19:2]

21 And a mighty angel took up a stone like a great millstone, and cast *it* into the sea, saying, Thus with violence shall *that* great city Babylon be thrown down, and shall be found no more at all. 22And the voice of harpers, and musicians, and of pipers, and trumpeters, shall be heard no more at all in thee; and no craftsman, of whatsoever craft *he be,* shall be found any more in thee; and the sound of a millstone shall be heard no more at all in thee; 23And the light of a candle shall shine no more at all in thee; and the voice of the bridegroom and of the bride shall be heard no more at all in thee: for thy merchants were the great men of the earth; for by thy sorceries were all nations deceived. 24And in her was found the blood of prophets, and of saints, and of all that were slain upon the earth. [ch. 17:6; Jer. 51:49]

The marriage supper of the Lamb

19 And after these *things* I heard a great voice of much people in heaven, saying, Alleluia; Salvation, and glory, and honour, and power, unto the Lord our God: 2For true and righteous *are* his judgments: for he hath judged the great whore, which did corrupt the earth with her fornication, and hath avenged the blood of his servants at her hand. 3And again they said, Alleluia. And her smoke rose up for ever and ever. 4And the four

and twenty elders and the four beasts fell down and worshipped God that sat on the throne, saying, Amen; Alleluia. 5And a voice came out of the throne, saying, Praise our God, all ye his servants, and ye that fear him, both small and great. 6And I heard as *it were* the voice of a great multitude, and as the voice of many waters, and as the voice of mighty thunderings, saying, Alleluia: for the Lord God Omnipotent reigneth. 7Let us be glad and rejoice, and give honour to him: for the marriage of the Lamb is come, and his wife hath made herself ready. 8And to her was granted that she should be arrayed in fine linen, clean and white: for the fine linen is the righteousness of saints. 9And he saith unto me, Write, Blessed *are* they which are called unto the marriage supper of the Lamb. And he saith unto me, These are the true sayings of God. 10And I fell at his feet to worship him. And he said unto me, See *thou do it* not: I am thy fellowservant, and of thy brethren that have the testimony of Jesus: worship God: for the testimony of Jesus is the spirit of prophecy. [ch. 22:8; Acts 10:26; ch. 22:9; 1 John 5:10; ch. 12:17]

The beast and false prophet

11 And I saw heaven opened, and behold a white horse; and he that sat upon him *was* called Faithful and True, and in righteousness he doth judge and make war. 12His eyes *were* as a flame of fire, and on his head *were* many crowns; and he had a name written, that no *man* knew, but he himself. 13And

he *was* clothed with a vesture dipt in blood: and his name is called The Word of God. 14And the armies which were in heaven followed him upon white horses, clothed in fine linen, white and clean. 15And out of his mouth goeth a sharp sword, that with it he should smite the nations: and he shall rule them with a rod of iron: and he treadeth the winepress of the fierceness and wrath of Almighty God. 16And he hath on *his* vesture and on his thigh a name written, KING OF KINGS, AND LORD OF LORDS. [ver. 12; Dan. 2:47; 1 Tim. 6:15; ch. 17:14]

17 And I saw an angel standing in the sun; and he cried with a loud voice, saying to all the fowls that fly in the midst of heaven, Come and gather yourselves together unto the supper of the great God; 18That ye may eat the flesh of kings, and the flesh of captains, and the flesh of mighty *men,* and the flesh of horses, and of them that sit on them, and the flesh of all *men,* both free and bond, both small and great. 19And I saw the beast, and the kings of the earth, and their armies, gathered together to make war against him that sat on the horse, and against his army. 20And the beast was taken, and with him the false prophet that wrought miracles before him, with which he deceived them that had received the mark of the beast, and them that worshipped his image. *These* both were cast alive into a lake of fire burning with brimstone. 21And the remnant were slain with the sword of him that sat

upon the horse, which *sword* proceeded out of his mouth: and all the fowls were filled with their flesh. [ver. 15; ver. 17,18; ch. 17:16]

The millennial reign

20 And I saw an angel come down from heaven, having the key of the bottomless *pit* and a great chain in his hand. 2And he laid hold on the dragon, *that* old serpent, which is the devil, and Satan, and bound him a thousand years, 3And cast him into the bottomless *pit,* and shut him up, and set a seal upon him, that he should deceive the nations no more, till the thousand years should be fulfilled: and after that he must be loosed a little season. [Dan. 6:17; ch. 12:9]

4 And I saw thrones, and they sat upon them, and judgment was given unto them: and *I saw* the souls of them that were beheaded for the witness of Jesus, and for the word of God, and which had not worshipped the beast, neither his image, neither had received *his* mark upon their foreheads, or in their hands; and they lived and reigned with Christ a thousand years. 5But the rest of the dead lived not again until the thousand years were finished. This *is* the first resurrection. 6Blessed and holy *is* he that hath part in the first resurrection: on such the second death hath no power, but they shall be priests of God and of Christ, and shall reign with him a thousand years. [ch. 2:11; Is. 61:6; 1 Pet. 2:9; ch. 1:6; ver. 4]

The loosing of Satan

7 And when the thousand years are expired, Satan shall be loosed

out of his prison, ⁸And shall go out to deceive the nations which are in the four quarters of the earth, Gog and Magog, to gather them together to battle: the number of whom *is* as the sand of the sea. ⁹And they went up on the breadth of the earth, and compassed the camp of the saints about, and the beloved city: and fire came down from God out of heaven, and devoured them. ¹⁰And the devil that deceived them was cast into the lake of fire and brimstone, where the beast and the false prophet *are*, and shall be tormented day and night for ever and ever. [ver. 8; ch. 19:20; ch. 14:10]

The great white throne judgment

11 And I saw a great white throne, and him that sat on it, from whose face the earth and the heaven fled *away;* and there was found no place for them. ¹²And I saw the dead, small and great, stand before God; and the books were opened: and another book was opened, which is *the book* of life: and the dead were judged out of those *things* which were written in the books, according to their works. ¹³And the sea gave up the dead which were in it; and death and hell delivered up the dead which were in them: and they were judged every man according to their works. ¹⁴And death and hell were cast into the lake of fire. This is the second death. ¹⁵And whosoever was not found written in the book of life was cast into the lake of fire. [ch. 19:20]

The new Jerusalem

21 And I saw a new heaven and a new earth: for the first heaven and the first earth were passed away; and there was no more sea. ²And I John saw the holy city, new Jerusalem, coming down from God out of heaven, prepared as a bride adorned for her husband. ³And I heard a great voice out of heaven saying, Behold, the tabernacle of God *is* with men, and he will dwell with them, and they shall be his people, and God himself shall be with them, *and be* their God. ⁴And God shall wipe away all tears from their eyes; and there shall be no more death, neither sorrow, nor crying, neither shall there be any more pain: for the former *things* are passed away. ⁵And he that sat upon the throne said, Behold, I make all *things* new. And he said unto me, Write: for these words are true and faithful. ⁶And he said unto me, It is done. I am Alpha and Omega, the beginning and the end. I will give unto him that is athirst of the fountain of the water of life freely. ⁷He that overcometh shall inherit all *things;* and I will be his God, and he shall be my son. ⁸But the fearful, and unbelieving, and the abominable, and murderers, and whoremongers, and sorcerers, and idolaters, and all liars, shall have their part in the lake which burneth with fire and brimstone: which is the second death. [1 Cor. 6:9; Gal. 5:19; Eph. 5:5; 1 Tim. 1:9; Heb. 12:14; ch. 20:14]

9 And there came unto me one of the seven angels which had the seven vials full of the seven last

plagues, and talked with me, saying, *Come* hither, I will shew thee the bride, the Lamb's wife. ¹⁰And he carried me away in the spirit to a great and high mountain, and shewed me *that* great city, the holy Jerusalem, descending out of heaven from God, ¹¹Having the glory of God: and her light *was* like unto a stone most precious, *even* like a jasper stone, clear as crystal; ¹²And had a wall great and high, and had twelve gates, and at the gates twelve angels, and names written *there*on, which are *the names* of the twelve tribes of the children of Israel: ¹³On the east three gates; on the north three gates; on the south three gates; and on the west three gates. ¹⁴And the wall of the city had twelve foundations, and in them the names of the twelve apostles of the Lamb. ¹⁵And he that talked with me had a golden reed to measure the city, and the gates thereof, and the wall thereof. ¹⁶And the city lieth foursquare, and the length is as large as the breadth: and he measured the city with the reed, twelve thousand furlongs. The length and the breadth and the height of it are equal. ¹⁷And he measured the wall thereof, an hundred *and* forty *and* four cubits, *according to* the measure of a man, that is, of *the* angel. ¹⁸And the building of the wall of it was *of* jasper: and the city *was* pure gold, like unto clear glass. ¹⁹And the foundations of the wall of the city *were* garnished with all *manner of* precious stones. The first foundation *was* jasper; the second, sapphire; the third, a chalcedony; the

fourth, an emerald; ²⁰The fifth, sardonyx; the sixth, sardius; the seventh, chrysolite; the eighth, beryl; the ninth, a topaz; the tenth, a chrysoprasus; the eleventh, a jacinth; the twelfth, an amethyst. ²¹And the twelve gates *were* twelve pearls; every several gate was of one pearl: and the street of the city *was* pure gold, as *it were* transparent glass. ²²And I saw no temple therein: for the Lord God Almighty and the Lamb are the temple of it. ²³And the city had no need of the sun, neither of the moon, to shine in it: for the glory of God did lighten it, and the Lamb *is* the light thereof. ²⁴And the nations of them which are saved shall walk in the light of it: and the kings of the earth do bring their glory and honour into it. ²⁵And the gates of it shall not be shut at all by day: for there shall be no night there. ²⁶And they shall bring the glory and honour of the nations into it. ²⁷And there shall in no wise enter into it any *thing* that defileth, neither *whatsoever* worketh abomination, or *maketh* a lie: but they which are written in the Lamb's book of life. [Is. 35:8; 52:1; 60:21; Joel 3:17; ch. 22:14; Phil. 4:3]

The water and tree of life

22 And he shewed me a pure river of water of life, clear as crystal, proceeding out of the throne of God and of the Lamb. ²In the midst of the street of it, and of either side of the river, *was there* the tree of life, which bare twelve *manner of* fruits, *and* yielded her fruit every month: and the leaves of the tree *were* for the healing of the nations. 3 And there shall be no more curse: but the throne of God and of the Lamb shall be in it; and his servants shall serve him: 4 And they shall see his face; and his name *shall be* in their foreheads. 5 And there shall be no night there; and they need no candle, neither light of the sun; for the Lord God giveth them light: and they shall reign for ever and ever. [ch. 21:23; Ps. 36:9; Dan. 7:27; Rom. 5:17; 2 Tim. 2:12]

Epilogue

6 And he said unto me, These sayings *are* faithful and true: and the Lord God of the holy prophets sent his angel to shew unto his servants *the things* which must shortly be done. 7 Behold, I come quickly: blessed *is* he that keepeth the sayings of the prophecy of this book. [ch. 3:11; ch. 1:3]

8 And I John saw these *things,* and heard *them.* And when I had heard and seen, I fell down to worship before the feet of the angel which shewed me these *things.* 9 Then saith he unto me, See *thou do it* not: for I am thy fellowservant, and of thy brethren the prophets, and of them which keep the sayings of this book: worship God. 10 And he saith unto me, Seal not the sayings of the prophecy of this book: for the time is at hand. 11 He that is unjust, let him be unjust still: and he which is filthy, let him be filthy still: and *he that is* righteous, let him be righteous still: and *he that is* holy, let him be

holy still. 12 And behold, I come quickly; and my reward *is* with me, to give every man according as his work shall be. 13 I am Alpha and Omega, the beginning and the end, the first and the last. 14 Blessed *are* they that do his commandments, that they may have right to the tree of life, and may enter in through the gates into the city. 15 For without *are* dogs, and sorcerers, and whoremongers, and murderers, and idolaters, and whosoever loveth and maketh a lie. [1 Cor. 6:9; Gal. 5:19; Col. 3:6; Phil. 3:2]

16 I Jesus have sent mine angel to testify unto you these *things* in the churches. I am the root and the offspring of David, *and* the bright and morning star. 17 And the Spirit and the bride say, Come. And let him that heareth say, Come. And let him that is athirst come. And whosoever will, let him take the water of life freely. 18 For I testify unto every *man* that heareth the words of the prophecy of this book, If any *man* shall add unto these *things,* God shall add unto him the plagues that are written in this book: 19 And if any *man* shall take away from the words of the book of this prophecy, God shall take away his part out of the book of life, and out of the holy city, and *from* the *things* which are written in this book. 20 He which testifieth these *things* saith, Surely I come quickly. Amen. Even so, come, Lord Jesus. 21 The grace of our Lord Jesus Christ *be* with you all. Amen.

The
Psalms and Proverbs

The Book of
Psalms

The way of the righteous

1 Blessed *is* the man that walketh not in the counsel of the ungodly, nor standeth in the way of sinners, nor sitteth in the seat of the scornful. ²But his delight *is* in the law of the LORD; and in his law doth he meditate day and night. ³And he shall be like a tree planted by the rivers of water, that bringeth forth his fruit in his season; his leaf also shall not wither; and whatsoever he doeth shall prosper. ⁴The ungodly *are* not so: but *are* like the chaff which the wind driveth away. ⁵Therefore the ungodly shall not stand in the judgment, nor sinners in the congregation of the righteous. ⁶For the LORD knoweth the way of the righteous: but the way of the ungodly shall perish. [Ps. 37:18; 2 Tim. 2:19]

The triumph of the king

2 Why do the heathen rage, and the people imagine a vain *thing?* ²The kings of the earth set themselves, and the rulers take counsel together, against the LORD, and against his anointed, *saying,* ³Let us break their bands asunder, and cast away their cords from us. ⁴He that sitteth in the heavens shall laugh: the LORD shall have them in derision. ⁵Then shall he speak unto them in his wrath, and vex them in his sore displeasure. ⁶Yet have I set my king upon my holy hill of Zion. ⁷I will declare the decree: the LORD hath said unto me, Thou *art* my Son; *this* day have I begotten thee. ⁸Ask

of me, and I shall give *thee* the heathen *for* thine inheritance, and the uttermost parts of the earth *for* thy possession. ⁹Thou shalt break them with a rod of iron; thou shalt dash them in pieces like a potter's vessel. ¹⁰Be wise now therefore, O ye kings: be instructed, ye judges of the earth. ¹¹Serve the LORD with fear, and rejoice with trembling. ¹²Kiss the Son, lest he be angry, and ye perish *from* the way, when his wrath is kindled but a little: blessed *are* all they that put their trust in him. [John 5:23; Rev. 6:16; Ps. 34:8; Is. 30:18; Rom. 9:33]

Confidence facing the enemy

A Psalm of David, when he fled from Absalom his son.

3 LORD, how are they increased that trouble me! many *are* they that rise up against me. ²Many *there be* which say of my soul, *There is* no help for him in God. Selah. ³But thou, O LORD, *art* a shield for me; my glory, and the lifter up of mine head. ⁴I cried unto the LORD *with* my voice, and he heard me out of his holy hill. Selah. ⁵I laid me down and slept; I awaked; for the LORD sustained me. ⁶I will not be afraid of ten thousands of people, that have set *themselves* against me round about. ⁷Arise, O LORD; save me, O my God: for thou hast smitten all mine enemies *upon* the cheek bone; thou hast broken the teeth of the ungodly. ⁸Salvation *belongeth* unto the LORD: thy blessing *is* upon thy people. Selah. [Is. 43:11]

Thoughts in the night

To the chief Musician on Neginoth,
A Psalm of David.

4 Hear me when I call, O God of my righteousness: thou hast enlarged me *when I was* in distress; have mercy upon me, and hear my prayer. 2O ye sons of men, how long *will ye turn* my glory into shame? *how long* will ye love vanity, *and* seek after leasing? Selah. 3But know that the LORD hath set apart *him that is* godly for himself: the LORD will hear when I call unto him. 4Stand in awe, and sin not: commune with your own heart upon your bed, and be still. Selah. 5Offer the sacrifices of righteousness, and put your trust in the LORD. 6*There be* many that say, Who will shew us *any* good? LORD, lift thou up the light of thy countenance upon us. 7Thou hast put gladness in my heart, more than *in* the time *that* their corn and their wine increased. 8I will both lay me down in peace, and sleep: for thou, LORD, only makest me dwell in safety. [Ps. 3:5; Lev. 25:18]

A morning prayer

To the chief Musician upon Nehiloth,
A Psalm of David.

5 Give ear to my words, O LORD, consider my meditation. 2Hearken unto the voice of my cry, my King, and my God: for unto thee will I pray. 3My voice shalt thou hear *in* the morning, O LORD; *in* the morning will I direct *my prayer* unto thee, and will look up. 4For thou *art* not a God that hath pleasure in wickedness:

neither shall evil dwell *with* thee. 5The foolish shall not stand in thy sight: thou hatest all workers of iniquity. 6Thou shalt destroy them that speak leasing: the LORD will abhor the bloody and deceitful man. 7But *as for* me, I will come *into* thy house in the multitude of thy mercy: *and* in thy fear will I worship toward thy holy temple. 8Lead me, O LORD, in thy righteousness because of mine enemies; make thy way straight before my face. 9For *there is* no faithfulness in their mouth; their inward *part is* very wickedness; their throat *is* an open sepulchre; they flatter with their tongue. 10Destroy thou them, O God; let them fall by their own counsels; cast them out in the multitude of their transgressions; for they have rebelled against thee. 11But let all those that put their trust in thee rejoice: let them ever shout for joy, because thou defendest them: let them also that love thy name be joyful in thee. 12For thou, LORD, wilt bless the righteous; *with* favour wilt thou compass him as *with* a shield.

Prayer for mercy during trouble

To the chief Musician on Neginoth upon
Sheminith, A Psalm of David.

6 O LORD, rebuke me not in thine anger, neither chasten me in thy hot displeasure. 2Have mercy upon me, O LORD; for I *am* weak: O LORD, heal me; for my bones are vexed. 3My soul is also sore vexed: but thou, O LORD, how long? 4Return, O LORD, deliver my soul: O save me for thy mercy's sake. 5For in death *there is* no remembrance of thee: in the grave who shall give thee thanks? 6I am weary with my groaning; all the night make I my bed to swim; I water my couch with my tears. 7Mine eye is consumed because of grief; it waxeth old because of all mine enemies. 8Depart from me, all ye workers of iniquity; for the LORD hath heard the voice of my weeping. 9The LORD hath heard my supplication; the LORD will receive my prayer. 10Let all mine enemies be ashamed and sore vexed: let them return *and* be ashamed suddenly.

The prayer of a wronged man

Shiggaion of David, which he sang unto the LORD, concerning the words of Cush the Benjamite.

7 O LORD my God, in thee do I put my trust: save me from all them that persecute me, and deliver me: 2Lest he tear my soul like a lion, rending *it* in pieces, while *there is* none to deliver. 3O LORD my God, if I have done this; if there be iniquity in my hands; 4If I have rewarded evil *unto* him that was at peace with me; (yea, I have delivered him that without cause is mine enemy:) 5Let the enemy persecute my soul, and take *it;* yea, let him tread down my life upon the earth, and lay mine honour in the dust. Selah. 6Arise, O LORD, in thine anger, lift up thyself because of the rage of mine enemies: and awake for me *to* the judgment *that* thou hast commanded. 7So shall the congregation of the people compass thee about: for their sakes therefore return thou on high. 8The LORD shall judge the people:

judge me, O LORD, according to my righteousness, and according to mine integrity *that is* in me. 9O let the wickedness of the wicked come to an end; but establish the just: for the righteous God trieth the hearts and reins. 10My defence *is* of God, which saveth the upright in heart. 11God judgeth the righteous, and God is angry *with the wicked* every day. 12If he turn not, he will whet his sword; he hath bent his bow, and made it ready. 13He hath also prepared for him the instruments of death; he ordaineth his arrows against the persecutors. 14Behold, he travaileth with iniquity, and hath conceived mischief, and brought forth falsehood. 15He made a pit, and digged it, and is fallen into the ditch *which* he made. 16His mischief shall return upon his own head, and his violent dealing shall come down upon his own pate. 17I will praise the LORD according to his righteousness: and will sing *praise* to the name of the LORD most High.

God's glory and man's honour

To the chief Musician upon Gittith, A Psalm of David.

8 O LORD our Lord, how excellent *is* thy name in all the earth! who hast set thy glory above the heavens. 2Out of the mouth of babes and sucklings hast thou ordained strength because of thine enemies, that *thou* mightest still the enemy and the avenger. 3When I consider thy heavens, the work of thy fingers, the moon and the stars, which thou hast ordained; 4What *is* man, that thou art mindful of him? and the son of man, that thou visitest him? 5For thou hast made him a little lower than the angels, and hast crowned him *with* glory and honour. 6Thou madest him to have dominion over the works of thy hands; thou hast put all *things* under his feet: 7All sheep and oxen, yea, and the beasts of the field; 8The fowl of the air, and the fish of the sea, *and whatsoever* passeth *through* the paths of the seas. 9O LORD our Lord, how excellent *is* thy name in all the earth! [ver. 1]

Praise to God for deliverance

To the chief Musician upon Muth-labben, A Psalm of David.

9 I will praise *thee,* O LORD, with my whole heart; I will shew forth all thy marvellous works. 2I will be glad and rejoice in thee: I will sing *praise* to thy name, O thou most High. 3When mine enemies are turned back, they shall fall and perish at thy presence. 4For thou hast maintained my right and my cause; thou satest in the throne judging right. 5Thou hast rebuked the heathen, thou hast destroyed the wicked, thou hast put out their name for ever and ever. 6O thou enemy, destructions are come to a perpetual end: and thou hast destroyed cities; their memorial is perished *with* them. 7But the LORD shall endure for ever: he hath prepared his throne for judgment. 8And he shall judge the world in righteousness, he shall minister judgment to the people in uprightness. 9The LORD also will be a refuge for the op-

pressed, a refuge in times of trouble. 10And they that know thy name will put their trust in thee: for thou, LORD, hast not forsaken them that seek thee. 11Sing *praises* to the LORD, which dwelleth in Zion: declare among the people his doings. 12When he maketh inquisition for blood, he remembereth them: he forgetteth not the cry of the humble. 13Have mercy upon me, O LORD; consider my trouble *which I suffer* of them that hate me, thou that liftest me up from the gates of death: 14That I may shew forth all thy praise in the gates of the daughter of Zion: I will rejoice in thy salvation. 15The heathen are sunk down in the pit *that* they made: in the net which they hid is their own foot taken. 16The LORD is known *by* the judgment *which* he executeth: the wicked is snared in the work of his own hands. Higgaion. Selah. 17The wicked shall be turned into hell, *and* all the nations that forget God. 18For the needy shall not alway be forgotten: the expectation of the poor shall *not* perish for ever. 19Arise, O LORD; let not man prevail: let the heathen be judged in thy sight. 20Put them in fear, O LORD: *that* the nations may know themselves *to be but* men. Selah.

God hears and acts

10 Why standest thou afar off, O LORD? *why* hidest thou *thyself* in times of trouble? 2The wicked in *his* pride doth persecute the poor: let them be taken in the devices that they have imagined. 3For the wicked boasteth of his heart's desire, and blesseth the covetous, *whom* the LORD abhorreth. ⁴The wicked, through the pride of his countenance, will not seek *after God:* God *is* not *in* all his thoughts. ⁵His ways are always grievous; thy judgments *are* far above out of his sight: *as for* all his enemies, he puffeth at them. ⁶He hath said in his heart, I shall not be moved: for *I shall* never *be* in adversity. ⁷His mouth is full *of* cursing and deceit and fraud: under his tongue *is* mischief and vanity. ⁸He sitteth in the lurking places of the villages: in the secret places doth he murder the innocent: his eyes are privily set against the poor. ⁹He lieth in wait secretly as a lion in his den: he lieth in wait to catch the poor: he doth catch the poor, when he draweth him into his net. ¹⁰He croucheth, *and* humbleth himself, that the poor may fall by his strong *ones.* ¹¹He hath said in his heart, God hath forgotten: he hideth his face; he will never see *it.* ¹²Arise, O LORD; O God, lift up thine hand: forget not the humble: ¹³Wherefore doth the wicked contemn God? he hath said in his heart, Thou wilt not require *it.* ¹⁴Thou hast seen *it;* for thou beholdest mischief and spite, to requite *it* with thy hand: the poor committeth *himself* unto thee; thou art the helper of the fatherless. ¹⁵Break thou the arm of the wicked and the evil *man:* seek out his wickedness *till* thou find none. ¹⁶The LORD *is* King for ever and ever: the heathen are perished out of his land. ¹⁷LORD, thou hast heard the desire of the humble: thou wilt prepare their heart, thou wilt cause

thine ear to hear: ¹⁸To judge the fatherless and the oppressed, that the man of the earth may no more oppress. [Ps. 82:3]

The LORD our refuge

To the chief Musician, *A Psalm* of David.

11 In the LORD put I my trust: how say ye to my soul, Flee *as* a bird *to* your mountain? ²For lo, the wicked bend *their* bow, they make ready their arrow upon the string, that *they* may privily shoot at the upright in heart. ³If the foundations be destroyed, what can the righteous do? ⁴The LORD *is* in his holy temple, the LORD'S throne *is* in heaven: his eyes behold, his eyelids try, the children of men. ⁵The LORD trieth the righteous: but the wicked and him that loveth violence his soul hateth. ⁶Upon the wicked he shall rain snares, fire and brimstone, and a horrible tempest: *this shall be* the portion of their cup. ⁷For the righteous LORD loveth righteousness; his countenance doth behold the upright. [Ps. 45:7]

Good thoughts for bad times

To the chief Musician upon Sheminith, A Psalm of David.

12 Help, LORD; for the godly *man* ceaseth; for the faithful fail from among the children of men. ²They speak vanity every one with his neighbour: *with* flattering lips *and* with a double heart do they speak. ³The LORD shall cut off all flattering lips, *and* the tongue that speaketh proud *things:* ⁴Who have said, With our tongue will we prevail; our lips *are* our own: who *is* lord over us? ⁵For the oppression of the poor, for the sighing of the needy, now will I arise, saith the LORD; I will set *him* in safety *from him that* puffeth at him. ⁶The words of the LORD *are* pure words: *as* silver tried in a furnace of earth, purified seven times. ⁷Thou shalt keep them, O LORD, thou shalt preserve them from this generation for ever. ⁸The wicked walk on every side, when the vilest men are exalted.

The deserted soul

To the chief Musician, A Psalm
of David.

13 How long wilt thou forget me, O LORD? for ever? how long wilt thou hide thy face from me? ²How long shall I take counsel in my soul, *having* sorrow in my heart daily? how long shall mine enemy be exalted over me? ³Consider *and* hear me, O LORD my God: lighten mine eyes, lest I sleep the *sleep of* death; ⁴Lest mine enemy say, I have prevailed against him; *and* those that trouble me rejoice when I am moved. ⁵But I have trusted in thy mercy; my heart shall rejoice in thy salvation. ⁶I will sing unto the LORD, because he hath dealt bountifully with me.

The fate of the fool

To the chief Musician, *A Psalm*
of David.

14 The fool hath said in his heart, *There is* no God. They are corrupt, they have done abominable works, *there is* none that doeth good. ²The LORD looked down from heaven upon the children of men, to see if there were *any* that did understand, *and* seek God. ³They are all gone aside, they are *all* together become filthy: *there is* none that doeth good, no, not one. ⁴Have all the workers of iniquity no knowledge? who eat up my people *as* they eat bread, *and* call not upon the LORD. ⁵There were they in great fear: for God *is* in the generation of the righteous. ⁶You have shamed the counsel of the poor, because the LORD *is* his refuge. [Ps. 9:9]

7 O that the salvation of Israel *were* come out of Zion! when the LORD bringeth back the captivity of his people, Jacob shall rejoice, *and* Israel shall be glad. [Ps. 53:6; Job 42:10]

The happiness of the holy

A Psalm of David.

15 LORD, who shall abide in thy tabernacle? who shall dwell in thy holy hill? ²He that walketh uprightly, and worketh righteousness, and speaketh the truth in his heart. ³*He that* backbiteth not with his tongue, nor doeth evil to his neighbour, nor taketh up a reproach against his neighbour. ⁴In whose eyes a vile *person* is contemned; but he honoureth them that fear the LORD. *He that* sweareth to *his own* hurt, and changeth not. ⁵*He that* putteth not out his money to usury, nor taketh reward against the innocent. He that doeth these *things* shall never be moved. [2 Pet. 1:10]

Joy in God's presence

Michtam of David.

16 Preserve me, O God: for in thee do I put my trust. ²O my soul, thou hast said unto the LORD, Thou art my Lord: my goodness extendeth not to thee; ³But to the saints that are in the earth, and to the excellent, in whom is all my delight. ⁴Their sorrows shall be multiplied that hasten after another god: their drink offerings of blood will I not offer, nor take up their names into my lips. ⁵The LORD is the portion of mine inheritance and of my cup: thou maintainest my lot. ⁶The lines are fallen unto me in pleasant places; yea, I have a goodly heritage. ⁷I will bless the LORD, who hath given me counsel: my reins also instruct me in the night seasons. ⁸I have set the LORD always before me: because he is at my right hand, I shall not be moved. ⁹Therefore my heart is glad, and my glory rejoiceth: my flesh also shall rest in hope. ¹⁰For thou wilt not leave my soul in hell; neither wilt thou suffer thine Holy One to see corruption. ¹¹Thou wilt shew me the path of life: in thy presence is fulness of joy; at thy right hand there are pleasures for evermore. [Mat. 7:14]

Deliverance from the wicked

A Prayer of David.

17 Hear the right, O LORD, attend unto my cry, give ear unto my prayer, that goeth not out of feigned lips. ²Let my sentence come forth from thy presence; let thine eyes behold the things that are equal. ³Thou hast proved mine heart; thou hast visited me in the night; thou hast tried me, and shalt find nothing; I am purposed that my mouth shall not transgress. ⁴Concerning the works of men, by the word of thy lips I have kept me from the paths of the destroyer. ⁵Hold up my goings in thy paths, that my footsteps slip not. ⁶I have called upon thee, for thou wilt hear me, O God: incline thine ear unto me, and hear my speech. ⁷Shew thy marvellous lovingkindness, O thou that savest by thy right hand them which put their trust in thee from those that rise up against them. ⁸Keep me as the apple of the eye, hide me under the shadow of thy wings, ⁹From the wicked that oppress me, from my deadly enemies, who compass me about. ¹⁰They are inclosed in their own fat: with their mouth they speak proudly. ¹¹They have now compassed us in our steps: they set their eyes bowing down to the earth; ¹²Like as a lion that is greedy of his prey, and as it were a young lion lurking in secret places. ¹³Arise, O LORD, disappoint him, cast him down: deliver my soul from the wicked, which is thy sword: ¹⁴From men which are thy hand, O LORD, from men of the world, which have their portion in this life, and whose belly thou fillest with thy hid treasure: they are full of children, and leave the rest of their substance to their babes. ¹⁵As for me, I will behold thy face in righteousness: I shall be satisfied, when I awake, with thy likeness. [1 John 3:2; Ps. 4:6,7; 16:11]

Calling upon God in distress

To the chief Musician, *A Psalm* of David the servant of the LORD, who spake unto the LORD the words of this song in the day *that* the LORD delivered him from the hand of all his enemies, and from the hand of Saul: And he said,

18 I will love thee, O LORD, my strength. ²The LORD *is* my rock, and my fortress, and my deliverer; my God, my strength, in whom I will trust; my buckler, and the horn of my salvation, *and* my high tower. ³I will call upon the LORD, who is *worthy* to be praised: so shall I be saved from mine enemies. ⁴The sorrows of death compassed me, and the floods of ungodly men made me afraid. ⁵The sorrows of hell compassed me about: the snares of death prevented me. ⁶In my distress I called upon the LORD, and cried unto my God: he heard my voice out of his temple, and my cry came before him, *even* into his ears. ⁷Then the earth shook and trembled; the foundations also of the hills moved and were shaken, because he was wroth. ⁸There went up a smoke out of his nostrils, and fire out of his mouth devoured: coals were kindled by it. ⁹He bowed the heavens also, and came down: and darkness *was* under his feet. ¹⁰And he rode upon a cherub, and did fly: yea, he did fly upon the wings of the wind. ¹¹He made darkness his secret place; his pavilion round about him *were* dark waters *and* thick clouds of the skies. ¹²At the brightness *that was* before him his thick clouds passed, hail-*stones* and coals of fire. ¹³The LORD also thundered in the heavens, and the Highest gave his voice; hail-*stones* and coals of fire. ¹⁴Yea, he sent out his arrows, and scattered them; and he shot out lightnings, and discomfited them. ¹⁵Then the channels of waters were seen, and the foundations of the world were discovered at thy rebuke, O LORD, at the blast of the breath of thy nostrils. ¹⁶He sent from above, he took me, he drew me out of many waters. ¹⁷He delivered me from my strong enemy, and from them which hated me: for they were too strong for me. ¹⁸They prevented me in the day of my calamity: but the LORD was my stay. ¹⁹He brought me forth also into a large place; he delivered me, because he delighted in me. ²⁰The LORD rewarded me according to my righteousness; according to the cleanness of my hands hath he recompensed me. ²¹For I have kept the ways of the LORD, and have not wickedly departed from my God. ²²For all his judgments *were* before me, and I did not put away his statutes from me. ²³I was also upright before him, and I kept myself from mine iniquity. ²⁴Therefore hath the LORD recompensed me according to my righteousness, according to the cleanness of my hands in his eyesight. ²⁵With the merciful thou wilt shew thyself merciful; with an upright man thou wilt shew thyself upright; ²⁶With the pure thou wilt shew thyself pure; and with the froward thou wilt shew thyself froward. ²⁷For thou wilt save the afflicted people; but wilt bring down high looks. 28For thou wilt light my candle: the LORD my God will enlighten my darkness. 29For by thee I have run through a troop; and by my God have I leaped over a wall. 30As for God, his way is perfect: the word of the LORD is tried: he is a buckler to all those that trust in him. 31For who is God save the LORD? or who is a rock save our God? 32It is God that girdeth me with strength, and maketh my way perfect. 33He maketh my feet like hinds' feet, and setteth me upon my high places. 34He teacheth my hands to war, so that a bow of steel is broken by mine arms. 35Thou hast also given me the shield of thy salvation: and thy right hand hath holden me up, and thy gentleness hath made me great. 36Thou hast enlarged my steps under me, that my feet did not slip. 37I have pursued mine enemies, and overtaken them: neither did I turn again till they were consumed. 38I have wounded them that they were not able to rise: they are fallen under my feet. 39For thou hast girded me with strength unto the battle: thou hast subdued under me those that rose up against me. 40Thou hast also given me the necks of mine enemies; that I might destroy them that hate me. 41They cried, but there was none to save them: even unto the LORD, but he answered them not. 42Then did I beat them small as the dust before the wind: I did cast them out as the dirt in the streets. 43Thou hast delivered me from the strivings of the people; and thou hast made me the head of the heathen: a people whom I have

not known shall serve me. 44As soon as they hear of me, they shall obey me: the strangers shall submit themselves unto me. 45The strangers shall fade away, and be afraid out of their close places. 46The LORD liveth; and blessed be my rock; and let the God of my salvation be exalted. 47It is God that avengeth me, and subdueth my people under me. 48He delivereth me from mine enemies: yea, thou liftest me up above those that rise up against me: thou hast delivered me from the violent man. 49Therefore will I give thanks unto thee, O LORD, among the heathen, and sing praises unto thy name. 50Great deliverance giveth he to his king; and sheweth mercy to his anointed, to David, and to his seed for evermore. [Ps. 144:10]

The works and word of God

To the chief Musician, A Psalm of David.

19 The heavens declare the glory of God; and the firmament sheweth his handywork. 2Day unto day uttereth speech, and night unto night sheweth knowledge. 3There is no speech nor language, where their voice is not heard. 4Their line is gone out through all the earth, and their words to the end of the world. In them hath he set a tabernacle for the sun, 5Which is as a bridegroom coming out of his chamber, and rejoiceth as a strong man to run a race. 6His going forth is from the end of the heaven, and his circuit unto the ends of it: and there is nothing hid from the heat thereof.

7 The law of the LORD *is* perfect, converting the soul: the testimony of the LORD *is* sure, making wise the simple. 8 The statutes of the LORD *are* right, rejoicing the heart: the commandment of the LORD *is* pure, enlightening the eyes. 9 The fear of the LORD *is* clean, enduring for ever: the judgments of the LORD *are* true *and* righteous altogether. 10 More to be desired *are they* than gold, yea, than much fine gold: sweeter also than honey and the honeycomb. 11 Moreover by them *is* thy servant warned: *and* in keeping of them *there is* great reward. 12 Who can understand *his* errors? cleanse thou me from secret *faults.* 13 Keep back thy servant also from presumptuous *sins;* let them not have dominion over me: then shall I be upright, and I shall be innocent from *the* great transgression. 14 Let the words of my mouth, and the meditation of my heart, be acceptable in thy sight, O LORD, my strength, and my redeemer. [Is. 47:4]

A prayer for the king

To the chief Musician, A Psalm of David.

20 The LORD hear thee in the day of trouble; the name of the God of Jacob defend thee; 2 Send thee help from the sanctuary, and strengthen thee out of Zion; 3 Remember all thy offerings, and accept thy burnt sacrifice. Selah. 4 Grant thee according to thine own heart, and fulfil all thy counsel. 5 We will rejoice in thy salvation, and in the name of our God we will set up *our* banners: the LORD fulfil all thy petitions. 6 Now

know I that the LORD saveth his anointed; he will hear him from his holy heaven with the saving strength of his right hand. 7 Some *trust* in chariots, and some in horses: but we will remember the name of the LORD our God. 8 They are brought down and fallen: but we are risen, and stand upright. 9 Save, LORD: let the king hear us when we call.

Splendor and success of the king

To the chief Musician, A Psalm of David.

21 The king shall joy in thy strength, O LORD; and in thy salvation how greatly shall he rejoice! 2 Thou hast given him his heart's desire, and hast not withholden the request of his lips. Selah. 3 For thou preventest him *with* the blessings of goodness: thou settest a crown of pure gold on his head. 4 He asked life of thee, *and* thou gavest *it* him, *even* length of days for ever and ever. 5 His glory *is* great in thy salvation: honour and majesty hast thou laid upon him. 6 For thou hast made him most blessed for ever: thou hast made him exceeding glad with thy countenance. 7 For the king trusteth in the LORD, and through the mercy of the most High he shall not be moved. 8 Thine hand shall find out all thine enemies: thy right hand shall find out those that hate thee. 9 Thou shalt make them as a fiery oven in the time of thine anger: the LORD shall swallow them up in his wrath, and the fire shall devour them. 10 Their fruit shalt thou destroy from the earth, and their seed

from among the children of men. 11For they intended evil against thee: they imagined a mischievous device, *which* they are not able *to perform.* 12Therefore shalt thou make them turn their back, *when* thou shalt make ready *thine arrows* upon thy strings against the face of them. 13Be thou exalted, LORD, in thine own strength: *so* will we sing and praise thy power.

A cry of anguish

To the chief Musician upon Aijeleth Shahar, A Psalm of David.

22 My God, my God, why hast thou forsaken me? *why art thou so* far from helping me, *and from* the words of my roaring? 2O my God, I cry in the daytime, but thou hearest not; and in the night season, and am not silent. 3But thou *art* holy, O thou that inhabitest the praises of Israel. 4Our fathers trusted in thee: they trusted, and thou didst deliver them. 5They cried unto thee, and were delivered: they trusted in thee, and were not confounded. 6But I *am* a worm, and no man; a reproach of men, and despised of the people. 7All they that see me laugh me to scorn: they shoot out the lip, they shake the head, *saying,* 8He trusted on the LORD *that* he would deliver him: let him deliver him, seeing he delighted in him. 9But thou *art* he that took me out of the womb: thou didst make me hope *when I was* upon my mother's breasts. 10I was cast upon thee from the womb: thou *art* my God from my mother's belly. 11Be not far from me; for trouble *is* near;

for *there is* none to help. 12Many bulls have compassed me: strong *bulls* of Bashan have beset me round. 13They gaped upon me *with* their mouths, *as* a ravening and a roaring lion. 14I am poured out like water, and all my bones are out of joint: my heart is like wax; it is melted in the midst of my bowels. 15My strength is dried up like a potsherd; and my tongue cleaveth *to* my jaws; and thou hast brought me into the dust of death. 16For dogs have compassed me: the assembly of the wicked have inclosed me: they pierced my hands and my feet. 17I may tell all my bones: they look *and* stare upon me. 18They part my garments among them, and cast lots upon my vesture. 19But be not thou far *from me,* O LORD: O my strength, haste thee to help me. 20Deliver my soul from the sword; my darling from the power of the dog. 21Save me from the lion's mouth: for thou hast heard me from the horns of the unicorns. [2 Tim. 4:17; Is. 34:7]

A song of praise

22 I will declare thy name unto my brethren: in the midst of the congregation will I praise thee. 23Ye that fear the LORD, praise him; all ye the seed of Jacob, glorify him; and fear him, all ye the seed of Israel. 24For he hath not despised nor abhorred the affliction of the afflicted; neither hath he hid his face from him; but when he cried unto him, he heard. 25My praise *shall be* of thee in the great congregation: I will pay my vows before them that fear him. 26The meek shall eat and

be satisfied: they shall praise the LORD that seek him: your heart shall live for ever. 27 All the ends of the world shall remember and turn unto the LORD: and all the kindreds of the nations shall worship before thee. 28 For the kingdom *is* the LORD'S: and *he is* the governor among the nations. 29 All *they that be* fat upon earth shall eat and worship: all they that go down to the dust shall bow before him: and none can keep alive his own soul. 30 A seed shall serve him; it shall be accounted to the Lord for a generation. 31 They shall come, and shall declare his righteousness unto a people that *shall be* born, that he hath done *this*. [Ps. 78:6]

The shepherd psalm

A *Psalm* of David.

23 The LORD *is* my shepherd; I shall not want. 2 He maketh me to lie down in green pastures: he leadeth me beside the still waters. 3 He restoreth my soul: he leadeth me in the paths of righteousness for his name's sake. 4 Yea, though I walk through the valley of the shadow of death, I will fear no evil: for thou *art* with me; thy rod and thy staff they comfort me. 5 Thou preparest a table before me in the presence of mine enemies: thou anointest my head with oil; my cup runneth over. 6 Surely goodness and mercy shall follow me all the days of my life: and I will dwell in the house of the LORD for ever.

Song to the King of glory

A Psalm of David.

24 The earth *is* the LORD'S, and the fulness thereof; the world, and they that dwell therein. 2 For he hath founded it upon the seas, and established it upon the floods. 3 Who shall ascend into the hill of the LORD? and who shall stand in his holy place? 4 He that hath clean hands, and a pure heart; who hath not lift up his soul unto vanity, nor sworn deceitfully. 5 He shall receive the blessing from the LORD, and righteousness from the God of his salvation. 6 This *is* the generation of them that seek him, that seek thy face, O Jacob. Selah. [Ps. 27:8]

7 Lift up your heads, O ye gates; and be ye lift up, ye everlasting doors; and the King of glory shall come in. 8 Who *is* this King of glory? the LORD strong and mighty, the LORD mighty *in* battle. 9 Lift up your heads, O ye gates; even lift *them* up, ye everlasting doors; and the King of glory shall come in. 10 Who is this King of glory? The LORD of hosts, he *is* the King of glory. Selah.

Prayer for guidance and protection

A *Psalm* of David.

25 Unto thee, O LORD, do I lift up my soul. 2 O my God, I trust in thee: let me not be ashamed, let not mine enemies triumph over me. 3 Yea, let none that wait on thee be ashamed: let them be ashamed which transgress without cause. 4 Shew me thy ways, O LORD; teach me thy paths. 5 Lead me in thy truth, and teach me: for thou *art* the God of my salvation; on thee do I wait all the day. ⁶Remember, O LORD, thy tender mercies and thy lovingkindnesses; for they *have been* ever of old. ⁷Remember not the sins of my youth, nor my transgressions: according to thy mercy remember thou me for thy goodness' sake, O LORD. ⁸Good and upright *is* the LORD: therefore will he teach sinners in the way. ⁹The meek will he guide in judgment: and the meek will he teach his way. ¹⁰All the paths of the LORD *are* mercy and truth unto such as keep his covenant and his testimonies. ¹¹For thy name's sake, O LORD, pardon mine iniquity; for it *is* great. ¹²What man *is* he that feareth the LORD? him shall he teach in the way *that* he shall choose. ¹³His soul shall dwell at ease; and his seed shall inherit the earth. ¹⁴The secret of the LORD *is* with them that fear him; and he will shew them his covenant. ¹⁵Mine eyes *are* ever towards the LORD; for he shall pluck my feet out of the net. ¹⁶Turn thee unto me, and have mercy upon me; for I *am* desolate and afflicted. ¹⁷The troubles of my heart are enlarged: O bring thou me out of my distresses. ¹⁸Look upon mine affliction and my pain; and forgive all my sins. ¹⁹Consider mine enemies; for they are many; and they hate me *with* cruel hatred. ²⁰O keep my soul, and deliver me: let me not be ashamed; for I put my trust in thee. ²¹Let integrity and uprightness preserve me; for I wait on thee. ²²Redeem Israel, O God, out of all his troubles. [Ps. 130:8]

The basis of judgment
A Psalm of David.

26 Judge me, O LORD; for I have walked in mine integrity: I have trusted also in the LORD; *therefore* I shall not slide. ²Examine me, O LORD, and prove me; try my reins and my heart. ³For thy lovingkindness *is* before mine eyes: and I have walked in thy truth. ⁴I have not sat with vain persons, neither will I go in with dissemblers. ⁵I have hated the congregation of evildoers; and will not sit with the wicked. ⁶I will wash mine hands in innocency: so will I compass thine altar, O LORD: ⁷That *I* may publish with the voice of thanksgiving, and tell of all thy wondrous works. ⁸LORD, I have loved the habitation of thy house, and the place where thine honour dwelleth. ⁹Gather not my soul with sinners, nor my life with bloody men: ¹⁰In whose hands *is* mischief, and their right hand is full *of* bribes. ¹¹But *as for* me, I will walk in mine integrity: redeem me, and be merciful unto me. ¹²My foot standeth in an even place: in the congregations will I bless the LORD. [Ps. 40:2; Ps. 27:11; Ps. 111:1]

David's song of confidence
A Psalm of David.

27 The LORD *is* my light and my salvation; whom shall I fear? the LORD *is* the strength of my life; of whom shall I be afraid? ²When the wicked, *even* mine enemies and my foes, came upon me to eat up my flesh, they stumbled and fell. ³Though a host should encamp against me, my heart shall not fear: though war should rise against me, in this *will* I *be* confident. ⁴One *thing* have I desired of the LORD, that will I seek after; that I may dwell in the house of the LORD all the days of my life, to behold the beauty of the LORD, and to inquire in his temple. ⁵For in the time of trouble he shall hide me in his pavilion: in the secret of his tabernacle shall he hide me; he shall set me up upon a rock. ⁶And now shall mine head be lifted up above mine enemies round about me: therefore will I offer in his tabernacle sacrifices of joy; I will sing, yea, I will sing *praises* unto the LORD. [Ps. 3:3]

7 Hear, O LORD, *when* I cry *with* my voice: have mercy also upon me, and answer me. ⁸*When thou saidst,* Seek ye my face; my heart said unto thee, Thy face, LORD, will I seek. ⁹Hide not thy face *far* from me; put not thy servant away in anger: thou hast been my help; leave me not, neither forsake me, O God of my salvation. ¹⁰When my father and my mother forsake me, then the LORD will take me up. ¹¹Teach me thy way, O LORD, and lead me in a plain path, because of mine enemies. ¹²Deliver me not over unto the will of mine enemies: for false witnesses are risen up against me, and such as breathe out cruelty. ¹³*I had fainted,* unless I had believed to see the goodness of the LORD in the land of the living. ¹⁴Wait on the LORD: be of good courage, and he shall strengthen thine heart: wait, I say, on the LORD.

A prayer for help

A Psalm of David.

28 Unto thee will I cry, O LORD, my rock; be not silent to me: lest, *if* thou be silent to me, I become like them that go down into the pit. ²Hear the voice of my supplications, when I cry unto thee, when I lift up my hands toward thy holy oracle. ³Draw me not away with the wicked, and with the workers of iniquity, which speak peace to their neighbours, but mischief *is* in their hearts. ⁴Give them according to their deeds, and according to the wickedness of their endeavours: give them after the work of their hands; render to them their desert. ⁵Because they regard not the works of the LORD, nor the operation of his hands, he shall destroy them, and not build them up. [Is. 5:12]

6 Blessed *be* the LORD, because he hath heard the voice of my supplications. ⁷The LORD *is* my strength and my shield; my heart trusted in him, and I am helped: therefore my heart greatly rejoiceth; and with my song will I praise him. ⁸The LORD *is* their strength, and he *is* the saving strength of his anointed. ⁹Save thy people, and bless thine inheritance: feed them also, and lift them up for ever. [Deut. 9:29; Ezra 1:4]

The LORD of the thunderstorm

A Psalm of David.

29 Give unto the LORD, O ye mighty, give unto the LORD glory and strength. ²Give unto the LORD the glory due unto his name; worship the LORD in the beauty of holiness. ³The voice of the LORD *is* upon the waters: the God of glory thundereth: the LORD *is* upon many waters. ⁴The voice of the LORD *is* powerful; the voice of the LORD *is* full of majesty. ⁵The voice of the LORD breaketh the cedars; yea, the LORD breaketh the cedars of Lebanon. ⁶He maketh them also to skip like a calf; Lebanon and Sirion like a young unicorn. ⁷The voice of the LORD divideth the flames of fire. ⁸The voice of the LORD shaketh the wilderness; the LORD shaketh the wilderness of Kadesh. ⁹The voice of the LORD maketh the hinds to calve, and discovereth the forests: and in his temple doth every one speak of *his* glory. ¹⁰The LORD sitteth upon the flood; yea, the LORD sitteth King for ever. ¹¹The LORD will give strength unto his people; the LORD will bless his people with peace. [Ps. 28:8]

The LORD my helper

A Psalm *and* Song *at* the dedication of the house of David.

30 I will extol thee, O LORD; for thou hast lifted me up, and hast not made my foes to rejoice over me. ²O LORD my God, I cried unto thee, and thou hast healed me. ³O LORD, thou hast brought up my soul from the grave: thou hast kept me alive, that I should not go down *to* the pit. ⁴Sing unto the LORD, O ye saints of his, and give thanks at the remembrance of his holiness. ⁵For his anger *endureth but* a moment; in his favour *is* life: weeping may endure for a night, but joy *cometh* in the morning. ⁶And in my prosperity I said, I shall never be moved. ⁷LORD, by thy favour thou hast made my mountain to stand strong: thou didst hide thy face, *and* I was troubled. ⁸I cried to thee, O LORD; and unto the LORD I made supplication. ⁹What profit *is there* in my blood, when I go down to the pit? Shall the dust praise thee? shall it declare thy truth? ¹⁰Hear, O LORD, and have mercy upon me: LORD, be thou my helper. ¹¹Thou hast turned for me my mourning into dancing: thou hast put off my sackcloth, and girded me *with* gladness; ¹²To the end that *my* glory may sing *praise* to thee, and not be silent. O LORD my God, I will give thanks unto thee for ever.

My times are in thy hand

To the chief Musician, A Psalm of David.

31 In thee, O LORD, do I put my trust; let me never be ashamed: deliver me in thy righteousness. ²Bow down thine ear to me; deliver me speedily: be thou my strong rock, for a house of defence to save me. ³For thou *art* my rock and my fortress; therefore for thy name's sake lead me, and guide me. ⁴Pull me out of the net that they have laid privily for me: for thou *art* my strength. ⁵Into thine hand I commit my spirit: thou hast redeemed me, O LORD God of truth. ⁶I have hated them that regard lying vanities: but I trust in the LORD. ⁷I will be glad and rejoice in thy mercy: for thou hast considered my trouble; thou hast known my soul in adversities; 8And hast not shut me up into the hand of the enemy: thou hast set my feet in a large room. 9Have mercy upon me, O LORD, for I am in trouble: mine eye is consumed with grief, *yea*, my soul and my belly. 10For my life is spent with grief, and my years with sighing: my strength faileth because of mine iniquity, and my bones are consumed. 11I was a reproach among all mine enemies, but especially among my neighbours, and a fear to mine acquaintance: they that did see me without fled from me. 12I am forgotten as a dead man out of mind: I am like a broken vessel. 13For I have heard the slander of many: fear *was* on every side: while they took counsel together against me, they devised to take away my life. 14But I trusted in thee, O LORD: I said, Thou *art* my God. 15My times *are* in thy hand: deliver me from the hand of mine enemies, and from them that persecute me. 16Make thy face to shine upon thy servant: save me for thy mercy's sake. 17Let me not be ashamed, O LORD; for I have called upon thee: let the wicked be ashamed, *and* let them be silent in the grave. 18Let the lying lips be put to silence; which speak grievous things proudly and contemptuously against the righteous. 19O how great *is* thy goodness, which thou hast laid up for them that fear thee; *which* thou hast wrought for them that trust in thee before the sons of men! 20Thou shalt hide them in the secret of thy presence from the pride of man: thou shalt keep them secretly in a pavilion from the strife of tongues. 21Blessed *be* the LORD: for he hath shewed me his marvellous kindness in a strong city. 22For I said in my haste, I am cut off from before thine eyes: nevertheless thou heardest the voice of my supplications when I cried unto thee. 23O love the LORD, all ye his saints: *for* the LORD preserveth the faithful, and plentifully rewardeth the proud doer. 24Be of good courage, and he shall strengthen your heart, all ye that hope in the LORD. [Ps. 27:14]

A prayer during distress

A Psalm of David, Maschil.

32 Blessed *is* he whose transgression *is* forgiven, whose sin *is* covered. 2Blessed *is* the man unto whom the LORD imputeth not iniquity, and in whose spirit *there is* no guile. 3When I kept silence, my bones waxed old through my roaring all the day long. 4For day and night thy hand was heavy upon me: my moisture is turned into the drought of summer. Selah. 5I acknowledged my sin unto thee, and mine iniquity have I not hid. I said, I will confess my transgressions unto the LORD; and thou forgavest the iniquity of my sin. Selah. 6For this shall every one *that is* godly pray unto thee in a time when thou mayest be found: surely in the floods of great waters they shall not come nigh unto him. 7Thou *art* my hiding place; thou shalt preserve me from trouble; thou shalt compass me about *with* songs of deliverance. Selah. 8I will instruct thee and teach thee in the way which thou shalt go: I will guide thee with mine eye. 9Be ye not as the horse, *or* as the mule, *which have* no understanding: whose mouth must be held in with bit and bridle, lest *they* come near unto thee. 10Many sorrows *shall be* to the wicked: but he that trusteth in the LORD, mercy shall compass him about. [Rom. 2:9; Prov. 16:20]

11 Be glad in the LORD, and rejoice, ye righteous: and shout for joy, all *ye that are* upright in heart. [Ps. 64:10]

The LORD provides and delivers

33 Rejoice in the LORD, O ye righteous: *for* praise is comely for the upright. 2Praise the LORD with harp: sing unto him with the psaltery *and* an instrument of ten strings. 3Sing unto him a new song; play skilfully with a loud noise. 4For the word of the LORD *is* right; and all his works *are done* in truth. 5He loveth righteousness and judgment: the earth is full *of* the goodness of the LORD. 6By the word of the LORD were the heavens made; and all the host of them by the breath of his mouth. 7He gathereth the waters of the sea together as a heap: he layeth up the depth in storehouses. 8Let all the earth fear the LORD: let all the inhabitants of the world stand in awe of him. 9For he spake, and it was *done;* he commanded, and it stood fast. 10The LORD bringeth the counsel of the heathen to nought: he maketh the devices of the people of none effect. 11The counsel of the LORD standeth for ever, the thoughts of his heart to all generations. 12Blessed *is* the nation whose God *is* the LORD; *and* the people *whom* he hath chosen for his own inheritance. 13The LORD looketh from heaven; he beholdeth all the sons of men. 14From the place of his habitation he looketh upon all the inhabitants of the earth. 15He fashioneth their hearts alike; he considereth all their works. 16There is no king saved by the multitude of a host: a mighty *man* is not delivered by much strength. 17A horse *is* a vain thing for safety: neither shall he deliver *any* by his great strength. 18Behold, the eye of the LORD *is* upon them that fear him, upon them that hope in his mercy; 19To deliver their soul from death, and to keep them alive in famine. 20Our soul waiteth for the LORD: he *is* our help and our shield. 21For our heart shall rejoice in him, because we have trusted in his holy name. 22Let thy mercy, O LORD, be upon us, according as we hope in thee.

A psalm of praise and trust

A *Psalm* of David, when he changed his behaviour before Abimelech; who drove him away, and he departed.

34 I will bless the LORD at all times: his praise *shall* continually *be* in my mouth. 2My soul shall make her boast in the LORD: the humble shall hear *thereof,* and be glad. 3O magnify the LORD with me, and let us exalt his name together. 4I sought the LORD, and he heard me, and delivered me from all my fears. 5They looked unto him, and were lightened: and their faces were not ashamed. 6This poor *man* cried, and the LORD heard *him*, and saved him out of all his troubles. 7The angel of the LORD encampeth round about them that fear him, and delivereth them. 8O taste and see that the LORD *is* good: blessed *is* the man *that* trusteth in him. 9O fear the LORD, ye his saints: for *there is* no want to them that fear him. 10The young lions do lack, and suffer hunger: but they that seek the LORD shall not want any good *thing.* 11Come, ye children, hearken unto me: I will teach you the fear of the LORD. 12What man *is he that* desireth life, *and* loveth *many* days, that *he* may see good? 13Keep thy tongue from evil, and thy lips from speaking guile. 14Depart from evil, and do good; seek peace, and pursue it. 15The eyes of the LORD *are* upon the righteous, and his ears *are open* unto their cry. 16The face of the LORD *is* against them that do evil, to cut off the remembrance of them from the earth. 17*The righteous* cry, and the LORD heareth, and delivereth them out of all their troubles. 18The LORD *is* nigh unto them that are of a broken heart; and saveth such as be of a contrite spirit. 19Many *are* the afflictions of the righteous: but the LORD delivereth him out of them all. 20He keepeth all his bones: not one of them is broken. 21Evil shall slay the wicked: and they that hate the righteous shall be desolate. 22The LORD redeemeth the soul of his servants: and none of them that trust in him shall be desolate. [1 Ki. 1:29; Ps. 71:23]

A plea for judgment

A Psalm of David.

35 Plead *my cause,* O LORD, with them that strive with me: fight against them that fight against me. 2Take hold of shield and buckler, and stand up for mine help. 3Draw out also the spear, and stop *the way* against them that persecute me: say unto my soul, I *am* thy salvation. 4Let them be confounded and put to shame that seek after my soul: let them be turned back and brought to confusion that devise my hurt. 5Let them be as chaff before the wind: and let the angel of the LORD chase *them.* 6Let their way be dark and slippery: and let the angel of the LORD persecute them. 7For without cause have they hid for me their net *in* a pit, *which* without cause they have digged for my soul. 8Let destruction come upon him at unawares; and let his net that he hath hid catch himself: into that *very* destruction let him fall. 9And my soul shall be joyful in the LORD: it shall rejoice in his salvation. 10All my bones shall say, LORD, who *is* like unto thee, which deliverest the poor from him that is too strong for him, yea, the poor and the needy from him that spoileth him? 11False witnesses did rise up; they laid to my charge *things* that I knew not. 12They rewarded me evil for good *to* the spoiling of my soul. 13But *as for* me, when they were sick, my clothing *was* sackcloth: I humbled my soul with fasting; and my prayer returned into mine own bosom. 14I behaved myself as though *he had been* my friend *or* brother: I bowed down heavily, as one that mourneth for his mother. 15But in mine adversity they rejoiced, and gathered themselves together: *yea,* the abjects gathered themselves together against me, and I knew *it* not; they did tear *me,* and ceased not: 16With hypocritical mockers in feasts, *they* gnashed upon me *with* their teeth. 17Lord, how long wilt thou look on? rescue my soul from their destructions, my darling from the lions. 18I will give thee thanks in the great congregation: I will praise thee among much people. 19Let not them that are mine enemies wrongfully rejoice over me: *neither* let them wink *with* the eye that hate me without a cause. 20For they speak not peace: but they devise deceitful matters against *them that are* quiet in the land. 21Yea, they opened their mouth wide against me, *and* said, Aha, aha, our eye hath seen *it.* 22*This* thou hast seen, O LORD: keep not silence: O Lord, be not far from me. 23Stir up thyself, and awake to my judgment, *even* unto my cause, my God and my Lord. 24Judge me, O LORD my God, according to thy righteousness; and let them not rejoice over me. 25Let them not say in their hearts, Ah, so would we have it: let them not say, We have swallowed him up. 26Let them be ashamed and brought to confusion together that rejoice at mine hurt: let them be clothed with shame and dishonour that magnify *themselves* against me. 27Let them shout for joy, and be glad, that favour my righteous cause: yea, let them say continually, Let the LORD be magnified, which hath pleasure in the prosperity of his servant. 28And my tongue shall speak of thy righteousness *and* of thy praise all the day long.

Wickedness confronts God's love

To the chief Musician, *A Psalm* of David the servant of the LORD.

36 The transgression of the wicked saith within my heart, *that there is* no fear of God before his eyes. 2For he flattereth himself in his own eyes, until his iniquity be found to be hateful. 3The words of his mouth *are* iniquity and deceit: he hath left off to be wise, *and* to do good. 4He deviseth mischief upon his bed; he setteth himself in a way *that is* not good; he abhorreth not evil. 5Thy mercy, O LORD, *is* in the heavens; *and* thy faithfulness *reacheth* unto the clouds. 6Thy righteousness *is* like the great mountains; thy judgments *are* a great deep: O LORD, thou preservest man and beast. 7How excellent *is* thy lovingkindness, O God! therefore the children of men put their trust under the shadow of thy wings. 8They shall be abundantly satisfied with the fatness of thy house; and thou shalt make them drink *of* the river of thy pleasures. 9For with thee *is* the fountain of life: in thy light shall we see light. 10O continue thy lovingkindness unto them that know thee; and thy righteousness to the upright in heart. 11Let not the foot of pride come against me, and let not the hand of the wicked remove me. 12There are the workers of iniquity fallen: they are cast down, and shall not be able to rise.

Blessings to the righteous

A Psalm of David.

37 Fret not thyself because of evildoers, neither be thou envious against the workers of iniquity. 2For they shall soon be cut down like the grass, and wither as the green herb. [Ps. 90:5,6]

3 Trust in the LORD, and do good; *so* shalt thou dwell in the land, and verily thou shalt be fed. 4Delight thyself also in the LORD; and he shall give thee the desires of thine heart. [Is. 58:14]

5 Commit thy way unto the LORD; trust also in him; and he shall bring *it* to pass. 6And he shall bring forth thy righteousness as the light, and thy judgment as the noonday. [Job 11:17]

7 Rest in the LORD, and wait patiently for him: fret not thyself because of him who prospereth *in* his way, because of the man who bringeth wicked devices to pass. [Lam. 3:26]

8 Cease from anger, and forsake wrath: fret not thyself in any wise to do evil. 9For evildoers shall be cut off: but those that wait upon the LORD, they shall inherit the earth. 10For yet a little while, and the wicked *shall* not *be*: yea, thou shalt diligently consider his place, and it *shall* not *be*. 11But the meek shall inherit the earth; and shall delight themselves in the abundance of peace. [Mat. 5:5]

12 The wicked plotteth against the just, and gnasheth upon him with his teeth. 13The Lord shall laugh at him: for he seeth that his day is coming. [Ps. 2:4; 1 Sam. 26:10]

14 The wicked have drawn out the sword, and have bent their bow, to cast down the poor and needy, *and* to slay such as be of upright conversation. 15Their sword shall enter into their own heart, and their bows shall be broken. [Ps. 9:16]

16 A little that a righteous *man* hath *is* better than the riches of many wicked. 17For the arms of the wicked shall be broken: but the LORD upholdeth the righteous. [Ps. 10:15]

18 The LORD knoweth the days of the upright: and their inheritance shall be for ever. 19They shall not be ashamed in the evil time: and in the days of famine they shall be satisfied. [Ps. 33:19]

20 But the wicked shall perish, and the enemies of the LORD *shall be* as the fat of lambs: they shall consume; into smoke shall they consume *away*. [Ps. 102:3]

21 The wicked borroweth, and payeth not again: but the righteous sheweth mercy, and giveth. 22For such as be blessed of him shall inherit the earth; and they that be cursed of him shall be cut off. [Prov. 3:33]

23 The steps of a *good* man are ordered by the LORD: and he delighteth in his way. 24Though he fall, he shall not be utterly cast down: for the LORD upholdeth *him* with his hand. [Prov. 24:16]

25 I have been young, and *now* am old; yet have I not seen the righteous forsaken, nor his seed

begging bread. 26*He is* ever merciful, and lendeth; and his seed *is* blessed. [Deut. 15:8]

27 Depart from evil, and do good; and dwell for evermore. 28For the LORD loveth judgment, and forsaketh not his saints; they are preserved for ever: but the seed of the wicked shall be cut off. 29The righteous shall inherit the land, and dwell therein for ever. [Prov. 2:21]

30 The mouth of the righteous speaketh wisdom, and his tongue talketh of judgment. 31The law of his God *is* in his heart; none of his steps shall slide. [Deut. 6:6]

32 The wicked watcheth the righteous, and seeketh to slay him. 33The LORD will not leave him in his hand, nor condemn him when he is judged. [2 Pet. 2:9; Ps. 109:31]

34 Wait on the LORD, and keep his way, and he shall exalt thee to inherit the land: when the wicked are cut off, thou shalt see *it*. [Ps. 27:14; Ps. 52:5,6]

35 I have seen the wicked in great power, and spreading himself like a green bay tree. 36Yet he passed away, and lo, he *was* not: yea, I sought him, but he could not be found. [Job 20:5]

37 Mark the perfect *man,* and behold the upright: for the end of *that* man *is* peace. 38But the transgressors shall be destroyed together: the end of the wicked shall be cut off. [Ps. 1:4]

39 But the salvation of the righteous *is* of the LORD: *he is* their strength in the time of trouble. 40And the LORD shall help them, and deliver them: he shall deliver

them from the wicked, and save them, because they trust in him. [Is. 31:5; 1 Chr. 5:20]

The burden of suffering

A Psalm of David, to bring to remembrance.

38 O LORD, rebuke me not in thy wrath: neither chasten me in thy hot displeasure. 2For thine arrows stick fast in me, and thy hand presseth me sore. 3*There is* no soundness in my flesh because of thine anger; neither *is there any* rest in my bones because of my sin. 4For mine iniquities are gone *over* mine head: as a heavy burden they are *too* heavy for me. 5My wounds stink *and* are corrupt because of my foolishness. 6I am troubled; I am bowed down greatly; I go mourning all the day long. 7For my loins are filled *with* a loathsome *disease:* and *there is* no soundness in my flesh. 8I am feeble and sore broken: I have roared by reason of the disquietness of my heart. 9Lord, all my desire *is* before thee; and my groaning is not hid from thee. 10My heart panteth, my strength faileth me: as for the light of mine eyes, it also is gone from me. 11My lovers and my friends stand aloof from my sore; and my kinsmen stand afar off. 12They also that seek after my life lay snares *for me:* and they that seek my hurt speak mischievous things, and imagine deceits all the day long. 13But I, as a deaf *man,* heard not; and *I was* as a dumb *man that* openeth not his mouth. 14Thus I was as a man that heareth not, and in whose mouth *are* no reproofs.

15For in thee, O LORD, do I hope: thou wilt hear, O Lord my God. 16For I said, *Hear me,* lest *otherwise* they should rejoice over me: when my foot slippeth, they magnify *themselves* against me. 17For I *am* ready to halt, and my sorrow *is* continually before me. 18For I will declare mine iniquity; I will be sorry for my sin. 19But mine enemies *are* lively, *and* they are strong: and they that hate me wrongfully are multiplied. 20They also that render evil for good are mine adversaries; because I follow *the thing that* good *is.* 21Forsake me not, O LORD: O my God, be not far from me. 22Make haste to help me, O Lord my salvation.

In time of trouble

To the chief Musician, *even* to Jeduthun, A Psalm of David.

39 I said, I will take heed to my ways, that *I* sin not with my tongue: I will keep my mouth with a bridle, while the wicked *is* before me. 2I was dumb *with* silence, I held my peace, *even* from good; and my sorrow was stirred. 3My heart was hot within me, while I was musing the fire burned: *then* spake I with my tongue,

4 LORD, make me to know mine end, and the measure of my days, what it *is; that* I may know how frail I *am.* 5Behold, thou hast made my days *as* a handbreadth; and mine age *is* as nothing before thee: verily every man at his best state *is* altogether vanity. Selah.

6 Surely every man walketh in a vain shew: surely they are disqui-

eted in vain: he heapeth up *riches,* and knoweth not who shall gather them. 7And now, Lord, what wait I for? my hope *is* in thee. 8Deliver me from all my transgressions: make me not the reproach of the foolish. 9I was dumb, I opened not my mouth; because thou didst *it.* 10Remove thy stroke away from me: I am consumed by the blow of thine hand. 11When thou with rebukes dost correct man for iniquity, thou makest his beauty to consume away like a moth: surely every man *is* vanity. Selah. [Job 13:28]

12 Hear my prayer, O LORD, and give ear unto my cry; hold not thy peace at my tears: for I *am* a stranger with thee, *and* a sojourner, as all my fathers *were.* 13O spare me, that I may recover strength, before I go hence, and be no more. [Job 10:20; Job 14:10]

Delight in the will of the Lord

To the chief Musician, A Psalm of David.

40 I waited patiently for the LORD; and he inclined unto me, and heard my cry. 2He brought me up also out of a horrible pit, out of the miry clay, and set my feet upon a rock, *and* established my goings. 3And he hath put a new song in my mouth, *even* praise unto our God: many shall see *it,* and fear, and shall trust in the LORD. 4Blessed *is that* man that maketh the LORD his trust, and respecteth not the proud, nor such as turn aside to lies. 5Many, O LORD my God, *are* thy wonderful works *which* thou hast done, and thy thoughts *which are* to us-ward: they cannot be reckoned up in order unto thee: *if* I would declare and speak *of them,* they are more than can be numbered. 6Sacrifice and offering thou didst not desire; mine ears hast thou opened: burnt offering and sin offering hast thou not required. 7Then said I, Lo, I come: in the volume of the book *it is* written of me, 8I delight to do thy will, O my God: yea, thy law *is* within my heart. 9I have preached righteousness in the great congregation: lo, I have not refrained my lips, O LORD, thou knowest. 10I have not hid thy righteousness within my heart; I have declared thy faithfulness and thy salvation: I have not concealed thy lovingkindness and thy truth from the great congregation. 11Withhold not thou thy tender mercies from me, O LORD: let thy lovingkindness and thy truth continually preserve me. 12For innumerable evils have compassed me about: mine iniquities have taken hold upon me, so that I am not able to look *up;* they are more than the hairs of mine head: therefore my heart faileth me. 13Be pleased, O LORD, to deliver me: O LORD, make haste to help me. 14Let them be ashamed and confounded together that seek after my soul to destroy it; let them be driven backward and put to shame that wish me evil. 15Let them be desolate for a reward of their shame that say unto me, Aha, aha! 16Let all those that seek thee rejoice and be glad in thee: let such as love thy salvation say continually, The LORD be magnified. 17But I *am* poor and

needy; *yet* the Lord thinketh upon me: thou *art* my help and my deliverer; make no tarrying, O my God. [Ps. 70:5]

Psalm of the compassionate

To the chief Musician, A Psalm of David.

41 Blessed *is* he that considereth the poor: the LORD will deliver him in time of trouble. 2The LORD will preserve him, and keep him alive; *and* he shall be blessed upon the earth: and thou wilt not deliver him unto the will of his enemies. 3The LORD will strengthen him upon the bed of languishing: thou wilt make all his bed in his sickness. 4I said, LORD, be merciful unto me: heal my soul; for I have sinned against thee. 5Mine enemies speak evil of me, When shall he die, and his name perish? 6And if he come to see *me,* he speaketh vanity: his heart gathereth iniquity to itself; *when* he goeth abroad, he telleth *it.* 7All that hate me whisper together against me: against me do they devise my hurt. 8An evil disease, *say they,* cleaveth fast unto him: and *now* that he lieth he shall rise up no more. 9Yea, mine own familiar friend, in whom I trusted, which did eat *of* my bread, hath lift up *his* heel against me. 10But thou, O LORD, be merciful unto me, and raise me up, that I may requite them. 11By this I know that thou favourest me, because mine enemy doth not triumph over me. 12And *as for* me, thou upholdest me in mine integrity, and settest me be-

fore thy face for ever. [Job 36:7; Ps. 34:15]

13 Blessed *be* the LORD God of Israel from everlasting, and to everlasting. Amen, and Amen. [Ps. 106:48]

Yearning for God

To the chief Musician, Maschil, for the sons of Korah.

42 As the hart panteth after the water brooks, so panteth my soul after thee, O God. ²My soul thirsteth for God, for the living God: when shall I come and appear before God? ³My tears have been my meat day and night, while *they* continually say unto me, Where *is* thy God? ⁴When I remember these *things,* I pour out my soul in me: for I had gone with the multitude, I went with them to the house of God, with the voice of joy and praise, *with* a multitude that kept holyday. ⁵Why art thou cast down, O my soul? and *why* art thou disquieted in me? hope thou in God: for I shall yet praise him *for* the help of his countenance. [ver. 11; Lam. 3:24]

6 O my God, my soul is cast down within me: therefore will I remember thee from the land of Jordan, and of the Hermonites, from the hill Mizar. ⁷Deep calleth unto deep at the noise of thy waterspouts: all thy waves and thy billows are gone over me. ⁸Yet the LORD will command his lovingkindness in the daytime, and in the night his song *shall be* with me, *and my* prayer unto the God of my life. ⁹I will say unto God my rock, Why hast thou forgotten me? why

go I mourning because of the oppression of the enemy? ¹⁰*As* with a sword in my bones, mine enemies reproach me; while they say daily unto me, Where *is* thy God? ¹¹Why art thou cast down, O my soul? and why art thou disquieted within me? hope thou in God: for I shall yet praise him, *who is* the health of my countenance, and my God. [Ps. 43:5]

A plea for judgment

43 Judge me, O God, and plead my cause against an ungodly nation: O deliver me from the deceitful and unjust man. ²For thou *art* the God of my strength: why dost thou cast me off? why go I mourning because of the oppression of the enemy? ³O send out thy light and thy truth: let them lead me; let them bring me unto thy holy hill, and to thy tabernacles. ⁴Then will I go unto the altar of God, unto God my exceeding joy: yea, upon the harp will I praise thee, O God my God. ⁵Why art thou cast down, O my soul? and why art thou disquieted within me? hope in God: for I shall yet praise him, *who is* the health of my countenance, and my God. [Ps. 42:5,11]

Appeal to God for deliverance

To the chief Musician for the sons of Korah, Maschil.

44 We have heard with our ears, O God, our fathers have told us, *what* work thou didst in their days, in the times of old. ²*How* thou didst drive out the heathen *with* thy hand, and plantedst them; *how* thou didst afflict the people, and cast them out. ³For they got not the land in possession by their own sword, neither did their own arm save them: but thy right hand, and thine arm, and the light of thy countenance, because thou hadst a favour unto them. ⁴Thou *art* my King, O God: command deliverances for Jacob. ⁵Through thee will we push down our enemies: through thy name will we tread them under that rise up against us. ⁶For I will not trust in my bow, neither shall my sword save me. ⁷But thou hast saved us from our enemies, and hast put them to shame that hated us. ⁸In God we boast all the day long, and praise thy name for ever. Selah. [Ps. 34:2; Jer. 9:24]

9 But thou hast cast off, and put us to shame; and goest not forth with our armies. ¹⁰Thou makest us to turn back from the enemy: and they which hate us spoil for themselves. ¹¹Thou hast given us like sheep appointed for meat; and hast scattered us among the heathen. ¹²Thou sellest thy people for nought, and dost not increase *thy wealth* by their price. ¹³Thou makest us a reproach to our neighbours, a scorn and a derision to them that are round about us. ¹⁴Thou makest us a byword among the heathen, a shaking of the head among the people. ¹⁵My confusion *is* continually before me, and the shame of my face hath covered me, ¹⁶For the voice of him that reproacheth and blasphemeth; by reason of the enemy and avenger. ¹⁷All this is come upon us; yet have we not for-

gotten thee, neither have we dealt falsely in thy covenant. ¹⁸Our heart is not turned back, neither have our steps declined from thy way; ¹⁹Though thou hast sore broken us in the place of dragons, and covered us with the shadow of death. ²⁰If we have forgotten the name of our God, or stretched out our hands to a strange god; ²¹Shall not God search this out? for he knoweth the secrets of the heart. ²²Yea, for thy sake are we killed all the day long; we are counted as sheep for the slaughter. ²³Awake, why sleepest thou, O Lord? arise, cast *us* not off for ever. ²⁴Wherefore hidest thou thy face, *and* forgettest our affliction and our oppression? ²⁵For our soul is bowed down to the dust: our belly cleaveth unto the earth. ²⁶Arise for our help, and redeem us for thy mercy's sake.

The king's marriage

To the chief Musician upon Shoshannim, for the sons of Korah, Maschil, A Song of loves.

45 My heart is inditing a good matter: I speak of the things which I have made touching *the* king: my tongue *is* the pen of a ready writer. ²Thou art fairer than the children of men: grace is poured into thy lips: therefore God hath blessed thee for ever. ³Gird thy sword upon *thy* thigh, O *most* mighty, *with* thy glory and thy majesty. ⁴And *in* thy majesty ride prosperously because of truth and meekness *and* righteousness; and thy right hand shall teach thee terrible *things.* ⁵Thine arrows *are* sharp in the heart of the king's enemies; *whereby* the people fall under thee. 6Thy throne, O God, *is* for ever and ever: the sceptre of thy kingdom *is* a right sceptre. 7Thou lovest righteousness, and hatest wickedness: therefore God, thy God, hath anointed thee *with* the oil of gladness above thy fellows. 8All thy garments *smell of* myrrh, and aloes, *and* cassia, out of the ivory palaces, *where*by they have made thee glad. 9Kings' daughters *were* among thy honourable *women:* upon thy right hand did stand the queen in gold of Ophir. 10Hearken, O daughter, and consider, and incline thine ear; forget also thine own people, and thy father's house; 11So shall the king greatly desire thy beauty: for he *is* thy Lord; and worship thou him. 12And the daughter of Tyre *shall be there* with a gift; *even* the rich among the people shall intreat thy favour. 13The king's daughter *is* all glorious within: her clothing *is* of wrought gold. 14She shall be brought unto the king in raiment of needlework: the virgins her companions that follow her *shall be* brought unto thee. 15With gladness and rejoicing shall they be brought: they shall enter into the king's palace. 16Instead of thy fathers shall be thy children, whom thou mayest make princes in all the earth. 17I will make thy name to be remembered in all generations: therefore shall the people praise thee for ever and ever.

The presence of God in calamity

To the chief Musician for the sons of Korah, A Song upon Alamoth.

46 God *is* our refuge and strength, a very present help in trouble. 2Therefore will not we fear, though the earth be removed, and though the mountains be carried into the midst of the sea; 3Though the waters thereof roar *and* be troubled, *though* the mountains shake with the swelling thereof. Selah. [Ps. 93:3,4]

4 *There is* a river, the streams whereof shall make glad the city of God, the holy *place* of the tabernacles of the most High. 5God *is* in the midst of her; she shall not be moved: God shall help her, *and that* right early. 6The heathen raged, the kingdoms were moved: he uttered his voice, the earth melted. 7The Lord of hosts *is* with us; the God of Jacob *is* our refuge. Selah.

8 Come, behold the works of the Lord, what desolations he hath made in the earth. 9He maketh wars to cease unto the end of the earth; he breaketh the bow, and cutteth the spear in sunder; he burneth the chariot in the fire. 10Be still, and know that I *am* God: I will be exalted among the heathen, I will be exalted in the earth. 11The Lord of hosts *is* with us; the God of Jacob *is* our refuge. Selah.

God the King of the earth

To the chief Musician, A Psalm for the sons of Korah.

47 O clap *your* hands, all ye people; shout unto God with the voice of triumph. 2For the

LORD most High *is* terrible; *he is* a great King over all the earth. ³He shall subdue the people under us, and the nations under our feet. ⁴He shall choose our inheritance for us, the excellency of Jacob whom he loved. Selah. [1 Pet. 1:4]

5 God is gone up with a shout, the LORD with the sound of a trumpet. ⁶Sing *praises* to God, sing *praises:* sing *praises* unto our King, sing *praises.* ⁷For God *is* the King of all the earth: sing ye *praises* with understanding. ⁸God reigneth over the heathen: God sitteth upon the throne of his holiness. ⁹The princes of the people are gathered together, *even* the people of the God of Abraham: for the shields of the earth *belong* unto God: he is greatly exalted. [Ps. 89:18]

A song to mount Zion

A Song *and* Psalm for the sons of Korah.

48 Great *is* the LORD, and greatly to be praised in the city of our God, *in* the mountain of his holiness. ²Beautiful for situation, the joy of the whole earth, *is* mount Zion, *on* the sides of the north, the city of the great King. ³God is known in her palaces for a refuge. ⁴For lo, the kings were assembled, they passed by together. ⁵They saw *it, and* so they marvelled; they were troubled, *and* hasted away. ⁶Fear took hold upon them there, *and* pain, as of a woman in travail. ⁷Thou breakest the ships of Tarshish with an east wind. ⁸As we have heard, so have we seen in the city of the LORD of hosts, in the city of our God: God will establish it for ever. Selah.

⁹We have thought of thy lovingkindness, O God, in the midst of thy temple. ¹⁰According to thy name, O God, so *is* thy praise unto the ends of the earth: thy right hand is full *of* righteousness. ¹¹Let mount Zion rejoice, let the daughters of Judah be glad, because of thy judgments. ¹²Walk about Zion, and go round about her: tell the towers thereof. ¹³Mark ye well her bulwarks, consider her palaces; that ye may tell *it* to the generation following. ¹⁴For this God *is* our God for ever and ever: he will be our guide *even* unto death.

The folly of trusting riches

To the chief Musician, A Psalm for the sons of Korah.

49 Hear this, all ye people; give ear, all ye inhabitants of the world: ²Both low and high, rich and poor, together. ³My mouth shall speak of wisdom; and the meditation of my heart *shall be of* understanding. ⁴I will incline mine ear to a parable: I will open my dark saying upon the harp. ⁵Wherefore should I fear in the days of evil, *when* the iniquity of my heels shall compass me about? ⁶They that trust in their wealth, and boast themselves in the multitude of their riches; ⁷None *of them* can by any means redeem *his* brother, nor give to God a ransom for him: ⁸(For the redemption of their soul is precious, and it ceaseth for ever:) ⁹That he should still live for ever, *and* not see corruption. ¹⁰For he seeth *that* wise *men* die, likewise the fool and the brutish person perish, and leave their wealth to others. 11Their inward *thought is, that* their houses *shall continue* for ever, *and* their dwelling places to all generations; they call *their* lands after their own names. 12Nevertheless man *being* in honour abideth not: he is like the beasts *that* perish. 13This their way *is* their folly: yet their posterity approve their sayings. Selah. 14Like sheep they are laid in the grave; death shall feed *on* them; and the upright shall have dominion over them in the morning; and their beauty shall consume *in* the grave from their dwelling. 15But God will redeem my soul from the power of the grave: for he shall receive me. Selah. 16Be not thou afraid when one is made rich, when the glory of his house is increased; 17For when he dieth he shall carry nothing away: his glory shall not descend after him. 18Though whiles he lived he blessed his soul: and *men* will praise thee, when thou doest well to thyself. 19He shall go to the generation of his fathers; they shall never see light. 20Man *that is* in honour, and understandeth not, is like the beasts *that* perish. [Eccl. 3:19]

True and false religion

A Psalm of Asaph.

50 The mighty God, *even* the LORD, hath spoken, and called the earth from the rising of the sun unto the going down thereof. 2Out of Zion, the perfection of beauty, God hath shined. 3Our God shall come, and shall not keep silence: a fire shall devour before him, and it shall be very tempestuous round about him. 4He shall call to the heavens from above, and to the earth, that *he* may judge his people. 5Gather my saints together unto me; those that have made a covenant with me by sacrifice. 6And the heavens shall declare his righteousness: for God *is* judge himself. Selah. [Ps. 75:7]

7 Hear, O my people, and I will speak; O Israel, and I will testify against thee: I *am* God, *even* thy God. 8I will not reprove thee for thy sacrifices or thy burnt offerings, *to have been* continually before me. 9I will take no bullock out of thy house, *nor* he goats out of thy folds. 10For every beast of the forest *is* mine, *and* the cattle upon a thousand hills. 11I know all the fowls of the mountains: and the wild beasts of the field *are* mine. 12If I were hungry, I would not tell thee: for the world *is* mine, and the fulness thereof. 13Will I eat the flesh of bulls, or drink the blood of goats? 14Offer unto God thanksgiving; and pay thy vows unto the most High: 15And call upon me in the day of trouble: I will deliver thee, and thou shalt glorify me. [Job 22:27; Ps. 22:23]

16 But unto the wicked God saith, What hast thou to do to declare my statutes, or *that* thou shouldest take my covenant in thy mouth? 17Seeing thou hatest instruction, and castest my words behind thee. 18When thou sawest a thief, then thou consentedst with him, and hast been partaker with adulterers. 19Thou givest thy mouth to evil, and thy tongue fram-

eth deceit. ²⁰Thou sittest *and* speakest against thy brother; thou slanderest thine own mother's son. ²¹These *things* hast thou done, and I kept silence; thou thoughtest that I was altogether *such a one* as thyself: *but* I will reprove thee, and set *them* in order before thine eyes. ²²Now consider this, ye that forget God, lest I tear *you* in pieces, and *there be* none to deliver. ²³Whoso offereth praise glorifieth me: and to him that ordereth *his* conversation *aright* will I shew the salvation of God. [Ps. 27:6; Gal. 6:16]

The penitent's psalm

To the chief Musician, A Psalm of David, when Nathan the prophet came unto him, after he had gone in to Bathsheba.

51 Have mercy upon me, O God, according to thy lovingkindness: according unto the multitude of thy tender mercies blot out my transgressions. ²Wash me throughly from mine iniquity, and cleanse me from my sin. ³For I acknowledge my transgressions: and my sin *is* ever before me. ⁴Against thee, thee only, have I sinned, and done *this* evil in thy sight: that thou mightest be justified when thou speakest, *and* be clear when thou judgest. ⁵Behold, I was shapen in iniquity; and in sin did my mother conceive me. ⁶Behold, thou desirest truth in the inward parts: and in the hidden *part* thou shalt make me to know wisdom. ⁷Purge me with hyssop, and I shall be clean: wash me, and I shall be whiter than snow. ⁸Make me to hear joy and gladness; *that* the bones *which* thou hast broken may rejoice. ⁹Hide thy face from my sins, and blot out all mine iniquities. ¹⁰Create in me a clean heart, O God; and renew a right spirit within me. ¹¹Cast me not away from thy presence; and take not thy holy Spirit from me. ¹²Restore unto me the joy of thy salvation; and uphold me *with thy* free spirit. ¹³*Then* will I teach transgressors thy ways; and sinners shall be converted unto thee. ¹⁴Deliver me from bloodguiltiness, O God, thou God of my salvation: *and* my tongue shall sing aloud of thy righteousness. ¹⁵O Lord, open thou my lips; and my mouth shall shew forth thy praise. ¹⁶For thou desirest not sacrifice; else would I give *it:* thou delightest not in burnt offering. ¹⁷The sacrifices of God *are* a broken spirit: a broken and a contrite heart, O God, thou wilt not despise. [Ps. 34:18; Is. 57:15]

18 Do good in thy good pleasure unto Zion: build thou the walls of Jerusalem. ¹⁹Then shalt thou be pleased with the sacrifices of righteousness, with burnt offering and whole *burnt offering:* then shall they offer bullocks upon thine altar. [Ps. 4:5; Mal. 3:3]

The fate of the wicked

To the chief Musician, Maschil, *A Psalm* of David, when Doeg the Edomite came and told Saul, and said unto him, David is come to the house of Ahimelech.

52 Why boastest thou thyself in mischief, O mighty *man?* the goodness of God *endureth* continually. ²Thy tongue deviseth mischiefs; like a sharp rasor, working deceitfully. ³Thou lovest evil more than good; *and* lying rather than to speak righteousness. Selah. ⁴Thou lovest all devouring words, O thou deceitful tongue. ⁵God shall likewise destroy thee for ever, he shall take thee away, and pluck thee out of *thy* dwelling place, and root thee out of the land of the living. Selah. ⁶The righteous also shall see, and fear, and shall laugh at him: ⁷Lo, *this is* the man *that* made not God his strength; but trusted in the abundance of his riches, *and* strengthened himself in his wickedness. ⁸But I *am* like a green olive tree in the house of God: I trust in the mercy of God for ever and ever. ⁹I will praise thee for ever, because thou hast done *it:* and I will wait on thy name; for *it is* good before thy saints. [Ps. 54:6]

The fate of the fool

To the chief Musician upon Mahalath, Maschil, *A Psalm* of David.

53 The fool hath said in his heart, There *is* no God. Corrupt are they, and have done abominable iniquity: *there is* none that doeth good. ²God looked down from heaven upon the children of men, to see if there were *any* that did understand, that did seek God. ³Every one of them is gone back, they are altogether become filthy; *there is* none that doeth good, no, not one. ⁴Have the workers of iniquity no knowledge? who eat up my people *as* they eat bread: they have not called upon God. ⁵There were they in great fear, *where* no fear was: for God

hath scattered the bones of him that encampeth *against* thee: thou hast put *them* to shame, because God hath despised them. [Lev. 26:17; Ezek. 6:5]

6 O that the salvation of Israel *were come* out of Zion! When God bringeth back the captivity of his people, Jacob shall rejoice, *and* Israel shall be glad. [Ps. 14:7]

A prayer for deliverance

To the chief Musician on Neginoth, Maschil, *A Psalm* of David, when the Ziphims came and said to Saul, Doth not David hide himself with us?

54 Save me, O God, by thy name, and judge me by thy strength. ²Hear my prayer, O God; give ear to the words of my mouth. ³For strangers are risen up against me, and oppressors seek after my soul: they have not set God before them. Selah. ⁴Behold, God *is* mine helper: the Lord *is* with them that uphold my soul. ⁵He shall reward evil unto mine enemies: cut them off in thy truth. ⁶I will freely sacrifice unto thee: I will praise thy name, O LORD; for *it is* good. ⁷For he hath delivered me out of all trouble: and mine eye hath seen *his desire* upon mine enemies. [Ps. 59:10]

The LORD will sustain

To the chief Musician on Neginoth, Maschil, *A Psalm* of David.

55 Give ear to my prayer, O God; and hide not thyself from my supplication. ²Attend unto me, and hear me: I mourn in my complaint, and make a noise; ³Because of the voice of the enemy, because of the oppression of the wicked: for they cast iniquity upon me, and in wrath they hate me. ⁵My heart is sore pained within me: and the terrors of death are fallen upon me. ⁵Fearfulness and trembling are come upon me, and horror hath overwhelmed me. ⁶And I said, O that I had wings like a dove, *for then* would I fly away, and be at rest. ⁷Lo, *then* would I wander far off, *and* remain in the wilderness. Selah. ⁸I would hasten my escape from the windy storm *and* tempest.

9 Destroy, O Lord, *and* divide their tongues: for I have seen violence and strife in the city. ¹⁰Day and night they go about it upon the walls thereof: mischief also and sorrow *are* in the midst of it. ¹¹Wickedness *is* in the midst thereof: deceit and guile depart not from her streets. ¹²For *it was* not an enemy *that* reproached me; then I could have borne *it:* neither *was it* he that hated me *that* did magnify *himself* against me; then I would have hid myself from him: ¹³But *it was* thou, a man mine equal, my guide, and mine acquaintance. ¹⁴We took sweet counsel together, *and* walked unto the house of God in company. ¹⁵Let death seize upon them, *and* let them go down quick *into* hell: for wickedness *is* in their dwellings, *and* among them. ¹⁶As *for* me, I will call upon God; and the LORD shall save me. ¹⁷Evening, and morning, and at noon, will I pray, and cry aloud: and he shall hear my voice. ¹⁸He hath delivered my soul in peace from the battle *that was* against me: for there were

many with me. ¹⁹God shall hear, and afflict them, even he that abideth of old. Selah. Because they have no changes, therefore they fear not God. ²⁰He hath put forth his hands against such as be at peace with him: he hath broken his covenant. ²¹*The words of* his mouth were smoother than butter, but war *was* in his heart: his words were softer than oil, yet *were* they drawn swords. ²²Cast thy burden upon the LORD, and he shall sustain thee: he shall never suffer the righteous to be moved. ²³But thou, O God, shalt bring them down into the pit of destruction: bloody and deceitful men shall not live out half their days; but I will trust in thee.

[Ps. 5:6; Job 15:32; Prov. 10:27; Eccl. 7:17]

A song for the distressed

To the chief Musician upon Jonath-elem-rechokim, Michtam of David, when the Philistines took him in Gath.

56 Be merciful unto me, O God: for man would swallow me up; he fighting daily oppresseth me. ²Mine enemies would daily swallow *me* up: for *they be* many that fight against me, O thou *most* High. ³*What* time I am afraid, I will trust in thee. ⁴In God I will praise his word, in God I have put my trust; I will not fear what flesh can do unto me. [Ps. 118:6; Is. 31:3]

5 Every day they wrest my words: all their thoughts *are* against me for evil. ⁶They gather themselves together, they hide themselves, they mark my steps, when they wait for my soul. ⁷Shall they escape by iniquity? in *thine*

anger cast down the people, O God. 8Thou tellest my wanderings: put thou my tears into thy bottle: *are they* not in thy book? 9When I cry *unto thee*, then shall mine enemies turn back: this I know; for God *is* for me. 10In God will I praise *his* word: in the Lord will I praise *his* word. 11In God have I put my trust: I will not be afraid what man can do unto me.

12 Thy vows *are* upon me, O God: I will render praises unto thee. 13For thou hast delivered my soul from death: *wilt* not *thou deliver* my feet from falling, that *I* may walk before God in the light of the living? [Ps. 116:8; Job 33:30]

The mercy and truth of God

To the chief Musician, Al-taschith, Michtam of David, when he fled from Saul in the cave.

57 Be merciful unto me, O God, be merciful unto me: for my soul trusteth in thee: yea, in the shadow of thy wings will I make my refuge, until *these* calamities be overpast. 2I will cry unto God most High; unto God that performeth *all things* for me. 3He shall send from heaven, and save me *from* the reproach of him that would swallow me up. Selah. God shall send forth his mercy and his truth. 4My soul *is* among lions: *and* I lie *even among* them that are set on fire, *even* the sons of men, whose teeth *are* spears and arrows, and their tongue a sharp sword. 5Be thou exalted, O God, above the heavens; *let* thy glory *be* above all the earth. [Ps. 108:5]

6 They have prepared a net for my steps; my soul is bowed down: they have digged a pit before me, into the midst whereof they are fallen *themselves*. Selah. 7My heart is fixed, O God, my heart is fixed: I will sing and give praise. 8Awake up, my glory; awake, psaltery and harp: I *myself* will awake early. 9I will praise thee, O Lord, among the people: I will sing unto thee among the nations. 10For thy mercy *is* great unto the heavens, and thy truth unto the clouds. 11Be thou exalted, O God, above the heavens: *let* thy glory *be* above all the earth. [ver. 5]

The punishment of the wicked

To the chief Musician, Al-taschith, Michtam of David.

58 Do ye indeed speak righteousness, O congregation? do ye judge uprightly, O ye sons of men? 2Yea, in heart you work wickedness; you weigh the violence of your hands in the earth. 3The wicked are estranged from the womb: they go astray as soon as they be born, speaking lies. 4Their poison *is* like the poison of a serpent: *they are* like the deaf adder *that* stoppeth her ear; 5Which will not hearken to the voice of charmers, charming *never so* wisely. 6Break their teeth, O God, in their mouth: break out the great teeth of the young lions, O Lord. 7Let them melt away as waters *which* run continually: *when* he bendeth *his bow to shoot* his arrows, let them be as cut in pieces. 8As a snail *which* melteth, let *every one of them* pass away: *like* the untimely birth of a woman, *that* they may not see the sun. ⁹Before your pots can feel the thorns, he shall take them away as with a whirlwind, both living, and in *his* wrath. ¹⁰The righteous shall rejoice when he seeth the vengeance: he shall wash his feet in the blood of the wicked. ¹¹So that a man shall say, Verily *there is* a reward for the righteous: verily he is a God that judgeth in the earth. [Ps. 92:15]

Triumph over enemies

To the chief Musician, Al-taschith, Michtam of David; when Saul sent, and they watcht the house to kill him.

59 Deliver me from mine enemies, O my God: defend me from them that rise up against me. ²Deliver me from the workers of iniquity, and save me from bloody men. ³For lo, they lie in wait for my soul: the mighty are gathered against me; not *for* my transgression, nor *for* my sin, O Lord. ⁴They run and prepare themselves without *my* fault: awake to help me, and behold. ⁵Thou therefore, O Lord God *of* hosts, the God of Israel, awake to visit all the heathen: be not merciful to any wicked transgressors. Selah.

6 They return at evening: they make a noise like a dog, and go round about the city. ⁷Behold, they belch out with their mouth: swords *are* in their lips: for who, *say they,* doth hear? ⁸But thou, O Lord, shalt laugh at them; thou shalt have all the heathen in derision. ⁹*Because of* his strength will I wait upon thee: for God *is* my defence. [Ps. 62:2]

10 The God of my mercy shall prevent me: God shall let me see *my desire* upon mine enemies. ¹¹Slay them not, lest my people forget: scatter them by thy power; and bring them down, O Lord our shield. ¹²*For* the sin of their mouth *and* the words of their lips let them even be taken in their pride: and for cursing and lying *which* they speak. ¹³Consume *them* in wrath, consume *them,* that they *may* not *be:* and let them know that God ruleth in Jacob unto the ends of the earth. Selah.

14 And at evening let them return; *and* let them make a noise like a dog, and go round about the city. [ver. 6]

15 Let them wander up and down for meat, and grudge if they be not satisfied. ¹⁶But I will sing of thy power; yea, I will sing aloud of thy mercy in the morning: for thou hast been my defence and refuge in the day of my trouble. ¹⁷Unto thee, O my strength, will I sing: for God *is* my defence, *and* the God of my mercy. [Ps. 18:1]

Prayer for national deliverance

To the chief Musician upon Shushan-eduth, Michtam of David, to teach; when he strove with Aram-naharaim and with Aram-zobah, when Joab returned, and smote of Edom in the valley of salt twelve thousand.

60 O God, thou hast cast us off, thou hast scattered us, thou hast been displeased; O turn thyself to us again. ²Thou hast made the earth to tremble; thou hast broken it: heal the breaches thereof; for it shaketh. ³Thou hast shewed thy people hard *things:* thou hast made us to drink the wine *of* astonishment. ⁴Thou hast given a banner to them that fear thee, that *it* may be displayed because of the truth. Selah. ⁵That thy beloved may be delivered; save *with* thy right hand, and hear me. ⁶God hath spoken in his holiness; I will rejoice, I will divide Shechem, and mete out the valley of Succoth. ⁷Gilead *is* mine, and Manasseh *is* mine; Ephraim also *is* the strength of mine head; Judah *is* my lawgiver; ⁸Moab *is* my washpot; over Edom will I cast out my shoe: Philistia, triumph thou because of me. [2 Sam. 8:1]

9 Who will bring me *into* the strong city? who will lead me *into* Edom? ¹⁰*Wilt* not thou, O God, *which* hadst cast us off? and *thou,* O God, *which* didst not go out with our armies? ¹¹Give us help from trouble: for vain *is* the help of man. ¹²Through God we shall do valiantly: for he *it is that* shall tread down our enemies. [Num. 24:18]

The prayer of a troubled heart

To the chief Musician upon Neginah,
A Psalm of David.

61 Hear my cry, O God; attend unto my prayer. ²From the end of the earth will I cry unto thee, when my heart is overwhelmed: lead me to the rock *that* is higher than I. ³For thou hast been a shelter for me, *and* a strong tower from the enemy. ⁴I will abide in thy tabernacle for ever: I will trust in the covert of thy wings. Selah. ⁵For thou, O God, hast heard my vows: thou hast given *me* the heritage of those that fear thy name. ⁶Thou wilt prolong the king's life: *and* his years as many generations. ⁷He shall abide before God for ever: O prepare mercy and truth, *which* may preserve him. ⁸So will I sing *praise* unto thy name for ever, that I may daily perform my vows.

Confidence in God

To the chief Musician, to Jeduthun,
A Psalm of David.

62 Truly my soul waiteth upon God: from him *cometh* my salvation. ²He only *is* my rock and my salvation; *he is* my defence; I shall not be greatly moved. ³How long will ye imagine mischief against a man? ye shall be slain all of you: as a bowing wall *shall ye be, and as* a tottering fence. ⁴They only consult to cast *him* down from his excellency: they delight in lies: they bless with their mouth, but they curse inwardly. Selah. [Ps. 28:3]

5 My soul, wait thou only upon God; for my expectation *is* from him. ⁶He only *is* my rock and my salvation: *he is* my defence; I shall not be moved. ⁷In God *is* my salvation and my glory: the rock of my strength, *and* my refuge, *is* in God. ⁸Trust in him at all times; ye people, pour out your heart before him: God *is* a refuge for us. Selah. [1 Sam. 1:15; Lam. 2:19]

9 Surely men of low degree *are* vanity, *and* men of high degree *are* a lie: to be laid in the balance, they *are* altogether *lighter* than vanity.

¹⁰Trust not in oppression, and become not vain in robbery: if riches increase, set not *your* heart *upon them*. ¹¹God hath spoken once; twice have I heard this; that power *belongeth* unto God. ¹²Also unto thee, O Lord, *belongeth* mercy: for thou renderest to *every* man according to his work. [Mat. 16:27]

The thirsty soul

A Psalm of David, when he was in the wilderness of Judah.

63 O God, thou *art* my God; early will I seek thee: my soul thirsteth for thee, my flesh longeth for thee, in a dry and thirsty land, where no water is; ²To see thy power and thy glory, so *as* I have seen thee in the sanctuary. ³Because thy lovingkindness *is* better than life, my lips shall praise thee. ⁴Thus will I bless thee while I live: I will lift up my hands in thy name. ⁵My soul shall be satisfied as *with* marrow and fatness; and my mouth shall praise *thee with* joyful lips: ⁶When I remember thee upon my bed, *and* meditate on thee in the *night* watches. ⁷Because thou hast been my help, therefore in the shadow of thy wings will I rejoice. ⁸My soul followeth hard after thee: thy right hand upholdeth me. ⁹But those *that* seek my soul, to destroy *it*, shall go into the lower parts of the earth. ¹⁰They shall fall by the sword: they shall be a portion for foxes. ¹¹But the king shall rejoice in God; every one that sweareth by him shall glory: but the mouth of them that speak lies shall be stopped. [Deut. 6:13]

Appeal for aid against enemies

To the chief Musician, A Psalm of David.

64 Hear my voice, O God, in my prayer: preserve my life from fear of the enemy. ²Hide me from the secret counsel of the wicked; from the insurrection of the workers of iniquity: ³Who whet their tongue like a sword, *and* bend *their bows to shoot* their arrows, *even* bitter words: ⁴That *they* may shoot in secret at the perfect: suddenly do they shoot at him, and fear not. ⁵They encourage themselves *in* an evil matter: they commune of laying snares privily; they say, Who shall see them? ⁶They search out iniquities; they accomplish a diligent search: both the inward *thought* of every one *of them*, and the heart, *is* deep. ⁷But God shall shoot at them *with* an arrow; suddenly shall they be wounded. ⁸So they shall make their own tongue to fall upon themselves: all that see them shall flee away. ⁹And all men shall fear, and shall declare the work of God; for they shall wisely consider of his doing. ¹⁰The righteous shall be glad in the LORD, and shall trust in him; and all the upright in heart shall glory.

God's provisions for the earth

To the chief Musician, A Psalm *and* Song of David.

65 Praise waiteth for thee, O God, in Zion: and unto thee shall the vow be performed. ²O thou that hearest prayer, unto thee shall all flesh come. ³Iniquities prevail against me: *as for* our transgressions, thou shalt purge them away. 4Blessed *is the man whom* thou choosest, and causest to approach *unto thee, that* he may dwell *in* thy courts: we shall be satisfied with the goodness of thy house, *even* of thy holy temple. [Ps. 33:12; Ps. 4:3; Ps. 36:8]

5 *By* terrible *things* in righteousness wilt thou answer us, O God of our salvation; *who art* the confidence of all the ends of the earth, and of them that are afar off *upon* the sea: 6Which by his strength setteth fast the mountains; *being* girded with power: 7Which stilleth the noise of the seas, the noise of their waves, and the tumult of the people. 8They also that dwell in the uttermost parts are afraid at thy tokens: thou makest the outgoings of the morning and evening to rejoice.

9 Thou visitest the earth, and waterest it: thou greatly enrichest it *with* the river of God, *which* is full *of* water: thou preparest them corn, when thou hast so provided for it. 10*Thou* waterest the ridges thereof abundantly: *thou* settlest the furrows thereof: thou makest it soft with showers: thou blessest the springing thereof. 11Thou crownest the year with thy goodness; and thy paths drop fatness. 12They drop *upon* the pastures of the wilderness: and the little hills rejoice on every side. 13The pastures are clothed with flocks; the valleys also are covered over with corn; they shout for joy, they also sing. [Is. 55:12]

God's power and works

To the chief Musician, A Song *or* Psalm.

66

Make a joyful noise unto God, all ye lands: 2Sing forth the honour of his name: make his praise glorious. 3Say unto God, How terrible *art thou in* thy works! through the greatness of thy power shall thine enemies submit themselves unto thee. 4All the earth shall worship thee, and shall sing unto thee; they shall sing *to* thy name. Selah. 5Come and see the works of God: *he is* terrible *in his* doing toward the children of men. 6He turned the sea into dry *land:* they went through the flood on foot: there did we rejoice in him. 7He ruleth by his power for ever; his eyes behold the nations: let not the rebellious exalt themselves. Selah. 8O bless our God, ye people, and make the voice of his praise to be heard: 9Which holdeth our soul in life, and suffereth not our feet to be moved. 10For thou, O God, hast proved us: thou hast tried us, as silver is tried. 11Thou broughtest us into the net; thou laidst affliction upon our loins. 12Thou hast caused men to ride over our heads; we went through fire and through water: but thou broughtest us out into a wealthy *place.* [Is. 51:23; Is. 43:2]

13 I will go *into* thy house with burnt offerings: I will pay thee my vows, 14Which my lips have uttered, and my mouth hath spoken, when I was in trouble. 15I will offer unto thee burnt sacrifices of fatlings, with the incense of rams; I will offer bullocks with goats.

Selah. 16Come *and* hear, all ye that fear God, and I will declare what he hath done for my soul. 17I cried unto him *with* my mouth, and *he was* extolled with my tongue. 18If I regard iniquity in my heart, the Lord will not hear *me:* 19*But* verily God hath heard *me;* he hath attended to the voice of my prayer. 20Blessed *be* God, which hath not turned away my prayer, nor his mercy from me.

God governs the nations

To the chief Musician on Neginoth, A Psalm *or* Song.

67 God be merciful unto us, and bless us; *and* cause his face to shine upon us; Selah. 2That thy way may be known upon earth, thy saving health among all nations. 3Let the people praise thee, O God; let all the people praise thee. 4O let the nations be glad and sing for joy: for thou shalt judge the people righteously, and govern the nations upon earth. Selah. 5Let the people praise thee, O God; let all the people praise thee. 6*Then* shall the earth yield her increase; *and* God, *even* our own God, shall bless us. 7God shall bless us; and all the ends of the earth shall fear him.

The God of Israel

To the chief Musician, A Psalm *or* Song of David.

68 Let God arise, let his enemies be scattered: let them also that hate him flee before him. 2As smoke is driven away, *so* drive *them* away: as wax melteth before the fire, *so* let the wicked

perish at the presence of God. 3But let the righteous be glad; let them rejoice before God: yea, let them exceedingly rejoice. 4Sing unto God, sing *praises to* his name: extol him that rideth upon the heavens by his name JAH, and rejoice before him. 5A father of the fatherless, and a judge of the widows, *is* God in his holy habitation. 6God setteth the solitary in families: he bringeth out those which are bound with chains: but the rebellious dwell *in* a dry *land.* [1 Sam. 2:5; Ps. 107:4-7; Acts 12:6; Ps. 107:34]

7 O God, when thou wentest forth before thy people, when thou didst march through the wilderness; Selah. 8The earth shook, the heavens also dropped at the presence of God: *even* Sinai itself *was moved* at the presence of God, the God of Israel. 9Thou, O God, didst send a plentiful rain, whereby thou didst confirm thine inheritance, when it was weary. 10Thy congregation hath dwelt therein: thou, O God, hast prepared of thy goodness for the poor. [Deut. 26:5; Ps. 74:19]

11 The Lord gave the word: great *was* the company of those that published *it.* 12Kings of armies did flee apace: and she that tarried at home divided the spoil. 13Though ye have lien among the pots, *yet shall ye be as* the wings of a dove covered with silver, and her feathers with yellow gold. 14When the Almighty scattered kings in it, it was *white as* snow in Salmon. [Josh. 10:10]

15 The hill of God *is as* the hill of Bashan; a high hill *as* the hill of Bashan. 16Why leap ye, ye high

hills? *this is* the hill *which* God desireth to dwell in; yea, the LORD
will dwell *in it* for ever. ¹⁷The chariots of God *are* twenty thousand,
even thousands of angels: the Lord
is among them, *as in* Sinai, in the
holy *place.* ¹⁸Thou hast ascended
on high, thou hast led captivity
captive: thou hast received gifts for
men; yea, *for* the rebellious also,
that the LORD God might dwell
among them. [Eph. 4:8; Judg. 5:12; Acts
2:4,33; 1 Tim. 1:13; Ps. 78:60]

19 Blessed *be* the Lord, *who*
daily loadeth us *with benefits, even*
the God of our salvation. Selah.
²⁰*He that is* our God *is* the God of
salvation; and unto GOD the Lord
belong the issues from death. ²¹But
God shall wound the head of his
enemies, *and* the hairy scalp of
such a one as goeth on still in his
trespasses. ²²The Lord said, I will
bring again from Bashan, I will
bring *my people* again from the
depths of the sea: ²³That thy foot
may be dipped in the blood of
thine enemies, *and* the tongue of
thy dogs in the same. [Ps. 58:10; 1 Ki.
21:19]

24 They have seen thy goings,
O God; *even* the goings of my God,
my King, in the sanctuary. ²⁵The
singers went before, the players on
instruments *followed* after; among
them were the damsels playing
with timbrels. ²⁶Bless ye God in
the congregations, *even* the Lord,
from the fountain of Israel. ²⁷There
is little Benjamin *with* their ruler,
the princes of Judah *and* their
council, the princes of Zebulun,
and the princes of Naphtali. ²⁸Thy
God hath commanded thy

strength: strengthen, O God, that
which thou hast wrought for us.
²⁹Because of thy temple at
Jerusalem shall kings bring presents unto thee. ³⁰Rebuke the company of spearmen, the multitude of
the bulls, with the calves of the
people, *till every one* submit himself with pieces of silver: scatter
thou the people *that* delight in war.
³¹Princes shall come out of Egypt;
Ethiopia shall soon stretch out her
hands unto God. [Is. 19:21; 45:14; Ps.
44:20]

32 Sing unto God, ye kingdoms
of the earth; O sing *praises unto*
the Lord; Selah. ³³To him that
rideth upon the heavens of heavens, *which were* of old; lo, he doth
send out his voice, *and that* a
mighty voice. ³⁴Ascribe ye
strength unto God: his excellency
is over Israel, and his strength *is* in
the clouds. ³⁵O God, *thou art* terrible out of thy holy places: the God
of Israel *is* he that giveth strength
and power unto *his* people. Blessed
be God. [Ps. 76:12]

The prayer for deliverance

To the chief Musician upon
Shoshannim, *A Psalm* of David.

69

Save me, O God; for the
waters are come in unto
my soul. ²I sink in deep mire,
where *there is* no standing: I am
come into deep waters, where the
floods overflow me. ³I am weary of
my crying: my throat is dried: mine
eyes fail while *I* wait for my God.
⁴They that hate me without a
cause are more than the hairs of
mine head: they that would destroy me, *being* mine enemies

wrongfully, are mighty: then I restored *that* which I took not away. 5O God, thou knowest my foolishness; and my sins are not hid from thee. 6Let not them that wait on thee, O Lord GOD of hosts, be ashamed for my sake: let not those that seek thee be confounded for my sake, O God of Israel. 7Because for thy sake I have borne reproach; shame hath covered my face. 8I am become a stranger unto my brethren, and an alien unto my mother's children. 9For the zeal of thine house hath eaten me up; and the reproaches of them that reproached thee are fallen upon me. 10When I wept, *and chastened* my soul with fasting, that was to my reproach. 11I made sackcloth also my garment; and I became a proverb to them. 12They that sit in the gate speak against me; and *I was* the song of the drunkards. 13But *as for* me, my prayer *is* unto thee, O LORD, *in* an acceptable time: O God, in the multitude of thy mercy hear me, in the truth of thy salvation. 14Deliver me out of the mire, and let me not sink: let me be delivered from them that hate me, and out of the deep waters. 15Let not the waterflood overflow me, neither let the deep swallow me up, and let not the pit shut her mouth upon me. 16Hear me, O LORD; for thy lovingkindness *is* good: turn unto me according to the multitude of thy tender mercies. 17And hide not thy face from thy servant; for I am in trouble: hear me speedily. 18Draw nigh unto my soul, *and* redeem it: deliver me because of mine enemies.

19 Thou hast known my reproach, and my shame, and my dishonour: mine adversaries *are* all before thee. 20Reproach hath broken my heart; and I am full of heaviness: and I looked *for some* to take pity, but *there was* none; and for comforters, but I found none. 21They gave me also gall for my meat; and in my thirst they gave me vinegar to drink. 22Let their table become a snare before them: and *that which should have been* for *their* welfare, *let it become* a trap. 23Let their eyes be darkened, that *they* see not; and make their loins continually to shake. 24Pour out thine indignation upon them, and let thy wrathful anger take hold of them. 25Let their habitation be desolate; *and* let none dwell in their tents. 26For they persecute *him* whom thou hast smitten; and they talk to the grief of those whom thou hast wounded. 27Add iniquity unto their iniquity: and let them not come into thy righteousness. 28Let them be blotted out of the book of the living, and not be written with the righteous. [Ex. 32:32; Phil. 4:3; Ezek. 13:9]

29 But I *am* poor and sorrowful: let thy salvation, O God, set me up on high. 30I will praise the name of God with a song; and will magnify him with thanksgiving. 31*This* also shall please the LORD better than an ox *or* bullock that hath horns *and* hoofs. 32The humble shall see *this, and* be glad: and your heart shall live that seek God. 33For the LORD heareth the poor, and despiseth not his prisoners. 34Let the heaven and earth praise him, the

seas, and every *thing* that moveth therein. [Ps. 96:11; 148:1; Is. 44:23; Is. 55:12]

35 For God will save Zion, and will build the cities of Judah: that they may dwell there, and have it in possession. 36The seed also of his servants shall inherit it: and they that love his name shall dwell therein. [Ps. 102:28]

Deliverance from persecutors

To the chief Musician, *A Psalm* of David, to bring to remembrance.

70 Make haste, O God, to deliver me; make haste to help me, O LORD. 2Let them be ashamed and confounded that seek after my soul: let them be turned backward, and put to confusion, that desire my hurt. 3Let them be turned back for a reward of their shame that say, Aha, aha. 4Let all those that seek thee rejoice and be glad in thee: and let such as love thy salvation say continually, Let God be magnified. 5But I *am* poor and needy: make haste unto me, O God: thou *art* my help and my deliverer; O LORD, make no tarrying. [Ps. 40:17; Ps. 141:1]

The prayer of an aged man

71 In thee, O LORD, do I put my trust: let me never be put to confusion. 2Deliver me in thy righteousness, and cause me to escape: incline thine ear unto me, and save me. 3Be thou my strong habitation, whereunto *I* may continually resort: thou hast given commandment to save me; for thou *art* my rock and my fortress. [Ps. 31:2,3; 44:4]

4 Deliver me, O my God, out of the hand of the wicked, out of the hand of the unrighteous and cruel man. 5For thou *art* my hope, O Lord GOD: *thou art* my trust from my youth. 6By thee have I been holden up from the womb: thou art he that took me out of my mother's bowels: my praise *shall be* continually of thee. 7I am as a wonder unto many; but thou *art* my strong refuge. 8Let my mouth be filled *with* thy praise *and with* thy honour all the day. 9Cast me not off in the time of old age; forsake me not when my strength faileth. 10For mine enemies speak against me; and they that lay wait for my soul take counsel together, 11Saying, God hath forsaken him: persecute and take him; for *there is* none to deliver *him*. 12O God, be not far from me: O my God, make haste for my help. 13Let them be confounded *and* consumed that are adversaries to my soul; let them be covered *with* reproach and dishonour that seek my hurt. 14But I will hope continually, and will yet praise thee more and more. 15My mouth shall shew forth thy righteousness *and* thy salvation all the day; for I know not the numbers *thereof*. 16I will go in the strength of the Lord GOD: I will make mention of thy righteousness, *even* of thine only. 17O God, thou hast taught me from my youth: and hitherto have I declared thy wondrous works. 18Now also when I am old and grayheaded, O God, forsake me not; until I have shewed thy strength unto *this* generation, *and* thy power to every

one *that* is to come. ¹⁹Thy righteousness also, O God, *is* very high, who hast done great *things*: O God, who *is* like unto thee! ²⁰*Thou,* which hast shewed me great and sore troubles, shalt quicken me again, and shalt bring me up again from the depths of the earth. ²¹Thou shalt increase my greatness, and comfort me on every side. ²²I will also praise thee with the psaltery, *even* thy truth, O my God: unto thee will I sing with the harp, O thou Holy One of Israel. ²³My lips shall greatly rejoice when I sing unto thee; and my soul, which thou hast redeemed. ²⁴My tongue also shall talk of thy righteousness all the day long: for they are confounded, for they are brought unto shame, that seek my hurt.

A prayer for the king

A Psalm for Solomon.

72 Give the king thy judgments, O God, and thy righteousness unto the king's son. ²He shall judge thy people with righteousness, and thy poor with judgment. ³The mountains shall bring peace to the people, and the little hills, by righteousness. ⁴He shall judge the poor of the people, he shall save the children of the needy, and shall break in pieces the oppressor. ⁵They shall fear thee as long as the sun and moon endure, throughout all generations. ⁶He shall come down like rain upon the mown grass: as showers that water the earth. ⁷In his days shall the righteous flourish; and abundance of peace so long as the moon endureth. ⁸He shall have dominion also from sea to sea, and from the river unto the ends of the earth. ⁹They that dwell in the wilderness shall bow before him; and his enemies shall lick the dust. ¹⁰The kings of Tarshish and *of* the isles shall bring presents: the kings of Sheba and Seba shall offer gifts. ¹¹Yea, all kings shall fall down before him: all nations shall serve him. ¹²For he shall deliver the needy when he crieth; the poor also, and *him* that hath no helper. ¹³He shall spare the poor and needy, and shall save the souls of the needy. ¹⁴He shall redeem their soul from deceit and violence: and precious shall their blood be in his sight. ¹⁵And he shall live, and to him shall be given of the gold of Sheba: prayer also shall be made for him continually; *and* daily shall he be praised. ¹⁶There shall be a handful of corn in the earth upon the top of the mountains; the fruit thereof shall shake like Lebanon: and *they* of the city shall flourish like grass of the earth. ¹⁷His name shall endure for ever: his name shall be continued as long as the sun: and *men* shall be blessed in him: all nations shall call him blessed. [Ps. 89:36; Gen. 12:3; Jer. 4:2; Luke 1:48]

18 Blessed *be* the LORD God, the God of Israel, who only doeth wondrous *things*. ¹⁹And blessed *be* his glorious name for ever: and let the whole earth be filled *with* his glory; Amen, and Amen. [Neh. 9:5; Num. 14:21; Hab. 2:14]

20 The prayers of David the son of Jesse are ended.

God delivers the righteous

A Psalm of Asaph.

73 Truly God *is* good to Israel, *even* to such as are of a clean heart. ²But *as for* me, my feet were almost gone; my steps had well nigh slipt. ³For I was envious at the foolish, *when* I saw the prosperity of the wicked. ⁴For *there are* no bands in their death: but their strength *is* firm. ⁵They *are* not in trouble *as other* men; neither are they plagued like *other* men. ⁶Therefore pride compasseth them about as a chain; violence covereth them *as* a garment. ⁷Their eyes stand out with fatness: they have more than heart could wish. ⁸They are corrupt, and speak wickedly *concerning* oppression: they speak loftily. ⁹They set their mouth against the heavens, and their tongue walketh through the earth. ¹⁰Therefore his people return hither: and waters of a full *cup* are wrung out to them. ¹¹And they say, How doth God know? and is there knowledge in the most High? [Job 22:13]

12 Behold, these *are* the ungodly, who prosper in the world; they increase *in* riches. ¹³Verily I have cleansed my heart *in* vain, and washed my hands in innocency. ¹⁴For all the day long have I been plagued, and chastened every morning. ¹⁵If I say, I will speak thus; behold, I should offend *against* the generation of thy children. ¹⁶When I thought to know this, it *was* too painful for me; ¹⁷Until I went into the sanctuary of God; *then* understood I their end.

¹⁸Surely thou didst set them in slippery *places:* thou castedst them down into destruction. ¹⁹How are they *brought* into desolation, as *in* a moment! they are utterly consumed with terrors. ²⁰As a dream when *one* awaketh; *so,* O Lord, when *thou* awakest, thou shalt despise their image. [Job 20:8; Ps. 90:5]

21 Thus my heart was grieved, and I was pricked *in* my reins. ²²So foolish *was* I, and ignorant: I was *as* a beast before thee. ²³Nevertheless I *am* continually with thee: thou hast holden *me* by my right hand. ²⁴Thou shalt guide me with thy counsel, and afterward receive me *to* glory. ²⁵Whom have I in heaven *but thee?* and *there is* none upon earth *that* I desire besides thee. ²⁶My flesh and my heart faileth: *but* God *is* the strength of my heart, and my portion for ever. ²⁷For lo, they that are far from thee shall perish: thou hast destroyed all them that go a whoring from thee. ²⁸But *it is* good for me to draw near to God: I have put my trust in the Lord GOD, that *I* may declare all thy works. [Heb. 10:22]

A plea for relief

Maschil of Asaph.

74 O God, why hast thou cast *us* off for ever? *why* doth thine anger smoke against the sheep of thy pasture? ²Remember thy congregation, *which* thou hast purchased of old; the rod of thine inheritance, *which* thou hast redeemed; this mount Zion, wherein thou hast dwelt. ³Lift up thy feet unto the perpetual desolations; *even* all *that* the enemy hath done wickedly in the sanctuary. 4Thine enemies roar in the midst of thy congregations; they set up their ensigns *for* signs. 5*A man* was famous according as he had lifted up axes upon the thick trees. 6But now they break down the carved work thereof at once with axes and hammers. 7They have cast fire into thy sanctuary, they have defiled *by casting down* the dwelling place of thy name to the ground. 8They said in their hearts, Let us destroy them together: they have burnt up all the synagogues of God in the land. 9We see not our signs: *there is* no more any prophet: neither *is there* among us any that knoweth how long. 10O God, how long shall the adversary reproach? shall the enemy blaspheme thy name for ever? 11Why withdrawest thou thy hand, even thy right hand? pluck *it* out of thy bosom. 12For God *is* my King of old, working salvation in the midst of the earth. 13Thou didst divide the sea by thy strength: thou brakest the heads of the dragons in the waters. 14Thou brakest the heads of leviathan in pieces, *and* gavest him *to be* meat to the people inhabiting the wilderness. 15Thou didst cleave the fountain and the flood: thou driedst up mighty rivers. 16The day *is* thine, the night also *is* thine: thou hast prepared the light and the sun. 17Thou hast set all the borders of the earth: thou hast made summer and winter. 18Remember this, *that* the enemy hath reproached, O LORD, and *that* the foolish people have blasphemed thy name. 19O deliver not the soul

of thy turtledove unto the multitude *of the wicked:* forget not the congregation of thy poor for ever. 20Have respect unto the covenant: for the dark places of the earth are full *of* the habitations of cruelty. 21O let not the oppressed return ashamed: let the poor and needy praise thy name. 22Arise, O God, plead thine own cause: remember how the foolish *man* reproacheth thee daily. 23Forget not the voice of thine enemies: the tumult of those that rise up against thee increaseth continually.

The justice of God

To the chief Musician, Al-taschith,
A Psalm *or* Song of Asaph.

75 Unto thee, O God, do we give thanks, *unto thee* do we give thanks: for *that* thy name *is* near thy wondrous works declare.

2 When I shall receive the congregation I will judge uprightly. 3The earth and all the inhabitants thereof *are* dissolved: I bear up the pillars of it. Selah. 4I said unto the fools, Deal not foolishly: and to the wicked, Lift not up the horn: 5Lift not up your horn on high: speak *not* with a stiff neck. 6For promotion *cometh* neither from the east, nor from the west, nor from the south. 7But God *is* the judge: he putteth down one, and setteth up another. 8For in the hand of the LORD *there is* a cup, and the wine is red; it is full *of* mixture; and he poureth out of the same: but the dregs thereof, all the wicked of the earth shall wring *them* out, *and* drink *them.* 9But I will declare for

ever; I will sing *praises* to the God of Jacob. ¹⁰All the horns of the wicked also will I cut off; *but* the horns of the righteous shall be exalted. [Ps. 101:8; Jer. 48:25; Ps. 89:17; 148:14]

The victorious power of God

To the chief Musician on Neginoth,
A Psalm *or* Song of Asaph.

76 In Judah *is* God known: his name *is* great in Israel. ²In Salem also is his tabernacle, and his dwelling place in Zion. ³There brake he the arrows of the bow, the shield, and the sword, and the battle. Selah. [Ps. 46:9; Ezek. 39:9]

4 Thou *art* more glorious *and* excellent than the mountains of prey. ⁵The stouthearted are spoiled, they have slept their sleep: and none of the men of might have found their hands. ⁶At thy rebuke, O God of Jacob, both the chariot and horse *are* cast into a dead sleep. ⁷Thou, *even* thou, *art* to be feared: and who may stand in thy sight when once thou art angry? ⁸Thou didst cause judgment to be heard from heaven; the earth feared, and was still, ⁹When God arose to judgment, to save all the meek of the earth. Selah. [Ps. 9:7-9; 72:4]

10 Surely the wrath of man shall praise thee: the remainder of wrath shalt thou restrain. ¹¹Vow, and pay unto the Lᴏʀᴅ your God: let all that be round about him bring presents unto him that ought to be feared. ¹²He shall cut off the spirit of princes: *he is* terrible to the kings of the earth. [Ps. 68:35]

The call to God for help

To the chief Musician, to Jeduthun,
A Psalm of Asaph.

77 I cried unto God *with* my voice, *even* unto God *with* my voice; and he gave ear unto me. ²In the day of my trouble I sought the Lord: my sore ran in the night, and ceased not: my soul refused to be comforted. ³I remembered God, and was troubled: I complained, and my spirit was overwhelmed. Selah. [Ps. 143:4]

4 Thou holdest mine eyes waking: I am *so* troubled that I cannot speak. ⁵I have considered the days of old, the years of ancient times. ⁶I call to remembrance my song in the night: I commune with mine own heart: and my spirit made diligent search. ⁷Will the Lord cast off for ever? and will he be favourable no more? ⁸Is his mercy clean gone for ever? doth *his* promise fail for evermore? ⁹Hath God forgotten to be gracious? hath he in anger shut up his tender mercies? Selah. [Is. 49:15]

10 And I said, This *is* my infirmity: *but I will remember* the years of the right hand of the most High. ¹¹I will remember the works of the Lᴏʀᴅ: surely I will remember thy wonders of old. ¹²I will meditate also of all thy work, and talk of thy doings. ¹³Thy way, O God, *is* in the sanctuary: who *is* so great a God as *our* God? ¹⁴Thou *art* the God that doest wonders: thou hast declared thy strength among the people. ¹⁵Thou hast with *thine* arm redeemed thy people, the sons of Jacob and Joseph. Selah. [Ex. 6:6; Deut. 9:29]

16 The waters saw thee, O God, the waters saw thee; they were afraid: the depths also were troubled. 17The clouds poured out water: the skies sent out a sound: thine arrows also went abroad. 18The voice of thy thunder *was* in the heaven: the lightnings lightened the world: the earth trembled and shook. 19Thy way *is* in the sea, and thy path in the great waters, and thy footsteps are not known. 20Thou leddest thy people like a flock by the hand of Moses and Aaron. [Ex. 13:21; Is. 63:11,12]

God's guidance of his people

Maschil of Asaph.

78 Give ear, O my people, to my law: incline your ears to the words of my mouth. 2I will open my mouth in a parable: I will utter dark sayings of old: 3Which we have heard and known, and our fathers have told us. 4We will not hide *them* from their children, shewing to the generation to come the praises of the LORD, and his strength, and his wonderful works that he hath done. [Deut. 6:7; Joel 1:3; Ex. 13:8,14]

5 For he established a testimony in Jacob, and appointed a law in Israel, which he commanded our fathers, that *they* should make them known to their children: 6That the generation to come might know *them, even* the children *which* should be born; *who* should arise and declare *them* to their children: 7That they might set their hope in God, and not forget the works of God, but keep his commandments: 8And might not

be as their fathers, a stubborn and rebellious generation; a generation *that* set not their heart aright, and whose spirit was not stedfast with God. 9The children of Ephraim, *being* armed, *and* carrying bows, turned *back* in the day of battle. 10They kept not the covenant of God, and refused to walk in his law; 11And forgat his works, and his wonders that he had shewed them. 12Marvellous things did he in the sight of their fathers, in the land of Egypt, *in* the field of Zoan. 13He divided the sea, and caused them to pass through; and he made the waters to stand as a heap. 14In the daytime also he led them with a cloud, and all the night with a light of fire. 15He clave the rocks in the wilderness, and gave *them* drink as *out of* the great depths. 16He brought streams also out of the rock, and caused waters to run down like rivers. [Deut. 9:21]

17 And they sinned yet more against him by provoking the most High in the wilderness. 18And they tempted God in their heart by asking meat for their lust. 19Yea, they spake against God; they said, Can God furnish a table in the wilderness? 20Behold, he smote the rock, that the waters gushed out, and the streams overflowed; can he give bread also? can he provide flesh for his people? [Num. 20:11]

21 Therefore the LORD heard *this,* and was wroth: so a fire was kindled against Jacob, and anger also came up against Israel; 22Because they believed not in God, and trusted not in his salvation: 23Though he had commanded the

clouds from above, and opened the doors of heaven, 24And had rained down manna upon them to eat, and had given them *of* the corn of heaven. 25Man did eat angels' food: he sent them meat to the full. 26He caused an east wind to blow in the heaven: and by his power he brought in the south wind. 27He rained flesh also upon them as dust, and feathered fowls like as the sand of the sea: 28And he let *it* fall in the midst of their camp, round about their habitations. 29So they did eat, and were well filled: for he gave them their own desire; 30They were not estranged from their lust. But while their meat *was* yet in their mouths, 31The wrath of God came upon them, and slew the fattest of them, and smote down the chosen *men* of Israel. 32For all this they sinned still, and believed not for his wondrous works. 33Therefore their days did he consume in vanity, and their years in trouble. 34When he slew them, then they sought him: and they returned and inquired early after God. 35And they remembered that God *was* their rock, and the high God their redeemer. 36Nevertheless they did flatter him with their mouth, and they lied unto him with their tongues. 37For their heart was not right with him, neither were they stedfast in his covenant. 38But he, *being* full of compassion, forgave *their* iniquity, and destroyed *them* not: yea, many a time turned he his anger away, and did not stir up all his wrath. 39For he remembered that they *were but* flesh; a wind that passeth away,

and cometh not again. [Ps. 103:14; John 3:6; Job 7:7,16]

40 How oft did they provoke him in the wilderness, *and* grieve him in the desert! 41Yea, they turned *back* and tempted God, and limited the Holy One of Israel. 42They remembered not his hand: nor the day when he delivered them from the enemy. 43How he had wrought his signs in Egypt, and his wonders in the field of Zoan: 44And had turned their rivers into blood; and their floods, *that* they could not drink. 45He sent divers sorts *of flies* among them, which devoured them; and frogs, which destroyed them. 46He gave also their increase unto the caterpillar, and their labour unto the locust. 47He destroyed their vines with hail, and their sycomore trees with frost. 48He gave up their cattle also to the hail, and their flocks to hot thunderbolts. 49He cast upon them the fierceness of his anger, wrath, and indignation, and trouble, *by* sending evil angels *among them.* 50He made a way to his anger; he spared not their soul from death, but gave their life over to the pestilence; 51And smote all the firstborn in Egypt; the chief of *their* strength in the tabernacles of Ham: 52But made his own people to go forth like sheep, and guided them in the wilderness like a flock. 53And he led them on safely, so that they feared not: but the sea overwhelmed their enemies. 54And he brought them to the border of his sanctuary, *even to* this mountain, *which* his right hand had purchased. 55He cast out the

heathen also before them, and divided them an inheritance by line, and made the tribes of Israel to dwell in their tents. ⁵⁶Yet they tempted and provoked the most high God, and kept not his testimonies: ⁵⁷But turned *back,* and dealt unfaithfully like their fathers: they were turned aside like a deceitful bow. ⁵⁸For they provoked him to anger with their high places, and moved him to jealousy with their graven images. ⁵⁹When God heard *this,* he was wroth, and greatly abhorred Israel: ⁶⁰So that he forsook the tabernacle of Shiloh, the tent *which* he placed among men; ⁶¹And delivered his strength into captivity, and his glory into the enemy's hand. ⁶²He gave his people over also unto the sword; and was wroth with his inheritance. ⁶³The fire consumed their young men; and their maidens were not given to marriage. ⁶⁴Their priests fell by the sword; and their widows made no lamentation. ⁶⁵Then the Lord awaked as one out of sleep, *and* like a mighty *man* that shouteth by reason of wine. ⁶⁶And he smote his enemies in the hinder parts: he put them to a perpetual reproach. ⁶⁷Moreover he refused the tabernacle of Joseph, and chose not the tribe of Ephraim: ⁶⁸But chose the tribe of Judah, the mount Zion which he loved. ⁶⁹And he built his sanctuary like high *palaces,* like the earth which he hath established for ever. ⁷⁰He chose David also his servant, and took him from the sheepfolds: ⁷¹From following the *ewes* great with young he brought him to feed Jacob his people, and Israel his inheritance. ⁷²So he fed them according to the integrity of his heart; and guided them by the skilfulness of his hands. [1 Ki. 9:4]

A lament for Jerusalem

A Psalm of Asaph.

79 O God, the heathen are come into thine inheritance; thy holy temple have they defiled; they have laid Jerusalem on heaps. ²The dead bodies of thy servants have they given *to be* meat unto the fowls of the heaven, the flesh of thy saints unto the beasts of the earth. ³Their blood have they shed like water round about Jerusalem; and *there was* none to bury *them.* ⁴We are become a reproach to our neighbours, a scorn and derision to them that are round about us. ⁵How long, LORD? wilt thou be angry, for ever? shall thy jealousy burn like fire? ⁶Pour out thy wrath upon the heathen that have not known thee, and upon the kingdoms that have not called upon thy name. ⁷For they have devoured Jacob, and laid waste his dwelling place. ⁸O remember not against us former iniquities: let thy tender mercies speedily prevent us: for we are brought very low. ⁹Help us, O God of our salvation, for the glory of thy name: and deliver us, and purge away our sins, for thy name's sake. ¹⁰Wherefore should the heathen say, Where *is* their God? let him be known among the heathen in our sight *by* the revenging of the blood of thy servants which is shed. ¹¹Let the sighing of the prisoner come before thee, according to the greatness of thy power: preserve thou those that are appointed to die; 12 And render unto our neighbours sevenfold into their bosom their reproach, wherewith they have reproached thee, O Lord. 13 So we thy people and sheep of thy pasture will give thee thanks for ever: we will shew forth thy praise to all generations. [Ps. 74:1; 95:7; Is. 43:21]

A call to God for help

To the chief Musician upon
Shoshannim-Eduth, A Psalm of Asaph.

80 Give ear, O Shepherd of Israel, thou that leadest Joseph like a flock; thou that dwellest *between* the cherubims, shine forth. 2 Before Ephraim and Benjamin and Manasseh stir up thy strength, and come and save us. 3 Turn us again, O God, and cause thy face to shine; and we shall be saved. [Lam. 5:21; Num. 6:25; Ps. 4:6]

4 O LORD God *of* hosts, how long wilt thou be angry against the prayer of thy people? 5 Thou feedest them with the bread of tears; and givest them tears to drink *in great* measure. 6 Thou makest us a strife unto our neighbours: and our enemies laugh among themselves. 7 Turn us again, O God *of* hosts, and cause thy face to shine; and we shall be saved.

8 Thou hast brought a vine out of Egypt: thou hast cast out the heathen, and planted it. 9 Thou preparedst *room* before it, and didst cause it to take deep root, and it filled the land. 10 The hills were covered *with* the shadow of it, and the boughs thereof *were like* the

goodly cedars. 11 She sent out her boughs unto the sea, and her branches unto the river.

12 Why hast thou *then* broken down her hedges, so that all they which pass by the way do pluck her? 13 The boar out of the wood doth waste it, and the wild beast of the field doth devour it. 14 Return, we beseech thee, O God *of* hosts: look down from heaven, and behold, and visit this vine; 15 And the vineyard which thy right hand hath planted, and the branch *that* thou madest strong for thyself.

16 *It is* burnt with fire, *it is* cut down: they perish at the rebuke of thy countenance. 17 Let thy hand be upon the man of thy right hand, upon the son of man *whom* thou madest strong for thyself. 18 So will not we go *back* from thee: quicken us, and we will call upon thy name. 19 Turn us again, O LORD God *of* hosts, cause thy face to shine; and we shall be saved.

God's goodness to Israel

To the chief Musician upon Gittith,
A Psalm of Asaph.

81 Sing aloud unto God our strength: make a joyful noise unto the God of Jacob. 2 Take a psalm, and bring hither the timbrel, the pleasant harp with the psaltery. 3 Blow up the trumpet in the new moon, in the time appointed, on our solemn feast day. 4 For this *was* a statute for Israel, *and* a law of the God of Jacob. 5 This he ordained in Joseph *for* a testimony, when he went out through the land of Egypt: *where* I heard a language that I understood not. [Ps. 114:1]

6 I removed his shoulder from the burden: his hands were delivered from the pots. 7Thou calledst in trouble, and I delivered thee; I answered thee in the secret place of thunder: I proved thee at the waters of Meribah. Selah. 8Hear, O my people, and I will testify unto thee: O Israel, if thou wilt hearken unto me; 9There shall no strange god be in thee; neither shalt thou worship any strange god. 10I am the LORD thy God, which brought thee out of the land of Egypt: open thy mouth wide, and I will fill it. 11But my people would not hearken to my voice; and Israel would none of me. 12So I gave them up unto their own heart's lust: and they walked in their own counsels. 13O that my people had hearkened unto me, and Israel had walked in my ways! 14I should soon have subdued their enemies, and turned my hand against their adversaries. 15The haters of the LORD should have submitted themselves unto him: but their time should have endured for ever. 16He should have fed them also with the finest of the wheat: and with honey out of the rock should I have satisfied thee. [Deut. 32:14; Job 29:6]

Unjust judgments rebuked
A Psalm of Asaph.

82 God standeth in the congregation of the mighty; he judgeth among the gods. 2How long will ye judge unjustly, and accept the persons of the wicked? Selah. 3Defend the poor and fatherless: do justice to the afflicted and needy. 4Deliver the poor and needy: rid them out of the hand of the wicked. 5They know not, neither will they understand; they walk on in darkness: all the foundations of the earth are out of course. 6I have said, Ye are gods; and all of you are children of the most High. 7But ye shall die like men, and fall like one of the princes. 8Arise, O God, judge the earth: for thou shalt inherit all nations. [Mic. 7:2,7; Ps. 2:8; Rev. 11:15]

Prayer for Israel's defence
A Song or Psalm of Asaph.

83 Keep not thou silence, O God: hold not thy peace, and be not still, O God. 2For lo, thine enemies make a tumult: and they that hate thee have lift up the head. 3They have taken crafty counsel against thy people, and consulted against thy hidden ones. 4They have said, Come, and let us cut them off from being a nation; that the name of Israel may be no more in remembrance. 5For they have consulted together with one consent: they are confederate against thee: 6The tabernacles of Edom, and the Ishmaelites; of Moab, and the Hagarenes; 7Gebal, and Ammon, and Amalek; the Philistines with the inhabitants of Tyre; 8Assur also is joined with them: they have holpen the children of Lot. Selah.

9 Do unto them as unto the Midianites; as to Sisera, as to Jabin, at the brook of Kison: 10Which perished at En-dor: they became as dung for the earth. 11Make their

nobles like Oreb, and like Zeeb: yea, all their princes as Zebah, and as Zalmunna: 12Who said, Let us take to ourselves the houses of God in possession. 13O my God, make them like a wheel; as the stubble before the wind. 14As the fire burneth a wood, and as the flame setteth the mountains on fire; 15So persecute them with thy tempest, and make them afraid with thy storm. 16Fill their faces with shame; that they may seek thy name, O LORD. 17Let them be confounded and troubled for ever; yea, let them be put to shame, and perish: 18That men may know that thou, whose name alone is JEHOVAH, art the most High over all the earth. [Ps. 59:13; Ex. 6:3; Ps. 92:8]

Longing for the sanctuary

To the chief Musician upon Gittith, A Psalm for the sons of Korah.

84 How amiable are thy tabernacles, O LORD of hosts! 2My soul longeth, yea, even fainteth for the courts of the LORD: my heart and my flesh crieth out for the living God. 3Yea, the sparrow hath found a house, and the swallow a nest for herself, where she may lay her young, even thine altars, O LORD of hosts, my King, and my God.

4 Blessed are they that dwell in thy house: they will be still praising thee. Selah. 5Blessed is the man whose strength is in thee; in whose heart are the ways of them. 6Who passing through the valley of Baca make it a well; the rain also filleth the pools. 7They go from strength to strength, every one of them in Zion appeareth before God. [Prov. 4:18; Deut. 16:16]

8 O LORD God of hosts, hear my prayer: give ear, O God of Jacob. Selah. 9Behold, O God our shield, and look upon the face of thine anointed. 10For a day in thy courts is better than a thousand. I had rather be a doorkeeper in the house of my God, than to dwell in the tents of wickedness. 11For the LORD God is a sun and shield: the LORD will give grace and glory: no good thing will he withhold from them that walk uprightly. 12O LORD of hosts, blessed is the man that trusteth in thee. [Ps. 2:12]

Prayer for mercy to Israel

To the chief Musician, A Psalm for the sons of Korah.

85 LORD, thou hast been favourable unto thy land: thou hast brought back the captivity of Jacob. 2Thou hast forgiven the iniquity of thy people, thou hast covered all their sin. Selah. 3Thou hast taken away all thy wrath: thou hast turned thyself from the fierceness of thine anger.

4 Turn us, O God of our salvation, and cause thine anger towards us to cease. 5Wilt thou be angry with us for ever? wilt thou draw out thine anger to all generations? 6Wilt thou not revive us again: that thy people may rejoice in thee? 7Shew us thy mercy, O LORD, and grant us thy salvation.

8 I will hear what God the LORD will speak: for he will speak peace unto his people, and to his saints: but let them not turn again to folly. 9Surely his salvation is nigh them

that fear him; that glory may dwell in our land. ¹⁰Mercy and truth are met together; righteousness and peace have kissed *each other.* ¹¹Truth shall spring out of the earth; and righteousness shall look down from heaven. ¹²Yea, the LORD shall give *that which is* good; and our land shall yield her increase. ¹³Righteousness shall go before him; and shall set *us* in the way of his steps. [Ps. 89:14]

Prayer for deliverance

A Prayer of David.

86 Bow down thine ear, O LORD, hear me: for I *am* poor and needy. ²Preserve my soul; for I *am* holy: O thou my God, save thy servant that trusteth in thee. ³Be merciful unto me, O LORD: for I cry unto thee daily. ⁴Rejoice the soul of thy servant: for unto thee, O Lord, do I lift up my soul. ⁵For thou, Lord, *art* good, and ready to forgive; and plenteous in mercy unto all them that call upon thee. ⁶Give ear, O LORD, unto my prayer; and attend to the voice of my supplications. ⁷In the day of my trouble I will call upon thee: for thou wilt answer me. ⁸Among the gods *there is* none like unto thee, O Lord; neither *are there any works* like unto thy works. ⁹All nations whom thou hast made shall come and worship before thee, O Lord; and shall glorify thy name. ¹⁰For thou *art* great, and doest wondrous *things:* thou *art* God alone. ¹¹Teach me thy way, O LORD; I will walk in thy truth: unite my heart to fear thy name. ¹²I will praise thee, O Lord my

God, with all my heart: and I will glorify thy name for evermore. ¹³For great *is* thy mercy toward me: and thou hast delivered my soul from the lowest hell. ¹⁴O God, the proud are risen against me, and the assemblies of violent *men* have sought after my soul; and have not set thee before them. ¹⁵But thou, O Lord, *art* a God full of compassion, and gracious, longsuffering, and plenteous in mercy and truth. ¹⁶O turn unto me, and have mercy upon me; give thy strength unto thy servant, and save the son of thine handmaid. ¹⁷Shew me a token for good; that they which hate me may see *it,* and be ashamed: because thou, LORD, hast holpen me, and comforted me.

Privileges of living in Zion

A Psalm *or* Song for the sons of Korah.

87 His foundation *is* in the holy mountains. ²The LORD loveth the gates of Zion more than all the dwellings of Jacob. ³Glorious *things* are spoken of thee, O city of God. Selah. [See Is. 60]

4 I will make mention of Rahab and Babylon to them that know me: behold Philistia, and Tyre, with Ethiopia; this *man* was born there. ⁵And of Zion it shall be said, This and that man was born in her: and the Highest himself shall establish her. ⁶The LORD shall count, when he writeth *up* the people, *that* this *man* was born there. Selah. ⁷As well the singers as the players on instruments *shall be there:* all my springs *are* in thee.

Prayer in the face of death

A Song or Psalm for the sons of Korah.
To the chief Musician upon Mahalath
Leannoth, Maschil of Heman
the Ezrahite.

88 O LORD God of my salvation, I have cried day and
night before thee: ²Let my prayer
come before thee: incline thine ear
unto my cry; ³For my soul is full of
troubles: and my life draweth nigh
unto the grave. ⁴I am counted with
them that go down into the pit: I
am as a man that hath no strength:
⁵Free among the dead, like the
slain that lie in the grave, whom
thou rememberest no more: and
they are cut off from thy hand.
⁶Thou hast laid me in the lowest
pit, in darkness, in the deeps. ⁷Thy
wrath lieth hard upon me, and
thou hast afflicted me with all thy
waves. Selah. [Ps. 42:7]

8 Thou hast put away mine acquaintance far from me; thou hast
made me an abomination unto
them; I am shut up, and I cannot
come forth. ⁹Mine eye mourneth
by reason of affliction: LORD, I have
called daily upon thee, I have
stretched out my hands unto thee.
¹⁰Wilt thou shew wonders to the
dead? shall the dead arise and
praise thee? Selah. [Ps. 6:5; Is. 38:18]

11 Shall thy lovingkindness be
declared in the grave? or thy faithfulness in destruction? ¹²Shall thy
wonders be known in the dark?
and thy righteousness in the land
of forgetfulness? ¹³But unto thee
have I cried, O LORD; and in the
morning shall my prayer prevent
thee. ¹⁴LORD, why castest thou off
my soul? why hidest thou thy face
from me? ¹⁵I am afflicted and ready
to die from my youth up: while I
suffer thy terrors I am distracted.
¹⁶Thy fierce wrath goeth over me;
thy terrors have cut me off. ¹⁷They
came round about me daily like
water; they compassed me about
together. ¹⁸Lover and friend hast
thou put far from me, and mine acquaintance into darkness. [Job 19:13]

God's covenant with David

Maschil of Ethan the Ezrahite.

89 I will sing of the mercies
of the LORD for ever: with
my mouth will I make known thy
faithfulness to all generations. ²For
I have said, Mercy shall be built up
for ever: thy faithfulness shalt thou
establish in the very heavens. ³I
have made a covenant with my
chosen, I have sworn unto David
my servant, ⁴Thy seed will I stablish for ever, and build up thy
throne to all generations. Selah.
[Luke 1:33]

5 And the heavens shall praise
thy wonders, O LORD: thy faithfulness also in the congregation of the
saints. ⁶For who in the heaven can
be compared unto the LORD? who
among the sons of the mighty can
be likened unto the LORD? ⁷God is
greatly to be feared in the assembly
of the saints, and to be had in reverence of all them that are about
him. ⁸O LORD God of hosts, who is
a strong LORD like unto thee? or to
thy faithfulness round about thee?
⁹Thou rulest the raging of the sea:
when the waves thereof arise, thou
stillest them. ¹⁰Thou hast broken
Rahab in pieces, as one that is

slain; thou hast scattered thine enemies with thy strong arm. [11]The heavens *are* thine, the earth also *is* thine: *as for* the world and the fulness thereof, thou hast founded them. [12]The north and the south thou hast created them: Tabor and Hermon shall rejoice in thy name. [13]Thou hast a mighty arm: strong is thy hand, *and* high is thy right hand. [14]Justice and judgment *are* the habitation of thy throne: mercy and truth shall go before thy face. [15]Blessed *is* the people that know the joyful sound: they shall walk, O LORD, in the light of thy countenance. [16]In thy name shall they rejoice all the day: and in thy righteousness shall they be exalted. [17]For thou *art* the glory of their strength: and in thy favour our horn shall be exalted. [18]For the LORD *is* our defence; and the Holy One of Israel *is* our king. [19]Then thou spakest in vision to thy holy one, and saidst, I have laid help upon *one that is* mighty; I have exalted *one* chosen out of the people. [20]I have found David my servant; with my holy oil have I anointed him: [21]With whom my hand shall be established: mine arm also shall strengthen him. [22]The enemy shall not exact upon him; nor the son of wickedness afflict him. [23]And I will beat down his foes before his face, and plague them that hate him. [24]But my faithfulness and my mercy *shall be* with him: and in my name shall his horn be exalted. [25]I will set his hand also in the sea, and his right hand in the rivers. [26]He shall cry unto me, Thou *art* my Father, my God, and the rock of my salvation. [27]Also I will make him *my* firstborn, higher than the kings of the earth. [28]My mercy will I keep for him for evermore, and my covenant *shall* stand fast with him. [29]His seed also will I make *to endure* for ever, and his throne as the days of heaven. [30]If his children forsake my law, and walk not in my judgments; [31]If they break my statutes, and keep not my commandments; [32]Then will I visit their transgression with the rod, and their iniquity with stripes. [33]Nevertheless my lovingkindness will I not utterly take from him, nor suffer my faithfulness to fail. [34]My covenant will I not break, nor alter the thing that is gone out of my lips. [35]Once have I sworn by my holiness that I will not lie unto David. [36]His seed shall endure for ever, and his throne as the sun before me. [37]It shall be established for ever as the moon, and *as* a faithful witness in heaven. Selah.

38 But thou hast cast off and abhorred, thou hast been wroth with thine anointed. [39]Thou hast made void the covenant of thy servant: thou hast profaned his crown *by casting it* to the ground. [40]Thou hast broken down all his hedges; thou hast brought his strong holds to ruin. [41]All that pass by the way spoil him: he is a reproach to his neighbours. [42]Thou hast set up the right hand of his adversaries; thou hast made all his enemies to rejoice. [43]Thou hast also turned the edge of his sword, and hast not made him to stand in the battle. [44]Thou hast made his glory to cease, and cast his throne down to

the ground. 45The days of his youth hast thou shortened: thou hast covered him with shame. Selah.

46 How long, LORD? wilt thou hide thyself, for ever? shall thy wrath burn like fire? 47Remember how short my time is: wherefore hast thou made all men in vain? 48What man *is he that* liveth, and shall not see death? shall he deliver his soul from the hand of the grave? Selah. [Ps. 49:9; Heb. 11:5]

49 Lord, where *are* thy former lovingkindnesses, *which* thou swarest unto David in thy truth? 50Remember, Lord, the reproach of thy servants; *how* I do bear in my bosom *the reproach of* all the mighty people; 51Wherewith thine enemies have reproached, O LORD; wherewith they have reproached the footsteps of thine anointed. [Ps. 74:22]

52 Blessed *be* the LORD for evermore. Amen, and Amen. [Ps. 41:13]

Eternal God and mortal man

A Prayer of Moses the man of God.

90 Lord, thou hast been our dwelling place in all generations. 2Before the mountains were brought forth, or ever thou hadst formed the earth and the world, even from everlasting to everlasting, thou *art* God. 3Thou turnest man to destruction; and sayest, Return, ye children of men. 4For a thousand years in thy sight *are but* as yesterday when it is past, and *as* a watch in the night. 5Thou carriest them away as with a flood; they are *as* a sleep: in the morning *they are* like grass *which*

groweth up. 6In the morning it flourisheth, and groweth up; in the evening it is cut down, and withereth. 7For we are consumed by thine anger, and by thy wrath are we troubled. 8Thou hast set our iniquities before thee, our secret *sins* in the light of thy countenance. 9For all our days are passed away in thy wrath: we spend our years as a tale *that is told.* 10The days of our years *are* threescore years and ten; and if by reason of strength *they be* fourscore years, yet *is* their strength labour and sorrow; for it is soon cut off, and we fly away. 11Who knoweth the power of thine anger? even according to thy fear, *so is* thy wrath. 12So teach *us* to number our days, that we may apply our hearts *unto* wisdom. 13Return, O LORD, how long? and let it repent thee concerning thy servants. 14O satisfy us early *with* thy mercy; that we may rejoice and be glad all our days. 15Make us glad according to the days *wherein* thou hast afflicted us, *and* the years *wherein* we have seen evil. 16Let thy work appear unto thy servants, and thy glory unto their children. 17And let the beauty of the LORD our God be upon us: and establish thou the work of our hands upon us; yea, the work of our hands establish thou it. [Ps. 27:4; Is. 26:12]

The security of the godly

91 He that dwelleth in the secret place of the most High shall abide under the shadow of the Almighty. 2I will say of the LORD, *He is* my refuge and my fortress: my God; in him will I trust. 3Surely he shall deliver thee from the snare of the fowler, *and* from the noisome pestilence. 4He shall cover thee with his feathers, and under his wings shalt thou trust: his truth *shall be thy* shield and buckler. 5Thou shalt not be afraid for the terror by night; *nor* for the arrow *that* flieth by day; 6*Nor* for the pestilence *that* walketh in darkness; *nor* for the destruction *that* wasteth at noonday. 7A thousand shall fall at thy side, and ten thousand at thy right hand; *but* it shall not come nigh thee. 8Only with thine eyes shalt thou behold and see the reward of the wicked. 9Because thou hast made the LORD, *which is* my refuge, *even* the most High, thy habitation; 10There shall no evil befall thee, neither shall *any* plague come nigh thy dwelling. 11For he shall give his angels charge over thee, to keep thee in all thy ways. 12They shall bear thee up in *their* hands, lest thou dash thy foot against a stone. 13Thou shalt tread upon the lion and adder: the young lion and the dragon shalt thou trample under feet.

14 Because he hath set his love upon me, therefore will I deliver him: I will set him on high, because he hath known my name. 15He shall call upon me, and I will answer him: I *will be* with him in trouble; I will deliver him, and honour him. 16*With* long life will I satisfy him, and shew him my salvation.

Praise for the LORD's goodness

A Psalm *or* Song for the sabbath day.

92 *It is a* good *thing* to give thanks unto the LORD, and to sing *praises* unto thy name, O most High: 2To shew forth thy lovingkindness in the morning, and thy faithfulness every night, 3Upon an instrument of ten strings, and upon the psaltery; upon the harp with a solemn sound. [1 Chr. 23:5; Ps. 33:2]

4 For thou, LORD, hast made me glad through thy work: I will triumph in the works of thy hands. 5O LORD, how great are thy works! *and* thy thoughts are very deep. 6A brutish man knoweth not; neither doth a fool understand this. 7When the wicked spring as the grass, and when all the workers of iniquity do flourish; *it is* that they shall be destroyed for ever: 8But thou, LORD, *art most* high for evermore. 9For lo, thine enemies, O LORD, for lo, thine enemies shall perish; all the workers of iniquity shall be scattered. 10But my horn shall thou exalt like *the horn of* an unicorn: I shall be anointed with fresh oil. 11Mine eye also shall see *my desire* on mine enemies, *and* mine ears shall hear *my desire* of the wicked that rise up against me. 12The righteous shall flourish like the palm tree: he shall grow like a cedar in Lebanon. 13Those that be planted in the house of the LORD shall flourish in the courts of our God. 14They shall still bring forth fruit in old age; they shall be fat and flourishing; 15To shew that the LORD *is* upright: *he is* my rock, and *there is*

no unrighteousness in him. [Deut. 32:4; Rom. 9:14]

The majesty of the LORD

93 The LORD reigneth, he is clothed with majesty; the LORD is clothed with strength, *wherewith* he hath girded himself: the world also is stablished, *that* it cannot be moved. 2 Thy throne is established of old: thou *art* from everlasting. 3 The floods have lifted up, O LORD, the floods have lifted up their voice; the floods lift up their waves. 4 The LORD on high *is* mightier than the noise of many waters, *yea, than* the mighty waves of the sea. 5 Thy testimonies are very sure: holiness becometh thine house, O LORD, for ever.

An appeal for God to avenge

94 O LORD God, to whom vengeance belongeth; O God, to whom vengeance belongeth, shew thyself. 2 Lift up thyself, thou judge of the earth: render a reward to the proud. [Ps. 7:6; Gen. 18:25]

3 LORD, how long shall the wicked, how long shall the wicked triumph? 4 *How long* shall they utter *and* speak hard *things? and* all the workers of iniquity boast themselves? 5 They break in pieces thy people, O LORD, and afflict thine heritage. 6 They slay the widow and the stranger, and murder the fatherless. 7 Yet they say, The LORD shall not see, neither shall the God of Jacob regard *it.* [Ps. 10:11]

8 Understand, ye brutish among the people: and ye fools, when will ye be wise? 9 He that planted the ear, shall he not hear? he that formed the eye, shall he not see? 10 He that chastiseth the heathen, shall not he correct? he that teacheth man knowledge, *shall not he know?* 11 The LORD knoweth the thoughts of man, that they *are* vanity. 12 Blessed *is* the man whom thou chastenest, O LORD, and teachest him out of thy law; 13 That *thou* mayest give him rest from the days of adversity, until the pit be digged for the wicked. 14 For the LORD will not cast off his people, neither will he forsake his inheritance. 15 But judgment shall return unto righteousness: and all the upright in heart shall follow it.

16 Who will rise up for me against the evildoers? *or* who will stand up for me against the workers of iniquity? 17 Unless the LORD *had been* my help, my soul had almost dwelt *in* silence. 18 When I said, My foot slippeth; thy mercy, O LORD, held me up. 19 In the multitude of my thoughts within me thy comforts delight my soul. 20 Shall the throne of iniquity have fellowship *with* thee, which frameth mischief by a law? 21 They gather themselves together against the soul of the righteous, and condemn the innocent blood. 22 But the LORD is my defence; and my God *is* the rock of my refuge. 23 And he shall bring upon them their own iniquity, and shall cut them off in their own wickedness; *yea,* the LORD our God shall cut them off. [Ps. 7:16; Prov. 2:22]

A call to praise the Lord

95 O come, let us sing unto the Lord: let us make a joyful noise to the rock of our salvation. 2Let us come before his presence with thanksgiving, *and* make a joyful noise unto him with psalms. 3For the Lord *is* a great God, and a great King above all gods. 4In his hand *are* the deep places of the earth: the strength of the hills *is* his also. 5The sea *is* his, and he made it: and his hands formed the dry *land.* 6O come, let us worship and bow down: let us kneel before the Lord our Maker. 7For he *is* our God; and we *are* the people of his pasture, and the sheep of his hand. To day if ye will hear his voice, 8Harden not your heart, as *in* the provocation, *and* as *in* the day of temptation in the wilderness: 9When your fathers tempted me, proved me, and saw my work. 10Forty years long was I grieved with *this* generation, and said, It *is* a people that do err in *their* heart, and they have not known my ways: 11*Unto* whom I sware in my wrath that they should not enter into my rest. [Heb. 4:3,5]

A call to worship the Lord

96 O sing unto the Lord a new song: sing unto the Lord, all the earth. 2Sing unto the Lord, bless his name; shew forth his salvation from day to day. 3Declare his glory among the heathen, his wonders among all people. 4For the Lord *is* great, and greatly to be praised: he *is* to be feared above all gods. 5For all the gods of the nations *are* idols: but the Lord made the heavens. 6Honour and majesty *are* before him: strength and beauty *are* in his sanctuary. 7Give unto the Lord, O ye kindreds of the people, give unto the Lord glory and strength. 8Give unto the Lord the glory due unto his name: bring an offering, and come into his courts. 9O worship the Lord in the beauty of holiness: fear before him, all the earth. 10Say among the heathen *that* the Lord reigneth: the world also shall be established *that* it shall not be moved: he shall judge the people righteously. 11Let the heavens rejoice, and let the earth be glad; let the sea roar, and the fulness thereof. 12Let the field be joyful, and all that *is* therein: then shall all the trees of the wood rejoice 13Before the Lord, for he cometh, for he cometh to judge the earth: he shall judge the world with righteousness, and the people with his truth. [Rev. 19:11]

The Lord's power and dominion

97 The Lord reigneth; let the earth rejoice; let the multitude of isles be glad *thereof.* 2Clouds and darkness *are* round about him: righteousness and judgment *are* the habitation of his throne. 3A fire goeth before him, and burneth up his enemies round about. 4His lightnings enlightened the world: the earth saw, and trembled. 5The hills melted like wax at the presence of the Lord, at the presence of the Lord of the whole earth. 6The heavens declare his righteousness, and all the people see his glory. 7Confounded be all they that serve graven images, that boast themselves of idols: worship him, all ye gods. 8Zion heard, and was glad, and the daughters of Judah rejoiced, because of thy judgments, O LORD. 9For thou, LORD, *art* High above all the earth: thou art exalted far above all gods. 10Ye that love the LORD, hate evil: he preserveth the souls of his saints; he delivereth them out of the hand of the wicked. 11Light is sown for the righteous, and gladness for the upright in heart. 12Rejoice in the LORD, ye righteous; and give thanks at the remembrance of his holiness. [Ps. 33:1; 30:4]

Praise to a righteous LORD

A Psalm.

98 O sing unto the LORD a new song; for he hath done marvellous *things:* his right hand, and his holy arm, hath gotten him the victory. 2The LORD hath made known his salvation: his righteousness hath he openly shewed in the sight of the heathen. 3He hath remembered his mercy and his truth toward the house of Israel: all the ends of the earth have seen the salvation of our God. 4Make a joyful noise unto the LORD, all the earth: make a loud noise, and rejoice, and sing *praise.* 5Sing unto the LORD with the harp; with the harp, and the voice of a psalm. 6With trumpets and sound of cornet make a joyful noise before the LORD, the King. 7Let the sea roar, and the fulness thereof; the world, and they that dwell therein. 8Let the floods clap *their* hands: let the hills be joyful together 9Before the LORD; for he cometh to judge the earth: with righteousness shall he judge the world, and the people with equity. [Ps. 96:10]

Praise to a holy God

99 The LORD reigneth; let the people tremble: he sitteth *between* the cherubims; let the earth be moved. 2The LORD *is* great in Zion; and he *is* high above all the people. 3Let them praise thy great and terrible name; *for* it *is* holy.

4 The king's strength also loveth judgment; thou dost establish equity, thou executest judgment and righteousness in Jacob. 5Exalt ye the LORD our God, and worship at his footstool; *for* he *is* holy. [Ps. 132:7; Lev. 19:2]

6 Moses and Aaron among his priests, and Samuel among them that call upon his name; they called upon the LORD, and he answered them. 7He spake unto them in the cloudy pillar: they kept his testimonies, and the ordinance *that* he gave them. 8Thou answeredst them, O LORD our God: thou wast a God that forgavest them, though thou tookest vengeance of their inventions. 9Exalt the LORD our God, and worship at his holy hill; for the LORD our God *is* holy. [Ps. 34:3]

A song of praise and joy

A Psalm of praise.

100 Make a joyful noise unto the LORD, all ye lands. 2Serve the LORD with gladness: come before his presence with singing. 3Know ye that the

LORD he *is* God: *it is* he *that* hath made us, and not we ourselves; *we are* his people, and the sheep of his pasture. ⁴Enter *into* his gates with thanksgiving, *and* into his courts with praise: be thankful unto him, *and* bless his name. ⁵For the LORD *is* good; his mercy *is* everlasting; and his truth *endureth* to all generations. [Ps. 136:1]

A perfect heart

A Psalm of David.

101 I will sing of mercy and judgment: unto thee, O LORD, will I sing. ²I will behave myself wisely in a perfect way. O when wilt thou come unto me? I will walk within my house with a perfect heart. ³I will set no wicked thing before mine eyes: I hate the work of them that turn aside; *it* shall not cleave to me. ⁴A froward heart shall depart from me: I will not know a wicked *person.* ⁵Whoso privily slandereth his neighbour, him will I cut off: him that hath a high look and a proud heart will not I suffer. ⁶Mine eyes *shall be* upon the faithful of the land, that *they* may dwell with me: he that walketh in a perfect way, he shall serve me. ⁷He that worketh deceit shall not dwell within my house: he that telleth lies shall not tarry in my sight. ⁸I will early destroy all the wicked of the land; that *I* may cut off all wicked doers from the city of the LORD. [Ps. 75:10; Jer. 21:12; Ps. 48:2,8]

God's years and man's days

A Prayer of the afflicted, when he is overwhelmed, and poureth out his complaint before the LORD.

102 Hear my prayer, O LORD, and let my cry come unto thee. ²Hide not thy face from me in the day *when* I am in trouble; incline thine ear unto me: in the day *when* I call answer me speedily. ³For my days are consumed like smoke, and my bones are burnt as a hearth. ⁴My heart is smitten, and withered like grass; so that I forget to eat my bread. ⁵By reason of the voice of my groaning my bones cleave to my skin. ⁶I am like a pelican of the wilderness: I am like an owl of the desert. ⁷I watch, and am as a sparrow alone upon the housetop. ⁸Mine enemies reproach me all the day; *and* they that are mad against me are sworn against me. ⁹For I have eaten ashes like bread, and mingled my drink with weeping, ¹⁰Because of thine indignation and thy wrath: for thou hast lifted me up, and cast me down. ¹¹My days *are* like a shadow that declineth; and I am withered like grass. [Eccl. 6:12; Is. 40:6-8; Jas. 1:10]

12 But thou, O LORD, shalt endure for ever; and thy remembrance unto all generations. ¹³Thou shalt arise, *and* have mercy upon Zion: for the time to favour her, yea, the set time, is come. ¹⁴For thy servants take pleasure in her stones, and favour the dust thereof. ¹⁵So the heathen shall fear the name of the LORD, and all the kings of the earth thy glory. ¹⁶When the LORD shall build up

Zion, he shall appear in his glory. [17] He will regard the prayer of the destitute, and not despise their prayer. [18] This shall be written for the generation to come: and the people which *shall be* created shall praise the LORD. [19] For he hath looked down from the height of his sanctuary; from heaven did the LORD behold the earth; [20] To hear the groaning of the prisoner; to loose those that are appointed to death; [21] To declare the name of the LORD in Zion, and his praise in Jerusalem; [22] When the people are gathered together, and the kingdoms, to serve the LORD. [23] He weakened my strength in the way; he shortened my days. [24] I said, O my God, take me not away in the midst of my days: thy years *are* throughout all generations. [25] Of old hast thou laid the foundation of the earth: and the heavens *are* the work of thy hands. [26] They shall perish, but thou shalt endure: yea, all of them shall wax old like a garment; as a vesture shalt thou change them, and they shall be changed: [27] But thou *art* the same, and thy years shall have no end. [28] The children of thy servants shall continue, and their seed shall be established before thee. [Ps. 69:36]

The benefits of the LORD

A Psalm of David.

103 Bless the LORD, O my soul: and all that is within me, *bless* his holy name. [2] Bless the LORD, O my soul, and forget not all his benefits: [3] Who forgiveth all thine iniquities; who healeth all thy diseases; [4] Who redeemeth thy life from destruction; who crowneth thee *with* lovingkindness and tender mercies; [5] Who satisfieth thy mouth with good *things; so that* thy youth is renewed like the eagle's. [Is. 40:31]

6 The LORD executeth righteousness and judgment for all that are oppressed. [7] He made known his ways unto Moses, his acts unto the children of Israel. [8] The LORD *is* merciful and gracious, slow to anger, and plenteous in mercy. [9] He will not always chide: neither will he keep *his anger* for ever. [10] He hath not dealt with us after our sins; nor rewarded us according to our iniquities. [11] For as the heaven is high above the earth, *so* great is his mercy toward them that fear him. [12] As far as the east is from the west, *so* far hath he removed our transgressions from us. [13] Like as a father pitieth *his* children, *so* the LORD pitieth them that fear him. [14] For he knoweth our frame; he remembereth that we *are* dust. [15] *As for* man, his days *are* as grass: as a flower of the field, so he flourisheth. [16] For the wind passeth over it, and it is gone; and the place thereof shall know it no more. [17] But the mercy of the LORD *is* from everlasting to everlasting upon them that fear him, and his righteousness unto children's children; [18] To such as keep his covenant, and to those that remember his commandments to do them. [Deut. 7:9]

19 The LORD hath prepared his throne in the heavens; and his kingdom ruleth over all. [20] Bless the LORD, ye his angels, that excel

in strength, that do his commandments, hearkening unto the voice
of his word. 21 Bless ye the LORD, all
ye his hosts; ye ministers of his,
that do his pleasure. 22 Bless the
LORD, all his works in all places of
his dominion: bless the LORD,
O my soul.

God the creator of the earth

104 Bless the LORD, O my
soul. O LORD my God,
thou art very great; thou art
clothed with honour and majesty.
2 Who coverest *thyself with* light as
with a garment: who stretchest out
the heavens like a curtain: 3 Who
layeth the beams of his chambers
in the waters: who maketh the
clouds his chariot: who walketh
upon the wings of the wind: 4 Who
maketh his angels spirits; his ministers a flaming fire: 5 *Who* laid the
foundations of the earth, *that* it
should not be removed for ever.
6 Thou coveredst it *with* the deep
as *with* a garment: the waters stood
above the mountains. 7 At thy rebuke they fled; at the voice of thy
thunder they hasted away. 8 They
go up *by* the mountains; they
down *by* the valleys unto the place
which thou hast founded for them.
9 Thou hast set a bound *that* they
may not pass over; *that* they turn
not again to cover the earth. 10 He
sendeth the springs into the valleys, *which* run among the hills.
11 They give drink to every beast of
the field: the wild asses quench
their thirst. 12 By them shall the
fowls of the heaven have their
habitation, *which* sing among the
branches. 13 He watereth the hills

from his chambers: the earth is satisfied with the fruit of thy works.
14 He causeth the grass to grow for
the cattle, and herb for the service
of man: that *he* may bring forth
food out of the earth; 15 And wine
that maketh glad the heart of man,
and oil to make *his* face to shine,
and bread *which* strengtheneth
man's heart. 16 The trees of the
LORD are full *of sap;* the cedars of
Lebanon, which he hath planted;
17 Where the birds make their
nests: *as for* the stork, the fir trees
are her house. 18 The high hills *are*
a refuge for the wild goats; *and* the
rocks for the conies. 19 He appointed the moon for seasons: the sun
knoweth his going down. 20 Thou
makest darkness, and it is night:
wherein all the beasts of the forest
do creep *forth.* 21 The young lions
roar after *their* prey, and seek their
meat from God. 22 The sun ariseth,
they gather themselves together,
and lay them down in their dens.
23 Man goeth forth unto his work
and to his labour until the evening.
24 O LORD, how manifold are thy
works! in wisdom hast thou made
them all: the earth is full *of* thy
riches. 25 *So is* this great and wide
sea, wherein *are* things creeping
innumerable, both small and great
beasts. 26 There go the ships: *there*
is that leviathan, *whom* thou hast
made to play therein. 27 These wait
all upon thee; that *thou* mayest
give *them* their meat in due season. 28 *That* thou givest them they
gather: thou openest thine hand,
they are filled *with* good. 29 Thou
hidest thy face, they are troubled:
thou takest away their breath, they

die, and return to their dust. 30Thou sendest forth thy spirit, they are created: and thou renewest the face of the earth. [Is. 32:15; Ezek. 37:9]

31 The glory of the LORD shall endure for ever: the LORD shall rejoice in his works. 32He looketh on the earth, and it trembleth: he toucheth the hills, and they smoke. 33I will sing unto the LORD as long as I live: I will sing praise unto my God while I have my being. 34My meditation of him shall be sweet: I will be glad in the LORD. 35Let the sinners be consumed out of the earth, and let the wicked be no more. Bless thou the LORD, O my soul. Praise ye the LORD. [Ps. 37:38; Prov. 2:22]

The LORD remembers his covenant

105 O give thanks unto the LORD; call upon his name: make known his deeds among the people. 2Sing unto him, sing psalms unto him: talk ye of all his wondrous works. 3Glory ye in his holy name: let the heart of them rejoice that seek the LORD. 4Seek the LORD, and his strength: seek his face evermore. 5Remember his marvellous works that he hath done; his wonders, and the judgments of his mouth; 6O ye seed of Abraham his servant, ye children of Jacob, his chosen. 7He is the LORD our God: his judgments are in all the earth. 8He hath remembered his covenant for ever, the word which he commanded to a thousand generations. 9Which covenant he made with Abraham, and his

oath unto Isaac; 10And confirmed the same unto Jacob for a law, and to Israel for an everlasting covenant: 11Saying, Unto thee will I give the land of Canaan, the lot of your inheritance: 12When they were but a few men in number; yea, very few, and strangers in it. 13When they went from one nation to another, from one kingdom to another people; 14He suffered no man to do them wrong: yea, he reproved kings for their sakes; 15Saying, Touch not mine anointed, and do my prophets no harm. 16Moreover, he called for a famine upon the land: he brake the whole staff of bread. 17He sent a man before them, even Joseph, who was sold for a servant: 18Whose feet they hurt with fetters: he was laid in iron: 19Until the time that his word came: the word of the LORD tried him. 20The king sent and loosed him; even the ruler of the people, and let him go free. 21He made him lord of his house, and ruler of all his substance: 22To bind his princes at his pleasure; and teach his senators wisdom. 23Israel also came into Egypt; and Jacob sojourned in the land of Ham. 24And he increased his people greatly; and made them stronger than their enemies. 25He turned their heart to hate his people, to deal subtilly with his servants. 26He sent Moses his servant; and Aaron whom he had chosen. 27They shewed his signs among them, and wonders in the land of Ham. 28He sent darkness, and made it dark; and they rebelled not against his word. 29He turned their waters into blood, and slew their fish. 30Their land brought forth frogs in abundance, in the chambers of their kings. 31He spake, and there came divers sorts *of flies, and* lice in all their coasts. 32He gave them hail *for* rain, *and* flaming fire in their land. 33He smote their vines also and their fig trees; and brake the trees of their coasts. 34He spake, and the locusts came, and caterpillars, and that without number, 35And did eat up all the herbs in their land, and devoured the fruit of their ground. 36He smote also all the firstborn in their land, the chief of all their strength. 37He brought them forth also with silver and gold: and *there was* not *one* feeble *person* among their tribes. 38Egypt was glad when they departed: for the fear of them that fell upon them. 39He spread a cloud for a covering; and fire to give light in the night. 40*The people* asked, and he brought quails, and satisfied them *with* the bread of heaven. 41He opened the rock, and the waters gushed out; they ran in the dry *places like* a river. 42For he remembered his holy promise, *and* Abraham his servant. 43And he brought forth his people with joy, *and* his chosen with gladness: 44And gave them the lands of the heathen: and they inherited the labour of the people; 45That they might observe his statutes, and keep his laws. Praise ye the LORD. [Deut. 4:1; 6:21-25]

God's mercy to Israel

106 Praise ye the LORD. O give thanks unto the LORD; for *he is* good: for his mercy *endureth* for ever. 2Who can utter

the mighty acts of the LORD? *who* can shew forth all his praise? 3Blessed *are* they that keep judgment, *and* he that doeth righteousness at all times. 4Remember me, O LORD, with the favour *that thou bearest* unto thy people: O visit me with thy salvation; 5That *I* may see the good of thy chosen, that *I* may rejoice in the gladness of thy nation, that *I* may glory with thine inheritance. 6We have sinned with our fathers, we have committed iniquity, we have done wickedly. 7Our fathers understood not thy wonders in Egypt; they remembered not the multitude of thy mercies; but provoked *him* at the sea, *even* at the Red sea. 8Nevertheless he saved them for his name's sake, that *he* might make his mighty power to be known. 9He rebuked the Red sea also, and it was dried up: so he led them through the depths, as *through* the wilderness. 10And he saved them from the hand of him that hated *them,* and redeemed them from the hand of the enemy. 11And the waters covered their enemies: there was not one of them left. 12Then believed they his words; they sang his praise. 13They soon forgat his works; they waited not for his counsel: 14But lusted exceedingly in the wilderness, and tempted God in the desert. 15And he gave them their request; but sent leanness into their soul. 16They envied Moses also in the camp, *and* Aaron the saint of the LORD. 17The earth opened and swallowed up Dathan, and covered the company of Abiram. 18And a fire was kindled in their company; the flame burnt up the wicked. ¹⁹They made a calf in Horeb, and worshipped the molten image. ²⁰Thus they changed their glory into the similitude of an ox that eateth grass. ²¹They forgat God their saviour, which had done great *things* in Egypt; ²²Wondrous works in the land of Ham, *and* terrible *things* by the Red sea. ²³Therefore he said that *he* would destroy them, had not Moses his chosen stood before him in the breach, to turn away his wrath, lest *he* should destroy *them*. ²⁴Yea, they despised the pleasant land, they believed not his word: ²⁵But murmured in their tents, *and* hearkened not unto the voice of the LORD. ²⁶Therefore he lifted up his hand against them, to overthrow them in the wilderness: ²⁷To overthrow their seed also among the nations, and to scatter them in the lands. ²⁸They joined themselves also unto Baal-peor, and ate the sacrifices of the dead. ²⁹Thus they provoked *him* to anger with their inventions: and the plague brake in upon them. ³⁰Then stood up Phinehas, and executed judgment: and *so* the plague was stayed. ³¹And *that* was counted unto him for righteousness unto all generations for evermore. ³²They angered *him* also at the waters of strife, so that it went ill with Moses for their sakes: ³³Because they provoked his spirit, so that he spake unadvisedly with his lips. ³⁴They did not destroy the nations, *concerning* whom the LORD commanded them: ³⁵But were mingled among the heathen, and learned their works. ³⁶And they served their idols: which were a snare unto them. ³⁷Yea, they sacrificed their sons and their daughters unto devils, ³⁸And shed innocent blood, *even* the blood of their sons and of their daughters, whom they sacrificed unto the idols of Canaan: and the land was polluted with blood. ³⁹Thus were they defiled with their own works, and went a whoring with their own inventions. ⁴⁰Therefore was the wrath of the LORD kindled against his people, insomuch that he abhorred his own inheritance. ⁴¹And he gave them into the hand of the heathen; and they that hated them ruled over them. ⁴²Their enemies also oppressed them, and they were brought into subjection under their hand. ⁴³Many times did he deliver them; but they provoked *him* with their counsel, and were brought low for their iniquity. ⁴⁴Nevertheless he regarded their affliction, when he heard their cry: ⁴⁵And he remembered for them his covenant, and repented according to the multitude of his mercies. ⁴⁶He made them also to be pitied of all those that carried them captives.

[Ezra 9:9; Jer. 42:12]

47 Save us, O LORD our God, and gather us from among the heathen, to give thanks unto thy holy name, *and* to triumph in thy praise. ⁴⁸Blessed *be* the LORD God of Israel from everlasting to everlasting: and let all the people say, Amen. Praise ye the LORD. [Ps. 41:13]

The LORD's goodness to men

107 O give thanks unto the LORD, for *he is* good: for his mercy *endureth* for ever. 2Let the redeemed of the LORD say *so,* whom he hath redeemed from the hand of the enemy; 3And gathered them out of the lands, from the east, and from the west, from the north, and from the south. [Ps. 106:47]

4 They wandered in the wilderness in a solitary way; they found no city to dwell in. 5Hungry and thirsty, their soul fainted in them. 6Then they cried unto the LORD in their trouble, *and* he delivered them out of their distresses. 7And he led them forth by the right way, that *they* might go to a city of habitation. 8Oh that *men* would praise the LORD *for* his goodness, and *for* his wonderful works to the children of men! 9For he satisfieth the longing soul, and filleth the hungry soul *with* goodness. [Ps. 34:10; Luke 1:53]

10 Such as sit in darkness and in the shadow of death, *being* bound in affliction and iron; 11Because they rebelled against the words of God, and contemned the counsel of the most High: 12Therefore he brought down their heart with labour; they fell down, and *there was* none to help. 13Then they cried unto the LORD in their trouble, *and* he saved them out of their distresses. 14He brought them out of darkness and the shadow of death, and brake their bands in sunder. 15Oh that *men* would praise the LORD *for* his goodness, and *for* his wonderful works to the

children of men! 16For he hath broken the gates of brass, and cut the bars of iron in sunder. [Is. 45:2]

17 Fools because of their transgression, and because of their iniquities, are afflicted. 18Their soul abhorreth all *manner of* meat; and they draw near unto the gates of death. 19Then they cry unto the LORD in their trouble, he saveth them out of their distresses. 20He sent his word, and healed them, and delivered *them* from their destructions. 21Oh that *men* would praise the LORD *for* his goodness, and *for* his wonderful works to the children of men! 22And let them sacrifice the sacrifices of thanksgiving, and declare his works with rejoicing. [Lev. 7:12; Ps. 116:17; Heb. 13:15; Ps. 9:11; 73:28; 118:17]

23 They that go down to the sea in ships, that do business in great waters; 24These see the works of the LORD, and his wonders in the deep. 25For he commandeth, and raiseth the stormy wind, which lifteth up the waves thereof. 26They mount up to the heaven, they go down again to the depths: their soul is melted because of trouble. 27They reel to and fro, and stagger like a drunken *man,* and are at their wit's end. 28Then they cry unto the LORD in their trouble, and he bringeth them out of their distresses. 29He maketh the storm a calm, so that the waves thereof are still. 30Then are they glad because they be quiet; so he bringeth them unto their desired haven. 31Oh that *men* would praise the LORD *for* his goodness, and *for* his wonderful works to the children of

men! 32Let them exalt him also in the congregation of the people, and praise him in the assembly of the elders. [Ps. 22:22,25]

33 He turneth rivers into a wilderness, and the watersprings into dry ground; 34A fruitful land into barrenness, for the wickedness of them that dwell therein. 35He turneth the wilderness into a standing water, and dry ground into watersprings; 36And there he maketh the hungry to dwell, that they may prepare a city for habitation; 37And sow the fields, and plant vineyards, which may yield fruits of increase. 38He blesseth them also, so that they are multiplied greatly; and suffereth not their cattle to decrease. 39Again, they are minished and brought low through oppression, affliction, and sorrow. 40He poureth contempt upon princes, and causeth them to wander in the wilderness, where there is no way. 41Yet setteth he the poor on high from affliction, and maketh him families like a flock. 42The righteous shall see it, and rejoice: and all iniquity shall stop her mouth. 43Whoso is wise, and will observe these things, even they shall understand the lovingkindness of the LORD. [Ps. 64:9; Jer. 9:12; Hos. 14:9]

A song of confidence in God

A Song or Psalm of David.

108 O God, my heart is fixed; I will sing and give praise, even with my glory. 2Awake, psaltery and harp: I myself will awake early. 3I will praise thee, O LORD, among the people:

and I will sing *praises* unto thee among the nations. 4For thy mercy *is* great above the heavens: and thy truth *reacheth* unto the clouds. 5Be thou exalted, O God, above the heavens: and thy glory above all the earth. [Ps. 57:5,11]

6 That thy beloved may be delivered; save *with* thy right hand, and answer me. 7God hath spoken in his holiness; I will rejoice, I will divide Shechem, and mete out the valley of Succoth. 8Gilead *is* mine; Manasseh *is* mine; Ephraim also *is* the strength of mine head; Judah *is* my lawgiver; 9Moab *is* my washpot; over Edom will I cast out my shoe; over Philistia will I triumph.

10 Who will bring me *into* the strong city? who will lead me into Edom? 11*Wilt* not *thou,* O God, *who* hast cast us off? and wilt not thou, O God, go forth with our hosts? 12Give us help from trouble: for vain *is* the help of man. 13Through God we shall do valiantly: for he *it is that* shall tread down our enemies. [Ps. 60:12]

A cry to God for help

To the chief Musician, A Psalm of David.

109 Hold not thy peace, O God of my praise; 2For the mouth of the wicked and the mouth of the deceitful are opened against me: they have spoken against me *with* a lying tongue. 3They compassed me about also *with* words of hatred; and fought against me without a cause. 4For my love they are my adversaries: but I *give myself unto* prayer. 5And they have rewarded me evil for good, and hatred for my love. ⁶Set thou a wicked *man* over him: and let Satan stand at his right hand. ⁷When he shall be judged, let him be condemned: and let his prayer become sin. ⁸Let his days be few; *and* let another take his office. ⁹Let his children be fatherless, and his wife a widow. ¹⁰Let his children be continually vagabonds, and beg: let them seek *their bread* also out of their desolate places. ¹¹Let the extortioner catch all that he hath; and let the strangers spoil his labour. ¹²Let there be none to extend mercy unto him: neither let there be any to favour his fatherless children. ¹³Let his posterity be cut off; *and* in the generation following let their name be blotted out. ¹⁴Let the iniquity of his fathers be remembered with the LORD; and let not the sin of his mother be blotted out. ¹⁵Let them be before the LORD continually, that he may cut off the memory of them from the earth. ¹⁶Because that he remembered not to shew mercy, but persecuted the poor and needy man, that *he* might even slay the broken in heart. ¹⁷As he loved cursing, so let it come *unto* him: as he delighted not in blessing, so let it be far from him. ¹⁸As he clothed himself with cursing like as with his garment, so let it come into his bowels like water, and like oil into his bones. ¹⁹Let it be unto him as the garment *which* covereth *him,* and for a girdle wherewith he is girded continually. ²⁰*Let* this *be* the reward of mine adversaries from the LORD, and of them that speak evil against my soul.

²¹ But do thou for me, O GOD the Lord, for thy name's sake: because thy mercy *is* good, deliver thou me. ²²For I *am* poor and needy, and my heart is wounded within me. ²³I am gone like the shadow when it declineth: I am tossed up and down as the locust. ²⁴My knees are weak through fasting; and my flesh faileth of fatness. ²⁵I became also a reproach unto them: *when* they looked upon me they shaked their heads. ²⁶Help me, O LORD my God: O save me according to thy mercy: ²⁷That they may know that this *is* thy hand; *that* thou, LORD, hast done it. ²⁸Let them curse, but bless thou: when they arise, let them be ashamed; but let thy servant rejoice. ²⁹Let mine adversaries be clothed with shame, and let them cover *themselves with* their own confusion, as *with* a mantle. ³⁰I will greatly praise the LORD with my mouth; yea, I will praise him among the multitude. ³¹For he shall stand at the right hand of the poor, to save *him* from those that condemn his soul. [Ps. 16:8; 73:23]

The king as priest and victor

A Psalm of David.

110 The LORD said unto my Lord, Sit thou at my right hand, until I make thine enemies thy footstool. ²The LORD shall send the rod of thy strength out of Zion: rule thou in the midst of thine enemies. ³Thy people *shall be* willing in the day of thy power, in the beauties of holiness from the womb of the morning: thou hast the dew of thy youth. ⁴The LORD hath sworn, and will not repent, Thou *art* a priest for ever after the order of Melchizedek. 5The Lord at thy right hand shall strike through kings in the day of his wrath. 6He shall judge among the heathen, he shall fill *the places with* the dead bodies; he shall wound the heads over many countries. 7He shall drink of the brook in the way: therefore shall he lift up the head. [Is. 53:12]

The LORD's wonderful works

111 Praise ye the LORD. I will praise the LORD with *my* whole heart, in the assembly of the upright, and *in* the congregation. 2The works of the LORD *are* great, sought out of all them that have pleasure therein. 3His work *is* honourable and glorious: and his righteousness endureth for ever. 4He hath made his wonderful works to be remembered: the LORD *is* gracious and full of compassion. 5He hath given meat unto them that fear him: he will ever be mindful of his covenant. 6He hath shewed his people the power of his works, that *he* may give them the heritage of the heathen. 7The works of his hands *are* verity and judgment; all his commandments *are* sure. 8They stand fast for ever and ever, *and* are done in truth and uprightness. 9He sent redemption unto his people: he hath commanded his covenant for ever: holy and reverend *is* his name. 10The fear of the LORD *is* the beginning of wisdom: a good understanding have all they that do

his commandments: his praise endureth for ever. [Eccl. 12:13]

The prosperity of the righteous

112 Praise ye the LORD. Blessed *is* the man *that* feareth the LORD, *that* delighteth greatly in his commandments. 2His seed shall be mighty upon earth: the generation of the upright shall be blessed. 3Wealth and riches *shall be* in his house: and his righteousness endureth for ever. 4Unto the upright there ariseth light in the darkness: *he is* gracious, and full of compassion, and righteous. 5A good man sheweth favour, and lendeth: he will guide his affairs with discretion. 6Surely he shall not be moved for ever: the righteous shall be in everlasting remembrance. 7He shall not be afraid of evil tidings: his heart is fixed, trusting in the LORD. 8His heart *is* established, he shall not be afraid, until he see *his desire* upon his enemies. 9He hath dispersed, he hath given to the poor; his righteousness endureth for ever; his horn shall be exalted with honour. 10The wicked shall see *it,* and be grieved; he shall gnash *with* his teeth, and melt away: the desire of the wicked shall perish. [Luke 13:28; Ps. 37:12; 58:7,8; Prov. 11:7]

A hymn of praise to God

113 Praise ye the LORD. Praise, O ye servants of the LORD, praise the name of the LORD. 2Blessed be the name of the LORD from this time forth and for evermore. 3From the rising of the sun unto the going down of the same the LORD'S name *is* to be praised. 4The LORD *is* high above all nations, *and* his glory above the heavens. 5Who *is* like unto the LORD our God, who dwelleth on high, 6Who humbleth *himself* to behold *the things that are* in heaven, and in the earth? 7He raiseth up the poor out of the dust, *and* lifteth the needy out of the dunghill; 8That *he* may set *him* with princes, *even* with the princes of his people. 9He maketh the barren *woman* to keep house, *to be* a joyful mother of children. Praise ye the LORD. [1 Sam. 2:5; Ps. 68:6; Is. 54:1; Gal. 4:27]

The God of the exodus

114 When Israel went out of Egypt, the house of Jacob from a people of strange language; 2Judah was his sanctuary, *and* Israel his dominion. [Ex. 6:7; Deut. 27:9]

3 The sea saw *it,* and fled: Jordan was driven back. 4The mountains skipped like rams, *and* the little hills like lambs. [Ps. 29:6; 68:16]

5 What ailed thee, O thou sea, that thou fleddest? thou Jordan, *that* thou wast driven back? 6Ye mountains, *that* ye skipped like rams; *and* ye little hills, like lambs?

7 Tremble, thou earth, at the presence of the Lord, at the presence of the God of Jacob; 8Which turned the rock *into* a standing water, the flint into a fountain of waters. [Ex. 17:6; Num. 20:11; Ps. 107:35]

To God alone belongs glory

115 Not unto us, O LORD, not unto us, but unto thy name give glory, for thy mercy, *and* for thy truth's sake. 2Wherefore should the heathen say, Where *is* now their God? [Ps. 42:3,10; 79:10; Joel 2:17]

3 But our God *is* in the heavens: he hath done whatsoever he pleased. 4Their idols *are* silver and gold, the work of men's hands. 5They have mouths, but they speak not: eyes have they, but they see not: 6They have ears, but they hear not: noses have they, but they smell not: 7They *have* hands, but they handle not: feet *have* they, but they walk not: neither speak they through their throat. 8They that make them are like unto them; *so is* every one that trusteth in them. [Ps. 135:18; Is. 44:9-11]

9 O Israel, trust thou in the LORD: he *is* their help and their shield. 10O house of Aaron, trust in the LORD: he *is* their help and their shield. 11Ye that fear the LORD, trust in the LORD: he *is* their help and their shield.

12 The LORD hath been mindful of us: he will bless *us;* he will bless the house of Israel; he will bless the house of Aaron. 13He will bless them that fear the LORD, *both* small and great. 14The LORD shall increase you more and more, you and your children. 15You *are* blessed of the LORD which made heaven and earth. [Gen. 14:19; 1:1; Ps. 96:5]

16 The heaven, *even* the heavens, *are* the LORD'S: but the earth hath he given to the children of

men. 17The dead praise not the LORD, neither any that go down into silence. 18But we will bless the LORD from this time forth and for evermore. Praise the LORD. [Ps. 113:2; Dan. 2:20]

Deliverance from death

116 I love the LORD, because he hath heard my voice and my supplications. 2Because he hath inclined his ear unto me, therefore will I call upon him as long as I live. 3The sorrows of death compassed me, and the pains of hell gat hold upon me: I found trouble and sorrow. 4Then called I upon the name of the LORD; O LORD, I beseech thee, deliver my soul. 5Gracious is the LORD, and righteous; yea, our God is merciful. 6The LORD preserveth the simple: I was brought low, and he helped me. 7Return unto thy rest, O my soul; for the LORD hath dealt bountifully with thee. 8For thou hast delivered my soul from death, mine eyes from tears, and my feet from falling. 9I will walk before the LORD in the land of the living. 10I believed, therefore have I spoken: I was greatly afflicted: 11I said in my haste, All men are liars. [Ps. 31:22; Rom. 3:4]

12 What shall I render unto the LORD for all his benefits towards me? 13I will take the cup of salvation, and call upon the name of the LORD. 14I will pay my vows unto the LORD now in the presence of all his people. 15Precious is the sight of the LORD is the death of his saints. 16Oh LORD, truly I am thy servant; I am thy servant, and the son of thy handmaid: thou hast loosed my bonds. 17I will offer to thee the sacrifice of thanksgiving, and will call upon the name of the LORD. 18I will pay my vows unto the LORD now in the presence of all his people, 19In the courts of the LORD's house, in the midst of thee, O Jerusalem. Praise ye the LORD. [Ps. 96:8; 100:4]

Praise for God's steadfast love

117 O praise the LORD, all ye nations: praise him, all ye people. 2For his merciful kindness is great toward us: and the truth of the LORD endureth for ever. Praise ye the LORD. [Ps. 100:5]

The LORD's mercy

118 O give thanks unto the LORD; for he is good: because his mercy endureth for ever. 2Let Israel now say, that his mercy endureth for ever. 3Let the house of Aaron now say, that his mercy endureth for ever. 4Let them now that fear the LORD say, that his mercy endureth for ever.

5 I called upon the LORD in distress: the LORD answered me, and set me in a large place. 6The LORD is on my side; I will not fear: what can man do unto me? 7The LORD taketh my part with them that help me: therefore shall I see my desire upon them that hate me. 8It is better to trust in the LORD than to put confidence in man. 9It is better to trust in the LORD than to put confidence in princes. 10All nations compassed me about: but in the name of the LORD will I destroy them. 11They compassed me

about; yea, they compassed me about: but in the name of the LORD I will destroy them. ¹²They compassed me about like bees; they are quenched as the fire of thorns: for in the name of the LORD I will destroy them. ¹³Thou hast thrust sore at me that *I* might fall: but the LORD helped me. ¹⁴The LORD *is* my strength and song, and is become my salvation. ¹⁵The voice of rejoicing and salvation *is* in the tabernacles of the righteous: the right hand of the LORD doeth valiantly. ¹⁶The right hand of the LORD is exalted: the right hand of the LORD doeth valiantly. ¹⁷I shall not die, but live, and declare the works of the LORD. ¹⁸The LORD hath chastened me sore: but he hath not given me over unto death. ¹⁹Open to me the gates of righteousness: I will go into them, *and* I will praise the LORD: ²⁰This gate of the LORD, into which the righteous shall enter. ²¹I will praise thee: for thou hast heard me, and art become my salvation. ²²The stone *which* the builders refused is become the head *stone* of the corner. ²³This is the LORD'S doing; it is marvellous in our eyes. ²⁴This *is* the day *which* the LORD hath made; we will rejoice and be glad in it. ²⁵Save now, I beseech thee, O LORD: O LORD, I beseech thee, send now prosperity. ²⁶Blessed *be* he that cometh in the name of the LORD: we have blessed you out of the house of the LORD. ²⁷God *is* the LORD, which hath shewed us light: bind the sacrifice with cords, *even* unto the horns of the altar. ²⁸Thou *art* my God, and I will praise thee: *thou art* my God, I

will exalt thee. ²⁹O give thanks unto the LORD; for *he is* good: for his mercy *endureth* for ever. [ver. 1]

Keepers of God's law

א ALEPH.

119

Blessed *are* the undefiled in the way, who walk in the law of the LORD. ²Blessed *are* they that keep his testimonies, *and that* seek him with the whole heart. ³They also do no iniquity: they walk in his ways. ⁴Thou hast commanded *us* to keep thy precepts diligently. ⁵O that my ways were directed to keep thy statutes! ⁶Then shall I not be ashamed, when I have respect unto all thy commandments. ⁷I will praise thee with uprightness of heart, when I shall have learned thy righteous judgments. ⁸I will keep thy statutes: O forsake me not utterly.

Purity, the fruit of the law

ב BETH.

9 Wherewithal shall a young man cleanse his way? by taking heed *thereto* according to thy word. ¹⁰With my whole heart have I sought thee: O let me not wander from thy commandments. ¹¹Thy word have I hid in mine heart, that I might not sin against thee. ¹²Blessed *art* thou, O LORD: teach me thy statutes. ¹³With my lips have I declared all the judgments of thy mouth. ¹⁴I have rejoiced in the way of thy testimonies, as *much as* in all riches. ¹⁵I will meditate in thy precepts, and have respect unto thy ways. ¹⁶I will de-

light myself in thy statutes: I will not forget thy word. [Ps. 1:2]

Eyes to see God's law

ג GIMEL.

17 Deal bountifully with thy servant, *that* I may live, and keep thy word. 18 Open thou mine eyes, that I may behold wondrous *things* out of thy law. 19 I *am* a stranger in the earth: hide not thy commandments from me. 20 My soul breaketh for the longing *that it hath* unto thy judgments at all times. 21 Thou hast rebuked the proud *that are* cursed, which do err from thy commandments. 22 Remove from me reproach and contempt; for I have kept thy testimonies. 23 Princes also did sit *and* speak against me: *but* thy servant did meditate in thy statutes. 24 Thy testimonies also *are* my delight *and* my counsellers. [ver. 77,92]

Prayer for understanding the law

ד DALETH.

25 My soul cleaveth unto the dust: quicken thou me according to thy word. 26 I have declared my ways, and thou heardest me: teach me thy statutes. 27 Make me to understand the way of thy precepts: so shall I talk of thy wondrous works. 28 My soul melteth for heaviness: strengthen thou me according unto thy word. 29 Remove from me the way of lying: and grant me thy law graciously. 30 I have chosen the way of truth: thy judgments have I laid *before me.* 31 I have stuck unto thy testimonies: O LORD, put me not to shame. 32 I will

run the way of thy commandments, when thou shalt enlarge my heart. [1 Ki. 4:29; Is. 60:5; 2 Cor. 6:11]

Living the LORD's way

ה HE.

33 Teach me, O LORD, the way of thy statutes; and I shall keep it *unto* the end. 34 Give me understanding, and I shall keep thy law; yea, I shall observe it with *my* whole heart. 35 Make me to go in the path of thy commandments; for therein do I delight. 36 Incline my heart unto thy testimonies, and not to covetousness. 37 Turn away mine eyes from beholding vanity; *and* quicken thou me in thy way. 38 Stablish thy word unto thy servant, who *is* devoted to thy fear. 39 Turn away my reproach which I fear: for thy judgments *are* good. 40 Behold, I have longed after thy precepts: quicken me in thy righteousness. [ver. 20; ver. 25,37]

Salvation through God's law

ו VAU.

41 Let thy mercies come also *unto* me, O LORD, *even* thy salvation, according to thy word. 42 So shall I have wherewith to answer him that reproacheth me: for I trust in thy word. 43 And take not the word of truth utterly out of my mouth; for I have hoped in thy judgments. 44 So shall I keep thy law continually for ever and ever. 45 And I will walk at liberty: for I seek thy precepts. 46 I will speak of thy testimonies also before kings, and will not be ashamed. 47 And I will delight myself in thy com-

mandments, which I have loved.
48My hands also will I lift up unto
thy commandments, which I have
loved; and I will meditate in thy
statutes. [ver. 15]

Comfort in God's law

ז ZAIN.

49 Remember the word unto
thy servant, upon which thou hast
caused me to hope. 50This *is* my
comfort in my affliction: for thy
word hath quickened me. 51The
proud have had me greatly in derision: *yet* have I not declined from
thy law. 52I remembered thy judgments of old, O LORD; and have
comforted myself. 53Horror hath
taken hold upon me because of the
wicked that forsake thy law. 54Thy
statutes have been my songs in the
house of my pilgrimage. 55I have
remembered thy name, O LORD, in
the night, and have kept thy law.
56This I had, because I kept thy
precepts.

The LORD our portion

ח CHETH.

57 *Thou art* my portion,
O LORD: I have said that *I* would
keep thy words. 58I intreated thy
favour with *my* whole heart: be
merciful unto me according to thy
word. 59I thought on my ways, and
turned my feet unto thy testimonies. 60I made haste, and de-
layed not to keep thy commandments. 61The bands of the wicked
have robbed me: *but* I have not forgotten thy law. 62At midnight I will
rise to give thanks unto thee because of thy righteous judgments.

63I *am* a companion of all *them* that
fear thee, and of them that keep
thy precepts. 64The earth, O LORD,
is full *of* thy mercy: teach me thy
statutes. [Ps. 33:5; ver. 12,26]

God's law taught by affliction

ט TETH.

65 Thou hast dealt well with
thy servant, O LORD, according
unto thy word. 66Teach me good
judgment and knowledge: for I
have believed thy commandments.
67Before I was afflicted I went
astray: but now have I kept thy
word. 68Thou *art* good, and doest
good; teach me thy statutes. 69The
proud have forged a lie against me:
but I will keep thy precepts with
my whole heart. 70Their heart is as
fat as grease; *but* I delight *in* thy
law. 71*It is* good for me that I have
been afflicted; that I might learn
thy statutes. 72The law of thy
mouth *is* better unto me than thousands of gold and silver. [Ps. 19:10;
Prov. 8:10,11,19]

Confidence in the law

י JOD.

73 Thy hands have made me
and fashioned me: give me understanding, that I may learn thy commandments. 74They that fear thee
will be glad when they see me; because I have hoped in thy word. 75I
know, O LORD, that thy judgments
are right, and *that* thou *in* faithfulness hast afflicted me. 76Let, I pray
thee, thy merciful kindness be for
my comfort, according to thy word
unto thy servant. 77Let thy tender
mercies come *unto* me, that I may

live: for thy law *is* my delight. 78Let the proud be ashamed; for they dealt perversely with me without a cause: *but* I will meditate in thy precepts. 79Let those that fear thee turn unto me, and those that have known thy testimonies. 80Let my heart be sound in thy statutes; that I be not ashamed.

A longing for comfort

ב CAPH.

81 My soul fainteth for thy salvation: *but* I hope in thy word. 82Mine eyes fail for thy word, saying, When wilt thou comfort me? 83For I am become like a bottle in the smoke; *yet* do I not forget thy statutes. 84How many *are* the days of thy servant? when wilt thou execute judgment on them that persecute me? 85The proud have digged pits for me, which *are* not after thy law. 86All thy commandments *are* faithful: they persecute me wrongfully; help thou me. 87They had almost consumed me upon earth; but I forsook not thy precepts. 88Quicken me after thy lovingkindness; so shall I keep the testimony of thy mouth. [ver. 40]

God's unchangeable law

ל LAMED.

89 For ever, O LORD, thy word *is* settled in heaven. 90Thy faithfulness *is* unto all generations: thou hast established the earth, and it abideth. 91They continue *this* day according to thine ordinances: for all *are* thy servants. 92Unless thy law *had been* my delights, I should then have perished in mine afflic-

tion. 93I will never forget thy precepts: for with them thou hast quickened me. 94I *am* thine, save me; for I have sought thy precepts. 95The wicked have waited for me to destroy me: *but* I will consider thy testimonies. 96I have seen an end of all perfection: *but* thy commandment *is* exceeding broad. [Mat. 5:18]

The love of God's law

מ MEM.

97 O how love I thy law! it *is* my meditation all the day. 98Thou *through* thy commandments hast made me wiser than mine enemies: for they *are* ever with me. 99I have more understanding than all my teachers: for thy testimonies *are* my meditation. 100I understand more than the ancients, because I keep thy precepts. 101I have refrained my feet from every evil way, that I might keep thy word. 102I have not departed from thy judgments: for thou hast taught me. 103How sweet are thy words unto my taste! *yea, sweeter* than honey to my mouth! 104Through thy precepts I get understanding: therefore I hate every false way. [ver. 128]

God's law a lamp to the feet

נ NUN.

105 Thy word *is* a lamp unto my feet, and a light unto my path. 106I have sworn, and I will perform *it,* that *I* will keep thy righteous judgments. 107I am afflicted very much: quicken me, O LORD, according unto thy word. 108Accept, I be-

seech thee, the freewill offerings of my mouth, O LORD, and teach me thy judgments. ¹⁰⁹My soul *is* continually in my hand: yet do I not forget thy law. ¹¹⁰The wicked have laid a snare for me: yet I erred not from thy precepts. ¹¹¹Thy testimonies have I taken as an heritage for ever: for they *are* the rejoicing of my heart. ¹¹²I have inclined mine heart to perform thy statutes alway, *even unto* the end. [ver. 33]

God's law a hiding place

ס SAMECH.

113 I hate *vain* thoughts: but thy law do I love. ¹¹⁴Thou *art* my hiding place and my shield: I hope in thy word. ¹¹⁵Depart from me, ye evildoers: for I will keep the commandments of my God. ¹¹⁶Uphold me according unto thy word, that I may live: and let me not be ashamed of my hope. ¹¹⁷Hold thou me up, and I shall be safe: and I will have respect unto thy statutes continually. ¹¹⁸Thou hast trodden down all them that err from thy statutes: for their deceit *is* falsehood. ¹¹⁹Thou puttest away all the wicked of the earth *like* dross: therefore I love thy testimonies. ¹²⁰My flesh trembleth for fear of thee; and I am afraid of thy judgments. [Hab. 3:16]

The psalmist loves God's law

ע AIN.

121 I have done judgment and justice: leave me not to mine oppressors. ¹²²Be surety for thy servant for good: let not the proud oppress me. ¹²³Mine eyes fail for thy salvation, and for the word of thy righteousness. ¹²⁴Deal with thy servant according unto thy mercy, and teach me thy statutes. ¹²⁵I *am* thy servant; give me understanding, that I may know thy testimonies. ¹²⁶*It is* time for *thee*, LORD, to work: *for* they have made void thy law. ¹²⁷Therefore I love thy commandments above gold; yea, above fine gold. ¹²⁸Therefore I esteem all *thy* precepts concerning all *things* to be right; *and* I hate every false way. [ver. 104]

The psalmist keeps God's law

פ PE.

129 Thy testimonies *are* wonderful: therefore doth my soul keep them. ¹³⁰The entrance of thy words giveth light; it giveth understanding unto the simple. ¹³¹I opened my mouth, and panted: for I longed for thy commandments. ¹³²Look thou upon me, and be merciful unto me, as thou usest to do unto those that love thy name. ¹³³Order my steps in thy word: and let not any iniquity have dominion over me. ¹³⁴Deliver me from the oppression of man: so will I keep thy precepts. ¹³⁵Make thy face to shine upon thy servant; and teach me thy statutes. ¹³⁶Rivers of waters run down mine eyes, because they keep not thy law. [Jer. 9:1; Ezek. 9:4]

God's law is true

צ TZADDI.

137 Righteous *art* thou, O LORD, and upright *are* thy judgments. ¹³⁸Thy testimonies *that* thou hast commanded *are* righteous and very

faithful. 139My zeal hath consumed me, because mine enemies have forgotten thy words. 140Thy word *is* very pure: therefore thy servant loveth it. 141I *am* small and despised: *yet* do not I forget thy precepts. 142Thy righteousness *is* an everlasting righteousness, and thy law *is* the truth. 143Trouble and anguish have taken hold on me: *yet* thy commandments *are* my delights. 144The righteousness of thy testimonies *is* everlasting: give me understanding, and I shall live. [ver. 34,73]

A cry for salvation

ק KOPH.

145 I cried with *my* whole heart; hear me, O LORD: I will keep thy statutes. 146I cried unto thee; save me, and I shall keep thy testimonies. 147I prevented the dawning of the morning, and cried: I hoped in thy word. 148Mine eyes prevent the *night* watches, that *I* might meditate in thy word. 149Hear my voice according unto thy lovingkindness: O LORD, quicken me according to thy judgment. 150They draw nigh that follow after mischief: they are far from thy law. 151Thou *art* near, O LORD; and all thy commandments *are* truth. 152Concerning thy testimonies, I have known of old that thou hast founded them for ever. [Luke 21:33]

Keeping God's law in adversity

ר RESH.

153 Consider mine affliction, and deliver me: for I do not forget thy law. 154Plead my cause, and deliver me: quicken me according to thy word. 155Salvation *is* far from the wicked: for they seek not thy statutes. 156Great *are* thy tender mercies, O LORD: quicken me according to thy judgments. 157Many *are* my persecutors and mine enemies; *yet* do I not decline from thy testimonies. 158I beheld the transgressors, and was grieved: because they kept not thy word. 159Consider how I love thy precepts: quicken me, O LORD, according to thy lovingkindness. 160Thy word *is* true *from* the beginning: and every one of thy righteous judgments *endureth* for ever. [1 Sam. 24:11]

Peace in keeping God's law

ש SCHIN.

161 Princes have persecuted me without a cause: but my heart standeth in awe of thy word. 162I rejoice at thy word, as one that findeth great spoil. 163I hate and abhor lying: *but* thy law do I love. 164Seven *times* a day do I praise thee because of thy righteous judgments. 165Great peace have they which love thy law: and nothing *shall* offend them. 166LORD, I have hoped for thy salvation, and done thy commandments. 167My soul hath kept thy testimonies; and *I* love them exceedingly. 168I have kept thy precepts and thy testimonies: for all my ways *are* before thee. [Prov. 5:21]

A prayer for understanding

ת TAU.

169 Let my cry come near before thee, O LORD: give me under-

standing according to thy word. 170Let my supplication come before thee: deliver me according to thy word. 171My lips shall utter praise, when thou hast taught me thy statutes. 172My tongue shall speak of thy word: for all thy commandments *are* righteousness. 173Let thine hand help me; for I have chosen thy precepts. 174I have longed for thy salvation, O LORD; and thy law *is* my delight. 175Let my soul live, and it shall praise thee; and let thy judgments help me. 176I have gone astray like a lost sheep; seek thy servant; for I do not forget thy commandments. [Is. 53:6]

A prayer for deliverance
A Song of degrees.

120 In my distress I cried unto the LORD, and he heard me. 2Deliver my soul, O LORD, from lying lips, *and* from a deceitful tongue. 3What shall be given unto thee? or what shall be done unto thee, thou false tongue? 4Sharp arrows of the mighty, with coals of juniper. 5Woe is me, that I sojourn *in* Mesech, *that* I dwell in the tents of Kedar! 6My soul hath long dwelt with him that hateth peace. 7I *am* for peace: but when I speak, they *are* for war.

Help from the LORD
A Song of degrees.

121 I will lift up mine eyes unto the hills, from whence cometh my help. 2My help *cometh* from the LORD, which made heaven and earth. 3He will not suffer thy foot to be moved: he that keepeth thee will not slumber.

4Behold, he that keepeth Israel shall neither slumber nor sleep. 5The LORD *is* thy keeper: the LORD *is* thy shade upon thy right hand. 6The sun shall not smite thee by day, nor the moon by night. 7The LORD shall preserve thee from all evil: he shall preserve thy soul. 8The LORD shall preserve thy going out and thy coming in from this time forth, and *even* for evermore. [Deut. 28:6]

The peace of Jerusalem
A Song of degrees of David.

122 I was glad when they said unto me, Let us go *into* the house of the LORD. 2Our feet shall stand within thy gates, O Jerusalem. 3Jerusalem *is* builded as a city that is compact together: 4Whither the tribes go up, the tribes of the LORD, *unto* the testimony of Israel, to give thanks unto the name of the LORD. 5For there are set thrones of judgment, the thrones of the house of David. [Deut. 17:8; 2 Chr. 19:8]

6 Pray for the peace of Jerusalem: they shall prosper that love thee. 7Peace be within thy walls, *and* prosperity within thy palaces. 8For my brethren and companions' sakes, I will now say, Peace *be* within thee. 9Because of the house of the LORD our God I will seek thy good. [Neh. 2:10]

A song of confidence in God
A Song of degrees.

123 Unto thee lift I up mine eyes, O thou that dwellest in the heavens. 2Behold, as the eyes of servants *look* unto the hand of their masters, *and* as the eyes of a maiden unto the hand of her mistress; so our eyes *wait* upon the LORD our God, until that he have mercy upon us. ³Have mercy upon us, O LORD, have mercy upon us: for we are exceedingly filled *with* contempt. ⁴Our soul is exceedingly filled *with* the scorning of those that are at ease, *and with* the contempt of the proud.

God's deliverance

A Song of degrees of David.

124

If *it had* not *been* the LORD who was on our side, now may Israel say; ²If *it had* not *been* the LORD who was on our side, when men rose up against us: ³Then they had swallowed us up quick, when their wrath was kindled against us: ⁴Then the waters had overwhelmed us, the stream had gone over our soul: ⁵Then the proud waters had gone over our soul. ⁶Blessed *be* the LORD, who hath not given us *as* a prey to their teeth. ⁷Our soul is escaped as a bird out of the snare of the fowlers: the snare is broken, and we are escaped. ⁸Our help *is* in the name of the LORD, who made heaven and earth. [Ps. 121:2; Gen. 1:1; Ps. 134:3]

The LORD the protector

A Song of degrees.

125

They that trust in the LORD *shall be* as mount Zion, *which* cannot be removed, *but* abideth for ever. ²*As* the mountains *are* round about Jerusalem, so the LORD *is* round about his people from henceforth even for ever.

³For the rod of the wicked shall not rest upon the lot of the righteous; lest the righteous put forth their hands unto iniquity. ⁴Do good, O LORD, unto *those that be* good, and to *them that are* upright in their hearts. ⁵As for such as turn aside *unto* their crooked ways, the LORD shall lead them forth with the workers of iniquity: *but* peace *shall be* upon Israel. [Prov. 2:15; Ps. 128:6]

Zion's captivity

A Song of degrees.

126

When the LORD turned again the captivity of Zion, we were like them that dream. ²Then was our mouth filled *with* laughter, and our tongue *with* singing: then said they among the heathen, The LORD hath done great things for them. ³The LORD hath done great things for us; *whereof* we are glad. ⁴Turn again our captivity, O LORD, as the streams in the south. ⁵They that sow in tears shall reap in joy. ⁶He that goeth forth and weepeth, bearing precious seed, shall doubtless come again with rejoicing, bringing his sheaves *with him*.

The vanity of work without God

A Song of degrees for Solomon.

127

Except the LORD build the house, they labour in vain that build it: except the LORD keep the city, the watchman waketh *but* in vain. ²*It is* vain for you to rise up early, to sit up late, to eat the bread of sorrows: *for* so he giveth his beloved sleep. ³Lo, children *are* an heritage of the LORD: *and* the fruit of the womb *is* *his* reward. ⁴As arrows *are* in the hand of a mighty *man; so are* children of the youth. ⁵Happy *is* the man that hath his quiver full of them: they shall not be ashamed, but they shall speak with the enemies in the gate. [Job 5:4; Prov. 27:11]

The God-fearing family

A Song of degrees.

128 Blessed *is* every one that feareth the LORD; that walketh in his ways. ²For thou shalt eat the labour of thine hands: happy *shalt* thou be, and *it shall be* well with thee. ³Thy wife *shall be* as a fruitful vine by the sides of thine house: thy children like olive plants round about thy table. ⁴Behold, that thus shall the man be blessed that feareth the LORD. ⁵The LORD shall bless thee out of Zion: and thou shalt see the good of Jerusalem all the days of thy life. ⁶Yea, thou shalt see thy children's children, *and* peace upon Israel. [Gen. 50:23; Job 42:16; Ps. 125:5]

Israel's enemies

A Song of degrees.

129 Many a time have they afflicted me from my youth, may Israel now say: ²Many a time have they afflicted me from my youth: yet they have not prevailed against me. ³The plowers plowed upon my back: they made long their furrows. ⁴The LORD *is* righteous: he hath cut asunder the cords of the wicked.

5 Let them all be confounded and turned back that hate Zion. ⁶Let them be as the grass upon the housetops, which withereth afore it groweth up: ⁷Wherewith the mower filleth not his hand; nor he that bindeth sheaves his bosom. ⁸Neither do they which go by say, The blessing of the LORD *be* upon you: we bless you in the name of the LORD. [Ruth 2:4; Ps. 118:26]

Waiting on the LORD

A Song of degrees.

130 Out of the depths have I cried unto thee, O LORD. ²Lord, hear my voice: let thine ears be attentive to the voice of my supplications. ³If thou, LORD, shouldest mark iniquities, O Lord, who shall stand? ⁴But *there is* forgiveness with thee, that thou mayest be feared. ⁵I wait for the LORD, my soul doth wait, and in his word do I hope. ⁶My soul *waiteth* for the Lord more than they that watch for the morning: *I say, more than* they that watch for the morning. [Ps. 119:147]

7 Let Israel hope in the LORD: for with the LORD *there is* mercy, and with him *is* plenteous redemption. ⁸And he shall redeem Israel from all his iniquities. [Ps. 103:3,4; Mat. 1:21]

A song of the humble

A Song of degrees of David.

131 LORD, my heart is not haughty, nor mine eyes lofty: neither do I exercise myself in great *matters,* or in *things* too high for me. ²Surely I have behaved and quieted myself, as a child that is weaned of his mother: my soul *is even* as a weaned child. ³Let Israel hope in the LORD from henceforth and for ever. [Ps. 130:7]

The promise to David and Zion
A Song of degrees.

132 LORD, remember David, *and* all his afflictions: ²How he sware unto the LORD, *and* vowed unto the mighty *God* of Jacob; ³Surely I will not come into the tabernacle of my house, nor go up into my bed; ⁴I will not give sleep to mine eyes, *or* slumber to mine eyelids, ⁵Until I find out a place for the LORD, a habitation for the mighty *God* of Jacob. ⁶Lo, we heard *of* it at Ephratah: we found it in the fields of the wood. ⁷We will go into his tabernacles: we will worship at his footstool. ⁸Arise, O LORD, into thy rest; thou, and the ark of thy strength. ⁹Let thy priests be clothed *with* righteousness; and let thy saints shout for joy. ¹⁰For thy servant David's sake turn not away the face of thine anointed.

11 The LORD hath sworn *in* truth unto David; he will not turn from it; Of the fruit of thy body will I set upon thy throne. ¹²If thy children will keep my covenant and my testimony that I shall teach them, their children also shall sit upon thy throne for evermore. ¹³For the LORD hath chosen Zion; he hath desired it for his habitation. ¹⁴This *is* my rest for ever: here will I dwell; for I have desired it. ¹⁵I will abundantly bless her provision: I will satisfy her poor *with* bread. ¹⁶I will also clothe her priests with salvation: and her saints shall shout aloud for joy.

¹⁷There will I make the horn of David to bud: I have ordained a lamp for mine anointed. ¹⁸His enemies will I clothe with shame: but upon himself shall his crown flourish. [Ps. 35:26; 109:29]

Brotherly unity
A Song of degrees of David.

133 Behold, how good and how pleasant *it is* for brethren to dwell together in unity. ²*It is* like the precious ointment upon the head, that ran down upon the beard, *even* Aaron's beard: that went down to the skirts of his garments; ³As the dew of Hermon, *and as the dew* that descended upon the mountains of Zion: for there the LORD commanded the blessing, *even* life for evermore. [Deut. 4:48; Lev. 25:21; Deut. 28:8; Ps. 42:8]

Blessing for the night watch
A Song of degrees.

134 Behold, bless ye the LORD, all ye servants of the LORD, which by night stand in the house of the LORD. ²Lift up your hands *in* the sanctuary, and bless the LORD. [1 Tim. 2:8]

3 The LORD that made heaven and earth bless thee out of Zion. [Ps. 124:8; 128:5; 135:21]

Praise to the LORD

135 Praise ye the LORD. Praise ye the name of the LORD; praise *him,* O ye servants of the LORD. ²Ye that stand in the house of the LORD, in the courts of the house of our God, ³Praise the LORD; for the LORD *is* good: sing *praises* unto his name; for *it is* pleasant. 4For the LORD hath chosen Jacob unto himself, *and* Israel for his peculiar treasure. 5For I know that the LORD *is* great, and *that* our Lord *is* above all gods. 6Whatsoever the LORD pleased, *that* did he in heaven, and in earth, in the seas, and all deep places. 7He causeth the vapours to ascend from the ends of the earth; he maketh lightnings for the rain; he bringeth the wind out of his treasuries. 8Who smote the firstborn of Egypt, both of man and beast. 9*Who* sent tokens and wonders into the midst of thee, O Egypt, upon Pharaoh, and upon all his servants. 10Who smote great nations, and slew mighty kings; 11Sihon king of the Amorites, and Og king of Bashan, and all the kingdoms of Canaan: 12And gave their land *for* an heritage, an heritage unto Israel his people. 13Thy name, O LORD, *endureth* for ever; *and* thy memorial, O LORD, throughout all generations. 14For the LORD will judge his people, and he will repent himself concerning his servants. [Deut. 32:36]

15 The idols of the heathen *are* silver and gold, the work of men's hands. 16They have mouths, but they speak not; eyes have they, but they see not; 17They have ears, but they hear not; neither is there *any* breath in their mouths. 18They that make them are like unto them: *so is* every one that trusteth in them.

19 Bless the LORD, O house of Israel: bless the LORD, O house of Aaron: 20Bless the LORD, O house of Levi: ye that fear the LORD, bless the LORD. 21Blessed *be* the LORD out of Zion, which dwelleth *at* Jerusalem. Praise ye the LORD. [Ps. 134:3]

A litany of God's wonders

136

O give thanks unto the LORD; for *he is* good: for his mercy *endureth* for ever. 2O give thanks unto the God of gods: for his mercy *endureth* for ever. 3O give thanks to the Lord of lords: for his mercy *endureth* for ever. 4To him who alone doeth great wonders: for his mercy *endureth* for ever. 5To him that by wisdom made the heavens: for his mercy *endureth* for ever. 6To him that stretched out the earth above the waters: for his mercy *endureth* for ever. 7To him that made great lights: for his mercy *endureth* for ever: 8The sun to rule by day: for his mercy *endureth* for ever: 9The moon and stars to rule by night: for his mercy *endureth* for ever. 10To him that smote Egypt in their firstborn: for his mercy *endureth* for ever: 11And brought out Israel from among them: for his mercy *endureth* for ever: 12With a strong hand, and with a stretched out arm: for his mercy *endureth* for ever. 13To him which divided the Red sea into parts: for his mercy *endureth* for ever: 14And made Israel to pass through the midst of it: for his mercy *endureth* for ever: 15But overthrew Pharaoh and his host in the Red sea: for his mercy *endureth* for ever. 16To him which led his people through the wilderness: for his mercy *endureth* for ever. 17To him which smote great kings: for his mercy *endureth* for ever: 18And slew famous kings: for his mercy *endureth* for ever: 19Sihon king of the Amorites: for his mercy *endureth* for ever: 20And Og the king of Bashan: for his mercy *endureth* for ever: 21And gave their land for an heritage: for his mercy *endureth* for ever: 22*Even* an heritage unto Israel his servant: for his mercy *endureth* for ever. 23Who remembered us in our low estate: for his mercy *endureth* for ever: 24And hath redeemed us from our enemies: for his mercy *endureth* for ever. 25Who giveth food to all flesh: for his mercy *endureth* for ever. 26O give thanks unto the God of heaven: for his mercy *endureth* for ever.

Captives in Babylon

137 By the rivers of Babylon, there we sat down, yea, we wept, when we remembered Zion. 2We hanged our harps upon the willows in the midst thereof. 3For there they that carried us away captive required of us a song; and they that wasted us *required of us* mirth, *saying,* Sing us *one* of the songs of Zion. 4How shall we sing the LORD's song in a strange land? 5If I forget thee, O Jerusalem, let my right hand forget *her cunning.* 6If I do not remember thee, let my tongue cleave to the roof of my mouth; if I prefer not Jerusalem above my chief joy. 7Remember, O LORD, the children of Edom *in* the day of Jerusalem; who said, Rase *it,* rase *it, even* to the foundation thereof. 8O daughter of Babylon, who art *to be* de-stroyed; happy *shall he be,* that rewardeth thee as thou hast served us. 9Happy *shall he be* that taketh and dasheth thy little ones against the stones. [Is. 13:16]

The LORD a faithful God

A Psalm of David.

138 I will praise thee with my whole heart: before the gods will I sing *praise* unto thee. 2I will worship toward thy holy temple, and praise thy name for thy lovingkindness and for thy truth: for thou hast magnified thy word above all thy name. 3In the day when I cried thou answeredst me, *and* strengthenedst me *with* strength in my soul. 4All the kings of the earth shall praise thee, O LORD, when they hear the words of thy mouth. 5Yea, they shall sing in the ways of the LORD: for great *is* the glory of the LORD. 6Though the LORD *be* high, yet hath he respect unto the lowly: but the proud he knoweth afar off. 7Though I walk in the midst of trouble, thou wilt revive me: thou shalt stretch forth thine hand against the wrath of mine enemies, and thy right hand shall save me. 8The LORD will perfect that which concerneth me: thy mercy, O LORD, *endureth* for ever: forsake not the works of thine own hands. [Ps. 57:2; Phil. 1:6; Job 10:3,8]

The prayer of a believing heart

To the chief Musician, A Psalm of David.

139 O LORD, thou hast searched me, and known *me.* 2Thou knowest my downsitting and mine uprising, thou understandest my thought afar off. ³Thou compassest my path and my lying down, and art acquainted *with* all my ways. ⁴For *there is* not a word in my tongue, *but* lo, O LORD, thou knowest it altogether. ⁵Thou hast beset me behind and before, and laid thine hand upon me. ⁶*Such* knowledge *is* too wonderful for me; it is high, I cannot attain unto it. [Job 42:3; Ps. 40:5]

7 Whither shall I go from thy spirit? or whither shall I flee from thy presence? ⁸If I ascend up *into* heaven, thou *art* there: if I make my bed in hell, behold, thou *art* there. ⁹*If* I take the wings of the morning, *and* dwell in the uttermost parts of the sea; ¹⁰Even there shall thy hand lead me, and thy right hand shall hold me. ¹¹If I say, Surely the darkness shall cover me; even the night *shall be* light about me. ¹²Yea, the darkness hideth not from thee; but the night shineth as the day: the darkness and the light *are* both alike *to thee.* [Job 34:22]

13 For thou hast possessed my reins: thou hast covered me in my mother's womb. ¹⁴I will praise thee; for I am fearfully and wonderfully made: marvellous *are* thy works; and *that* my soul knoweth right well. ¹⁵My substance was not hid from thee, when I was made in secret, *and* curiously wrought in the lowest parts of the earth. ¹⁶Thine eyes did see my substance, yet being unperfect; and in thy book all *my members* were written, *which* in continuance were fashioned, when *as yet there was* none of them. ¹⁷How precious also

are thy thoughts unto me, O God: how great is the sum of them! ¹⁸*If* I should count them, they are more in number than the sand: when I awake, I am still with thee.

19 Surely thou wilt slay the wicked, O God: depart from me therefore, ye bloody men. ²⁰For they speak against thee wickedly, *and* thine enemies take *thy name* in vain. ²¹Do not I hate them, O LORD, that hate thee? and am not I grieved with those that rise up against thee? ²²I hate them *with* perfect hatred: I count them mine enemies. ²³Search me, O God, and know my heart: try me, and know my thoughts: ²⁴And see if *there be any* wicked way in me, and lead me in the way everlasting. [Ps. 5:8]

For protection against enemies

To the chief Musician, A Psalm of David.

140 Deliver me, O LORD, from the evil man: preserve me from the violent man; ²Which imagine mischiefs in *their* heart; continually are they gathered together *for* war. ³They have sharpened their tongues like a serpent; adder's poison *is* under their lips. Selah. [Ps. 58:4]

4 Keep me, O LORD, from the hands of the wicked; preserve me from the violent man; who have purposed to overthrow my goings. ⁵The proud have hid a snare for me, and cords; they have spread a net by the way side; they have set grins for me. [Jer. 18:22]

6 I said unto the LORD, Thou *art* my God: hear the voice of my supplications, O LORD. ⁷O GOD the

Lord, the strength of my salvation, thou hast covered my head in the day of battle. 8Grant not, O LORD, the desires of the wicked: further not his wicked device; *lest* they exalt themselves. Selah. [Deut. 32:27]

9 *As for* the head of those that compass me about, let the mischief of their own lips cover them. 10Let burning coals fall upon them: let them be cast into the fire; into deep pits, *that* they rise not up again. 11Let not an evil speaker be established in the earth: evil shall hunt the violent man to overthrow *him.*

12 I know that the LORD will maintain the cause of the afflicted, *and* the right of the poor. 13Surely the righteous shall give thanks unto thy name: the upright shall dwell in thy presence.

Conduct amidst trial

A Psalm of David.

141 LORD, I cry unto thee: make haste unto me; give ear unto my voice, when I cry unto thee. 2Let my prayer be set forth before thee *as* incense; *and* the lifting up of my hands *as* the evening sacrifice. 3Set a watch, O LORD, before my mouth; keep the door of my lips. 4Incline not my heart to *any* evil thing, to practise wicked works with men that work iniquity: and let me not eat of their dainties. [Prov. 23:6]

5 Let the righteous smite me; *it shall be* a kindness: and let him reprove me; *it shall be* an excellent oil, *which* shall not break my head: for yet my prayer also *shall be* in their calamities. 6When their

judges are overthrown in stony places, they shall hear my words; for they are sweet. 7Our bones are scattered at the grave's mouth, as when one cutteth and cleaveth *wood* upon the earth.

8 But mine eyes *are* unto thee, O GOD the Lord: in thee is my trust; leave not my soul destitute. 9Keep me from the snare *which* they have laid for me, and the grins of the workers of iniquity. 10Let the wicked fall into their own nets, whilst that I withal escape. [Ps. 35:8]

The prisoner's prayer

Maschil of David; A Prayer when he was in the cave.

142 I cried unto the LORD *with* my voice; with my voice unto the LORD did I make my supplication. 2I poured out my complaint before him; I shewed before him my trouble. 3When my spirit was overwhelmed within me, then thou knewest my path. In the way wherein I walked have they privily laid a snare for me. 4I looked *on my* right hand, and beheld, but *there was* no man that would know me: refuge failed me; no man cared for my soul. 5I cried unto thee, O LORD: I said, Thou *art* my refuge *and* my portion in the land of the living. 6Attend unto my cry; for I am brought very low: deliver me from my persecutors; for they are stronger than I. 7Bring my soul out of prison, that *I* may praise thy name: the righteous shall compass me about; for thou shalt deal bountifully with me. [Ps. 34:2; Ps. 13:6]

The prayer of a soul in distress
A Psalm of David.

143 Hear my prayer, O LORD, give ear to my supplications: in thy faithfulness answer me, *and* in thy righteousness. ²And enter not into judgment with thy servant: for in thy sight shall no *man* living be justified. ³For the enemy hath persecuted my soul; he hath smitten my life down to the ground; he hath made me to dwell in darkness, as those that have been long dead. ⁴Therefore is my spirit overwhelmed within me; my heart within me is desolate. ⁵I remember the days of old; I meditate on all thy works; I muse on the work of thy hands. ⁶I stretch forth my hands unto thee: my soul *thirsteth* after thee, as a thirsty land. Selah. [Ps. 88:9; 63:1]

7 Hear me speedily, O LORD: my spirit faileth: hide not thy face from me, lest I be like unto them that go down into the pit. ⁸Cause me to hear thy lovingkindness in the morning; for in thee do I trust: cause me to know the way wherein I should walk; for I lift up my soul unto thee. ⁹Deliver me, O LORD, from mine enemies: I flee unto thee to hide me. ¹⁰Teach me to do thy will; for thou *art* my God: thy spirit *is* good; lead me into the land of uprightness. ¹¹Quicken me, O LORD, for thy name's sake: for thy righteousness' sake bring my soul out of trouble. ¹²And of thy mercy cut off mine enemies, and destroy all them that afflict my soul: for I *am* thy servant. [Ps. 54:5]

The warrior's psalm
A Psalm of David.

144 Blessed *be* the LORD my strength, which teacheth my hands to war, *and* my fingers to fight: ²My goodness, and my fortress; my high tower, and my deliverer; my shield, and *he* in whom I trust; who subdueth my people under me.

3 LORD, what *is* man, that thou takest knowledge of him? *or* the son of man, that thou makest account of him? ⁴Man is like to vanity: his days *are* as a shadow that passeth away. ⁵Bow thy heavens, O LORD, and come down: touch the mountains, and they shall smoke. ⁶Cast forth lightning, and scatter them: shoot out thine arrows, and destroy them. ⁷Send thine hand from above; rid me, and deliver me out of great waters, from the hand of strange children; ⁸Whose mouth speaketh vanity, and their right hand *is* a right hand of falsehood. ⁹I will sing a new song unto thee, O God: upon a psaltery *and* an instrument of ten strings will I sing *praises* unto thee. ¹⁰*It is he* that giveth salvation unto kings: who delivereth David his servant from the hurtful sword. ¹¹Rid me, and deliver me from the hand of strange children, whose mouth speaketh vanity, and their right hand *is* a right hand of falsehood:

12 That our sons *may be* as plants grown up in their youth; *that* our daughters *may be* as corner stones, polished *after* the similitude of a palace: ¹³*That* our garners *may be* full, affording all

manner of store: *that* our sheep may bring forth thousands and ten thousands in our streets: 14*That* our oxen *may be* strong to labour; *that there be* no breaking in, nor going out; that *there be* no complaining in our streets. 15Happy *is that* people, that is in such a case: *yea,* happy *is that* people, whose God *is* the LORD. [Ps. 33:12]

The goodness of the LORD

David's *Psalm of* praise.

145 I will extol thee, my God, O king; and I will bless thy name for ever and ever. 2Every day will I bless thee; and I will praise thy name for ever and ever. 3Great *is* the LORD, and greatly to be praised; and his greatness *is* unsearchable. 4One generation shall praise thy works to another, and shall declare thy mighty acts. 5I will speak of the glorious honour of thy majesty, and of thy wondrous works. 6And *men* shall speak of the might of thy terrible acts: and I will declare thy greatness. 7They shall abundantly utter the memory of thy great goodness, and shall sing of thy righteousness.

8 The LORD *is* gracious, and full of compassion; slow to anger, and of great mercy. 9The LORD *is* good to all: and his tender mercies *are* over all his works. 10All thy works shall praise thee, O LORD; and thy saints shall bless thee. 11They shall speak of the glory of thy kingdom, and talk of thy power; 12To make known to the sons of men his mighty acts, and the glorious majesty of his kingdom. 13Thy kingdom *is* an everlasting king-dom, and thy dominion *endureth* throughout all generations. [1 Tim. 1:17]

14 The LORD upholdeth all that fall, and raiseth up all those that be bowed down. 15The eyes of all wait upon thee; and thou givest them their meat in due season. 16Thou openest thine hand, and satisfiest the desire of every living thing. 17The LORD *is* righteous in all his ways, and holy in all his works. 18The LORD *is* nigh unto all them that call upon him, to all that call upon him in truth. 19He will fulfil the desire of them that fear him: he also will hear their cry, and will save them. 20The LORD preserveth all them that love him: but all the wicked will he destroy. 21My mouth shall speak the praise of the LORD: and let all flesh bless his holy name for ever and ever.

An exhortation to trust God

146 Praise ye the LORD. Praise the LORD, O my soul. 2While I live will I praise the LORD: I will sing *praises* unto my God while I have *any* being. 3Put not your trust in princes, *nor* in the son of man, in whom *there is* no help. 4His breath goeth forth, he returneth to his earth; in that *very* day his thoughts perish. 5Happy *is* he that *hath* the God of Jacob for his help, whose hope *is* in the LORD his God: 6Which made heaven, and earth, the sea, and all that therein is: which keepeth truth for ever: 7Which executeth judgment for the oppressed: which giveth food to the hungry. The LORD looseth the prisoners: 8The LORD openeth *the eyes of* the blind: the LORD raiseth them that are bowed down: the LORD loveth the righteous: ⁹The LORD preserveth the strangers; he relieveth the fatherless and widow: but the way of the wicked he turneth upside down. ¹⁰The LORD shall reign for ever, *even* thy God, O Zion, unto all generations. Praise ye the LORD. [Ex. 15:18; Ps. 10:16]

The might and grace of the LORD

147 Praise ye the LORD: for *it is* good to sing *praises* unto our God; for *it is* pleasant; *and* praise is comely. ²The LORD doth build up Jerusalem: he gathereth together the outcasts of Israel. ³He healeth the broken in heart, and bindeth up their wounds. ⁴He telleth the number of the stars; he calleth them all *by their* names. ⁵Great *is* our Lord, and of great power: his understanding *is* infinite. ⁶The LORD lifteth up the meek: he casteth the wicked down to the ground. ⁷Sing unto the LORD with thanksgiving; sing *praise* upon the harp unto our God: ⁸Who covereth the heaven with clouds, who prepareth rain for the earth, who maketh grass to grow *upon* the mountains. ⁹He giveth to the beast his food, *and* to the young ravens which cry. ¹⁰He delighteth not in the strength of the horse: he taketh not pleasure in the legs of a man. ¹¹The LORD taketh pleasure in them that fear him, in those that hope in his mercy. ¹²Praise the LORD, O Jerusalem; praise thy God, O Zion. ¹³For he hath strength-

ened the bars of thy gates; he hath blessed thy children within thee. ¹⁴He maketh peace *in* thy borders, *and* filleth thee *with* the finest of the wheat. ¹⁵He sendeth forth his commandment *upon* earth: his word runneth very swiftly. ¹⁶He giveth snow like wool: he scattereth the hoarfrost like ashes. ¹⁷He casteth forth his ice like morsels: who can stand before his cold? ¹⁸He sendeth out his word, and melteth them: he causeth his wind to blow, *and* the waters flow. ¹⁹He sheweth his word unto Jacob, his statutes and his judgments unto Israel. ²⁰He hath not dealt so with any nation: and *as for his* judgments, they have not known them. Praise ye the LORD. [Rom. 3:1,2]

Nature's praise of the LORD

148 Praise ye the LORD. Praise ye the LORD from the heavens: praise him in the heights. ²Praise ye him, all his angels: praise ye him, all his hosts. ³Praise ye him, sun and moon: praise him, all ye stars of light. ⁴Praise him, ye heavens of heavens, and ye waters that *be* above the heavens. ⁵Let them praise the name of the LORD: for he commanded, and they were created. ⁶He hath also stablished them for ever and ever: he hath made a decree which shall not pass. [Ps. 89:37; Jer. 33:25]

7 Praise the LORD from the earth, ye dragons, and all deeps: ⁸Fire, and hail; snow, and vapour; stormy wind fulfilling his word: ⁹Mountains, and all hills; fruitful trees, and all cedars: ¹⁰Beasts, and

all cattle; creeping things, and flying fowl: [11]Kings of the earth, and all people; princes, and all judges of the earth: [12]Both young men, and maidens; old men, and children: [13]Let them praise the name of the LORD: for his name alone *is* excellent; his glory *is* above the earth and heaven. [14]He also exalteth the horn of his people, the praise of all his saints; *even* of the children of Israel, a people near unto him. Praise ye the LORD. [Ps. 75:10; Ps. 149:9; Eph. 2:17].

The LORD's love of Israel

149

Praise ye the LORD. Sing unto the LORD a new song, *and* his praise in the congregation of saints. [2]Let Israel rejoice in him that made him: let the children of Zion be joyful in their King. [3]Let them praise his name in the dance: let them sing *praises* unto him with the timbrel and harp. [4]For the LORD taketh pleasure in his people: he will beautify the meek with salvation. [5]Let the saints be joyful in glory: let them sing aloud upon their beds. [6]Let the high *praises* of God *be* in their mouth, and a twoedged sword in their hand; [7]To execute vengeance upon the heathen, *and* punishments upon the people; [8]To bind their kings with chains, and their nobles with fetters of iron; [9]To execute upon them the judgment written: this honour have all his saints. Praise ye the LORD. [Deut. 7:1,2; Ps. 148:14]

Let every thing praise the LORD

150

Praise ye the LORD. Praise God in his sanctuary: praise him in the firmament of his power. [2]Praise him for his mighty acts: praise him according to his excellent greatness. [3]Praise him with the sound of the trumpet: praise him with the psaltery and harp. [4]Praise him with the timbrel and dance: praise him with stringed instruments and organs. [5]Praise him upon the loud cymbals: praise him upon the high sounding cymbals. [6]Let every *thing that hath* breath praise the LORD. Praise ye the LORD.

Proverbs

The purpose of Proverbs

1 The proverbs of Solomon the son of David, king of Israel.
[1 Ki. 4:32; Eccl. 12:9]

2 To know wisdom and instruction; to perceive the words of understanding; 3To receive the instruction of wisdom, justice, and judgment, and equity; 4To give subtilty to the simple, to the young man knowledge and discretion. 5A wise *man* will hear, and will increase learning; and a man of understanding shall attain unto wise counsels: 6To understand a proverb, and the interpretation; the words of the wise, and their dark sayings. [Ps. 78:2]

Warnings against violence

7 The fear of the LORD *is* the beginning of knowledge: *but* fools despise wisdom and instruction. 8My son, hear the instruction of thy father, and forsake not the law of thy mother: 9For they *shall be* an ornament of grace unto thy head, and chains about thy neck. 10My son, if sinners entice thee, consent thou not. 11If they say, Come with us, let us lay wait for blood, let us lurk privily for the innocent without cause: 12Let us swallow them up alive as the grave; and whole, as those that go down into the pit: 13We shall find all precious substance, we shall fill our houses *with* spoil: 14Cast in thy lot among us; let us all have one purse: 15My son, walk not thou in the way with them; refrain thy foot from their path: 16For their feet run to evil, and make haste to shed blood. 17Surely in vain the net *is* spread in the sight of any bird. 18And they lay wait for their own blood; they lurk privily for their own lives. 19So *are* the ways of every one that is greedy of gain; *which* taketh away the life of the owners thereof. [1 Tim. 6:10]

Result of rejecting wisdom

20 Wisdom crieth without; she uttereth her voice in the streets: 21She crieth in the chief place of concourse, in the openings of the gates: in the city she uttereth her words, *saying,* 22How long, ye simple ones, will ye love simplicity? and the scorners delight in their scorning, and fools hate knowledge? 23Turn you at my reproof: behold, I will pour out my spirit unto you, I will make known my words unto you. [Joel 2:28]

24 Because I have called, and ye refused; I have stretched out my hand, and no man regarded; 25But ye have set at nought all my counsel, and would none of my reproof: 26I also will laugh at your calamity; I will mock when your fear cometh; 27When your fear cometh as desolation, and your destruction cometh as a whirlwind; when distress and anguish cometh upon you: 28Then shall they call upon me, but I will not answer; they shall seek me early, but they shall not find me: 29For that they hated knowledge, and did not choose the fear of the LORD: 30They would

none of my counsel: they despised all my reproof. 31Therefore shall they eat of the fruit of their own way, and be filled with their own devices. 32For the turning away of the simple shall slay them, and the prosperity of fools shall destroy them. 33But whoso hearkeneth unto me shall dwell safely, and shall be quiet from fear of evil. [Ps. 25:12; 112:7]

The reward of wisdom

2 My son, if thou wilt receive my words, and hide my commandments with thee; 2So that *thou* incline thine ear unto wisdom, *and* apply thine heart to understanding; 3Yea, if thou criest after knowledge, *and* liftest up thy voice for understanding; 4If thou seekest her as silver, and searchest for her as *for* hid treasures; 5Then shalt thou understand the fear of the LORD, and find the knowledge of God. 6For the LORD giveth wisdom: out of his mouth *cometh* knowledge and understanding. 7He layeth up sound wisdom for the righteous: *he is* a buckler to them that walk uprightly. 8*He* keepeth the paths of judgment, and preserveth the way of his saints. 9Then shalt thou understand righteousness, and judgment, and equity; *yea*, every good path.

10 When wisdom entereth into thine heart, and knowledge is pleasant unto thy soul; 11Discretion shall preserve thee, understanding shall keep thee: 12To deliver thee from the way of the evil *man*, from the man that speaketh froward things; 13Who leave the paths of uprightness, to walk in the ways of darkness; 14Who rejoice to do evil, *and* delight in the frowardness of the wicked; 15Whose ways *are* crooked, and *they* froward in their paths: 16To deliver thee from the strange woman, *even* from the stranger *which* flattereth with her words; 17Which forsaketh the guide of her youth, and forgetteth the covenant of her God. 18For her house inclineth unto death, and her paths unto the dead. 19None that go *unto* her return *again*, neither take they hold of the paths of life. 20That thou mayest walk in the way of good *men*, and keep the paths of the righteous. 21For the upright shall dwell *in* the land, and the perfect shall remain in it. 22But the wicked shall be cut off from the earth, and the transgressors shall be rooted out of it. [Job 18:17; Ps. 37:28]

The blessing of wisdom

3 My son, forget not my law; but let thine heart keep my commandments: 2For length of days, and long life, and peace, shall they add to thee. 3Let not mercy and truth forsake thee: bind them about thy neck; write them upon the table of thine heart: 4So shalt thou find favour and good understanding in the sight of God and man. [Rom. 14:18]

5 Trust in the LORD with all thine heart; and lean not unto thine own understanding. 6In all thy ways acknowledge him, and he shall direct thy paths. [1 Chr. 28:9; Jer. 10:23]

7 Be not wise in thine own

eyes: fear the LORD, and depart from evil. 8It shall be health to thy navel, and marrow to thy bones. [Job 21:24]

9 Honour the LORD with thy substance, and with the firstfruits of all thine increase: 10So shall thy barns be filled *with* plenty, and thy presses shall burst out with new wine. [Deut. 28:8]

11 My son, despise not the chastening of the LORD; neither be weary of his correction: 12For whom the LORD loveth he correcteth; even as a father the son *in whom* he delighteth. [Deut. 8:5]

13 Happy *is* the man *that* findeth wisdom, and the man *that* getteth understanding. 14For the merchandise of it *is* better than the merchandise of silver, and the gain thereof than fine gold. 15She *is* more precious than rubies: and all the things thou canst desire are not to be compared unto her. 16Length of days *is* in her right hand; and in her left hand riches and honour. 17Her ways *are* ways of pleasantness, and all her paths *are* peace. 18She *is* a tree of life to them that lay hold upon her: and happy *is* every one that retaineth her. 19The LORD by wisdom hath founded the earth; by understanding hath he established the heavens. 20By his knowledge the depths are broken up, and the clouds drop down the dew. [Gen. 1:9; Deut. 33:28; Job 36:28]

21 My son, let not them depart from thine eyes: keep sound wisdom and discretion: 22So shall they be life unto thy soul, and grace to thy neck. 23Then shalt thou walk *in* thy way safely, and thy foot shall not stumble. 24When thou liest down, thou shalt not be afraid: yea, thou shalt lie down, and thy sleep shall be sweet. 25Be not afraid of sudden fear, neither of the desolation of the wicked, when it cometh. 26For the LORD shall be thy confidence, and shall keep thy foot from being taken.

27 Withhold not good from them to whom it is due, when it is in the power of thine hand to do *it*. 28Say not unto thy neighbour, Go, and come again, and to morrow I will give; when thou hast it by thee. 29Devise not evil against thy neighbour, seeing he dwelleth securely by thee. 30Strive not with a man without cause, if he have done thee no harm. 31Envy thou not the oppressor, and choose none of his ways. 32For the froward *is* abomination to the LORD: but his secret *is* with the righteous. 33The curse of the LORD *is* in the house of the wicked: but he blesseth the habitation of the just. 34Surely he scorneth the scorners: but he giveth grace unto the lowly. 35The wise shall inherit glory: but shame shall be the promotion of fools.

The command to obtain wisdom

4 Hear, ye children, the instruction of a father, and attend to know understanding. 2For I give you good doctrine, forsake you not my law. 3For I was my father's son, tender and only *beloved* in the sight of my mother. 4He taught me also, and said unto me, Let thine heart retain my words: keep my commandments, and live. 5Get wisdom, get understanding: forget

it not; neither decline from the words of my mouth. 6Forsake her not, and she shall preserve thee: love her, and she shall keep thee. 7Wisdom *is* the principal thing; *therefore* get wisdom: and with all thy getting get understanding. 8Exalt her, and she shall promote thee: she shall bring thee to honour, when thou dost embrace her. 9She shall give to thine head an ornament of grace: a crown of glory shall she deliver *to* thee. [ch. 1:9; 3:22]

10 Hear, O my son, and receive my sayings; and the years of thy life shall be many. 11I have taught thee in the way of wisdom; I have led thee in right paths. 12When thou goest thy steps shall not be straitened; and when thou runnest, thou shalt not stumble. 13Take fast hold of instruction; let *her* not go: keep her; for she *is* thy life.

14 Enter not into the path of the wicked, and go not in the way of evil men. 15Avoid it, pass not by it, turn from it, and pass away. 16For they sleep not, except they have done mischief; and their sleep is taken away, unless they cause *some* to fall. 17For they eat the bread of wickedness, and drink the wine of violence. 18But the path of the just *is* as the shining light, that shineth more and more unto the perfect day. 19The way of the wicked *is* as darkness: they know not at what they stumble. [1 Sam. 2:9; Job 18:5,6; Is. 59:9,10; Jer. 23:12; John 12:35]

20 My son, attend to my words; incline thine ear unto my sayings. 21Let them not depart from thine eyes; keep them in the midst of thine heart. 22For they *are* life unto those that find them, and health to all their flesh. 23Keep thy heart with all diligence; for out of it *are* the issues of life. 24Put away from thee a froward mouth, and perverse lips put far from thee. 25Let thine eyes look right on, and let thine eyelids look straight before thee. 26Ponder the path of thy feet, and let all thy ways be established. 27Turn not *to* the right hand nor *to* the left: remove thy foot from evil. [Deut. 5:32; 28:14; Josh. 1:7; Is. 1:16; Rom. 12:9]

Warning against unchastity

5 My son, attend unto my wisdom, *and* bow thine ear to my understanding: 2That *thou* mayest regard discretion, and *that* thy lips may keep knowledge. 3For the lips of a strange *woman* drop *as* a honeycomb, and her mouth *is* smoother than oil: 4But her end is bitter as wormwood, sharp as a twoedged sword. 5Her feet go down *to* death; her steps take hold on hell. 6Lest thou shouldest ponder the path of life, her ways are moveable, *that* thou canst not know *them.* 7Hear me now therefore, O ye children, and depart not from the words of my mouth. 8Remove thy way far from her, and come not nigh the door of her house: 9Lest thou give thine honour unto others, and thy years unto the cruel: 10Lest strangers be filled *with* thy wealth; and thy labours *be* in the house of a stranger; 11And thou mourn at the last, when thy flesh and thy body are consumed, 12And say, How have I hated instruction, and my heart despised reproof; 13And have not obeyed

the voice of my teachers, nor inclined mine ear to them that instructed me! 14I was almost in all evil in the midst of the congregation and assembly.

15 Drink waters out of thine own cistern, and running waters out of thine own well. 16Let thy fountains be dispersed abroad, *and* rivers of waters in the streets. 17Let them be only thine own, and not strangers' with thee. 18Let thy fountain be blessed: and rejoice with the wife of thy youth. 19*Let her be as* the loving hind and pleasant roe; let her breasts satisfy thee at all times; and be thou ravisht always with her love. 20And why wilt thou, my son, be ravisht with a strange *woman,* and embrace the bosom of a stranger? 21For the ways of man *are* before the eyes of the LORD, and he pondereth all his goings. 22His own iniquities shall take the wicked himself, and he shall be holden with the cords of his sins. 23He shall die without instruction; and in the greatness of his folly he shall go astray. [Job 4:21; 36:12]

Warnings against idleness

6 My son, if thou be surety for thy friend, *if* thou hast stricken thy hand with a stranger, 2Thou art snared with the words of thy mouth, thou art taken with the words of thy mouth, 3Do this now, my son, and deliver thyself, when thou art come into the hand of thy friend; go, humble thyself, and make sure thy friend. 4Give not sleep to thine eyes, nor slumber to thine eyelids. 5Deliver thyself as a roe from the hand *of the hunter,* and as a bird from the hand of the fowler.

6 Go to the ant, thou sluggard; consider her ways, and be wise: 7Which having no guide, overseer, or ruler, 8Provideth her meat in the summer, *and* gathereth her food in the harvest. 9How long wilt thou sleep, O sluggard? when wilt thou arise out of thy sleep? 10*Yet* a little sleep, a little slumber, a little folding of the hands to sleep: 11So shall thy poverty come as one that travelleth, and thy want as an armed man. [ch. 10:4]

Warning against sowing discord

12 A naughty person, a wicked man, walketh *with* a froward mouth. 13He winketh with his eyes, he speaketh with his feet, he teacheth with his fingers; 14Frowardness *is* in his heart, he deviseth mischief continually; he soweth discord. 15Therefore shall his calamity come suddenly; suddenly shall he be broken without remedy. [Jer. 19:11; 2 Chr. 36:16]

16 These six *things* doth the LORD hate: yea, seven *are* an abomination unto him: 17A proud look, a lying tongue, and hands that shed innocent blood, 18A heart that deviseth wicked imaginations, feet that be swift in running to mischief, 19A false witness *that* speaketh lies, and he that soweth discord among brethren. [Ps. 27:12; ver. 14]

Warning against adultery

20 My son, keep thy father's commandment, and forsake not the law of thy mother: 21Bind them continually upon thine heart, *and*

tie them about thy neck. 22When thou goest, it shall lead thee; when thou sleepest, it shall keep thee; and when thou awakest, it shall talk *with* thee. 23For the commandment *is* a lamp; and the law *is* light; and reproofs of instruction *are* the way of life: 24To keep thee from the evil woman, from the flattery of the tongue of a strange *woman.* 25Lust not after her beauty in thine heart; neither let her take thee with her eyelids. 26For by means of a whorish woman *a man is brought* to a piece of bread: and the adulteress will hunt for the precious life. 27Can a man take fire in his bosom, and his clothes not be burnt? 28Can one go upon hot coals, and his feet not be burnt? 29So he that goeth in to his neighbour's wife; whosoever toucheth her shall not be innocent. 30*Men* do not despise a thief, if he steal to satisfy his soul when he is hungry; 31But *if* he be found, he shall restore sevenfold; he shall give all the substance of his house. 32*But* whoso committeth adultery with a woman lacketh understanding: he *that* doeth it destroyeth his own soul. 33A wound and dishonour shall he get; and his reproach shall not be wiped away. 34For jealousy *is* the rage of a man: therefore he will not spare in the day of vengeance. 35He will not regard any ransom; neither will he rest content, though thou givest many gifts.

7 My son, keep my words, and lay up my commandments with thee. 2Keep my commandments, and live; and my law as the apple of thine eye. 3Bind them upon thy fingers, write them upon the table of thine heart. 4Say unto wisdom, Thou *art* my sister; and call understanding *thy* kinswoman: 5That *they* may keep thee from the strange woman, from the stranger *which* flattereth with her words. 6For at the window of my house I looked through my casement, 7And beheld among the simple ones, I discerned among the youths, a young man void of understanding, 8Passing through the street near her corner; and he went the way to her house, 9In the twilight, in the evening, in the black and dark night: 10And behold, there met him a woman *with* the attire of a harlot, and subtil of heart. 11(She *is* loud and stubborn; her feet abide not in her house: 12Now *is* she without, now in the streets, and lieth in wait at every corner.) 13So she caught him, and kissed him, and with an impudent face said unto him, 14*I have* peace offerings with me; *this* day have I payed my vows. 15Therefore came I forth to meet thee, diligently to seek thy face, and I have found thee. 16I have deckt my bed *with* coverings of tapestry, *with* carved *works, with* fine linen of Egypt. 17I have perfumed my bed *with* myrrh, aloes, and cinnamon. 18Come, let us take our fill of love until the morning: let us solace ourselves with loves. 19For the goodman *is* not at home, he is gone a long journey: 20He hath taken a bag of money with him, *and* will come home at the day appointed. 21With her much fair speech she

caused him to yield, with the flattering of her lips she forced him. 22He goeth after her straightway, as an ox goeth to the slaughter, or as a fool to the correction of the stocks; 23Till a dart strike through his liver; as a bird hasteth to the snare, and knoweth not that it *is* for his life. [Eccl. 9:12]

24 Hearken unto me now therefore, O ye children, and attend to the words of my mouth. 25Let not thine heart decline to her ways, go not astray in her paths. 26For she hath cast down many wounded: yea, many strong *men have been* slain by her. 27Her house *is* the way to hell, going down to the chambers of death. [ch. 2:18; 5:5; 9:18]

The call of wisdom

8 Doth not wisdom cry? and understanding put forth her voice? 2She standeth in the top of high places by the way, *in* the places of the paths. 3She crieth at the gates, at the entry of the city, *at* the coming in at the doors. 4Unto you, O men, I call; and my voice *is* to the sons of man. 5O ye simple, understand wisdom: and, ye fools, be ye of an understanding heart. 6Hear, for I will speak of excellent things; and the opening of my lips *shall be* right things. 7For my mouth shall speak truth; and wickedness *is* an abomination to my lips. 8All the words of my mouth *are* in righteousness; *there is* nothing froward or perverse in them. 9They *are* all plain to him that understandeth, and right to them that find knowledge. 10Receive my instruction, and not sil-

ver; and knowledge rather than choice gold. 11For wisdom *is* better than rubies; and all the things that may be desired are not to be compared to it. [Job 28:15; Ps. 19:10; 119:127; ch. 3:14,15; 4:5,7; 16:16]

12 I wisdom dwell *with* prudence, and find out knowledge of witty inventions. 13The fear of the LORD *is* to hate evil: pride, and arrogancy, and the evil way, and the froward mouth, do I hate. 14Counsel *is* mine, and sound wisdom: I *am* understanding; I have strength. 15By me kings reign, and princes decree justice. 16By me princes rule, and nobles, *even* all the judges of the earth. 17I love them that love me; and those that seek me early shall find me. 18Riches and honour *are* with me; *yea,* durable riches and righteousness. 19My fruit *is* better than gold, yea, than fine gold; and my revenue than choice silver. 20I lead in the way of righteousness, in the midst of the paths of judgment: 21That *I* may cause those that love me to inherit substance; and I will fill their treasures.

22 The LORD possessed me *in* the beginning of his way, before his works of old. 23I was set up from everlasting, from the beginning, or ever the earth was. 24When *there were* no depths, I was brought forth; when *there were* no fountains abounding with water. 25Before the mountains were settled, before the hills was I brought forth: 26While as yet he had not made the earth, nor the fields, nor the highest part of the dust of the world. 27When he pre-

pared the heavens, I *was* there: when he set a compass upon the face of the depth: 28When he established the clouds above: when *he* strengthened the fountains of the deep: 29When he gave to the sea his decree, that the waters should not pass his commandment; when he appointed the foundations of the earth: 30Then I was by him, *as* one brought up *with him:* and I was daily *his* delight, rejoicing always before him; 31Rejoicing in the habitable part of his earth; and my delights *were* with the sons of men. [Ps. 16:3]

32 Now therefore hearken unto me, O ye children: for blessed *are they that* keep my ways. 33Hear instruction, and be wise, and refuse *it* not. 34Blessed *is* the man that heareth me, watching daily at my gates, waiting at the posts of my doors. 35For whoso findeth me findeth life, and shall obtain favour of the LORD. 36But he that sinneth *against* me wrongeth his own soul: all they that hate me love death. [ch. 20:2]

Wisdom and folly contrasted

9 Wisdom hath builded her house, she hath hewn out her seven pillars: 2She hath killed her beasts; she hath mingled her wine; she hath also furnished her table. 3She hath sent forth her maidens: she crieth upon the highest places of the city, 4Whoso *is* simple, let him turn in hither: *as for* him that wanteth understanding, she saith to him, 5Come, eat of my bread, and drink of the wine *which* I have mingled. 6Forsake the foolish, and

live; and go in the way of understanding. 7He that reproveth a scorner getteth to himself shame: and he that rebuketh a wicked *man* getteth himself a blot. 8Reprove not a scorner, lest he hate thee: rebuke a wise *man,* and he will love thee. 9Give *instruction* to a wise *man,* and he will be yet wiser: teach a just *man,* and he will increase in learning. 10The fear of the LORD *is* the beginning of wisdom: and the knowledge of the holy *is* understanding. 11For by me thy days shall be multiplied, and the years of thy life shall be increased. 12If thou be wise, thou shalt be wise for thyself: but *if* thou scornest, thou alone shalt bear *it.* [Job 35:6,7; ch. 16:26]

13 A foolish woman *is* clamorous: *she is* simple, and knoweth nothing. 14For she sitteth at the door of her house, on a seat in the high places of the city, 15To call passengers who go right *on* their ways: 16Whoso *is* simple, let him turn in hither: and *as for* him that wanteth understanding, she saith to him, 17Stolen waters are sweet, and bread *eaten* in secret is pleasant. 18But he knoweth not that the dead *are* there; *and that* her guests *are* in the depths of hell. [ch. 2:18]

Proverbs of Solomon

10 The proverbs of Solomon. A wise son maketh a glad father: but a foolish son *is* the heaviness of his mother. 2Treasures of wickedness profit nothing: but righteousness delivereth from death. 3The LORD will not suffer the soul of the righteous to famish:

but he casteth away the substance of the wicked. 4He becometh poor that dealeth *with* a slack hand: but the hand of the diligent maketh rich. 5He that gathereth in summer *is* a wise son: *but* he that sleepeth in harvest *is* a son that causeth shame. 6Blessings *are* upon the head of the just: but violence covereth the mouth of the wicked. 7The memory of the just *is* blessed: but the name of the wicked shall rot. 8The wise in heart will receive commandments: but a prating fool shall fall. 9He that walketh uprightly walketh surely: but he that perverteth his ways shall be known. 10He that winketh *with* the eye causeth sorrow: but a prating fool shall fall. 11The mouth of a righteous *man is* a well of life: but violence covereth the mouth of the wicked. 12Hatred stirreth up strifes: but love covereth all sins. 13In the lips of him that hath understanding wisdom is found: but a rod *is* for the back of him that is void of understanding. 14Wise *men* lay up knowledge: but the mouth of the foolish *is* near destruction. 15The rich *man's* wealth *is* his strong city: the destruction of the poor *is* their poverty. 16The labour of the righteous *tendeth* to life: the fruit of the wicked to sin. 17He *is in* the way of life that keepeth instruction: but he that refuseth reproof erreth. 18He that hideth hatred *with* lying lips, and he that uttereth a slander, *is* a fool. 19In the multitude of words there wanteth not sin: but he that refraineth his lips *is* wise. 20The tongue of the just *is as* choice silver: the heart of

the wicked *is* little worth. 21The lips of the righteous feed many: but fools die for want of wisdom. 22The blessing of the LORD, it maketh rich, and he addeth no sorrow with it. 23It is as sport to a fool to do mischief: but a man of understanding hath wisdom. 24The fear of the wicked, it shall come *upon* him: but the desire of the righteous shall be granted. 25As the whirlwind passeth, so *is* the wicked no *more:* but the righteous *is* an everlasting foundation. 26As vinegar to the teeth, and as smoke to the eyes, so *is* the sluggard to them that send him. 27The fear of the LORD prolongeth days: but the years of the wicked shall be shortened. 28The hope of the righteous *shall be* gladness: but the expectation of the wicked shall perish. 29The way of the LORD *is* strength to the upright: but destruction *shall be* to the workers of iniquity. 30The righteous shall never be removed: but the wicked shall not inhabit the earth. 31The mouth of the just bringeth forth wisdom: but the froward tongue shall be cut out. 32The lips of the righteous know what is acceptable: but the mouth of the wicked *speaketh* frowardness.

11 A false balance *is* abomination to the LORD: but a just weight *is* his delight. 2When pride cometh, then cometh shame: but with the lowly *is* wisdom. 3The integrity of the upright shall guide them: but the perverseness of transgressors shall destroy them. 4Riches profit not in the day of wrath: but righteousness deliv-

ereth from death. 5The righteousness of the perfect shall direct his
way: but the wicked shall fall by
his own wickedness. 6The righteousness of the upright shall deliver them: but transgressors shall
be taken in their own naughtiness.
7When a wicked man dieth, *his* expectation shall perish: and the
hope of unjust *men* perisheth.
8The righteous is delivered out of
trouble, and the wicked cometh in
his stead. 9A hypocrite with *his*
mouth destroyeth his neighbour:
but through knowledge shall the
just be delivered. 10When it goeth
well with the righteous, the city rejoiceth: and when the wicked perish, *there is* shouting. 11By the
blessing of the upright the city is
exalted: but it is overthrown by the
mouth of the wicked. 12He that is
void of wisdom despiseth his
neighbour: but a man of understanding holdeth his peace. 13A
talebearer revealeth secrets: but he
that is of a faithful spirit concealeth
the matter. 14Where no counsel *is,*
the people fall: but in the multitude of counsellers *there is* safety.
15He that is surety for a stranger
shall smart *for it:* and he that
hateth suretiship *is* sure. 16A gracious woman retaineth honour:
and strong *men* retain riches.
17The merciful man doeth good to
his own soul: but *he that is* cruel
troubleth his own flesh. 18The
wicked worketh a deceitful work:
but *to* him that soweth righteousness *shall be* a sure reward. 19As
righteousness *tendeth* to life: so he
that pursueth evil *pursueth it* to his
own death. 20They *that are* of a

froward heart *are* abomination
unto the LORD: but *such as are* upright in *their* way *are* his delight.
21*Though* hand *join* in hand, the
wicked shall not be unpunished:
but the seed of the righteous shall
be delivered. 22*As* a jewel of gold
in a swine's snout, *so is* a fair
woman which is without discretion. 23The desire of the righteous
is only good: *but* the expectation of
the wicked *is* wrath. 24There is
that scattereth, and yet increaseth;
and *there is* that withholdeth more
than is meet, but *it tendeth* to
poverty. 25The liberal soul shall be
made fat: and he that watereth
shall be watered also himself. 26He
that withholdeth corn, the people
shall curse him: but blessing *shall
be* upon the head of him that selleth *it.* 27He that diligently seeketh
good procureth favour: but he that
seeketh mischief, it shall come
unto him. 28He that trusteth in his
riches shall fall: but the righteous
shall flourish as a branch. 29He that
troubleth his own house shall inherit the wind: and the fool *shall
be* servant to the wise of heart.
30The fruit of the righteous *is* a
tree of life; and he that winneth
souls *is* wise. 31Behold, the righteous shall be recompensed in the
earth: much more the wicked and
the sinner. [Jer. 25:29]

12 Whoso loveth instruction
loveth knowledge: but he
that hateth reproof *is* brutish. 2A
good *man* obtaineth favour of the
LORD: but a man of wicked devices
will he condemn. 3A man shall not
be established by wickedness: but
the root of the righteous shall not

be moved. 4A virtuous woman *is* a crown to her husband: but she that maketh ashamed *is* as rottenness in his bones. 5The thoughts of the righteous *are* right: *but* the counsels of the wicked *are* deceit. 6The words of the wicked *are* to lie in wait *for* blood: but the mouth of the upright shall deliver them. 7The wicked *are* overthrown, and *are* not: but the house of the righteous shall stand. 8A man shall be commended according to his wisdom: but he that is of a perverse heart shall be despised. 9*He that is* despised, and hath a servant, *is* better than he that honoureth himself, and lacketh bread. 10A righteous *man* regardeth the life of his beast: but the tender mercies of the wicked *are* cruel. 11He that tilleth his land shall be satisfied *with* bread: but he that followeth vain *persons is* void of understanding. 12The wicked desireth the net of evil *men:* but the root of the righteous yieldeth *fruit.* 13The wicked is snared by the transgression of *his* lips: but the just shall come out of trouble. 14A man shall be satisfied *with* good by the fruit of *his* mouth: and the recompence of a man's hands shall be rendered unto him. 15The way of a fool *is* right in his own eyes: but he that hearkeneth unto counsel *is* wise. 16A fool's wrath is presently known: but a prudent *man* covereth shame. 17*He that* speaketh truth sheweth forth righteousness: but a false witness sheweth deceit. 18There is that speaketh like the piercings of a sword: but the tongue of the wise *is* health. 19The lip of truth

shall be established for ever: but a lying tongue *is* but for a moment. 20Deceit *is* in the heart of them that imagine evil: but to the counsellers of peace *is* joy. 21There shall no evil happen to the just: but the wicked shall be filled *with* mischief. 22Lying lips *are* abomination to the LORD: but they that deal truly *are* his delight. 23A prudent man concealeth knowledge: but the heart of fools proclaimeth foolishness. 24The hand of the diligent shall bear rule: but the slothful shall be under tribute. 25Heaviness in the heart of man maketh it stoop: but a good word maketh it glad. 26The righteous *is* more excellent than his neighbour: but the way of the wicked seduceth them. 27The slothful *man* roasteth not that which he took in hunting: but the substance of a diligent man *is* precious. 28In the way of righteousness *is* life; and *in* the pathway *thereof there is* no death.

13 A wise son *heareth his* father's instruction: but a scorner heareth not rebuke. 2A man shall eat good by the fruit of *his* mouth: but the soul of the transgressors *shall eat* violence. 3He that keepeth his mouth keepeth his life: *but* he that openeth wide his lips shall have destruction. 4The soul of the sluggard desireth, and *hath* nothing: but the soul of the diligent shall be made fat. 5A righteous *man* hateth lying: but a wicked *man* is loathsome, and cometh to shame. 6Righteousness keepeth *him that is* upright in the way: but wickedness overthroweth the sinner. 7There is that maketh himself rich, yet *hath* nothing: *there is* that maketh himself poor, yet *hath* great riches. 8The ransom of a man's life *are* his riches: but the poor heareth not rebuke. 9The light of the righteous rejoiceth: but the lamp of the wicked shall be put out. 10Only by pride cometh contention: but with the well advised *is* wisdom. 11Wealth *gotten* by vanity shall be diminished: but he that gathereth by labour shall increase. 12Hope deferred maketh the heart sick: but *when* the desire cometh, *it is* a tree of life. 13Whoso despiseth the word shall be destroyed: but he that feareth the commandment shall be rewarded. 14The law of the wise *is* a fountain of life, to depart from the snares of death. 15Good understanding giveth favour: but the way of transgressors *is* hard. 16Every prudent *man* dealeth with knowledge: but a fool layeth open *his* folly. 17A wicked messenger falleth into mischief: but a faithful ambassador *is* health. 18Poverty and shame *shall be to* him that refuseth instruction: but he that regardeth reproof shall be honoured. 19The desire accomplished is sweet to the soul: but *it is* abomination to fools to depart from evil. 20He that walketh with wise *men* shall be wise: but a companion of fools shall be destroyed. 21Evil pursueth sinners: but to the righteous good shall be repayed. 22A good *man* leaveth an inheritance to *his* children's children: and the wealth of the sinner *is* laid up for the just. 23Much food *is in* the tillage of the poor: but there is *that is* destroyed for want of judgment. 24He that spareth his rod hateth his son: but he that loveth him chasteneth him betimes. 25The righteous eateth to the satisfying of his soul: but the belly of the wicked shall want. [Ps. 34:10; 37:3]

14 Every wise woman buildeth her house: but the foolish plucketh it down with her hands. 2He that walketh in his uprightness feareth the LORD: but he that is perverse in his ways despiseth him. 3In the mouth of the foolish *is* a rod of pride: but the lips of the wise shall preserve them. 4Where no oxen *are,* the crib *is* clean: but much increase *is* by the strength of the ox. 5A faithful witness will not lie: but a false witness will utter lies. 6A scorner seeketh wisdom, and *findeth it* not: but knowledge *is* easy unto him that understandeth. 7Go from the presence of a foolish man, when thou perceivest not *in him* the lips of knowledge. 8The wisdom of the prudent *is* to understand his way: but the folly of fools *is* deceit. 9Fools make a mock at sin: but among the righteous *there is* favour. 10The heart knoweth his own bitterness; and a stranger doth not intermeddle with his joy. 11The house of the wicked shall be overthrown: but the tabernacle of the upright shall flourish. 12There is a way which seemeth right unto a man, but the end thereof *are* the ways of death. 13Even in laughter the heart is sorrowful; and the end of that mirth *is* heaviness. 14The backslider in heart shall be filled with his own ways: and a good man *shall be satisfied* from himself. 15The simple believeth every word: but the prudent *man* looketh well to his going. 16A wise *man* feareth, and departeth from evil: but the fool rageth, and *is* confident. 17He that is soon angry dealeth foolishly: and a man of wicked devices is hated. 18The simple inherit folly: but the prudent are crowned *with* knowledge. 19The evil bow before the good; and the wicked at the gates of the righteous. 20The poor is hated even of his own neighbour: but the rich *hath* many friends. 21He that despiseth his neighbour sinneth: but he that hath mercy on the poor, happy *is* he. 22Do they not err that devise evil? but mercy and truth *shall be to* them that devise good. 23In all labour there is profit: but the talk of the lips *tendeth* only to penury. 24The crown of the wise *is* their riches: *but* the foolishness of fools *is* folly. 25A true witness delivereth souls: but a deceitful *witness* speaketh lies. 26In the fear of the LORD *is* strong confidence: and his children shall have a place of refuge. 27The fear of the LORD *is* a fountain of life, to depart from the snares of death. 28In the multitude of people *is* the king's honour: but in the want of people *is* the destruction of the prince. 29He that is slow to wrath *is* of great understanding: but *he that is* hasty of spirit exalteth folly. 30A sound heart *is* the life of the flesh: but envy the rottenness of the bones. 31He that oppresseth the poor reproacheth his Maker: but he that honoureth him hath mercy on the

poor. 32The wicked is driven away in his wickedness: but the righteous hath hope in his death. 33Wisdom resteth in the heart of him that hath understanding: but *that which is* in the midst of fools is made known. 34Righteousness exalteth a nation: but sin *is* a reproach to any people. 35The king's favour *is* toward a wise servant: but his wrath is *against* him that causeth shame. [Mat. 24:45]

15 A soft answer turneth away wrath: but grievous words stir up anger. 2The tongue of the wise useth knowledge aright: but the mouth of fools poureth out foolishness. 3The eyes of the LORD *are* in every place, beholding the evil and the good. 4A wholesome tongue *is* a tree of life: but perverseness therein *is* a breach in the spirit. 5A fool despiseth his father's instruction: but he that regardeth reproof is prudent. 6In the house of the righteous *is* much treasure: but in the revenues of the wicked *is* trouble. 7The lips of the wise disperse knowledge: but the heart of the foolish *doeth* not so. 8The sacrifice of the wicked *is* an abomination to the LORD: but the prayer of the upright *is* his delight. 9The way of the wicked *is* an abomination unto the LORD: but he loveth him that followeth after righteousness. 10Correction *is* grievous unto him that forsaketh the way: *and* he that hateth reproof shall die. 11Hell and destruction *are* before the LORD: how much more then the hearts of the children of men? 12A scorner loveth not one that reproveth him: neither will he go unto the wise.

13 A merry heart maketh a cheerful countenance: but by sorrow of the heart the spirit *is* broken. 14 The heart of him that hath understanding seeketh knowledge: but the mouth of fools feedeth on foolishness. 15 All the days of the afflicted *are* evil: but *he that is* of a merry heart *hath* a continual feast. 16 Better *is* little with the fear of the LORD than great treasure and trouble therewith. 17 Better *is* a dinner of herbs where love is, than a stalled ox and hatred therewith. 18 A wrathful man stirreth up strife: but *he that is* slow to anger appeaseth strife. 19 The way of the slothful *man is* as a hedge of thorns: but the way of the righteous *is* made plain. 20 A wise son maketh a glad father: but a foolish man despiseth his mother. 21 Folly *is* joy to *him that is* destitute of wisdom: but a man of understanding walketh uprightly. 22 Without counsel purposes *are* disappointed: but in the multitude of counsellors *they* are established. 23 A man hath joy by the answer of his mouth: and a word *spoken* in due season, how good *is it!* 24 The way of life *is* above to the wise, that *he* may depart from hell beneath. 25 The LORD will destroy the house of the proud: but he will establish the border of the widow. 26 The thoughts of the wicked *are* an abomination to the LORD: but *the words of* the pure *are* pleasant words. 27 He that is greedy of gain troubleth his own house; but he that hateth gifts shall live. 28 The heart of the righteous studieth to answer: but the mouth of the wicked poureth out evil *things.* 29 The LORD *is* far from the wicked: but he heareth the prayer of the righteous. 30 The light of the eyes rejoiceth the heart: *and* a good report maketh the bones fat. 31 The ear that heareth the reproof of life abideth among the wise. 32 He that refuseth instruction despiseth his own soul: but he that heareth reproof getteth understanding. 33 The fear of the LORD *is* the instruction of wisdom; and before honour *is* humility. [ch. 1:7; ch. 18:12]

16 The preparations of the heart in man, and the answer of the tongue, *is* from the LORD. 2 All the ways of a man *are* clean in his own eyes; but the LORD weigheth the spirits. 3 Commit thy works unto the LORD, and thy thoughts shall be established. 4 The LORD hath made all *things* for himself: yea, even the wicked for the day of evil. 5 Every one *that is* proud in heart *is* an abomination to the LORD: *though* hand *join* in hand, he shall not be unpunished. 6 By mercy and truth iniquity is purged: and by the fear of the LORD *men* depart from evil. 7 When a man's ways please the LORD, he maketh even his enemies to be at peace with him. 8 Better *is* a little with righteousness than great revenues without right. 9 A man's heart deviseth his way: but the LORD directeth his steps. 10 A divine sentence *is* in the lips of the king: his mouth transgresseth not in judgment. 11 A just weight and balance *are* the LORD'S: all the weights of the bag *are* his work. 12 *It is* an abomination to kings to commit wickedness: for the throne is established by righteousness. 13Righteous lips *are* the delight of kings; and *they* love him that speaketh right. 14The wrath of a king *is as* messengers of death: but a wise man will pacify it. 15In the light of the king's countenance *is* life; and his favour *is* as a cloud of the latter rain. 16How much better *is it* to get wisdom than gold! and to get understanding rather to be chosen than silver! 17The highway of the upright *is* to depart from evil: he that keepeth his way preserveth his soul. 18Pride *goeth* before destruction, and a haughty spirit before a fall. 19Better *it is to be* of an humble spirit with the lowly, than to divide the spoil with the proud. 20He that handleth a matter wisely shall find good: and whoso trusteth in the LORD, happy *is* he. 21The wise in heart shall be called prudent: and the sweetness of the lips increaseth learning. 22Understanding *is* a wellspring of life unto him that hath it: but the instruction of fools *is* folly. 23The heart of the wise teacheth his mouth, and addeth learning to his lips. 24Pleasant words *are as* a honeycomb, sweet to the soul, and health to the bones. 25There is a way that seemeth right unto a man, but the end thereof *are* the ways of death. 26He that laboureth laboureth for himself; for his mouth craveth it of him. 27An ungodly man diggeth up evil: and in his lips *there is* as a burning fire. 28A froward man soweth strife: and a whisperer separateth chief friends. 29A violent man enticeth his neighbour, and leadeth him into the way *that is* not good. 30He shutteth his eyes to devise froward things: moving his lips he bringeth evil to pass. 31The hoary head *is* a crown of glory, *if it* be found in the way of righteousness. 32He that is slow to anger *is* better than the mighty; and he that ruleth his spirit than he that taketh a city. 33The lot is cast into the lap; but the whole disposing thereof *is* of the LORD.

17 Better *is* a dry morsel, and quietness therewith, than a house full *of* sacrifices with strife. 2A wise servant shall have rule over a son that causeth shame, and shall have part of the inheritance among the brethren. 3The fining pot *is* for silver, and the furnace for gold: but the LORD trieth the hearts. 4A wicked doer giveth heed to false lips; *and* a liar giveth ear to a naughty tongue. 5Whoso mocketh the poor reproacheth his Maker: *and* he that is glad at calamities shall not be unpunished. 6Children's children *are* the crown of old men; and the glory of children *are* their fathers. 7Excellent speech becometh not a fool: much less do lying lips a prince. 8A gift *is as* a precious stone in the eyes of him that hath it: whithersoever it turneth, it prospereth. 9He that covereth a transgression seeketh love; but he that repeateth a matter separateth very friends. 10A reproof entereth more into a wise *man* than an hundred stripes into a fool. 11An evil *man* seeketh only rebellion: therefore a cruel messenger shall be sent against him. 12Let a bear robbed of her whelps

meet a man, rather than a fool in his folly. ¹³Whoso rewardeth evil for good, evil shall not depart from his house. ¹⁴The beginning of strife *is as* when one letteth out water: therefore leave off contention, before *it* be meddled with. ¹⁵He that justifieth the wicked, and he that condemneth the just, even they both *are* abomination to the LORD. ¹⁶Wherefore *is there* a price in the hand of a fool to get wisdom, seeing *he hath* no heart *to it?* ¹⁷A friend loveth at all times, and a brother is born for adversity. ¹⁸A man void of understanding striketh hands, *and* becometh surety in the presence of his friend. ¹⁹He loveth transgression that loveth strife: *and* he that exalteth his gate seeketh destruction. ²⁰He that hath a froward heart findeth no good: and he that hath a perverse tongue falleth into mischief. ²¹He that begetteth a fool *doeth* it to his sorrow: and the father of a fool hath no joy. ²²A merry heart doeth good *like* a medicine: but a broken spirit drieth the bones. ²³A wicked *man* taketh a gift out of the bosom to pervert the ways of judgment. ²⁴Wisdom *is* before him that hath understanding; but the eyes of a fool *are* in the ends of the earth. ²⁵A foolish son *is* a grief to his father, and bitterness to her that bare him. ²⁶Also to punish the just *is* not good, *nor* to strike princes for equity. ²⁷He that hath knowledge spareth his words: *and* a man of understanding is of an excellent spirit. ²⁸Even a fool, when he holdeth his peace, is counted wise: *and* he that shutteth his lips

is esteemed a man of understanding. [Job 13:5]

18 Through desire a man, having separated himself, seeketh *and* intermeddleth with all wisdom. ²A fool hath no delight in understanding, but that his heart may discover itself. ³When the wicked cometh, *then* cometh also contempt, and with ignominy reproach. ⁴The words of a man's mouth *are as* deep waters, *and* the wellspring of wisdom *as* a flowing brook. ⁵*It is* not good to accept the person of the wicked, to overthrow the righteous in judgment. ⁶A fool's lips enter into contention, and his mouth calleth for strokes. ⁷A fool's mouth *is* his destruction, and his lips *are* the snare of his soul. ⁸The words of a talebearer *are* as wounds, and they go down *into* the innermost parts of the belly. ⁹He also that is slothful in his work *is* brother to him that is a great waster. ¹⁰The name of the LORD *is* a strong tower: the righteous runneth into it, and is safe. ¹¹The rich *man's* wealth *is* his strong city, and as a high wall in his own conceit. ¹²Before destruction the heart of man is haughty, and before honour *is* humility. ¹³He that answereth a matter before he heareth *it*, it *is* folly and shame unto him. ¹⁴The spirit of a man will sustain his infirmity; but a wounded spirit who can bear? ¹⁵The heart of the prudent getteth knowledge; and the ear of the wise seeketh knowledge. ¹⁶A man's gift maketh room for him, and bringeth him before great *men*. ¹⁷*He that is* first in his own cause *seemeth* just;

but his neighbour cometh and searcheth him. 18The lot causeth contentions to cease, and parteth between the mighty. 19A brother offended *is harder to be won* than a strong city: and *their* contentions *are* like the bars of a castle. 20A man's belly shall be satisfied with the fruit of his mouth; *and with* the increase of his lips shall he be filled. 21Death and life *are* in the power of the tongue: and they that love it shall eat the fruit thereof. 22*Whoso* findeth a wife findeth a good *thing*, and obtaineth favour of the LORD. 23The poor useth intreaties; but the rich answereth roughly. 24A man that hath friends must shew himself friendly: and there is a friend *that* sticketh closer than a brother. [ch. 17:17]

19 Better *is* the poor that walketh in his integrity, than *he that is* perverse in his lips, and *is* a fool. 2Also, *that* the soul *be* without knowledge, *it is* not good; and he that hasteth with *his* feet, sinneth. 3The foolishness of man perverteth his way: and his heart fretteth against the LORD. 4Wealth maketh many friends; but the poor is separated from his neighbour. 5A false witness shall not be unpunished, and *he that* speaketh lies shall not escape. 6Many will intreat the favour of the prince: and every *man is* a friend to him that giveth gifts. 7All the brethren of the poor do hate him: how much more do his friends go far from him! he pursueth *them with* words, *yet* they *are* wanting *to him.* 8He that getteth wisdom loveth his own soul: he that keepeth understanding shall find good. 9A false witness shall not be unpunished, and *he that* speaketh lies shall perish. 10Delight *is* not seemly for a fool; much less for a servant to have rule over princes. 11The discretion of a man deferreth his anger; and *it is* his glory to pass over a transgression. 12The king's wrath *is* as the roaring of a lion; but his favour *is* as dew upon the grass. 13A foolish son *is* the calamity of his father: and the contentions of a wife *are* a continual dropping. 14House and riches *are* the inheritance of fathers: and a prudent wife *is* from the LORD. 15Slothfulness casteth into a deep sleep; and an idle soul shall suffer hunger. 16He that keepeth the commandment keepeth his own soul; *but* he that despiseth his ways shall die. 17He that hath pity upon the poor lendeth unto the LORD; and that which he hath given will he pay him again. 18Chasten thy son while there is hope, and let not thy soul spare for his crying. 19*A man* of great wrath *shall* suffer punishment: for if thou deliver *him,* yet thou must do *it* again. 20Hear counsel, and receive instruction, that thou mayest be wise in thy latter end. 21*There are* many devices in a man's heart; nevertheless the counsel of the LORD, that shall stand. 22The desire of a man *is* his kindness: and a poor *man is* better than a liar. 23The fear of the LORD *tendeth* to life: and *he that hath it* shall abide satisfied; he shall not be visited *with* evil. 24A slothful *man* hideth his hand in *his* bosom, and will not so much as bring it to his mouth again. 25Smite a scorner, and the simple will beware: and reprove one that hath understanding, *and* he will understand knowledge. 26He that wasteth *his* father, *and* chaseth away *his* mother, *is* a son that causeth shame, and bringeth reproach. 27Cease, my son, to hear the instruction *that causeth* to err from the words of knowledge. 28An ungodly witness scorneth judgment: and the mouth of the wicked devoureth iniquity. 29Judgments are prepared for scorners, and stripes for the back of fools. [ch. 26:3]

20 Wine *is* a mocker, strong drink *is* raging: and whosoever is deceived thereby is not wise. 2The fear of a king *is* as the roaring of a lion: *whoso* provoketh him to anger sinneth *against* his own soul. 3*It is* an honour for a man to cease from strife: but every fool will be meddling. 4The sluggard will not plow by reason of the cold; therefore shall he beg in harvest, and *have* nothing. 5Counsel in the heart of man *is like* deep water; but a man of understanding will draw it out. 6Most men will proclaim every one his own goodness: but a faithful man who can find? 7The just *man* walketh in his integrity: his children *are* blessed after him. 8A king that sitteth in the throne of judgment scattereth *away* all evil with his eyes. 9Who can say, I have made my heart clean, I am pure from my sin? 10Divers weights, *and* divers measures, both of them *are* alike abomination to the LORD. 11Even a child is known by his do-

ings, whether his work *be* pure, and whether *it be* right. 12The hearing ear, and the seeing eye, the LORD hath made even both of them. 13Love not sleep, lest thou come to poverty; open thine eyes, *and* thou shalt be satisfied *with* bread. 14*It is* naught, *it is* naught, saith the buyer: but when he is gone his way, then he boasteth. 15There is gold, and a multitude of rubies: but the lips of knowledge *are* a precious jewel. 16Take his garment that is surety *for* a stranger: and take a pledge of him for a strange *woman.* 17Bread of deceit *is* sweet to a man; but afterwards his mouth shall be filled *with* gravel. 18Every purpose is established by counsel: and with good advice make war. 19He that goeth about *as* a talebearer revealeth secrets: therefore meddle not with him that flattereth *with* his lips. 20Whoso curseth his father or his mother, his lamp shall be put out in obscure darkness. 21An inheritance *may be* gotten hastily at the beginning; but the end thereof shall not be blessed. 22Say not thou, I will recompense evil; *but* wait on the LORD, and he shall save thee. 23Divers weights *are* an abomination unto the LORD; and a false balance *is* not good. 24Man's goings *are* of the LORD; how can a man then understand his own way? 25*It is* a snare to the man *who* devoureth *that which is* holy, and after vows to make inquiry. 26A wise king scattereth the wicked, and bringeth the wheel over them. 27The spirit of man *is* the candle of the LORD, searching all the inward parts of the belly. 28Mercy and truth preserve the king: and his throne is upholden by mercy. 29The glory of young men *is* their strength: and the beauty of old men *is* the gray head. 30The blueness of a wound cleanseth away evil: so *do* stripes the inward parts of the belly.

21 The king's heart *is* in the hand of the LORD, *as* the rivers of water: he turneth it whithersoever he will. 2Every way of a man *is* right in his own eyes: but the LORD pondereth the hearts. 3To do justice and judgment *is* more acceptable to the LORD than sacrifice. 4A high look, and a proud heart, *and* the plowing of the wicked, *is* sin. 5The thoughts of the diligent *tend* only to plenteousness; but *of* every one that is hasty only to want. 6The getting of treasures by a lying tongue *is* a vanity tossed to and fro of them that seek death. 7The robbery of the wicked shall destroy them; because they refuse to do judgment. 8The way of man *is* froward and strange: but *as for* the pure, his work *is* right. 9It *is* better to dwell in a corner of the housetop, than with a brawling woman in a wide house. 10The soul of the wicked desireth evil: his neighbour findeth no favour in his eyes. 11When the scorner is punished, the simple is made wise: and when the wise is instructed, he receiveth knowledge. 12The righteous *man* wisely considereth the house of the wicked: *but God* overthroweth the wicked for *their* wickedness. 13Whoso stoppeth his ears at the cry of the poor, he also shall cry himself, but shall not be heard. 14A gift in secret pacifieth anger: and a reward in the bosom strong wrath. 15It *is* joy to the just to do judgment: but destruction *shall be* to the workers of iniquity. 16The man that wandereth out of the way of understanding shall remain in the congregation of the dead. 17He that loveth pleasure *shall be* a poor man: he that loveth wine and oil shall not be rich. 18The wicked *shall be* a ransom for the righteous, and the transgressor for the upright. 19It *is* better to dwell in the wilderness, than with a contentious and an angry woman. 20There *is* treasure to be desired and oil in the dwelling of the wise; but a foolish man spendeth it up. 21He that followeth after righteousness and mercy findeth life, righteousness, and honour. 22A wise *man* scaleth the city of the mighty, and casteth down the strength of the confidence thereof. 23Whoso keepeth his mouth and his tongue keepeth his soul from troubles. 24Proud *and* haughty scorner *is* his name, who dealeth in proud wrath. 25The desire of the slothful killeth him; for his hands refuse to labour. 26He coveteth greedily all the day long: but the righteous giveth and spareth not. 27The sacrifice of the wicked *is* abomination: how much more, *when* he bringeth it with a wicked mind? 28A false witness shall perish: but the man that heareth, speaketh constantly. 29A wicked man hardeneth his face: but *as for* the upright, he directeth his way. 30There *is* no wisdom nor understanding nor counsel against the LORD. 31 The horse *is* prepared against the day of battle: but safety *is* of the LORD. [Ps. 3:8]

22 A *good* name *is* rather to be chosen than great riches, *and* loving favour rather than silver and gold. 2 The rich and poor meet together: the LORD *is* the Maker of them all. 3 A prudent *man* foreseeth the evil, and hideth himself: but the simple pass on, and are punished. 4 By humility *and* the fear of the LORD *are* riches, and honour, and life. 5 Thorns *and* snares *are* in the way of the froward: he that doth keep his soul shall be far from them. 6 Train up a child in the way he should go: and when he is old, he will not depart from it. 7 The rich ruleth over the poor, and the borrower *is* servant to the lender. 8 He that soweth iniquity shall reap vanity: and the rod of his anger shall fail. 9 He that hath a bountiful eye shall be blessed; for he giveth of his bread to the poor. 10 Cast out the scorner, and contention shall go out; yea, strife and reproach shall cease. 11 He that loveth pureness of heart, *for* the grace of his lips the king *shall be* his friend. 12 The eyes of the LORD preserve knowledge, and he overthroweth the words of the transgressor. 13 The slothful *man* saith, *There is* a lion without, I shall be slain in the streets. 14 The mouth of strange *women is* a deep pit: he that is abhorred of the LORD shall fall therein. 15 Foolishness *is* bound in the heart of a child; *but* the rod of correction shall drive it far from him. 16 He that oppresseth the poor to increase his *riches, and* he that giveth to the rich, *shall* surely *come* to want.

Hear the words of the wise

17 Bow down thine ear, and hear the words of the wise, and apply thine heart unto my knowledge. 18 For *it is* a pleasant *thing* if thou keep them within thee; they shall withal be fitted in thy lips. 19 That thy trust may be in the LORD, I have made known to thee *this* day, even *to* thee. 20 Have not I written to thee excellent things in counsels and knowledge, 21 That *I* might make thee know the certainty of the words of truth; that *thou* mightest answer the words *of* truth to them that send *unto* thee? [Luke 1:3,4; 1 Pet. 3:15]

22 Rob not the poor, because he *is* poor: neither oppress the afflicted in the gate: 23 For the LORD will plead their cause, and spoil the soul of those that spoiled them. 24 Make no friendship with an angry man; and with a furious man thou shalt not go: 25 Lest thou learn his ways, and get a snare to thy soul. 26 Be not thou *one* of them that strike hands, *or* of them that are sureties for debts. 27 If thou hast nothing to pay, why should he take away thy bed from under thee? 28 Remove not the ancient landmark, which thy fathers have set. [Deut. 19:14]

29 Seest thou a man diligent in his business? he shall stand before kings; he shall not stand before mean *men.*

23 When thou sittest to eat with a ruler, consider diligently what *is* before thee: 2 And put a knife to thy throat, if thou *be* a man given to appetite. ³Be not desirous of his dainties: for they *are* deceitful meat. ⁴Labour not to be rich: cease from thine own wisdom. ⁵Wilt thou set thine eyes upon that which is not? for *riches* certainly make themselves wings; they fly away as an eagle *toward* heaven.

6 Eat thou not the bread of *him that hath* an evil eye, neither desire thou his dainty meats: ⁷For as he thinketh in his heart, so *is* he: Eat and drink, saith he to thee; but his heart *is* not with thee. ⁸The morsel *which* thou hast eaten shalt thou vomit up, and lose thy sweet words. ⁹Speak not in the ears of a fool: for he will despise the wisdom of thy words. ¹⁰Remove not the old landmark; and enter not into the fields of the fatherless: ¹¹For their Redeemer *is* mighty; he shall plead their cause with thee. ¹²Apply thine heart unto instruction, and thine ears to the words of knowledge. ¹³Withhold not correction from the child: for *if* thou beatest him with the rod, he shall not die. ¹⁴Thou shalt beat him with the rod, and shalt deliver his soul from hell.

15 My son, if thine heart be wise, my heart shall rejoice, even mine. ¹⁶Yea, my reins shall rejoice, when thy lips speak right things. ¹⁷Let not thine heart envy sinners: but *be thou* in the fear of the LORD all the day long. ¹⁸For surely there is an end; and thine expectation shall not be cut off. ¹⁹Hear thou, my son, and be wise, and guide thine heart in the way. ²⁰Be not amongst winebibbers; amongst ri-

otous eaters of flesh: ²¹For the drunkard and the glutton shall come to poverty: and drowsiness shall clothe *a man* with rags.

22 Hearken unto thy father that begat thee, and despise not thy mother when she is old. ²³Buy the truth, and sell *it* not; *also* wisdom, and instruction, and understanding. ²⁴The father of the righteous shall greatly rejoice: and he that begetteth a wise *child* shall have joy of him. ²⁵Thy father and thy mother shall be glad, and she that bare thee shall rejoice. ²⁶My son, give me thine heart, and let thine eyes observe my ways. ²⁷For a whore *is* a deep ditch; and a strange *woman is* a narrow pit. ²⁸She also lieth in wait as *for* a prey, and increaseth the transgressors among men. [ch. 7:12; Eccl. 7:26]

29 Who hath woe? who hath sorrow? who hath contentions? who hath babbling? who hath wounds without cause? who hath redness of eyes? ³⁰They that tarry long at the wine; they that go to seek mixt wine. ³¹Look not thou upon the wine when it is red, when it giveth his colour in the cup, *when* it moveth itself aright. ³²At the last it biteth like a serpent, and stingeth like an adder. ³³Thine eyes shall behold strange *women*, and thine heart shall utter perverse things. ³⁴Yea, thou shalt be as he that lieth down in the midst of the sea, or as he that lieth upon the top of a mast. ³⁵They have stricken me, *shalt thou say, and* I was not sick; they have beaten me, *and* I felt *it* not: when shall I awake? I will seek it yet again. [Jer. 5:3; Eph. 4:19]

24

Be not thou envious against evil men, neither desire to be with them. ²For their heart studieth destruction, and their lips talk of mischief. ³Through wisdom is a house builded; and by understanding it is established: ⁴And by knowledge shall the chambers be filled *with* all precious and pleasant riches. ⁵A wise man *is* strong; yea, a man of knowledge increaseth strength. ⁶For by wise counsel thou shalt make thy war: and in multitude of counsellers *there is* safety. ⁷Wisdom *is* too high for a fool: he openeth not his mouth in the gate. ⁸He that deviseth to do evil shall be called a mischievous person. ⁹The thought of foolishness *is* sin: and the scorner *is* an abomination to men. ¹⁰If thou faint in the day of adversity, thy strength *is* small. ¹¹If thou forbear to deliver *them that are* drawn unto death, and *those that are* ready to be slain; ¹²If thou sayest, Behold, we knew it not; doth not he that pondereth the heart consider *it?* and he that keepeth thy soul, doth *not* he know *it?* and shall *not* he render to *every* man according to his works? ¹³My son, eat thou honey, because *it is* good; and the honeycomb, *which is* sweet to thy taste: ¹⁴So shall the knowledge of wisdom be unto thy soul: when thou hast found *it,* then there shall be a reward, and thy expectation shall not be cut off. ¹⁵Lay not wait, O wicked *man,* against the dwelling of the righteous; spoil not his resting place: ¹⁶For a just *man* falleth seven *times,* and riseth up *again:* but the

wicked shall fall into mischief. ¹⁷Rejoice not when thine enemy falleth, and let not thine heart be glad when he stumbleth: ¹⁸Lest the LORD see *it,* and it displease him, and he turn away his wrath from him. ¹⁹Fret not thyself because of evil *men,* neither be thou envious at the wicked; ²⁰For there shall be no reward to the evil *man;* the candle of the wicked shall be put out. ²¹My son, fear thou the LORD and the king: *and* meddle not with them that are given to change: ²²For their calamity shall rise suddenly; and who knoweth the ruin of them both?

Sayings of the wise

23 These *things* also *belong* to the wise. *It is* not good to have respect of persons in judgment. ²⁴He that saith unto the wicked, Thou *art* righteous; him shall the people curse, nations shall abhor him: ²⁵But to them that rebuke *him* shall be delight, and a good blessing shall come upon them. ²⁶*Every* man shall kiss *his* lips that giveth a right answer. ²⁷Prepare thy work without, and make it fit for thyself in the field; and afterwards build thine house. ²⁸Be not a witness against thy neighbour without cause; and deceive not with thy lips. ²⁹Say not, I will do so to him as he hath done to me: I will render to the man according to his work. [Mat. 5:39]

30 I went by the field of the slothful, and by the vineyard of the man void of understanding; ³¹And lo, it was all grown over *with* thorns, *and* nettles had covered

the face thereof, and the stone wall thereof was broken down. ³²Then I saw, *and* considered *it* well: I looked upon *it, and* received instruction. ³³Yet a little sleep, a little slumber, a little folding of the hands to sleep: ³⁴So shall thy poverty come *as* one that travelleth; and thy want as an armed man.

More proverbs of Solomon

25 These *are* also proverbs of Solomon, which the men of Hezekiah king of Judah copied out. [1 Ki. 4:32]

2 *It is* the glory of God to conceal a thing: but the honour of kings *is* to search out a matter. ³The heaven for height, and the earth for depth, and the heart of kings *is* unsearchable. ⁴Take away the dross from the silver, and there shall come forth a vessel for the finer. ⁵Take away the wicked *from* before the king, and his throne shall be established in righteousness. ⁶Put not forth thyself in the presence of the king, and stand not in the place of great *men:* ⁷For better *it is* that it be said unto thee, Come up hither; than that thou shouldest be put lower in the presence of the prince whom thine eyes have seen. ⁸Go not forth hastily to strive, lest *thou know not* what to do in the end thereof, when thy neighbour hath put thee to shame. ⁹Debate thy cause with thy neighbour *himself;* and discover not a secret *to* another: ¹⁰Lest he that heareth *it* put thee to shame, and thine infamy turn not away.

11 A word fitly spoken *is like* apples of gold in pictures of silver. ¹²As an earring of gold, and an ornament of fine gold, *so is* a wise reprover upon an obedient ear. ¹³As the cold of snow in the time of harvest, *so is* a faithful messenger to them that send him: for he refresheth the soul of his masters. ¹⁴Whoso boasteth himself of a false gift *is like* clouds and wind without rain. ¹⁵By long forbearing is a prince persuaded, and a soft tongue breaketh the bone. ¹⁶Hast thou found honey? eat so much as is sufficient for thee, lest thou be filled there*with,* and vomit it. ¹⁷Withdraw thy foot from thy neighbour's house; lest he be weary *of* thee, and *so* hate thee. ¹⁸A man that beareth false witness against his neighbour *is* a maul, and a sword, and a sharp arrow. ¹⁹Confidence in an unfaithful *man* in time of trouble *is like* a broken tooth, and a foot out of joint. ²⁰As he that taketh away a garment in cold weather, *and as* vinegar upon nitre, so *is* he that singeth songs to a heavy heart. ²¹If thine enemy *be* hungry, give him bread to eat; and if he *be* thirsty, give him water to drink: ²²For thou shalt heap coals of fire upon his head, and the LORD shall reward thee. ²³The north wind driveth away rain: so *doth* an angry countenance a backbiting tongue. ²⁴It is* better to dwell in a corner of the housetop, than with a brawling woman and in a wide house. ²⁵As cold waters to a thirsty soul, so *is* good news from a far country. ²⁶A righteous *man* falling down before the wicked *is as* a

troubled fountain, and a corrupt spring. ²⁷*It is* not good to eat much honey: so *for men* to search their own glory *is not* glory. ²⁸He that *hath* no rule over his own spirit *is like* a city *that is* broken down, *and* without walls. [ch. 16:32]

26 As snow in summer, and as rain in harvest, so honour *is* not seemly for a fool. ²As the bird by wandering, as the swallow by flying, so the curse causeless shall not come. ³A whip for the horse, a bridle for the ass, and a rod for the fools' back. ⁴Answer not a fool according to his folly, lest thou also be like unto him. ⁵Answer a fool according to his folly, lest he be wise in his own conceit. ⁶He that sendeth a message by the hand of a fool cutteth off the feet, *and* drinketh damage. ⁷The legs of the lame are not equal: so *is* a parable in the mouth of fools. ⁸As *he that* bindeth a stone in a sling, so *is* he that giveth honour to a fool. ⁹*As* a thorn goeth up into the hand of a drunkard, so *is* a parable in the mouth of fools. ¹⁰The great *God* that formed all *things* both rewardeth the fool, and rewardeth transgressors. ¹¹As a dog returneth to his vomit, *so* a fool returneth to his folly. ¹²Seest thou a man wise in his own conceit? *there is* more hope of a fool than of him. ¹³The slothful *man* saith, There is a lion in the way; a lion *is* in the streets. ¹⁴*As* the door turneth upon his hinges, so *doth* the slothful upon his bed. ¹⁵The slothful hideth his hand in *his* bosom; it grieveth him to bring it again to his mouth. ¹⁶The sluggard *is* wiser in his own

conceit than seven *men* that can render a reason.

17 He that passeth by, *and* meddleth with strife *belonging* not to him, *is like* one that taketh a dog by the ears. ¹⁸As a mad *man* who casteth firebrands, arrows, and death, ¹⁹So *is* the man *that* deceiveth his neighbour, and saith, Am not I in sport? ²⁰Where no wood is, *there* the fire goeth out: so where *there is* no talebearer, the strife ceaseth. ²¹*As* coals *are* to burning coals, and wood to fire; so *is* a contentious man to kindle strife. ²²The words of a talebearer *are* as wounds, and they go down *into* the innermost parts of the belly. ²³Burning lips and a wicked heart *are like* a potsherd covered with silver dross. ²⁴He that hateth dissembleth with his lips, and layeth up deceit within him; ²⁵When he speaketh fair, believe him not: for *there are* seven abominations in his heart. ²⁶*Whose* hatred is covered by deceit, his wickedness shall be shewed before the *whole* congregation. ²⁷Whoso diggeth a pit shall fall therein: and he that rolleth a stone, it will return upon him. ²⁸A lying tongue hateth *those that are* afflicted by it; and a flattering mouth worketh ruin.

27 Boast not thyself of to morrow; for thou knowest not what a day may bring forth. ²Let another *man* praise thee, and not thine own mouth; a stranger, and not thine own lips. ³A stone *is* heavy, and the sand weighty; but a fool's wrath *is* heavier than them both. ⁴Wrath *is* cruel, and anger *is* outrageous; but who is able to stand before envy? 5Open rebuke *is* better than secret love. 6Faithful *are* the wounds of a friend; but the kisses of an enemy *are* deceitful. 7The full soul loatheth a honeycomb; but *to* the hungry soul every bitter *thing is* sweet. 8As a bird that wandereth from her nest, so *is* a man that wandereth from his place. 9Ointment and perfume rejoice the heart: so *doth* the sweetness of a man's friend by hearty counsel. 10Thine own friend, and thy father's friend, forsake not; neither go *into* thy brother's house in the day of thy calamity: *for* better *is* a neighbour *that is* near than a brother far off. [ch. 17:17]

11 My son, be wise, and make my heart glad, that I may answer him that reproacheth me. 12A prudent *man* foreseeth the evil, *and* hideth himself; *but* the simple pass on, *and* are punished. 13Take his garment that is surety *for* a stranger, and take a pledge of him for a strange *woman.* 14He that blesseth his friend with a loud voice, rising early in the morning, it shall be counted a curse to him. 15A continual dropping in a very rainy day and a contentious woman are alike. 16Whosoever hideth her, hideth the wind, and the ointment of his right hand, *which* bewrayeth *itself.* 17Iron sharpeneth iron; so a man sharpeneth the countenance of his friend. 18Whoso keepeth the fig tree shall eat the fruit thereof: so he that waiteth on his master shall be honoured. 19As *in* water face *answereth* to face, so the heart of

man to man. 20Hell and destruction are never full; so the eyes of man are never satisfied. 21As the fining pot for silver, and the furnace for gold; so *is* a man to his praise. 22Though thou shouldest bray a fool in a mortar among wheat with a pestle, *yet* will not his foolishness depart from him. [Jer. 5:3]

23 Be thou diligent to know the state of thy flocks, *and* look well to thy herds. 24For riches *are* not for ever: and doth the crown *endure* to every generation? 25The hay appeareth, and the tender grass sheweth itself, and herbs of the mountains are gathered. 26The lambs *are* for thy clothing, and the goats *are* the price of the field. 27And *thou shalt have* goats' milk enough for thy food, for the food of thy household, and *for* the maintenance for thy maidens.

28

The wicked flee when no man pursueth: but the righteous are bold as a lion. 2For the transgression of a land many *are* the princes thereof: but by a man of understanding *and* knowledge the state *thereof* shall be prolonged. 3A poor man that oppresseth the poor *is like* a sweeping rain which leaveth no food. 4They that forsake the law praise the wicked: but such as keep the law contend with them. 5Evil men understand not judgment: but they that seek the Lord understand all *things.* 6Better *is* the poor that walketh in his uprightness, than he *that is* perverse in *his* ways, though he *be* rich. 7Whoso keepeth the law *is* a wise son: but he that is a companion of riotous *men* shameth his father. 8He that by usury and unjust gain increaseth his substance, he shall gather it for him that will pity the poor. 9He that turneth away his ear from hearing the law, even his prayer *shall be* abomination. 10Whoso causeth the righteous to go astray in an evil way, he shall fall himself into his own pit: but the upright shall have good *things* in possession. 11The rich man *is* wise in his own conceit; but the poor that hath understanding searcheth him out. 12When righteous *men* do rejoice, *there is* great glory: but when the wicked rise, a man is hidden. 13He that covereth his sins shall not prosper: but whoso confesseth and forsaketh *them* shall have mercy. 14Happy *is* the man that feareth alway: but he that hardeneth his heart shall fall into mischief. 15*As* a roaring lion, and a ranging bear; *so is* a wicked ruler over the poor people. 16The prince that wanteth understanding *is* also a great oppressor: *but* he that hateth covetousness shall prolong *his* days. 17A man that doeth violence to the blood of *any* person shall flee to the pit; let no man stay him. 18Whoso walketh uprightly shall be saved: but *he that is* perverse in *his* ways shall fall at once. 19He that tilleth his land shall have plenty *of* bread: but he that followeth after vain *persons* shall have poverty enough. 20A faithful man shall abound with blessings: but he that maketh haste to be rich shall not be innocent. 21To have respect of persons *is* not good: for

for a piece of bread *that* man will transgress. 22He that hasteth to be rich *hath* an evil eye, and considereth not that poverty shall come *upon* him. 23He that rebuketh a man, afterwards shall find more favour than he that flattereth with the tongue. 24Whoso robbeth his father or his mother, and saith, *It is* no transgression; the same *is* the companion of a destroyer. 25He that is of a proud heart stirreth up strife: but he that putteth his trust in the LORD shall be made fat. 26He that trusteth in his own heart *is* a fool: but whoso walketh wisely, he shall be delivered. 27He that giveth unto the poor *shall* not lack: but he that hideth his eyes shall have many a curse. 28When the wicked rise, men hide themselves: but when they perish, the righteous increase. [ver. 12; Job 24:4]

29 He, that being often reproved hardeneth *his* neck, shall suddenly be destroyed, and that without remedy. 2When the righteous are in authority, the people rejoice: but when the wicked beareth rule, the people mourn. 3Whoso loveth wisdom rejoiceth his father: but he that keepeth company with harlots spendeth *his* substance. 4The king by judgment stablisheth the land: but he that receiveth gifts overthroweth it. 5A man that flattereth his neighbour spreadeth a net for his feet. 6In the transgression of an evil man *there is* a snare: but the righteous doth sing and rejoice. 7The righteous considereth the cause of the poor: *but* the wicked regardeth not to know *it*. 8Scornful men bring a city into a snare: but wise *men* turn away wrath. ⁹If a wise man contendeth with a foolish man, whether he rage or laugh, *there is* no rest. ¹⁰The bloodthirsty hate the upright: but the just seek his soul. ¹¹A fool uttereth all his mind: but a wise *man* keepeth it in *till* afterwards. ¹²If a ruler hearken to lies, all his servants *are* wicked. ¹³The poor and the deceitful man meet together: the LORD lighteneth both their eyes. ¹⁴The king that faithfully judgeth the poor, his throne shall be established for ever. ¹⁵The rod and reproof give wisdom: but a child left *to himself* bringeth his mother to shame. ¹⁶When the wicked are multiplied, transgression increaseth: but the righteous shall see their fall. ¹⁷Correct thy son, and he shall give thee rest; yea, he shall give delight unto thy soul. ¹⁸Where *there is* no vision, the people perish: but he that keepeth the law, happy *is* he. ¹⁹A servant will not be corrected by words: for though he understand he will not answer. ²⁰Seest thou a man that is hasty in his words? *there is* more hope of a fool than of him. ²¹He that delicately bringeth up his servant from a child shall have him become *his* son at the length. ²²An angry man stirreth up strife, and a furious man aboundeth in transgression. ²³A man's pride shall bring him low: but honour shall uphold the humble in spirit. ²⁴Whoso is partner with a thief hateth his own soul: he heareth cursing, and bewrayeth *it* not. ²⁵The fear of man bringeth a snare: but whoso putteth his trust

in the LORD shall be safe. ²⁶Many seek the ruler's favour; but *every* man's judgment *cometh* from the LORD. ²⁷An unjust man is an abomination to the just: and *he that is* upright in the way *is* abomination to the wicked.

Observations of Agur

30 The words of Agur the son of Jakeh, *even* the prophecy: the man spake unto Ithiel, even unto Ithiel and Ucal.

2 Surely I *am* more brutish than *any* man, and have not the understanding of a man. ³I neither learned wisdom, nor have the knowledge of the holy. ⁴Who hath ascended up *into* heaven, or descended? who hath gathered the wind in his fists? who hath bound the waters in a garment? who hath established all the ends of the earth? what *is* his name, and what *is* his son's name, if thou canst tell? [John 3:13; Job 38:4; Ps. 104:3; Is. 40:12]

5 Every word of God *is* pure: he *is* a shield unto them that put their trust in him. ⁶Add thou not unto his words, lest he reprove thee, and thou be found a liar. [Deut. 4:2; Rev. 22:18]

7 Two *things* have I required of thee; deny me *them* not before I die: ⁸Remove far from me vanity and lies: give me neither poverty nor riches; feed me with food convenient for me: ⁹Lest I be full, and deny *thee*, and say, Who *is* the LORD? or lest I be poor, and steal, and take the name of my God *in vain.* [Deut. 8:12]

10 Accuse not a servant unto his master, lest he curse thee, and

thou be found guilty. 11There is a generation that curseth their father, and doth not bless their mother. 12There is a generation that are pure in their own eyes, and yet is not washed from their filthiness. 13There is a generation, O how lofty are their eyes! and their eyelids are lifted up. 14There is a generation, whose teeth are as swords, and their jaw teeth as knives, to devour the poor from off the earth, and the needy from among men. [Job 29:17; Ps. 52:2; Ps. 14:4; Amos 8:4]

15 The horseleach hath two daughters, crying, Give, give. There are three things that are never satisfied, yea, four things say not, It is enough: 16The grave; and the barren womb; the earth that is not filled with water; and the fire that saith not, It is enough. [ch. 27:20; Hab. 2:5]

17 The eye that mocketh at his father, and despiseth to obey his mother, the ravens of the valley shall pick it out, and the young eagles shall eat it. [Gen. 9:22; Lev. 20:9; ch. 20:20; 23:22]

18 There be three things which are too wonderful for me, yea, four which I know not: 19The way of an eagle in the air; the way of a serpent upon a rock; the way of a ship in the midst of the sea; and the way of a man with a maid. 20Such is the way of an adulterous woman; she eateth, and wipeth her mouth, and saith, I have done no wickedness.

21 For three things the earth is disquieted, and for four which it cannot bear: 22For a servant when he reigneth; and a fool when he is filled with meat; 23For an odious woman when she is married; and a handmaid that is heir to her mistress.

24 There be four things which are little upon the earth, but they are exceeding wise: 25The ants are a people not strong, yet they prepare their meat in the summer; 26The conies are but a feeble folk, yet make they their houses in the rocks; 27The locusts have no king, yet go they forth all of them by bands; 28The spider taketh hold with her hands, and is in kings' palaces.

29 There are three things which go well, yea, four are comely in going: 30A lion which is strongest among beasts, and turneth not away for any; 31A greyhound; a he goat also; and a king, against whom there is no rising up.

32 If thou hast done foolishly in lifting up thyself, or if thou hast thought evil, lay thine hand upon thy mouth. 33Surely the churning of milk bringeth forth butter, and the wringing of the nose bringeth forth blood: so the forcing of wrath bringeth forth strife.

Words of king Lemuel

31 The words of king Lemuel, the prophecy that his mother taught him.

2 What, my son? and what, the son of my womb? and what, the son of my vows? 3Give not thy strength unto women, nor thy ways to that which destroyeth kings. 4It is not for kings, O Lemuel, it is not for kings to drink wine; nor for princes strong drink: 5Lest

they drink, and forget the law, and pervert the judgment of any of the afflicted. 6Give strong drink unto him that is ready to perish, and wine unto those that be of heavy hearts. 7Let him drink, and forget his poverty, and remember his misery no more. 8Open thy mouth for the dumb in the cause of all such as are appointed to destruction. 9Open thy mouth, judge righteously, and plead the cause of the poor and needy. [Lev. 19:15; Deut. 1:16; Job 29:12; Is. 1:17; Jer. 22:16]

The virtuous woman

10 Who can find a virtuous woman? for her price *is* far above rubies. 11The heart of her husband doth *safely* trust in her, so that he shall have no need of spoil. 12She will do him good and not evil all the days of her life. 13She seeketh wool, and flax, and worketh willingly with her hands. 14She is like the merchant's ships; she bringeth her food from afar. 15She riseth also while *it is* yet night, and giveth meat to her household, and a portion to her maidens. 16She considereth a field, and buyeth it: with the fruit of her hands she planteth a vineyard. 17She girdeth her loins with strength, and strengtheneth her arms. 18She perceiveth that her merchandise *is* good: her candle goeth not out by night. 19She layeth her hands to the spindle, and her hands hold the distaff. 20She stretcheth out her hand to the poor; yea, she reacheth forth her hands to the needy. 21She is not afraid of the snow for her household: for all her household *are* clothed with scarlet. 22She maketh herself coverings of tapestry; her clothing *is* silk and purple. 23Her husband is known in the gates, when he sitteth among the elders of the land. 24She maketh fine linen, and selleth *it;* and delivereth girdles unto the merchant. 25Strength and honour *are* her clothing; and she shall rejoice in time to come. 26She openeth her mouth with wisdom; and in her tongue *is* the law of kindness. 27She looketh well to the ways of her household, and eateth not the bread of idleness. 28Her children arise up, and call her blessed; her husband *also,* and he praiseth her. 29Many daughters have done virtuously, but thou excellest them all. 30Favour *is* deceitful, and beauty *is* vain: *but* a woman that feareth the LORD, she shall be praised. 31Give her of the fruit of her hands; and let her own works praise her in the gates.

Key Bible Promises

| God's Promise of:

His Love: . . . . Isaiah 54:10; Jeremiah 31:3–4a;
Matthew 10:30–31; John 3:16; 15:9, 13;
1 John 4:9

His Forgiveness: . . . . . 2 Chronicles 7:14; Psalm 103:8–12;
Jeremiah 31:34; Luke 15:3–7; Acts
10:43; Ephesians 1:7; 1 John 1:9

His Salvation: . . . . Psalm 37:39–40; Isaiah 25:9; Matthew
1:21; Acts 16:31; Ephesians 2:8;
Hebrews 7:25

His Holy Spirit: . . . . . . Joel 2:29; Luke 11:13; John 14:16–17;
Acts 2:38; Romans 8:11

His Peace: . . . . Psalm 29:11; Isaiah 26:3; John 14:27;
Romans 5:1–2; Ephesians 2:14;
2 Thessalonians 3:16

His Joy: . . . . Psalm 16:11; 90:14; John 15:10–11;
16:22; 1 Peter 1:8

His Freedom: . . . . Psalm 119:32; 146:7; John 8:34–36;
Romans 6:6, 14, 20–22; 2 Corinthians
3:17

His Encouragement: . . . Jeremiah 29:11; 2 Thessalonians
2:16–17; 1 Peter 2:9

His Blessing: . . . . Psalm 128:5–6; Ezekiel 34:26; John
1:16; 10:10; Romans 8:28; Ephesians 1:3

His Presence: . . . . Joshua 1:5; Psalm 46:1, 7; Matthew 18:20;
28:20; John 6:37; Romans 8:38–39

Everlasting Life: . . . . . Job 19:25–27; John 3:16; 6:40; 10:28;
1 Corinthians 15:51–52; 1 Thessalonians
4:17

Growth: . . . . Psalm 92:12, 14; 2 Corinthians 3:18;
Ephesians 4:14–15; Philippians 1:6

Excellence: . . . . Joshua 1:7; Matthew 20:26–28; John
14:12; 15:15–16

Strength: . . . . Psalm 73:25–26; Isaiah 40:29, 31;
Ephesians 3:20; 2 Thessalonians 3:3;
1 Peter 5:10

Answered Prayer: . . . . Psalm 65:2, 5; Matthew 7:7–11; 21:22;
1 Peter 3:12; 1 John 5:14–15

Christ's Return: . . . . . John 14:2–3; Acts 1:11; 1 Thessalonians
4:16–17; Revelation 1:7

| God's Promise When You:

Feel Guilty: . . . . 2 Samuel 14:14; Psalm 130:3–4; Romans 8:1–2; 1 Corinthians 6:11; Ephesians 3:12; Hebrews 10:22–23

Feel Dejected: . . . . . . Psalm 130:7; Matthew 11:28–30; Romans 8:26–27; Hebrews 4:16; James 4:8, 10

Feel Despair: . . . . Psalm 119:116; Isaiah 57:15; Jeremiah 32:17; Hebrews 10:35

Are Disappointed: . . . . . Psalm 22:4–5; Matthew 19:25–26; Ephesians 3:20

Are Depressed: . . . . Deuteronomy 31:8; Psalm 34:18; Isaiah 49:13–15; Romans 5:5

Are Persecuted: . . . . . . Genesis 50:20; Psalm 37:1–2; Matthew 5:10–12; 2 Corinthians 4:8–12; 2 Timothy 1:11–12; 1 Peter 3:13–14

Are Anxious: . . . . Psalm 55:22; Isaiah 41:13; Matthew 6:25; 11:28–29; Philippians 4:6–7; 1 Peter 5:7

Are Filled with Longing: Psalm 37:4; 84:11; 103:5; Luke 12:29–31

Are Sick: . . . . Psalm 23:4; 73:26; Isaiah 57:18; Matthew 8:16–17; John 16:33; Romans 8:37–39; James 5:14–15

Are Impatient: . . . . Psalm 27:13–14; 37:7, 9; Romans 2:7; 1 Timothy 1:16; Hebrews 6:12; 2 Peter 3:9

Are Confused: . . . . Psalm 32:8; Isaiah 42:16; John 8:12; 14:27; 1 Corinthians 2:15–16; James 1:5

Are Tempted: . . . . Job 23:10–11; 1 Corinthians 10:13; Hebrews 2:18; 4:15–16; James 1:2–4, 13–14; 1 Peter 5:8–10

Are Weak: . . . . Psalm 72:13; Isaiah 41:10; Romans 8:26; 1 Corinthians 1:7–9; 2 Corinthians 4:7–9; 12:9–10

Are Afraid: . . . . Psalm 4:8; 23:4; Isaiah 35:4; Romans 8:37–39; 2 Corinthians 1:10; 2 Timothy 1:7; Hebrews 13:6

Are in Need: . . . . Isaiah 58:11; John 6:35; 2 Corinthians 9:10–11; Ephesians 3:20–21; Philippians 4:19

Obey: . . . . Matthew 16:27; John 8:31–32; 14:21,
                                    23; James 1:25
Grieve: . . . . Psalm 119:50, 76–77; Jeremiah 31:13;
                                    Matthew 5:4; John 16:20–22;
                                    1 Thessalonians 4:13–14; Revelation
                                    21:3–4
Suffer: . . . . Psalm 34:19; Nahum 1:7; John 16:33;
                                    Romans 8:16–17; 1 Peter 2:20–21;
                                    4:12–13
Fail: . . . . Joshua 1:9; Romans 3:23–24; 5:8
Doubt: . . . . Psalm 34:22; 11:25–26; Romans 4:5;
                                    1 John 4:15–16

I God's Promises When:

You Need Comfort: . . . . Isaiah 12; 40:1–11; Jeremiah
                                        31:10–13; 2 Corinthians
                                        1:3–7; 7:6–13
You Need Assurance of Salvation: Psalm 91:14–16; Micah
                                        7:18–20; John 3:14–21;
                                        11:25–26; Acts 16:31–34;
                                        1 John 5:9–13
*You Wonder about Your Spiritual
Gifts:* . . . . Romans 12:3–8;
                                        1 Corinthians 1:4–9;
                                        12:1–14:25; 1 Peter
                                        4:10–11
*You Desire to Learn How to
Pray:* . . . . 2 Chronicles 20:5–12;
                                        20:5–12; Matthew 6:5–15;
                                        Mark 11:22–25; Luke
                                        18:9–14; Philippians 4:6–7
You Have Been Cheated: . . . . . Matthew 18:15–17;
                                        1 Corinthians 6:1–8
*You Need to Control Your
Tongue:* . . . . Psalm 39:1; Proverbs
                                        10:18–20; Matthew 15:11;
                                        James 3:1–12
You Have Been Quarreling: . . . . Genesis 13:5–11; Psalm 133;
                                        Ephesians 4:1–6; 4:25–27;
                                        2 Timothy 2:14–26; James
                                        4:1–12

You Desire Revenge: . . . . Deuteronomy 32:35; Psalm
94:1; Proverbs 25:21–22;
Matthew 5:38–42; Romans
12:17–21; 1 Thessalonians
5:15; 1 Peter 3:8–19

You Struggle with Laziness: . . . . Proverbs 6:6–11; 10:4–5;
Ephesians 5:15–16;
1 Thessalonians 4:11–12;
2 Thessalonians 3:6–15

You Struggle with Lust: . . . . Deuteronomy 22:22–24;
Matthew 5:27–30; Romans
7:7–25; 13:8–14;
1 Corinthians 6:15–20;
Galatians 5:16–17; James
1:13–18

You Struggle with Addiction: . . . Psalm 18:28–36; Proverbs
20:1, 23:29–35; Romans
6:1–23; 12:1–2; 1 Corinthians
6:12–20; Philippians 3:17–4:1

You Struggle with Apathy: . . . . . Matthew 25:1–13; Luke
12:35–48; 1 Thessalonians
5:1–11; Revelation 3:1–6,
15–22

You Are Prone to Judge Others: . Matthew 7:1–5; 1 Corinthians
4:1–5; James 2:1–13; 4:11–12

You Are in a Position of
Responsibility: . . . . Proverbs 3:21–27;
1 Corinthians 16:13–14;
Galatians 6:9–10

You Are Establishing a New
Home: . . . . Joshua 24:15; Matthew
7:24–27; Ephesians 5:22–6:4;
Colossians 3:18–21; 1 Peter
3:1–7

You Are Challenged by the
Enemy: . . . . Joshua 1:6–9; Psalm 56:1–4;
Romans 8:38–39;
2 Corinthians 4:7–18;
Ephesians 6:10–18;
2 Timothy 4:6–8

You Are Tempted to Be Bitter: . . Proverbs 16:32; 1 Corinthians
13; Ephesians 4:29–5:2;
Hebrews 12:14–15

You Are Tempted to Neglect Public
Worship: .... Exodus 20:8–11; Psalm
                            95:1–7; Acts 2:42–47;
                            Hebrews 10:24–25

You Are Angry: .... Genesis 4:1–12; Psalm 4:4;
                            Matthew 5:21–22; 18:21–35;
                            Ephesians 4:25–5:2; James
                            1:19–21

You Are Jealous: .... Numbers 12:1–15; Galatians
                            5:13–15, 19–21; James
                            3:13–18

You Are Proud: .... Proverbs 8:12–13; Mark
                            10:35–45; Romans 12:3;
                            Philippians 2:1–11

You Are Greedy: .... Psalm 10; Ecclesiastes 2:1–11;
                            Luke 12:13–21; 2 Corinthians
                            9:7–14; Ephesians 5:3–7;
                            1 John 3:16–18

Your Faith Needs Strengthening: .. Genesis 15:1–6; Proverbs
                            3:5–8; Romans 5:1–11;
                            1 Corinthians 9:24–27;
                            Hebrews 10:19–25, 35–39;
                            11:1, 6

Things Are Going Well: .... Job 31:24–28; Proverbs 15:27;
                            1 Timothy 6:18–19; Hebrews
                            13:5

Seeking God's Direction: ...... 1 Kings 3:6–14; Romans
                            12:1–3; Ephesians 5:15–17;
                            Colossians 1:9–12; James
                            1:5–6

The Future Seems Hopeless: .... Isaiah 54:1–7; Lamentations
                            3:19–24; 1 Corinthians
                            15:20–28; 1 Peter 1:3–9; 5:10;
                            Revelation 11:15–19

The World Seems Enticing: .... Genesis 3:1–7; Ecclesiastes
                            2:1–11; 2 Corinthians
                            6:14–7:1; James 1:26–27;
                            4:4–10; 1 John 2:15–17

Others Disagree with You: ..... Matthew 7:1–5; Romans
                            12:16–21; 14:1–15:7

Others Have Sinned Against You: .. Genesis 50:15–20; Matthew
                            6:14–15; 18:21–35; Colossians
                            3:12–14; James 2:13

Harmony of the Gospels

	Matthew	Mark	Luke	John
The Deity of Jesus				1:1–5
Announcement of the Birth of John the Baptist			1:5–25	
The Betrothal of the Virgin Mary	1:18		1:27	
The Announcement of the Birth of Jesus			1:26–38	
Mary Visits Elizabeth			1:39–56	
Joseph's Dream	1:20–25			
The Birth of John the Baptist			1:57–80	
The Birth of Jesus			2:1–7	
The Visit by the Shepherds			2:8–20	
The Circumcision and Naming of Jesus			2:21	
The Presentation in the Temple			2:22–29	
The Genealogy of Jesus	1:1–17		3:23–38	
The Visit of the Wise Men	2:1–12			
The Flight to Egypt	2:13–15			
The Massacre of the Infants	2:16–18			
The Return from Egypt	2:19–23		2:39	
The Boy Jesus in the Temple			2:46	
With the Teachers in the Temple			2:46–50	
Youth of Jesus			2:51	
The Preaching of John the Baptist	3:1–4	1:1–8	3:1–18	1:6–15
Baptism by John	3:6	1:5	3:21	
The First Testimony of the Baptist to Christ	3:11–12	1:7–8		1:29–34
The Baptism of Jesus	3:13–17	1:9–11	3:21–22	
The Temptation of Jesus	4:1–11	1:12–13	4:1–13	
John the Baptist's Testimony to Himself				1:19–28
The Call of the First Disciples	4:18–22	1:16–20	5:1–11	1:37–51
First Miracle at Cana				2:1–11

	Matthew	Mark	Luke	John
Visit to Capernaum				2:12
Cleansing of the Temple	21:12–13	11:15–17	19:45–46	2:13–23
Nicodemus				3:1–21
The Final Witness of the Baptist				3:22–36
The Samaritan Woman				4:1–42
The Return to Galilee				4:43–45
The Second Sign at Cana				4:46–54
The Cure on a Sabbath				5:1–47
Imprisonment of John the Baptist	4:12; 14:3	1:14–15		3:24
The Beginning of the Galilean Ministry	4:12–17	1:14–15	4:14–15	
The Rejection at Nazareth	13:54–58	6:1–4	4:16–27	
Jesus Preaches at Capernaum	4:13–17			
The Cure of a Man with an Unclean Spirit		1:23–27	4:33–36	
The Cure of Peter's Mother-in-law	8:14–15	1:29–31	4:38–39	
Other Healings	8:16–17	1:32–34	4:40–41	
Circuit through Galilee		1:38–39	4:42–44	
The Cleansing of a Leper	8:1–4	1:40–45	5:12–18	
Retirement for Solitary Prayer		1:45	5:16	
The Healing of a Paralytic	9:1–8	2:1–12	5:18–25	
Call of Matthew	9:9–17	2:13–22	5:27–39	
Ministering to a Great Multitude	4:23–25		6:17–19	
Picking Grain on the Sabbath	12:1–8	2:23–28	6:1–5	
The Man with the Withered Hand	12:9–14	3:1–6	6:6–11	
Retirement for Solitary Prayer			6:12	
The Mission of the Twelve	10:1–4	3:13–19; 6:7–13	6:13–16; 9:1–6	
The Sermon on the Mount	5:1—7:29		6:20–49	
The Healing of the Centurion's Servant	8:5–13		7:1–10	

	Matthew	Mark	Luke	John
The Raising of the Widow's Son			7:11–17	
The Messengers from John the Baptist	11:2–19		7:18–35	
The Pardon of the Sinful Woman			7:36–50	
The Beatitudes	5:2–12		6:20–26	
Galilean Women Follow Jesus			8:1–3	
Jesus and Beelzebul	12:22–28	3:23–30	11:14–23	
Blasphemy against the Holy Spirit	12:31–32			
The Return of the Unclean Spirit	12:43–45	11:24–26		
The True Family of Jesus	12:46–50	3:31–35	8:19–21	
The Parable of the Sower	13:1–9	4:1–9; 4:14–20	8:6–8; 8:11–15	
The Parable of the Tares among the Wheat	13:24–30			
The Parable of the Mustard Seed	13:31–32	4:30–32	13:18–19	
The Parable of the Leaven	13:33		13:20–21	
The Parable of the Lamp	5:15	4:21	8:16; 11:33	
The Parable of the Buried Treasure	13:44			
The Parable of the Fine Pearl	13:45–46			
The Parable of the Thrown Net	13:47–48			
The Calming of the Storm at Sea	8:24–27	4:37–41	8:23–25	
The Healing of the Gadarene Demoniacs	8:28–34	5:1–20	8:26–39	
The Parable of the Bridegroom	9:15			
The Parable of the New Cloth	9:16	2:21	5:36	
The Parable of the New Wine in Old Bottles	9:17	2:22	5:37–38	
Miracles: Jairus' Daughter and the Woman with the Flow of Blood	9:18–26	5:22–43	8:41–56	
The Healing of Two Blind Men	9:27–31			
The Healing of a Mute Person	9:32–34			

	Matthew	Mark	Luke	John
The Mission of the Twelve	10:1–4	6:7–12	9:1–6	
Herod's Opinion of Jesus	14:1–12	6:14–29	9:7–9	
The Return of the Twelve and the Feeding of the Five Thousand	14:13–21	6:31–44	9:10–17	6:1–14
The Walking on the Water	14:22–33	6:47–52		6:16–21
The Bread of Life Discourse				6:22–65
Retirement for Solitary Prayer	14:23	6:46		
The Tradition of the Elders	15:1–20	7:1–23		
The Canaanite Woman's Faith	15:24–29	7:24–30		
The Healing of Many People	15:29–31			
The Feeding of the Four Thousand	15:32–39	8:1–9		
The Demand for a Sign: Weather	16:1–4	8:11–13	12:54–56	
The Leaven of the Pharisees and Sadducees	16:5–12	8:14–21		
Peter's Confession of Christ	16:13–20	8:27–30	9:18–20	
The First Prediction of the Passion	16:21–23	8:31–38	9:22–27	
The Transfiguration of Jesus	17:1–8	9:2–8	9:28–36	
The Healing of a Boy with a Demon	17:14–21	9:14–25	9:37–43	
The Second Prediction of the Passion	17:22–23	9:30–32	9:43–45	
Payment of the Temple Tax	17:24–27			
The Greatest in the Kingdom	18:1–5	9:33–37	9:46–48	
The Parable of the Lost Sheep	18:10–14		15:1–7	
A Person Who Sins	18:15–20		17:3–4	
A Lesson on Self-denial	18:18			
The Parable of the Unforgiving Servant	18:23–35			
The Departure for Jerusalem			9:51–52	
The Jealousy of the Samaritans			9:53	
The Anger of James and John			9:54–56	
The Festival of Tabernacles				7:1–10

	Matthew	Mark	Luke	John
The Cleansing of the Temple	21:12–17	11:15–18		
The Lesson of the Fig Tree	21:20–22	11:20–25		
The Authority of Jesus Questioned	21:23–27	11:27–33	20:1–8	
The Parable of the Two Sons	21:28–32			
The Parable of the Tenants	21:33–46	12:1–12	20:9–19	
The Wedding Banquet	22:1–14		14:15–24	
Paying Taxes to the Emperor	22:15–22	12:13–17	20:20–26	
The Question about the Resurrection	22:23–33	12:18–27	20:27–39	
The Greatest Commandment	22:34–40	12:28–34	11:25–28	
The Question about David's Son	22:41–46	12:35–37	20:41–44	
Denunciation of the Scribes and Pharisees	23:1–33	12:38–40	11:37–54	
The Poor Widow's Contribution		12:41–44	21:1–4	
The Coming of Jesus' Hour				12:20–23
The Destruction of the Temple Foretold	24:1–2	13:1–3		
The Parable of the Ten Virgins	25:1–13		19:11–27	
The Judgement of the Nations	25:31–46			
The Conspiracy Against Jesus	26:3–5	14:1–2	22:1–2	
The Betrayal by Judas	26:14–16	14:10–11	22:3–6	18:2–5
Preparation of the Passover	26:17–19	14:12–16	22:7–13	
The Washing of the Disciples' Feet				13:1–17
The Lord's Supper	26:26	14:22	22:14	
The Betrayal Foretold	26:21	14:18	22:21	13:21
The Giving of the Piece of Bread				13:26–27
The Departure of Judas				13:30
Peter's Denial Predicted	26:31–35	14:27–31	22:21–23	13:36
Blessing the Cup	26:27–28	14:23–24	22:17	
Last Supper Discourses				14:1–14
The Prayer of Jesus				17:1–26
The Hymn	26:30	14:26		

	Matthew	Mark	Luke	John
The Agony in the Garden	26:36; 26:44	14:32–42	22:39–46	18:1
Jesus is Comforted by the Angel			22:43–44	
The Sleep of the Apostles	26:40–45	14:37–41	22:45–46	
The Betrayal and Arrest of Jesus	26:47–50	14:43–45	22:47	18:1–14
Peter Smites Malchus	26:51	14:47	22:50	18:10
Jesus Heals the Ear of Malchus			22:51	
Jesus Forsaken by His Disciples	26:56	14:50		
Jesus Led to Annas				18:12–13
Jesus before the Sanhedrin	26:57	14:53	22:66	
Peter Follows Jesus	26:58	14:54	22:55	18:15
The High Priest's Adjuration	26:63	14:61	22:66	
Jesus Condemned	26:66–67	14:64–65	22:70–71	
Peter's Denial of Jesus	26:69–75	14:66–72	22:54–62	18:17–27
Jesus before Pilate	27:1	15:1	23:1	18:28
The Death of Judas	27:3			
Pilate Comes out to the People				18:29
Pilate Speaks to Jesus Privately				18:33
Mockery by the Soldiers	27:27	15:15	22:63–65	19:1
Jesus Crowned with Thorns	27:29	15:17		19:2
Jesus Exhibited by Pilate				19:5
Jesus Questioned by Pilate	27:11	15:2	23:2	
Jesus Sent by Pilate to Herod			23:6–11	
The Sentence of Death	27:15	15:6	23:17	19:12–16
Pilate Receives a Message from his Wife	27:19			
Pilate Washes His Hands	27:24			
Pilate Releases Barnabas	27:26	15:15	23:25	
Pilate Delivers Jesus to Be Crucified	27:26	15:15	23:25	19:16
The Way of the Cross	27:32	15:21	23:26	
The Crucifixion	27:33–44	15:22–32	23:33–43	19:17–30

	Matthew	Mark	Luke	John
The Death of Jesus	27:45–56	5:33–41	23:44–49	
The Burial of Jesus	27:57–61	15:42–47	23:50–56	19:38–42
The Guard at the Tomb	27:62–66			
The Resurrection of Jesus	28:1–10	16:1–8	24:1–12	20:1–10
The Report of the Guards	28:11–15			
The Appearance to Mary Magdalene		16:9		20:14
The Appearance to the Women Returning Home	28:9			
The Appearance to Two Disciples Going to Emmaus		16:12	24:13–32	
The Appearance to Peter			24:34	
The Appearance to the Disciples in Jerusalem			24:36	20:19
The Appearance to the Eleven Apostles		16:14		
The Appearance to Thomas				20:27
The Appearance to the Seven Disciples				21:1–22
Jesus and Peter				21:15–19
The Commissioning of the Disciples		28:16–20	16:14	
The Ascension of Jesus		16:19–20	24:50–43	

Miracles of the
New Testament

| Miracles Associated with the Birth of Jesus

Conception by Elisabeth, Luke 1:18, 24, 25.
The incarnation of Jesus, Matt. 1:18–25; Luke 1:26–80.
The appearance of the star of Bethlehem, Matt. 2:1–9.
The deliverance of Jesus, Matt. 2:13–23.

| Miracles of Jesus

Water made wine, John 2:1–11.
Heals the nobleman's son, John 4:46–54.
Draught of fishes, Luke 5:1–11.
Heals the demoniac, Mark 1:23–26; Luke 4:33–36.
Heals Peter's mother-in-law, Matt. 8:14–17; Mark 1:29–31;
    Luke 4:38, 39.
Cleanses the leper, Matt. 8:1–4; Mark 1:40–45; Luke 5:12–15.
Heals the paralytic, Matt. 9:1–8; Mark 2:1–12; Luke 5:17–26.
Healing of the invalid, John 5:1–15.
Restoring the withered hand, Matt. 12:9–13; Mark 3:1–5;
    Luke 6:6–11.
Restores the centurion's servant, Matt. 8:5–13; Luke 7:1–10.
Raises the widow's son to life, Luke 7:11–16.
Heals a demoniac, Matt. 12:22–37; Mark 3:11; Luke 11:14, 15.
Stills the storm, Matt. 8:23–27; 14:32; Mark 4:35–41;
    Luke 8:22–25.
Casts devils out of two Gadarenes, Matt. 8:28–34; Mark 5:1–20;
    Luke 8:26–39.
Raises from the dead the daughter of Jairus, Matt. 9:18, 19, 23–26;
    Mark 5:22–24, 35–43; Luke 8:41, 42, 49–56.
Cures the woman with the issue of blood, Matt. 9:20–22;
    Mark 5:25–34; Luke 8:43–48.
Restores two blind men to sight, Matt. 9:27–31.
Heals a demoniac, Matt. 9:32, 33.
Feeds five thousand people, Matt. 14:15–21; Mark 6:35–44;
    Luke 9:12–17; John 6:5–14.
Walks on the sea, Matt. 14:22–33; Mark 6:45–52; John 6:16–21.
Heals the daughter of the Syrophenician woman, Matt. 15:21–28;
    Mark 7:24–30.
Feeds four thousand people, Matt. 15:32–39; Mark 8:1–9.
Restores one deaf and mute, Mark 7:31–37.

Restores a blind man, Mark 8:22–26.
Restores seizuring child, Matt. 17:14–21; Mark 9:14–29;
   Luke 9:37–43.
Tribute money obtained from a fish's mouth, Matt. 17:24–27.
Restores ten lepers, Luke 17:11–19.
Opens the eyes of a one born blind, John 9.
Raises Lazarus from the dead, John 11:1–46.
Heals the woman with the spirit of infirmity, Luke 13:10–17.
Cures one with dropsy, Luke 14:1–6.
Restores two blind men near Jericho, Matt. 20:29–34;
   Mark 10:46–52; Luke 18:35–43.
Curses a fig tree, Matt. 21:17–22; Mark 11:12–14, 20–24.
Heals the ear of Malchus, Luke 22:49–51.
Second draught of fishes, John 21:6.

| Miracles of the Disciples of Jesus

By the seventy, Luke 10:17–20.
By other disciples, Mark 9:39; John 14:12
By the apostles, Acts 3:6, 12, 13, 16; 4:10, 30; 9:34, 35; 16:18.
Peter cures the sick, Acts 5:15, 16;
   Aeneas, Acts 9:34;
   raises Dorcas, Acts 9:40;
   causes the death of Ananias and Sapphira, Acts 5:5, 10.
Peter and John cure a lame man, Acts 3:2–11.
Peter and other apostles delivered from prison, Acts 5:19–23;
   12:6–11; 16:26.
Philip carried away by the Spirit, Acts 8:39.
Paul strikes Elymas with blindness, Acts 13:11;
   heals a cripple, Acts 14:10;
   casts out evil spirits, and cures sick, Acts 16:18; 19:11, 12; 28:8, 9;
   raises Eutychus to life, Acts 20:9–12;
   shakes a viper off his hand, Acts 28:5.
Paul cured of blindness, Acts 9:3–6, 17, 18.

Parables of the New Testament

| Parables of Jesus

The wise and foolish builders, Matt. 7:24–27; Luke 6:47–49.
Two debtors, Luke 7:41–47.
The rich fool, Luke 12:16–21.
The servants waiting for their Lord, Luke 12:35–40.
Barren fig tree, Luke 13:6–9.
The sower, Matt. 13:3–9, 18–23; Mark 4:1–9, 14–20;
   Luke 8:5–8, 11–15.
The tares, Matt. 13:24–30, 36–43.
Seed growing secretly, Mark 4:26–29.
Mustard seed, Matt. 13:31, 32; Mark 4:30–32; Luke 13:18, 19.
Leaven, Matt. 13:33; Luke 13:20, 21.
Hidden treasure, Matt. 13:44.
Pearl of great price, Matt. 13:45, 46.
Drawn net, Matt. 13:47–50.
Unmerciful servant, Matt. 18:23–35.
Good Samaritan, Luke 10:30–37.
Friend at midnight, Luke 11:5–8.
Good shepherd, John 10:1–16.
Great supper, Luke 14:15–24.
Lost sheep, Matt. 18:12–14; Luke 15:3–7.
Lost piece of money, Luke 15:8–10.
The prodigal and his brother, Luke 15:11–32.
The unjust steward, Luke 16:1–9.
Rich man and Lazarus, Luke 16:19–31.
Pleading widow, Luke 18:1–8.
Pharisee and tax collector, Luke 18:9–14.
Labourers in the vineyard, Matt. 20:1–16.
The pounds, Luke 19:11–27.
The two sons, Matt. 21:28–32.
Wicked tenant farmers, Matt. 21:33–44; Mark 12:1–12;
   Luke 20:9–18.
Marriage of the king's son, Matt. 22:1–14.
Fig tree leafing, Matt. 24:32, 33; Mark 13:28, 29.
Man taking a far journey, Mark 13:34–37.
Ten virgins, Matt. 25:1–13.
Talents, Matt. 25:14–30.
The vine, John 15:1–17.

| Parables in the Acts and Epistles

The sheet let down from heaven in Peter's vision, Acts 10:10–16.
The two covenants, Gal. 4:22–31.
The mercenary soldier, 2 Tim. 2:3, 4.
The athlete, 2 Tim. 2:5.
Husbandman, 2 Tim. 2:6.
Furnished house, 2 Tim. 2:20, 21.
Looking-glass, Jas. 1:23–25.

How to Become a Christian

The central theme of the Bible is God's love for you and for all people. This love was revealed when Jesus Christ, the Son of God, came into the world as a human being, lived a sinless life, died on the cross, and rose from the dead. Because Christ died, your sins can be forgiven, and because He conquered death you can have eternal life. You can know for sure what will become of you after you die.

You have probably heard the story of God's love referred to as the "Gospel." The word Gospel simply means "Good News." The Gospel is the Good News that, because of what Christ has done, we can be forgiven and can live forever.

But this gift of forgiveness and eternal life cannot be yours unless you willingly accept it. God requires an individual response from you. The following verses from the Bible show God's part and yours in this process:

GOD'S LOVE IS REVEALED IN THE BIBLE

"For God so loved the world, that he gave his only begotten Son, that whosoever believeth in him should not perish, but have everlasting life."—John 3:16 (KJV)

God loves you. He wants to bless your life and make it full and complete. And He wants to give you a life which will last forever, even after you experience physical death.

WE ARE SINFUL

"For all have sinned, and come short of the glory of God."— Romans 3:23 (KJV)

You may have heard someone say, "I'm only human—nobody's perfect." This Bible verse says the same thing: We are all sinners. We all do things that we know are wrong. And that's why we feel estranged from God—because God is holy and good, and we are not.

SIN HAS A PENALTY

"For the wages of sin is death."—Romans 6:23 (KJV)

Just as criminals must pay the penalty for their crimes, sinners must pay the penalty for their sins. If you continue to sin, you will pay the penalty of spiritual death: You will not only die physically; you will also be separated from our holy God for all eternity. The Bible teaches that those who choose to remain separated from God will spend eternity in a place called hell.

CHRIST HAS PAID OUR PENALTY!

"But God commendeth his love toward us, in that, while we were yet sinners, Christ died for us."—Romans 5:8 (KJV)

The Bible teaches that Jesus Christ, the sinless Son of God, has paid the penalty for all your sins. You may think you have to lead a good life and do good deeds before God will love you. But the Bible says that Christ loved you enough to die for you, even when you were rebelling against Him.

SALVATION IS A FREE GIFT

"For by grace are ye saved through faith; and that not of yourselves: it is the gift of God: not of works, lest any man should boast."—Ephesians 2:8-9 (KJV)

The word grace means "undeserved favor." It means God is offering you something you could never provide for yourself: forgiveness of sins and eternal life, God's gift to you is free. You do not have to work for a gift. All you have to do Is joyfully receive it, Believe with all your heart that Jesus Christ died for you!

CHRIST IS AT YOUR HEART'S DOOR

"Behold, I stand at the door, and knock: if any man hear my voice, and open the door, I will come in to him, and will sup with him, and he with me."—Revelation 3:20 (KJV)

Jesus Christ wants to have a personal relationship with you. Picture, if you will, Jesus Christ standing at the door of your heart (the door of your emotions, intellect and will). Invite Him in; He is waiting for you to receive Him into your heart and life.

YOU MUST RECEIVE HIM

"But as many as received him, to them gave he power to become the sons of God, even to them that believe on his name:"—John 1:12 (KJV)

When you receive Christ into your heart you become a child of God, and have the privilege of talking to Him in prayer at any time about anything. The Christian life is a personal relationship to God through Jesus Christ. And best of all, it is a relationship that will last for all eternity.

Used by permission from the Billy Graham Evangelistic Association

If you have followed these steps and have received Christ into your life, look for a local church and tell the pastor that you have made this decision. If possible, also tell the person who gave you this New Testament. They will be happy to help you take the next steps in your new life in Christ.